From Text to Context

ↄ Ismar Schorsch

FROM
TEXT TO
CONTEXT

The Turn to History in
Modern Judaism

Brandeis University Press
Published by University Press of New England
Hanover and London

Brandeis University Press
Published by University Press of New England,
Hanover, NH 03755
Printed in the United States of America
5   4   3   2   1
cip data appear at the end of the book

The preparation and publication of this
volume was made possible by a grant
from the Memorial Foundation for
Jewish Culture.

(continued next page)

To the memory of

LEOPOLD ZUNZ (1794–1886)

in whose shadow we still stand

Contents

Preface

For the past twenty years, the genesis, diffusion, impact, and meaning of modern Jewish historiography have been at the core of my research agenda. The present collection of essays brings together many of the preliminary studies which were meant to test my ideas and pave the way to mature and synthetic work. Some, like those on Nahman Krochmal and Moritz Steinschneider, have been omitted as too technical even for this volume. Unfortunately, my election as Chancellor of the Jewish Theological Seminary of America in 1986 prevented me from reaching the stage of comprehensive synthesis. So it is with a sense of muted delight that I assemble what has been completed into a single volume.

In the course of my research, I have received assistance from many quarters. During the academic year 1980–81, I enjoyed the support of a yearlong fellowship from the National Endowment for the Humanities. I also benefited several times from stipends awarded me by the Memorial Foundation for Jewish Culture.

I owe a debt of special gratitude to the staffs of the archives in which I labored to discover and decipher the unpublished papers and documents pertaining to the *Wissenschaft* movement: The Library of the Jewish Theological Seminary of America, The Leo Baeck Institute in New York, The Jewish National and University Library in Jerusalem, The Central Archives for the History of the Jewish People in Jerusalem, and the Deutsches Zentralarchiv in Merseburg. Their archivists facilitated my quest with skill, understanding, and interest.

Throughout these long years of research, the Seminary not only provided me with time off, but even more important, with a community of scholars invested in my project. I am cognizant of the extent to which a scholar's place of work impacts on his or her research agenda. Had I chosen to pursue my academic career at an American university, I suspect that my research would have remained focused on the external history of the Jewish experience. The Seminary setting encouraged and abetted my fascination with the turn to historical thinking in modern Judaism. The nature of that turn, with its assertion of the right of free inquiry and its impact on Jewish self-understanding, is very much an integral part of the history of the Seminary itself. From the outset, the Seminary, committed to training a rabbinate imbued with historical consciousness and halakhic fidelity, served as one of the main channels for the transfer of critical Jewish scholarship from Europe to America. It remains dedicated to the proposition that *Wissenschaft* and values are not inimical.

In addition I am grateful for the subvention toward publication that I received from the Seminary's Maxwell and Fannie E. Abbell Research Fund.

I also wish to express my warm thanks to the Tauber Institute and its distinguished director, Professor Jehuda Reinharz, for their readiness to publish my essays as a book.

And finally, an inadequate word of gratitude and affection for my wife, Sally, whose companionship has been a lifelong boon.

New York City   I.S.
June 18, 1993
22 Sivan 5753

Acknowledgments

Grateful acknowledgment is made to the following for permission to reprint previously published material by Ismar Schorsch:

American Jewish Congress: "Zacharias Frankel and the European Origins of Conservative Judaism," originally published in *Judaism*, 1981. Reprinted by permission.

Israel Museum: "Art as Social History: Moritz Oppenheim and the German Jewish Vision of Emancipation," originally published in *Moritz Oppenheim: The First Jewish Painter*, 1983. Reprinted by permission.

Jewish Theological Seminary of America: "Ideology and History in the Age of Emancipation," originally published in *The Structure of Jewish History and Other Essays* by Heinrich Graetz, translated and edited by Ismar Schorsch, 1975; "The Place of Jewish Studies in Contemporary Scholarship," originally published in *The State of Jewish Studies*, edited by Shaye J. D. Cohen and Edward L. Greenstein, 1990. Reprinted by permission.

Leo Baeck Institute (London): "Emancipation and the Crisis of Religious Authority: The Emergence of the Modern Rabbinate," originally published in *Revolution and Evolution: 1848 in German-Jewish History*, 1981; "German Judaism: From Confession to Culture" originally published in *Die Juden im Nationalsozialistischen Deutschland: The Jews in Nazi Germany 1933–1943*, edited by Arnold Paucker, 1986; "German Antisemitism in the Light of Post-War Historiography," 1974; "From Wolfenbüttel to Wissenschaft: The Divergent Paths of Isaac M. Jost and Leopold Zunz," 1977; "The Leo Baeck Institute: Continuity amid Desolation," 1980; "The Religious Parameters of Wissenschaft: Jewish Academics at Prussian Universities," 1980; "The Emergence of Historical Consciousness in Modern Judaism," 1983; "Breakthrough into the Past: The Verein für Cultur und Wissenschaft der Juden," 1988; "The Myth of Sephardic Supremacy," 1989; "The Ethos of Modern Jewish Scholarship," 1990; "Scholarship in the Service of Reform," 1990; and "History as Consolation," 1992; originally published in the *Leo Baeck Institute Year Book*. Reprinted with the kind permission of Dr. Arnold Paucker (Editor 1970–1992).

Leo Baeck Institute (New York): "On the History of the Political Judgment of the Jew," originally published as a *Leo Baeck Memorial Lecture,* 1976. Reprinted by permission.

Macmillan Publishing Company: "Jewish Studies from 1818 to 1919," reprinted from *The Encyclopedia of Religion,* edited by Mircea Eliade and published by Macmillan Publishing Company. © 1986 by Macmillan Publishing Company, a division of Macmillan, Inc. All rights reserved. Used by permission of the publisher.

Abbreviations

AZJ	*Allgemeine Zeitung des Judentums*
CAHJP	The Central Archives for the History of the Jewish People, Jerusalem
DZAM	Deutsches Zentralarchiv, Merseburg
INJ	*Der Israelit des neunzehnten Jahrhunderts*
JJGL	*Jahrbuch für jüdische Geschichte und Literatur*
JJLG	*Jahrbuch der jüdisch-literarischen Gesellschaft*
JNUL	The Jewish National and University Library, Jerusalem
LBIYB	*Leo Baeck Institute Year Book*
LBIA	Leo Baeck Institute Archives, New York
MGWJ	*Monatsschrift für Geschichte und Wissenschaft des Judentums*
TZW	*Der Treue Zions-Wächter*
WZJT	*Wissenschaftliche Zeitschrift für jüdische Theologie*
ZGJD	*Zeitschrift für die Geschichte der Juden in Deutschland*
ZRIJ	*Zeitschrift für die religiosen Interessen des Judentums*
ZWJ	*Zeitschrift für die Wissenschaft des Judentums,* Berlin 1822–1823

From Text to Context

ဢ 1

Introduction

When Heinrich Graetz finally came to write of the century from Mendelssohn to the revolutions of 1848, with its quickening pace of change for European Jewry, he chose to title this fourth period of Jewish history as "the time of growing self-consciousness."[1] The heading expressed his conviction that the turn to history was even more basic than the attainment of equal rights. While both effected a dramatic release from medieval shackles, the heady recovery of the Jewish past filled Jews with pride and self-confidence. Their growing appreciation for the pathos of Jewish history, for the power of Jewish values and ideas, and for the persistence of the Jewish people countered the blandishments of assimilation. To unfurl the antiquity of Judaism created new grounds for a sense of sacred obligation.

Graetz may have overestimated the binding power of historical consciousness. To my mind, he did not exaggerate its centrality. The cumulative effects of *Wissenschaft des Judentums* (the scientific study of Judaism) was to make historical thinking the dominant universe of discourse in Jewish life and historians its major intellectual figures.

The evidence for this startling transformation is simply legion, from the enormous impact of Graetz's own work to the universal acclaim accorded Gershom Scholem's lifelong exposition of Jewish mysticism. The classic disputes of the modern era over emancipation, religious reform, antisemitism, Zionism, and the nature of Judaism are redolent with facts, tools, and perspectives drawn from the realm of Jewish history. Intellectual leadership came from the ranks of historians like Leopold Zunz, Abraham Geiger, Simon Dubnov, Yosef Klausner, Yehezkel Kaufmann, Ben Zion Dinur, Yitzhak Baer, Simon Rawidowicz, and Salo W. Baron. Strikingly, Jewish philosophy remained a decidedly secondary and impoverished field throughout, while some of its major practitioners like Kaufmann Kohler, Hermann Cohen, Martin Buber, and Mordecai Kaplan were heavily influenced by the findings of historical research.

Graetz had not erred. The turn to history reshaped the Jewish mind and the *Wissenschaft* movement proved to be German Jewry's most far-reaching legacy. No intellectual history of the Jews in the modern period can be written without the Science of Judaism as its centerpiece.

The year 1994 marks the two-hundredth anniversary of the birth of its founder, Leopold Zunz. In the absence of the full-scale biography he so richly deserves, I have chosen to dedicate this volume of essays to his memory. The tribute is not artificial or forced, for his persona pervades my work. Years of intimate contact have persuaded me that Zunz may just have been the most important German Jew of the nineteenth century, a figure of Mendelssohnian proportions. No one else quite matches his seminal role in the probing, recasting, and defending of Judaism. In an age of constant political intrusion and anguished intellectual disorder, he fought for Judaism on many fronts: to reconstruct the synagogue service, rabbinate, and sermon, to stem the tide of radical reform, to advance the cause of political liberalism and counter antisemitism, to revamp the contours of Jewish education, and to gain an academic setting for the study of Judaism, all while never letting up on his lifelong dedication to scholarship.

He was a many-sided man of fierce passion and meticulous detail, of wounding wit and excessive sensitivity, of intense Jewish pride and lofty humanism. For a Jewish world set adrift by emancipation, he offered a new type of religious leadership: the historian.

Under the most adverse of personal circumstances, Zunz singlehandedly led the assault on Judaism's non-historical mode of thought. He grasped fully the revolutionary import of the ideas of individuality and development which constituted the core of the new German historicism. He adroitly wielded its threefold methodology in the study of ancient texts: the quest for critical editions, the practice of philological exegesis, and finally, the need for contextual and comparative analysis. Midrash would no longer be allowed to pass for history.

With this equipment Zunz forged a new paradigm to correct, account for, and generate the data of Jewish history. He conceptualized the entire expanse of Jewish studies with pellucid clarity, endowed it with its resonate name, and set the highest standards for its conduct. For his own work, he chose with remarkable prescience to write the history of the synagogue, the institution that would emerge in the emancipation era as the most important public arena for the expression of Jewish identity. The factual detail, architectonic power, and intensity of purpose which always mark his scholarship combined to inspire generations of young disciples down to the present.

Zunz worked with a sense of mission and cultivated the novelty and significance of his career. He saved the scraps from his work desk—the diary, notes, drafts, and letters which accumulated over a sixty-year period of productivity—out of conviction that they were indispensable for the future historian of the stormy origins of modern Jewish scholarship. The literary remains of his multiple roles, smuggled out of Germany just before the outbreak of World War II and preserved today in Jerusalem in the archives of the Jewish National and University Library, bespeak a confident sense of self.

Just how valuable a repository I discovered nearly two decades ago during a memorable sabbatical in Jerusalem, when I had the leisure to entomb myself in that faded world of Gothic script. Zunz's vast collection of tantalizing morsels and official documents richly confirms what he once said to an admiring young colleague: "Those who have read my books are far from knowing me."[2] His personal papers offer the commentary to his printed work, a glimpse of the issues and agony, the controversy and intent that provoked and informed specific pieces of research. Poring over those neglected fragments, I realized the full depth of Zunz's engagement with his time as well as with his subject matter and the fascinating interplay between the two. It was during that year that I decided that no deep or comprehensible history of *Wissenschaft* could be written without going into the numerous collections of unpublished papers left behind by its important practitioners and scattered around the world. The footnotes to my essays are testimony to that plan of action; the incomplete state of my work, to the size of the task.

In the early phases of the movement, *Wissenschaft* scholars were a continental fraternity of isolated and beleaguered literati who rarely met face to face. Corresponding with each other in Hebrew or German stretched a lifeline of mutual support across distances not easily traversed, and thus left revealing deposits to be mined by later generations. Though they often clashed ideologically, they still shared information, ideas, and manuscripts. Toward the end of the century, their intellectual heirs, quite conscious of the stature of the founding polymaths, began to publish their letters.

It is from that vast repository of letters, published and unpublished, that the social and intellectual history of European *Wissenschaft* will eventually be crafted. They shed light on the power of the academic imperative, the loneliness of the scholarly vocation, the impediments to systematic research, the difficulty in finding suitable employment and the complexity of personal ties. They help to trace the stages of the institutionalization of *Wissenschaft* in Germany and its transmission to Russia. Above all, they highlight the ideological ferment that struggled for expression in the dense but authoritative rhetoric of modern scholarship.

As intellectual history and not just historiography, the study of *Wissenschaft* excavates the underlying subtext of scholarly works by contextualizing their authors. From the outset I was partisan to the view of Friedrich Meinecke

that historical truth is not something given from the start, which has only to be freed from certain accidental veils, but is something that has to be newly created by constant fresh attempts on the part of the researching mind, whose subjectivity is quite as often a source of power as it is a hindrance in the acquisition of knowledge.[3]

Engagement thus gives rise to both strengths and weaknesses, to insight and distortion, to power and polemics. My design was never to register merely the exponential growth in historical knowledge, much as that does fascinate me, but to fathom the urgent present-mindedness that shaped and applied it. *Wissenschaft* furnished the tools to restore or remake a Judaism cut loose from its moorings by unimagined new knowledge, enemies, and alternatives.

It surely continued to perform that vital function in eastern Europe. The death of Graetz in 1891 prompted Simon Dubnov, after years of vacillation, to choose his calling. On New Year's Day 1892 he confided in his diary: "My purpose in life has been made clear: the popularization of the historical knowledge of Jewry with a special emphasis on the history of Russian Jews. I have become a missionary of history. For the sake of this purpose I have renounced literary criticism and journalism."[4] And as a missionary Dubnov detested pedantry. "The essence of historicism," he told his students, "lies in apprehending the past with the immediacy of the current moment and in thinking of the contemporary world historically."[5]

That same year he published a Hebrew manifesto which enunciated a sweeping program of historical research for Russian Jewry. If "Nahpesa ve-Nahkora" (Let Us Search and Investigate) resembled Zunz's famous essay of 1818, "Etwas über die rabbinische Literatur" (Concerning Rabbinic Literature), it actually came to replicate and complement the work of Graetz. For Dubnov it was no longer tribal or religious bonds that united the Jewish people, but historical consciousness alone. He pleaded for the founding of a Russian Jewish historical society that would create the neglected field of Russian Jewish history and impel a nationwide search for Hebrew sources such as the official record books of Jewish communities and their fraternal societies.[6]

Dubnov had begun on the path that would soon take him to the discovery of the *kahal,* the self-governing medieval communal institution which embodied Jewish autonomy, dignity, and national consciousness. In contrast to Zunz who had posited the synagogue as the historical vehicle of Jewish continuity, and Graetz who had failed to identify any such over-arching construct, Dubnov would seize what was still close at hand in eastern Europe, the *kahal* as the political seedbed for ethnic identity. Eventually Dubnov would give concrete expression to the national sentiment of medieval Jewry which had been averred but never shown by Graetz. For good reason: the spirit of emancipation in Germany militated against any definition of Jewishness that was other than religious.

What endowed Dubnov's call and leadership with success was the simultaneous translation into Hebrew of Graetz's stirring *Geschichte der Juden* (History of the Jews) by Shaul Pinhas Rabinowitz. The transition from *Haskalah* (enlightenment) to *Wissenschaft* in Russia was already well underway. In the preface to the third edition of his translation (surely a sign of its popularity) which began to appear in 1899, Rabinowitz declared:

From the time when the first volume of this work was published (in 1888), the house of Israel in Russia and other lands, where the children of the prophets and sages had not forgotten the language spoken by their ancestors for more than a thousand years, fell in love with the history of the Jewish people.[7]

By way of confirmation, it may be noted that when Ahad Ha'am, Dubnov's close friend and ideological adversary, launched his Zionist cultural journal *Ha-Shiloah* in 1897, the Hebrew language no longer served as a mere conduit for general culture but as an independent medium for national self-understanding. Historical discourse would shed abundant new light on the development and creativity of the Jewish people. The conceptual arena for the disputations to come was ready.

As a pivotal historian and publicist for nearly fifty years, Dubnov inspired the turn to Jewish history in eastern Europe on a wide front. He promoted the study of Jewish folklore and ethnography as a national pastime and the recording of Jewish suffering in dark times as a sacred task. S. Anski's eyewitness account of the fate of Galician Jewry in World War I, Eliyahu Cherikover's tracking of the Ukrainian pogroms during the Russian Revolution and the personal diaries and secret archives of Polish Jews in the ghettos during the Holocaust all bear the imprint of Dubnov's final words in Riga in 1941 which bespoke his lifelong creed: "People, do not forget. Speak of this, people; record it all."[8] For Dubnov the cultivation of Jewish history offered not only insight into the meaning of contemporary events, but also the promise of ultimate victory over Haman and his minions.

He worked from the bottom up in a secular national vein. His cause was to raise the history of the Jews in eastern Europe from oblivion and to reveal that the scepter of autonomy had never left the descendants of Judah. Indeed, self-government constituted the necessary soil for the cultural hegemony of successive centers of Jewish life. His was a grand and moving conceptualization of Jewish history charged with ideological import, that reinforced the position of historical thought at the very heart of the debate over the modern Jewish condition.[9]

But Jewish history supplied the message no less than the medium. In 1893 Dubnov wrote that "at present the fulcrum of Jewish national being lies in historical consciousness."[10] The claim suggests that for many a secularized Jew in both the East and the West the turn to history gradually spawned an ethnic attachment that might replace the religious content and renew the communal ties of an attenuated Jewish identity. It certainly did for Dubnov. The recovery of the past, disseminated through Jewish art, literature and eventually museums, evoked a bevy of emotions that replenished Jewish pride. Historical consciousness served to soften the self-centeredness fostered by emancipation. The unparalleled record of Jewish suffering and achievement challenged the prevailing narcissism.

It would take us too far afield to marshal all the evidence for the formative role of Jewish history in the shaping of the multiple identities of modern Jews. My essay on the power of the Sephardic mystique among emancipated German Jews is merely a striking case in point. But one could cite just as readily the vitality of "the lachrymose conception" of Jewish history in the modern Jewish psyche, or the role of the Maccabees, Masada, and archaeology in Israeli culture, or the grip of the Holocaust on the contemporary American Jewish scene. Museums like Beit ha-Tefutzot in Tel Aviv, the Israel Museum and Yad va-Shem in Jerusalem, the Jewish Museum in New York, and now the United States Holocaust Memorial Museum in Washington are fonts of historical facts, images, and conceptualizations for popular consumption. Moreover, the proliferation of academic positions in North America and Western Europe, including Germany, assures an escalating pace of fresh research and thought.

In short, emancipation altered the nature of Jewish memory; it did not destroy it. Nor is the change as far-reaching as one might think. Judaism had historicized itself long before the modern era by shifting the arena of God's presence from nature to history and infusing its liturgical calendar with historical rationales. Historical consciousness was always the substratum of Jewish identity. If it is diluted and eroded by now the fault lies less with history than historians. In the words of Zunz: "Wherever art goes under, the artists have preceded it."[11] When wielded by a master like Scholem, history can still transform the mind of an age.

NOTES

1. Heinrich Graetz, *Geschichte der Juden*, XI, 2nd ed., Leipzig, 1900, p. 1.

2. Solomon Schechter, *Studies in Judaism*, third series, Philadelphia, 1945, p. 84.

3. Friedrich Meinecke, *Historism*, trans. by J. E. Anderson, London, 1972, p. 64.

4. Sophie Dubnov-Erlich, *The Life and Work of S. M. Dubnov*, Bloomington and Indianapolis, 1991, p. 99. On Dubnov's tortuous, youthful quest for his own space, see Robert M. Seltzer, "Coming Home: The Personal Basis of Simon Dubnov's Ideology," *AJS Review*, I (1976), pp. 283–301.

5. *Ibid.*, p. 166.

6. Published in *Pardes* (Hebrew), I (1892), ed. by Y. H. Ravnitzki, pp. 221–242.

7. Heinrich Graetz, *Divrei Yemei Yisrael*, trans. by Saul Pinchas Rabinowitz, I, Warsaw, 1890 (the preface to the 3rd ed. is inserted and dated 1899).

8. Sophie Dubnov-Erlich, p. 247.

9. On Dubnov's influence, see Jonathan Frankel, "Assimilation and the Jews in Nineteenth-century Europe: Toward a New Historiography," in *Assimilation and Community*, edited by Jonathan Frankel and Steven J. Zipperstein, Cambridge and New York, 1992, pp. 1–37.

10. Simon Dubnow, *Nationalism and History*, edited by Koppel S. Pinson, Philadelphia, 1958, p. 265.

11. Leopold Zunz, *Gesammelte Schriften*, II, Berlin, 1875, p. 190.

Emancipation and Its Aftermath

❧ 2

Emancipation and the
Crisis of Religious Authority:
The Emergence of the
Modern Rabbinate

In 1841 the *Culturverein*, a Berlin-based society founded one year earlier to encourage talented Jews to direct their energies to the neglected fields of Jewish culture and scholarship, offered the substantial prize of 200 Thalers to the author of the best monograph on the subject "What was, is, and should the rabbi be?" Two years later, with no bidders, the *Culturverein* trimmed its sails and abbreviated the topic to a study of the institution since 1782. A brief introduction devoted to the preceding centuries would suffice. But the second contest proved no more productive than the first. Not a single hungry historian ventured to try his hand and the prize went unawarded.[1]

Non-events, however, are not always insignificant. Occasionally they may serve to pinpoint the center of a bewildering panorama. The still-born brain child of the *Culturverein* is an instructive case in point, for the topic selected aimed at the heart of the religious dilemmas tormenting Central European Jewry since the onset of the emancipation process. The steady improvement in legal status with its welcome expansion of opportunities for economic, educational and social integration had confronted both the individual Jew and the organized community with an unprecedented convergence of pressures for religious accommodation. The manifold need to diminish Jewish otherness chipped away at a sacred life style tested and toughened by recurring adversity. The mounting tension between ancient loyalties and new opportunities quickly provoked a crisis in religious authority, which compounded the confusion. The rabbinate, which had reached the zenith of its institutional development in late medieval Ashkenazic Jewry, suddenly saw its authority challenged from diverse quarters. While government officials curtailed its powers and weighed its utility as an agent for social change within the Jewish community, Jews of culture and money moved to outflank it. The German rabbinate itself became in the early decades of the nineteenth century a bitterly contested prize, as competing parties fought to shape it in accord with their program. By the 1840s the transformation was widespread and irreversible. The entrance of Jews into German society had created the modern rabbinate, a professional elite in consonance with the social context in which it operated.

The agenda put forth by the *Culturverein,* in short, was intended to illuminate a major consequence of emancipation. It was formulated on both occasions by none other than Leopold Zunz, the moving spirit of the *Verein* until 1844 when it began to divert its energies to Reform.[2] After an abortive career as a *Prediger* in Berlin in the early twenties, Zunz had retained an abiding interest in the rabbinate and his critical views were to contribute to its transformation.[3] The silence that greeted both topics suggests not only that few contemporaries could match Zunz's learning, but also that most fell far short of his acute understanding of their own turbulent era.

I

The familiar is always difficult to define, for we lack the distance necessary for abstraction. Precisely because the modern rabbinate is so central to the conduct of Jewish life outside Israel it is advisable to begin our study of its genesis by establishing how German Jews redefined the institution in its transitional stage. Often what is self-evident conceals a tortuous history of ambiguity.

To fully appreciate the new, let us begin with a glance at the old. Hirschel Levin was the last Chief Rabbi (*Oberlandesrabbiner*) of Berlin. He assumed office in 1784, after having served in Glogau, Metz, Halberstadt, and London, and died in 1800. Two years before his death, he addressed a petition directly to the King of Prussia, Friedrich Wilhelm III, requesting that his duties be lightened because of age and infirmities. Specifically he sought to be relieved of handling cases of wardship and of issuing responsa to the many *halakhic* questions directed to him. To drive home the validity of his request, Levin stipulated the taxing responsibilities of his office, which called for the vigor of a healthy man in the prime of life:

It requires, in addition to the most exacting execution of all religious prescriptions, an ever watchful eye for maintaining the purity of the faith among the nation settled here, resolution of all related questions and doubts, responsibility for the continuation of talmudic learning, and finally the most extensive jurisdiction over a large number of juridical cases arising among the nation such as inheritance, divorce, etc.[4]

The entire document graphically depicts the well-known fact that the traditional Ashkenazic rabbi at the end of the eighteenth century still functioned primarily in a juridical capacity as an expositor of Jewish civil and religious law. Levin fulfilled that role with such learning, tolerance, and nobility that he even earned the lasting admiration of David Friedländer, who, as we shall see, abhorred the rabbinic type that Levin represented.[5]

A variety of official and personal documents from the early decades of the nineteenth century illustrated how quickly the extension of even partial emancipation opened the way to decisive modifications in the rabbinic office, although it must not be overlooked that the process of transformation had been set in motion long before, at the moment when the spirit of absolutism prompted rulers to begin curbing the judicial and coercive powers of the rabbinate.[6] I have intentionally stayed away from governmental edicts on the rabbinate, which will be analyzed in a later context, in an effort to define the institution in terms of what was actually happening on the local level rather than in terms of what was expected at the level of government.

A letter of 1828 written by Nathan Marcus Adler to Gottschalk Ballin, the head of the Jewish community in Oldenburg where Adler was being considered for the position of Chief Rabbi of the duchy, offers a striking contrast to the picture painted by Levin but thirty years before: "For beside the duties of preaching, running the school, [and] answering questions related to the synagogue and to ritual and ceremonial laws, the functions of the rabbi consist of weddings, divorces, translation of Hebrew documents [and] certification of ritual slaughterers . . ."[7]

When Adler received his appointment from the government a few months later, he became the first German rabbi with a doctorate. Both his rabbinic and university training had been acquired in Würzburg, where the renowned Talmudist Abraham Bing taught many young aspirants for the rabbinate. Oldenburg was the first rabbinic position for both Adler (1828–1830) and his successor Samson Raphael Hirsch (1830–1841), and their combined early careers provide ample evidence that the emergence of the modern rabbinate was not a development restricted to the nascent Reform movement.[8]

The earliest instance of this shift in priorities attached to the office occurred in the largest Jewish community in the German states. In 1821 the Ashkenazic *Kehillah* of Hamburg numbering well over 6,000 Jews appointed Isaak Bernays to serve as its religious leader with the title *Hakham*. The community had been without a rabbi since 1812. In the interval it had suffered the formation within its ranks of a dissident Reform *Tempelverein*, which by 1820 had hired the services of two *Prediger,* Eduard Kley and Gotthold Salomon, both with doctorates, and precipitated a liturgical controversy of international scope.[9] In the person of Bernays the *Kehillah* found a man whose training foreshadowed the future. Beyond the customary *halakhic* expertise, testified to by ordination from Abraham Bing, he had acquired a rare mastery of the entire range of Jewish literature.[10] Even rarer for this early period, he had attended the universities of Würzburg and Munich, without completing the doctorate, attaining a level of secular knowledge which a Christian professor of theology at Munich, who recommended him to Hamburg, claimed he had on occasion seen in a Christian but never in a Jew.[11]

The contract between Bernays and the board clearly reflected the impact of changing social conditions on the character of his office. He was specifically forbidden to rebuke, deprive of charity, or punish any native or foreign Jew for religious transgressions. He was expected to preach in German in the synagogue on all fast days and festivals and to assume responsibility for the educational institutions of the community. Finally, the contract emphasized that Bernays would exercise no jurisdiction over matters of civil law. Throughout, the contract designated the office in a new vocabulary befitting its transformation. Bernays was referred to as a "geistlicher Beamter," a term appropriated from the established churches, while the Sephardic title *Hakham* was unquestionably meant to convey the discontinuity between the new Hamburg rabbi and his predecessors.[12]

Less novel but still a departure was the job description of the rabbinic post in Breslau as formulated in the communal statutes revised in the mid-twenties. Though an impeccable character and undisputed mastery of the talmudic corpus were still the overriding qualifications, the community now also sought a man with knowledge of German adequate for the preparation of reports requested by the government. In addition to the traditional semi-annual *halakhic* lectures preceding the Day of Atonement and Passover, the rabbi was now instructed to deliver every month an edifying address of a religious and moral nature in the largest synagogue of the community. He was also expected to supervise the religious schools of the community and finally to regard visiting the sick and comforting the dying as one of his most sacred obligations.

Salomon Tiktin's own conception of the rabbinic office was far more restricted. In 1823 he had submitted to the provincial government a traditional definition limiting the office to the interpretation and administration of Jewish law. Rabbinic functions included responsibility for all matters pertaining to marriage, divorce, licensing of ritual slaughterers, preparation and sale of kosher meat, and government inquiries on Jewish law. The rabbi occasionally delivered sermons in conjunction with holidays but had nothing to do with teaching the young. Tiktin's adamant refusal to satisfy communal expectations for more than a decade and the determination to conduct his rabbinate in terms of his own pre-emancipation conception of the office led to a search in 1838 for a second rabbi better suited to meet the needs of a new generation.[13]

Backed by more than 120 of the educated and wealthy members of the community, including the members of the board, Dr. Wilhelm Freund, an educator by profession, wrote in February 1838 to Rabbi Salomon Herxheimer, the liberal Chief Rabbi of Anhalt–Bernburg who had received his doctorate at Marburg, inquiring as to his interest in the position. It is clear from the contents of this long and instructive letter that Herxheimer was the board's first choice. Geiger could not even be considered, because he was anathema to the Orthodox (*die Strenggläubigen*). What the board was now looking for contrasted sharply with what it had expected from the office but fifteen years before.

The requirements are 1) competent talmudic knowledge, where possible already officially exercised 2) university education, where possible evidenced by the doctorate 3) a competent oratorical ability (since our main synagogue has over 500 seats and holds 1,000 people) and finally 4) a strictly religious life style.[14]

The differences between the board and Tiktin were irreconcilable. In 1834 he had written to the board indignantly that no rabbi of an important community was ever required to deliver sermons (*Vorträge*) on a weekly basis. Moreover, his own experience had shown that an address laced with talmudic citations rarely edified or uplifted a congregation. When the board finally selected Geiger for the new position, Tiktin contended that a university education disqualified a man for the rabbinate, an argument which in Germany, as we shall see, was already well on its way to obsolescence.[15]

If Tiktin represented the rabbinic vintage of an earlier age, Geiger's first post in Wiesbaden (1832–1838) displayed all the earmarks of a new type of religious leadership. His contract called for him to preach in the synagogue and to dispense religious instruction daily to the older boys and girls of the community and made him responsible for supervising the conduct of worship and education.[16] His early letters from Wiesbaden confirm the scope of his work, the zest with which he pursued it, and the success he enjoyed. He preached every Saturday without difficulty, in part to teach German, in part to bring his congregation to appreciate "a rational service." He conducted weddings in the synagogue, accompanying each with a sermon. In the community school he taught the upper classes daily and supervised what went on in the lower ones. He also represented the community before the government, mediated conflicts between members of the community, and worked to improve the distribution of charity. Geiger concluded his letter of 29th December 1832 to his younger friend and soon-to-be colleague Elias Grünebaum with the comment that in Wiesbaden the rabbi is truly a "*Seelsorger.*"[17]

A few days later in a letter to his close friend Joseph Derenbourg, who was to shun the rabbinate for pure scholarship, much to Geiger's chagrin, Geiger reflected on the kind of education required of a modern rabbi (*ein gelehrter jüdischer Theologe*). He must acquire a broad and solid scholarly education, practical theological training especially in preaching, and an understanding of Judaism in its historical development. Of course, it was exactly the large dosage of academic exposure which tended to make the rabbinate for Geiger, and others, a discordant profession (*einen zwiegespaltenen Beruf*), impaled on the tension between the sacred habits of the multitude and the results of critical scholarship.[18]

The distance traveled in the reshaping of the rabbinate by the 1830s was incisively summed up in 1835 by the still unknown Zacharias Frankel, then serving the Bohemian town of Teplitz. Born in Prague into a wealthy and illustrious rabbinic family, Frankel went to Pest at the somewhat advanced age of twenty-four to gain his *Abitur* and doctorate.[19] In 1835 he composed a lengthy memorandum for a Teplitz government official describing the key religious institutions of the rabbinate, the synagogue, and the school. The statement in turn came to the attention of the Saxonian government, prompting it to invite Frankel in 1836 to become the

Chief Rabbi of the realm, with his seat in Dresden. The memorandum contains a systematic presentation of his views on the rabbinate and adumbrates his later campaign to restore it to its central role in Jewish life. Despite Frankel's attempt to invoke as many ancient and medieval precedents as he could find, the treatment is informed throughout by the realization that the modern rabbinate was the off-spring of emancipation.[20]

The functions of the modern rabbi were conceived by Frankel so broadly as to make him the dominant figure in the community. He was to teach both the young and the old, the latter by means of sermons and lectures. He was to supervise the administration of charity, the conduct of the synagogue, and the competence of other religious functionaries. Authority to perform marriages and to issue divorce papers (the *get*) was his alone. He was to comfort the suffering and to render opinions on questions of Jewish law. In sum, the rabbi constituted the lifeblood of the community. By representing a higher moral principle, the rabbi transformed the community into a spiritual whole. Those communities which chose to leave rabbinic positions vacant to facilitate their escape from talmudic constraints soon fell victim to fragmentation and chaos.

A new age likewise dictated modifications in rabbinic education. Frankel dismissed the exclusive concentration on talmudic studies along with its validating assumption that other bodies of knowledge were either false or irrelevant. Two considerations rendered a humanistic education indispensable for effective work in the rabbinate:

The young grow up acquainted with modern literature, and not infrequently with ancient as well. Jews pursue the arts and sciences with love. If the rabbi is to be respected as a learned man, he must be academically trained. To be intimately familiar with the Talmud is not enough; the Muses must also not be strange to him. Furthermore, his perception will be so purified by a faith combined with a pure and elevated philosophy that he will be able to combat firmly much superstition and nonsense, without weakening his attachment to the Law. He should stand at the head of the community not as a blind fanatic, but as a believer imbued by a lofty deity. This certainly lies within his calling! He should be the teacher and guide of the people. Would our age in fact take instruction from a man trained otherwise?[21]

At the same time. Frankel defended the continued centrality of talmudic studies. Mastery of German language and literature alone did not qualify a man to speak from the pulpit. Yet the era of the old *yeshivot* had passed; the young simply avoided them. Citing the example of the recently opened rabbinical school in Padua (1829), Frankel called for the opening of a broadly backed rabbinical seminary whose curriculum would comprise both humanistic and theological training and whose ordination would be relied upon to certify competence to provide religious leadership. Nearly two decades later Frankel would be invited to translate his vision into reality.

Frankel's discourse also touched on the third distinguishing feature of the modern rabbinate: the nature of its authority. The authority exercised by Hirschel Levin derived from a tangible, sacred, and comprehensive legal tradition. All his functions related to mediating the values and injunctions preserved in the corpus of rabbinic literature. That tradition was no less sacred for Frankel, but the age had reduced its stability and truncated its comprehensiveness. In its place Frankel invoked the universal category of religion. The rabbi had to be a man imbued with the spirit of God. "Religion can be taught only by a religious man."[22] Prayer flowed from the heart and not the mind, and it was feeling which constituted the core of religion. To be sure, Frankel meant religion as refracted through the Jewish experience, but Judaism proved to be more than its rabbinic crystallization. It was susceptible to modification from two directions: the collective will of the people and the wisdom of an advanced age. Talmudic literature now embodied but one of several sources of inspiration and instruction for rabbinic leadership. In an age rampant with secularization Frankel believed that religion in its Jewish guise should serve as the ultimate source of authority for the modern rabbinate.

The memorandum by Frankel has provided us with a commentary to the contractual descriptions of the rabbinate in transition, and like any good commentary, it has explicated and amplified our texts. Across Central Europe from Wiesbaden to Breslau, from Oldenburg to Teplitz, a type of rabbinic leadership had begun to emerge which distinctly differed from its late medieval counterpart in terms of function, education, and authority. The synagogue became the rabbi's principal arena and teaching Judaism, in whose name he spoke, his primary function. The courts and talmudic academies, in which he formerly exercised his expertise and power as transmitter of Jewish law, did not survive emancipation. As the last major public forum of Jewish religious life, the synagogue gained a centrality it had never enjoyed in medieval times. Nor did the medieval rabbi ever deign to conduct its operations. Emancipation transmuted Judaism into a religion and its place of worship inevitably became its dominant institutional expression. But in its formative stage, the synagogue was also an institution in flux that begged for leadership. The transformation of the rabbinate represented a momentous response to that power vacuum, because the ensuing dialectic invigorated both the synagogue and the rabbinate.

II

The remarkable historical fact about the modern rabbinate is the speed with which it came to prevail in all sectors of German Jewry. Measured by the acquisition of secular education, the most conspicuous mark of its practitioners, the modern rabbinate had become a permanent and prominent feature by mid-century. Without a doubt the decision to search for a university-educated rabbi who would adapt synagogue services and educational programs along German lines often polarized the members of the community, and yet the rapid erosion of the medieval rabbinate was a process that could neither be stemmed nor reversed. Writing in 1838 in firm support of Ludwig Philippson's recent proposal to raise funds for a Jewish theological faculty to be attached to a German university, Meyer Isler of Hamburg observed that the change in the character of rabbinic education had been so thoroughly welcomed by most of the communities in Germany

that I have no fear of being in error when I claim that throughout Germany, perhaps with the single exception of the most eastern region, no new rabbi in the last fifteen or twenty years has been appointed who has not more or less associated himself with this advance by adding Gymnasium and university studies to his talmudic training.[23]

The historical evidence seems to accord with Isler's assertion: by the 1840s the modern rabbinate was advancing steadily across Germany.

The evidence is of two kinds: statistical and attitudinal. The statistical data derive from the unmistakable stamp of the modern German rabbi: the achievement of the doctorate. A new type of rabbinic leadership had given rise to a corresponding revolution in professional training. Fortunately, it is easy to determine if a rabbi had earned a doctorate. In a society as rank-conscious as Germany's, if he had one, he flaunted it. His name rarely if ever appeared in print unadorned by his title. The Eastern European opponents of the modern rabbinate ingeniously turned the honorific into a sign of disgrace. By disdainfully referring to German rabbis only as doctors, they meant to belittle the extent of their talmudic knowledge.

A variety of fragmentary statistics gives some idea of the steady increase in the number of young men entering the rabbinate who equipped themselves with a university degree. The rabbinical conferences which spanned the decade from 1837 to 1847 provide one source of information. The following table makes clear how many in attendance were the product of a university education:[24]

Doctorates at Rabbinical Conferences

Conference	Date	Total No. of Rabbis	Doctorates	Percentage
Wiesbaden	1837	13	6	46
Braunschweig	1844	22	15	65
Frankfurt am Main	1845	28	19	68
Breslau	1846	24	13	54
Dresden (abortive)	1847	19	10	53

To be sure, there is considerable overlap in attendance among the first four conferences with their dominant Reform tone. Geiger and Herxheimer managed to participate in all four. Nevertheless, what is significant about those present with doctorates is that with the exception of Gotthold Salomon, whose doctorate still derived from the second decade, all had earned their degrees toward the end of the 1820s and after. A new generation versed in German culture and exposed to critical scholarship was entering the rabbinate.[25]

Frankel's abortive theologian's conference, enlarged to include laymen who were excluded from the Reform assemblies, would have brought together a more conservative cluster of rabbis from the same generational group as their Reform counterparts who had also graduated from a German university. A rabbi like Hirsch S. Hirschfeld, who occupied the pulpit in Wollstein (Poznań), had received his doctorate from the University of Berlin in 1836 and embarked on an ambitious literary project to expound the systems of rabbinic law and lore in German. A confirmed Hegelian as well as the son-in-law of Salomon Eger, to whom he dedicated his story of *midrashic* exegesis, he lived gracefully and creatively in two incongruous worlds.[26] In brief, the intention of Hirschfeld, Abraham Wolf, Michael Sachs, Levi Bodenheimer (who broke with the Reformers), Samuel Meyer, Jacob Levy (the later Aramaic lexicographer), Wolf Meisel, and I. A. Fränkel to cooperate with Frankel serves to counter the impression that the modern rabbinate was a Reform preserve, a thesis to which we shall return.

Sporadic reports on the rabbinate in contemporary Jewish newspapers by informed local correspondents constitute another source of statistical information. Bavaria, for example, with its Jewish population of 63,000 in 1843, second only in size to Prussia, was divided into 44 rabbinical districts. Since its draconic Jewry law of 1813, Bavaria had required of its rabbis extensive academic studies, without however stipulating the amount, and passage of a state-administered examination, which varied in difficulty from district to district. By 1847 exactly one-quarter of the Bavarian rabbinate, comprising eleven rabbis, had a university degree.[27] In Württemberg, with its tradition of well-educated Lutheran clergy, the government since 1828 had specifically demanded university study for its rabbis and in 1834 dismissed some 45 pre-emancipation rabbis unable to pass the new state examination. In 1847 the Jewish population of nearly 12,000 was served by twelve rabbis of whom six had completed a doctoral program.[28]

The most difficult rabbinate on which to obtain any information, alas, is that which served the largest segment of German Jewry. In 1843 Prussia included a Jewish population of 206,500 divided into 863 organized communities.[29] But since the government, as we shall see, treated the rabbis as non-persons, I have been unable to come up with official statistics on the size and composition of the rabbinate. A few stray facts must suffice. Writing in 1845, Frankel claimed that in all the seven eastern provinces of Prussia there were not eight academically trained rabbis. The *Prediger* he contemptuously divided into those who could and those who could not read Hebrew.[30] By 1847, however, Poznań alone with its 67-odd rabbis already had four university graduates including Hirschfeld in Wollstein, Schwabacher in Schwerin, Gebhardt in Gnesen, and Stein in Filehne.[31] Altogether I have tracked down twenty Prussian rabbis and preachers with doctorates in the

1840s in a community which may have totaled some 430 rabbis. Thus rabbis with doctorates in Prussia would have comprised as yet less than five percent of the total rabbinate.[32]

In all of Germany by 1847, I have been able to identify sixty-seven rabbis and preachers who had acquired the coveted university degree.[33] But the significance of this figure far transcends its size. First, nearly all of these men had finished their studies after 1830. The better part of their careers still lay ahead of them, while many of their older colleagues with much less secular education came from an earlier vintage. As they retired they would definitely not be replaced by men who resembled them in training. The days of the cultural autodidact in Germany were over. Equally important is the obvious fact that the body of university-trained rabbis was substantially larger than the number holding doctorates. Many young men of this first generation of modern rabbis had obtained the *Abitur* and spent time in a university without completing the degree. Men like Isaak Bernays, Samson Raphael Hirsch, Leopold Stein, and Bernhard Wechsler can hardly be classified as illiterate for having failed to achieve the doctorate! In states like Bavaria and Württemberg where state examinations certified rabbinic competence a doctorate was a luxury. In chaotic Prussia, on the other hand, the doctorate served as a surrogate for state certification. Finally, and no less obvious, was the pattern of rabbinic appointments. By the 1840s the large and middle-size communities—Hamburg, Stuttgart, Hanover, Cassel, Munich, Berlin, Breslau, Königsberg, Filehne, Wollstein, Gnesen, Dresden, Magdeburg, and Frankfurt am Main—had filled their pulpits with modern rabbis. A respectable percentage of German Jews was already being served by a new type of spiritual leader. His presence in smaller communities only underscored the direction of the trend and the degree of consensus. By midcentury leadership had passed to rabbis whose eloquence and culture testified to extensive formal education.

The attitudinal evidence in favor of our proposition that the modern rabbinate was fully operational in Germany by the 1840s is even more cogent than the statistical. The need for a secularly trained rabbinate was no longer a bone of contention between Reform and Orthodox. It is hard to imagine that the word "consensus" has any applicability in a decade so rife with religious controversy as the 1840s, but the evidence is incontrovertible that on the issue of formal secular education, Reform and Orthodox were joined in unexpected agreement. This consensus deserves emphasis and reflection because it contrasts so vividly with the attitude of East European Orthodoxy to secular education.

Typical is the Hebrew responsum written by Eliyahu Rogolar, the rabbi of Kalisch (in Congress Poland but on the Poznań border), to Zevi Lehren, the Amsterdam communal leader, following the rabbinical conference in Braunschweig. Besides condemning the *halakhic* innovations of the German rabbis, Rogolar delivered a brief against secular learning. He invoked the example of the revered scholar and saint, Eliyahu of Vilna, who had dabbled in secular studies only in his leisure hours and steadfastly warned against them. Talmudic studies, Rogolar insisted, were self-sufficient and irreconcilable with philosophy.[34] This principled resistance to secular studies was to frustrate every effort by the Russian government and the Jewish intelligentsia to modernize rabbinic education throughout the century. The conflict soon led to the extraordinary phenomenon of a dual rabbinate: a minority of official but unpopular rabbis literate in Russian but incompetent in Talmud intent on dislodging the dominant and still respected leadership trained in the insulated world of the *yeshivot*.[35]

At first glance it would appear as if the lines of battle in Germany in the 1840s were similarly drawn. In the aftermath of Braunschweig, whose tremors were felt across the continent, Orthodox leaders prompted by Lehren, among others, launched an international effort to repudiate the decisions of the conference. When the protest was published, it bore the weighty endorsement of 77 rabbinic signatures. Within a few months a second edition appeared with 116. But the number of signatories with doctorates remained constant at four, representing barely 3 percent of the later and larger figure, a percentage strikingly lower than that to be found at Braunschweig.

However, the actual import of this document runs counter to first impressions. The text itself lacks so much as a critical allusion to the validity of secular studies. Its criticism is directed solely at the *halakhic* record of the conference. The fact that the authors of the protest stayed clear of any principled attack against secular learning suggests its western provenance, a conclusion confirmed by the geographic distribution of the signatories. Whereas the second edition does not carry the name of a single Russian rabbi, it does contain the names of 46 German, 18 Viennese, Prague, and Moravian, 12 French, 2 Swiss, and 38 Hungarian rabbis, although the Hungarians agreed to sign only after they had persuaded the initiators of the protest to add a Hebrew translation to the German text, for "who would delight in teaching his son the holy tongue if he sees rabbis afraid to use their own language?" Equally significant is the fact that the only university graduates to sign the protest came from the German rabbinate. The correct point of reference is not the larger number of doctorates in the Reform camp, but the absence of any doctorates among Orthodox rabbis outside Germany. Like the rest of German Jewry, German Orthodoxy was rapidly diverging from its East European counterpart.[36]

Once again, one is struck by how early the divergence becomes evident. From the outset of the emancipation era in the early decades of the nineteenth century, the emerging leadership of West European Orthodoxy displayed surprising receptivity to the intrusion of secular learning. Whereas Bernays (b. 1791) and Jakob Ettlinger (b. 1798) both attended German universities, Seligmann Bär Bamberger (b. 1807) was self-taught, to the point where he could read Latin and Greek authors in the original. All three men preached and wrote in German. The mentor of Bernays and Ettlinger was Abraham Bing (b. 1752) who presided over the talmudic academy in Würzburg until 1839 and taught a good many of the first modern rabbis in Germany, despite their simultaneous attendance at the University of Würzburg. In 1833 Bing did appeal in vain to the Bavarian government to release prospective rabbis from the requirement of a university education, which seriously infringed on their talmudic studies. Yet even for Bing the objection was partial rather than total.[37]

In Berlin another survivor from the pre-emancipation rabbinate went well beyond Bing in an effort to integrate the two areas of study. Meyer Simon Weyl (b. 1744) succeeded Hirschel Levin as the chief occupant of the Berlin rabbinate in 1800. Nine years later he unhappily settled for the unwieldy title of Associate Chief Rabbi from a wary communal board reluctant to grant him too much rabbinic authority.[38] In November 1824 the aging Weyl unilaterally approached the Prussian Minister of Education and Religion with a proposal to answer one of the great problems of the age: the proper training of rabbis and teachers. Weyl submitted a plan to found a theological seminary that would serve and be financed by all of Prussian Jewry. Piqued by Weyl's failure to seek its counsel and approval, the board allowed the idea to languish with his death in February 1826.[39]

But what is noteworthy about this unapplauded venture was Weyl's profound grasp of the nature of his age. No enlightened nineteenth-century Jew expressed the relationship between social context and rabbinic education with more insight and cogency than this rabbinic "leftover" from an earlier era.

The Israelite in the Kingdom of Prussia has been given a new relationship (*Beziehung*). He is no longer merely a member of a religion; he has also become a member of the State, and he must be equipped with all the skills which his expanded role (*Beruf*) requires. It is therefore necessary that one depart from the narrow course (*Tendenz*) which has prevailed in Israelite seminaries up to now and also here to move forward with the demand of the age: namely, that in such an institution attention must henceforth be paid to all those educational subjects which are indispensable to the teacher of the people [the rabbi] and the teacher of the young, if they are to do their jobs worthily.[40]

Accordingly, Weyl recommended that in the seminary's preparatory class, which would extend over four years, students should devote twenty hours a week to religious subjects and eighteen hours to a program of secular studies to include German, French, Latin, geography, history, science, and mathematics. In the upper class, which would last another three years, prospective teachers and rabbis would be separated. While he did not spell out the rabbinic program, the future teachers would continue to study language, literature, philosophy, and pedagogy alongside their religious studies. Weyl's departing vision fully anticipated the institution of the modern rabbinate.[41]

No less prescient was Israel Deutsch (b. 1800), the rabbi of Beuthen, a Jewish community in Upper Silesia with more than 700 Jews in the early 1840s, which he served from 1829 until his death in 1853.[42] Without benefit of formal education, he gained a good command of German, though he never felt comfortable preaching in it, and a respectable degree of general culture. His fascinating correspondence with Abraham Muhr, an educated, well-known, and Jewishly learned businessman in Pless, not only represents a rare instance of dialogue between two men of increasingly divergent religious views, but also reveals a vivid picture of a deeply committed traditional rabbi pained by the pace and excesses of an age in flux.[43] With a fine sense of self-awareness, he admitted to Muhr in 1838: "I recognize in myself a hybrid. Part of the modern generation, though clothed in stiff, medieval garb, I differ from my own kind only in that I realize better what I need, what I lack."[44]

Deutsch was not averse to external improvements in Judaism like the sermon, confirmation, the organ, and decorum.[45] What he found contemptible among the Reformers was their motive, their irreverence, and their unbridled critical scholarship.[46] He preferred the gentle and respectful approach of an Azariah de Rossi.[47] Deutsch was even prepared to attend Frankel's conference in 1847, to the dismay of his Orthodox colleagues.[48] Above all, he believed that viable modifications could only be introduced by a new type of Orthodox leadership, religious to the core yet immersed in German culture.

Reform must therefore, if it is to be beneficial, come from the Orthodox, whose lives are not in contradiction to Scripture and Tradition. However at present, this is still impossible, because Orthodoxy still lacks a sufficient number of men who possess enough academic education (*wissenschaftliche Bildung*) in order to carry out reform properly. That we lack academically trained men stems from the fact that many believe that an academic education affects religion adversely and is irreconcilable with Orthodoxy. But many have now retreated from this view. Scholarship is no longer scorned. If Orthodoxy will not disappear in the interval, it will find in the next generation thoroughly educated adherents. And it will be reserved for them to set into motion that which we can only regard as a pious wish.[49]

By the 1840s German Orthodoxy had gained enough academically trained rabbis to found and sustain its first newspaper. The enormous religious ferment which marked and invigorated Jewish life during the decade preceding the Revolutions of 1848 spawned a number of short-lived journalistic ventures which covered the gamut of religious positions. There was no mistaking the identity of the *Treue Zions-Wächter*; it was militantly Orthodox, as its name implied. But it also bore the unmistakable imprint of its German context, despite the fact that it was actually published in Danish Altona. Its editor, Samuel Enoch, was a native of Hamburg who had studied rabbinics with Bernays, Bing, and Bodenheimer and received a doctorate from the University of Erlangen. In Altona he opened and directed a Jewish secondary school and worked closely with Jakob Ettlinger, whose German sermons he frequently published in his paper.[50] Although the circle of contributors to the *Treue Zions-Wächter* was rather limited, it did include a number of other rabbis with doctorates like the learned Benjamin Auerbach in Darmstadt who had obtained his degree from Marburg. German Orthodoxy had come of age; it was ready to employ the fruits of assimilation to defend the sanctity of Jewish law.

Given that setting, one is hardly surprised not to find in its pages any polemic against secular studies. Rabbi I. Löwenstein of Geilingen (Baden), who signed the Orthodox declaration against the Braunschweig conference and wrote vehemently against Reform, conceded that the Jew was not meant to vegetate in a ghetto. His religion was not hostile to science. On the contrary, he contended, only through confronting the world could his faith be tested and strengthened. True science and religion had always enriched each other.[51] Accordingly, when Enoch issued a call for building an Orthodox rabbinical seminary in July 1846 he proposed that it combine both religious and profane studies. Out of a nine-hour day, three hours were to be allotted to German style, philosophy, homiletics, mathematics, history, and geography. The goal was to equip the prospective rabbi with all the secular education necessary for his job.[52] It is worth noting that Enoch's carefully drawn proposal evoked not a single response.

But to focus exclusively on the issue of secular studies is to obscure growing differences between Reform and Orthodox over related issues. Accepting the validity of a general education did not mean according it the same valence as given by Reform advocates. The writers of the Zions-Wächter were consistently unwilling to grant it parity with the talmudic studies necessary for the rabbinate. Enoch significantly designated secular studies in his proposal as ancillary (Hilfswissen-schaften), and they were to be taught in the controlled environment of a seminary. At the same time, the Orthodox mounted a campaign to reassert the centrality of traditional Jewish learning. The study of philology and philosophy no more qualified a man to be a doctor than it did to be a rabbi.[53] The heart of the rabbinate still consisted of administering Jewish law in such areas as ritual slaughtering, the writing of sacred texts, ritual bathing, marriage and divorce, and all others in which it was still operable. Piety and talmudic learning were the qualities a community should look for when searching for a rabbi, and these were precisely the attributes conspicuously absent among Reform rabbis.[54]

The Orthodox shift in emphasis impinged on another fundamental problem: the process of certification. How could a community be protected from hiring a rabbinic candidate whose oratorical skills and university degree belied a meager mastery of sacred texts? The granting of rabbinic ordination had traditionally crowned a fruitful personal relationship between student and teacher, and its efficacy rested on communal trust in the reputation of the mentor. Though emancipation had hobbled the system by closing the academies in Germany and rupturing the ties to the East, it remained functional. When poverty drove Zunz in the 1830s to look for a pulpit, he was forced to acquire ordination, despite his scholarly credentials, from Aaron Chorin, the venerable Hungarian Reformer.[55] The institution of Prediger whose responsibilities were restricted to synagogue and school was an innovation intended, among other things, to circumvent the need for talmudic certification. But the plethora of halakhic modifications adopted and proclaimed by the rabbinical conferences of the 1840s mobilized the Orthodox to call for revamping the slovenly procedure of certifying the talmudic qualification of candidates for the rabbinate. What drew a number of Orthodox rabbis to announce their willingness to attend Frankel's abortive Dresden conference was the possibility of forming a national rabbinical board to certify prospective rabbis.[56] Clearly the insistence on proper rabbinic credentials was meant to challenge the legitimacy of Reform leadership.

The Reform, of course, were not oblivious to the problem of certification. It was simply subsumed under the larger issue of the proper locus for future rabbinic education. With the dream of a Jewish theological faculty at a German university, Geiger and Philippson hoped to duplicate the institutional model of German Protestantism which since the Reformation had used the university as the training ground for its ministers.[57] The inclusion of Jewish studies in the university structure would accord the field a level of respect it could not hope to attain in the framework of a separate seminary along Catholic lines. Even more, such academic integration would transform the traditional mode of Jewish study into a critical and historical discipline. The canons of nineteenth-century scholarship would govern both the humanistic and Judaic components of a rabbi's training. The proponents of the seminary option from Weyl and Frankel to the *Zions-Wächter* were less taken by the glamor of university accreditation and more eager for a religious ambiance in which the traditional study of classical texts would still prevail.[58] But even the latter option was distinctly German. Esriel Hildesheimer, who had obtained his doctorate from the University of Halle in 1845 with a dissertation on the proper method of interpreting Scripture, invested a superhuman effort in his attempt to create a modern rabbinical seminary with a large quotient of secular studies in Eisenstadt in the 1850s and 1860s, yet the German transplant did not take.[59] Ironically, the German university, so inhospitable to Jewish studies, imprinted its indelible stamp on all three German seminaries. What came to separate them was not their brand of scholarship but the degree of *halakhic* observance.

But in the 1840s this outcome was far from self-evident. In fact in 1842 German Jewry was treated to a controversy which rendered explicit the most disruptive implication of university education for rabbis. In that year Geiger had published the first of a series of scholarly essays designed to undermine the exegetical base of Judaism's *halakhic* superstructure. Succeeding generations of rabbinic sages, he contended, displayed ever less evidence of understanding the plain sense of Scripture and were guilty of deriving countless religious injunctions and practices from Scripture through the most forced and arbitrary kind of exegetical reasoning.[60] Geiger's provocation prompted his Orthodox opposition—Salomon Tiktin, Salomon Eger, David and Israel Deutsch, among others—to challenge the right of a rabbi to unrestricted free inquiry. In the words of Tiktin: "How can a man who denies the tradition and publicly ridicules the principles of the Talmud exercise functions whose correct execution rests entirely on traditional stipulations?"[61]

That question had been wracking German Protestantism at least since 1830 when the powerful conservative *Evangelische Kirchenzeitung* of Hengstenberg had launched its counter-offensive against the rational theologians who dominated the Protestant theological faculties of Prussian universities. While the king would not then agree to purge those professors who undermined the sacred texts and dogmas of the Church, he made it clear to his minister of religion that all new academic appointments were to be theologically orthodox.[62] During the next two decades government-backed theological orthodoxy recaptured the theological faculties, compelled pastors to accept the official creed, and drove thousands of liberal Protestants into the ranks of dissenters. Until 1848 religious controversy frequently served as the medium for the expression of political discontent.[63]

In Breslau, the board decided to submit the Orthodox challenge to the German rabbinate. The formulation of the question caught the potential conflict between the rational ethos of the university and the dogmatic claims of the tradition inherent in the training of a modern rabbi. The board asked: "Whether Jewish theology could tolerate scholarly treatment, unrestricted research, or if the traditional statutes as preserved in the Talmud may not be touched or even investigated?"[64]

This discomforting question elicited a range of deeply felt responses of which the board saw fit to publish seventeen that were unequivocally affirmative. The statistics are significant. Ten were written by rabbis with doctorates; only three were written by men born before 1800, and Joseph Maier of Stuttgart clearly belonged to the new generation; except for Chorin in Arad and Holdheim in Schwerin, all the respondents came from western and southern Germany. In short, the confrontation exhibited regional, educational, and generational differences as well as religious ones.

The respondents tended to affirm both horns of the dilemma: the historic right in Judaism to express independent opinions and the continued validity of Jewish law. Their efforts to reconcile the tension took a variety of forms. Holdheim and Abraham Kohn of Austria argued that research is personal and permissible, but that altering the law can only be done in concert. Geiger never presumed to refashion Judaism single-handedly according to the results of his research.[65] That is why, Moses Gutmann of Bavaria observed, the Orthodox were utterly unable to impugn the piety of Geiger's personal life.[66] Kohn also drew attention to the precedent of the medieval Jewish exegetes who constantly interpreted the plain sense of Scripture contrary to *halakhic* derivations.[67] On the other hand, Herxheimer added, when the rabbi was asked what the law in a particular matter is, it was not his subjective view that was being sought but rather the law as codified.[68] David Einhorn made the same distinction using the example of the civil servant who administers many a law whose wisdom he may dispute.[69] In contrast Mendel Hess, the editor of the radical *Israelit*, restricted the rabbi's freedom of action by warning that he can only teach what the people are capable of understanding. He must never impose his views on an ill-equipped community.[70] In sum, the liberal members of the modern rabbinate passionately defended the freedom of inquiry they had learned to value and exercise at the university. To have done less, Bernhard Wechsler of Oldenburg feared, would have meant to drive the best minds out of the rabbinate.[71] At the same time, however, they avowed the need to subordinate individual views to the collective will of Jewish law. By implication, the soon-to-be-convened rabbinical conferences would provide a welcome instrument to transcend the limitations of the individual to effect change.

Zacharias Frankel did not submit a statement to the Breslau board, but it is possible to gain an approximate idea of his position through an essay by Wolf Landau which took up the question in the pages of Frankel's *Zeitschrift* in 1845. A native of Dresden, Landau had received his doctorate in 1839 from the University of Leipzig and his rabbinic ordination in 1845 from Frankel. He was employed by the Dresden Jewish community as a teacher and upon Frankel's departure would become its rabbi. Thus Landau was both physically and religiously close to Frankel.[72] Deeply troubled by the allegedly high-handed treatment of *halakhic* material by Chorin, Holdheim, and Geiger, he struggled to formulate several principles which should govern rabbinic behavior. First, a rabbi must believe in the divine origin and eternal validity of the Bible. Second, he must accept tradition, defined as that body of law extrapolated by the rabbis from Scripture in which there is consensus as to the substance of the law, if not to its exegetical derivation. In both categories of Jewish law, Landau was prepared to grant full freedom of inquiry, provided that the observance of the law continued, for in neither was he ready to countenance *halakhic* change. Only in the area of rabbinic ordinances was change permissible. A man unwilling to avow these principles was unfit for the rabbinate. Instead Landau called for university-trained men steeped in all the sources of Jewish history who would speak of Judaism with authenticity and reverence from the pulpit and in the classroom.[73]

The Orthodox view on the right of free inquiry was stated with clarity and pathos by Israel Deutsch, one of the instigators of the original attack against Geiger. Muhr had criticized him for denouncing Geiger rather than refuting him with scholarship. He answered with disarming candor:

You say we should have rebutted in a scholarly manner. Now before you, friend, who know that I never attended school, it is of no consequence if I freely admit that I do not know how one begins to wage a fight in a scholarly manner. In my simplicity I believed that every discipline (*Wissenschaft*) has its own sources, authorities and axioms, concerning which it need not give any further reckoning and at which point one must cease questioning. Tradition, however, has no other guarantee for it than the tradition itself. Its sources and authorities are its transmitters, with the Jewish tradition therefore the Talmud alone. Scholarship here means to prove from the Talmud what the tradition says about itself. This we did, if not fully, at least sufficiently. Or should we have demonstrated the tradition philosophically?[74]

This response closely approximated the stance previously taken by Samson Raphael Hirsch and subsequently by the *Zions-Wächter.* Having made its peace with the demand for university-trained rabbis, German Orthodoxy likewise faced the consequences. Initially it sought to seal off hermetically the study of sacred texts from all outside sources and new methods. But that would not be its last response to the challenge of modern scholarship. [75]

III

If the modern rabbinate was operating widely in Germany by the 1840s, then it is self-evident that the Breslau Rabbinical Seminary, opened in 1854, must be seen as the consequence and not the cause of this development. By the time funds became available for the creation of a seminary in Germany, the function, education, and authority of the modern rabbi had been worked out. What Breslau did indeed provide was a stable institutional setting in which to develop the Jewish component of rabbinic education: a curriculum corresponding somewhat more fully to the totality of Jewish religious creativity and cautiously infused by the critical spirit of *Wissenschaft*. [76] Even less significant in the emergence of the modern rabbinate were the earlier rabbinical seminaries in Padua and Metz, opened in 1829, which simply did not live up to their promise. The *Ecole Rabbinique* for decades was hardly distinguishable from the old Metz *yeshivah* whose site it occupied, while the *Collegio Rabbinico* merely exhibited the trappings of a comprehensive curriculum and a critical approach. [77] In brief, the modern rabbinate is not the creation of a school but the product of a milieu, and this insight brings us to the ultimate and most elusive historical question: namely, why did the modern rabbinate arise in Germany?

Certainly both the French and Austrian governments appreciated the centrality of rabbinic leadership in Jewish society and moved quickly to transform and co-opt it to accelerate the process of assimilation. The quasi-governmental system of consistories imposed by Napoleon in 1808 radically redefined the functions and educational prerequisites of the rabbi and even set up machinery to ensure at least partial compliance. [78] In Austria, Emperor Francis I announced in 1820 his intention of soon requiring that every new rabbinic candidate should demonstrate by examination a thorough philosophic as well as Jewish education. [79] But lack of determined government enforcement in both post-emancipation France and pre-emancipation Austria allowed the training of rabbis to proceed unreformed. Neither edicts nor assimilation alone were enough to set the stage for the emergence of the modern rabbinate.

It is a convergence of factors that seems to make the institution indigenous to the German states. Operating in a legal context of partial emancipation, the German rabbinate was simultaneously exposed to a powerful and persistent anticlericalism within the Jewish community, to government pressure in a variety of forms, and to the pervasive influence of the German university. The convergence of these diverse factors on the rabbinate produced a revolution in the nature of religious leadership.

The violent anticlericalism which erupted in German Jewry at the end of the eighteenth century with the glimmer of emancipation went far beyond the well-known literary outbursts by educated malcontents.[80] It quickly assumed the character of a coordinated assault for control of the two communal institutions over which traditional rabbinic supervision had usually been minimal—the elementary school and the synagogue. Far sooner than the rabbis, their critics sensed that with the shrinkage of communal parameters and the loosening of communal bonds these institutions would become the dominant forums of Jewish religious expression. Across Germany from Breslau to Seesen, Jews from the ranks of the young and the wealthy cooperated to build tuition-free schools (*Freischulen*) and conduct German services free of rabbinic control. Often education and worship took place in the same building, on different days, with the *Lehrer* serving as *Prediger.* The very effort to create an office of *Prediger* in cities like Berlin, Leipzig, Königsberg, and Hamburg and to fill it with men learned in Judaism but university-educated bespoke a maneuver, to outflank the traditional rabbinate. But the laymen who organized these dissident temple associations were not about to grant their *Prediger* exclusive authority in matters of religion either. As the 1817 statutes of the Hamburg *Tempelverein* stipulated, the *Prediger* enjoyed merely a consultative role in deliberations pertaining to the service of his office. Only in cases where the board of four members was deadlocked would the *Prediger* be allowed to cast the deciding vote.[81]

In the larger communities the forces of anticlericalism were often powerful enough to attack the institution of the rabbinate directly. Thus when the post of Chief Rabbi fell vacant in Breslau in 1793, in Berlin in 1801, in Hamburg in 1812, in Königsberg in 1813, in Glogau in 1816, and in Poznań in 1846, they succeeded each time in preventing the office from being filled again and in forcing the next rabbinic appointment to settle for a lesser title.[82]

In an authoritarian state intra-group conflict is inevitably played out on the level of government. Anti-rabbinic forces thus soon moved to enlist official support to break the power of the traditional rabbinate. Specifically they tried to minimize its significance by depicting an archaic institution with restricted and peripheral functions. In 1819 David Friedländer, the central figure of the anticlerical movement from the start, published a devastating critique of the traditional rabbinate. He stressed that the rabbi did not bear the slightest resemblance to pastor or priest. With no sacramental powers, the rabbi was merely *primus inter pares,* a knowledgeable consultant in matters of Jewish law, invested with no greater authority than that of any learned layman. He played no role whatsoever in performing circumcisions, conducting services, offering moral guidance, teaching the young, visiting the sick and dying, and administering charity. Hence to revere the rabbi as the sole religious authority in Jewish life was not only an error in fact, but, because of his conservative bent, precluded any prospect for reform.[83]

Exactly one year later the Saxon government turned to Ruben Gumpertz, another member of the Berlin Jewish patriciate, for information on the duties and position of the rabbi in Prussia, and received a précis of the Friedländer portrait. A disciple of Mendelssohn, a close friend of Friedländer and Jacobson, and a relative of Zunz, Gumpertz summarized the critique in a derogation that would reverberate in Prussian circles for the next century: "Quite properly and fittingly, therefore, one could call the rabbis . . . kosher supervisors (*Kauscherwächter*), since, as indicated above, their functions relate primarily to decisions regarding permitted and forbidden foods, the kashrut of foods and drinks and what pertains to them."

Ironically, as we shall see, the Gumpertz memorandum became the basis of Prussian policy toward the rabbinate, while the Saxon regime chose to ignore it.[84]

To forestall that eventuality, Simon Weyl, Berlin's last leading rabbi to be drawn from the ranks of the medieval rabbinate, submitted to the Prussian Minister of Religion in 1826 his own lengthy statement. Weyl, who had requested and received from the Ministry a copy of the notorious Gumpertz memorandum, accused it of being infested with Friedländer's bile. His own brief on behalf of the centrality of traditional rabbinic leadership, despite its total dissimilarity to the Christian ministry which he admitted, had no other purpose than

to counter the false views, put forth recently by men whose intentions are to belittle the rabbis in the eyes of adult Jews who are uninformed and without religious knowledge. Thereby they hope to create an opening for unworthy religious ideas and to spread a spirit of sectarianism, which, because it does not recognize positive religion, seeks to create new forms for new false teachings.[85]

Weyl understood what was at stake. Who exercised the authority to effect the religious accommodations dictated by emancipation? The energy invested to dismiss the importance of the rabbinate spoke volumes about its dominant and obstructive position.

It is important, however, not to miss the genuine religious impulse which at least partially fueled this struggle for power in a period of bewildering transition. The pointed ridicule of the culinary duties of a truncated medieval rabbinate along with the general conviction that rabbinic leadership bore no resemblance to the Christian clergy bespoke a set of new expectations. Emancipation had begun to alter the conception of religion as well as the legal status of Jews. Increasingly confined to the synagogue, the religious experience should uplift, edify, and ennoble. The preoccupation with the aesthetics of worship and the spoken word denoted a radical shift in emphasis from outwardness to inwardness, from executing a prescribed action to experiencing a mood. A rabbinate, excluded from the synagogue and presiding over ritual matters no longer perceived to have the slightest connection with religion, offended Jews who had been conditioned to look for spiritual edification from their religious leaders rather than legal expertise. The irreverent words of Gotthold Salomon, who can scarcely be dismissed as an irreligious personality, to his colleague and counterpart Isaak Noah Mannheimer in Vienna in 1830 indicate both the wide extent and religious roots of this revulsion:

You really have nothing to do with strictly rabbinical functions? Right? You really need not concern yourself with stomachs, or cows and oxen, wild fowl or poultry, or with women and their [ritual] baths? We should express it openly, that these tasks must be fully separated from the office of teacher and preacher, and a special man should be assigned to them just as to the [biblical] scapegoat. As long as this does not happen, the hands and feet of the better and enlightened rabbis will be bound. Every stomach and slaughter expert must remain subordinate to the rabbi . . . but the rabbi himself must not get involved with these things.[86]

This sustained and varied assault from within certainly accelerated the demise of the medieval rabbinate and helped to pave the way for the development of new forms of religious leadership. But in the long run the rebellion proved to be a mixed blessing for the modern rabbinate in Germany, for it left behind a legacy of deep suspicion toward every assertion of rabbinic prerogative. Such heady ideas as the egalitarian nature of Judaism and the dispensability of rabbinic authority continued to plague the modern heirs of the medieval rabbinate as they sought to solidify their own control over religious life.

Two disparate efforts by them to consolidate rabbinic authority in the 1840s ran into serious lay opposition. The first arose in conjunction with the protracted courtship of Zacharias Frankel by Berlin. As we have seen from the forceful articulation of his views in 1835, Frankel was determined to regain for the modern rabbi the dignity and preeminence once enjoyed by his medieval ancestor. By 1838 the Berlin board was ready to invite him to fill its top rabbinic post which had been held vacant since the death of Weyl in 1826. But Frankel was not prepared to consider leaving Dresden till the autumn of 1841. In the negotiations which followed Frankel drove a hard bargain. He insisted on being recognized as the highest religious authority in the community, on receiving a life contract and a salary of 2,500 Thalers plus a parsonage to obviate any need for outside income, and on gaining official government endorsement. As supreme religious authority, Frankel claimed the exclusive right to submit synagogal reforms to the board for approval, control over all the community's educational institutions including the teachers' seminary run by Zunz, and exclusive authority to sanction marriages. Despite the cost in terms of money and power, the board approved Frankel's election in September 1842 as Berlin's first *Oberrabbiner* in more than four decades. At this juncture Frankel held out for the unattainable—official appointment by the Prussian government. Finally, on 6th February 1843, Frankel sent off a proud and forthright letter to the Minister of Religion expressing his dismay at the deteriorating status of Prussian Jewry. He appealed to Eichhorn to begin to correct this appalling situation by officially investing him with the authority to serve as Chief Rabbi of Berlin. Since Eichhorn would offer no more than a mere confirmation of his election, Frankel made the momentous decision to stay in Dresden.[87]

The entire performance by Frankel can be understood only against the back-drop of more than sixty years of rampant anticlericalism. Frankel's excessive de-mands were designed to counter the abhorrence of rabbinic supremacy which still ran deep among the members of the board. His close friend Joseph Muhr, the banker and older brother of Abraham Muhr in Pless who had been so instrumental in engineering his election in the first place, had informed him of the dominant influence of the publisher Moritz Veit, and Frankel regarded Veit as an uninformed political Jew completely insensitive to traditional Jewish forms of religious ex-pression.[88] His fears were not misplaced, for Veit was indeed an inveterate foe of what he termed rabbinic despotism. As he caustically wrote to Johann Jacoby in May 1841, "the priestly yen for power finds room under the hats of doctors just as easily as under Polish fur caps."[89] Veit was convinced that his vision of unhin-dered religious progress could only be guaranteed through a presbyterial form of government in which bishop and presbyters shared power. Though a member of the board, the rabbi should have but one vote. Frankel's proposal smacked of an episcopal hierarchy.[90] Not assured of victory in advance, Frankel backed off to await more favorable conditions to advance his cause.

The second noteworthy assertion of rabbinic preeminence of the decade came with the well-known rabbinical conferences. On the one hand, they were a symp-tom of growing professional consciousness. Ludwig Philippson urged his young, cultured colleagues to view themselves as religious professionals. Like other emerg-ing professionals—doctors, apothecaries, scientists, lawyers, philologians, Protes-tant pastors, farmers, and industrialists—the rabbis should convene annually to enhance their work. Toward that end, attendance was restricted to rabbis, associate rabbis, and preachers.[91] On the other hand, the conferences came in the wake of a spate of radical declarations on the nature of Judaism by lay groups which max-imized the degree of historical discontinuity, and consequently the conferences amounted to a rabbinic counter-attack to reclaim exclusive authority to speak on religious matters.[92] But the conferences also coincided with a period of mounting pressure in Prussian society for a liberalization of church rule. Through the con-gregations and national councils of the Protestant Friends and the German Cath-olics and the officially but briefly backed synodal reorganization of the Lutheran Church, laymen were fighting for a greater voice in shaping church policy and doctrine.[93] The intent of the rabbinical conferences ran headlong into the egali-tarian spirit sweeping the German religious scene.

Veit made it bluntly clear to his close friend Michael Sachs, whom he had brought to Berlin as associate rabbi after the Frankel fiasco, that he was not to attend the Braunschweig conference. It was precisely his lack of involvement in rabbinic politics that made Sachs appealing to Berlin. Religious leadership had to be a cooperative venture on all levels. Locally the rabbi served as theological consultant of the board in its spiritual work; nationally a synodal structure better accorded with the temper of Prussian Jewry. Sachs heeded his advice.[94]

The most vociferous lay backers of the synod model organized themselves into the Berlin Reform association and issued a national call for a synod composed of deputies elected by the educated Jews of Prussia. Its mandate would be to revive Judaism by bringing it once again into accord with the beliefs and practices of its adherents. The association recognized neither a binding theology nor a dominant clergy. Moreover, professional obligations precluded the rabbis from revamping Judaism themselves:

The synod should not teach but give us Judaism. The rabbis as such cannot do that; they are condemned to teach us; to teach us with a shrug of the shoulder that which they might well be quite disinclined to give us. They stand between us and the Law as unfree judicial representatives whom the harsh law may pain but which they must still enunciate.[95]

Despite a variety of tacks, the synod proposal failed to find much resonance outside Berlin. Within its own bailiwick, the association made Holdheim, whom it employed in April 1847, subservient to the will of the board. It conceded only that he be invited to participate with a right to vote in all sessions dealing with religious affairs.[96]

The criticism of the rabbinical conferences from the right also questioned the exclusion of learned laymen. Raphael Kirchheim of Frankfurt, who had translated and published Rapoport's passionate Hebrew rebuke, taunted the rabbis for the fixation on their title while trampling the teachings of rabbinism. The Prophets and early talmudic sages themselves would have been disqualified from attending, for neither held official clerical posts. Abraham Adler, the *Prediger* in Worms, responded disingenuously that considerations of space dictated admitting only professionals.[97] The criticism prompted Frankel to open his abortive counter-conference to theologians, men of Jewish learning regardless of their employment, and he beseeched Zunz personally to honor the assembly with his presence, to no avail. In consonance with his democratic convictions, Zunz would participate only if deputized by a constituency.[98]

The relentless pressure from within the Jewish community by the detractors of the rabbinate was complemented by substantial pressure from without in the form of government policy. The crossfire decisively impaired the institution's ability to hold out against modernization. Autocratic regimes throughout Europe from Napoleon to the Czar recognized the centrality of the rabbinate in the pre-emancipation community and moved to harness its authority to prepare Jews for integration. The policy was lucidly formulated by Secretary of State Schroetter in the lengthy deliberations which preceded the Prussian edict of emancipation of

1812: "Because of the great influence which the rabbis have over the community, it is necessary to ensure that educated and, what follows naturally from this, tolerant people be elected as rabbis."[99]

Accordingly, Schroetter urged that every applicant for a rabbinic post must give evidence of having spent three years at a university studying philosophy and Semitic languages.[100]

Although the Prussian government ignored his counsel, its intent was subsequently implemented by other German states. The most instructive example is that of Bavaria. In 1813 it became one of the first German regimes to insist that future rabbis acquire extensive academic training. In 1826 it effectively closed the large and famous *yeshivah* in Fürth when it forced the faculty to incorporate secular studies into the curriculum. Still more significant than the stipulation of educational requirements was their enforcement through state examinations, which were regionally administered. Thus in Upper Franconia every rabbinic applicant was subjected to a battery of tests which covered Greek, Latin, logic, metaphysics, moral and religious philosophy, pedagogy, history, exegesis of the Old Testament, homiletics, and Jewish history, philosophy, and liturgy and which usually took eight to ten days to complete.[101]

The imposition of state examinations constituted the key element in the rapid transformation of the Bavarian rabbinate, despite the basically rural and traditional character of the population that it served. By comparison, the French rabbinate lagged decades behind. Indeed, the French government since 1820 had required that every candidate for a rabbinic post had to be fluent in French and familiar with Latin and Greek. Nevertheless, though such a level of education fell far short of the *baccalauréat*, the graduates of the *Ecole Rabbinique* rarely reached it during the school's thirty-year sojourn in Metz. The decisive difference between France and Bavaria was the absence of enforcement. Neither the French government nor the Central Consistory ever sought to devise a system of examinations to disqualify candidates with insufficient education.[102] Academic standards without enforcement sank to the level of sage counsel.

The Bavarian combination of enforced requirements provided the model for much of Germany. The Electorate of Hesse, Württemberg, Baden, the Duchy of Saxony, and Frankfurt am Main set up machinery to examine candidates for the rabbinate while states like Mecklenburg-Schwerin, Nassau, Oldenburg, and the Duchy of Hesse were satisfied with evidence of academic training.[103] In sum, firm government intervention applied effective leverage to modify the nature of rabbinic education.

Prussia of course stands out as the obvious exception to this pattern. Its policy toward the rabbinate from the emancipation edict of 1812 through the Jewry law of 1847 was marked by studied neglect. Though it shared the intent of other German states, to orchestrate the assimilation of its Jewish population, it chose not to coopt the rabbinate as an instrument of state policy. On the contrary, by the sudden

and total removal of every external prop it hoped to weaken the religious cohesiveness of the Jewish community and to intensify the centrifugal pressure. In
thirty-nine paragraphs the edict of emancipation mentioned the office exactly
twice and alluded to it once. Rabbis were deprived of whatever judicial authority
they had left; foreign Jews were denied the right to become rabbis in Prussia; and
by implication weddings were lifted from rabbinic jurisdiction. The rabbinate,
much like the organized Jewish community, had been set adrift to fend for itself.[104]

The Gumpertz memorandum not only signified an unexpected endorsement
for the Prussian government of its hands-off policy toward the rabbinate from the
Jewish side but also provided the basis for a disabling extension. Since the nature
of religious leadership in Judaism differed fundamentally from that which prevailed
in Christianity, the government embarked on a policy to deny the rabbinate any
opportunity to recast its image by appropriating terminology from the Christian
ministry. A tacit alliance between the government and the anticlerical camp led
by Friedländer had locked the Prussian rabbinate into a petrified mold.

Over the next quarter century a series of government rescripts prevented the
institution from asserting its spiritual character. As expounders of law whose opinions Jews were not even obliged to accept, the rabbis lacked the attributes which
would qualify them to be classified as clerics.[105] Not being teachers of religion in
the Christian sense, they did not merit the honor, when elected to office, of government confirmation.[106] Despite Weyl's learned protest, the Minister of Religion
decided that marriages could be solemnized without them, since they were not
endowed with any *potestas ecclesiastica*.[107] In the 1840s Eichhorn issued orders forbidding rabbis to use the Protestant titles *Geistlicher* or *Prediger* or to wear the clerical
garb of pastors.[108] In 1846 Eichhorn, already hard at work on the pending Jewry
law, articulated the motivation behind government policy with a candor that only
bureaucratic secrecy permits. The statement cleanly disconnected the conflicting
strategies of both sides in the emancipation struggle:

Modern Judaism visibly strives to appropriate the terms peculiar to the Christian
Church and its institutions and to imitate the forms of the Christian service. If we
could assume that thereby a convergence and a gradual conversion to Christianity
would be prepared, then it would be in the interest of the Christian Church to
advance that striving in every way. It is however more than doubtful if in fact it
does not achieve exactly the opposite, insofar as one is satisfied with the form while
the content is thereafter tossed aside just as before.[109]

A specific objective is often rendered more desirable through denial than persuasion. How often does deprivation stimulate a drive to over-compensate! The
intent of Prussian policy was not to transform the medieval rabbinate but to discredit it. The effect, however, was precisely the opposite: to galvanize Jewish efforts
to renovate the institution along the lines of the Protestant clergy. The doctorate
came to certify what the State withheld. Even astute Christian observers perceived
that in Prussia the degree functioned as a surrogate for state certification. In 1846

the Dean of Breslau's Faculty of Philosophy informed Eichhorn that ". . . the larger communities in the cities demand now of every applicant for a rabbinic post that he acquire a doctorate, because they regard this step as a form of state examination and thereby persuade themselves as to a candidate's competence . . ."[110]

The government's stance on the rabbinate derived from the same source as its policy on religious reform: a contempt for the spiritual claims of Judaism. By preserving religious forms which no longer accorded with the tastes and needs of Jews integrating into German society, the government hoped to accelerate and finalize the process of alienation. In the early 1840s the government did finally give up its oppressive defense of Orthodoxy, but it continued to abide by its policy toward the rabbinate.[111] The Jewry law of 1847 codified that policy and determined the status of the rabbi in Prussia till the formal dissolution of the Jewish community by the Nazis in 1938.

It is doubtful if there ever was a Jewry law more painstakingly prepared than the comprehensive Prussian legislation of 1847. Nearly six years in the making and involving every level of government, the law generated an archive of data on the condition of Prussian Jewry, a deluge of inter-office memoranda exposing the line-up of bureaucratic attitudes, and a bevy of Jewish petitions betraying the wide diversity of religious attachments and social aspirations.[112] Among other things, the law set out to order the chaotic internal affairs of the local Jewish community by meticulously stipulating its rules of governance. The First United Diet, "Prussia's first *Reichstag*," did manage to temper somewhat the reactionary tone and substance of the draft which eventually emerged from the years of ministerial deliberation.[113] For example, it replaced the offensive political term *Judenschaft* for the local Jewish community with the religious term *Synagogengemeinde*.[114] Nevertheless, the final legislation still treated its subject as a body politic rather than a religious association.

The law created a strong, well-organized community on the local level without ever acknowledging its religious purpose or according recognition to the presence of religious leadership. An elected lay board exercised full control over all communal affairs and institutions, and it alone represented the community before the outside world.[115] The office of rabbi was mentioned only once when foreign Jews were forbidden to serve without prior acquisition of citizenship;[116] otherwise it was consistently submerged in the lifeless term *Kultusbeamten* (religious functionaries). Nor did the law require a community to hire a *Kultusbeamte* to conduct its religious life, whereas it did make it mandatory to employ the services of a *Religionslehrer* to instruct the young.[117] Even in connection with the performance of weddings, the law circumvented the rabbi with the unwieldy phrase *"der die Trauung vollziehende Jude"* (the Jew who performs the wedding).[118]

In its accompanying explanation of the draft submitted to the Diet, the government justified its concept of the rabbi as a sometime employee of the board. It contended that Judaism drew no distinction between laymen and clergy and recognized no man as a supreme religious authority. Neither the powers nor functions of rabbis corresponded to those exercised by Christian clergy. Specifically their presence at religious ceremonies was not required, and in general their authority was commensurate with the public confidence that their learning could inspire.[119]

Philippson, who denounced the entire piece of legislation as retrograde, was particularly piqued by the implicit denigration of the modern rabbinate:

In regard to the rabbis, the well-known Gumpertz memorandum of 1818 [sic], which reduces the rabbis to mere adjudicators of kosher and *trefa*, still constitutes the foundation. The changing times that demand of rabbis preaching, theological learning, teaching religion, and pastoral work, are passed over without notice and disregarded. Today when the smallest community demands of its *shochet* (ritual slaughterer) to be a rabbi, the State still regards the rabbi as a *shochet*. This is the legacy of the lifeless Twenties for Judaism.[120]

But the link between Gumpertz and 1847 was not quite as direct as Philippson implied. Gumpertz's message was mediated and reinforced by no less a formidable figure than Leopold Zunz, his second cousin and close friend, whose influence on the law in regard to the nature of religious leadership appears to have been decisive. It is ironic that a man who so detested Prussia's emancipation policy should have become such a vigorous ally in its campaign to thwart the development of effective rabbinic leadership. But the convergence of extremes effected a temporary alliance. Zunz's anticlericalism matched his abhorrence of Prussian illiberalism.[121]

The highest echelons of the Prussian government had been weighing seriously the advisability of a general Jewry law for the entire realm as far back as 1839,[122] and Zunz's career intersected its long prehistory several times. Although evidence is wanting, it is hard to escape the impression that the topic proposed by Zunz for the *Culturverein* prize essay of 1841, our point of departure, was not prompted by the political apprehension that future Prussian legislation might accord the rabbinate a centrality historically and theologically unwarranted. Two years later Zunz was invited by the board of the Poznań Jewish community to offer in writing his answers to nine involved questions relating to the conduct of Jewish religious life sent out by the Ministry of Religion to assist it in drafting the relevant sections of the pending Jewry law. On the subject of the rabbinate, Zunz sketched an institution of limited authority and function. The community elected a rabbi to interpret Jewish law, to supervise its ritual institutions, to handle all cases of marriage and divorce, and to teach Talmud. Whereas once his education was restricted to talmudic studies, today the rabbi must be trained as a theologian. Yet Zunz gave no hint that the modern rabbi preached or taught the young. In short, he was neither priest nor minister. His authority rested on trust in his expertise and piety, and in the event that trust vanished he was subject to dismissal.[123] Zunz personally sent copies of his response to the Ministries of Religion and Interior and was honored with acknowledgments from both.[124]

By 1845 these two ministries had swung into high gear in their preparatory work on a comprehensive Jewry law. This time the government turned to Zunz directly. On 27th February he was part of a delegation that also included Joseph Muhr, the president of the Berlin *Gemeinde*, and Julius Rubo, its longtime syndic, which had been invited by the Ministry of Interior to meet with two of its officials for the purpose of providing further reliable information on Jewish affairs. Zunz was probably accorded the honor on the basis of his scholarly stature, his official position as director of Berlin's teachers' seminary, and the instructive quality of his 1843 memorandum. According to the official written summary of that meeting, it is evident that the Gumpertz spirit pervaded the delegation's presentation. It had insisted that the only indispensable official for a Jewish community was a teacher (*Religionslehrer*). Judaism did not regard the rabbi as an official invested with church authority (*potestas ecclesiastica*). The conduct of worship services did not require his presence, and his authority was no greater than public confidence in him.[125] The summary of this meeting was eventually printed by the government in 1847 as part of an appendix to its official commentary justifying the draft submitted for consideration to the United Diet.[126] The government had found a far more learned Jewish adviser than Gumpertz to validate its calculated neglect of the rabbinate.

Muhr, Rubo, and Zunz met once again with the same two officials from the Ministry of Interior on 8th April. Finally in June they completed their own long-awaited memorandum on subjects covered during those two influential meetings. Again they emphasized the importance of the *Religionslehrer*, a man of broad Jewish learning, whose task was to instruct children of both sexes in Judaism. They called on the government to appoint examining commissions for each province to certify qualified teachers. In turning to the rabbi, the authors revealed the ultimate source of their antagonism to the office in any form and thereby clarified the basic issue:

Freedom of conscience must not be curtailed. Related to this is the fact that the synagogue (*der jüdische Kultus*) can no longer survive in the rigid forms of the Tradition. One or another board, or religious functionary may seek to introduce in their domain a change that accords with the [present] spiritual movement. This movement must not be restrained; indeed it cannot be restrained.[127]

For this reason the authors stressed the egalitarian nature of Judaism and the non-obligatory force of rabbinic pronouncements. Put differently, rapid religious accommodation necessitated a reduction in rabbinic power.

To handle the spread of religious strife which would ineluctably follow such a diffusion of authority, the authors proposed to establish a national commission to illuminate the issues of Jewish law and the local conditions involved in a communal fracas. The commission should consist of three *Kultusbeamten* (*Rabbiner, Religionslehrer, Prediger*) and six respected laymen, both groups to be appointed by the government, though synagogue boards should have the right to nominate a list of lay candidates. In an early draft the government adopted a modified form of this proposal, changing, among other things, the composition to five rabbis and four laymen.

Muhr, Rubo, and Zunz took umbrage at the redistribution of power and in a second memorandum, dated 6th July 1846, delivered a blistering attack against the rabbinate. In particular they advised that the term *Rabbiner* be omitted from the legislation, a counsel, as we have seen, accepted by the government. Their argumentation was twofold. First, it is a nondescript title without objective reality, arbitrarily bestowed on or appropriated by the most dissimilar people: any ancient or medieval Jewish author, any Jew who was author of a Hebrew book on Judaism, any Jew in Polish or Turkish garb who knows some Hebrew, any student of the Talmud, any man bearing the title *Morenu* (the traditional title of rabbinic ordination) whatever his livelihood, anyone employed by a community to perform the most diverse functions, and, finally and properly, men who have demonstrated the talmudic knowledge or professional competence to merit the title. Proof of the confusion, historical as well as substantive, surrounding the title is provided by the silence which greeted the prize essay contest of the *Culturverein* in 1841 and 1843. Second, the authors argued that the contemporary rabbinate can boast of few men conscious of their times and grounded in modern scholarship, who have tried to confront the dilemmas of the age in a scholarly way and by virtue of their learning and character have won the public's trust. Such men are more often to be found in the ranks of the non-professionals. The religious advances made to date owe little to the professional rabbinate.

On the make-up of the commission, the authors reaffirmed their previous stand. Independent laymen were more likely to deliver impartial opinions than members of a clerical guild dependent on, yet often in conflict with, their own community. Personal ties to colleagues in polarized communities would still further color their judgment.[128]

While the authors spoke as one throughout these three significant documents, the leading voice was unmistakably that of Zunz. The extensive knowledge, charged opinions, and laconic, apodictic style were transparently vintage Zunz. His impact on the final version of the law of 1847 was enormous. For its own very different reasons, the government chose to incorporate his guidelines: to play down the institution of the rabbinate, to delete the title *Rabbiner,* to employ the term *Kultusbeamte,* to give priority to the office of *Religionslehrer,* and to create a national commission for resolving communal dissension, although its composition was left more flexible than Zunz would have liked.[129] Indeed, Zunz spoke for many and that fact gave his voice still greater resonance. The boards of major communities like Breslau and Königsberg, though not Berlin, were so committed to the defense of "an unrestricted freedom of conscience, the independence of the individual community, and a complete integration of Jews with their Christian fellow citizens in all non-religious areas" that they were determined even to deny the rabbi a seat on the board.[130] The rabbinate stood athwart the path of unhampered religious reform. The uncharacteristic responsiveness of the Prussian government on this score to popular opinion, which stood in such marked contrast to its stubborn resistance to the groundswell of the 1840s in favor of full emancipation among key sectors of Prussian society, granted the anticlerical forces an irreversible victory. The modern rabbinate in Prussia was hamstrung at the very moment of its emergence.

The dramatic interplay between internal and external pressures on the medieval rabbinate throughout Germany in the first half of the nineteenth century was accompanied by yet a third decisive factor: the flowering of the German university. If anticlericalism and government policy were the jaws of the vise which ensnared the rabbinate, the university was the tool which effected the change. Testimony to its centrality in the transformation was the fact that the doctorate became the emblem of the modern rabbi.

When Renan declared after the Franco-Prussian War that the German universities had won the war, he paid tribute to the classical age of the institution.[131] Revitalized in the dark days following the Prussian collapse of 1806, the German university uniquely combined the task of teaching and research predicated on a belief in the unity of knowledge. The new preeminence of the philosophy faculty, which now trained the nation's Gymnasium teachers and also attracted the candidates for the rabbinate, bespoke a lofty commitment to broad, critical, disinterested humanistic studies intended primarily to cultivate the mind rather than to prepare for a profession.[132] Regardless of whether this German version of *Paedia* was ever tenable, it exercised a hypnotic influence on aspiring young Jews who by 1848 already constituted a percentage in the student population twice as large as that of Jews in the general population.[133]

Equally influential was the Protestant model of training clergy at a university rather than a seminary. Although the inclusion of practical theology into the curriculum of the theological faculty generated much debate, the State usually required of a theological student a three-year course of university study before he qualified for the first of two state examinations to gain admission to the ministry, a branch of the civil service.[134] In consequence, most candidates for the Protestant ministry did not stay to complete the doctorate.[135]

The significance of these societal forces on the formation of the modern rabbinate can best be appreciated by comparison to the French scene, where higher education in the German sense was unknown and the intellectual training of the parish priest remained rudimentary. The Revolution and Napoleon had chosen to dismantle rather than revitalize the decadent universities of the eighteenth century, replacing them with unintegrated faculties and special schools. The faculties of sciences and letters primarily licensed teachers for the *lycée* and administered the examination for the *baccalauréat*. The level of instruction was inferior, large areas of knowledge ignored, and research relegated to non-teaching institutes.[136] The theological faculties, of course, had been put out of business long before the Council of Trent which had transferred the training of priests to episcopal seminaries. In the nineteenth century both the *petits* and the *grands séminaires* in France were marked by a severe religious regimen, exclusion of secular studies, and uncritical study of sacred texts.[137] Thus the intellectual mediocrity of the French rabbinate for most of the century mirrored the secular and religious academic levels in French society.

In contrast, the German rabbinate emerged in a context marked by intellectual ferment, discipline, and excellence. The university in its great formative period after 1815 transformed traditional Jewish learning into German *Wissenschaft*; equally important it enabled the rabbinate to remain a scholarly profession. At its best the German experience of *Bildung* fused with the Jewish value of Torah study to create a life-long commitment to advance the frontiers of Jewish knowledge and self-understanding. The persistent exclusion of young Jewish scholars from university careers in Judaica enhanced the scholarly character of the German rabbinate. *Wissenschaft des Judentums* soon became the preserve of practicing rabbis because the rabbinate provided one of the few professional careers in which it could be pursued. While that consequence may have had its drawbacks for the dispassionate study of the Jewish past, it certainly heightened the intellectual vigor of the rabbinate. Soon enough, these diverse developments granted the modern rabbinate a scholarly stature that went far to offset the weakness of its legal position. As in the Middle Ages learning remained the ultimate source of religious authority.

APPENDIX

Rabbis with Doctorates in 1840s[138]

Name	University at which Degree Taken	Chief Rabbinic Mentor	Communities Served till 1848
1. Adler, Abraham	Bonn (1835)	in Karlsruhe	Worms
2. Adler, Lazar		Abraham Bing	Kissingen
3. Adler, Nathan M.	Erlangen (1828)	Abraham Bing	Oldenburg
			Hannover
4. Adler, Samuel	Giessen (1836)	Jakob Bamberger	Worms
			Alzey
5. Aub, Joseph			Bayreuth
6. Auerbach, Aron			Dept. of
			Rhein-Mosel
7. Auerbach, Benjamin H.	Marburg	L. Kalburg K. Bamberger	Darmstadt
8. Auerbach, I.			Frankfurt am Main
9. Bodenheimer, Levi	Würzburg (1828)	Abraham Bing Ascher Löb	Hildesheim Krefeld
10. Cohn, Salomon	Breslau (?)		Oppeln
11. Einhorn, David	München	in Fürth	Birkenfeld Schwerin
12. Enoch, Samuel	Erlangen (1832)	Isaak Bernays Abraham Bing	Kassel Altona

Name	University at which Degree Taken	Chief Rabbinic Mentor	Communities Served till 1848
13. Formstecher, Salomon	Giessen (1831)	in Offenbach	Offenbach
14. Fränkel, I. A.			Märkisch-Friedland
15. Frankel, Meyer			Witzenhausen
16. Frankel, Zacharias	Pest (1831)	in Prag	Teplitz Dresden
17. Frankfurter, Naftali			Lehrensteinfeld Braunsbach Hamburg
18. Gebhardt			Wreschen Gnesen
19. Geiger, Abraham	Marburg (1834)	Salomon Geiger	Wiesbaden Breslau
20. Güldenstein, Michael			Buchau
21. Gutmann, Moses	Erlangen		Redwitz
22. Haas, Moses			Hofgeismar
23. Herxheimer, Salomon	Marburg	Scheyer	Eschwege Bernburg
24. Herzfeld, Levi	Berlin (1836)	Samuel Eger	Braunschweig
25. Hess, Mendel			Stadt-Lengsfeld
26. Hildesheimer, Esriel	Halle (1846)	Jakob Ettlinger	Halle
27. Hirsch, Maier			Freudenthal Braunsbach
28. Hirsch, Samuel			Dessau Luxemburg
29. Hirschfeld, Hirsch S.	Berlin (1836)		Wollstein Gleiwitz
30. Hochstädter, Benjamin	Jena (1843)		Langenschwalbach
31. Holdheim, Samuel	Leipzig		Frankfurt a.d. Oder
32. Jellinek, Adolf	Leipzig		Leipzig
33. Jolowicz, Heymann			Marienwerder
34. Kämpf, Saul Isaac	Halle (1844)	Akiba Eger	Mecklenburg-Strelitz Prag
35. Klein			Stolp
36. Kley, Eduard			Hamburg
37. Landau, W.	Leipzig (1839)	Zacharias Frankel	Dresden
38. Landsberg, Meyer			Hildesheim
39. Levi, Benedict	Giessen (1828)	Koppel Bamberger	Giessen
40. Levi, Jacob	Halle (1845)	Akiba Eger	Rosenberg
41. Lewysohn, Ludwig	Halle (1843)		Frankfurt a.d. Oder
42. Lilienthal, Max	München (1837)	Hirsch Aub	Riga
43. Löwenmayer, M.	Erlangen		Salzburg
44. Löwi, Isaak	München		Fürth
45. Maier, Joseph	Tübingen	in Fürth	Stuttgart
46. Mainzer, Maier Aron			Weikersheim

Name	University at which Degree Taken	Chief Rabbinic Mentor	Communities Served till 1848
47. Mayer, Samuel	Tübingen	Klaus in Mannheim	Hechingen
48. Meisel, Wolf A.	Kiel (1841)	Jacob Oettinger	Stettin
49. Meyer, Samuel E.			Hannover
50. Neumann, Abraham	Giessen (1833)	in Fürth	Riga
51. Philippson, Ludwig	Jena (1833)	in Dresden	Magdeburg
52. Rohmann, Philipp	Würzburg	Abraham Bing	Kassel
53. Rothschild, David			Hamm
54. Saalschutz, Joseph	Königsberg (1824)		Wien Königsberg
55. Sachs, Michael	Berlin (1834)		Prag Berlin
56. Salomon, Gotthold			Hamburg
57. Schiller, Salomon M.			Eperjes Leipzig
58. Schlenker, Seligman			Regensburg
59. Schwabacher, Simeon L.	Tübingen (1841)		Prag Hamburg
60. Sobernheim, Isaak	Bonn (1834)		Bingen
61. Sommerfeld, Hermann			Elbing
62. Stein			Filehne
63. Ullmann, Lion	Giessen (1835)	Mengenberg N. Ellinger	Krefeld
64. Wälder, Abraham			Jebenhausen Berlichingen
65. Wassermann, Moses	Tübingen (1832)	Abraham Bing	Mühringen
66. Weiman, Elkan	Würzburg	Abraham Bing	Welbhausen
67. Wolf, Abraham A.	Giessen (1821)	Abraham Bing	Kopenhagen

NOTES

1. Leopold Zunz, *Gesammelte Schriften*, 3 vols., Berlin 1875–1876, II, p. 209; *Der Orient*, 1843, pp. 305–306. For the statutes of the *Culturverein*, see *Der Orient*, 1841, pp. 174–176.

2. Zunz, *op cit.*, p. 209. On Zunz's central role, see CAHJP, P 47 (letter by Muhr to Veit, 18th December 1840) and *Der Orient*, 1840, p. 199. On his withdrawal from the *Verein*, see JNUL, 4° 792/F-2, p. 36.

3. See the superb study by Alexander Altmann, "Zur Frühgeschichte der jüdischen Predigt in Deutschland: Leopold Zunz als Prediger," in *Year Book VI of the Leo Baeck Institute*, London 1961, pp. 3–59.

4. Moritz Stern, "Meyer Simon Weyl, der letzte kurbrandenburgische Landrabbiner," *Jeschurun*, XIII (1926), pp. 290–291. An instructive description of the power and status of the medieval rabbinate at its zenith is drawn by the worldly Italian rabbi Leon of Modena in his *History of the Rites, Customs, and Manners of Life of the Present*

Jews throughout the World, translated by Edmund Chilmead, London 1650, pp. 68–71:

> These men, that is to say, the *Cacham, Rab,* or *Morenu,* decide all controversies concerning the Things that are either Lawful or Prohibited, and all other Differences; they execute the Office of Publick Notaries, and give Sentence also in Civil Controversies; they Marry, and give Bills of Divorce; they Preach also, if they can; and are the Chief men in the Academies before mentioned; they have the uppermost Seats in their Synagogues, and in all Assemblies; and they punish those, that are Disobedient, with *Excommunication*; and there is generally great Respect shewed unto them in all Things. (pp. 69–70)

5. David Friedländer, *Ueber die Verbesserung der Israeliten im Königreich Pollen,* Berlin 1819, pp. xxxv–xxxvi. On the history of the medieval rabbinate, see Salo W. Baron, *The Jewish Community,* 3 vols., Philadelphia 1948, II, pp. 66–94.

6. In Prussia the first decisive step was taken by the 1750 General Patent of Frederick the Great which denied rabbis nearly all jurisdiction in civil cases and sharply curtailed their coercive powers in religious matters. (See Selma Stern, *Der Preussische Staat und die Juden,* Dritter Teil: "Die Zeit Friedrichs des Grossen," Zweite Abteilung: Akten, Tübingen 1971 [Schriftenreihe wissenschaftlicher Abhandlungen des Leo Baeck Instituts 24/2], pp. 118–133).

7. Leo Trepp, *Die Oldenburger Judenschaft,* Oldenburg 1973, p. 90.

8. *Ibid.,* pp. 88–207; Isaac Heinemann, "Samson Raphael Hirsch: The Formative Years of the Founder of Modern Orthodoxy," *Historia Judaica,* XIII (1951), pp. 29–54.

9. Helga Krohn, *Die Juden in Hamburg 1800–1850.* Frankfurt am Main 1967, pp. 9, 28–35.

10. In a letter dated 15th March 1833, Zunz asked his learned Hamburg friend Heimann Michael, the owner of the largest private Judaica collection left in Germany, whether he knew what Bernays thought of his recently published *Gottesdienstliche Vorträge der Juden?* Bernays had promised Zunz to read it and the latter obviously valued his judgment. (A[braham] Berliner, *Briefwechsel zwischen Heimann Michael und Leopold Zunz,* Sonderabdruck aus dem *JJLG,* IV, Frankfurt am Main 1907, p. 11).

11. Eduard Dukesz, "Zur Biographie des Chacham Isaak Bernays," *JJLG,* V (1907), p. 300.

12. *Ibid.,* pp. 302–304. Events in Poznań in 1815 seem dimly to anticipate the Hamburg scene of 1821. At that time the board moved quickly to bring the universally acclaimed talmudic scholar Akiba Eger to Poznań as Chief Rabbi. But it ran into some unexpected opposition from a determined minority which managed to extract several important concessions before it gave its consent. The opposition insisted that Eger should not be permitted to grant rabbinic ordination to unmarried adolescents. Talmudic studies comprised their entire formal education, and without some measure of secular education they were unfit to serve a German community. The opposition also succeeded in denying Eger the right to reprimand anyone publicly. His sermons were to be restricted to topics of general morality. Eger was the last great figure of the old Ashkenazic rabbinate in Germany. But even in "benighted" Poznań the winds of change had begun to blow. (See Philipp Bloch, "Die ersten Culturbestrebungen der jüdischen Gemeinde Posen," in *Jubelschrift zum siebzigsten Geburtstage des Professor Graetz,* Breslau 1887, pp. 202–208.)

13. CAHJP, P 17/437; *Bericht des Ober-Vorsteher-Collegii an die Mitglieder der hiesigen Israeliten-Gemeinde,* Breslau 1842, pp. 3–10.

14. CAHJP, P 46/4.

15. *Bericht des Ober-Vorsteher-Collegii,* p. 8; Ludwig Geiger (ed.), *Abraham Geiger: Leben und Lebenswerk,* Berlin 1910, p. 56.

16. *Ibid.,* p. 22.

17. Ludwig Geiger (ed.), *Abraham Geigers Nachgelassene Schriften,* V, Berlin 1878, pp. 75–76; *AZJ,* LX (1896), p. 81 (letter to Derenbourg, 18th February 1833).

18. *AZJ,* LX (1896), pp. 80, 188–189, 214.

19. Shaul Pinchas Rabinowitz, *Rabbi Zehariah Frankel* (in Hebrew), Warsaw 1898, pp. 21–23.

20. CAHJP, P 17/991. A copy of this significant manuscript of 57 pages is preserved in the large *Nachlass* of Moritz Stern, the former chief librarian of the Berlin *Gemeinde.* The extensive textual and explanatory notes, most likely prepared by Stern, indicate his intention to publish it. But the bibliography of his published works confirms that it never saw the light of day. (See Joseph Stern, *Moritz Stern, Bibliographie,* Jerusalem 1939.) My description of its genesis follows the reconstruction·by Stern from which I have no reason to diverge. My attention was drawn to Frankel's *Gutachten* by my friend Professor Michael A. Meyer of Hebrew Union College.

On Frankel's life-long commitment to revive the title and office of rabbi, see the testimony of his former student Moritz Güdemann in his tribute in *Zacharias Frankel Gedenkblätter zu seinem hundertsten Geburtstage,* edited by M. Brann, Breslau 1901, pp. 55–56.

21. CAHJP, P 17/991, pp. 17–18.

22. *Ibid.,* p. 20.

23. *AZJ,* II (1838), p. 154.

24. *AZJ,* LX (1896), p. 213; *Protocolle der ersten Rabbiner-Versammlung,* Braunschweig 1844, p. 1; *Protocolle und Aktenstücke der zweiten Rabbiner-Versammlung,* Frankfurt am Main 1845, p. 3; *Protocolle der dritten Versammlung deutscher Rabbiner,* Breslau 1847, p. 1; *Der Orient,* 1846, p. 237.

25. See Appendix.

26. Monika Richarz, *Der Eintritt der Juden in die akademischen Berufe: Jüdische Studenten und Akademiker in Deutschland 1678–1848,* Tübingen 1974 (Schriftenreihe wissenschaftlicher Abhandlungen des Leo Baeck Instituts 28), p. 99n., and *Der Orient* 1841, pp. 1–2. In the 1840s he wrote *Der Geist der talmudischen Auslegung der Bibel: Halachische Exegese,* Berlin 1840, and *Der Geist der ersten Schriftauslegungen: Die hagadische Exegese,* Berlin 1847. Regarding his plan for a Latin edition of the Talmud, see *Der Orient,* 1840, p. 185. A Catholic physician and close friend of Hirschfeld has left an intimate portrait of the man and his family. (Ulla Wolff-Frank, "Das Haus: Aus den Aufzeichnungen des Kreisphysikus Dr. E," *JJGL,* XXII [1919] pp. 132–158.)

27. See the illuminating analysis of state policy toward the rabbinate in Bavaria in *AZJ,* II (1838), pp. 473–474, 481–482, 485–488, 502, 509–510. Information on the educational level of individual rabbis is to be found in *Der Orient,* 1847, pp. 75–76, 81–82.

28. Paul Tänzer, *Die Rechtsgeschichte der Juden in Württemberg,* Berlin 1922, pp. 76–77; Aron Tänzer, *Die Geschichte der Juden in Württemberg,* Frankfurt am Main 1937, pp. 70–78; *AZJ,* XI (1847), pp. 724–726. The population statistics for Bavaria and Baden come from the *Vollständige Verhandlungen des Ersten Vereinigten Preussischen Landtages über die Emancipationsfrage der Juden,* Berlin 1847, p. xvi.

29. *AZJ,* X (1846), p. 118.

30. ZRIJ, II (1845), pp. 209–210.

31. *Der Orient,* 1847, pp. 290–291.

32. The mathematics behind this "guestimate" is simple enough. If Poznań's 135

organized Jewish communities had a total of 67 rabbis (*ibid.*) and the district of Oppeln in Upper Silesia had 42 communities with 20 rabbis (*Zur Judenfrage*, II [1844], p. 54), it means that the Prussian ratio of community to rabbi is approximately 2:1. Therefore, 863 organized communities in all of Prussia (*AZJ*, X [1846], p. 118) should have somewhere in the vicinity of 430 rabbis. For Prussian rabbis with doctorates, see the Appendix.

33. See Appendix.

34. Eliyahu Rogolar, *Yad Eliyahu* (in Hebrew) (Warsaw 1900), part one, pp. 32–35. I am indebted to my friend Professor Emanuel Etkes of The Hebrew University for bringing this *responsum* to my attention.

35. Azriel Shochat, *The "Crown Rabbinate" in Russia* (in Hebrew) (The University of Haifa 1975). Both the *Maskilim* and the government at various times called for importing modern rabbis from Germany until a native rabbinate along German lines could be produced (pp. 17, 20, 40). In fact, in the early 1860s the assimilated communities of Odessa and St. Petersburg brought Simeon L. Schwabacher and Abraham Neumann respectively to occupy their pulpits (pp. 64–66, 130).

36. The dual language protest was published in pamphlet form in 1845 under the title *Schelomet Emunei Yisrael*. The German text with the original 77 signatories was reprinted in *Der Orient*, 1845, pp. 100–103. The second edition with 116 signatories which I used is bound without title page together with the Seminary library's copy of Zevi Lehren and Aaron Prinz, *Torat ha-Kenaot*, Amsterdam 1845. The four German rabbis with doctorates were Nathan M. Adler, Aron Auerbach and his brother Benjamin Hirsch Auerbach (their father was Abraham Auerbach who also signed), and Meyer Fränkel. For the letter by Abraham Samuel Benjamin Sofer to Jakob Ettlinger, from which the quotation is taken, see Solomon Sofer (ed.), *Iggrot Sofrim*, Tel-Aviv 1970, III, pp. 6–8.

Although contemporaries credited the Amsterdam magnate Zevi Lehren with initiating the Orthodox protest (the opening paragraph of the aforementioned letter by Rogolar to Lehren; AZJ, IX [1845], pp. 125–126; Heinrich Graetz, *Geschichte der Juden*, XI, 2nd edn., Leipzig 1900, p. 517), there is some evidence to suggest the deep involvement of the Ettlinger circle in Altona. For example, on 7th March 1845 Samuel Enoch, the editor of the *Treue Zions-Wächter*, sent a draft of the forthcoming circular to Rabbi Loeb Schwab of Pest requesting his signature "im Namen eines zu diesem Behufe zusammengetretenen Comitee." (Leo Baeck Institute Archives, AR-7002, Appendix II; see also the aforementioned letter by Sofer to Ettlinger in response to a similar request.) In her unpublished doctoral dissertation, Judith Bleich has attempted to credit Ettlinger with the entire initiative. (*Jacob Ettlinger: His Life and Works*, New York University 1974, pp. 186–191.) In light of Lehren's *Torat ha-Kenaot*, which consists of 37 *responsa* to him condemning the Braunschweig conference, this revision is excessive. Rather, the protest appears to have been the product of a joint venture.

37. On Ettlinger, see *Encyclopaedia Judaica*, VI, Berlin 1930, col. 826; S. Eppenstein, "Leben und Wirken Dr. I. Hildesheimers," *Jeschurun*, VII (1920), pp. 276–278; and now the admirable biography by Bleich, *op. cit.*, pp. 242–261. On Bamberger, see *Rabbiner Seligman Bär Bamberger*, Würzburg 1897, pp. 6–7, 10–11, 16; Herz Bamberger, *Geschichte der Rabbiner der Stadt und des Bezirkes Würzburg*, Hamburg 1906), pp. 67–72; and Mordechai Eliav, "Ha-Rav Yitzhak Dov ha-Levi Bamberger. Ha-Ish u-Tekufato," *Sinai*, LXXXIV (1979), nos. 1–2, pp. 61–71. On Bing, see Herz Bamberger, *op cit.*, pp. 86–90.

38. Moritz Stern, *loc. cit.*, pp. 298–307, and Louis Lewin, *Geschichte der Juden in Lissa*, Pinne 1904, pp. 338–346.

39. Copies of some documents pertaining to the altercation between Weyl and the board are preserved in CAHJP, P 17/448. For the reconstruction of this instructive episode, see Michael Holzman, *Geschichte der jüdischen Lehrer-Bildungsanstalt in Berlin*, Berlin 1909, pp. 1–31.

40. *Ibid.*, p. 9.

41. *Ibid.*, pp. 18–23.

42. The population figure is given by Salomon Neumann, *Zur Statistik der Juden in Preussen von 1816 bis 1880*, Berlin 1884, p. 46.

43. *Proben aus dem literarischen Nachlasse des Herrn Israel Deutsch*, ed. by Abraham and David Deutsch, Gleiwitz 1855. The introduction contains a brief biography.

44. *Ibid.*, p. 43.

45. *Ibid.*, pp. 38, 54.

46. *Ibid.*, pp. 72, 77, 94, 102, 119, 120.

47. *Ibid.*, p.77.

48. *AZJ*, X (1846), p. 731; *Der Orient*, 1847, p. 3. Also his article in *Der Orient*, 1847, pp. 5–8 where he raised the issues which troubled him.

49. *Proben*, pp.62–63.

50. On Enoch, see *Israelitische Wochenschrift*, 1877, p. 40. He published the *Treue Zions-Wächter* from 1845 to 1854. Beginning with 1846 he and Ettlinger put out a Hebrew *Literaturblatt* entitled *Shomer Zion ha-Neeman* which was primarily restricted to the traditional mode of *halakhic* discourse but thereby drew contributors from Eastern Europe. A charming example of Ettlinger's sermonic style is "Israels Zeitrechnung nach Mondesumlaut," *TZW*, 1846, nos. 16–19.

51. *TZW*, 1846, p. 125.

52. *TZW*, 1846, pp. 241–245.

53. *TZW*, 1846, p. 34; 1847, p. 100.

54. *TZW*, 1847, pp. 97–101, 105–108.

55. S. Maybaum, "Aus dem Leben von Leopold Zunz," *Zwölfter Bericht über die Lehranstalt für die Wissenschaft des Judenthums in Berlin*, Berlin, 1894, pp. 19–29.

56. *Der Orient*, 1846, p. 274 and the Hebrew Beilage to no. 40. Originally scheduled for 21st–22nd October 1846, it was postponed upon request to the following spring (*Der Orient*, 1846, p. 293), but never materialized. The contemporary press provides only the most fragmentary evidence of the jockeying which took place behind the scenes. (For a good specimen, see *AZJ*, X (1846), pp. 492, 523.) The *TZW* repudiated the idea because Frankel had failed to sign the denunciation of the Braunschweig conference (1846, pp. 249–250; 1847, pp. 81–83). But reports did circulate at the time that Rabbi Salomon Eger of Poznań supported Frankel's scheme (*Der Orient*, 1847, p. 73), though this seems unlikely from Eger's own harsh words to his brother Abraham in a letter after the fact. According to him, Frankel's intended assembly frightened the Orthodox more than the three previous Reform conferences (Solomon Sofer, *op cit.*, I, p. 84), perhaps because, as we have seen, it threatened to split them.

57. Abraham Geiger, "Die Gründung einer jüdisch-theologischen Facultät," *WZJT*, II (1836), pp. 1–21; *AZJ*, I (1837), pp. 349–351; Friedrich Paulsen, *The German Universities and University Study*, trans. by Frank Thilly and William Elwang, New York 1906, p. 38. See also Salo W. Baron, "Jewish Studies at Universities: An Early Project," *Hebrew Union College Annual*, XLVI (1975), pp. 357–376.

58. See Michael A. Meyer, "Conflicting Views on the Training of Modern Rabbis in 19th-Century Germany" (in Hebrew), *Proceedings of the Sixth World Congress for Jewish Studies*, II, Jerusalem 1976, pp. 195–200.

59. Eppenstein, *op cit.*, pp. 290–299; Mordechai Eliav, "Torah im Derekh Eretz be-Hungaria," *Sinai*, LI (1962), pp. 127–142.

60. A. Geiger, "Das Verhältniss des natürlichen Schriftsinnes zur thalmudischen Schriftdeutung," *WZJT*, V (1844), pp. 53–81. It is evident from contemporary references that this essay appeared in early 1842 (*Proben*, pp. 3–4; Salomon A. Tiktin, *Darstellung des Sachverhältnisses*, Breslau 1842, p. 28).

61. *Ibid.*, p. 16.

62. Johannes B. Kissling, *Der deutsche Protestantismus*, 2 vols., Münster 1917, I, pp. 42–67; Robert M. Bigler, *The Politics of German Protestantism*, Berkeley–Los Angeles 1972, pp. 76–124.

63. Bigler, *op. cit.*, pp. 53–155; Hans Rosenberg, *Politische Denkströmungen im deutschen Vormärz*, Göttingen 1972, pp. 18–50.

64. *Rabbinische Gutachten über die Verträglichkeit der freien Forschung mit dem Rabbineramte*, 2 vols., Breslau 1842–1843, I, p. 16.

65. *Ibid.*, I, p. 76.

66. *Ibid.*, I, pp. 164–165.

67. *Ibid.*, I, p. 111.

68. *Ibid.*, I, p. 120.

69. *Ibid.*, I, p. 136.

70. *Ibid.*, I, pp. 157–159. See also his essay "Sind die neuen Rabbiner Heuchler?" in *Der Israelit*, 20th February 1842, pp. 29–31.

71. *Ibid.*, I, pp. 93–94.

72. Meyer Kayserling, *Bibliothek jüdischer Kanzelredner*, 2 vols., Berlin 1870–1872, II, p. 114.

73. Wolf Landau, "Anforderungen des Glaubens und der theologischen Wissenschaft an den Rabbiner," *ZRIJ*, II (1845), pp. 139–142, 182–190, 214–218. See also the lengthy refutation of Geiger's thesis by another member of Frankel's Dresden circle. M. Schwarzauer, in the *Literaturblatt des Orients*, 1842, nos. 17, 18, 19 and 25.

74. *Proben*, pp. 98–99. On his role in the *Gutachten* submitted by nine Upper Silesian rabbis in behalf of Tiktin (*Darstellung*, pp. 28–31), see *Proben*, pp. 3–4.

75. *TZW*, 1845, p. 19; Samson Raphael Hirsch, *The Nineteen Letters of Ben Uziel*, trans. by Bernard Drachman, New York 1942, pp. 169–209. On the divergence of Hildesheimer from the Hirsch position on *Wissenschaft*, see Mordechai Eliav (ed.), *Rabbiner Esriel Hildesheimer Briefe*, Jerusalem 1965, Veröffentlichung des Leo Baeck Instituts, pp. 207–216.

76. Markus Brann, *Geschichte des jüdisch-theologischen Seminars in Breslau*, Breslau 1904, Beilage I (Z. Frankels Organisationsplan ..).

77. For the *Ecole Rabbinique*, see Jules Bauer, *L'École rabbinique de France*, Paris n.d., and now the rich new material in Phyllis Cohen Albert, *The Modernization of French Jewry, Consistory and Community in the Nineteenth Century*, Hanover, New Hampshire, 1977. For the *Collegio Rabbinico*, see the careful study by Nikolaus Vielmetti, "Die Gründungsgeschichte des Collegio Rabbinico in Padua," Sonderdruck aus *Kairos*, Heft 1 (1970). I am indebted to my friend Professor Daniel Carpi of Tel-Aviv University for providing me with a copy of this essay.

78. Simeon J. Maslin, *Selected Documents of Napoleonic Jewry*, Cincinnati 1957, pp. 30–31, 98–101, 108–109, 113–121; Albert, *op. cit.*, pp. 143–150, 182–187.

79. A. F. Pribram, *Urkunden und Akten zur Geschichte der Juden in Wien*, 2 vols.,

Vienna 1918, II, pp. 305–306. More generally, G. Wolf, "Die Versuche zur Errichtung einer Rabbinerschule in Oesterreich," *ZGJD*, V (1892), pp. 27–53.

80. Israel Zinberg, *A History of Jewish Literature*, trans. by Bernard Martin, VIII, Cincinnati–New York 1976, pp. 96–126.

81. JNUL, 4° 792/D 25.

82. Markus Brann, "Geschichte des Landrabbinats in Schlesien," *Jubelschrift zum siebzigsten Geburtstage des Prof. Dr. H. Graetz*. Breslau 1887, pp. 262–267; *idem*, "Aus der Zeit von hundert Jahren," *MGWJ*, LIX (1915), pp. 135–136.

83. Friedländer, *op. cit.*, pp. xxxi–xxxix, 25–38.

84. *Zur Judenfrage*, II (1844), p. 215. In the 1840s Jewish spokesmen appreciated the influence of Gumpertz's memorandum on Prussian policy. That is why Wilhelm Freund, the editor, published it for the first time (*ibid.*, pp. 213–216) and added a rejoinder as well (*ibid.*, pp. 199–210). On Gumpertz, see David Kaufmann and Max Freudenthal, *Die Familie Gomperz*, Frankfurt am Main 1907, pp. 204–215. In Saxony, though not a civil servant, the rabbi did enjoy official recognition. His election was confirmed by the Minister of Religion and he could not be dismissed without the Minister's approval (*Zur Judenfrage*, II [1844], pp. 302–303).

85. CAHJP, P 17/447.

86. M. Rosenmann, "Briefe Gotthold Salomons an Isaak Noah Mannheimer," *JJGL*, XXII (1919), p. 78. It is equally important to note that Kant's philosophical repudiation of heteronomy as ethically worthless served to alienate many an educated Jew from traditional Judaism. For a typical example, see F. Eisenberg, *Staat und Religion, mit bes., Rücksicht auf die Stellung der Israeliten*, Leipzig 1844, pp. 148–156. This valuable book was brought to my attention by Dr. Max Gruenewald.

87. This fascinating episode was reconstructed by S. Bernfeld on the basis of the extensive correspondence between Joseph Muhr and Frankel which he published in a series of fourteen articles in the *AZJ*, LXII (1898), nos. 29–31, 33–34, 37, 39, 41, 45, 48–51.

88. *AZJ*, LXII (1898), p. 607. On Joseph Muhr, see Markus Brann, *Abraham Muhr: Ein Lebensbild*, 2nd edn. (n.p., n.d.), pp. 11–12.

89. Ludwig Geiger, "Zum Andenken an Moritz Veit," *MGWJ*, LII (1908), p. 528.

90. Ludwig Geiger (ed.), *Michael Sachs und Moritz Veit: Briefwechsel*, Frankfurt am Main 1897, p. 62.

91. *AZJ*, VIII (1844), pp. 26–27; *Protocolle der ersten Rabbiner-Versammlung*, p. 5.

92. Below, pp. 272–74.

93. Catherine Magill Holden, *A Decade of Dissent in Germany: An Historical Study of the Society of Protestant Friends and the German-Catholic Church, 1840–1848* (unpub. diss. Yale University, 1954); Gwendolyn Evans Jensen, "Official Reform in *Vormärz* Prussia: The Ecclesiastical Dimension," *Central European History*, VII (1974), pp. 137–158.

94. L. Geiger, *Sachs und Veit*, pp. 83–84.

95. *AZJ*, IX (1845), p. 376. See also *AZJ*, X (1846), pp. 505–508, 530–533, for lay reaction in Frankfurt am Main.

96. See the copy of his contract in CAHJP, P 43. Under the impact of the revolutionary climate, efforts to convene a nationwide synod were revived in 1848 in South-Western Germany. (See Jacob Toury, *Soziale und politische Geschichte der Juden in Deutschland 1847–1971*, Düsseldorf 1977, pp. 248–252.) Eisenberg, *op. cit.* (pp. 168–169) was also wary of rabbinic presumption to govern Jewish life unilaterally. The *Gemeinde*, he believed, should be run by a lay board in which the rabbi enjoyed but a single vote. In 1853 the radical Galician Reform leader Joshua Heschel

Schorr criticized Geiger in the pages of *Hehalutz* for having harmed the cause of Reform by inviting only rabbis to the conferences. The exclusion of competent laymen aroused suspicion that the rabbis were out to increase their power, while at the same time preventing some rabbis from speaking candidly for fear of losing their jobs (Joshua Schorr, *Selected Essays* [in Hebrew], ed. by Ezra Spicehandler, Jerusalem 1972, p. 84).

97. Abraham Adler, *Die sieben und siebzig sogenannten Rabbiner und die Rabbiner-Versammlung,* Mannheim 1845, pp. 10–11, 29. The Hebrew original and German translation by Kirchheim were published together under the title *Sendschreiben eines Rabbiners an die Rabbiner-Versammlung zu Frankfurt am Main,* Frankfurt am Main 1845.

98. The original *Aufruf* appeared in *Der Orient,* 1846, pp. 149–151. The letter to Zunz dated 21st June 1846 is in JNUL, G 12. Frankel answered Zunz's criticism indirectly in *ZRIJ,* III (1846), p. 340. Zunz had been peeved by Frankel's attempt to place the teachers' seminary under rabbinic supervision when he considered coming to Berlin as *Oberrabbiner* (Nahum N. Glatzer [ed.], *Leopold Zunz. Jude—Deutscher—Europäer: Ein jüdisches Gelehrtenschicksal des 19. Jahrhunderts in Briefen an Freunde,* Tübingen 1964 [Schriftenreihe wissenschaftlicher Abhandlungen des Leo Baeck Instituts II], pp. 217n. l. 223).

99. Ismar Freund, *Die Emanzipation der Juden in Preussen,* 2 vols., Berlin 1912, II, pp. 246–247.

100. *Ibid.,* p. 100.

101. Stefan Schwarz, *Die Juden in Bayern,* München–Wien 1963, p. 347. On the fate of the *yeshiva* in Fürth, see Isaak M. Jost, *Neuere Geschichte der Israeliten,* 3 vols., Breslau n.d., I, p. 132. Regarding Upper Franconia, see *AZJ,* II (1838), pp. 473–474. Actually the first German regime to require secular education of its rabbis was Baden in 1809. But this provision of its Jewry law was simply ignored until 1823 and even thereafter only fitfully implemented. In consequence, the Baden rabbinate of the 1840s remained undistinguished and poorly educated (*Israelitische Annalen,* 1839, pp. 392–393, 398–399, 413–414).

102. Bauer, *op. cit.,* pp. 20–23, 46–47, 50–52, 65–69; Albert, *op. cit.,* pp. 252–253.

103. Jost, *op. cit.,* I, pp. 98, 132–134, 146–158, 175, 214, 216–217, 223–224, 227–228, 260, 264.

104. Freund, *op. cit.,* II, pp. 455–459.

105. Jeremias Heinemann (Hrsg.), *Sammlung der die religiöse und bürgerliche Verfassung der Juden in den Königl. Preuss. Staaten betreffenden Gesetze, Verordnungen, Gutachten, Berichte und Erkenntnisse,* 2nd edn., Glogau 1813, reprinted Hildesheim 1976, p. 394.

106. *Ibid.,* pp. 396–397.

107. *Ibid.,* p. 275.

108. DZAM, Ministerium des Innern, Rep. 77 Tit. 415 Nr. 54; Rep. 77 Tit. 2 Gener. Nr. 28; Rep. 77 Tit. 30 Nr. 132.

109. DZAM, Ministerium des Innern, Rep. 77 Tit. 2 Gener. Nr. 28 p. 111 b.

110. Moritz Kalisch, *Die Judenfrage in ihrer wahren Bedeutung für Preussen,* Leipzig 1860, pp. 18–19.

111. The famous Cabinet Order of 9th December 1823 had quashed efforts at liturgical reform in Berlin and forestalled all similar efforts throughout Prussia for the next two decades (Ludwig Geiger, *Geschichte der Juden in Berlin,* 2 vols., Berlin 1871, I, pp. 164–168, II, pp. 210–234). The policy of intervention in Jewish religious affairs was finally abandoned by Eichhorn in late 1842 in the face of the ir-

reconcilable differences wracking the Jewish community in Breslau since Geiger's arrival (DZAM, Ministerium des Innern, Rep. 77 Tit. 1021 Breslau Nr. 32 vol. II; *AZJ*, VIII (1844), pp. 718–720).

112. Horst Fischer, *Judentum, Staat und Heer in Preussen im frühen 19. Jahrhundert: Zur Geschichte der staatlichen Judenpolitik*, Tübingen 1968 (Schriftenreihe wissenschaftlicher Abhandlungen des Leo Baeck Instituts 20), pp. 151–190; Herbert Strauss, "Pre-emancipation Prussian Policies towards the Jews 1815–1847," in *Year Book XI of the Leo Baeck Institute*, London 1966, pp. 107–137; *idem*, "Liberalism and Conservatism in Prussian Legislation for Jewish Affairs, 1815–1847," *Jubilee Volume dedicated to Curt C. Silberman*, ed. by Herbert A. Strauss and Hanns G. Reissner, New York 1969, pp. 114–132.

113. The title was bestowed by Reinhart Koselleck, *Preussen zwischen Reform und Revolution*, Stuttgart 1967, pp. 367, 368.

114. *AZJ*, XI (1847), p. 420.

115. *AZJ*, XI (1847), pp. 421–422.

116. *AZJ*, XI (1847), p. 454.

117. *AZJ*, XI (1847), pp. 423–424, 441.

118. *AZJ*, XI (1847), p. 445.

119. *Vollständige Verhandlungen*, p. xxvii.

120. *AZJ*, XI (1847), p. 372.

121. For an early and vehement expression of Zunz's hostility toward the contemporary occupants of the rabbinate, see his 1819 article "Geist der Rabbiner," republished by Ludwig Geiger in *AZJ*, LXXX (1916), pp. 413–414. This outburst was provoked by the uncompromising rabbinic rejection of the liturgical reforms initiated by the Hamburg *Tempelverein*. Zunz speaks of "contemporary rabbinism" as "a degenerate institution of ignorance, arrogance and fanaticism" (p. 413).

122. DZAM, Ministerium des Innern, Rep. 77 Tit. 30 Nr. 85, vol. II.

123. Zunz, *Gesammelte Schriften*, II, pp. 207–210. Zunz was not the only man to submit his views. Compare, for example, the response of Heymann Jolowicz, the *Prediger* in Marienwerder (*Der Israelit*, 1843, nos. 28–30).

124. JNUL, 4° 792/C-1.

125. CAHJP, P 2/55 B. Rubo's own views are more fully presented in his *Die Rechtsverhältnisse der jüdischen Gemeinden*, Berlin 1844, pp. 56–81. This learned tract was likewise prompted by the government's request for information on the religious affairs of the Jewish community.

126. DZAM, *Geheimes Zivilkabinett*, 2.2.1. Nr. 23681.

127. *Ibid.*, p. 93. Copy in JNUL, 4° 792 D-24a.

128. JNUL, 4° 792/D-24a.

129. The final version read: "The commission should . . . consist of nine religious functionaries or other men of the Jewish faith who enjoy the confidence of the Jewish community (*Judenschaft*) to which they belong (*AZJ*, XI [1847], p. 424). As far as I know, this commission was never activated. Contemporaries were not unaware of the influential role played by Muhr, Rubo, and Zunz (*Der Orient*, 1847, pp. 370–371).

130. See the illuminating correspondence between the boards of Berlin, Breslau, and Königsberg published by Hermann Vogelstein, "Zur Vorgeschichte des Gesetzes . . . vom 23. Juli 1847," *Zwei und vierzigster Bericht über den Religions-Unterricht der Synagogengemeinde zu Königsberg in Pr. für das Schuljahr 1908/1909*, Königsberg n.d., pp. 3–28. The quotation comes from a letter dated 14th June 1842 by the Königsberg board to its Berlin counterpart, p. 16. In contrast, Berlin and Veit firmly believed that the

rabbi should be a member of the board. (See Veit's extensive *Gutachten* on the government's draft in CAHJP, P 2/V 55 B.)

131. Theodore Zeldin, *France 1848–1945*, 2 vols., Oxford 1973–1977, II, p. 320.

132. Friedrich Paulsen, "Die deutsche Universität als Unterrichtsanstalt und als Werkstatte der wissenschaftlichen Forschung," *Gesammelte Pädagogische Abhandlungen*, Stuttgart–Berlin 1912, pp. 151–188.

133. Richarz, *op. cit.*, p. 93.

134. Bigler, *op. cit.*, p. 53; Paulsen, *The German Universities*, p. 336.

135. Richarz, *op. cit.*, p. 191.

136. Zeldin, *op. cit.*, II, pp. 316–345.

137. Paulsen, *The German Universities*, p. 48; Zeldin, *op. cit.*, II, pp. 994–1004.

138. This list was compiled from the primary sources and secondary literature on which this essay is based. I regret the lacunae that remain. My sources were not quite as obliging as I would have liked.

~ 3

The Religious Parameters of *Wissenschaft:* Jewish Academics at Prussian Universities

Jewish emancipation is a classic case of secularization. The revolutionary decision to abandon an entrenched policy of segregation for integration signaled a determination to resolve the question of Jewish status free of religious constraints. It bespoke the courage to fly in the face of a millennial Christian tradition which had progressively relegated the locus of Jewish existence to the periphery of society as separate and unequal. To invite Jews to enter society as equals meant to remove one more issue of public policy from church domination.[1]

But as an isolated measure emancipation was doomed to fail. It required the backing of a state prepared to restrict the institutional power of Christianity on a wide front. For what emancipation needed above all else was a social matrix in which religion had been neutralized. As long as religious interests retained the political capacity to shape policy in major sectors of society, Jews stood little chance of gaining legal equality or social integration. Long before Bruno Bauer concluded in 1842 that Jewish emancipation was unattainable in a state still dominated by Christianity, Moses Mendelssohn had foreseen that integrating Jews was predicated on transforming religion into a private matter. It was this realization which prompted him to devote the first half of his emancipation tract *Jerusalem* to an elaborate theoretical argument for removing religion from the public arena.[2]

The zigzag course of emancipation in Prussia and Germany down to 1914 amply confirms Mendelssohn's political sagacity. Its piecemeal extension and administrative subversion testify to the sad fact that governments eager to shore up their eroding position with the romantic ideology of the Christian state were singularly ill-equipped to carry out a Jewish policy inherently secular.

The self-contradictory nature of Prussian policy on Jews in the first half of the nineteenth century is especially manifest in the question of university employment. The liberal spirit which informed the famous emancipation edict of 1812 had, among many innovations, also declared Jews eligible for academic posts, a measure in full accord with the new secular ethos of *Wissenschaft* as embodied two years earlier in the University of Berlin. Unlike older surviving universities, its statutes enunciated no religious requirements for those invited to join its faculties. Similarly the statutes of the new interdenominational (*paritätische*) University of Breslau, which like those of Berlin were issued in 1816, stipulated no general religious conditions for its teaching personnel, though they did contain instructions to maintain a Catholic and Evangelical theology faculty as well as to appoint both a Catholic and Evangelical professor of philosophy.[3] At least in theory then, the revitalized Prussian university was to integrate a broad conception of scholarship with participatory learning in an atmosphere free of denominationalism.

During the ensuing decades, young Jews, often with little formal *Gymnasium* training, streamed into the universities, and most faculties of medicine and philosophy quickly divested commencement exercises of their religious character to award degrees to Jewish students. In consequence, by mid-century the percentage of Jews in German universities was already twice that of their percentage in the general population.[4] What often frustrated the upward mobility of Jewish graduates in Prussia and elsewhere was the absence of career opportunities in the public sector. Even the edict of 1812 had preferred to restrict state employment of Jews for the time being to the field of education, which below the university level, of course, was still conducted wholly along confessional lines and hence effectively closed to Jews.[5]

Thus when King Friedrich Wilhelm III personally decided on 18th August 1822 to deny Eduard Gans, the brilliant disciple of Hegel and intimate friend of Leopold Zunz, an appointment as associate professor of law, the last portal to the public sector was sealed. The promise of academic appointments to Jews, he stated cryptically, could not be effected "without great disruption" and should be withdrawn.[6]

In 1826 the ministry of education informed all Prussian universities that the King's decision applied even to the lowest rung of the academic ladder, the unsalaried position of instructor (*Privatdozent*), although that rank did not technically constitute a government appointment. The occasion was an inquiry from the Berlin philosophy faculty regarding Marcus Leo Frankenheim whom it had promoted in 1823. The faculty was now prepared to appoint him as an instructor in physics and mathematics, provided the step did not conflict with the spirit of the royal cabinet order of 18th August. The answer was unequivocal: "as long as he professes the Jewish religion, he may not be admitted to habilitate as an instructor."[7] The unrelenting enforcement of that policy for the next two decades prompted one contemporary to quip that in Prussia Jews were not even allowed to starve as *Privatdozenten*.[8]

The government, however, did unhappily allow the Academy of Sciences in 1842 to elect is first Jewish member since Mendelssohn to its section of physics and mathematics, a Dr. Riess, whose father was a Berlin banker. Although that honor carried with it the right to deliver lectures at the universities of Bonn and Berlin, thereby colliding with current policy, Eichhorn, the autocratic minister of education, felt quite certain that Riess had no intention of doing so. More important, in urging the King's approval, Eichhorn drew a basic distinction. Whereas religion was of little consequence for the Academy whose members engaged mainly in research in the natural sciences, it remained a prerequisite for the proper training of young men for a career in state service or in the church, which continued to be the primary function of university professors.[9] In sum, as long as that traditional view of the university prevailed, Jews could not advance beyond the level of students.

The issue was reopened by the government itself in 1847 as part of the new comprehensive Jewry law intended to complete, albeit in a restricted sense, the work of 1812.[10] The controversy set off by this issue alone deserves separate study because it illuminates such a broad horizon: the bureaucratic style of Prussian absolutism, the anti-Jewish animus of the professoriate, the Christian tone of the Prussian university and the religious parameters of its *Wissenschaft*.

The original impetus to reconsider Jewish suitability for academic office came paradoxically from no less a source than King Friedrich Wilhelm IV. An adherent of Karl Ludwig von Haller, the formidable theoretician of the medieval patrimonial state, the King came to the throne determined to hold the swelling forces of liberalism at bay by reinvigorating the alliance between throne and altar. Public life would be restored to a Christian foundation and Jews returned to a corporate status on the edge of Christian society.[11] Nevertheless, in reactivating the machinery to prepare a uniform Jewry law for the entire realm in 1841, he expressed a willingness to accord Jews a measure of reward for their academic achievements. Specifically, he raised the possibility of admitting them to the faculties of medicine and philosophy.[12] The royal cabinet (*Staatsministerium*) was less than enthusiastic with the idea. By a six-to-five vote it accepted the principle of admitting Jews to academic office.[13] What eventually emerged from the laborious and protracted preparation of the draft of the Jewry law was an elliptic concession hedged with restrictions. In those universities which by statute did not insist on religious qualifications, Jews could serve as instructors and associate professors in the fields of mathematics, science, and medicine.[14]

In the course of presenting the final draft for consultation in June 1847 to the United Diet, Prussia's first half-hearted stab at representative rule, the government spelled out the implications and rationale of this concession. The function of the university was not to transmit bare facts but to nurture spiritual growth. It enshrined the cultural treasures of a national life permeated by Christianity. Accordingly, four types of limitations were built into the text. First, no university would be compelled to violate its own statutes. The law would constitute no more than a recommendation. In fact, the government was fairly certain that of the six universities operating in Prussia, only the statutes of Berlin did not preclude employing Jews. Second, faculties of law and theology were not under discussion, since their subject matter self-evidently disqualified Jews. They could not teach church law, which the doctorate of jurisprudence included, nor even German law, which sprang from Christian roots, for genuine understanding was a function of spiritual kinship as well as intellect. Third, within the faculty of philosophy, Jews could not be entrusted with teaching classics, history, or philosophy, subjects whose ultimate meaning could be grasped only from a Christian point of view. Finally, Jews were still barred from the rank of professor in order to deny them access to the positions of dean or rector in which they would exercise authority over Christians. Just in case anyone thought otherwise, the draft reiterated explicitly that the rest of the educational system would continue to remain inaccessible to Jews. In essence, what was being offered amounted to an empty gesture, signifying neither a viable career option for aspiring Jewish scholars nor the slightest compromise of the Christian character of the Prussian educational system.[15]

In their deliberations on the provisions of this paragraph, both curiae of Prussia's first "*Reichstag*" found them too restrictive.[16] The conservative upper house of lords, while respecting existing university statutes, proposed to allow Jews also to teach philology and to attain the rank of full professor.[17] In contrast, the rebellious lower house led by *Landrat* Georg von Vincke of Westphalia and the Rhenish manufacturer and intellectual Gustav Mevissen, both of whom had previously advocated the extension of full emancipation, took the position that Jews be granted the right to teach all disciplines, except those which presupposed adherence to Christianity, and to fill all academic posts from instructor to rector. Mevissen, a self-educated Hegelian and co-founder of the radical *Rheinische Zeitung,* denounced the government for betraying Germany's greatest achievement in the modern era: the freeing of *Wissenschaft* from the tyranny of religious dogmatism: "Free scholarship exists only when it tosses aside all restraints, all presuppositions in its research, when it recognizes as correct and true only that which it has found by way of free inquiry."[18] Equally defiant was the lower house's unexpected vote to establish a chair for Jewish theology at a Prussian university. According Judaism its legitimate place in the cosmopolitan world of *Wissenschaft* would redound to the benefit of both.[19]

The stage was now set for one of the more bizarre episodes in the long and tortuous history of the Prussian bureaucracy. On 9th July 1847, several weeks before the actual promulgation of the new Jewry law in a version which did incorporate many of the modifications suggested by the more trustworthy upper house of the Diet, the senate and rector of the University of Berlin rushed off an apprehensive petition to the minister of education. The restrictive nature of university statutes throughout Prussia threatened to transform the magnanimous grant of university employment to Jews into a piece of special legislation pertaining only to Berlin. Since its statutes alone did not preclude hiring Jews *de jure,* Berlin would soon be overrun by young Jews bent on a career in the one public sector open to them. The consequences would aggravate an already troublesome situation. A falling enrollment coupled with an inflated teaching corps had reduced the student–teacher ratio to an all-time low of 8:1. That ratio, implied the petition, cut deeply into the faculty fees so vital to augmenting the inadequate salaries paid by the government. Moreover, Berlin would be denied the training benefits fostered by the mobility built into the *Privatdozent* system. It would become host to a growing number of Jewish instructors unable to teach elsewhere and with little prospect of advancement in Berlin. The time had come to raise the practice of *Wissenschaft* above the confines of religious parochialism. Certainly the University of Berlin, contended the senate, had nothing to regret in having adhered to that principle by appointing worthy Catholic scholars. Specifically, the senate called on Eichhorn to bring all university statutes into harmony with the intent of the new law.[20]

Indeed, the decision to open the academic market even partially to Jewish applicants could not have come at a more inopportune time. Prussian universities were still reeling from the sudden drop in student attendance which struck in the mid-1830s after nearly two decades of exhilarating growth. From 1829 to 1838 the total student population fell from 6,154 to 4,480.[21] In the winter semester of 1833–1834 student attendance at Berlin peaked at 2,001, a figure not attained again until the winter of 1862–1863.[22] By the summer of 1847, the number of matriculated students at Berlin had declined to 1,378[23] Hardest hit were the faculties of law and theology which soon began to lose their numerical advantage. The fate of theology at Berlin was typical, declining from an enrollment of 641 students in the winter of 1830–1831 to 214 in the summer semester of 1847.[24] Unable to absorb the graduates of these faculties in the crowded and unexpanding field of state service, the government took a variety of steps to curtail the overproduction of an academic proletariat.[25]

The inevitable consequence was an excess of university teachers even in the more stable faculties of medicine and philosophy. As early as 1843 the Berlin senate had vigorously protested to Eichhorn over the harmful results. It pleaded at that time to be consulted about future appointments, as it had not been in the past, and proposed to stiffen the qualifications for the rank of instructor. Still more radical was the suggestion to introduce a "numerus clausus" governing the number of instructors in each faculty. Eichhorn's agreement to the first two requests temporarily improved the stormy relations between the minister and the university.[26] Four years later the prospect of opening a tight market to Jewish competition threatened to aggravate a chronic condition.

Nevertheless, Eichhorn chose to react to the Berlin petition of 1847 with uncharacteristic restraint. He simply ignored its appeal for firm government intervention. Instead he handled the paragraph in question as a recommendation and proceeded to solicit the opinion of the entire academic establishment on two questions: to what extent did the statutes of one's university accord with the provisions of the new Jewry law, and, if not, was it advisable to change them? Eichhorn felt that the importance of the subject warranted a three-tier response from each university: first the individual opinion of each full professor, then the collective opinion of each faculty and finally the collective opinion of the senate. Thus, during the autumn and winter months of 1847–1848, the entire upper echelon of the Prussian professoriate was compelled to set aside time to formulating its views on Jews and Judaism, the university and *Wissenschaft*. [27] Ironically, a law intended to end the panoply of conflicting regulations pertaining to Jewish status throughout the country was so worded as to preserve that confusion in university life.

The government's own deep-seated ambivalence on the wisdom of allowing Jews to teach prompted an extraordinary display of diffidence toward an institution it generally dominated. Friedrich Wilhelm IV's campaign against "atheistic" Hegelianism had repeatedly violated the academic freedom of the university. In March 1842 Eichhorn revoked the right of Bruno Bauer to teach as an instructor in the Protestant theological faculty of Bonn after the talented but temperamental scholar had produced the first part of a Hegelian study repudiating the synoptic Gospels as valid evidence for the historical Jesus. Prior to the dismissal, Eichhorn had requested, for the first time ever, the written opinion of all six Protestant theological faculties in Prussia and then promptly ignored the results, which favored not removing Bauer by a margin of sixteen to eleven. Still more ominous for the survival of academic freedom was the prescription to all Protestant theological faculties which followed. Eichhorn reminded them of their primary responsibility to train pastors, and therefore the eternal truths of the Lutheran Church would define the boundaries of their research and teaching. [28] Bauer supplied the epitaph: "Precisely there where the labor of investigation is warranted, research is forbidden. Only in peripheral and unessential subjects is it permitted. The prisoner may stroll around in his prison; but the very idea that he might be in prison is prohibited." [29]

A few months later Eichhorn turned his fire on Hoffmann von Fallersleben. A full professor of German language and literature at Breslau since 1835, Hoffmann was summarily dismissed without pension for the political intent of his artless verse. In 1844, Karl Nauwerck, a *Privatdozent* in Berlin's philosophy faculty, met the same fate for his unwelcome political views, despite the strenuous effort of his colleagues to defend him. [30] Finally, mention should be made of Karl Schwarz, a young erstwhile Hegelian, who was suspended by Eichhorn from the theology faculty of Halle in February 1846 for speaking at a meeting of Protestant Friends in Halle and espousing the right to study the Bible without theological preconceptions. [31] In light of this record, respect for the academic integrity of the university was a sentiment in which the government indulged only when indifferent or uncertain.

The unprecedented inquiry on Jews as academics generated nearly 280 separate opinions, many of considerable length. Largely unpublished, this body of material represents a unique if unwieldy treasure-trove of attitudes on Jews and Judaism held by the most educated of all Prussian élites. [32] Mostly men of humble origin who were the first to benefit when talent became the key to an academic career, they were now asked whether that same criterion should be extended to the members of another disadvantaged group.[33] Beyond pique and prejudice stood the basic issues of the nature of *Wissenschaft* and the function of the university, topics that could hardly be treated without relating to the political philosophy of the government. Professors must have realized all too well that the survey gave the ministry of education a superb opportunity for scanning their political views. Consequently, it is hard to judge how many must have been cowed into muting or concealing their genuine feelings. Nor was the audience for which they wrote exactly passive. The unduly liberal views expressed by most members of Breslau's Lutheran theology faculty evoked a prompt inquiry by Eichhorn. He was quickly reassured that by the time the vote had reached the senate, several men had reconsidered.[34]

Nor was there any mistaking the government's political philosophy, for immediately after the deliberations of the Diet on the Jewry law, Friedrich Julius Stahl, its premier ideological apostle, published a series of essays in the *Evangelische Kirchenzeitung* expounding the conception of the Christian state and its relation to deism and Judaism. Reissued as a book, the text was referred to by several respondents.[35] Against the inroads of atheistic individualism from across the French border, Stahl defended the traditional political culture in which the ethos of biblical Christianity sanctified and guided the existing monarchical and corporate structures. State institutions were to manifest their Christian character, and political rights as opposed to civil rights could be extended only to believers. To call for a chair of Jewish theology was to request the state to disseminate religious error. Jews were thus disqualified from full participation on principle, not prejudice. The farrago that passed for Reform Judaism was neither tenable nor acceptable. Assimilation and conversion were the only road to equality. Till then, the only state service open to them would be as university teachers of indisputably non-Christian subjects. Like Prussian Jewry, the humanities remained unemancipated.[36]

In order to quantify the cumbersome results of Eichhorn's survey it is necessary to translate the original two-fold question, which delicately focused on the statutes of the university, into the unambiguous question whether Jews should be admitted according to the modest terms of the new law; that is, as instructors, associate, and full professors in the fields of medicine, mathematics, natural science, geography, and philology?[37] Since the government knew precisely the contents of all university statutes—in fact they had been published just a few years before in an exhaustive collection of statutes and regulations pertaining to the conduct of Prussian universities—the first question was substantively gratuitous.[38] Functionally, however, it gave many a chance to objectify and obscure their personal opposition by interpreting the statutes negatively. As Planck of Greifswald's legal faculty astutely observed, form and content were inseparable: ". . . if one finally wants progress in the matter, the form can no longer stand in its way, just as the introduction of a new law cannot be impeded by the existence of an older, contradictory one."[39] But judgment is called for in yet another way. Quite a few opinions, while espousing noble sentiments, were hedged with so many qualifications and preconditions that they amounted to a negative vote. For example, the senate of Greifswald conceded that its statutes did not explicitly exclude Jews. Nor was it necessary that every teacher be Christian in order to preserve the Christian character of the university. Yet by insisting that for every discipline in which a Jew be appointed, a Christian should be too, thereby guaranteeing students a choice, the senate actually answered the question negatively.[40] In short, my statistical analysis rests inescapably on a subjective though not arbitrary base.

In 1847 Prussia had six universities located in Berlin, Bonn, Breslau, Greifswald, Halle and Königsberg, and a Catholic academy in Münster with but two faculties, altogether a total of twenty-eight faculties. In terms of individual professors, 141 voted in favor of accepting Jews as colleagues, while 102, or 44 percent of those voting, came out against. Broken down by universities, the individual vote favored Jews at Berlin (47–15), Bonn (30–9), Greifswald (16–9), and Königsberg (19–9) but not at Breslau (18–21), Halle (11—29) or Münster (0–10). In terms of the collective vote of faculties, eleven favored admitting Jews, while fourteen, or 50 percent of all Prussian faculties, rejected the idea. Three faculties split. Broken down by disciplines, the negative vote consisted of all three Catholic theological faculties, three Lutheran, four legal, two medical, and two philosophical faculties. Conversely, three Lutheran, one legal, two medical, and five philosophical faculties voted to accept Jews. Finally, at the senate level, only Berlin, Bonn, and Königsberg stood ready to live with the new law, while the senates of Breslau, Greifswald, Halle, and Münster were not.[41]

The outcome can hardly be called a resounding vote of approval for the government's modest proposal, or for that matter for the principle of unfettered objective scholarship. With legal faculties tending to vote against and philosophical faculties in favor, a conflicted professoriate emerged even more conservative than the government. The unqualified stance of Cruse, of Königsberg's medical faculty, found only muted resonance among his colleagues: "In no religion, no country, no estate are outstanding minds so numerous as to make it possible to value faith, nationality, and estate when it comes to advancing scholarship and to disseminating it for the good of mankind."[42] Of course, many who favored the government's move were spared the need to expound their personal views. Their assignment was over when they took the position that the statutes of their university posed no obstacle.

In terms of a content analysis, it is possible to identify a medley of arguments brought forth in favor. First, the presence of a few Jews will not endanger the Christian character of the university.[43] Second, the step will serve to reduce the differences dividing a heterogeneous population.[44] Third, the history of Jewish suffering warrants compassion and Christian amends.[45] Fourth, the degree of assimilation generated by partial emancipation confirms the belief that Jewish defects were externally induced.[46] Fifth, the opportunity will help divert Jews from business.[47] Sixth, Jews have the talent to contribute; witness their achievements in Spain and the accomplishments of Spinoza and Mendelssohn.[48] Seventh, the law will reduce the career frustrations which drive bright young Jews to the left.[49] Eighth, no one should be disadvantaged because of his religion.[50] And finally, *Wissenschaft* itself must be emancipated from religion.[51] What did unite many government supporters with their colleagues on the other side, however, was a robust antipathy for Jews and Judaism and a conviction that their mutual disappearance must be the ultimate consequence of emancipation.[52]

The arguments against implementation were usually delivered with more passion and at greater length. They are noteworthy not for their originality but for their advocates.[53] The evidence accords with the unbroken history of antisemitism in modern Germany: education had little impact on prejudice. To begin with, the policy of piecemeal emancipation itself provided a convenient dodge. Legal faculties refused to countenance Jews teaching in their ranks as long as they were denied access to state service in general and the judiciary in particular.[54] Conversely, Protestant universities like Halle, whose statutes required that professors adhere to the Augsburg Confession, preferred to delay action until the effect of the new law on other universities became apparent.[55] Also widespread was the revulsion aroused by the perception of Jews as a hermetically insulated, tenaciously egoistic and unalterably alien nation.[56] This specter drove some despondent critics to advocate complete emancipation as the only remedy.[57]

Whatever Jews did opened them to attack. The orthodox were abused for subservience to the Talmud with its anti-Christian animus, degenerate morality, and obsessive ritualism.[58] The enlightened were deemed as dangerous atheists, men without character who dominated the press, polemicized against Christianity, and led the destructive movements of the day.[59]

Throughout these sundry objections against appointing Jews reverberated the conception of the university as a *corpus ecclesiasticum* whose ethical and scholarly message could be mediated only in a Christian atmosphere. Learning took place only when student and teacher shared the same religion, and the pursuit of knowledge required a Christian disposition.[60]

Yet the Prussian university was less Christian than Protestant, for Catholics were almost as disadvantaged as Jews. Of the seven Catholic universities (Trier, Bonn, Köln, Münster, Paderborn, Erfurt, and Breslau) operating at the end of the eighteenth century on land now belonging to Prussia, only a truncated Münster with faculties of theology and philosophy remained a Catholic institution.[61] Outside the Catholic theological faculties, Bonn and Breslau were hardly interdenominational. In 1842 the philosophy faculty at Bonn had a staff of nineteen full professors; exactly one was a Catholic. History, philosophy, Oriental languages, and philology were taught exclusively by Protestants.[62] At Berlin, Franz Bopp, who pioneered the comparative study of Sanskrit, was one of the few Catholic professors.[63] From Königsberg and Halle, Catholics were excluded by statute and from Greifswald until the 1840s by practice.[64] Shortly before Eichhorn's poll of the professoriate, the senate of Königsberg had dismissed a *Privatdozent* for joining the ranks of the German Catholic movement.[65]

This pervasive exclusion of Catholics complicated the Jewish issue in two ways. Some professors at Halle and Königsberg were horrified by the idea of opening their ranks to Jews while still excluding Catholics and insisted that both be admitted simultaneously.[66] But that meant entangling the Jewish proposal in a web of other animosities. On the other hand, Catholic professors, in addition to giving vivid expression to a traditional abhorrence of Judaism, feared that Jewish advances would come at their expense. One informed Catholic theologian at Breslau claimed that the ratio of Protestant to Catholic academics in Prussia was 10:1, whereas the ratio in the population stood at 3:2. Thus if the exclusivist statutes of other universities were allowed to stand, Jews would be appointed only at the inter-denominational schools, thereby eroding the Catholic position still further. The total number of Catholic *Privatdozenten* at Prussia's six universities did not exceed the number at Münster or Trier at the turn of the century.[67]

But Protestant professors feared the specter of Jewish competition no less than their Catholic colleagues. Certain code words recurred throughout the opinions. The moral indictment of Jewish egotism, arrogance, vanity, drive, industry, and pushiness masked economic anxiety.[68] In particular, the large Jewish population in Breslau and Silesia unnerved many academics at the provincial university there.[69] In 1840 the philosophy faculty had reinstituted a Christian oath prior to awarding the doctorate in order to reduce its Jewish enrollment.[70] In the medical faculty Jews constituted some 60 percent of the student population and Jews dominated the medical profession in Breslau.[71] In his statement the rector of the university, who personally favored implementing the provisions of the Jewry law, summarized the concern which prompted the majority of his men to vote against the government. The talent, wealth, and communal backing which Jewish academics enjoyed would quickly lead to a disruption of the harmony which prevailed in the faculties of medicine and philosophy.[72] It is quite clear that the response from Breslau betrayed the mentality of a guild. In less than half a century the opponents of emancipation had been forced by the pace of Jewish assimilation to switch their arguments from inferiority to superiority.

In sum, the survey of 1847 revealed the Prussian professoriate to be as ambivalent about Jewish emancipation as the rest of Prussian society. The mixed results suggest no widespread challenge to the cautious and equivocal approach set down by the government, with a sizable preference for even greater caution. Axiomatic to the entire discussion were the convictions that the university was a Christian institution and *Wissenschaft* a Christian enterprise. Jewish participation was by sufferance, not principle.

Events overtook the cumbersome review process even before the last of the opinions was submitted. By the time the rector and senate of Bonn convened on 4th April 1848 to formulate their views, Berlin was host to its first revolution, the King had withdrawn to Potsdam, recalled the United Diet, and was about to issue some liberal guidelines for a future constitution. Paragraph five of the proclamation of 6th April promised that political rights would no longer be restricted by religious considerations.[73] The Gordian knot had been cut. Not only were universities no longer closed to Jewish academics, the emancipation struggle itself seemed over. In July the ministry of education circulated a rescript to the effect that Jews henceforth were eligible for all academic posts except those which necessitated a Christian occupant.[74]

The appointment of three Jews as instructors during the same period of time seemed to confirm that law indeed governed reality. In October 1847, Berlin's medical faculty welcomed Robert Remak, a scientific polymath, who had been turned down four years earlier. In 1848 Jacob Bernays, a classical philologist, habilitated at Bonn and Joseph Saalschütz, a rabbi and Orientalist, did likewise at Königsberg, both in the faculty of philosophy.[75]

Yet once the regime had weathered the revolution, law and reality were quickly forced apart. In 1850 the legal faculties of Breslau and Berlin reiterated the longstanding objections to awarding a doctorate in jurisprudence to a Jew. The degree certified not only academic mastery of both civil and church law, but also moral commitment and spiritual kinship. To confer the doctorate on Jews would be to de-Christianize the discipline. Civil servants represented merely the external dignity of the state, but the doctor of law embodied the inner dignity of the secular and religious legal systems.[76]

An equally specious distinction was made by the ministerial cabinet at its meeting of 9th September 1851. It acknowledged that the royal proclamation of 6th April 1848 assured Jews of the opportunity to prepare themselves adequately for state service. But having demonstrated competence by passing a state examination gave them no right to any specific state job. The decision to appoint or reject an applicant lay entirely within the jurisdiction of the department chief, who of course was to assess qualifications irrespective of religion. That logical legerdemain would be invoked by Prussian officials well into the twentieth century in order to restrict the number of Jews entering state service to a trickle.[77]

As for academic employment, the fate of Jacob Bernays provides a poignant dénouement. The son of the orthodox if modern rabbi of Hamburg, Bernays was acknowledged to be among the most promising young classicists in all Germany. Immediately after having earned his doctorate at Bonn in 1848, he was invited by the faculty of philosophy to become an instructor, counter to its own regulations which required at least a two-year interval. During the next four years the faculty interceded annually with the government on his behalf for a special subvention to mitigate his poverty. The quality of his scholarship so impressed England's leading classicist that Oxford University invited him to prepare a new edition of Lucretius with a Latin commentary. By 1852 Bernays's meteoric career forced an inescapable test of the government's intention to abide by the provisions of the Jewry law of 1847 and the principles of 1848, though the reactionary climate was hardly conducive to a favorable outcome.

Bernays's letters of recommendation for promotion to the rank of associate professor were worthy of his impeccable credentials. One came from the King's longtime friend and ambassador to England, Freiherr Christian K. G. von Bunsen, who had been Bernays's host in London in 1851, and the other from Christian A. Brandis, his teacher and colleague at Bonn. Both men knew Bernays intimately and praised his piety and character as well as his scholarship. They stressed his religious orthodoxy, his respect for and knowledge of Christianity, his abhorrence of shallow rationalism, and his political conservatism.[78]

Unable to avoid a decision, the King turned in April 1852 to his minister of education, Karl Otto von Raumer, for counsel. By the end of June, Raumer obliged with a reasoned negative response. To his credit, he averred and recounted Bernays's ample qualifications. His objections rested on other grounds. With three full and two associate professors, the field of classical philology at Bonn was already crowded. More fundamental, however, Raumer argued for the Christian character of the Prussian university. If not explicitly expressed in the university's statutes, the relationship was always spelled out in its ancient documents of incorporation, and the mission of every university as a training ground for civil servants for church and state certainly implied it. The primary function of the classical philologist was to train the teachers of Prussia's Gymnasia. On both levels of education classical literature had to be Christianized by teaching it in such a way as not to undermine the Christian value system and thought patterns of the young. To assign that responsibility to a Jew was a dereliction of duty.[79] Denied promotion, Bernays went off reluctantly to Breslau to join the faculty of Zacharias Frankel's recently opened rabbinical seminary, a tiny haven for a handful of frustrated Jewish academics.[80]

With Raumer's policy statement we have come full circle. Though major consumers of *Wissenschaft*, Jews were denied the chance to become its producers and purveyors. Decades later, when academic employment did become available on a restricted basis, Jews were still systematically excluded throughout Germany from the rank of full professor and from the fields of law, literature, history, philosophy, classics, and Oriental studies.[81] The university as the apex of the educational system could not transcend its pervasive confessional character, and as a state institution it was often shackled by governments intent on exploiting religion to bolster their authority. In consequence, German governments repeatedly promised Jews in law what they would not deliver in practice and duplicity became normative. The duplicity which eventually facilitated the Nazi execution of the "Final Solution" had ample precedent in the history of the German bureaucracy's treatment of Jews. More basic, the continued centrality of religion in public life proved a potent factor in subverting emancipation and preserving the problematic status of Jews.

NOTES

1. The conception of secularization which informs this paragraph derives from Peter S. Berger, *The Sacred Canopy,* Anchor Books Edition, Garden City 1969, p. 107.

2. Moses Mendelssohn, *Jerusalem: oder über religiöse Macht und Judenthum,* Frankfurt am Main–Leipzig, 1787. For Bauer's views see his *Die Judenfrage,* Braunschweig 1843, pp. 19–20, 59–62.

3. Ismar Freund, *Die Emanzipation der Juden in Preussen,* 2 vols., Berlin 1912, II, p. 456. The statutes of Berlin and Breslau were printed in Johann F. W. Koch, *Die Preussischen Universitäten,* 2 vols., Berlin–Posen–Bromberg 1839–1840, I, pp. 41 ff. and pp. 318 ff. Although Bonn was founded in 1818 during the tail end of the liberal era, its statutes were not issued until 1827. Not surprisingly, therefore, they stress to a much greater extent than those of Berlin and Breslau the religious mission of the university and the connection of the Lutheran faculty to the church (Koch, *op. cit.,* I, pp. 190–191, 219–220).

4. Monika Richarz, *Der Eintritt der Juden in die akademischen Berufe: Jüdische Studenten und Akademiker in Deutschland 1678–1848,* Tübingen 1974 (Schriftenreihe wissenschaftlicher Abhandlungen des Leo Baeck Instituts 28), p. 93.

5. Freund, *op. cit.,* II, p. 456.

6. A copy of the King's order to Chancellor Hardenberg, Gans's benefactor, may be found in CAHJP, P 17/634. The decisive German phrase reads: "nicht ohne grosse Missverhältnisse zu veranlassen." On the episode see Hanns Günther Reissner, *Eduard Gans: Ein Leben im Vormärz,* Tübingen 1965 (Schriftenreihe wissenschaftlicher Abhandlungen des Leo Baeck Instituts 14), pp. 91–93. The phrase quoted by Reissner (p. 92) actually comes from the proclamation by the *Königliches Geheimes Staatsministerium* on 4th December 1822 and not the King's order of 18th August. The text of the proclamation was published by M. Kalisch, *Die Judenfrage,* Leipzig 1860, pp. 3–4.

7. The documents were published by Kalisch, pp. 4–5. Frankenheim was the first Jew to earn a doctorate from Berlin's philosophy faculty. By 1827 he had converted to Christianity, a step which eventually paid off in an associate professorship in mathematics at Breslau. (Richarz, *op. cit.,* p. 99, n. 40; Nahum N. Glatzer, *Leopold and Adelheid Zunz: An Account in Letters 1815–1885,* London 1958. Publication of the Leo Baeck Institute, p. 53; Heinrich Wuttke, ed., *Jahrbuch der deutschen Universitäten,* I, Leipzig 1842, p. 82.)

8. Richarz, *op. cit.,* pp. 210–211. On the plight of Prussia's *Privatdozenten,* see Erich G. C. Hahn, "The Junior Faculty in 'Revolt': Reform Plans for Berlin University in 1848," *The American Historical Review,* vol. 82 (1977), pp. 875–895.

9. The relevant documents were published by Kalisch, *op. cit.,* pp. 5–10.

10. The best treatment of the involved and protracted drafting of the Jewry law is by Horst Fischer, *Judentum, Staat und Heer in Preussen im frühen 19. Jahrhundert: Zur Geschichte der staatlichen Judenpolitik,* Tübingen 1968 (Schriftenreihe wissenschaftlicher Abhandlungen des Leo Baeck Instituts 20), pp. 151–190.

11. Ernst Rudolph Huber, *Deutsche Verfassungsgeschichte seit 1789,* 4 vols., Stuttgart 1957–1969, II, pp. 256–257; Fischer, *op. cit.,* pp. 151–157.

12. DZAM, *Geheimes Zivilkabinett*, 2.2.1, Nr. 23680.

13. DZAM, Rep. 90a, BIII2b, Nr. 6, Bd. 55.

14. The draft submitted by the government to the United Diet was printed at the beginning of *Vollständige Verhandlungen des ersten Vereinigten Preussischen Landtages über die Emancipationsfrage der Juden*, Berlin 1847, pp. i–x. Paragraph 35 included stipulations regarding university teaching (pp. v–vi).

15. *Ibid.*, pp. xxxvii–xxxix, 98–99, 328–333.

16. The designation "Reichstag" is applied by Reinhart Koselleck, *Preussen zwischen Reform und Revolution*, Stuttgart 1967, pp. 367–368.

17. *Vollständige Verhandlungen*, pp. 110–114.

18. *Ibid.*, p. 341. On Vincke and Mevissen, see their admiring younger contemporary Rudolf Haym, *Reden und Redner des ersten Vereinigten Preussischen Landtags*, Berlin 1847, pp. 55ff. and 225ff. Haym reprinted their addresses on the Jewry law (pp. 132–143, 253–259).

19. *Vollständige Verhandlungen*, p. 343. Ludwig Geiger's doubts as to whether a vote in plenum was ever taken on this proposal derived from a careless reading of the protocols. The text is unambiguous. (Ludwig Geiger, "Zunz im Verkehr mit Behorden und Hochgestellten," *Monatsschrift für Geschichte und Wissenschaft des Judentums*, vol. LX [1916], p. 334.)

20. Published by Kalisch, *op. cit.*, pp. 66–71.

21. Koselleck, *op. cit.*, p. 440, n. 174.

22. Max Lenz, *Geschichte der Königlichen Friedrich-Wilhelms-Universität zu Berlin*, 4 vols., Halle 1910–1918, II, pt. 1, p. 406.

23. Kalisch, *op. cit.*, p. 67.

24. Lenz, *op. cit.*, II, pt. 2, p. 105.

25. On the overproduction of university graduates, see Koselleck, *op. cit.*, pp. 438–440 and Lenore O'Boyle, "The Problem of an Excess of Educated Men in Western Europe, 1800–1850," *Journal of Modern History*, vol. XLII (1970), pp. 471–478.

26. Lenz, *op. cit.*, II, pt. 2, pp. 71–73.

27. Kalisch, *op. cit.*, p. 71–74.

28. Ernst Barnikol, *Bruno Bauer: Studien und Materialien*, Assen, Niederlande 1972, pp. 150, 157, 500–502. The entire episode was exhaustively studied by Barnikol, cf. pp. 136ff.

29. Bruno Bauer, *Die gute Sache der Freiheit*, Zurich–Winterthur 1842, p. 11. To counter public anger at Bauer's removal and to reaffirm the principle of free inquiry, the ministry of education permitted the Lutheran theological faculty of Bonn to publish all opinions submitted (Barnikol, *op. cit.*, p. 174–175). See *Gutachten der Evangelisch-theologischen Facultaten*, Berlin 1842.

30. On Hoffmann, see his autobiography, *Mein Leben*, 6 vols., Hannover 1868, IV, pp. 1–35. On Nauwerck, see Lenz, *op. cit.*, II, pt. 2, pp. 77–83.

31. See the exhaustive monograph by Ernst Barnikol, "Karl Schwarz (1812–1885) in Halle vor und nach 1848," *Wissenschaftliche Zeitschrift der Martin-Luther-Universität Halle-Wittenberg*, X (1961), pp. 550–558.

32. An instructive and representative selection was published by Kalisch, *op. cit.*, pp. 84–232. However, the bulk remains buried in the files of the Prussian *Kultusministerium* preserved in Merseburg. My discovery of them in July 1977 provided the impetus for this essay.

33. On the change in the social origins of German scholars in the first half of the nineteenth century, see Franz Schnabel, *Deutsche Geschichte im neunzehnten Jahrhun-*

dert, 4 vols., Freiburg im Breisgau 1933–1937, III, pp. 129–130, and Alexander Busch, *Die Geschichte des Privatdozenten,* Stuttgart 1959, pp. 43–53.

34. Kalisch, *op. cit.,* pp. 192–193.

35. For example, Voigt of Königsberg's philosophical faculty. See DZAM, Rep. 76Va. Sekt. 1, Tit. IV, Gen., Nr. 2a, Bd. II, pp. 66–71.

36. Friedrich Julius Stahl, *Der christliche Staat und sein Verhältniss zu Deismus und Judenthum: Eine durch die Verhandlungen des Vereinigten Landtags hervorgerufene Abhandlung,* Berlin 1847, especially pp. 20–30.

37. The stages in the emergence of the final text are laid out in the *Allgemeine Zeitung des Judentums,* 1847, pp. 443, 510.

38. Kosch, *op. cit.,* I, *passim.*

39. Rep. 76Va, Sekt. 1, Tit. IV, Gen., Nr. 2a, Bd. I, pp. 43–44. Planck was even ready to open the legal faculty to Jewish scholars, for if the study of law required religious affinity, how could Christian savants presume to understand Roman law? (pp. 40–43).

40. Kalisch, *op. cit.,* pp. 154–158.

41. The statistical summary is based on the *Gutachten* published by Kalisch, pp. 84–232 as well as those preserved in the following files in Merseburg: Rep. 76Va, Sekt. 1, Tit., IV, Gen., Nr. 2, Bd. I & II and Rep. 76Va, Sekt. 1, Tit. IV, Gen., Nr. 2a, Bd. I & II. Henceforth, when referring to this material, I will give only the number, volume, and page. Kalisch attempted no statistical analysis and erred in the case of Halle, which he thought refused to submit any *Gutachten.* Contemporary Jewish newspapers carried brief and sporadic, but generally accurate reports of the voting in different faculties and universities. (See *Die Allgemeine Zeitung des Judentums,* 1847, pp. 757, 759; and 1848, pp. 27, 71, 94.) Lenz's slanted discussion of the entire episode is restricted to Berlin (*Op. cit.,* II, pt. 2, pp. 168, 172.)

42. Kalisch, *op. cit.,* p. 199.

43. *Ibid.,* pp. 105–106 (Stahl), 188 (Berlin, phil. fac.). The view of Christian Julius Braniss, a Hegelian philosopher at Breslau and the teacher of Heinrich Graetz and other Jewish students preparing for the rabbinate, deserves special attention. He firmly advocated allowing Jews to teach at Breslau precisely because of his conviction that *Wissenschaft* was an inherently Christian mode of intellectual creativity. No Jew, no matter how distant from the dogmas of a church, could engage in *Wissenschaft* without being transformed by its essentially Christian spirit. (Nr. 2a, Bd. I, p. 275.) On Braniss's possible influence on Graetz, see Hans Liebeschütz, *Das Judentum im deutschen Geschichtsbild von Hegel bis Max Weber,* Tübingen 1967 (Schriftenreihe wissenschaftlicher Abhandlungen des Leo Baeck Instituts 17), pp. 139–140.

44. Kalisch, *op. cit.,* p. 188 (Berlin, phil. fac.); Nr. 2, Bd. I, pp. 196–197 (Königsberg Evang. fac.).

45. Kalisch, *op. cit.,* pp. 183–184; Nr. 2a, Bd. I, pp. 335–336 and Bd. II, pp. 80–81.

46. Nr. 2a, Bd. II, pp. 80–81.

47. Nr. 2a, Bd. II, pp. 129–130 (Christian A. Brandis).

48. Nr. 2a, Bd. I, p. 226 (Heinrich Middeldorpf of Breslau's Evang. fac. See his equally liberal defense of Bruno Bauer in *Gutachten,* pp. 72–77). Also Bd. II, pp. 123–124 (Georg W. Freytag). The favorable opinion of Freytag, the renowned Arabist and teacher of Abraham Geiger, Salomon Munk, Jacob Bernays, and other Jewish students, graphically illustrates the complexity of separating *Wissenschaft* from theology in an institution which served both of these jealous masters. While scholarship could only applaud the advantages to be gained from having Jews teach

Hebrew, Freytag was quick to point out that Christian interests precluded any possibility of allowing them to explicate texts drawn from the Old Testament. Indeed, there was widespread apprehension at the thought of admitting Jews generally into *"sprachwissenschaftliche Lehrfächer,"* because of the perceived inter-relatedness of philology, exegesis and *"Gesinnung."* (Nr. 2a, Bd. I, p. 119.)

49. Kalisch, *op. cit.*, p. 225; Nr. 2, Bd. I, pp. 216–217.

50. Nr. 2a, Bd. II, p. 90.

51. Kalisch, *op. cit.*, pp. 198–199; Nr. 2a, Bd. I, p. 115 and Bd. II, p. 137.

52. Kalisch, *op. cit.*, pp. 99–100; Nr. 2, Bd. I, pp. 196–197, 307; Nr. 2a, Bd. I, pp. 335–347 and Bd. II, pp. 86, 91, 160. The key word regarding ultimate expectations was *Verschmelzung*.

53. The same and similar arguments abound in Eleonore Sterling, *Judenhass: Die Anfange des politischen Antisemitismus in Deutschland (1815–1850)*, Frankfurt am Main 1969.

54. Nr. 2, Bd. I, pp. 109–111, 201–202; Nr. 2a, Bd. I, p. 265; Kalisch, *op. cit.*, p. 91.

55. Nr. 2, Bd. I, pp. 287, 319; Nr. 2a, Bd. I, p. 124.

56. The opinion of Gaupp of Breslau's legal faculty was typical:

Die Juden erscheinen aber nun vor allen Dingen als ein besonderes, durch ein Jahrhunderte lang geschlossenes Connubium nur in sich selbst fortgepflantztes Volk; ein Stückchen Orient was die Vorsehung in alle Länder des Occidents gestreut hat, was aber noch immer den Typus des Orients bewahrt. (Nr. 2a, Bd. I, p. 327.)

His colleague Purkinje of the medical faculty regarded the Jews as a race: "In anthropologischer Hinsicht betrachte ich die Juden als eine selbständige Race . . ." (Kalisch, *op. cit.*, p. 168). See also Nr. 2a, Bd. II, pp. 36, 160.

57. Nr. 2a, Bd. I, p. 265.

58. Nr. 2, Bd. I, pp. 232–234 (Catholic fac. of Bonn), 281; Nr. 2a, Bd. II, pp. 62–71.

59. Kalisch, *op. cit.*, pp. 88 (Neander), 109; Nr. 2, Bd. I, p. 233; Nr. 2a, Bd. I, pp. 35–36, 317–320; Nr. 2a, Bd. II, pp. 62–71, 86.

60. The psychological case was put succinctly by Wilhelm Esser, a professor of philosophy and classical philology at Münster: "Der Mensch lernt am besten von solchen Menschen, zu denen er sich hingezogen fühlt, bezüglich am besten von solchen, die in Ansehung der wichtigsten und heiligsten Dinge mit ihm dieselben Ueberzeugungen theilen." (Nr. 2a, Bd. I, p. 199.) Julius A. S. Wegscheider, Halle's most famous rationalist theologian, did advocate a change in the statutes of his university despite grave reservations: an observant Jew could never carry out the obligations of full membership in a Christian academic body while an irreligious Jew would exert a deleterious influence on students (Nr. 2, Bd. I, p. 281). His conservative colleague, Friedrich A. G. Tholuck, whose vote was negative, felt that no Jew, whatever his ilk, could teach history or philosophy.

Kann ein Jude, ohne sein Judenthum aufzugeben, mit Hegel das Christenthum für den Wendepunkt der Weltgeschichte, mit Schiller für die grösste welthistorische Begebenheit erklären? Und auch diejenigen, welche ihren religiösen Grundsätzen nach verpflichtet sind, das Christenthum nur als eine Verirrung der Menschheit zu betrachten, sollten von einem christlichen Staate als Lehrer der Geschichte und Philosophie angestellt werden können? (Nr. 2, Bd. I, p. 283.)

Georg F. Pohl, a professor of physics at Breslau, was equally adamant about their inability to teach the natural sciences properly.

Es wird hier hinreichend sein, zu bemerken, dass Natur und Geschichte, wie Körper und Seele, so innig miteinander verbunden sind, dass wer die Geschichte nicht versteht, noch weniger dahin zu gelangen vermag, die Natur würdig zu begreifen und zu deuten. . . . Eine jüdische Lebensanschauung ist eines solchen zum wirklichen Fortschritt erforderlichen Naturverständnisses noch weniger als des Verständnisses der Geschichte mächtig; sie löst ohne zu erlösen, sie zerstreut statt zu sammeln, sie führt statt zur Einigung, zum Zerwürfniss und Verfall, und die höheren christlichen Lehranstalten, welche die Stimme dieser Anschauung unter sich aufnehmen und walten lassen, werden, je weniger sie es vielleicht ahnen um so entschiedener die Blüthe ihrer Wirksamkeit dem Todeshauche des inneren Unterganges opfern. (Nr. 2a, Bd. I, pp. 271–272.)

See also Nr. 2a, Bd. I, pp. 18, 280–282, 287–288 and Kalisch, *op. cit.*, pp. 87–88.

61. Nr. 2a, Bd. I, p. 247.

62. Friedrich von Bezold, *Geschichte der Rheinischen Friedrich-Wilhelms-Universität*, Bonn 1920, p. 351.

63. Lenz, *op. cit.*, II, pt. I, pp. 281–282.

64. Several professors commented on the growth in the number of Catholic academics at Greifswald under Eichhorn's regime. See Nr. 2a, Bd. I, pp. 35–36, 118.

65. His name was Hiabowski. See Nr. 2a, Bd. II, p. 13.

66. For example, Gebser, Sieffert, and Lehnerdt of the Evangelical theological faculty at Königsberg (Nr. 2a, Bd. II, pp. 1–17) and De Witte, Henke, and Wunderlich of Halle's legal faculty (Nr. 2, Bd. I, pp. 288–291). The following declaration by Sieffert is representative:

Übrigens versteht es sich von selbst, dass bei einer etwaigen Aufhebung oder Modifizirung des Par. 105 unserer Statuten diese Modifizirung nicht etwa bloss zu Gunsten der Juden geschehen kann, sondern dann so gefasst werden muss, dass auch katholischen Dozenten zu den Stellen, welche nicht ihrer wesentlichen Natur und Bestimmung nach die evangelische Confession voraussetzen, der Zutritt offen sein muss, indem es eine schmähliche Herabwürdigung des einen Theils der christlichen Kirche durch den andern wäre, die dem Christenthum überhaupt beharrlich widerstrebenden Elemente unserer Staatsgesellschaft uns für verwandter und befreundeter zu erachten als die im Wesentlichen auf derselben christlichen Grundlage stehenden. (Nr. 2a, Bd. II, p. 11.)

67. This instructive *Gutachten* by Franz Karl Movers, professor of Old Testament exegesis, presented a cogent case against Prussian partiality. The fact that not a single Catholic university had survived Prussian expansion epitomized the fate of Catholicism in the Prussian state. See Nr. 2a, Bd I, pp. 247–248. Dieters of the legal faculty at Bonn claimed that young Catholics were avoiding an academic career for lack of opportunity. (Nr. 2a, Bd. II, pp. 105–106.) The scanty information available on the systematic exclusion of Catholics from an academic career in Prussia prior to 1870 was collected by Wilhelm Lossen, *Der Anteil der Katholiken am akademischen Lehramte in Preussen*, Köln 1901, pp. 4–11, 16–27, 162–164.

68. One typical example of this rhetoric should suffice. Gerlach of Halle's philosophical faculty reluctantly voted to implement the new law, but he feared the impact on the university of a style peculiar to Jews.

. . . sondern es wäre auch zu befürchten, dass unsere Universitäten bei der bekannten Industrie des jüdischen Volks und bei der Kecken Zudringlichkeit und Eitelkeit, die sich schon jetzt nicht selten an jungen jüdischen Literaten bemerklich macht, in kurzer Zeit von einem Geiste würden durchdrungen werden, der je rein jüdischer er ist, um so mehr zu dem christlichen in Antipathie steht. (Nr. 2, Bd. I, p. 300.)

69. Hans K. L. Barkow of Breslau was so firmly opposed to admitting Jews to his medical faculty that he wrote twice on the matter. As the following choice passage makes clear, it was Jewish style backed by Jewish power which frightened him.

Ich halte die Ansicht nur zu begründet, dass die Fakultät jüdisch werden wird, wenn die Schranken gelockert werden sollten, so lange der jetzige Geist unter den Juden fortdauert, und ich kann für ihre Zulassung nicht stimmen, so lange unausstehliche Arroganz und Eitelkeit, und eine Betriebsamkeit, welche zur Erreichung ihres vorgesteckten Ziels keine humane Rücksicht und keine Pietät kennt, bei ihnen vorwaltend ist, weil ich die Überzeugung habe, dass die Fakultät es nicht mit einzelnen Personlichkeiten, sondern mit der Judenschaft zu thun haben wird. (Kalisch, *op. cit.*, p. 186.)

70. Kalisch, *op. cit.*, pp. 10–21.

71. *Ibid.*, pp. 163, 176.

72. Nr. 2, Bd. I, p. 170. The historian Heinrich Leo spoke at length of the unscrupulous style of Eduard Gans to underscore the dangers inherent in opening the academic market place to Jews. An erstwhile Hegelian, bitter critic of Ranke and author of a history of the Jews, Leo had been at Berlin until 1827, when he secured a post in Halle. Though typical, his envious testimony betrays deep personal wounds.

. . . weil ein längeres freundliches Verhältniss zu dem verstorbenen Prof. Gans in Berlin mir einen deutlichen Einblick gewährt hat in die Mittel, deren ein Mann jüdischer Art, sobald er nicht wirklich im innersten Sinne sich mit christlichen und deutschen Empfindungen identificirt hat, fähig ist, um Anderen mit denen er concurrirt, das Feld zu verderben. Wie dieser es gegen Freunde ganz offen aussprach, dass er *à tout prix* Zuhörer neben Herrn von Savigny haben müsse, und er gegen seine Freunde gar kein Hehl hatte, dass er sowohl was den Geldpunkt betreffe es jedem annehmlicher zu machen suche bei ihm als bei einem Anderen zu hören,—als was das wissenschaftliche Object anbetraf, es geradehin aussprach, dass Zuhörer durch spannenden unterhaltenden Vortrag herbei gezogen werden müssten selbst wenn der Gegenstand des Vortrags dabei etwas zu kurz komme—so würden es mehr oder weniger alle jüdischen Docenten *vis à vis* ihrer christlichen Concurrenten machen. . . . Ich sehe in Folge der Zulassung von Juden allmälig eine völlige Degeneration der jetzigen academischen Stellungen kommen. *Ibid.*, p. 309.

On Leo, see Lenz, *op. cit.*, II, pt. 1, pp. 277–279. On Gans's skill as a lecturer, *ibid.*, p. 495.

73. Freund, *op. cit.*, II, p. 520.

74. Kalisch, *op. cit.*, p. 240.

75. *Der Orient*, 1847, p. 357; Lenz, *op. cit.*, II, pt. 2, pp. 166–168; Busch, *op. cit.*, pp. 153–154; Richarz, *op. cit.*, pp. 210–212. Related developments in Austria allow for an instructive comparison with Prussia. On 31st March 1848 the Austrian government issued an edict that henceforth no qualified person would be denied a university post because of religion. By September 1849 Wolfgang Wessely, probably the first Jew to earn a doctorate from the Catholic University of Prague, received an appointment as its associate professor of Hebrew language and literature with a salary of 600 florin. Two years later he received yet a second appointment to the university's legal faculty as an associate professor of law. By 1861 he reached the rank of full professor. In December 1849 Saul Isaak Kaempf, the *Prediger* of Prague's Reform synagogue, became a *Privatdozent* at the university in ancient Hebrew and Oriental languages. (Guido Kisch, *Die Prager Universität und die Juden 1348–1848*,

Mährisch-Ostrau 1935, pp. 60–68.) The contrast with Prussia is striking. Whereas the philosophical faculty of Berlin turned down Zunz's well-known appeal of 25th July 1848 to create a professorship of Jewish history and literature, its Catholic counterpart in Prague saw fit to invite two men to cover the field. (Geiger, *op. cit.*, pp. 334–347.)

76. Nr. 2, Bd. II, p. 9ff.

77. Nr. 2, Bd. II. The minutes read:

. . . dass aber die Erlangung dieser Qualification überhaupt noch kein Recht auf die Verleihung eines bestimmten Staatsamtes begründe, dass es vielmehr der Beurtheilung des betreffenden Departements Chefs bei Bewerbungen um ein bestimmtes Amt vorbehalten bleiben müsse, ob der Bewerber, ganze abgesehen von seinem religiösen Bekenntnisse, sich seiner Persönlichkeit und seinen Fähigkeiten nach für dieses Amt eigne.

The policy was publicly restated in the Prussian Chamber of Deputies by the minister of justice in 1901. (See my *Jewish Reactions to German Anti-Semitism, 1870–1914*, New York–London 1972, p. 151.)

78. Copies of the letters of recommendation are in Nr. 2, Bd. II, pp. 29–30. The biographical information is drawn primarily from these letters and the subsequent opinion of von Raumer. See also Hans J. Bach, *Jakob Bernays: Ein Beitrag zur Emanzipationsgeschichte der Juden und zur Geschichte des deutschen Geistes im neunzehnten Jahrhundert*, Tübingen 1974 (Schriftenreihe wissenschaftlicher Abhandlungen des Leo Baeck Instituts 30), pp. 108–117. Senate requests of the government for financial assistance for Bernays may be found in DZAM, Rep. 76Va, Sekt. 3, Tit. IV, Nr. 45, Bd. II, pp. 16, 119, 180.

79. DZAM, Rep. 76Va, Sekt. 3, Tit. IV, Nr. 45, Bd. II, pp. 51–54. Since this important memorandum was unknown to Bach, it is worthwhile quoting the crucial passage in the original.

Die Hauptaufgabe eines Professors der alten Sprachen besteht in Ausbildung der Philologen und Theologen, welche dereinst als Lehrer an unseren Gymnasien wirken sollen; der Unterricht in den alten Sprachen ist die Hauptbasis der Gymnasial-Bildung und wird es, das hoffe ich, bleiben, trotz der Angriffe, die er von realistisch-lichtfreundlicher wie von katholischer Seite mit gleicher Stärke zu erdulden hat. Von höchster Bedeutung ist es aber, dass der Unterricht der alten Sprachen auf Universitäten wie auf Gymnasien in einer Wiese stattfinde, welche der klassischen Bildung in dem Erziehungsgange der Jugend die rechte Stellung sichert, nicht als Gegensatz christlicher Gesinnung und Denkart sondern als ein wesentliches Moment ihrer Kräftigung. Bei aller Anerkennung, welche dem persönlichen Charakter eines Dozenten jüdischer Konfession zu zollen sein mag, kann ich nicht annehmen, dass er jenen Anforderungen zu entsprechen im Stande sey? Ich würde es vielmehr für höchst bedenklich erachten, durch Anstellung eines jüdischen Professors der alten Sprachen auf viele Jahre hin die Ausbildung von Gymnasiallehrern in einer Provinz in eine Hand zu legen, welche sonstiger Vorzüge ungeachtet, doch ausser Stande ist, für die Ausbildung christlicher Lehrer an christlichen Gymnasien die nöthigen Garantien zu geben. (pp. 53–54)

80. Bach, *op. cit.*, pp. 117–119.

81. See the important statistics collected by Bernhard Breslauer, *Die Zurücksetzung der Juden an den Universitäten Deutschlands*, Berlin 1911, and the recent essay by David L. Preston, "The German Jews in Secular Education, University Teaching, and Science: A Preliminary Inquiry," *Jewish Social Studies*, XXXVIII (1976), pp. 99–116. Friedrich Paulsen, the noted German authority on higher education at the end

of the century, was distressed by "the strong preponderance of Jews at the universities." (*The German Universities*, New York 1906, pp. 158–159.) In his autobiography
Paulsen related that the philosophy faculty of Berlin diverted him from philosophy
into education with an enticing offer as associate professor to forestall the unwelcome appointment of Moritz Lazarus to the field as full professor. (*An Autobiography*,
New York 1938, p. 253.)

4

The Myth of Sephardic Supremacy

With the advent of emancipation in Central Europe, German-speaking Jewry gradually unhinged itself from the house of Ashkenazic Judaism. Inclusion in the body politic sundered a religious unity born of common patrimony. Historians have tended to focus on the institutional expressions of this rupture—the repudiation of the educational system, the mode of worship, and the rabbinic leadership intrinsic to Ashkenazic Judaism—with special emphasis on the Western tastes and values which propelled the transformation of all areas of Jewish life. What has been singularly overlooked is the simultaneous quest for a Jewish paradigm which would ground institutional rebellion in Jewish soil. With surprising speed German Jews came to cultivate a lively bias for the religious legacy of Sephardic Jewry forged centuries before on the Iberian Peninsula, without which they would have cut loose from Judaism itself. The embrace of what had previously hovered but dimly on the liminal level of Ashkenazic consciousness enabled them to redefine their identity in a Jewish mode. The critique of Ashkenazic Judaism was leveled from the vantage point of a usable past. During the next two centuries, modern Jewish history would replay this dialectic of rebellion and renewal by recourse to the periphery of group consciousness, but not beyond, with some degree of regularity. Counter-history fed both the impulse for rejuvenation and the desire for continuity.

As construed by Ashkenazic intellectuals, the Sephardic image facilitated a religious posture marked by cultural openness, philosophic thinking, and an appreciation for the aesthetic. Like many a historical myth, it evoked a partial glimpse of a bygone age determined and colored by social need. Eventually, as we shall see, the Sephardic mystique came to operate in four distinct areas of Jewish life in nineteenth-century Germany—liturgy, synagogue architecture, literature, and scholarship. The romance with Spain offers yet another perspective on the degree to which German Jewry distanced itself from its East European origins.

I

The multifaceted interaction between Sephardic and Ashkenazic Judaism in the centuries following the Spanish expulsion has yet to be studied comprehensively. Still there is little doubt that beyond the world-wide influence of Lurianic *Kabbalah*, the religious culture of Spanish Jewry held but slight allurement for a self-sufficient and self-confident Ashkenazic Judaism in its age of spiritual ascendancy. Ashkenazic religious leadership in the second half of the sixteenth century began to turn its back on the rich rationalistic legacy of Spain—its biblical exegesis, grammatical research, and philosophic enterprise.[1] Typical of the growing assertiveness was the public attack delivered in 1559 by the chief rabbinic figure of Poznań in the synagogue on the sabbath before Passover, in which he defended the Talmud as the sole and infallible source of all the knowledge required of Jews and depicted the burning of the Talmud in Rome in 1553 by order of the Papacy as an expression of divine displeasure at the publication of Maimonides's *Guide of the Perplexed* in Venice two years before.[2] Similarly the Prague polymath David Gans in his historical chronicle *Zemah David* (The Shoot of David), of 1592, betrayed an unmistakable sense of Ashkenazic superiority by dryly juxtaposing the Sephardic tendency to convert in times of persecution with the alleged Ashkenazic resolve to embrace martyrdom.[3]

Throughout this period of cultural estrangement, however, there are traces of self-criticism within Ashkenazic Judaism that are inspired by Sephardic example. The fascination with Spain that comes to characterize the German-Jewish scene of the nineteenth century is a discontinuity with historical roots. The criticism is most often directed against the insular, ungraded, and adult-oriented educational system of the Ashkenazic world. While it is not clear that the educational reforms of a Jehuda Löw ben Bezalel (better known as the Maharal of Prague) in the sixteenth century were inspired by a Spanish model, the comments and proposals made by Shabbatai Sheftel Horowitz, Shabbatai Bass, and Zevi Hirsch Ashkenazi in the following two centuries were certainly informed by direct contact with the Sephardic Diaspora.[4]

Bass, who was born in 1641 in Poland and educated in Prague, spent five years in the quickening ambience of the Sephardic community of Amsterdam completing in 1680 his *Siftei Yeshenim* (The Lips of the Sleeping), the first bibliography of Hebraica prepared by a Jew. The significance of this work, for our purpose, goes well beyond his praise in the introduction of the graded and efficient Sephardic educational system he came to admire in Amsterdam. As an instrument of scholarship, the bibliography, with its 2,200 titles, provided the Hebrew reader for whom it was intended with a sense that Jewish literary creativity transcended the writing of legal codes, commentaries, and *responsa*. With the autodidact in mind, Bass stressed in his introduction the centrality of method and system in the mastery of any discipline. The ability to arrive at reliable conclusions, and not the mechanical assimilation of factual knowledge, was the mark of the true scholar.[5]

No less unusual for his time was Zevi Ashkenazi, the devout yet worldly father of Jacob Emden. Known by the Sephardic title *Hakham* (sage), Ashkenazi was born in Moravia in 1660, educated in Salonica, and for the rest of his life moved easily between the Ashkenazic and Sephardic orbits. His intellectual horizons, though, were distinctly Sephardic with a good command of European languages, secular learning, Jewish philosophy, and Hebrew grammar, all of which made him a life-long critic of the educational curriculum that prevailed in Central Europe.[6]

That same critique was substantially amplified in the middle of the eighteenth century by Isaac Wetzlar, a native of Lower Saxony and successful merchant with a solid rabbinic education, in his unpublished Yiddish ethical tract *Liebes Brief*. Whatever else his use of Yiddish may have betokened, it signaled a desire to deliver his indictment of Ashkenazic society to the largest possible audience. Wetzlar was discomfited by Gentile ridicule of Judaism, angered by the low quality of lay and rabbinic leadership, and envious of the orderliness and emphases of the Sephardic educational system. He extolled the study of Jewish philosophy, the decorum of the Sephardic synagogue, and its willingness to employ Spanish or Portuguese in communal worship. Consciousness of Sephardic practice, nurtured by at least one visit to Hamburg, with its still bustling Sephardic community, and perhaps else-where, had sensitized Wetzlar to shortcomings in his own Jewish world.[7] In fact, as the autobiography of Glückel of Hameln illustrates, frequent travel by Ashken-azic merchants and entrepreneurs in this age of mercantilism to the emporiums of Amsterdam and Hamburg and to international fairs provided an infectious source of exposure to the contrasting religious style of the Sephardic Diaspora.[8] In sum, then, it is possible to identify an unbroken if modest tradition of Ashkenazic self-criticism informed by a selective admiration for Spanish Judaism long before the emergence of a veritable Sephardic mystique in the last quarter of the eighteenth century.

The full-blown cultural critique of the *Haskalah* (German Jewry's ephemeral Hebraic version of the European Enlightenment) drew much of its validation, if not inspiration, directly from Spain. The advocacy of secular education, the curb-ing of talmudic exclusivity and the resumption of studies in Hebrew grammar, biblical exegesis, and Jewish philosophy, and the search for historical exemplars led to a quick rediscovery of Spanish models and achievements. Given the deep Ashkenazic aversion to any serious study of the Bible, Mendelssohn's extensive Hebrew commentary to the Pentateuch was no less of a revolutionary break than his German translation and relied heavily on the grammatical and exegetical spade-work of Spanish forerunners. The combined result of commentary and translation at least partially warranted Heine's arresting comparison of Mendelssohn to Luther by virtue of their common endeavor to restore the centrality of the biblical text to their respective religious cultures.[9]

A quintessential expression of the *Haskalah*'s repudiation of Poland for Spain may be found in a withering satire by Aaron Wolfsohn, a teacher in the modern Jewish school of Breslau and one of the editors of the movement's ailing Hebrew periodical *Hame'asef*. Serialized in its pages during 1794–1795, "Siḥa be-Eretz ha-Hayim" (A Conversation in Paradise) takes place in the heavenly abode on the day of Mendelssohn's death. Prior to his arrival, we are treated to a delicious exchange between a reluctant Maimonides and an uncouth Polish rabbi, whose two-year residence on a lower level of paradise has improved his Hebrew enough to discourse with the Sephardic sage. The rabbi is overjoyed at the chance to display his immense knowledge of Maimonides's twelfth-century codification of all of Jewish law before the author himself. After much badgering, Maimonides unhappily agrees to test his learning, but when he begins by asking whether God might be corporeal—a subject on which Maimonides's own rationalistic view had already given rise to bitter controversy—his Polish tormentor protests that he never wasted his time studying trivia, but only matters of import—the laws governing sacrifices, family purity, and financial affairs. In regard to the realm of theology, he firmly believed that lightning was created to punish the wicked and personally warded off its destructive force by placing salt on the four corners of his table and opening the book of Genesis.

When Mendelssohn finally arrives on the scene, he is affectionately embraced as an equal by a weary and perturbed Maimonides. In response to his urgent inquiry as to the reasons for the benighted condition of Ashkenazic Jews, Mendelssohn offers three: oppression which brought them to despise Gentile learning; the absence of legal consensus; and an abstruse and casuistic mode of learning. Wolfsohn concludes his satirical foray by having Moses himself come out to welcome Mendelssohn to paradise, thereby uniting in symbolic religious accord the three towering Moses figures of Jewish history. The scene graphically exemplified the deeper meaning of the *Haskalah*'s famous *bon mot* that "from Moses to Moses there was no one like Moses." Collapsing the Moses of Egypt and the Moses of Dessau into the Moses of Cordoba rendered the philosophic strain of Spanish Judaism both pristine and normative.[10]

A modicum of personal experience helped to fuel this flight of historical imagination. At one point Wolfsohn has Mendelssohn confess that it was only his discovery of Maimonides's *Guide* that extracted him from the ignorance and confusion of the talmudic world, and indeed for the entire generation of autodidacts, as Isaak Euchel stressed in his biography of Mendelssohn, the *Guide* served as the great intellectual emancipator.[11] It provided their first taste of secular knowledge and remained a model for a rational exposition of Judaism. There was nothing exceptional about the pious Jews of the city of Poznań forbidding the itinerant Salomon Maimon, whose very name testifies to his indebtedness to Maimonides, to introduce their children to the *Guide*.[12] If, in fact, the *Haskalah* is unthinkable without the *Guide*, then its republication in 1742 in Jessnitz, but a few miles away from

Dessau, after a hiatus of nearly two centuries amounted to a major breach in the intellectual defenses of Ashkenazic society. The glaring lack of even a single introductory rabbinic approbation underscores the official hostility to the venture, though Mendelssohn's own teacher of Talmud, David Fränkel, seems to have favored it covertly. Without question, however, the new edition of the *Guide*, with several commentaries and a glossary of foreign words, opened up a road for many an inquiring mind that would eventually terminate in the alluring vistas of the Enlightenment.[13]

Political considerations tended to reinforce the cultural attraction to Spain. The far more privileged, prosperous, and assimilated Sephardic Jews of Amsterdam, London, and Bordeaux served as the cutting edge of the campaign for emancipation. That role was already adumbrated by Isaac de Pinto, the respected Jewish *Philosophe* of Amsterdam, in his 1762 refutation of Voltaire's scurrilous encyclopaedia article on the Jews. In defending Judaism, de Pinto chided Voltaire for his blanket indictment of all Jews, which had totally obscured the vast economic, social, and cultural differences between Ashkenazim and Sephardim, clearly implying that the latter by virtue of their noteworthy accomplishments enjoyed a greater claim to admission into the body politic than their oppressed brethren. And, indeed, the resistance in revolutionary circles to the prospect of emancipating the Sephardic Jews of Bordeaux and the South in 1790 proved much less severe than that which forced a delay of yet another twenty months in granting emancipation to the larger number of far more alien Ashkenazim in Alsace and Lorraine.[14]

The import of events in France was not lost on young German-Jewish intellectuals engaged in their own struggle for significant equality, and they often cast their argument in terms of de Pinto. Thus, for example, Eduard Gans, the staunch and acute young Hegelian president of the ephemeral *Verein für Cultur und Wissenschaft der Juden (Culturverein)*, submitted a lengthy petition to the Prussian government in the spring of 1820 seeking official approval for the name and activities of his society. To enforce his contention that Judaism posed no threat to meeting the demands of good citizenship, Gans pointed to the enduring record of Spanish Jewry.

These Jews, resembling all others both physically and mentally but granted by the Arabs equality with Muslims, proceeded to plumb in concert all the known sciences of the day. . . . And they employed (in their writings) not Hebrew but Arabic. Indeed those Jews expelled from this land to France, Holland, Italy, and England, to the detriment of Spanish economic life, and their still living progeny have never formed the contrast to Christian society which was so striking in the other family of Jews kept intentionally apart. They are marked by less discrepancy in morality, purer speech, greater order in the synagogue, and in fact better taste.[15]

But a few years later the more prosaic Isaak Markus Jost, who had distanced himself from the messianic fervor of the *Culturverein* and who bore little affection for his own Ashkenazic culture, wrote in a late chapter of his multi-volume *Geschichte der Israeliten* that Spanish and German Jews, for all their agreement in matters of religion, "constitute practically distinct national groups" (*verschiedene Völkerstämme*).[16]

The preparedness of Napoleon in 1806 to reopen the issue within France of whether adherents of Judaism are even capable of citizenship augmented Sephardic prestige still further. His famous twelve questions and the rhetoric of his officials imposed a far-reaching distinction on Judaism that would become basic to the protracted emancipation debate in Central Europe. As formulated by the Sanhedrin in February 1807 in the preamble to its nine-point doctrinal and *halakhic* pronouncement, that distinction divided the provisions of Jewish law into two kinds—religious provisions that are eternal and political ones that obtained only for the period of Jewish statehood. In his invaluable transactions of the preceding Assembly of Notables, Diogene Tama, the secretary of the deputy from Bouches du Rhône, astutely linked this novel distinction in a general way to the figures of Don Isaac Abravanel and Maimonides. The former, he contended,

. . . establishes a judicious distinction between things essentially connected with religious dogmas, and those which have reference only to points of civil morals, which last are always susceptible of changes and modifications, according to the civil and political state of those whose happiness they have in view.[17]

Not only, then, were Sephardic Jews more worldly, but their conception of Judaism met the political needs of the modern age; though in truth this quite imprecise, essentially alien, but immensely useful distinction unveiled a powerful means for friend and foe alike to strip Judaism of any rite, restriction, or institution that was perceived to jeopardize the goal of integration.[18]

To consolidate this historical overview, we might say that the movements for *Haskalah* and emancipation had fanned a spark into a fire. A restricted tradition of self-criticism with a distinguished genealogy was about to erupt into a broad social force that would infuse the major expressions of an emergent Jewish subculture. A changing political context had ignited a growing rebellion against Polish Judaism, while the need for continuity and legitimacy begged for a new cultural paradigm.

II

The rapid diffusion of the Spanish mystique is attested to by its appearance in four distinct areas of Jewish culture in nineteenth-century Germany. The impulsion was not passed along from one to the other, but deriving from a common source penetrated simultaneously into the domains of liturgy, synagogue architecture, literature, and scholarship. The shift toward Spain was not gradual or sequential but sudden and ubiquitous.

With emancipation, as we have seen, the synagogue emerged for a time as the dominant area of Jewish expression, and it should come as no surprise to discover that the Spanish bias affected both its liturgy and architecture. Already Naftali Herz Wessely, whose admiration for the Sephardim of Amsterdam was born of personal experience, had contended in the fourth and final letter of his *Words of Peace and Truth* that the Sephardic pronunciation of Hebrew was grammatically preferable to the manner in which the Ashkenazim rendered it.[19] A generation later, the teachers and preachers who pioneered the development of a German rite adopted the Sephardic pronunciation for their "German synagogue."[20] Not a point of *halakhic* contention, the switch could be defended by Eliezer Liebermann in terms of grammatical propriety or by Moses Konitz of Ofen (Buda) in terms of demography—more than 7/8 of the Jewish world offers its prayers in the Hebrew of the Sephardim![21] But the ultimate motivation of this unnatural and self-conscious appropriation of Sephardic Hebrew was the desire to distinguish the sound of the sacred tongue from that of Yiddish, which these alienated Ashkenazic intellectuals regarded as a non-language that epitomized the abysmal state of Jewish culture.[22]

No less symptomatic of that degradation for them was the condition of the traditional German liturgy for festivals (the *Mahzor*), thickly overlaid with impenetrable Hebrew poems (*piyyutim*) composed by medieval sages and with mystical interpolations from the realm of Lurianic *Kabbalah*. At the turn of the century, its state of disrepair had prompted Wolf Heidenheim, the founder of a famous Jewish publishing house in the Frankfurt suburb of Rödelheim and one of the most anomalous and understudied figures of the German *Haskalah*, to undertake a new nine-volume edition of the German *Mahzor* with a semblance of a critical text, a lucid German translation (in Hebrew characters) and an expansive Hebrew commentary. Working entirely alone, Heidenheim hoped to rid the Hebrew text of innumerable corruptions, to illuminate the difficult vocabulary and abstruse allusions of the *piyyutim*, and to drive out of circulation the egregious older German translations available. The edition bespoke a heroic effort by an open-minded scholar, singularly free of any affinity for Spain, to restore and defend the religious grandeur of his own Ashkenazic liturgical tradition. Heidenheim regarded the rhyme and meter of Sephardic *piyyutim* as alien to Hebrew literature, which to his mind had always accorded priority to content over form. Accordingly, his commentary focused on the sources, grammar, and meaning of his texts and not on their literary quality. Overall, the project was clearly analogous to and perhaps even inspired by Mendelssohn's edition of the Pentateuch. Nevertheless, its import was more mixed. Whereas the religious tastes of the age militated against the retention of large chunks of *piyyutim* in the synagogue, Heidenheim's signal accomplishment would place all future students of the subject in his debt.[23]

In 1841 a second edition of the prayerbook of the Hamburg Temple, the most enduring and influential of the early "German synagogues," ignited a second broad controversy that betrayed yet another aspect of the preference for Spain within the synagogue. In addition to its transliteration of Hebrew according to the Sephardic pronunciation, which obviously still prevailed in the temple, the prayerbook comprised a parsimonious selection of *piyyutim*, drawn entirely from the Sephardic orbit.[24] Among other features, that rejection of native *piyyutim* familiar and sacred to German Jews for the utterly strange, though perhaps superior products of the Spanish synagogue also drew the ire of Zacharias Frankel of Dresden, whose differences with the Reform camp were beginning to crystallize. His espousal of liturgical continuity and familiarity over poetic quality indeed challenged the very operating principle if not underlying motive of the Hamburg circle and their allies.[25] Without the embrace of Sephardic culture, the rebellion against Ashkenaz was hardly possible. Gotthold Salomon and Abraham Geiger, who represented the old and new generation of Reform rabbinic leadership, both intoned in their defenses of the prayerbook the grammatical, literary, and philosophical superiority of Spanish religious poetry. The Ashkenazim were deemed inferior in all three respects and consequently the content of their poetry "baroque in the extreme and the language barbaric and monstrous."[26] Furthermore, Salomon protested his synagogue's living connection to the Sephardic tradition. The selection of *piyyutim* was neither academic nor arbitrary. "At the founding of the temple, our association counted quite a few respected Portuguese families among its most enthusiastic supporters."[27]

Basic to this preference for Spanish *piyyutim* was a general conception of what separated the liturgical creativity of medieval Sephardim and Ashkenazim first enunciated by Shlomo Yehudah Rapoport in 1827. His subsequent fame as one of the founders of the academic study of Judaism, despite his unassimilated origins in Eastern Galicia, made of his early observation a stock stereotype of the age. Rapoport claimed that "the religious poetry of the Sephardim was an instrument of communication between the soul and its Maker whereas that of the Ashkenazim, between the nation of Israel and its God."[28] The distinction served to endow Spanish Jewry with a sense of individualism. Its public worship did not muffle the anguish of the individual beneath the oppressive fate of the community, but rather facilitated the expression of his personal pain directly to God. Such immediacy not only lent a special intimacy to Spanish *piyyutim,* it also helped to blunt the frequent charge of dual loyalty.

The same year (1842) that the controversy over the Hamburg Temple prayer book reverberated through Central Europe, Leopold Dukes published a modest German introduction to the study of medieval Hebrew poetry, which elegantly elaborated and justified the substitution of a few choice specimens of Sephardic *piyyutim* in the synagogue for the entire Ashkenazic liturgical corpus. A native of Pressburg and a product of its famous *yeshivah,* Dukes was a scholarly autodidact who led an impoverished existence in Germany scouring archives for manuscripts pertaining to medieval Hebrew literature. *Zur Kenntnis der neuhebräischen religiösen Poesie* (Toward an Understanding of neo-Hebraic Religious Poetry) deepened the stereotypes. The unattractiveness of Ashkenazic religious poetry was a function of social context. Totally excluded from Christian society, the Jews of Franco-

Germany vegetated intellectually on a meager diet of rabbinic texts. The ungrammatical, unedifying, and artless nature of their poetry was but a mirror image of the curriculum on which they were nurtured. The human dimension of either Jew or Christian was denied a means of universal expression. In contrast, the open atmosphere and secular arena that obtained in Muslim Spain enriched its Jews with the chance to cultivate a thirst for knowledge as a source of truth and an appreciation for language as an instrument of power and beauty. Its poetry, consequently, is meticulously crafted, echoes universal themes, and laments national calamities with the gentleness of a lover. Historical research had been enlisted to serve the need to shift cultural paradigms.[29]

The external façade of the synagogue likewise bore the impress of the Sephardic bias. Emancipation, although incomplete, permitted German Jews for the first time to discard the inconspicuous, nondescript, and often unofficial status of their houses of worship. The magnificent edifices constructed in the course of the nineteenth century gave resounding public testimony to their confidence in the durability of emancipation and their pride in their religious distinctiveness. But the freedom to build synagogues posed a serious architectural challenge: no conscious tradition existed of what might constitute the most appropriate style for a Jewish sanctuary. The insecurity of medieval Jewish life had impeded the formation of such a tradition. After several decades of experimentation, Christian architects and Jewish communal boards arrived at a consensus that synagogues ought to be built in what became known as the Moorish style, and in the fifties and sixties imposing Moorish synagogues rose to grace the rapidly expanding Jewish communities of Leipzig, Frankfurt, Cologne, Mainz, Budapest, Vienna, and Berlin. Not till the end of the century, according to the leading scholar of this fascinating and long neglected subject, did the cresting tide of antisemitism in Germany induce communities to opt for an architectural style that lowered their public profile.

In his seminal work *Synagogen in Deutschland*, Harold Hammer-Schenk has suggested that the acceptance of a Moorish design, based largely on the mosques of North Africa and the Alhambra and not on any knowledge of the few medieval synagogues left in Spain, rested on two factors. The first was the conviction by historians that Arabic architecture, though distinctly inferior to Gothic, clearly foreshadowed later developments in Europe and therefore accorded perfectly with the prevailing Gentile perception of the relationship between Judaism and Christianity. Since Gothic was held to be quintessentially Christian, the synagogue was assigned a style that symbolized both its chronological and qualitative position in the history of religion. Moreover, and this was the second factor, Moorish architecture seemed to harmonize with the course of Jewish history as well by highlighting the oriental origins of the Jew although, as Hammer-Schenk realized, Jews in the process of Westernization were scarcely pleased at being reminded of their "primitive" ancestry. Consequently, the theory falls short of explaining the phenomenon. Communal boards, who always made the final decision over what style to employ, irrespective of the architect, were unlikely to choose one that accentuated both the inferiority and orientalism of Judaism.[30]

My own view, given the burden of this essay, should be clear. The appeal of Moorish architecture for the emancipated synagogue derived from its Spanish connection. It answered the need for a distinctive style precisely because it dovetailed so completely with the overriding Spanish bias of German Jewry. There was nothing oriental about the Arabs; without them Greek philosophy would never have reached the West. One was fully entitled to draw on the inspiration of Spain to renovate both the interior and the exterior of the synagogue. What more powerful symbol of the rupture with Ashkenazic culture than to build synagogues in the spirit of Spain!

The Sephardic mystique, however, extended well beyond the confines of the synagogue. Another facet of contemporary Jewish expression in which it played a formative role is the nascent and novel field of Jewish literature. This body of *belles lettres*, which represents an under-utilized source of insight for the social and intellectual historian of German Jewry, comprises works by writers born as Jews who used the medium of fiction or poetry either to air a problematic relationship to Judaism or to mediate it positively. What stands out is the degree to which writers of both types turned for their material to the Sephardic experience, which obliged them with equal bounty as a font of pride or self-criticism.

Heine's frequent recourse to that font is well known and has prompted one astute scholar to speak of his "Marrano pose." The designation is meant to capture not only his life-long fascination with Spain, but also his recurring identification with the fate of unwilling converts left no choice by a society bent on complete religious conformity. Heine was not beyond intimating a Spanish provenance for some of his own ancestors.[31] But the metaphor is also misleading, for Heine, the most celebrated and defiant convert of the century, never concealed his Jewish patrimony from his readership and his *oeuvre* is saturated with Jewish themes, animadversions, and memories. A figure of unique talent and complexity, Heine's preference for Spain is nevertheless typical.

In *Der Rabbi von Bacherach*, to cite but one example, the bias manifests itself in a paradoxical way. Begun before his conversion while still a member of the *Verein für Cultur und Wissenschaft der Juden*, this truncated novella represented the first effort by a German to mediate the religious beauty and historical pathos of Judaism through fiction. Heine's romantic nature protested the evisceration of both by the Hegelian scalpel of Gans, the *Culturverein's* chief conceptual surgeon. Judaism was a living organism subject to abuse and given to pain and not a set of unfeeling abstractions. That is the truth that Heine struggled to convey with the few Christian resources put at his disposal by Zunz. As the first chapter shows, it was not the worldly Judaism of Spain but the besieged and unyielding Judaism of Germany that Heine intended to evoke.[32] His choice was consistent with a remarkably sympathetic portrait of present-day Polish Jewry which he had published just one year earlier (1823), wherein he praised its spiritual wholeness and unconflicted character.[33] And yet the Spanish penchant could not be held at bay. Heine introduced into the story of Rabbi Abraham the utterly unhistorical fact of a medieval German rabbinical student spending some seven years of study in Spain. The asceticism of Ashkenazic Judaism is softened by the self-indulgence of the Sephardim, and one is tempted to explain Rabbi Abraham's subsequent flight with Sarah, his wife, from their crowded *seder* table just prior to a charge of ritual murder—an act so contrary to the Ashkenazic ethos of martyrdom but fully in tune with the surging spirit of individualism—as a consequence of the Spanish sojourn. Whatever the great descriptive merits of this chapter—which was probably the only one finished at Heine's conversion in 1825—it still embodied the self-conflict he had set out to transcend.[34]

Sephardic subject matter remained a staple of the early Jewish historical novel, a genre to whose development no one contributed more than Ludwig Philippson. Perhaps the most adept popular mediator of Judaism in nineteenth-century Germany, Philippson along with his brother Phöbus, a physician and talented writer, produced a large sample of historical novels meant to inspire respect and sympathy for Judaism. The drama usually unfolds at high speed on a familiar international stage; Jews are awash in persecution but abound in virtue, and the courtship of a Gentile paragon never manages to overcome the religious loyalty of an exquisite Jewish damsel. The ingredients for this formula, as in *Die Marannen* (1843), *Hispania und Jerusalem* (1843), and *Jakob Tirado* (1867), are often drawn from the stockpile of Sephardic history. Its massive appeal is epitomized in a memorable scene in *Die Marannen*, which is set in Granada in 1492 after the final defeat of the last Arab stronghold on the Iberian Peninsula. Don Isaac Abravanel appears before Ferdinand and Isabella to avert the immediate consequence of victory, the pending expulsion of Spanish Jewry. His argument is threefold: The Jews have lived in Spain since the destruction of Jerusalem's First Temple, longer than in any other country of Europe. They have cultivated the arts and sciences, which ennoble the human spirit. And they have never demeaned themselves by lapsing into petty trade or moneylending. "In the entire realm there is not a single grandee, hidalgo, or burger who is indebted to a Jew." If indeed Abravanel's words have a ring of contemporaneity to them, it is because the entire German-Jewish perception of Spanish Jewry was such a mix of present need and past reality.[35]

In Berthold Auerbach's first novel, a fictionalized life of Spinoza published in 1837, the myth is extended to Amsterdam, as it is in Philippson's *Jakob Tirado*, and facilitates the re-appropriation of Spinoza for Jewish history.[36] The book is the work of a young free-thinker who but recently abandoned the idea of devoting his life to the rabbinate, and it certainly is a brief for the supremacy of reason and the freedom of the individual. But for all his alienation from the theology and group primacy of Judaism, Auerbach portrays Spinoza as a reincarnation of Maimonides. As the young Spinoza is about to cross the intellectual threshold separating Judaism from mankind, the narrator exclaims: "Did not Maimonides already teach that the pious of all religions attain eternal salvation."[37] The implicit universalism of Sephardic rationalism is about to be rendered explicit. Despite the evident break, on a deeper level the secular messianism imputed by Auerbach to Spinoza seemed but a step along the cultural continuum from Cordoba to Amsterdam. Spinoza became the cultural hero of German Jews not only because they read him selectively, but also because he seemed to sum up the loftiest ideas of the Sephardic tradition.[38]

The fourth and final area pervaded by the Spanish bias is German Jewry's greatest and most enduring cultural achievement—the Science of Judaism (*Wissenschaft des Judentums*). Its relationship to that bias was dialectic: while historical research certainly did not set off the Spanish siren, its ready submission worked to enrich and enhance the resonance. The course of modern Jewish scholarship cannot be understood apart from the Spanish mystique and, in fact, no other area of modern Jewish culture remained under its sway as long. The purpose of our present discussion is merely to adumbrate the development and to show its consonance with the broader cultural scene.

Historical thinking in modern Judaism was nurtured on a Spanish diet. The most cogent proof for that assertion is the fact that the first two subfields to emerge—medieval Jewish philosophy and poetry—consisted primarily of texts produced by Spanish authors. Both *foci* represent an unforced extension of the *Haskalah*'s prior interest in the philosophy of Maimonides and the revival of Hebrew poetry. By the 1840s the pages of the weekly *Literaturblatt des Orients*, for a decade the most fecund forum of Jewish scholarly exchange in Central Europe, were teeming with the texts and studies of Jewish cultural creativity under Islam.[39] There is nothing fortuitous about the rash of German translations and paraphrases of the ethical and philosophic works of the likes of Bahya ibn Pakuda (1836), Maimonides (1838, 1839), Joseph Albo (1844), Saadia (1845), and Halevi (1853), often without benefit of manuscripts or in some cases the Arabic original.[40] The recovery of the medieval rationalist tradition rejected by Ashkenazic Judaism addressed both internal and external, religious and political needs.[41] Yet despite the impulse of extraneous concerns, the subfield of Jewish philosophy early on, thanks to the heroic scholarship of Salomon Munk, a Prussian expatriate in Paris, could boast of two of the crowning achievements of nineteenth-century Jewish *Wissenschaft*— the identification of Salomon ibn Gabirol as the unexpected author of a major eleventh-century Neoplatonic work, the *Fons Vitae* (*Mekor Hayim*), which till Munk was held to be the treatise of a non-Jewish philosopher (1846), and the publication and translation into French of the Arabic original of Maimonides's *Guide* (1856–1866).[42] Decades of spadework emboldened Munk to declare exactly what his Jewish audience yearned to hear: "Jews unquestionably shared with Arabs the distinction of having preserved and disseminated the science of philosophy during the centuries of barbarism and thereby having exercised on Europe for a long time a civilising influence."[43]

The early flowering of the study of medieval Hebrew poetry, as we have already glimpsed, was also indebted to Spanish soil. Scholarship fleshed out intuition. In this case the first serious work devoted to the history of Hebrew poetry did not come from a Jewish scholar but rather from a young conservative Lutheran academic at the University of Leipzig by the name of Franz Delitzsch, who was destined to become the greatest Christian Hebraist of the century. A modest study of immense sweep and lavish empathy, *Zur Geschichte der jüdischen Poesie*, unfurled a vision of an unbroken tradition of Hebrew poetry from the close of the Hebrew Canon down to the *Haskalah* and thus constituted a worthy sequel in subject and spirit to Herder's renowned analysis of biblical poetry published a half-century before.[44] Its relevance to our immediate concern is that Delitzsch fully betrayed the Spanish bias, which he either absorbed from Julius Fürst, his Hebrew mentor, or arrived at on his own. Indeed, his value-laden nomenclature strengthened the preference. He was the first scholar to bestow on specific periods of Spanish-Jewish poetry such glowing rubrics as "the golden age" (940–1040), "the silver age" (1040–1140), and "the age of roses among the thorns" (1140–1240?) and thereby to forge a literary classification that would long govern the field and even discolor the picture of the political and social context.[45] By way of contrast, he depicted the later medieval poetry of German Jews with all the animus of a typically alienated Ashkenazic intellectual.

Without civic freedom, without secure domicile, facing an ignorant, fanatical papal and monastic world, excluded from all public, useful activity and forced into the most menial and mindless occupations, Jews of the German Empire vegetated within the four ells of the *Halakhah* or the talmudic study halls and took refuge in the secret and mystical recesses of the *Kabbalah* . . . Thus the Jewish literature of the time, in comparison with that across the Pyrenees . . . bears the character of dark seclusion, of sorrowful and esoteric impenetrability, of tasteless and artless literary style and structure.[46]

A few years after the appearance of Delitzsch's book, the Sephardic mystique evoked a full-fledged study of the religious poetry of Spanish Jewry. Its author was Michael Sachs, a trained philologist and gifted translator who in 1844 had been chosen to become the first modern rabbinic leader of the burgeoning Jewish community in Berlin. More pertinent, he was an eloquent romantic completely at odds with the self-criticism and religious program of radical Reform whose strength in Germany was gaining. To confound the low self-esteem on which the movement was predicated, he sought to unveil and celebrate for a German audience some of the finest religious expressions of the Jewish spirit, a search that brought him quite naturally to Spain. And, as might be expected, his book of translations and exposition opened with a splendid German rendition of Ibn Gabirol's *Keter Malkhut* (the Royal Crown), whose poetic depiction of the cosmos from a religious perspective is a gem of Jewish universalism.[47]

Ironically, Sachs's monument to the religious creativity of Spanish Jewry owed much to the aid of an Italian romantic who battled for a lifetime against the very bias the book epitomized. In his letters to Sachs, Samuel David Luzzatto chided his slightly younger German colleague, with whom he generously shared his trove of manuscripts and incomparable knowledge of Hebrew, for avoiding the religious legacy of German Jewry. He disputed the alleged distinction by Rapoport between the poetry of Ashkenaz and Sepharad that informed Sachs's principle of selection. In the face of the still vast number of unpublished poems from both geographic sectors, the generalization simply did not hold.

And after what God has brought into my hands of these poems, it seems to me that the Sephardim composed more "national songs" than the Ashkenazim. Moreover, I've noticed that a sense of Israel's superiority, a love for its national concerns, a hatred of its enemies, a national enthusiasm and even fanaticism are no less evident in the poems of Sepharad than Ashkenaz . . . For in truth, what can a creature say to his Creator, if he avoids every expression of nationality and individuality? Philosophy and poetry are adversaries, and if we remove from the realm of poetry the spirit of zeal and hatred, then "who could endure its coldness?"[48]

But Sachs persisted in his plan to minimize the parochial and pointedly omitted from the book all specimens of Sephardic nationalism which Luzzatto had sent him.[49] Yet in the end, despite some larger and smaller reservations that Luzzatto aired in a generally favorable review when the book appeared, he warmly appreciated Sachs's religious conservatism: "Far be it for me to raise my sword against you [he wrote toward the end of the review], for you are an ornament for Judaism, and I shall always hope that if for now our hearts are not alike, someday they will unite."[50]

The power of Sachs's achievement did, however, touch the heart of an ailing Heine on the way to his "mattress grave." Without that book, Heine, reduced now to the state of "a poor Jew sick unto death, an emaciated image of wretchedness, an unhappy man," would never have written his epic poem "Jehuda ben Halevi."[51] In his notes to the poem he quotes Sachs verbatim, and even in its unfinished form, it gives the appearance of a poetic version of Sachs's Sephardic galaxy. But Heine's hero is the poem's namesake and in one memorable passage on Halevi's unique talent the two identities merge completely: The extraordinary poet graced by God sins neither in prose nor poetry. Responsible to God alone, he may be killed by the people, but they can never pass judgment on him.[52] Sachs had provided Heine with the inspiration he lacked years before when he began his *Rabbi of Bacherach*—a work of Jewish history that uplifted as well as informed.

Scholarship, like literature, soon moved to embellish the Sephardic mystique by appropriating the Diaspora created after the expulsion from Spain. The link was effected in 1859 by Moritz Meyer Kayserling in a study of the vernacular poetry of Sephardic exiles that may, in fact, have been intended as a complement to Sachs's initiative. Born in Hanover in 1829 and the son-in-law of Ludwig Philippson, Kayserling eventually became the liberal rabbi of Budapest and his generation's leading Jewish scholar of Sephardic Jewry. In this early work, boldly entitled *Sephardim: Romanische Poesien der Juden in Spanien* and cast in a rather militantly Jewish tone, Kayserling exults in the contributions of Sephardic *literati*, mainly in Amsterdam, to Spanish and Portuguese literature of the early modern period. The group portrait he crafts highlights the very traits that would resonate with a readership of Jews justifying emancipation to themselves and others. Persecution had not destroyed the aristocratic bearing, the cultural loyalty, the linguistic purity, and the alliance of religion with secular learning that had distinguished Spanish Jewry. Retention of an unadulterated language became a measure of character and culture, and worldliness tempered religious fanaticism. Without restraint or refinement, Kayserling dared to assert:

that [the Spanish and Portuguese Jews] were the first who united in themselves religion and science, maintaining both in equal measure. Their religious behavior was always so pure, so free of all hypocrisy, remaining forever one and the same, far removed from all incursions of vapid rationalizing, because it emerged united with science, which in turn kept it from ever losing its way. We must constantly acknowledge the benefit that wherever Spanish and Portuguese Jews settled, they spread culture, knowledge, and solid learning.[53]

The relevance of this cultural paradigm is not only blatant, but precludes any possible appreciation of the "anomalous" history of Sephardic mysticism.

Nevertheless, the historical canvas had been significantly broadened. Kayserling inaugurated the scholarly study of the Sephardic legacy in Amsterdam; he demonstrated the validity of a definition of Jewish literature that went beyond works by Jews in Hebrew; and finally he drew a number of inventive parallels between Mendelssohn and Manesseh ben Israel that solidified the Sephardic affinity of the Dessau sage by tracing it through Amsterdam.

But the study of Sephardim in Amsterdam could not break out of the conceptual grid created by the dominant periodization of the *Wissenschaft* circle. If Mendelssohn's persona and achievement signaled the "renaissance" of Judaism in the modern period, its "dark ages" had not set in until the extinction of Judaism in Spain. A chronological sequence is given a causal nexus: the triumph of rampant Rabbinism in Poland in the sixteenth century is made a consequence of the destruction of Spanish Jewry in the fifteenth century. And it is only with Mendelssohn's spiritualization of Judaism that the synthesis once forged in Spain is restored. Thus the Sephardic bias shapes the need to order the seamless continuum of Jewish history into meaningful and manageable structural units, and the resulting periodization long defied the accumulation of conflicting evidence.

An early and unsophisticated, but therefore instructive, example of this periodization is to be found in the 1820 *Vorlesungen über die neuere Geschichte der Juden* by

Salomon Löwisohn, which Zunz dismissed with cryptic sarcasm three years later.[54] Löwisohn, who died at the age of thirty-two in 1821, was a transitional figure—a Prague *Maskil* who came to Vienna in 1815 to work as a Hebrew editor in the press of Anton Schmid, and a talented Hebrew poet with more than a passing interest in Jewish history. His German tract is little more than a collection of *aperçus* on some of the more noteworthy figures of Jewish history in the Diaspora, usually selected from the Islamic or Sephardic orbit, and relies far too heavily on evidence culled from Latin chroniclers and Christian bibliographers. Of interest here is that while modern Jewish scholarship would soon repudiate his methodological naïveté, it would remain largely subservient to his periodization. Despite the attainments of the Sephardim in Amsterdam, and Löwisohn extols their famous synagogue as the most beautiful Jewish sanctuary since the Second Temple, he declares that the Spanish expulsion ushered in the most benighted period in Jewish history. As Enlightenment advanced in the Christian world, Jewry sank beneath the pall of Polish Judaism—its mounting burden of commandments and commentaries, its suffocating talmudism, its proliferating superstitions, and its antagonism to morality and secular learning—not to be redeemed until "that marvellous man [*Wundermann*], chosen by fate for a higher calling, until Mendelssohn came and effected that stunning revolution in the inner life of Israel, whose healing and glorious results are still not in full view."[55]

After three decades of critical research, the same periodization is still one of the few points in common between works as dissimilar as Ludwig Philippson's popular public lectures in 1847 on *Die Entwickelung der religiösen Idee im Judenthume, Christenthume und Islam* and Moritz Steinschneider's massively erudite encyclopedia essay of 1850 on *Jüdische Literatur.* Adversaries rather than colleagues, both men nevertheless treated the Spanish expulsion as a cultural watershed. For all that Steinschneider knew of the cultural productivity of Jews during the three centuries before his own, his uniformly harsh assessment of the quality of its diverse expressions concurred with the far less learned opinion offered by Philippson: "Longer than among the Arabs and Christians, a scientific impulse survived among the Jews till into the fifteenth century. Amid widespread persecutions, specifically the expulsion from Spain, it was extinguished."[56]

The import of this passage is that the demarcation is cultural. Not the loss of life or the trauma of suffering but the disappearance of a distinctive religious style is what blankets the next age in "darkness." The uniqueness of Sephardic Judaism on which this periodization rests is most evident when we look for its point of emergence, and by 1850 the cultural historians of the *Wissenschaft* movement—Zunz, Sachs, and Steinschneider in particular—had built a strong case for starting the period which ended with the collapse of Judaism on the Iberian Peninsula back in the eighth century. The triumph of Islam had brought the major centers of Jewish life within the ambience of a dynamic society in cultural ferment.[57] The confrontation between an unreflective, text-based, and inward-looking Judaism and a self-confident Islamic civilization fertilized by the legacy of Greece resulted in a transformation of Jewish thought patterns and modes of expression. The flowering of Jewish learning under Islam diminished the independent study of *Halakhah*, thereby increasing popular reliance on the *Geonim* (the heads of the rabbinic academies in Baghdad), and turned the undifferentiated and intuitive corpus of *midrash* (the vast literature of rabbinic exegesis of the Bible) into distinct and critical disciplines.[58] According to Steinschneider, whose historical survey of Jewish literature is predicated on this periodization, *"midrash* and *aggadah* were the emanation of the national spirit through the prevailing method of oral transmission. With the Arab-Greek culture, the spirit of the individual comes to the fore. Only now do writers, authors, and distinct disciplines actually arise."[59] What is more, Steinschneider was prepared to call this sustained leavening of rabbinic Judaism by the world of Islam Sephardic Judaism, after its dominant representatives— Spanish Jewry (*Sefarad* being the Hebrew term for Spain).[60] But in this instance, the metonymy is not just a figure of speech; it is the sanctification of an ideal type that is more symbol than substance. The Sephardic bias had rendered Spanish Jewry synonymous with an era of Jewish history that shamed the religious fanaticism and cultural narrowness of medieval Christendom. To see that era as ended by the Christian-inspired expulsion from Spain only confirmed the truth of the periodization.[61]

What should be equally evident by now is that the ultimate power and appeal of the Sephardic mystique in the age of emancipation derived from its Greek core.[62] In 1847 Luzzatto had admonished Steinschneider, at the outset of his scholarly career, not "to glorify and flaunt those Jews whose being was not truly Jewish but Greek or Arabic."[63] But the temptation was reinforced by need. Islamic civilization had fertilized Judaism with the philosophy and science of the Hellenic world and that link was vital to the process of Westernizing Judaism in the nineteenth century. The Sephardic mystique not only provided emancipated Jews with a source of pride and an instrument of rebellion, but also enabled them to recover a classical heritage in common with German culture. On one level, it was the Jewish equivalent of what one historian has called "the tyranny of Greece over Germany."[64] If our analysis has proven anything, it is that a literate German Jew was as likely to venerate the Sephardim as a Wilhelm von Humboldt the Greeks.

Our study of Greek history is therefore a matter quite different from our other historical studies. For us, the Greeks step out of the circle of history . . . Knowledge of the Greeks is not merely pleasant, useful or necessary for us—no, in the Greeks alone we find the ideal of that which we ourselves should like to be and produce.[65]

Substitute the word "Sephardim" for "Greeks" and the tribute could have come from any number of the people discussed in this chapter.

But on a deeper level, the resemblance rested on identity, for in Spain Islamic culture as conduit infused Judaism with a large dose of Greek rationalism. In 1841 at the end of a majestic survey of Jewish contributions to geographical literature,

Zunz elaborated on the Greek role in Jewish history. "Three times did Jews encounter the Hellenic spirit, the emancipator of nations." Besides the experience of his own day and the confrontation in the Greco-Roman world, Zunz spoke of the encounter under Islam.

When in the eighth century, the victorious Arabs were subdued by the books of the conquered, Syrian and Arabic authors introduced for a second time Greek knowledge among the Jews of Muslim countries: astronomy, philosophy, medicine, and by degrees geography. German and French Jews, in contrast, partook of the darkness of the Middle Ages, although they still retained advantages over the Christians, not only by virtue of a more ancient cultivation, but also by the gradual introduction and influence of the Hebrew-Arabic literature.[66]

Paradoxically, the contact with Islam had made Judaism part of the Western world.

NOTES

1. Chaim Hillel Ben-Sasson, *Hagut ve-Hanhagah*, Jerusalem 1959, pp. 13–16.

2. Philipp Bloch, "Der Streit um den More des Maimonides in der Gemeinde Posen um die Mitte des 16. Jahrhundert," in *MGWJ*, XXXXVII (1903), pp. 154–155, 167, 346.

3. David Gans, *Zemah David* (in Hebrew), ed. by Mordechai Breuer, Jerusalem 1983, pp. 133, 136–137.

4. Aharon Fritz Kleinberger, *The Educational Theory of the Maharal of Prague* (in Hebrew), Jerusalem 1962, pp. 90–192.

5. Shabbatai Bass, *Siftei Yeshenim* (in Hebrew), Amsterdam 1680, author's introduction. See also Shimeon Brisman, *A History and Guide to Judaic Bibliography*, Cincinnati–New York 1977, pp. 9–13. It is worth noting that both Bass and Naftali Herz Wessely in 1782 employed the same piquant rabbinic dictum to advance their respective views—"Any scholar without breeding is worth less than a carcass" (*Kol hakham she-ein bo daat, neveila tova himenu*—see *Midrash Wayyikra Rabbah*, ed. by Mordecai Margulies, 5 vols., Jerusalem 1953–1960, I, pp. 32–33). Bass chose to interpret the term *daat* to mean scholarly method which one can learn only from a teacher, as opposed to a body of knowledge which one can master alone. (*Siftei Yeshenim*, introd., pp. 4–5.) For Wessely, *daat* connoted secular knowledge which must be acquired by every Jew in addition to and prior to the knowledge of *Torah* incumbent upon him. (*Divrei Shalom ve-Emet*, 1st edn. [n.p.n.d.], end of chap. 1.) The changing social and political circumstances of Ashkenazic Jewry, and not the differences in interpretation, altered the import of the dictum and determined the different reactions.

6. Jakob Emden, *Megilat Sefer*, ed. by David Cahana (reprint Joseph Waldman, New York 1956), pp. 7–53, esp. p. 46.

7. Morris M. Faierstein, "The Liebes Brief. A Critique of Jewish Society in Germany (1749)," in *LBIYB XXVII* (1982), pp. 219–241.

8. Alfred Feilchenfeld (transl. and ed.), *Denkwürdigkeiten der Glückel von Hameln*, Berlin 1913, pp. 89–90, 116–118, 186–187, 190–191.

9. *Heinrich Heine. Säkularausgabe*, 27 vols. (in progress) (Berlin–Paris 1970ff.), VIII, p. 185.

10. *Hame'asef*, VII (1794–1795), pp. 54–67, 120–158, 203–227, 279–360. On the import of the *bon mot*, see James H. Lehmann, "Maimonides, Mendelssohn and

the Me'asfim: Philosophy and the Biographical Imagination in the Early Haskalah," in *LBIYB XX* (1975), pp. 101–103.

11. Aaron Wolfsohn, *Hame'asef, loc. cit.*, p. 210. Isaak Euchel, *Toldot Rabbenu he-Hakham Moshe ben Menahem,* Berlin 1788, p. 7.

12. Salomon Maimon, *An Autobiography,* transl. by J. Clark Murray, Boston 1888, p. 205.

13. Max Freudenthal, *Aus der Heimat Mendelssohns. Moses Benjamin Wulff und seine Familie, die Nachkommen des Moses Isserles,* Berlin 1900, pp. 218–221.

14. Isaac de Pinto, *Apologie pour la nation juive,* Amsterdam 1762; Frances Malino, *The Sephardic Jews of Bordeaux: Assimilation and Emancipation in Revolutionary France,* Alabama 1978.

15. JNUL Jerusalem, 4° 792/B–10, p. 36.

16. Isaak Markus Jost, *Geschichte der Israeliten,* 9 vols., Berlin 1820–1828, VIII, p. 309.

17. Diogene Tama, *Transactions of the Parisian Sanhedrin,* transl. by F. D. Kirwan, London 1807, p. 56. *Décisions Doctrinales du Grand Sanhédrin,* Paris 1812, pp. 6–8. I do think that this modern distinction between the enduring religious and temporary political components of Judaism derives a tenuous plausibility from a somewhat analogous distinction made by Maimonides in his *Guide* between the divine laws of the *Torah* which order the physical life of man in society and those which advance his individual spiritual perfection.

Know that as between these two aims, one is indubitably greater in nobility, namely, the welfare of the soul—I mean the procuring of correct opinions—while the second aim—I mean the welfare of the body—is prior in nature and time. The latter aim consists of the governance of the city and the well-being of the states of all its people according to their capacity. (Moses Maimonides, *The Guide of the Perplexed,* trans. by Shlomo Pines, Chicago 1964, p. 510)

18. For subsequent applications and elaborations of this distinction in Judaism, see Malino, *op. cit.*, pp. 92–93; *Protokolle der ersten Rabbiner-Versammlung zu Braunschweig,* Braunschweig 1844, pp. 63–69; and Samuel Holdheim, *Über die Autonomie der Rabbinen und das Princip der jüdischen Ehe,* 2nd. edn., Schwerin 1847.

19. Simha Assaf (ed.), *Mekorot le-Toldot ha-Hinukh be-Yisrael,* 4 vols., Tel-Aviv 1925–1942, I, p. 234.

20. Leopold Zunz, *Die gottesdienstlichen Vorträge der Juden,* 2nd edn., Frankfurt am Main 1892, p. 474.

21. Eliezer Liebermann, *Or Nogah,* Dessau 1818, part one, pp. 18–19; *Nogah ha-Zedek,* Dessau 1818, p. 27.

22. It should be noted that the close resemblance in pronunciation between the biblical Hebrew taught at German universities of the time and the Hebrew of the Sephardim no doubt bestowed a verisimilitude of correctness on the latter. (See Wilhelm Gesenius, *Hebräische Grammatik,* Halle 1813, pp. 6–13.) Thus it is not surprising to find Zunz transliterating the Hebraic texts of his sermons according to the model of academic Hebrew. (Leopold Zunz, *Predigten,* 2nd edn., Berlin 1846, pp. 17, 105, 157, 158, 198.) In a most interesting letter dated 4th October 1827, J. J. Bellermann, a well-known theologian, scholar, and director of the prestigious Berlin *Gymnasium zum grauen Kloster,* advised Zunz to teach the youngsters in the Jewish communal school over which Zunz presided the Sephardic pronunciation of Hebrew from the very beginning. Bellermann had been invited to observe a public examination of the children. While expressing his pleasure at the event, he did see fit to challenge the

retention of the "Polish pronunciation of Hebrew," because it managed to offend both the vowels and accents of the language. And in conjunction with the vowels, he pointed out the historical superiority of Sephardic Hebrew.

As you well know, the writings of learned Alexandrian Jews—in the Septuagint, Josephus, Philo, and Aquila—show that the Polish pronunciation is incorrect. . . . The learned Portuguese, Spanish, French and Italian Jews have the correct one. Why shouldn't the Jews of Berlin and in fact of Germany choose the better [of the two]? Especially Berlin Jewry which has already adopted so much that is correct? It would indisputably accrue to their honor, if they would offer other communities in this matter an example. (Ludwig Geiger, "Aus L. Zunz' Nachlass," *Zeitschrift für die Geschichte der Juden in Deutschland*, V (1892), pp. 256–257.)

23. Wolf Heidenheim (ed.), *Sefer Kerovot hu Makhzor*, 9 vols., Rödelheim 1800–1805, *Pesah*, "Vorbericht"; *Shemini Azeret ve-Simhat Torah*, "Ha-Piyut ve-ha-Paytanim," p. vi. See also Louis Lewin, "Materialien zu einer Biographie Wolf Heidenheims," *MGWJ*, XLIV (1900), pp. 127–138; XLV (1901), pp. 422–432, 549–558.

24. *Seder ha-Avodah: Gebetbuch für die öffentliche und häusliche Andacht nach dem Gebrauch des Neuen Israelitischen Tempels in Hamburg*, Hamburg 1841.

25. *Der Orient*, 1842, p. 64; *Literaturblatt des Orients*, 1842, cols. 366, 379–381.

26. Abraham Geiger, *Der Hamburger Tempelstreit*, Breslau 1842, p. 28.

27. Gotthold Salomon, *Sendschreiben an den Herrn Dr. Z. Frankel*, Hamburg 1842, p. 35.

28. *Bikurei ha-Itim*, VIII (1827), p. 184. Salomon refers to this passage in his own defense, p. 33.

29. Leopold Dukes, *Zur Kenntnis der neuhebräischen religiösen Poesie*, Frankfurt am Main 1842, pp. 16–29, 93, 133. The book is structured thematically, but most of the examples are taken from the Sephardic orbit.

30. Harold Hammer-Schenk, *Synagogen in Deutschland: Geschichte einer Baugattung im 19. und 20. Jahrhundert (1780–1933)*, 2 vols., Hamburg 1981, I, pp. 251–301. Cf. Hannelore Künzl, *Islamische Stilelemente im Synagogenbau des 19. und frühen 20. Jahrhunderts*, Frankfurt–Bern–New York–Nancy 1984, pp. 109–126.

31. Philipp F. Veit, "Heine: The Marrano Pose," *Monatshefte*, LXVI (1974), pp. 145–156.

32. See below, pp. 217–218.

33. S. S. Prawer, *Heine's Jewish Comedy: A Study of his Portraits of Jews and Judaism*, Oxford 1983, pp. 59–69.

34. *Heine: Säkularausgabe*, IX, pp. 56–57. Cf. Prawer, *op. cit.*, pp. 85–96.

35. Phöbus Philippson, *Die Marannen in Saron*, Phöbus and Ludwig Philippson, I, 2nd edn., Leipzig 1855, p. 92.

36. Berthold Auerbach, *Spinoza: Eine Denkerleben*, 2nd edn., Mannheim 1855; Ludwig Philippson, *Jakob Tirado*, Leipzig 1867.

37. Auerbach, *op. cit.*, p. 94. On the Maimonidean source and the later controversy on it, see James H. Lehmann, *loc. cit.*, pp. 92–93.

38. On Spinoza in the mind of German Jewry in the nineteenth and twentieth centuries, see Leo Strauss, *Spinoza's Critique of Religion*, New York 1965, pp. 15–31. On Auerbach, see Jacob Katz, "Berthold Auerbach's Anticipation of the German-Jewish Tragedy," *Hebrew Union College Annual*, LIII (1982), pp. 215–240.

39. Both *Der Orient* and the *Literaturblatt des Orients* appeared under the editorship of Julius Fürst from 1840 to 1851 and carried the subtitle *Berichte, Studien und Kritiken für jüdische Geschichte und Literatur.*

40. An excellent if not exhaustive overview of nineteenth- and twentieth-century German translations of medieval Jewish philosophical texts can be found in Aron Freimann, *Katalog der Judaica und Hebraica, Stadtbibliothek Frankfurt am Main*, 2nd edn., Graz 1968, pp. 335–340.

41. See the introduction of Simon Scheyer to his German translation of part three of Maimonides, *Guide of the Perplexed* entitled *Dalalat al Haiirin*, Frankfurt am Main 1838, where he intones the similarities between the era of Maimonides and his own. Religiously Scheyer moved rapidly from a state of devout Orthodoxy to one of total alienation. (See Abraham Geiger, *Nachgelassene Schriften*, 5 vols., Berlin 1875–1878, vol. V, p. 17.)

42. Salomon Munk, "Salomo Ibn Gebirol," *Literaturblatt des Orients*, 1846, cols. 721–727. S. Munk, *Le Guide des égarés traité de théologie et de philosophie par Moïse ben Maimoun dit Maimonide*, 3 vols., Paris 1856–1866.

43. S. Munk, *Philosophie und philosophische Schriftsteller der Juden*, transl. by Bernhard Beer, Leipzig 1852, p. 38.

44. Franz Delitzsch, *Zur Geschichte der jüdischen Poesie*, Leipzig 1836; Johann Gottfried von Herder, *Vom Geist der Ebraischen Poesie*, ed. by Karl Wilhelm Justi, 3rd edn., 2 vols., Leipzig 1825. Herder's great study of biblical poetry prompted a kindred biographer to name him evocatively the "Winkelmann of Hebrew poetry." (Quoted by Albert Lewkowitz, *Das Judentum und die geistigen Strömungen des 19. Jahrhunderts*, Breslau 1935, p. 183.)

45. Delitzsch, *op. cit.*, pp. 44–45.

46. *Ibid.*, pp. 79–80. As we have seen (above pp. 78–79), Dukes fully shared Delitzsch's critical opinion of the liturgical legacy of Ashkenazic Jewry, despite a spirited defense of it by Samuel Luzzatto in a letter to him dated 3rd May 1836. In terms of emotional intensity, literary imagination, and wealth of vocabulary, the Ashkenazim surpassed the Sephardim no less than Dante surpassed Tasso. Their faults were an excess of their virtues. (*S. D. Luzzatto's Hebräische Briefe*, ed. by Eisig Gräber, 9 vols., Przemysl 1882–1894, reprinted Jerusalem 1967 in 2 vols., pp. 336–337.) Luzzatto was among the most vigorous critics of the Sephardic mystique.

47. Michael Sachs, *Die religiöse Poesie der Juden in Spanien*, Berlin 1845, pp. 3–29.

48. *Luzzatto's Hebräische Briefe, op. cit.*, p. 779.

49. Thus Sachs omitted a splendid example of a messianic lament by Jehudah Halevi sent him by Luzzatto. (*Ibid.*, pp. 767–768.)

50. *Ozar Nechmad*, ed. by Ignaz Blumenfeld, II (1857), p. 27. See Luzzatto's poignant defense of his review to an irate Sachs in *Hebräische Briefe*, pp. 977–980. Luzzatto was also aggrieved because Sachs had cavalierly dismissed his failure to punctuate the Hebrew text of the poems provided by Luzzatto as a mechanical matter of minor import. Luzzatto had originally stipulated such punctuation as a condition for his assistance. (*Ibid.*, p. 767.)

51. Heine's self-description is translated by Prawer, *op. cit.*, p. 531.

52. *Heinrich Heine Werke*, 4 vols., ed. by Christoph Siegrist, Frankfurt am Main 1968, I, pp. 203–204, 521.

53. Moritz Kayserling, *Sephardim: Romanische Poesien der Juden*, Leipzig 1859, p. 137.

54. Salomon Löwisohn, *Vorlesungen über die neuere Geschichte der Juden*, Vienna 1820. Leopold Zunz, "Salomon ben Isaac, genannt Raschi," *ZWJ*, 1823, pp. 279 (with allusion to Löwisohn, *op. cit.*, p. 82), 281 (with allusion to Löwisohn, *op. cit.*, p. 80), 370 note 94 (with overt reference).

55. Löwisohn, *op. cit.*, p. 73. On Löwisohn, see Reuven Michael, "The Contri-

bution of *Sulamith* to Modern Jewish Historiography" (in Hebrew), *Zion*, XXXIX (1974), pp. 106–113.

56. Ludwig Philippson, *Die Entwickelung der religiösen Idee im Judenthume, Christenthume und Islam*, 2nd edn., Leipzig 1874, p. 132. Moritz Steinschneider, "Jüdische Literatur," in *Allgemeine Encyklopädie der Wissenschaften und Künste*, ed. by Ersch and Gruber, vol. 27, Leipzig 1850, pp. 358, 448, 453, 460. See also Kayserling, *op. cit.*, pp. 131–145.

57. Steinschneider, *loc. cit.*, p. 385.

58. *Ibid.*, pp. 385, 393.

59. *Ibid.*, p. 394.

60. *Ibid.*, p. 385.

61. See also Leopold Zunz, *Zur Geschichte und Literatur*, Berlin 1845, pp. 25–28; Sachs, *op. cit.*, pp. 159–161, 167–168, 180–195.

62. The growing Romantic fascination with Spain in Europe and America in the first half of the nineteenth century ("Oh, lovely Spain! renown'd, romantic land!"—Lord George Byron, *Childe Harold's Pilgrimage*, canto I, stanza 35) was, to be sure, a parallel cultural development which reinforced the Jewish bias. Byron's poetry, Juan Antonio Llorente's history of the Spanish Inquisition, Washington Irving's evocative historical narratives, and Owen Jones's magnificent folio edition of the *Plans, Elevation, Sections and Details of the Alhambra* (2 vols., London 1842) unfurled the drama, glory, and cruelty of medieval Spain. In 1837 William H. Prescott, a Boston Brahmin and man of letters, could claim in the preface to his stirring *History of the Reign of Ferdinand and Isabella, the Catholic of Spain* (3 vols., Boston 1838) that "English writers have done more for the illustration of Spanish history than for that of any other except their own." Despite the language barrier, Prescott's two sympathetic chapters on the history and fate of the Jews in Spain did not escape the attention of Zacharias Frankel, who was moved to translate and reprint them in his scholarly journal, *Zeitschrift für die religiösen Interessen des Judentums*, II (1845), pp. 485–486. The intent of my argument is not to discount the likely influence of these broader currents, but rather to point to what I regard as a deeper, specifically Jewish reason for the German-Jewish appropriation of the Sephardic legacy.

63. *Luzzatto's Hebräische Briefe, op. cit.*, p. 1031.

64. E. M. Butler, *The Tyranny of Greece over Germany*, Boston 1958, pp. 80–81.

65. Marianne Cowan, *Humanist Without Portfolio*, Detroit 1963, p. 79.

66. Leopold Zunz, "Essay on the Geographical Literature of the Jews," in A. Asher, *The Itinerary of Rabbi Benjamin of Tudela*, 2 vols., London–Berlin, 1841, II, p. 303. Translation slightly revised.

Art as Social History:
Moritz Oppenheim and
the German Jewish
Vision of Emancipation

The instant and astounding commercial success of the well-known paintings of traditional Jewish family life by Moritz Oppenheim is a phenomenon of artistic diffusion that begs for historical attention. That it has been utterly ignored, despite the abiding interest in Oppenheim's art, illustrates just once more the disparity between knowing and understanding.[1]

The complete series of twenty grisailles, depicting in the main Jewish religious practice in the German ghetto just prior to emancipation, falls into four general categories: the life cycle (6), the Sabbath (5), the festivals (6), and life outside the ghetto (3). Prompted by the Frankfurt art publisher Heinrich Keller, Oppenheim published his first portfolio of six photographic reproductions along with an evocative explanatory text by Leopold Stein in 1866. Two years later the portfolio had grown to fourteen pictures and by 1874 to eighteen.[2] According to an 1876 advertisement, a set of eighteen pictures could be bought in any one of four different sizes ranging in price from 24 to 162 marks, with the folder extra.[3] With the inclusion of *Hanukkah* and *Shavuot* in 1881, the portfolio format reached its final complement of twenty paintings.[4] Adding special luster to the entire enterprise was publication in 1867 and 1868 by the widely read German family magazine *Die Gartenlaube* of three of Oppenheim's paintings (*Beginning of Sabbath, Passover,* and *Sukkot*) accompanied by a rather effusive text.[5]

The first book version of the series, a handsome folio edition of twenty pictures and text, was printed by Keller in 1882, the year of Oppenheim's death, and sold for the substantial sum of 36 marks.[6] Four years later Keller issued a second edition and yet a third edition in 1901. In 1913 a fourth German edition of much smaller size but with a new text by Emil Levy, also a rabbi, came out in Berlin under the imprint of Louis Lamm.[7] In sum, with a publication record of untold portfolio editions and at least four bound editions over a span of forty-eight years, Oppenheim's *Bilder aus dem altjüdischen Familienleben* may well have been the most popular Jewish book ever published in Germany.

If further proof of popularity (not to speak of influence on the subsequent explosion of Jewish genre painting) be needed, it should be noted that at the same time the *Bilder* sold in book or portfolio, they were also mass-marketed in the form of postcards and decorated pewter and porcelain plates.[8]

Such a record of enthusiasm for this first nineteenth-century effort to portray Judaism through the medium of art locates Oppenheim's work squarely in the domain of social history. Its reception bespeaks a singular accord between artist and audience, providing the social historian with a rare opportunity to probe the state of Jewish consciousness in Germany in the half century before World War One. For what can one say with any degree of reliability about the values, beliefs, attitudes, and expectations of the inarticulate masses prior to the age of the scientific opinion poll? Historians are forever on the lookout for actions and artifacts, techniques and perspectives that might amplify their inaudible voice. This essay represents such an effort, based on the conviction that the Oppenheim phenomenon reveals a collective state of mind. It tells us something of the manner in which German Jewry conceived of emancipation, because it refracted a religious nostalgia fraught with political significance. Through his art Oppenheim delivered a political message that caught the consensus of German Jewry.

That message is best deciphered by the historian of German Jewry and not the historian of Jewish art. The paintings resonate with issues and attitudes that derive directly from the problematic status of an emancipated Judaism within an unemancipated society, and to view them only from the perspective of art history is akin to playing a stereo record through a mono system. Yet more is available to the Jewish historian than even a full awareness of the range of conflicts created by the process of integration. The intent of the artist is further illuminated by at least three contemporary texts which give a semblance of voice to his art.

The first, of course, is the descriptive commentary by Stein which skillfully blends a reverence for the pathos of Jewish history with an appreciation for the virtues of Judaism. In both tone and substance, Stein's text perfectly complements Oppenheim's art. The degree of harmony is not fortuitous. Both men resided in Frankfurt and had worked on the same liturgical commission for the editing of a new prayerbook in the late 1850s. Like Oppenheim, Stein spent his youth in the isolation of pre-modern Judaism and was endowed with a creative spirit that, in his case, expressed itself in poetry and drama as well as theology. By 1862 Stein had resigned his rabbinic post in Frankfurt of sixteen years amid a cloud of controversy and was evidently both available and suitable to assist Oppenheim.[9] The fact that the commentary is already an integral part of the initial portfolio suggests that Stein may actually have served as Oppenheim's religious consultant throughout the project. In tandem, they produced no less than a beautifully designed primer on Judaism, intended for Christian as well as Jew. To quote Stein:

The Christian world does not know Judaism very well and makes little effort to get to know it. Accordingly, these pictures are also of such great value for learning about Judaism, for they reveal in such an appealing way its most intimate spiritual life.[10]

The second text is a tribute to Oppenheim written by Gabriel Riesser in 1854 that rests solidly on a friendship of at least two decades.[11] Riesser had emerged dramatically as the political spokesman for German Jewry by virtue of his principled and pugnacious defense of the right to emancipation uncompromised by any religious surrender. The two men were linked publicly first in 1835 when a group of Baden Jews expressed their gratitude to Riesser for having bravely defended their political interests by presenting him with Oppenheim's handsome oil painting of a young Jewish soldier, who had volunteered for the War of Liberation, returning home on the Sabbath to his still observant family. What made the gift appropriate is that it epitomized Riesser's political ideology: loyalty to faith and fatherland were not in conflict.[12] More important for our purposes, it conveyed Oppenheim's own conviction. There is no evidence that it had been commissioned and Riesser testified in the essay that "The idea of this painting is one of the most deeply felt by the artist, sprung from the very core of his spiritual being."[13]

Given that degree of accord, the friendship deepened steadily. At the end of 1838 Oppenheim, a much sought after portraitist, did an oil painting of Riesser "out of pure friendship," bestowing it on his grateful family as a gift. The sitting took much longer than Riesser expected, because half-way through Oppenheim set aside his first try. But Riesser's patience was sustained by the character of his painter, whom he described in a letter as "a man with a first-rate mind, much experience and culture . . . with whom it is exceptionally pleasant to chat and who, while working diligently, is the one who pretty much keeps the conversation going."[14] Over the years the two men continued to remain in touch through correspondence that went far beyond a perfunctory exchange of greetings.[15] Thus Riesser did not exaggerate when he wrote in his 1854 tribute that he and Oppenheim "had long been united in a most intimate friendship constantly strengthened by mutuality of purpose and sentiment."[16]

In that tribute Riesser celebrated his friend as a quintessentially Jewish artist in the same sense that one can speak of a Christian artist, that is one who places his art in the service of his faith. Unlike his contemporaries, Oppenheim had not spurned his roots to seek renown and wealth in the world of German culture. Rather love and loyalty had moved him to commit his talent to dispelling the prejudice and ignorance which obscured the beauty of Judaism. A telling analogy drove home the point.

Just as Leah's son brings his forlorn mother the flowers he has chanced upon with which she might gain some affection, so does the faithful Jewish artist dedicate the flowers of his genius to his religion and its followers, that he might help thereby to soften the unwarranted antipathy and alienation and to advance the work of love and humanity.[17]

Indeed, the full truth of Riesser's encomium was yet to be realized. By 1854 Oppenheim had done relatively little in the way of "Jewish art." It may just be that Riesser's citation contributed to inspiring fulfillment, for within two years Oppenheim had completed his famous depiction of Lavater's attempt to convert Mendelssohn with Lessing looking on, and by the early 1860s he was at work on a number of the oil originals of the later gouaches.[18]

That the agenda of the 1860s reflected continuity of interest and not a new departure is unequivocally established by our third text, Oppenheim's own *Erinnerungen* composed in 1880, though not published until 1924 by his grandson Alfred Oppenheim. The literary quality of this charming memoir amply confirms Riesser's description of his friend and portraitist: its unpretentious author was a lively raconteur whose well-crafted stories ring with insight, irony, and compassion. Characteristically Oppenheim made no effort to conceal the selectivity of his recall or the restricted audience for which he wrote.

With these belated memoirs penned in 1880, primarily for my dear family as well as for a few friends, I have indeed forgotten much and have intentionally left much, in fact a great deal, unsaid. For these sketches should offer you only pleasant reminiscences.[19]

In truth, they offer much more. They reveal a painter with a lively sense of Jewishness who saw fit to devote a large part of his final testament not to matters of art but to religion. His life was recounted from a Jewish perspective and, consequently, serves to illuminate his art.

II

The most remarkable biographical fact in the life of this "first Jewish painter" in Germany is that his dramatic ascent from the ghetto of Hanau, where he was born in 1800, to the honorary title of professor bestowed on him in 1827 by the Grand Duke of Weimar at the recommendation of Goethe, did not pass through the portal of conversion.[20] In those early decades of partial emancipation, few talented Jews were prepared to deny themselves the unfolding career opportunities afforded by conversion. For most, like Abraham Mendelssohn, who was fated to provide the link between a famous father and a renowned son, religion meant little more than ethics, which could readily be wrapped in most any ceremonial garb.[21] Among aspiring Jewish painters, conversion assured talent its just reward, while the rising middle class, with its hunger for status and immortality, created an ever expanding market for portraiture. Eduard Magnus, the painter of Felix Mendelssohn and one of Berlin's most heralded portraitists, was born in Berlin in 1799 and baptized while yet a child.[22] In contrast, Eduard Bendemann, son of a Berlin banker and close friend of Felix Mendelssohn, converted in 1835 when he married the daughter of his famous Nazarene teacher Wilhelm Schadow, whom he eventually succeeded in 1859 as the director of the important Düsseldorf Academy. It is worth noting that the act of conversion was sandwiched in between Bendemann's grandiloquent artistic statements on the end of Jewish history—*The Jews Mourning in Babylon* (1832) and *Jeremiah at the Ruins of Jerusalem* (1836). These celebrated paintings express more than the pathos of destruction and exile; they imbue the year 587 B.C.E. with a finality that is distinctly Christian.[23]

Oppenheim chose to read Jewish history differently and eventually became a spokesman for the religion he refused to abandon. An age of waning communal constraints and universal disdain for Judaism inevitably transformed a posture of personal loyalty into a paradigmatic model. Like Moses Mendelssohn and Gabriel Riesser, Oppenheim was prepared to use his professional skills in defense of his religious convictions. A coherence between ancestral faith and cultural creativity is the conspicuous leitmotif of the memoir and suggests that Oppenheim was quite aware that the message of his Jewish art sprang from religious sentiments sown in childhood.

That childhood as recollected from a distance of seven decades conveys a family life in which piety and prosperity had not yet been torn asunder. The few clues provided by Oppenheim indicate that his family must have belonged to the wealthier members of the Hanau *Judengasse* with its approximately eighty Jewish dwellings.[24] The house was comfortably outfitted with expensive ceremonial objects, and Oppenheim's father, who probably was a merchant of some kind, seems to have had among his best customers local Christians of status and wealth. Despite a decline in the family's fortunes, resulting perhaps from the French occupation from 1806 to 1813, a change of which even the young Oppenheim was conscious, his father still managed to pay for tutors and a variety of schooling and to amass a dowry of several thousand gulden for his only daughter.[25] The relevance of this sparse economic information to Oppenheim's art may just be in the possibility that the distinctly bourgeois standard of living embodied in the family scenes of the *Bilder* is less a retrojection of nineteenth-century tastes than a reflection of the actual comfort of his parental home. For there is no question that Oppenheim dipped freely into his childhood memories for the material of his art.

The most striking proof of this dependence is his oil painting of 1878 entitled *A Jewish School for Infants*. According to Oppenheim, such a one-room school for toddlers from the ghetto constituted his earliest formal learning experience. The infants were confined to benches along the walls, until called up to learn the Hebrew alphabet from an elderly teacher seated in a large chair in the middle of the room. Barely able to reach the top of the table in front of him, they had to stand on a box to see the printed page from which he taught them. Oppenheim's verbal description of this scene fully matches the painting of 1878, including the tone of affectionate irony.[26]

In general, the Oppenheim paintings seem to be anchored in the religious atmosphere of his own childhood. The rhythm and ethos of traditional Judaism still governed both home and street. Holidays were observed with an eye to beauty and

Moritz's drawings decorated the *Succah*. Hard times did not curb the habit of giving charity. The formative personality in Oppenheim's young life was apparently his mother, a devout and decent woman who set the religious tone of the home. According to family tradition, she gave birth to Moritz at the end of a day-long religious fast (the tenth of Tevet). His abiding affection for her is evidenced not only in his anguish at the news of her death, while he is off pursuing an artistic career in Rome, but also in the moving tribute to her that he pens as an octagenarian in his memoir.[27] The caring and dignified women who grace Oppenheim's depiction of traditional family life are evidently drawn from vivid personal experience.

The childhood in Hanau coincided with the start of momentous changes in Jewish life, and the processes of emancipation and assimilation clearly impacted on the Oppenheim family. Most intriguing in Oppenheim's reconstruction of those years is the utter naturalness with which the family seems to have integrated. The agony of dissonance and alienation which so often characterized that first generation of Jews out of the ghetto is absent, or at least forgotten. Secular education, new forms of self-expression, and a Gentile ambience were appropriated without discarding traditional modes of piety. This unconflicted coexistence predated the French amelioration of 1806, for even Oppenheim's pious mother enjoyed German literature and an occasional visit to the theater, to which she often took Moritz. Still, one stepped outside the ghetto gates with trepidation. The young Oppenheim dreaded his weekly lesson in German calligraphy amid a class of unfriendly Christian children and his father forbade him ever to leave the ghetto to play with them. Yet after 1806 the family did not hesitate to send him to a *Gymnasium* to prepare for a possible career in medicine nor did it protest when he began to show a serious interest in becoming a painter.[28] How many modern Jewish painters from Eastern Europe realized their native talents only by ignoring the sometimes bitter opposition of parents still steeped in traditional Judaism![29] The harmony achieved in his parental home between what appeared to many as the polar opposites of Judaism and the German world would become the personal trademark of Oppenheim's own career as a Jewish painter.

If the memoir is to be believed, and it was not intended for publication, his education as a painter did not induce him to conceal his religious identity or to suppress his Jewish consciousness. While still in Hanau he gained entry to the art collection of a local count by virtue of his artistic promise. There he spent his weekdays copying the masters, while continuing to adhere to the dietary laws so strictly that on one early occasion when the countess went to the trouble of obtaining kosher meat for him, he awkwardly refused to touch it. Upon hearing the story, his parents seemed to approve, his very pious brother Isaac sang his praises outright, and his older brother Simon, already somewhat of a freethinker, slapped him in dismay.[30] If a delicate self-portrait can be dated to this period, his appearance bespoke his loyalties: a sensitive young man, distinctly Jewish, with a large skullcap and sidelocks neatly combed back over his ears.[31]

Sometime later in Munich, the next step on his artistic journey, he lodged and took his meals at a kosher inn. In addition to the 30 gulden provided him monthly by Simon, he began to paint portraits "a tout prix," though not on the Sabbath. At one point, his homesickness was relieved by a hundred page German letter in Hebrew characters which minutely described life in his beloved Hanau *Judengasse* "that could scarcely have been matched by a Kompert." The writer was his brother Herz who eventually married a Christian. From Munich Oppenheim went to Paris where his stay of several months at the studio of Jean Baptiste Regnault did not teach him much more than to overcome his inhibition at painting models in the nude.[32]

The decisive spurt to artistic maturity and public acclaim came during Oppenheim's four-year sojourn in Rome from 1821 to 1825, where he fell under the influence of the German Nazarenes and especially their leader Johann Friedrich Overbeck. According to Ferdinand Hiller, the composer and long-time friend of Oppenheim, he always regarded Overbeck's *oeuvre* with unrestrained enthusiasm.[33] However, it was not the monuments of Rome or the austere religious intensity of the Nazarenes or the dazzle of high German society in which he traveled that riveted the imagination of the aspiring Jewish painter, but rather the ancient and still oppressed Roman ghetto. Repeatedly he returned till he penetrated its layers of suspicion toward strangers. In time he was able to arrange for Sabbath meals in the ghetto; he observed its different rituals attentively, and bristled at the indignities to which its occupants were still subjected by the Church. Efforts to convert him by the Nazarenes merely reinforced his loyalties. He celebrated the simplicity, intimacy, and equality of the synagogue over against the ornate splendor, economic disparities, and hierarchical structure of Roman Catholicism.[34]

News of his mother's death sent him reeling in grief to the ghetto where he spent the seven-day period of intense mourning (the *Shiva*) among his coreligionists. Thereafter he relocated for a time to Naples to shake off his state of depression without giving up on finding a quorum of Jews in which to recite the Kaddish. More important, Naples provided the key to his future. The warm reception accorded him by Baron Carl Meyer von Rothschild created the ties which would eventually make Oppenheim the painter and art factotum of the Frankfurt Rothschilds. In 1825 Oppenheim left Italy and took up permanent residence in Frankfurt, where in time he became known as "the painter of the Rothschilds and the Rothschild of the painters."[35]

The purpose of this selective biographical excursus has been to illuminate the second half of that sobriquet. To be called "the Rothschild of the painters" surely meant that Oppenheim was the best in his field, but beyond that it also connoted the sense that excellence and notoriety were not gained at the expense of religion. Accomplishment in the larger world did not sever parochial moorings. As with the Rothschilds themselves, pride of ancestry remained, even as the degree of observance waned. There is no intention here to argue that Oppenheim abided by all the minutiae of Jewish law, though he probably observed much more than just the fast of Yom Kippur as reported by Hiller in his heartfelt obituary. The point is rather, as Hiller rightly stressed, that Judaism unquestionably played a large part in his life. Hiller defined "the special relationship" insightfully as "less of a faith or religion than a home (*Heimat*)."[36] For Oppenheim, and I dare say for many Jews of the modern era, Judaism was neither creedal nor behavioral but emotional—à sense of place, an organizing principle of reality acquired in childhood and anchored in filial piety. In depicting the sanctity of the Jewish home, Oppenheim avowed its centrality in the formation of religious sentiment, autobiographically and historically.

III

The global message of the Oppenheim *Bilder* was consciously put by Stein toward the end of the volume through a Riesser quotation. "The Jew of the nineteenth century seeks to be fair to the present but not to deny his past."[37] But to state the message so baldly is to miss the subtle indirection and nuanced effect with which it was delivered. The paintings were disarmingly didactic in their treatment of a diversity of themes once freighted with controversy. A bitterly contested emancipation had rendered the right of Judaism to survive highly problematic, and only our own familiarity with the paintings and distance from the period have dulled our senses to the issues. In other words, the complex message of the medium can best be explicated through a contextual analysis of its thematic strands. Appearances notwithstanding, there was nothing innocent or self-evident about the way Oppenheim worked. Stein rightfully called him "the thinking painter."[38]

As the title of the series indicates, the focus was the family and no less than thirteen of the twenty scenes related to the practice of Judaism in a family setting. The Jewish home had constituted the locus of Oppenheim's earliest venture into the genre mode, *The Return of the Volunteer,* and at the time Riesser in his verbose but thoughtful statement of acceptance stressed the significance of the choice: "Indeed the artist has chosen the right picture in order to bring vividly to mind our religion as formed thousands of years ago: the family (as) its sanctuary, parental love its symbol, father and mother its priests (*die Heiligen*)."[39] By the 1860s the cultural taste of middle-class Germans reinforced the choice. The era of the *Gartenlaube* was in full swing with the family as both its audience and program. A weekly with a large national circulation, it embarked on a program of gradual political liberalization through the edification of the family. Its handsomely illustrated pages provided a predigested fare of science, ethnography, fiction, poetry, history and politics, something for every member of the family delivered at a leisurely pace in florid, sentimental prose. The tone was reverential, the mood optimistic, and the cultural purview quite cosmopolitan.[40] Thus when Oppenheim conceived the idea of portraying Judaism graphically, there was no reason to alter the setting. The family was "in."

Beyond that, the family focus permitted Oppenheim to start from strength. Friend and foe alike had long agreed that the vigor and sanctity of family life was crucial to understanding Judaism religiously and historically. Hegel's deep insight into the character of the Hebrew Bible applied to much of pre-modern Judaism.

The individual never comes to the consciousness of independence; on that account we do not find among the Jews any belief in the immortality of the soul; for individuality does not exist in and for itself. But though in Judaism the *Individual* is not respected the *Family* has inherent value; for the worship of Jehovah is attached to the Family, and it is consequently viewed as a substantial existence.[41]

While the theological condition described by Hegel had been corrected by Rabbinic Judaism with the introduction of a belief in an afterlife, the subservience of the individual Jew to communal constraints remained a social reality throughout the medieval period.

In 1846 in a stirring historical drama on Uriel Acosta, the prolific Gentile author and acknowledged leader of the radical Young Germans Karl Gutzkow delivered a shuddering example of the once terrifying power of clerical authority in Jewish life. The power of the ancient truism that "the magic of the family is deeply rooted in our people" induced Acosta, the prototype of a nineteenth-century Jewish intellectual, to abandon his vision of truth, to forego flight, and to suffer the vengeance of the Rabbinic court in Amsterdam. Attachment to family led to intellectual castration and martyrdom. Yet the object of Gutzkow's controlled wrath was not the post-emancipation Jewish community but the reigning conservative alliance of throne and altar in Prussia.[42]

By mid-century political emancipation had transformed the medieval social reality, setting the individual Jew free to conduct his life in accord with the dictates of his conscience, and libido. Adherence to Jewish law had become entirely a matter of personal volition and religious practice, increasingly confined to the arena of the synagogue. Oppenheim appeared to counter these trends by recalling the importance of the family in the habituation of religious practice and the inculcation of moral values. Unbridled individual freedom could be moderated only by the revival of a living religion in the home. A Judaism restricted to the synagogue would soon resemble little more than a museum relic. Private practice had to correspond to public profession in order that inner commitment might supplant external compulsion.

As portrayed by Oppenheim, the traditional Jewish family was imbued with a love for learning. Living rooms are lined with shelves of sacred books and their study is an extension of worship. Older men remain in the synagogue long after the end of public prayer to immerse themselves in the perusal of timeless texts, whereas the home provides the forum in which the youngster is called upon to display the accomplishments of the classroom, on Saturday afternoons and on the occasion of his Bar-Mitzvah. The ghetto was not a community of illiterates, and even women, who as a rule were denied the benefit of formal religious education, were not strangers to the printed word. In one telling depiction of the tangible tranquility of the ghetto street on Saturday afternoon, Oppenheim prominently displayed the figure of a wizened grandmother poring over the scriptural lesson of the week in her personal copy of the *Ze'enah U-re'enah*, the Yiddish anthology of rabbinic homily and exegesis for women in the Ashkenazi world.[43]

The upshot of these details was to temper the collective "inferiority complex" which had set in with the first faint glimmer of a change in the locus of Jewish life, from the periphery of the body politic into its very midst. Beginning with Mendelssohn, Jewish leadership had adopted a program of self-improvement, predicated on the unquestioned cultural backwardness of the Jewish masses.[44] Oppenheim's portrayal softened the critique: perhaps uncultured, but not unlettered. The "oriental" heritage of Judaism may be alien and distasteful to Western sensibilities, but it is not objectively primitive. Nor is Yiddish proof of illiteracy. Obliquely Oppenheim made a case for the cerebral character of traditional Judaism.

With less restraint, he celebrated the dignity of the Jewish woman. She presided over the sanctuary in which the routine of daily life was sanctified by the practice of Judaism, and Oppenheim projected her as a commanding presence, a person of stature, wisdom, warmth, and piety. The nobility and harmony which marked the homes he painted were her accomplishment. From the very outset in his *Return of the Volunteer* Oppenheim assigned the mother pride of place by locating her at the very heart of the scene. Attention to her dominant religious role domestically yielded a more balanced judgment on the status of women in traditional Judaism than the wholesale indictment set forth by Abraham Geiger just a few years later in 1837.

Let there be not distinction from now on between the duties for men and women unless deriving from the natural laws governing the sexes; no assumption about the intellectual minority of women as though they were incapable of grasping the profound truths of religion; no institution of public worship either in terms of form or content, that would close the gates of the temple to women; no humiliation of women in the form of the marriage-service and no imposition of fetters which might easily come to destroy a woman's happiness.

But Geiger was a full century ahead of his time. The acquisition of political rights for women within the *Gemeinde* (the right to vote and be elected) had to precede the campaign for equality within the synagogue.[45] In contrast to Geiger, Oppenheim sensed that the absence of public equality in Jewish life did not simply mean religious nonage or historical insignificance. Through the agency of the family, women exerted constant influence on the course of Jewish survival. In the words of Stein on the studious grandmother with her Yiddish compendium: "Look carefully again at this lovable and loyal little old lady and the riddle will be unraveled, how the Jewish people (Volksstam) managed to avoid drowning amid its endless suffering—*the virtue of its women rescued it.*"[46]

If the family was crucial to the transmission of Judaism, it also served to refract the quality of both its moral and ritual dimensions. As focus for the entire series, the family lent itself to a visual discourse on the nature of Judaism. The subject begged for popular treatment, for the formidable and largely unreconciled opposition to emancipation in Germany had rested much of its case on a relentlessly derogatory view of Judaism. Could adherents of such a religion become useful and trustworthy citizens? Many Jews, who likewise identified with this critique, suffered from grave doubts.[47]

Oppenheim's traditional family exemplified the loftiness of Jewish morality. In a variety of settings, he demonstrated the sanctity and wholesomeness of matrimony in Judaism, grounded in religious commitment and governed by mutual respect and affection. The purpose of marriage was to have children and they abounded in these paintings. Only one, depicting the observance of a *Yahrzeit* somewhere during the Franco-Prussian War, was without the presence of even a single Jewish child, for obvious reasons. Observance is a family affair and children of all ages are included. The cultivation of a lasting love for Judaism is the ultimate goal of a recurring pageantry of ritual. Children are not only an object of endless pleasure and pride but more deeply a source of consolation: they symbolize the future of Judaism. In turn, whether the occasion is solemn or festive, the relationship toward them is marked by tenderness.

Equally significant, Oppenheim stressed that tenderness extended beyond the immediate members of the family. The frequent figure of the Polish Jew with his distinctive garb in paintings like *Sabbath Eve, Sabbath Afternoon, Close of Sabbath,* and *Passover* bespoke the openness and hospitality of the traditional Jewish home. In fact, concern for the stranger transcended the Jewish world. In *The Village Vendor,* a picture to which we shall return, Oppenheim prominently displayed a Jewish youngster accompanying his father about to journey forth for the week giving charity to a barefoot German adolescent. There is no double standard here: want, regardless of creed, deserves to be alleviated.

On the quality of Jewish morality, Oppenheim's art took issue with Kant's philosophy, which had denied moral worth to any act dictated externally. Only acts which derive from the self-legislating capacity of rational man, from the autonomy of his individual will can lay claim to the title of ethical behavior. Kant's philosophic attack against the very idea of a heteronomous moral system, while threatening all revealed religion, posed a special challenge to Judaism with its thoroughly legal character. To Kant it seemed heteronomy incarnate, a statutory corpus imposed for political ends. Lacking ethical intent, Judaism proliferated forms of soulless piety. In consequence, Kant refused to grant it the name religion or even a place in the history of religion.[48]

Given the source, the substance of this harsh indictment was to reverberate down through the next two centuries to Moritz Lazarus, Hermann Cohen, and beyond. The import of Oppenheim's work was to restore Judaism to the status of religion. The moral norms embodied in the traditional family certainly had their roots in external prescription, but the ease and grace of their enactment testified persuasively as to the degree of internalization. Not the source but the whole-hearted acceptance of norms measured the worth of an ethical act, even in the noumenal world. In the phenomenal world illustrated by Oppenheim, the spon-taneous and natural expression of the moral virtues pointed to a successful tran-sition from heteronomy to autonomy.[49]

On the quality of Jewish ritual, Oppenheim produced even more evidence to refute the charge of "mechanical worship."[50] Indeed, many Jews shared and am-plified the charge, even as they defended the integrity of Jewish morality.[51] Op-penheim's art served to dissolve the prevailing conception of law and piety as polar opposites. As lived in the traditional Jewish home, prescribed ritual was neither dreary nor oppressive, observed only out of guilt; nor was it the antithesis of joy, beauty, or serenity. Rather it constituted the uplifting medium of expression for genuine religious sentiment and a set of colorful symbols for conveying ultimate meaning. Nowhere was this inner spirituality more effectively shown than in Op-penheim's portrayal of the final moments in the synagogue before the start of Yom Kippur: a myriad of telling details summed up the solemnity of the hour and the state of individual preparedness.[52]

In the process of averring Judaism as religion, Oppenheim touched upon some very specific and highly charged issues. For example, he communicated the sense of Jewish unity which had prevailed prior to the rupture of emancipation. In one picture there is the ubiquitous charity box for the Holy Land, in another a Pales-tinian emissary probably working the Diaspora for funds.[53] And in many, as noted before, there is the Polish guest, whose honorable welcome in German homes sug-gested the common language, shared religious practice, and frequent intercourse which had once joined the disparate sectors of the Ashkenazi world.[54] Emanci-pation in the West had inflicted a bifurcation that turned kinsmen into adversaries.

Similarly provocative was the circumcision scene which introduced the entire series. While that choice may seem quite natural, given the fact that the first six paintings depict the life cycle, it must be remembered that circumcision was a rite that offended the sensibilities of many an educated German Jew who regarded it as a primitive vestige of an oriental religion. Some even refused to have sons cir-cumcised while insisting on their Jewishness and their right to be registered as members of the *Gemeinde*. Clearly the matter touched on basic questions of self-definition and status and consequently remained a bone of public contention from the time of the Frankfurt Reform Association in 1843 to the Augsburg Synod of 1871.[55] In 1866, some three years after Oppenheim had completed the original oil painting of the circumcision scene, sixty-six Viennese Jewish doctors submitted a brief against the rite to the board of the Vienna Jewish community, claiming among other things that the operation fated Jewish children to be physically weaker than their Christian counterparts and curtailed the lifespan of Jewish males.[56]

Indeed, Oppenheim did give heed to contemporary sensibilities. His oblique representation focused merely on the *dramatis personae* prior to the baby's arrival, in striking contrast to Bernard Picart's indelicate engraving of some 130 years earlier where the exposed child is center stage with legs held forcibly apart and foreskin about to be clipped. Furthermore, Oppenheim, unlike Picart, located the ceremony visibly in the synagogue after the morning service, and the place bestowed the meaning. Circumcision is a religious act, neither barbaric nor hygienic, which defines status. Not private birth but public initiation marks a male's entry into the covenant of Judaism.[57]

In his treatment of the marriage ceremony, Oppenheim again appeared intent to underscore the religious nature of the occasion. Despite the fact that this time the locus was outside the synagogue, in accordance with late medieval Ashkenazi practice, the presence of a rabbinic officiant from eastern Europe draped in a prayer shawl, the serious demeanor of bride and groom, and the display of two decanters of wine projected the solemnity of a religious act, exactly the mood which Picart's raucous version of a Jewish wedding had failed to convey.[58] Given the widespread view that a Jewish marriage was not more than a civil act concluding an economic arrangement, the point was by no means idle. Samuel Holdheim, the most consistent and therefore extreme Reformer of the century, had devoted an entire book in 1843 to the argument that both legally and historically matters of personal status in Jewish law belong to the civil realm and hence should be relinquished to the jurisdiction of the state.[59] Berthold Auerbach disseminated the same view in his widely read novel *Dichter und Kaufmann* where he offered the following interpretation of the Jewish wedding:

. . . their marriages (i.e., of Jewish beggars on the road) were consummated on the country roads by the simple transfer of a ring and the presence of two witnesses. Such a marriage was perfectly lawful according to the original principles of the Jewish religion, for marriage, as a purely civil contract, needed no clergyman, and even by the clergy was not consecrated in the synagogues, but outside under a canopy stretched for the purpose.[60]

It was to counter this uncomplimentary impression that early in the nineteenth century German Jews began to transfer their weddings into the synagogue and to embellish them with an edifying address. Precisely because of the resemblance to Christian practice, Hungarian Orthodoxy, but not German, repudiated even this minimal change in custom.[61] Its unbroken insularity spared it the need to establish the spirituality of Judaism. Without the intrusion of self-consciousness, the familiar was still self-evident. But Oppenheim addressed acculturated German Jews who had to defend their right to remain different. His extraordinary success in creating a visual panoply of moments of Jewish piety made his work an effective instrument for correcting Christian as well as Jewish biases.

The didactic art of Oppenheim accomplished not only a transvaluation of traditional Judaism but also a rehabilitation of the ghetto in which it was practiced. Chronologically most of the scenes were placed in the closing decades of the eighteenth century when residence was still restricted to the ghetto and emancipation, but a chimera. The vision of that ghetto conjured up by the artist's eye, however, hardly accorded with the prevailing image. Oppenheim's ghettos did not loom as the embodiment of Jewish cultural inferiority, social backwardness, economic sterility, and moral depravity as contended so vehemently by the early opponents of emancipation and the Maskilim. In the spirit of Heine's *Sabbath Princess,* Oppenheim painted the ghetto as a refuge of civility and sanctity in an uncivilized world, an oasis in which the Jew, forced to seek his livelihood in hostile terrain, returned to restore body and soul. In his comment on *The Village Vendor* Stein struck the same note: "In the ghetto in which they were locked up nightly and turned into city prisoners, there they were actually free, uplifted by an ennobling feeling of self-worth."[62] Moreover, Oppenheim's vendor was neither a hawker nor a huckster, but a respectable, well-dressed traveling merchant whose bearing betokened probity and integrity. The ghetto was a community permeated with middle-class values, a transcendent rhythm, and a sense of superiority. Closing the gates meant excluding an inferior way of life. Stein cited the revealing response of one former ghetto dweller when asked what it felt like to be locked in over the weekend? " 'What?' explained the jovial old man. 'They locked us in? Not at all! We locked them out.' "[63]

Rehabilitation of the pre-emancipation ghetto, therefore, was an exercise in reconciliation. To Jews but a generation or two out of the ghetto Oppenheim proclaimed that such humble origins were not a badge of shame or a source of character defects. The unabated virulence of German resistance to Jewish aspirations were not to be explained in terms of vestigial traits from the ghetto which impaired Jewish behavior. The appropriate attitude toward the immediate past was pride and not embarrassment. Oppenheim had set out to create a usable past, one that might spare Jews the enervating waste involved in repressing the ghetto experience. In consequence, Adolph Kohut could report at the turn of the century in his popular one-volume *Geschichte der deutschen Juden*: "With amazement does the world now realize that the ghetto was not only filled with dark walls and narrow alleys, but also with an abundance of poetry and spirit."[64]

If Oppenheim's *Bilder* open in the ghetto of the eighteenth century, they close unmistakably in the emancipation of the nineteenth. The final three paintings of *The Village Vendor, Yahrzeit Service,* and *The Return of the Volunteer* seem carefully designed and selected to recapitulate a major theme implicit throughout the series: the compatibility of Judaism with the demands of citizenship. They deal not merely with the life of the individual Jew outside the ghetto, but the emergence of Judaism from the ghetto. Thus both substantively and chronologically they constitute a fitting denouement. They proclaim overtly that the adherents of Judaism are unequivocally suited for admission into the body politic, for as Oppenheim had shown with such pathos and insight, Jews are neither misanthropes, nor subversives, nor parasites. The compatibility of their twin allegiance to religion and country was deftly enunciated already in *The Village Vendor,* a poignant vignette suggesting the larger phenomenon of transition from the periphery of civil society to its center. As the vendor leaves his home he kisses the mezuzah while his son treats a wandering Christian youth to an act of charity. The very simultaneity of the two acts on the threshold of entering the outside world symbolized the lack of conflict between the disparate sets of obligations.

In a striking detail of an earlier picture in the series, *The Rabbi's Blessing,* Oppenheim alluded to the ample experience of medieval Jewry in reconciling the dictates of multiple loyalties. The synagogue in which the sage blessed the youngster after a Sabbath morning service has a pillar displaying a large plaque with the traditional Hebrew prayer for the welfare of the Gentile ruler just above a padlocked charity box for Jews in Jerusalem. Their close proximity in the sanctuary denoted the degree of compatibility.

For the modern world, however, the ultimate test of compatibility was the battlefield, and emancipated Jewry hastened to allay all doubts. In 1807 the Paris Sanhedrin granted Jews in the military, whether at the front or not, a blanket dispensation from the gamut of religious obligations for the duration of their service, and in 1846 the Breslau Rabbinical Conference exempted soldiers and civil servants from the manifold duties of Sabbath observance.[65] But the intent of Oppenheim's final two pictures on Jews in the military was not to reiterate or amplify those anxious declarations. On the contrary, he seemed eager to demonstrate that even the absorbing demands of wartime did not require a total suspension of Jewish loyalty. The issue, of course, was not military service alone, but the uncompromising conception of citizenship. In his reflections on *The Returning Volunteer,* Riesser had emphasized the symbolic character of the painting: "We see in the youthful warrior the inspired love for the fatherland coupled with the fervent adherence to the religious life of his family to whose bosom he returns."[66] Some thirty years later when Oppenheim returned to the painting to prepare the grissaille for the printed portfolio, he heightened its effect: the young soldier now bears a distinctively Jewish physiognomy, carries his arm in a sling testifying to service on the battlefield, and has an admiring sister with head demurely covered who no longer looks like his lover.[67]

Oppenheim's assertiveness went beyond a claim for compatibility to a denial of subordination. Piety and patriotism were co-equal, that is the vision of emancipation enunciated in his rendition of a *Yahrzeit* observance during the Franco-Prussian War. A ragtag Minyan of German soldiers in a French farmhouse brings the war to a momentary halt. Even in the midst of battle Judaism claims its rights. Not what has to be surrendered but what can be preserved is the focus. Oppenheim assumes compatibility and urges self-respect. Reverence for one's ancestors is a declaration of the right to be different, of a conception of citizenship that did not curb freedom of religion, of a vision of society based on cultural pluralism.[68]

The point of this essay has been to contend that this idea of emancipation was not the isolated view of a Gabriel Riesser or a Moritz Oppenheim but the public credo of German Jewry. Oppenheim translated Riesser's emancipation ideology into the medium of art and the unprecedented acclaim for both men is testimony to its diffusion. Nearly all the paintings were completed in the decade of the 1860s as the final legal barriers to full emancipation were being dismantled across Germany, and their serene, sentimental mood betrays the hopefulness of the age as well as the sunny disposition of the artist. Ignored is the pain and precariousness of Jewish existence with Tisha B'Av, the fast day commemorating the destruction of the temples in Jerusalem, conspicuously missing.[69] Yet at least part of the immense popularity of the series is directly attributable to the renewed virulence and ominous dimensions of antisemitism in Germany at the end of the 1870s. It is hardly an accident of publishing history that Oppenheim's *Bilder* in book form went through two quick editions in the 1880s at a time when confidence in the permanence and quality of emancipation began to waver. Stein's sober comment on *The Return of the Volunteer* suddenly gained a distressing relevance: "May the broken arm not symbolize the shattered expectations of the Jews nor the cross (the iron cross on the young soldier's chest) the return of the 'Christian state.'"[70] Both the medium and the message serve to fortify the resolve of an anxious community. Counsel delivered in a decade of hope had become consolation for a decade of gloom: political equality was not to be secured through religious suicide. With Oppenheim, Jewish iconography emerged as a wholly new and unexpected resource in the battle to preserve Jewish identity.

One telling piece of external evidence, also drawn from the field of Jewish iconography, to confirm this reading of Oppenheim and his audience. Some time after the Franco-Prussian War an anonymous artist created a commemorative panel of the Yom Kippur services held for Jewish soldiers of the German army on the 5th and 6th of October 1870 outside the besieged city of Metz. Again it is the mass production and broad appeal of this artifact of folk art which attract the attention of the social historian. The scene is a valley with a large assembly of Jewish soldiers standing in reverential pose and fervent prayer, facing a small mound with a simple wooden ark, a large box serving as a table, and a cantor with *tallit* leading the services. In the distance lies Metz dominated by a single church spire and up on the hill, barely visible, a line of German soldiers guarding their praying comrades in arms throughout the day. In the corners of the panel is a consecutive poetic rendition of the event in which we are told that 1200 Jewish soldiers participated, while along the top in both Hebrew and German appears the resonant verse from the prophet Malachi: "Do we not all have one father; did not one God create us all?"[71]

Investigation into the literary sources on the war experience quickly reveals that the panel depicts a pious myth, but which, like all myth, is redolent with existential meaning. The facts of the matter are more modest, though not less significant. As a result of inquiries from two sides—Jewish soldiers in the field and the rabbinate of Mannheim—permission was granted to a rabbinic intern from Mannheim by the commanding general of the First Army Corps, von Manteuffel, to conduct services during Yom Kippur running a total of 7½ hours. Held in two small adjoining rooms and without benefit of a Torah scroll, the services attracted some 150 Jewish military personnel. According to one grateful participant the religious intensity was extraordinary: "Not one of us ever prayed with such ardent devotion in the most magnificent temple back home as in this small, humble room with its broken-down door, knocked-out windows, and walls riddled by shells."[72]

However, historical significance had little to do with size or fervor. The occasion marked a rare instance in which the Prussian government extended a token of official sanction to the practice of Judaism. Unlike the wars against Denmark in 1864 and Austria in 1866, this war had coincided with the fall festivals of the Jewish calendar and the demand for chaplains and services was not only an expression of religious need but also of political aspiration. Jewish spokesmen were coming to realize that in a country of established churches, genuine emancipation had to comprise equal status for Jews and Judaism. The government's long-standing policy of denying status and support to the religious institutions and spiritual leaders of Judaism unfurled for all to see its contempt for the religion of its Jewish citizens. The gesture of Manteuffel and the subsequent appointment by the government of three civilian Jewish chaplains seemed to augur a radical change in official policy.[73]

By enlarging freely on the details of the event, the commemorative panel created a myth laden with political symbolism. First, it vividly conveyed a sense of the large number of Jews who had served their country, a figure which Ludwig Philippson, the venerable editor of Germany's oldest Jewish newspaper, had energetically set out to determine right after the war. With the cooperation of Jewish communal officials he quickly compiled and published a preliminary master list containing the names of 2531 Jewish soldiers, along with a special list of 83 whose wounds had earned them the iron cross.[74] The effort was inspired as much by the desire to demonstrate to the government the objective need for Jewish chaplains as by eagerness to exhibit to all the depth of Jewish patriotism. For the artist, the setting of a service provided the only way to construe a visual image of the aggregate number of Jews in the army.

At the same time, the imposing size of that service of 1200 Jewish soldiers reinforced the official nature of the occasion. Army headquarters had seen fit to release these men from duty, to treat their religious sensibilities with no less respect and concern than it showed for those of its Catholic and Protestant soldiers. Jews had indeed contributed mightily to the unification of Germany and the service at Metz was emblematic of the hoped-for extension of full legitimacy and equality to Judaism in the new empire.

Finally, the panel symbolized a vision of emancipation that asserted the right to retain and cultivate Jewish loyalties. If even on the battlefield Jews were not compelled to forego their religious needs, in fact to satisfy them made them better soldiers, then certainly once back in society they had every right to preserve their religious affiliation, in fact doing so made them better citizens. As both the verse from the Hebrew Bible and the line of Christian soldiers standing watch suggest, it was a vision of civic unity based on religious diversity, a diversity itself rooted in and curbed by the consciousness of ultimate theological accord. The body politic had neither the right nor the power to obliterate the religious expression of deep historical loyalties.

The paintings of Oppenheim and the Metz commemorative reflect how far German Jewry had come since the hasty and servile dispensation of the French Sanhedrin. The issue was no longer the need to relinquish but the right to retain. Self-respect had begun to replace fear. A protracted struggle for admission and equality had crystalized a vision of emancipation which not only provided a framework for Jewish survival but also made a contribution to the political theory of the modern state.

IV

The source of Oppenheim's inspiration no less than the significance of its execution is a question that likewise transcends the parameters of art history. To be sure, his genre and historical paintings were entirely in tune with the prevailing Biedermeier appetite for depiction of the past as expressed in the meticulous work of Adolf von Menzel, the irreverent art of Karl Spitzweg, and the maudlin illustrations of the *Gartenlaube*. Moreover, we should not discount the influence of the Nazarenes who offered Oppenheim a powerful model for the rejuvenation of art and religion through mutual interaction. Long years after his sojourn in Italy, Oppenheim was still on intimate terms with Philip Veit, the son of Dorothea Schlegel and grandson of Moses Mendelssohn, a devout Catholic, and a leading practitioner of Christian art.[75]

However, the purpose to which the medium was put ultimately derived from Jewish sources and they go well beyond the fond recollection of childhood memories. For Oppenheim, unlike Heine, Judaism remained a living presence, an existential fact which readied him to embrace the justice of Riesser's campaign. The first portfolio appeared just three years after Riesser's death in 1863 and, read correctly, took up the cudgels for the same cause. Whereas Riesser had contended for Judaism's political right to equality and survival, Oppenheim produced the evidence for the authenticity and dignity of its religious life.

But in this regard, he was not the first. Others in the field of literature had preceded him and their work in fact provides the most illuminating context in which to locate the genesis of his Jewish art. In the mid-decades of the nineteenth century a cluster of young Jewish authors writing in German began to create a genre of ghetto short story and novel whose stance and tone marked a dramatic break with the unrelieved polemical thrust of *Haskalah* and Yiddish literature on the same subject. Born in the shadow of the ghetto and working quite independently of each other, men like Leopold Kompert, Aron Bernstein, Salomon Kohn, Ludwig Philippson, Marcus Lehmann, and briefly Berthold Auerbach used the vehicle of fiction to capture the pathos and drama and virtue of the disappearing social microcosm from which they hailed. The ghetto had been blamed for so much, yet understood by so few. With empathy and insight they wrote of Jewish life across Central Europe in the century prior to emancipation, each one about the region he knew best. Through a skillful blend of story, dialogue, and description they conveyed a vivid sense of the ghetto's assorted inhabitants, inner tranquility, ethical nobility, quiet heroism, intellectual elitism, rich family life, language, and folklore without concealing its darker sides or the tensions of transition. These were not novels of rebellion, demolition, or didactic enlightenment, bristling with satire and sarcasm, but rather retrospectives done with warm hues and gentle irony. The novels defied the unabated German, and often Jewish, rhetoric on the need to obliterate the baleful effects of ghetto degeneracy and bespoke a renewal of self-respect based on reconciliation with the immediate past.

The absence of any monographic treatment of the literary accomplishment of these mid-century writers and others reflects the failure to appreciate the basic change in attitude their works embody.[76] The positive valence given to late medieval Ashkenazi Judaism directly contravened the penchant for self-definition in terms of Sephardi Judaism and the conviction that the two centuries before emancipation constituted the nadir of European Jewish history. Both perceptions—of Sephardi superiority rooted in worldliness and Ashkenazi inferiority grounded in insularity—expressed the profound alienation of emancipated German Jewish intellectuals from their own religious heritage. Even Heine who made an abortive effort at some slight correction of the imbalance in his *Der Rabbi von Bacherach* could not suppress his Sephardi preference.[77] The founders of *Wissenschaft des Judentums* wore the same cognitive spectacles and turned first to exhuming the poetic and philosophic monuments of Spanish Jewry or their Islamic Jewish prototypes. The young Zunz soon became cognizant of the prevailing distortion and devoted much of his scholarly output to the rehabilitation of rabbinic culture in medieval Ashkenaz, but even he despised its later epigoni.[78] Reconciliation had to await the literary imagination, which discovered the beauty of the ghetto's inner life. Based on personal experience and collective memory, the writers of *Ghettogeschichten* conjured up the world of the simple Jew.

It should be evident by now that this proliferating literature, which began with

Auerbach's popular *Dichter und Kaufmann* in 1839 and in many ways is the Jewish analogue of his *Schwarzwälder Dorfgeschichten* of 1843, commended itself as a fertile source for Oppenheim's *Bilder.* The striking affinities in subject and perspective strongly suggest influence. But the evidence is even more concrete and cogent. In perusing this literature with the paintings in mind, one soon comes across literary scenes which seem to have served as the very blueprint for specific pictorial compositions. For example, Bernstein's Posen ghetto drawn so tenderly in *Vögele, der Maggid,* abounds with cats, as do most of Oppenheim's family scenes.[79] Similarly, Bernstein's playful rumination on the Shabbos nap as the immediate and ineluctable consequence of the soporific effect of *kugel* may have been translated by Oppenheim into the slumbering figure of the father at the table after dinner in his *Sabbath Afternoon.*[80] A still more apparent literary parallel was Auerbach's description of the *Dorfgeher's* exit on Sunday morning kissing the mezuzah as his wife prays fervently for his safety in the background—the same two details showing up later in Oppenheim's composition.[81]

Finally, and most convincing of all because of the anomaly of the detail, is the literary base for Oppenheim's *Sabbath Eve.* What stands out in this painting is the unorthodox manner in which the father blesses his two daughters upon returning home from the synagogue. Instead of blessing each one separately with two hands upon the head, he blesses them simultaneously with one hand upon each. The change in practice seems to have been lifted out of a Kompert story from 1846, where the reason becomes evident. There the father is rushed by son and daughter as he enters the house, each one striving to be the first one blessed. In Solomonic fashion, he quickly resolves an instance of troublesome sibling rivalry by extending one hand to each child and blessing them together.[82]

Oppenheim's reliance on literary sources is not surprising. As a pioneer in the artistic portrayal of Jewish life, he had no immediate models. Where could he turn for help in conceptualizing and composing his paintings? As he began to work he must have read or reread authors who in a different medium were striving toward similar objectives: a reconciliation with the past and the enrichment of collective memory. What he accomplished spawned a tradition of Jewish genre painting and yielded an unexpected addition to the depleted forces of Jewish cohesion.

NOTES

1. Within the last decade four exhibitions devoted to Oppenheim have been held: at the Washington Hebrew Congregation (1974), Yeshiva University Museum (1977), the Jewish Museum (1981), and the Israel Museum (1983). See the resulting essays by Manuela Hoelterhoff, *A Monograph on the Works and Life of Moritz Oppenheim* (Washington 1974); Alfred Werner, *Families and Feasts: Paintings by Oppenheim and Kaufmann* (New York, 1977); Norman L. Kleeblatt, *The Paintings of Moritz Oppenheim* (New York, 1981). My own essay appeared first in the handsome catalogue of the Israel Museum exhibition curated by Elisheva Cohen, *Moritz Oppenheim: The First Jewish Painter* (Jerusalem, 1983).

2. Moritz Oppenheim, *Errinerungen*, edited by Alfred Oppenheim (Frankfurt am Main, 1924), pp. 114–15 (Nachwort).

3. J. Schwanthaler, *Professor M. Oppenheim's Bilder aus dem altjüdischen Familienleben poetisch dargestellt* (Frankfurt am Main, 1876), on back cover. Published by Heinrich Keller, this collection of 18 poems was probably commissioned to be sold along with the portfolio.

4. The Klau Library of HUC-JIR in Cincinnati has a copy of the 1881 portfolio inscribed by Simon Wolf, the well-known Jewish lawyer and lobbyist, to his wife on August 26, 1881. The title beneath each painting was printed in German, English, French, and occasionally even in Hebrew.

5. *Die Gartenlaube*, 1867, pp. 313–19; 1868, pp. 628–32.

6. *Erinnerungen*, p. 115. The price is mentioned in the advertisement carried by the *Israelitsche Wochenschrift*, 1882, p. 284. The Klau Library of HUC-JIR possesses a copy of this now rare first edition: *Moritz Oppenheim, Bilder aus dem altjüdischen Familienleben nach Original-Gemälden. Mit Einführung und Erläuterungen von Leopold Stein* (Frankfurt am Main, 1882). Despite the unsubstantiated claims of several recent writers on Oppenheim, that the first book edition of the *Bilder* was published in 1881, I prefer the testimony of Alfred Oppenheim cited above. Moreover, I have been unable to find even a trace of a copy of such an edition anywhere, whereas I have managed to find copies of the German book editions of 1882, 1886, 1901, and 1913.

7. For this essay I have made use of the 1886 edition. There are no page numbers and the Roman numerals refer to the numbers assigned each painting.

8. The Archives of the Leo Baeck Institute in New York (2798) preserve a set of 20 *Postkarten* published in Frankfurt with titles in four languages. My guess is that they were printed sometime between 1900 and 1914. The information regarding the plates I owe to my friend Prof. Richard Cohen of the Hebrew University and several German acquaintances. The *Israelitische Wochenschrift*, 1882, p. 116, reported in its obituary on Oppenheim that his *Bilder* "had become a staple of the export and art business."

Contemporary written appreciations of the *Bilder* are not lacking though difficult to track down. Those I have found are in the *Allgemeine Zeitung des Judentums*, 1870, p. 225; 1882, p. 226; *Der Israelit*, 1882, erste Beilage zu Nr. 12, pp. 289–90 (claiming that the *Yahrzeit Service* was based on an actual happening during the Franco-Prussian War); and Emil Lehmann, *Gesammelte Schriften*, 2nd ed. (Dresden, n.d.), p. 224.

As for German Jewish genre painters directly inspired by Oppenheim, see Hermann Junker, "Fortsetzung der Oppenheim'schen Bilder aus dem jüdischen Leben," *Populär-wissenschaftliche Monatsblätter,* ed. by Adolf Brüll, 1885, pp. 9–12, and Wilhelm Thielmann, *Aus der Synagoge: Nach der Natur Gezeichnet* (a portfolio edition of ten graphic sketches published about 1899 by Heinrich Keller).

In the spring of 1900, on the occasion of the 100th anniversary of Oppenheim's birth, a large retrospective comprising 142 works was held in Frankfurt. (*Katalog der Ausstellung von Werken des Professor Moritz Oppenheim zur Feier seines 100. Geburtstages im Frankfurter Kunstverein vom 22. April bis 13. Mai 1900*).

However, by the opening of the pathbreaking Ausstellung jüdischer Künstler in Berlin on Nov. 17, 1907, with some 160 paintings by 70 Jewish artists, the sentimental style of Oppenheim had fallen into disrepute and his work barely represented. (See G. Kutna in *Ost und West*, 1908, col. 24.)

9. On Stein, see Harry W. Ettelson, "Leopold Stein," *Year Book of the Central Con-*

ference of American Rabbis, XXI (1911), pp. 306–27. On the liturgical commission, Jacob J. Petuchowski, *Prayerbook Reform in Europe* (New York, 1968), p. 157.

10. *Bilder,* XV.

11. Gabriel Riesser, "Moritz Oppenheim: Biographische Skizze," *Jahrbuch des Nützlichen und Unterhaltenden für Israeliten,* ed. by K. Klein, 1854, pp. 9–25 (appendix to *Volks-Kalendar und Jahrbuch für Israeliten auf das Jahr 5614* (1854). In 1865 Livius Fürst, the son of Julius Fürst, published a similarly laudatory though mainly derivative evaluation of Oppenheim in the *Illustrirte Monatshefte für des gesammten Interessen des Judentums,* I (Vienna, 1865), pp. 17–24. On Riesser, see Moshe Rinott, "Gabriel Riesser—Fighter for Jewish Emancipation," *LBIYB* VII (1962), pp. 11–38.

12. *Gabriel Riesser's Gesammelte Schriften,* ed. by M. Isler, 4 vols. (1867–1868), I, p. 163.

13. Riesser, *Jahrbuch,* p. 18.

14. Riesser's *Gesammelte Schriften,* I, p. 293.

15. Elisheva Cohen, "Moritz Daniel Oppenheim," *Bulletin des Leo Baeck Instituts,* XVI–XVII (1977–78), p. 43 n. 2. According to Ms. Cohen, Oppenheim's *Nachlass* at the Israel Museum sheds no light on the genesis of his *Bilder* (p. 70). Nine of the letters (2 by Oppenheim to Riesser and 7 by Riesser to Oppenheim) have now been published by E. Cohen, *Moritz Oppenheim: The First Jewish Painter,* pp. 65–77.

16. Riesser, *Jahrbuch,* p. 22. Years later in his *Erinnerungen,* Oppenheim spoke with affection, pride, and wit of his long departed friend (pp. 86–88).

17. *Ibid.,* p. 11.

18. *Katalog der Ausstellung Oppenheim,* pp. 10–11, 15. In 1862 Oppenheim also painted in oil the *Raub des Mortara-Kindes* (*Erinnerungen,* p. 121).

19. *Erinnerungen,* p. 96.

20. The accolade is cited by Christine von Kohl in *Monumenta Judaica, Handbuch* (Cologne, 1963), p. 476. The correct year of Oppenheim's birth was established by E. Cohen, p. 42, and is confirmed by the *Katalog der Ausstellung Oppenheim.*

21. Eric Werner, *Mendelssohn: A New Image of the Composer and His Age* (London, 1963), pp. 28–44.

22. Karl Schwartz, *Jewish Artists of the 19th and 20th Centuries* (New York, 1949), p. 25; Käte Gläser, *Das Bildnis im Berliner Biedermeier* (Berlin, 1932?), pp. 26–27, 58–59.

23. *Monumenta Judaica,* pp. 479–80; Adolph Kohut, *Berühmte israelitische Männer und Frauen,* 2 vols. (Leipzig–Reudnitz, n.d.), I, pp. 260–63; S. Kirschstein, *Juedische Graphiker aus der Zeit von 1625–1825* (Berlin, 1918), p. 29; Cecil Roth, ed., *Jewish Art: An Illustrated History* (New York, Toronto, London, 1961), cols. 544–45.

24. The size of the ghetto is given by Paul Arnsberg, *Die jüdischen Gemeinden in Hessen,* 2 vols. (Frankfurt am Main, 1971), I, p. 320.

25. *Erinnerungen,* pp. 7, 18–19.

26. *Ibid.,* pp. 8, 119.

27. *Ibid.,* pp. 5–8, 14, 42–43.

28. *Ibid.,* pp. 10–13.

29. For example, E. M. Lilien (*Ost und West,* 1901, col. 519); Stanislaus Bender (*Sammelmappe Stan: Bender,* 12th ed. [Frankfurt am Main, n.d.], introduction); and Chaim Soutine (*Schwarz,* pp. 187–89).

30. *Erinnerungen,* p. 16.

31. E. Cohen, *Bulletin,* p. 46.

32. *Erinnerungen,* pp. 20–25, 28.

33. Ferdinand Hiller, "Der Maler Moritz Oppenheim in Frankfurt am Main," *Erinnerungsblätter* (Cologne, 1884), p. 122.

34. *Erinnerungen*, pp. 32–43, 55–56.

35. *Ibid.*, pp. 44–47, 74–75. The accolade is on p. 75.

36. Hiller, pp. 121–22.

37. *Bilder*, XX.

38. *Ibid.*, V.

39. Riesser's *Gesammelte Schriften*, IV, p. 719.

40. Ernest K. Bramsted, *Aristocracy and the Middle-Classes in Germany*, revised ed. (Chicago and London, 1967), pp. 203–16; Heinz Klüter, ed., *Facsimile Querschnitt durch die Gartenlaube* (Stuttgart and Vienna, 1963); Henry Wassermann, "Jews and Judaism in the Gartenlaube," *LBIYB*, XXIII (1978), pp. 47–60. (The treatment of Oppenheim is condescending and the reference to the *Gartenlaube* erroneous [p. 51 n. 15].)

41. Georg Wilhelm Friedrich Hegel, *The Philosophy of History* (Dover Publications, New York, 1956), p. 197.

42. *Gutzkows Werke*, ed. by Peter Müller, II (Leipzig and Vienna, n.d.). The quotation is on p. 86.

43. *Bilder: Das Verhören, Bar-Mizwa-Vortrag, Sabbath-Nachmittag, Der Segen des Rabbi, Sabbath-Ruhe auf der Gasse*.

44. Alexander Altmann, *Moses Mendelssohn* (Philadelphia, 1973), pp. 344, 368–72.

45. Abraham Geiger, "Die Stellung des weiblichen Geschlechtes in dem Judentume unserer Zeit," *Wissenschaftliche Zeitschrift für jüdische Theologie*, III (1837), pp. 13–14. On the later period, see Marion Kaplan, *The Jewish Feminist Movement in Germany* (Westport, Conn., and London, 1979), pp. 147–68.

46. *Bilder*, X.

47. Bramsted, pp. 132–49; Jacob Katz, *From Prejudice to Destruction, Anti-Semitism, 1700–1933* (Cambridge, Mass., 1980), pp. 147–220.

48. Immanuel Kant, *Religion within the Limits of Reason Alone* (Harper Torchbooks, N.Y., 1960), pp. 115–20; Emil L. Fackenheim, *Encounters between Judaism and Modern Philosophy* (Philadelphia, 1973), pp. 39–43.

49. *Ibid.*, pp. 43–53.

50. Kant, p. 118.

51. For example, David Friedländer, Solomon Maimon, Lazarus Bendavid, and Saul Ascher. See Michael A. Meyer, *The Origins of the Modern Jew* (Detroit, 1967).

52. *Bilder: Am Vorabend des Sühnetages*.

53. *Bilder: Der Segen des Rabbi, Das Wochen-oder Pfingst-Fest*.

54. *Bilder: Die Trauung, Freitag Abend, Sabbath-Nachmittag, Sabbath Ausgang, Der Oster-Abend, Am Vorabend des Sühnetages*.

55. W. Gunther Plaut, ed., *The Rise of Reform Judaism* (New York, 1963), pp. 206–11.

56. *Referate über die der ersten israelitischen Synode zu Leipzig überreichten Anträge* (Berlin, 1871), pp. 196–97. The contemporary Jewish newspapers were replete with discussions of circumcision. (For a sample, see the *Allgemeine Zeitung des Judentums*, 1869, pp. 693–97; 1870, pp. 429–31.)

57. *The Ceremonies and Religions of the Various Nations of the Known World*, I, *Containing the Ceremonies of the Jews and the Roman Catholics* with copper plates by Bernard Picart (London, 1733), facing p. 80. Oppenheim's painting was discreetly entitled *Der Gevatter erwartet das Kind*.

58. *Bilder: Die Trauung; The Ceremonies*, I, facing p. 239.

59. Samuel Holdheim, *Ueber die Autonomie der Rabbinen und das Princip der jüdischen Ehe* (Schwerin, 1843).

60. Berthold Auerbach, *Poet and Merchant*, trans. by Charles T. Brooks (New York, 1877), p. 2.

61. Yekutiel Yehuda Grünewald, *A Contribution to the History of the Religious Reformation in Germany and Hungary: Hamaharam Shick and his Time* (Hebrew) (Jerusalem, 1972), pp. 65–66.

62. *Bilder,* XVIII.

63. *Ibid.,* XVIII.

64. Adolph Kohut, *Geschichte der deutschen Juden* (Belrin, 1898), p. 799.

65. *Décisions doctrinales du Grande Sanhédrin* (Paris, 1898; reprinted Jerusalem, 1958), p. 46; David Philipson, *The Reform Movement in Judaism*, rev. ed. (New York, 1931), p. 213.

66. Riesser's *Gesammelte Schriften*, IV, p. 721.

67. The original oil painting is at the Jewish Museum in New York. I am grateful to Dr. Fred Grubel for pointing out to me how noticeably it differs from the grissaille.

68. *Bilder: Die Jahrzeit* (Minian); also above note 8.

69. For example the truly gargantuan American edition (17" × 21") of Oppenheim's *Bilder* published by Louis Edward Levy, *The Jewish Year* (Philadephia, 1895), made one striking addition to the set of 20: the gripping portrayal of Tisha B'Av by Leopold Horovitz entitled *Mourning for Jerusalem*.

70. *Bilder,* XX.

71. An exemplar is preserved in the archives of the Leo Baeck Institute (1223–1). Another was shown by The Jewish Museum, New York in its exhibition "Fabric of Jewish Life: Textiles from the Jewish Museum Collection" (New York, 1977), p. 127. Again I have been told by German Jews that the commemorative panel was found in many Jewish homes. The verse from Malachi is 2:10.

72. *Allgemeine Zeitung des Judentums*, 1870, pp. 823–25 (quotation p. 824); 857–61, 873–74, 893.

73. Ismar Schorsch, *Jewish Reactions to German Anti-Semitism* (New York and Philadelphia, 1972), p. 27.

74. *Gedenkbuch an den deutsch-französischen Krieg von 1870–71 für die deutschen Israeliten* (Bonn, 1871). *Allgemeine Zeitung des Judentums*, 1871, pp. 495–96.

75. *Erinnerungen*, pp. 88–90. Despite his discomfort each time he saw the daughter of Mendelssohn make the sign of the cross when putting her grandson to bed, Oppenheim preserved his friendship with Veit by avoiding any discussion of religion.

76. The available analyses are both general and antiquated. See for example Gustav Karpeles, *Geschichte der jüdischen Literatur,* 2 vols. (Belrin, 1886), pp. 1133–37; Meyer Waxman, *A History of Jewish Literature*, 5 vols. (New York and London, 1960), IV, pp. 576–90; Joel Müller, "Leopold Kompert als jüdischer Geschichtsschreiber," *Populär-wissenschaftliche Monatsblätter,* 1888, pp. 193–96, 217–20; 249–51, 265–73; Karl Emil Franzos, "Leopold Kompert," *Jahrbuch für jüdische Geschichte und Literatur* IX (1906), pp. 147–60; and the introduction by Stefan Hock to *Leopold Komperts sämtliche Werke*, 10 vols. (Leipzig, n.d.), I. Franzos stands apart from this group in both background and attitude.

77. Philippe F. Veit, "Heine: The Marrano Pose," *Monatshefte*, LXVI (1974), pp. 145–56.

78. See below, pp. 245–254.

79. Aron Bernstein, *Vögele, der Maggid: Mendel Gibbor* (Berlin, 1860), I, pp. 40, 47.

80. *Ibid.,* p. 78.

81. Auerbach, p. 23.

82. Leopold Kompert, *Aus dem Ghetto,* 3rd ed. (Leipzig, 1887), p. 15. I do wish to note that Alfred Werner in one aside did connect Oppenheim with Kompert but failed to develop the promise of his insight. (A. Werner, "Oppenheim: A Rediscovery," *Midstream,* 1974, p. 55.)

6

On the History of
the Political Judgment
of the Jew

In the field of historical inquiry, accepted patterns of thought often interfere with new empirical research. The conceptual equipment a historian brings to explore unknown terrain may just be unsuited for the task and serve to distort rather than delineate the contours of his topic. The proper understanding of many a new subject has been long delayed by an instinctive application of well-worn notions that make it difficult to approach the subject at hand without blinders. Should those notions about the past also be in error, the difficulty in studying a new topic is twice compounded. It may thus take sometimes a generation or two before historians are able to free themselves from the strait jacket of earlier conceptualizations in order to conduct their research in terms dictated by the subject itself.

Rarely has a subject appeared to confirm so conclusively a prevailing perception of the past as in the case of the Nazi extermination of European Jewry. The isolation, helplessness, and disorientation experienced by Jews caught in the Nazi maelstrom seem to bear out the contention that in the Diaspora Jews were destined to remain the passive victims of historical circumstances beyond their control. At the end of his still overwhelming study of the Final Solution, Raul Hilberg unhesitatingly invoked "a two-thousand-year-old experience" to account for the absence of Jewish resistance.[1]

For the first time in the history of Western civilization the perpetrators had overcome all administrative and moral obstacles to a killing operation. For the first time, also, the Jewish victims—caught in the strait jacket of their history—plunged themselves physically and psychologically into catastrophe. The destruction of the Jews was thus no accident.[2]

I should like to express my gratitude to my mentor and friend, Chancellor Gerson D. Cohen, for enhancing this essay with his learning and wisdom.

Consequently, the ultimate explanation for a Jewish response which unwittingly abetted Nazi objectives is to be found in the nature of Jewish history rather than in the nature of the Nazi assault. Jewish behavior during the Holocaust becomes thereby but one instance of a general view of the Diaspora experience.

That Hilberg who is neither a Jewish historian nor a Zionist should have recourse to this view is perhaps the most convincing evidence as to the extent of its dominance. And indeed the most cursory historiographical survey will quickly reveal the diverse quarters and variety of forms in which the view is to be found. Like most of the regnant conceptualizations about the Jewish past, this one too has its genesis in the historical creativity of nineteenth-century *Wissenschaft*. Amid the pressure of the emancipation struggle, Jewish advocates and historians divested exilic Judaism of any trace of political history. What survived the final demise of the Jewish state was a religious community with a universal mandate to teach mankind the loftiest known form of ethical monotheism. The lands of the dispersion, and not Palestine, now became the only legitimate arena for the conduct of Jewish life.

Whereas this part of the reconstruction of Jewish history was meant to disarm Christian opponents of emancipation as well as to shore up Jewish loyalties to Judaism, the continued emphasis on the unbroken suffering of the exilic experience was intended to strengthen the claim for equality. Contemporary Jewish faults were not evidence of innate depravity but only the scars left by more than a millennium of Christian oppression. It was this exclusive emphasis on the twin themes of persecution and martyrdom that reduced the political history of Diaspora Jewry to little more than the passive endurance of endless violence. The deeply engaged scholars of the emancipation era had produced a secularized version of the older religious concept of *Galut*.[3]

In the early decades of the twentieth century this perception of the Diaspora experience became central to a number of seminal if disparate statements about Jewish history. For example, two men as dissimilar as Max Weber and Franz Rosenzweig arrived independently and simultaneously at very similar formulations. Though Weber's empathetic and value-free sociology summed up the best of the German academic tradition, it did teeter at the brink of relativism, and Rosenzweig, who had mastered that tradition at the feet of Friedrich Meinecke, dared to reject it for a highly subjective mode of theological thought.[4] Toward the end of his trenchant study of Israelite religion, Weber offered some observations on the nature of the Diaspora Jewish community. Following Wellhausen, he stressed the priestly role in transforming post-exilic Judaism from a national polity into a religious community, while disregarding the potent expressions of national vitality that punctuated the period of the Second Commonwealth. Above all, he designated this self-imposed and ritually effected segregation as the condition of a pariah community. Jewish scholars might carp at what actually had become the prevailing

Protestant thesis about the origins of this pariah community, but there can be little doubt about the fact that the resonances of Weber's term accorded perfectly with their own perception of Jewish fate in the Middle Ages.[5]

What Weber put sociologically, Rosenzweig articulated theologically. In many ways a spokesman for a resurgent German Orthodoxy, Rosenzweig turned his back on nineteenth-century Jewish *Wissenschaft* and its evolutionary model of Judaism. Instead, he ventured a bold non-temporal portrayal of a thoroughly ahistorical Judaism. The key to the survival, essence, and mission of Judaism lay in its existence outside the parameters of history. As a spiritual nation the Jews exhibited a uniquely non-historical relationship to the usual constituent factors of nationality—law, language, and land. By sacrificing its temporal existence, Judaism served to embody for Jews and to hold out for mankind messianic redemption. In regard to our immediate concern what must be stressed is that in his flight from *Wissenschaft*, Rosenzweig ironically reinforced in a profound way the dominant non-political view of Diaspora history.[6]

That view gained still wider currency when it was seized by the ideologues of the Zionist renaissance and turned with devastating effect on the defenders of Western-style emancipation. The paradoxical fact is that both Zionists and emancipationists for different reasons shared the same grim perception of the Jewish Middle Ages; what divided them so deeply was rather the question of whether that dark period was over. Against the background of the brutal failure of the Jewish policy of the czarist regime, Zionism delivered a passionate critique of Jewish powerlessness.

No document states that indictment more radically than the Hebrew short story by Haim Hazaz entitled "The Sermon." When the awkward and inarticulate Yudka overcomes his trepidation to address the central committee of his kibbutz, the Jewish people has at last found one of its own to ventilate its true feelings. The hesitant speech by Yudka is a blunt rejection of all exilic history, a subject that should be expunged from the textbooks of our children.

Because we didn't make our own history, the goyim made it for us. Just as they used to put out our candles on Sabbath, milk our cows and light our oven on Sabbath, so they made our history for us to suit themselves, and we took it from them as it came.[7]

A closer look at the nature of this imposed history reveals an endless repetition of "oppression, defamation, persecution, and martyrdom . . . That's what's in it, and nothing more! After all, it's . . . it's . . . it bores you to death, it's just plain dull!"[8] By the time he's finished Yudka has repudiated Judaism itself, its paralyzing legalism, its messianic passivity, and its rootless existence. Zionism is no less than a break with the past. "When a man can no longer be a Jew, he becomes a Zionist."[9]

One of the conduits through which this non-political view of Jewish history was diffused in America was the work of Hannah Arendt. As early as 1944 in an essay entitled "The Jew as Pariah: A Hidden Tradition," she applied Max Weber's thesis in an effort to relate at least part of the creativity of four Jewish writers and artists to their personal experience of pariahdom.[10] A year later she moved from the artistic to the political consequences of the pariah legacy. She now turned with vengeance on the Zionist movement in a broad, biting critique of its political judgment and nerve. The upshot of her pungent analysis was that the Zionists were consistently guilty of the very same political obtuseness and timidity for which they roundly condemned their opponents.[11] In *The Origins of Totalitarianism*, Arendt expanded her charge into a general indictment of all Jewish political sagacity. A two-thousand-year condition of powerlessness had atrophied the political capacity of the Jews. In consequence, Jewish leadership since the emancipation had blindly committed itself to a tragic alliance with the nation-state that would eventually lead to the destruction of both.[12] In sum, a decade before Hilberg's book, Arendt had implicitly put forth the proposition that the victims of the Final Solution were partially responsible for their fate. Jewish history had transformed the descendants of the prophets into pariahs incapable of sound political judgment.[13]

The purpose of this excursion into modern Jewish historiography is not to duck the issue whether Jews did or did not resist the Nazis, but rather to emphasize the extent to which our perception and articulation of the problem are conditioned by certain ingrained notions about Jewish history which themselves are not beyond question. Indeed, what I have tried to suggest is that the non-political view of Diaspora history was itself conditioned by an identifiable set of historical circumstances and refurbished and redeployed by scholars and ideologues of a later age. Tracing the genesis of the conventional wisdom was meant to challenge its validity. On the factual level, the Hilberg version of the Arendt thesis has rightly provoked a torrent of research intent on showing the nature and extent of Jewish resistance; on the interpretive level, however, it has yet failed to stimulate a fresh examination of Jewish political history.

II

At the outset, two theoretical observations are in order regarding the common view so clearly mirrored in the works of Arendt and Hilberg. First, the Jews in the Diaspora do have a political history, for political history is not a function of land, but of legal status and group cohesiveness. For much of their Diaspora experience the Jews constituted a state within a state precisely because they were distinguished by both. Furthermore, that status and cohesiveness gave rise to major institutions of self-government whose responsibility it was to administer the internal and external or, if you please, the domestic and foreign affairs of the community. For the purpose of our analysis we shall restrict our use of the term political history to the external affairs of the Jewish community, but even in that limited sense it is not easy to exclude internal matters, for often internal policies were dictated by external considerations. A case in point would be the widespread sumptuary laws of medieval Jewish communities which were designed to control the display of Jewish wealth so as not to excite Gentile envy.[14] Jewish leaders clearly sensed that economic grievances often fueled the fires of religious hatred.[15]

Beyond the insistence on a political dimension to Jewish history, it should also be observed initially that survival as a dynamic, creative and cohesive minority evokes a presumption of political sagacity of a fairly high order. The refuse pile of history confirms that national survival is a rare achievement. To be sure, the determination of medieval Jews to persist against all odds was rooted in deep faith, and where that faith weakened, as it did in fourteenth- and fifteenth-century Spain, so did the will to persist.[16] But religious commitment without political sagacity is about as effective as brawn without brain. To depoliticize Jewish history is to make survival either mystifying or fortuitous. In contrast, I would like to argue that studied politically Jews have displayed over time an unusual ability to identify their collective interests, to assess the possibilities for action, to locate allies, to organize and deploy their resources, and to learn from their failures and mistakes. Moreover, Jewish political history evinces the existence of distinct policies for survival carefully formulated and consciously transmitted from generation to generation. While most of my examples will be drawn from the modern period, the nature of the prevailing view dictates that I devote a few remarks first to the political strategy of medieval Jewry.

As we have seen, the perception of Diaspora history in terms of powerlessness and passivity rests heavily on the medieval experience. In truth, however, these terms are simply inadequate for understanding medieval political strategy, because they submerge every trace of consciousness and initiative. A more appropriate term for the subject would be political quietism, which is meant to designate a calculated policy of cooperation with established authorities on the basis of utility. What Jews needed most in Christian Europe was protection from the mob, whether driven by greed or bigotry, and they usually managed to acquire it by offering their talents, connections, and resources to the dominant power in the territory they sought to inhabit. The agreement was usually finalized in the form of a written charter which granted Jews communal autonomy and physical protection in return for their economic service.[17] What deserves special emphasis though is the fact that this alliance with authority did not derive solely from an assessment of the unstable conditions of feudal Europe. It was also the political legacy of rabbinic Judaism worked out in the dark decades following the last of the daring rebellions against Imperial Rome. No matter how justified by Roman provocation, the rebellions proved a disastrous exercise in futility which endangered the status of Jews throughout the empire and weakened the centrality of Palestinian leadership. In consequence, rabbinic leadership of the second and third centuries expunged the symbol of Masada from the collective memory and glorified instead the figure of Rabban Yohanan ben Zakkai, whose sober political judgment had been vindicated by the Zealots' crushing defeat. As their power grew, the rabbis effected a fundamental change in political policy away from military resistance to political quietism. Toward that end, they condemned messianic speculation, inculcated respect for the ruling authorities, and suppressed the example of Maccabean military prowess.[18]

This religiously reinforced political policy, which permeated much of the evolving corpus of rabbinic literature, was conveniently and cogently summarized early in the Middle Ages in a historical work that was destined to become the major medieval Jewish source of information about the period of the Second Commonwealth. Written in lucid Biblical prose, *Yosephon* was probably composed by a Jew from southern Italy somewhere between the years 900 and 965. The primary source, though not the only one, from which Joseph ben Gurion, the purported author, drew his material seems to have been Latin translations of *The Jewish War and Jewish Antiquities* by Josephus, hence the eventual resemblance in name.[19] In retelling the story of the first great uprising against Rome which ended in the destruction of the Temple, the author fully shared the anti-Zealot bias of his namesake. Coupled with an admiration for the heroism and martyrdom of the Zealots is an intense disapproval of their revolt. The uprising is portrayed as a rejection of God's will. In the hierarchical structure of nature, one part is always subservient to another. The Fourth Kingdom, like all great empires, is ordained by God, and the mandate of Jewish leadership is to assure survival through submission. Interlaced throughout this political message is also a rich array of religious consolations.[20] Nevertheless, what stands out is that European Jewry was heir to a political policy forged in the wake of catastrophic failure and perfectly suited to its own precarious minority status in a feudal Christian society.

The national expulsions of the thirteenth, fourteenth, and fifteenth centuries gravely challenged the underlying assumptions of this policy of quietism. A brief aside by Abravanel in the middle of one of his messianic tracts of consolation written after 1492 suggests that at least some contemporary Jewish leaders realized the implications. Abravanel correctly distinguished between persecutions and expulsions in terms of their source rather than size. Persecutions welled up from below. They gave vent to the fury of the mob and usually ran counter to government policy. On the other hand, expulsions derived from above as an official act of state, and signified a repudiation and not a temporary breakdown of the alliance based on mutual interests between the Jewish polity and the central authorities.[21]

That the agony of repeated expulsion did not bring about a fundamental reappraisal of Jewish political strategy in the turbulent two centuries which followed the Spanish expulsion may perhaps best be accounted for by the geographically and economically expanding world into which Jews were thrown. Both sets of circumstances created an ethos of mercantilism freed of religious constraints that granted Jews the mobility and opportunities to relocate with relative ease. And thus despite the military and messianic paroxysms of David Reubeni in the sixteenth and Shabbatai Zevi in the seventeenth century, Jewish leadership preferred to reformulate its medieval argument of economic utility in terms of the new era. Simone Luzzatto's 1638 Italian tract on behalf of the economic utility and religious civility of Venetian Jewry is only the most complete and sophisticated example we have of this refurbished Jewish argument, but there can be little doubt that Jews used the same effective appeal to the economic interests of increasingly secularized governments to gain entry into Holland, England, and the rising absolute states of central Europe.[22]

Thus a proper reading of even medieval Jewish history, I suggest, reveals a conscious political tradition. Jews may indeed have been pariahs, but never powerless to exert a measure of influence on the forces shaping their destiny. In our preoccupation with the parameters set by the dominant institutions of non-Jewish society, we must not lose sight of the assessments made and initiatives taken by Jewish leadership. That Jews came through the precarious insecurity of extended exile is testimony to the intelligence and effectiveness with which they conducted their foreign affairs.

III

In comparison with the medieval period, modern Jewish history exhibits political as well as religious diversity. What emancipationists and Zionists did share was a common determination to end the state of *Galut*. By the end of the eighteenth century, that state was no longer marked by recurring waves of persecution and expulsion, but rather by a mountain of suffocating regulations, which undercut the very mercantilist objectives of European absolutism. Innumerable restrictions and excessive taxation had reduced the ever increasing masses of Ashkenazic Jewry to abject poverty. These conditions dictated a major shift in Jewish strategy.

When Mendelssohn eventually rose to speak out publicly on behalf of the adherents of Judaism, he unequivocally sided with the forces for change. Unlike Dohm, he did not plead for an amelioration of Jewish status out of prudential considerations; on the contrary, he demanded the extension of full equality on the basis of principle. The intent of his lengthy excursus into political theory which constitutes the first and more important half of *Jerusalem* is to establish the principle that the state has no theoretical right to demand religious reforms in return for an improvement of status. In effect he set forth an elaborate theoretical argument for the separation of church and state. In the process he totally abandoned the traditional Jewish line of argumentation in terms of utility. Equality was a right and not a reward. *Jerusalem* is therefore a tract of revolutionary import.[23] Amelioration was perhaps still possible through an alliance with the absolute state; emancipation, however, could become a reality only in a liberal state based on law. Within the context of Jewish political history, the fight for emancipation meant a challenge to established authority not seen since the rebellions against Rome.

The political realignment of the Jews with the forces for change had actually begun a century before in two cases of resettlement. Jews entered both Holland and England by exploiting the occasion of a victorious revolution. In the Low Lands the House of Orange had just thrown off the Spanish yoke and across the Channel Cromwell had driven out the Stuarts. Both groups of insurgents were eager to attract the financial resources at the disposal of Jewish exiles from the Iberian Peninsula.[24] In the broad wake of the French Revolution, that nexus between emancipation and a change in the political order became a European common-place. The long-delayed emancipation of Russian Jewry in 1917 only underscores the fact that any radical improvement in Jewish status required the overthrow of the *ancien régime*.

As the nineteenth century wore on, the continued denial of emancipation in its varied forms intensified Jewish opposition to those in power. The degree of militancy must be measured by what Jewish leaders did and not what they said, for often they couched a defiant posture in the most conciliatory terms. A proto-typical example of this political style was the resistance manifested by the Parisian Assembly of Notables to Napoleon. Of all the questions he foisted on them in his determination to reconsider the wisdom of emancipation, only one really impinged on the future survival of the Jewish community: whether Judaism allowed for intermarriage. Napoleon's intent was clear: emancipation required the dissolution of Jewish group identity. And yet, while the delegates profusely protested their identity with France and their love of Frenchmen, they refused to condone the practice of intermarriage. On the issue that counted, they stood firm, even against Napoleon.[25] Similarly, when in the early 1840s Frederick William IV of Prussia unveiled the retrogressive idea of reimposing a medieval corporate structure on Prussian Jewry, he was met with such a barrage of petitions and protests from the Jewish community that he soon withdrew his proposal.[26] The departure from the traditional Jewish alliance with those in power marked by these instances of col-lective action is confirmed by Jacob Toury's analysis of Jewish political behavior in *Vormärz* Germany. According to his rough estimate, by the 1840s some 46 per-cent of the Jewish population and about 82 percent of the Jews active in politics identified with the liberals and those still further to the left.[27]

It must be noted, however, that the first figure in particular indicated a still sizable preference for the prevailing political order. Not all Jews recognized as early or as clearly as did Leopold Zunz that Jewish emancipation was predicated on the triumph of political liberalism.[28] Or perhaps precisely because the fight for eman-cipation had set the Jewish community on a collision course with the guardians of traditional society, many refused to discard the medieval alliance with estab-lished authority. The most consistent adherents of the medieval policy in the mod-ern era were the Orthodox. The most traditional sector of the Jewish community also practiced the most conservative politics. For decades its leaders dissociated themselves from the struggle for emancipation for fear of its religious consequences.

The historical significance of Samson Raphael Hirsch rests on the political import of his message as much as on its religious content. For the first time, an Orthodox leader not only welcomed the challenge of emancipation, but as the events of 1848 in Austria would show, was willing to fight for it with courage and vigor.[29] But such militancy did not typify the politics of his later followers, who often preferred the Catholic Center to the Protestant liberals and rarely fought the antisemites.[30] Perhaps the most striking instance of Orthodoxy's political conservatism comes from inter-war Poland where the Agudas Yisroel, the political spokesman for Polish Hasidism, maintained a close alliance with the Polish regime, despite repeated betrayal, until the infamous restriction on Jewish ritual slaughtering in 1936 drove it into furious opposition.[31]

If then the struggle for emancipation radicalized the political strategy of much of the organized Jewish community, the constant need to defend emancipation often called forth bold and imaginative action. The very formation of the Alliance Israélite Universelle in 1860 served to repudiate the passionate renunciation by the Parisian Assembly of Notables of all links of kinship to Jews outside France. Taking advantage of the imperialistic foreign policy of the Second Empire, the founders sought to export emancipation and thereby strengthen its roots at home. The survival of oppression abroad stirred not only deep ancestral ties but also sound political instinct: like a communicable disease, antisemitism was highly infectious. In the system of minorities treaties following World War One, emancipated Jewry in the West capped a long diplomatic campaign to secure the freedom and equality of Jews in the East through the force of international law.[32]

Domestically Jews also organized to defend their interests. While the German Centralverein (1893) and the American Jewish Committee (1906) differed in origins, structure, and tactics, they both benefited in their early stages from intelligent, energetic, and courageous leadership. Men like Maximilian Horwitz, Eugen Fuchs, Jacob Schiff, and Louis Marshall deserve to be included among the great statesmen of Jewish history. None of them held back from challenging their respective governments in order to protect or advance Jewish interests. The early record compiled by the American Jewish Committee on this score is unmatched by that of any other ethnic immigrant group of the time. In addition to effecting the abrogation of the long-standing commerce and navigation treaty with Russia in 1912, its leaders single-handedly blocked the growing body of restrictionists for nearly a decade from passing a literacy test that would have effectively excluded most Jewish immigrants from eastern Europe.[33] To the same end, namely to keep the gates of America open, Jacob Schiff conceived, implemented, financed, and fought for his Galveston movement, a rare and sophisticated attempt at organized immigration which eventually led in 1910 to an explosive confrontation between Schiff and the Secretary of Commerce and Labor.[34]

IV

The inevitable political result of the emancipation struggle, either to attain it or to defend it, was that it committed Jews to a vision of an open society based on law in which people were judged on merit. Moreover, their historical experience had uniquely prepared them to succeed in such a setting. They had no attachment to the political structure of the past with its plethora of oppressive restrictions; they had gained ample economic experience by virtue of constantly proving their economic usefulness; and they harbored a deep reverence for learning, albeit religious. In consequence, even in countries where this vision was only partially realized, Jews displayed an awesome pattern of upward mobility.

But political and economic freedom had its victims at both ends of the social ladder, who mourned the passing of medieval society with its stable and secure corporate, hierarchical structure. Losers in the unstoppable transition to modernity, they soon came to fear and despise the Jews who emerged as its primary beneficiaries. Nineteenth-century antisemitism certainly continued to be nourished by the subterranean sources of religious animosity but it also assumed all the earmarks of a political and economic backlash. The most direct and sustained attack on Jewish aspirations came from the right as part of its desperate campaign to thwart the creation of a liberal capitalistic society. The Nazi-inspired Holocaust may thus be seen as the final supreme effort by the right to turn back the clock by annihilating those whom it perceived to be the progenitors of an abhorrent world.[35]

Long before the ultimate Nazi backlash to emancipation, some Jews had already succumbed to despair over the prospects of ever realizing it. Since the creation of a Jewish state *ex nihilo* must count, among other things, as one of the great diplomatic achievements in modern history, we can hardly conclude our reflections without trying to locate the place of Zionist diplomacy within the larger history of Jewish political sagacity. In its rejection of emancipation as the way to end the state of Jewish suffering, the Zionist movement also turned its back on the confrontation politics of the emancipationists. Regardless of the revolutionary significance of the Zionist message within the Jewish community, its political strategy in the national and international arenas entailed cooperation with recognized loci of power. If the political strategy of the emancipationists bore some resemblance to the defiance of authority exhibited by the Jews of antiquity, then Zionist foreign policy heralded a return to the medieval alliance with authority.

At the outset, political Zionism concentrated, to the exclusion of almost every other concern or program, in a frenetic search for allies. While the setting was new, the drama had all the earmarks of a replay of many a medieval scene: a lonely Jewish intercessor pleading for rights of residence for his people before the seat of power. Like his medieval forerunners, Herzl was in pursuit of a charter, a document which would legally define the rights of settlement and thereby protect Jewish settlers from the capricious mood of the indigenous population. What Herzl could

offer in return was not much more than the utilitarian arguments of his predecessors. Depending on his audience, Herzl could expound the benefits of a Jewish
homeland as a welcome reduction of domestic unrest, as a means to save the ailing
Ottoman Empire and curtail Russian expansion, or as the creation of a cultural
and economic sphere of influence in the Middle East for a deserving European
backer. Herzl had intuited what medieval Jews had learned through long experience: that a given constellation of conditions could create a convergence of interests
between two disparate polities. In short, because of the Jews' anomalous demographic situation, Zionism was compelled to pursue a conservative political
policy.[36]

The trick, of course, was to identify and exploit such a constellation. Herzl had
been granted a glimpse of the promised land, but he could not conquer it. That
the task was eventually accomplished with supreme skill by one of Herzl's bitterest
young critics adds an ironic touch to the history of political Zionism. But the
Balfour Declaration reflected merely a temporary convergence of interests. The
tragedy of Weizmann's subsequent leadership stemmed at least in part from his
reluctance to recognize how contrary to British national interests the Declaration
really was and to modify Zionist policy accordingly.[37] Nevertheless, without the
cover of the Declaration and the infusion from the Nazi onslaught, the Yishuv
would never have gained the critical mass necessary to defend its fledgling state
on the battlefield. Under the leadership of Ben-Gurion, war became an extension
of diplomacy and Zionism reverted to the revolutionary politics of the Second
Commonwealth.

The similarity between Zionism and the medieval Jewish experience extends
even beyond a common political strategy to a common political objective. Underlying the idea of a Jewish homeland was a basic preference for the segregation of
the medieval ghetto. The dispiriting resurgence of antisemitism in the last quarter
of the nineteenth century confirmed the long-unspoken fear of many Jews that a
lasting and honorable integration was a bitter illusion. But what was the alternative? In an age of nationalism, it was obviously no longer possible to return to the
separate corporate structure of the ghetto. New conditions dictated a new form of
segregation. The Jewish state became the functional equivalent of the medieval
Kehilla.

Furthermore, what appealed to early Zionists like Moshe Lilienblum in the East
and Max Nordau in the West, before Zionism became entangled in a full-scale
rebellion against Judaism, was the autonomy of the medieval Jewish community
and the sense of dignity which came with independence. Unlike their emancipated
progeny, medieval Jews never suffered from pangs of inferiority.[38]

It is no accident, I think, that when the Balfour Declaration came and the Yishuv set about to form its institutions of self-government, what began to emerge
was a replica of a medieval *Kehillah*. At first, in fact, membership in the Knesset

Yisrael, the Jewish Community of Palestine, was to be compulsory, as it had once been in the traditional *Kehillah*, but the British rejected the idea. The major organs of the Community like the Chief Rabbinate and its Council, the Elected Assembly, and the National Council closely paralleled the governing institutions of a *Kehilla*, not merely because the British sought to impose a religious character on Palestinian Jewry, but also because these were the basic political structures known to the members of both the old indigenous Yishuv and the immigrants from eastern Europe.[39] In sum, a political analysis of Zionist history reveals far more affinity with medieval models than Zionist rhetoric would ever suggest.

V

As if you haven't already suspected it, my lecture this evening does have a hidden agenda. Put boldly, I have been bent on challenging the notions that the condition of Jewish powerlessness ended only in 1948 or that Jewish political sagacity emerged first in 1897 not only because they are a distortion of the past, but also because they are a disservice to the present. The millennial record of the Jews is a vast repository of political experience and wisdom acquired under the most divergent and adverse conditions. Unfortunately, in a highly politicized, volatile, and cynical world, Jewish survival continues to hang in the balance as precariously as ever. To deny or debunk the political dimension of Jewish history is to discard a potential resource, a luxury we can ill afford.

I am fully conscious that it is no longer fashionable to study history for pragmatic reasons. When Machiavelli wrote on Livy, he was so preoccupied with the political lessons for his own day that he never sensed how unreliable a source on early Roman history Livy actually was. And yet contemporary students of Jewish history, with all their lip service to critical and dispassionate scholarship, often write on Jewish political history in undisguised judgmental terms. Ideological presuppositions and outmoded conceptualizations continue to blur their vision.[40] But the subject is too important for such flawed treatment. The objective study of Jewish political history is no longer just an end in itself; its results must also serve as a source of instruction and stimulation for Jewish civil servants, communal leaders, politicians, and statesmen in the Diaspora and Israel who bear the awesome responsibility to secure the Jewish future.

NOTES

1. Raul Hilberg, *The Destruction of the European Jews* (Chicago, 1961), p. 666.

2. *Ibid.*, p. 669.

3. Salo Baron, "Ghetto and Emancipation," *The Menorah Journal*, XIV (June 1928), pp. 515–526.

4. Nahum N. Glatzer, *Franz Rosenzweig: His Life and Thought* (New York, 1953), pp. 94–98.

5. Max Weber, *Ancient Judaism,* trans. by Hans H. Gerth and Don Martindale (Glencoe, Illinois, 1952), pp. 336–355. On the ideological overtones of this scholarly debate, see Ismar Schorsch, *Jewish Reactions to German Anti-Semitism, 1870–1914* (New York, 1972), pp. 169–177, and Uriel Tal, "Theologische Debatte um das 'Wesen' des Judentums," in *Juden im Wilhelminischen Deutschland 1890–1914,* edited by Werner E. Mosse and Arnold Paucker (Tübingen, 1976), pp. 599–632.

6. See, for example, Franz Rosenzweig, "Geist und Epochen der jüdischen Geschichte," in his *Kleinere Schriften* (Berlin, 1937), pp. 12–25; also Alexander Altmann, "Franz Rosenzweig on History," in his *Studies in Religious Philosophy and Mysticism* (London, 1969), pp. 275–291.

7. Haim Hazaz, "The Sermon," in *Israeli Stories: A Selection of the Best Contemporary Hebrew Writing,* edited by Joel Blocker (New York, 1962), p. 69.

8. *Ibid.,* p. 70.

9. *Ibid.,* p. 82.

10. Hannah Arendt, "The Jew as Pariah: A Hidden Tradition," *Jewish Social Studies,* VI (1944), pp. 99–122.

11. *Idem,* "Zionism Reconsidered," *The Menorah Journal,* XXXIII (1945), pp. 162–196.

12. *Idem, The Origins of Totalitarianism,* 2nd ed. (Meridian Books, New York 1958), pp. 3–120.

13. The proposition was subsequently made explicitly in her *Eichmann in Jerusalem* (The Viking Press, New York, 1968), pp. 112–134. But it is important to recognize that indictment as an extension and specification of her own general theory of Jewish political obtuseness and not merely as the consequence of Hilberg's influence.

14. Salo W. Baron, *The Jewish Community,* II (Philadelphia, 1948), pp. 301–307.

15. See, for example, the high degree of awareness reflected in the works of two keen sixteenth-century observers, Samuel Usque, *Consolation for the Tribulations of Israel,* trans. by Martin A. Cohen (Philadelphia, 1965), pp. 168, 177, 185, 192, and 198, and Solomon ibn Verga, *Shevet Yehudah,* edited by Ezriel Shohet (Jerusalem, 1947), pp. 30–31.

16. Heinrich Graetz, *Geschichte der Juden,* VIII, 4th ed. (Leipzig, n.d.), pp. 424–425; Yitzhak Baer, *A History of the Jews in Christian Spain,* II (Philadelphia, 1966), pp. 253–259.

17. Salo W. Baron, *A Social and Religious History of the Jews,* 18 vols. (New York & Philadelphia, 1952–1983), IV, pp. 3–88.

18. *Ibid.,* II, pp. 89–128; M. Avi–Yonah, *The Jews of Palestine* (New York, 1976), pp. 64–71; Jonathan A. Goldstein, "The Hasmonaeans: The Dynasty of God's Resisters," *Harvard Theological Review,* LXI (1975), pp. 53–58.

19. David Flusser, "The Author of the Book of Yosephon: His Personality and his Age" (Hebrew), *Zion* XVIII (1953), pp. 109–126.

20. Yitzhak Baer, "The Hebrew Yosephon" (Hebrew), in *Sefer Dinaburg,* edited by Y. Baer *et al.* (Jerusalem, 1949), pp. 178–205.

21. Isaac Abravanel, *Sefer Yeshuot Meshiho* (Jerusalem, 1967), p. 46.

22. Simha Luzzatto, *Ma' amar al Yehudei Venetziah,* trans. by Dan Latis (Jerusalem, 1951). Actually in the case of sixteenth- and seventeenth-century Venice, Jews skillfully employed the argument of economic utility in the context of a declining economic power. (See Ben Ravid, "The Establishment of the Ghetto Vecchio of Venice, 1541," in *Proceedings of the Sixth World Congress of Jewish Studies,* II [Jerusalem, 1975], pp. 153–167 and *idem,* "The First Charter of the Jewish Merchants of Venice, 1589,"

in *A.J.S. Review,* I [1976], pp. 187–222.) For other examples from the age of early capitalism when Jews couched their appeals for settlement in strictly economic terms, see Menasseh ben Israel, *The Humble Addresses,* in *Menasseh ben Israel's Mission to Oliver Cromwell,* edited by Lucien Wolf (London, 1901), pp. 75–89 and Hermann Kellenbenz, *Sephardim an der unteren Elbe* (Wiesbaden, 1958), pp. 30–32. The importance of the Jewish role in the economic history of the period is refreshingly argued by Fernand Braudel, *The Mediterranean,* II (New York, 1973), pp. 802–826.

23. Moses Mendelssohn, *Jerusalem and Other Jewish Writings,* trans. by Alfred Jospe (New York, 1969); Alexander Altmann, "The Philosophical Roots of Moses Mendelssohn's Plea for Emancipation," *Jewish Social Studies,* XXXVI (1974), pp. 191–202.

24. Herbert I. Bloom, *The Economic Activities of the Jews of Amsterdam in the Seventeenth and Eighteenth Centuries* (reprinted New York, 1969), pp. xi–xviii, 5, 8, 21; Menna Prestwich, "Diplomacy and Trade in the Protectorate," *The Journal of Modern History,* XXII (1950), p. 116.

25. Jacob Katz, *Out of the Ghetto* (Cambridge, Mass., 1973), pp. 140–141.

26. Horst Fischer, *Judentum, Staat und Heer in Preussen im frühen 19. Jahrhundert* (Tübingen, 1968), pp. 151–166.

27. Jacob Toury, *Die politischen Orientierungen der Juden in Deutschland* (Tübingen, 1966), p. 27.

28. See the preface to his *Die gottensdienstlichen Vorträge der Juden* (Berlin, 1832).

29. Samson Raphael Hirsch, *The Nineteen Letters of Ben Uziel,* trans. by Bernard Drachman (New York, 1942), pp. 85, 164–170; Salo W. Baron, "The Revolution of 1848 and Jewish Scholarship," in *Proceedings of the American Academy of Jewish Research,* XX (1951), pp. 34–42.

30. Toury, pp. 246–261.

31. Ezra Mendelsohn, "The Dilemma of Jewish Politics in Poland: Four Responses," in *Jews and Non-Jews in Eastern Europe 1918–1945,* edited by Bela Vago and George L. Mosse (New York & Jerusalem, 1974), pp. 209–214.

32. André Chouraqui, *Cent Ans d'histoire: l'Alliance Israélite Universelle et la renaissance juive contemporaine, 1860–1960* (Paris, 1965); Oscar Janowsky, *The Jews and Minority Rights, 1898–1919* (New York, 1933).

33. On the history of the Centralverein before 1914, see Schorsch, *Jewish Reactions to German Anti-Semitism, 1870–1914,* pp. 103ff., and Arnold Paucker, "Zur Problematik einer jüdischen Abwehrstrategie in der deutschen Gesellschaft," in *Juden im Wilhelminischen Deutschland 1890–1914,* pp. 479–548. On the history of the Committee, see Naomi W. Cohen, *Not Free To Desist* (Philadelphia, 1972). The fight against the restrictions is told in depth by Judith Goldstein, "The Politics of Ethnic Pressure: The American Jewish Committee as Lobbyist, 1906–1917" (unpublished Ph.D. dissertation, Columbia University, 1972).

34. Bernard Marinbach, *Galveston: Ellis Island of the West* (Albany, 1983).

35. George L. Mosse, *The Crisis of German Ideology* (New York, 1964); Peter G. J. Pulzer, *The Rise of Political Anti-Semitism in Germany and Austria* (New York, 1964); Werner Jochmann, "Die Ausbreitung des Antisemitismus," in *Deutsches Judentum in Krieg und Revolution, 1916–1923,* edited by Werner E. Mosse and Arnold Paucker (Tübingen, 1971), pp. 409–510.

36. Alex Bein, *Theodor Herzl* (Philadelphia, 1956).

37. Barnet Litvinoff, *Weizmann, Last of the Patriarchs* (New York, 1976).

38. Moses Lilienblum, *Kol Kitvei Moshe Lilienblum,* IV (Odessa, 1913), pp. 48, 92; Arthur Hertzberg, ed., *The Zionist Idea* (Garden City, N.Y., 1959), pp. 237–238.

39. Moshé Burstein, *Self-Government of the Jews in Palestine since 1900* (Tel Aviv, 1934); Gerson D. Cohen, *Aliyah* (New York, 1968), p. 17.

40. See, for instance, Michael R. Marrus, *The Politics of Assimilation* (Oxford, 1971); Jehuda Reinharz, *Fatherland or Promised Land* (Ann Arbor, Michigan, 1975); Sidney M. Bolkosky, *The Distorted Image* (New York, 1975).

ᴄᴈ 7

German Antisemitism
in the Light of Post-War
Historiography

Among the many responses set off by the near annihilation of
European Jewry a generation ago, one of the most tangible has been an unabated
interest in the study of German antisemitism. The connection is epitomized by
the career of Léon Poliakov, who in 1951 published the earliest comprehensive
history of the Holocaust and subsequently undertook to write a still unfinished
multi-volume *History of Antisemitism*, whose ultimate objective is to explore the
nexus between the Christian perception of the Jew and the Final Solution of the
Nazis.[1]

Since the Second World War the historical literature on the subject of German
antisemitism has grown to impressive proportions, and despite the recent disjointed broad broadside by Geoffrey Barraclough against the liberal preoccupation
with the origins of Nazism,[2] there is little prospect that Jewish historians will soon
outgrow their existential concern with the roots and role of Nazi antisemitism.
And rightly so, for much remains to be uncovered and explained. But it is time
to take stock, to assess the achievements of a quarter-century of conceptualization and research in order to formulate the agenda at least for the immediate
future.

To impose a semblance of order on this unwieldy body of literature, I should
like to organize the material into general works on antisemitism which impinge
on the German phenomenon and specific studies of German antisemitism itself.
Whereas the first category breaks down into interpretations that are either religious
or political in character, the second category consists of interpretations that are
basically either socio-economic or ideological. Though I would be the first to acknowledge the distortion inherent in any such overarching construct, I do think it
is not only a useful device but also accords in some measure with the conceptual
trends that have emerged in the historiography of the subject.

I

The initial attempt to account for the Holocaust sought to invoke the known to explain the unique; namely, to apply the general theory regarding the Christian origins of antisemitism to the German case. The Nazi assault upon the Jews did not erupt in a vacuum but within the context of an animosity that had been cultivated systematically by Christianity for nearly two millennia. Theologically, legally, and culturally Christianity had effectively rendered the Jews hateful.

Two widespread assumptions made this application relatively simple. The first was a rather monolithic conception of medieval Jewish existence in terms of insecurity, degradation, and persecution. This uniformly bleak view of Diaspora history, which became dominant in nineteenth-century Jewish scholarship and reflected all the strains of the emancipation struggle, identified religious bigotry as the causative agent and the Church as its chief purveyor. Accompanying this assumption was a second, related to the continuity between medieval and modern antisemitism. Despite the differences in rhetoric and form, the phenomenon was perceived to be still fundamentally Christian and religious.

One of the earliest cogent statements of this thesis was delivered by Joshua Trachtenberg at the height of the war in his learned and stimulating study of the utterly negative image of the Jew fostered by the Church and accepted by the masses in the late Middle Ages. In a variety of forms, the Christian world gave expression to its perception of the Jew as the accomplice of Satan, the master of sorcery and the source of all heresy.[3]

Nearly two decades later, Raul Hilberg incorporated this thesis in his monumental work on *The Destruction of the European Jews*. In the opening chapter cryptically entitled "Precedents," Hilberg ignored the evolution of antisemitism in modern Germany and the turbulent decades of the Weimar Republic in order to emphasize the canonical antecedents of Nazi legislation. Though deliberately skirting the complex problem of causation, Hilberg clearly intended to imply that there was nothing accidental about the parallels. "The German Nazis, then, did not discard the past; they built upon it. They did not begin a development; they completed it."[4] Since the Holocaust this interpretation has been passionately reiterated and elaborated by Jews and non-Jews alike—Jules Isaac, Malcolm Hay, Friedrich Heer, and A. Roy Eckardt to name only the most important.[5]

Yet despite the elegance of its simplicity and the appeal of its argument, this approach to modern antisemitism in general and the German case in particular, with its emphasis on the continuity of religious hatred, stirs some grave doubts. To question it is not to deny the existence or vitality of religious tensions in the modern era.[6] Few historians would be so naïve as to imagine that with the achievement of emancipation in the nineteenth century, age-old sentiments simply withered overnight. At the end of the century, German government officials, not to mention large sectors of German public opinion, still gave sufficient credence to the medieval canard of ritual murder to entertain the idea seriously when it was revived in connection with the unsolved murders of a five-year-old boy in Xanten in 1891 and of a teen-age boy in Konitz in 1900.[7] Furthermore, it is quite evident that both before and after the First World War, the attitudes of German Conservatives toward the Jews derived primarily from medieval religious roots.[8]

What is at issue here is the significance to be assigned to Christian prejudice in the evolution of German antisemitism that culminated in the Nazis. After twenty-five years of research, it can no longer be singled out as the root cause for the collapse of emancipation in Germany. At the most, it deserves to be considered as one component of a complex matrix.

To make Christian antisemitism the root cause is to render the Final Solution inexplicable, for Christianity never called for the extermination of the Jews. Had this been its official policy, the Jews would hardly have survived the Middle Ages. On the contrary, the theology and policy of the Church protected Jews in medieval society through the extension of a limited form of toleration. In Rome where the Papacy reigned supreme till 1871, the Jewish community represented "the oldest uninterrupted Jewish settlement in Europe."[9] As long as Jews chose to reject the Church's message of salvation, at times delivered with irresistible force, they were assured in theory of the right to survive in conditions befitting the lowly state of their religion.[10] In contrast, only an ideology which designated Jews as unredeemable could generate a system for their total annihilation.

Likewise, the two assumptions posited by the theory of Christian culpability are historically questionable. Long before the Second World War, Salo Baron, who has revised our understanding of so many aspects of Jewish history, began to challenge the regnant view of the Middle Ages, which he aptly dubbed "the lachrymose conception of Jewish history." Pointing out its function within the context of the emancipation struggle, Baron marshaled an impressive body of evidence to show that Jews actually enjoyed a comparatively high legal status in medieval society, marked by long periods of tranquillity. Hatred did not constantly govern Jewish–Christian relations nor was persecution the lot of every generation. And the violence which did punctuate this extended era of coexistence was by no means incited solely by religious passions.[11] In short, there is nothing one-sided or inevitable about the treatment of Jews in medieval Christendom that could serve to explain their execution at the hands of the Nazis.

In addition, the emphasis on continuity ignores the staggering differences between the two periods. Perhaps the most germane to our discussion is the precipitous decline in the power of religion in the modern era. Since the Renaissance, an inexorable process of secularization had emancipated one sector of society after another from the shackles of religious domination. To acknowledge this retreat of Christianity on every front, while attributing to it on the Jewish question an influence it rarely enjoyed in the Middle Ages, simply makes no sense. It would be more plausible to argue, as did Eva Reichmann, that the collapse of Christianity, with its commitment to Jewish survival, endangered rather than enhanced the status of the Jews.[12] The hallmark of modern antisemitism is its secular idiom and in this case the medium is the message.

As early as 1940, on the threshold of the Final Solution, Maurice Samuel, the gifted commentator on Jewish life, intuited many of the difficulties with the religious interpretation of modern antisemitism. In a remarkable way *The Great Hatred* anticipated many of the conclusions arrived at more dispassionately after the war. Samuel unerringly sensed the uniqueness of the phenomenon. He insisted that antisemitism lay at the heart of Nazi ideology and that on the deepest level it represented a deadly revolt against the intolerably demanding morality of the Judeo-Christian tradition. It was merely safer to attack the Judeo part of the hyphenate. Samuel did not mince words in his denunciation of liberals who stubbornly refused to face the ominous implications of the Nazi assault.[13]

A far more original general interpretation of modern antisemitism appeared in 1951 with the publication of Hannah Arendt's now justly famous *The Origins of Totalitarianism*.[14] With immense learning and unusual conceptual power, the author set out to unravel the origins and dynamics of a new political system of absolute power committed to the relentless pursuit of world domination and based on the atomized masses left by the disintegration of the nation-state. In the best tradition of Hegelian thought, the analysis consists of a thesis, an antithesis and a synthesis. The *leitmotif* of modern European history is the fate of the nation-state: its formation, its demise at the hands of the masses and its replacement by a totalitarian system. The catalyst in this dialectic is capitalism. Unfortunately, as in most Hegelian paradigms, the parts are better than the whole. The impressive theoretical superstructure often rests precariously on the flimsiest factual foundation.

Among the most novel aspects of Hannah Arendt's analysis is the prominence attributed to the Jews in both the nation- and the totalitarian state: in the former as co-founder and in the latter as victim. Of course there is nothing accidental about this symmetry. If the totalitarian state is construed as the revolt of the rootless masses against a political system which grants them neither equality nor security, then the Jews as the most vulnerable representatives of that system will obviously bear the brunt of the attack. Their annihilation was the ultimate price for an alliance which Jews had struck at the dawn of the nation-state, when they placed their economic resources at the disposal of the absolute princes. The money of Jewish purveyors and financiers helped to build the nation-state, and their descendants died at the hands of its destroyers.

The basic trouble with this theory of modern Jewish history, which assumes a necessary equality between cause and effect, is its continental scope. Had it been rigorously confined to Central Europe, it would have gained in substance what it might have lost in brilliance, though even here the evidence does not warrant the apodictic tone of the argument.

Nevertheless, the study represents a breakthrough on at least two counts as far as our subject is concerned. First, it argues for the fundamental difference between medieval and modern antisemitism. The latter is a distinctly political antagonism which derives not from the radical change in status effected by emancipation but rather from the alliance struck by Jews with the ruling authorities of the nation-state: ". . . each class of society which came into a conflict with the state as such became antisemitic because the only social group which seemed to represent the state were the Jews."[15] The real nineteenth-century precursors of the Nazis were the pan-Germans who in their tribal nationalism sought both to transcend the geographic limitations of the nation-state and to eradicate the Jews. "It has been one of the most unfortunate facts in the history of the Jewish people that only its enemies, and almost never its friends, understood that the Jewish question was a political one."[16] With this pungent proposition, Hannah Arendt challenged the students of modern antisemitism to consider the non-religious roots of the Jewish question.

Her second contribution to the subject is less explicit but equally far-reaching. The unmistakable implication of the structure and thesis of her book is that the Jews stand astride the very center of the history of modern Europe. The opening third of her analysis is not called "the emergence of the nation-state" but simply "antisemitism," a choice that must mean that the course of modern European history can never be fully fathomed without a proper grasp of the Jewish dimension. The seminal role of the Jews provoked deep feelings of ambivalence and resentment which in turn exerted a decisive influence on the fate of the nation-state. The ironic twist in her point of view is striking. Whereas earlier generations of Jewish historians had proclaimed the universal importance of their subject matter in terms of Jewish contribution to civilization, Hannah Arendt implied, at least for the modern era, that actual significance was bestowed by the nature of Gentile reactions.[17] Antisemitism, and not Jewish creativity, is the point at which the co-ordinates of Jewish and general history converge. Her shift in emphasis served to alert the scholarly world to antisemitism as a key to the understanding of Germany's tumultuous history during the last two centuries, and since the appearance of her provocative book some German historians have attempted to integrate the theme into their larger canvas.[18]

II

It is only to be expected that the most substantive contributions to the study of German antisemitism since the war should have come from specialists who have restricted their work to the German scene. For a very good reason, as we shall try to indicate later, the initial thrust was in terms of a socio-economic interpretation. The two classic studies of this genre as well as the volume by Hannah Arendt, which all appeared within a span of two years, clearly suggest that the prevailing conception of Nazism at the time did not as yet allow for an ideological approach.

In 1949 Paul Massing, one of the few important non-Jewish associates of the former Frankfurt Institute of Social Research, now based at Columbia, published a pioneering study of political antisemitism in Germany in the last quarter of the nineteenth century. Despite his disenchantment with communism during the Stalin purges and his foolhardy act of withdrawal from party membership on a visit to Moscow in 1937, he authored a refined socialist exposition of the events.[19] Massing interprets the sudden power wielded by conservative and racial forms of antisemitism in the German political arena from the mid-seventies to the mid-nineties as primarily a product of economic crisis. The unexpected and protracted depression which afflicted the new German state created the acute social tensions that provided antisemitism with its electoral appeal. Whether hawked by the Conservatives or the far more radical demagogues of racism, its main support came from the aggrieved *Mittelstand* of the cities and the countryside. The economic recovery after 1895 cut short this first trial run of political antisemitism. Internally the socialists now loomed as a far greater threat, and beyond that nationalism had seized the public imagination.

After twenty-five years, Massing's penetrating and judicious study of the rise and impact of political antisemitism before the turn of the century remains unsurpassed. One may question a somewhat excessive and arbitrary use of the concept of the *Mittelstand*. The ultimate economic fate of school teachers, university students, and professors is quite dissimilar from that of peasants, artisans, and shopkeepers even if for a time their incomes are equally low. The virulent antisemitism of the former does not readily lend itself to the same economic interpretation as the latter. Still the connection between economic malaise and the initial eruption of political antisemitism asserted by Massing has been substantiated by subsequent research.[20]

A second line of investigation adopted by Massing has proved equally fruitful. His interest went well beyond the cluster of small and unstable antisemitic parties to study also the influence which their crude ideology and vulgar rhetoric exerted on the political behavior of the major parties. Specifically he showed that the Conservatives were perfectly willing to utilize antisemitism to gain the mass base necessary to return to power. In the last decade the works of Jacob Toury and Ernest Hamburger have further illuminated this kind of interaction by tracing the impact of antisemitism on the center and left of the political spectrum. The National Liberals and Progressives ceased to nominate Jews for the *Reichstag* and Prussian *Landtag*. Their reluctance effected a dramatic shift to the left in the party affiliation of Jews in the *Reichstag*. Whereas during the first decade of the Empire the majority were National Liberals, during the last two decades they had become Social Democrats.[21]

The real question, however, is whether the level of animosity toward the Jews in German society declined with the arrest of political antisemitism after 1895. There is a growing amount of evidence to indicate that it merely assumed new forms as it succeeded in permeating society at large. This is perhaps the most valuable insight in Peter Pulzer's more recent coverage of the same ground. Despite a sweeping political interpretation which would seem to be inadequately rooted in the data and an assumption that antisemitism was strictly the preserve of the German right, Pulzer did realize that "the decline in the virulence of organised party antisemitism was matched by its increasing pervasion of social life, semi-political bodies, and ideological and economic pressure groups."[22] If anything, the intense nationalism of the pan-German type deepened the isolation of German Jewry.

Finally, it ought to be noted that the evocative title of Massing's book, *Rehearsal for Destruction*, suggests more of a causal nexus between the failure of political antisemitism at the end of the nineteenth century and its success in the thirties than he ever established. Massing was not preoccupied with continuity. His intent was to study the political consequences of economic calamity only in round one, when both fanatics and manipulators found antisemitism to be an effective palliative. But the implication is clear: similar circumstances would breed the same reaction pattern.[23]

Eva Reichmann's *Hostages of Civilisation*, which came out a year after Massing's work, fully shared its underlying thesis: the primacy of economic factors. In scope, method and concern, it differed markedly. Eva Reichmann was one of the intellectual spokesmen of German Jewry's massive defense organization, the *Central-verein deutscher Staatsbürger jüdischen Glaubens*, and her book still echoes the debates between Zionists and non-Zionists before and after the war over the viability of Jewish existence outside a Jewish state.[24] Her book is intended as an argument in defense of emancipation. The catastrophe of German Jewry was *sui generis* and cannot be cited as evidence to prove the failure of the entire emancipation experiment. Even in Germany emancipation was brought down not by the weight of an unbroken antisemitic tradition, but by a convergence of extraordinary conditions.

Eva Reichmann's argument is buttressed by an array of analytic concepts drawn from the fields of history, sociology, and psychology. The key difference between the antisemitism of the nineteenth century and that of the twentieth is the waning of the objective causes. The first flush of emancipation had given rise to a vertical type of immigration, and the lack of assimilation which marked the masses emerging from the ghetto inevitably created severe inter-group tensions. But by the twentieth century with Jews now indistinguishable from their neighbors, the survival of antisemitism could no longer be explained in terms of Jewish defects and differences. It derived instead directly from the Nazis, who ruthlessly exploited the relics of inter-group tensions to woo the masses with symbols and bonanzas that concealed the intractable reality. The vulgarity of Nazi antisemitism was part of their unabashed readiness to gratify the passions of a weary and desperate people, humiliated by defeat and impoverished by the Depression. Influenced by Freud's

Civilization and Its Discontents, Eva Reichmann depicted the Germans as angry and aggressive hostages bound by the shackles of civilization. The style and substance of the Nazi program provided exactly the emotional release and instinct gratification for which the masses yearned. In short, emancipation in Germany fell victim to a unique collective explosion of the death instinct.

The obvious difficulty with this early venture into psycho-history is, of course, the problem of verification. What kind of evidence is available to establish the decisive role of such elusive constructs and who needs the additional explanation if the economic theory suffices to account for the data? If Eva Reichmann's utilization of Freud cannot be defended on that score, at least it bespoke the recognition that historians must also face the disturbing fact that the primitive, coarse and vicious propaganda poured out by the Nazis ceased to appall the sensibilities of civilized people. The normal restraints of civil society had been leveled by a cascade of unmatched vituperation, while the Nazi vote continued to soar. Moreover, she sensed that the debilitated condition of Christianity, rather than enhancing Jewish prospects for full integration, had gravely reduced the power of the collective superego to repress the Nazi onslaught.

With Eva Reichmann's work the need to go beyond the strictly socio-economic interpretation becomes apparent. What hindered students of German antisemitism was the prevailing perception of Nazism. As long as Nazism was understood as a non-ideological movement and as long as its Jew-hatred was regarded merely as a cold-blooded tactic for political advantage, Jewish historians would continue to stress economic and political factors and to locate the roots of the Holocaust in our own century. The early studies of German antisemitism, which we have considered, definitely reflected the regnant view of Nazism as the incarnation of the will to power, inspired by the vision of permanent revolution and unhindered by ideological commitment. In 1939 Hermann Rauschning, Hitler's former confidant, had stridently warned the West about the nihilistic revolution sweeping Germany, and despite the intemperate and crude challenge by Peter Viereck two years later, Rauschning's non-ideological analysis exercised the imagination of historians for the next three decades. Neither Hannah Arendt nor Alan Bullock transcended this demonic view of Nazism. Their profound works continued to posit a perception in which ideology only disguised the naked pursuit of power. Sheer opportunism was the tactical expression of ideological bankruptcy.[25]

The publication in 1956 of *Er ist wie Du* by Eleonore Sterling, who was to die twelve years later at the age of forty-three, heralded a new era of research.[26] A sophisticated, multi-level study of the ideological antecedents and functional equivalents of Nazi antisemitism in the first half of the nineteenth century, the volume broke new ground both methodologically as well as substantively. To measure the attitudes of German society toward the Jews, Eleonore Sterling discarded the usual method of generalizing on the basis of the published legacy of a few renowned figures and rummaged through the archives to exhume the petitions, pamphlets, newspapers, and correspondence that preserved the sentiments of countless middlebrows. The evidence led her to conclude that neither the emancipation of the Jews nor the secularization of society served to dismantle the intense medieval prejudices against the Jews, which she depicted in terms taken straight from Trachtenberg. To be sure, the antagonism was no longer anchored in the religious moorings which had once made it the misguided expression of sincere faith. But as it became unfastened it was deliberately or unconsciously appropriated to vent a host of contemporary political, economic, and intellectual grievances.

Eleonore Sterling claimed that for disparate reasons and in different guises antisemitism suited the needs of nearly every sector of German society in a tumultuous period of transition. For the conservatives, medieval Christian antisemitism was redeployed in defense of political feudalism. For the liberals and radicals, a secular critique of Judaism helped to reassert the deep-rooted sense of Christian superiority in non-religious terms. In the case of the lower classes, a violent *völkisch* Jew-hatred that pressed for expulsion, resettlement, racial purification, and extermination relieved the resentment of the powerless. In the context of national frustration and economic dislocation, antisemitism proved the ideal diversionary tactic to protect those in power from the wrath of those upon whom it weighed most heavily. Because of their own acute ambivalence, the liberals did nothing to counter the illusion that the millennium would dawn with the destruction of the Jews.

Indeed, the heart of Eleonore Sterling's book is the politicization of antisemitism, a pattern of German politics already developed in the first half of the nineteenth century. The recurring use of antisemitism as a bogus remedy for the ills of an ailing society says something about the nature of political culture in Germany. Long before the Nazis, a reaction pattern had been formed and an ideological tradition cultivated that predisposed a troubled society to repeatedly opt for the same incredibly simplistic solution. A primitive mechanism of problem solving had been foisted upon a naïve and immature body politic.

Part of this naïveté may well stem, as Fritz Stern has contended, from an ingrained cultural bias against political life.[27] What is the nature of politics in a society whose educated élite scorns and shuns the political arena as debasing? Stern himself has deftly shown the kind of infantile political wisdom of which the unpolitical German was capable.[28] The cliché-ridden leap from cultural pessimism to military conquest, political hegemony and national regeneration epitomized a pervasive and enduring state of mind, incisively depicted by Nietzsche: "Weariness that wants to reach the ultimate with one leap, with one fatal leap, a poor ignorant weariness that does not want to want any more: this created all gods and other worlds."[29] It comes as no surprise that in the German ideology of the conservative revolution the Jew enjoyed a seat of honor. In typically simplistic fashion, he was cast as the symbol of modernity: the purveyor of civilization and the enemy of culture.

Three years after Stern first called attention to the intoxicating nature and wide appeal of the Germanic ideology as a partial answer to why Hitler repelled so few educated Germans in his bid for power, George Mosse renewed the investigation in *The Crisis of German Ideology*.[30] But whereas Stern had recreated the spirit, style, and substance of this ideology through the medium of biography, Mosse attempted to distill it directly from a disparate array of nineteenth- and twentieth-century primary sources. What emerges is an amorphous conceptual construct known by the name of *"völkisch* ideology" that runs the risk of becoming a kind of intellectual "grab bag" into which a host of antimodern "isms" are somewhat haphazardly thrown. Essentially it is a backward-looking, corporate, and élitist view of society, based on soil and *Volk* and laden with mystical tendencies and racist rhetoric. Mosse sees antisemitism as the most direct expression of *völkisch* ideology. The cultural pessimism of the middle class which fed the ideology was effectively diverted from the real issues in the direction of the Jews, the perfect foil.

In the turmoil after the war, the ever-widening institutionalization of *völkisch* ideology paved the way for Hitler. Specifically, Hitler's obsession with the Jews crystallized a diffuse sentiment into a perfect instrument for mobilizing the masses. Unlike most scholars, Mosse boldly argues that it was precisely Nazi antisemitism which gained it mass support. In their political naïveté, the Germans again grabbed for the usual sham solution to unresolved problems: the elimination of the Jews would rectify the humiliations and injustices of a detested society. Nazi antisemitism offered the ideal middle-class revolution: nothing would change. Instead, in their flight from reality, the Germans plunged into the abyss of totalitarianism.

Recently, Werner Jochmann's monographic study of the explosive upsurge of antisemitism during the traumatic years from 1916 to 1923 has reinforced much of Mosse's trenchant analysis.[31] Launched first by pan-German and *völkisch* circles, the attack against the Jews spread and intensified in direct consequence of national humiliation and social disintegration. By the time of its dissolution in June 1922 after the murder of Rathenau, *Der Deutschvölkische Schutz- und Trutz-Bund* had become not only the most radical antisemitic organization in the Weimar Republic, but with its 530 local chapters and 200,000 members also the largest.[32] In varying degrees, its brand of antisemitism infected ever larger numbers of students, teachers, professors, veterans, pastors, editors, journalists, civil servants, shop owners, commercial employees, and women. On the basis of extensive archival research, Jochmann concluded that by 1923, while "one large part of the population hated and despised the Jews, the other, just barely the majority, had either inwardly given them up or displayed no inclination to get involved on their behalf."[33] It was the old pattern all over again: instead of turning on those responsible for losing the war and unleashing the chaos, the Germans were induced to take out their frustration against their traditional enemies.[34]

In 1969 the ideological study of German antisemitism was significantly advanced by the publication of Uriel Tal's *Judaism and Christianity in the "Second Reich" 1870–1914.*[35] On the basis of many new archival sources, Tal carried Sterling's attitudinal and ideological analysis of the German middlebrow forward into the era of the Bismarckian state. Not only did he succeed in demonstrating the wide currency of three distinct types of antisemitism, but he also expounded the intellectual infrastructure of each one with profound insight. At least in part that penetration derives from a refusal to treat ideas merely as a reflex of socio-economic conditions. The antisemitic ideas of conservative, liberal, and racist ideologues addressed a range of genuine intellectual, religious, and emotional needs and constituted an integral part of a coherent world view.

Tal's assumption and method score their most notable success in his searching analysis of the nature and roots of the liberal antagonism toward Jewish survival after emancipation. Long ignored by Jewish historians because of its basically latent character and because of their own liberal commitments, this tension cannot readily be reduced to non-ideological factors. With a wealth of data and sheer analytic power, Tal probes the state of mind of German liberals at the end of the century. Precisely because they shared so fully the same set of rational humanistic, secular, and political values as their Jewish counterparts, Christian liberals felt their own identity threatened by the continued existence of an assimilated Jewish community. Despite their insistence on a separation of church and state, they offered a non-pluralistic vision of society no less hostile to Jewish aspirations for group survival than that of the conservatives. The humanistic study of the Gospels would infuse the educational system and the figure of Jesus would serve as an ethical exemplar, with the result that German culture would be permeated with the ethos of an enlightened Christianity.

This critical appraisal of German liberalism is really part of a post-Holocaust re-examination of European liberalism and its forerunners, by Jewish scholars disillusioned by the silence of the liberal world during the thirties and forties. In their quest for a new society, advocates of the enlightenment and liberalism had certainly effected the emancipation of Western European Jewry, but what had inhibited their twentieth-century disciples from protesting its revocation and from rising against the murder of its chief beneficiaries? Since the intuitive response by Maurice Samuel, historians like Eliyahu Cherikover, Eleonore Sterling, Arthur Hertzberg, Shmuel Ettinger, Jacob Katz, and Uriel Tal have reopened the study of French *philosophes* and *Jacobins* and German liberals with regard to the Jewish question only to discover that the very same men who proposed the emancipation of the Jew harbored a decidedly negative image of him and a strong antipathy toward his religion. It was hoped that emancipation would quickly lead to the disappearance of European Jewry.[36]

This deep-seated intellectual ambivalence of German liberals has been confirmed in the social realm by Jacob Katz's pioneering study of *Jews and Freemasons in Europe 1723–1939.*[37] Primarily limited to the German scene, it provides ample documentation on the tremendous reluctance of the rising middle class which dominated Freemasonry to admit aspiring Jews of the same class to its exclusive lodges. The protracted and unsuccessful struggle of Jews to gain entry into the ranks of German Masonry mirrored their struggle for full admission into German society. As legal barriers tumbled, they were effectively replaced by social impediment. Christianity remained an inseparable component of the German movement. It is no accident that the first German lodge of B'nai B'rith was founded by Jews who had been driven out of Masonic lodges in the 1870s and 1880s.[38]

Besides the older forms of antisemitism of the conservatives and liberals, Tal also focuses on the new ideological superstructure erected by the racist antisemites. What he adds to the earlier studies of Stern and Mosse is a profound analysis of the implicit and explicit anti-Christian motifs inherent in the racist attack on the Jews. During the period of the Empire, they had still to be muted, for undisguised they were simply too radical for the German electorate. By the time of the Nazis, these motifs were not only baldly invoked but entirely acceptable. At the end of his analysis, Tal suggests that Houston Stewart Chamberlain played the major role in crystallizing and legitimizing this Aryan version of Christianity and thereby transmitting it from the pre-war to the post-war generation, an insight fully confirmed by Geoffrey Field's important Columbia doctoral dissertation on "H. St. Chamberlain: Prophet of Bayreuth."[39]

In recent years other sectors of German society have also begun to receive the attention of scholars interested in measuring their attitudes toward Jews. Hermann Greive, for example, has shown the extensive anti-Jewish sentiments among Catholics during the Weimar period, which became increasingly susceptible to reformulation in racist terms.[40] Hans-Helmuth Knütter and George Mosse have in different ways probed deeply the reservations and ambivalences felt toward Jews on the left among unaffiliated intellectuals of the *Weltbühne* type or card-carrying members of the Socialist party. To a great extent, the tension flowed from a combination of ideological presuppositions and objective economic realities. The upshot was that Jews received only limited support from the left in their confrontation with Nazi antisemitism.[41] Since no group in Germany fully escaped infection by antisemitism, the Jews could find temporary allies only among those Germans who disliked them least.

III

In retrospect, the achievement of a quarter-century of intensive research on German antisemitism is impressive. The visceral Jew-hatred of the Nazis was not fortuitous but the culmination of a chronic and endemic condition of German society. Intellectual historians have unearthed a massive quantity of evidence depicting an extraordinary diversity of anti-Jewish ideologies. German society was blanketed by overlapping critiques of Jews and Judaism. Each sector leveled its attack from its own ideological vantage point. The consequence was that German Jewry lived in a society in which no party held an ideology that could accept Jewish aspirations for group survival. In no other European society were Jewish–Christian relations shaped by such a comprehensive superstructure of ideological antisemitism. While this oppressive superstructure certainly did not predetermine the demise of German Jewry, it effectively rendered the Germans insensate when the sentence was progressively carried out.

If the vital legacy of *völkisch* ideology helps to explain "why so few of the educated, civilised classes recognised Hitler as the embodiment of evil,"[42] then the tortuous history of German antisemitism may suggest why the abusive and scurrilous version of the Nazis did not alienate the Germans when they still had a choice. Extended exposure to vituperative ideological Jew-hatred had desensitized them to the ominous possibility of translating words into actions. As the Nazis revoked emancipation and deported Jews, the pervasive negative predisposition of their German neighbors inhibited them from risking the consequences of protest.

What remains to be explained is why the medieval animosity toward Jews, with which every European society entered the modern era, was not dissipated in Germany, but rather sustained, transmuted, and intensified, thereby lending itself to exploitation in times of stress. The answer may lie partially in the ambiguous record of the major institution of German society, the state, which as yet has been generally ignored by students of antisemitism. The reluctance, equivocation, and reversals with which German governments enacted emancipation and the administrative discrimination to which Jewish citizens were subsequently subjected served to keep alive and reinforce the prejudices of German society. As Wilhelm von Humboldt presciently recognized in 1809 at the very outset of the emancipation process: "Gradual emancipation merely emphasises the segregation which it desires to abolish in all matters that are not repealed and even doubles it, precisely because the new and greater freedom attracts attention toward the disabilities that remain and thus serves to defeat its own aim."[43]

Exactly one hundred and seven years later, at the height of a war that German Jewry thought would irrefutably establish its claim to complete acceptance, the Prussian Minister of War saw fit to subject the Jews to a special head-count to ensure that they were serving the Fatherland in proper numbers.[44] The persistence of such overt acts of discrimination from above, especially in a society as respectful of authority as Germany, repeatedly provided a model for the entire population. The failure of the state to resolve decisively the ambiguities of Jewish status preserved a major structural flaw in German society that ultimately led under severe stress to catastrophic results. Our next task should be to reconstruct the theory and reality of governmental policy toward the Jews throughout the modern period, in all areas where the state was required to deal with Jews as individuals or as a group. The emerging pattern may have much to tell us about the reason for the enduring prominence of antisemitism in German society.[45]

NOTES

1. Léon Poliakov, *Bréviaire de la haine*, Paris 1951; *idem, Histoire de l'antisémitisme*, 3 vols., Paris 1955–1968.
2. Geoffrey Barraclough, in *The New York Review of Books*, 19th October, 2nd November, 16th November, 1972.
3. Joshua Trachtenberg, *The Devil and the Jew*, New Haven 1943.
4. Raul Hilberg, *The Destruction of the European Jews*, Chicago 1961, p. 4.
5. Jules Isaac, *Jesus and Israel*, trans. by Sally Gran, New York 1971; *idem, Genèse de l'antisémitisme*, Paris 1956; *idem, The Teaching of Contempt*, trans. by Helen Weaver, New York 1964. Malcolm Hay, *The Foot of Pride*, Boston 1950. Friedrich Heer, *God's First Love*, trans. by Geoffrey Skelton, New York 1970. A. Roy Eckardt, *Elder and Younger Brothers*, New York 1967; *idem, Your People, My People*, New York 1974.
6. Salo W. Baron, *Modern Nationalism and Religion*, New York 1960.
7. Ismar Schorsch, *Jewish Reactions to German Anti-Semitism 1870–1914*, New York 1972, 104–105, 150.
8. Werner Jochmann, "Die Ausbreitung des Antisemitismus," in *Deutsches Judentum in Krieg und Revolution 1916–1923*. Ein Sammelband herausgegeben von Werner E. Mosse unter Mitwirkung von Arnold Paucker, Tübingen 1971 (Schriftenreihe wissenschaftlicher Abhandlungen des Leo Baeck Instituts 25), pp. 487–492.
9. Salo W. Baron, *A Social and Religious History of the Jews*, 1st ed., 3 vols., New York 1937, II, p. 47.
10. An informative, incisive, and judicious survey of the evolution and complexity of Church policy toward the Jews is provided by Baron, *A Social and Religious History of the Jews*, 2nd rev. ed., 15 vols., New York 1952–1973, IV, pp. 3–149; IX, pp. 3–192.
11. Salo W. Baron, "Ghetto and Emancipation," in *Menorah Journal* XIV (1928), pp. 515–526; *idem, A Social and Religious History of the Jews*, 1st ed., II, pp. 3–86; *idem*, "The Jewish Factor in Medieval Civilization," in *Proceedings of the American Academy for Jewish Research* XII (1942), pp. 34–44; *idem, A Social and Religious History of the Jews*, 2nd ed., XI.
12. Eva G. Reichmann, *Hostages of Civilisation*, London 1950, pp. 74–82.
13. Maurice Samuel, *The Great Hatred*, New York 1948.
14. Hannah Arendt, *The Origins of Totalitarianism*, New York 1958.
15. *Ibid.*, p. 25.
16. *Ibid.*, p. 56.
17. A typical specimen of this apologetically inspired literature is Joseph Jacobs, *Jewish Contributions to Civilization*, Philadelphia 1919.
18. Ernst Nolte, *Three Faces of Fascism*, New York 1969; Helmut Krausnick *et al., Anatomy of the SS State*, London 1968; Karl Dietrich Bracher, *The German Dictatorship*, New York 1970; Eberhard Jäckel, *Hitlers Weltanschauung*, Tübingen 1969. The absence of any serious discussion of German antisemitism is a striking omission in Ralf Dahrendorf's stimulating *Society and Democracy in Germany*, New York 1969.
19. Paul W. Massing, *Rehearsal for Destruction*, New York 1949. The biographical data is provided by Martin Jay's superb intellectual history of the Frankfurt school, *The Dialectical Imagination*, Boston 1973, pp. 34, 170–171.
20. Hans Rosenberg, *Grosse Depression und Bismarckzeit*, Berlin 1967.
21. Jacob Toury, *Die politischen Orientierungen der Juden in Deutschland: Von Jena bis Weimar*, Tübingen 1966 (Schriftenreihe wissenschaftlicher Abhandlungen des Leo

Baeck Instituts 15), pp. 192–201; Ernest Hamburger, "One Hundred Years of Emancipation," in *LBIYB XIV* (1969), pp. 19–21.

22. Peter G. J. Pulzer, *The Rise of Political Anti-Semitism in Germany and Austria*, New York 1964, p. 219.

23. Massing, *Rehearsal for Destruction*, p. 109.

24. For the pre-war debate in which Eva Reichmann was personally involved see Werner E. Mosse, "Der Niedergang der Weimarer Republik und die Juden" and Kurt Loewenstein, "Die inner-jüdische Reaktion auf die Krise der deutschen Demokratie," in *Entscheidungsjahr 1932: Zur Judenfrage in der Endphase der Weimarer Republik. Ein Sammelband herausgegeben von Werner E. Mosse unter Mitwirkung von Arnold Paucker*, Tübingen 1965, 1966 (Schriftenreihe wissenschaftlicher Abhandlungen des Leo Baeck Instituts 13), pp. 43–49, 381–382.

25. Hermann Rauschning, *The Revolution of Nihilism*, New York 1939, especially part one. Peter Viereck, *Metapolitics*, rev. ed., New York 1965. On Rauschning's influence on the historical profession, see also Klaus Hildebrand, "Hitlers Ort in der Geschichte des preussisch-deutschen Nationalstaates," *Historische Zeitschrift*, vol. 217 (Dec. 1973), p. 595. As for the historians themselves, see Hannah Arendt, *The Origins of Totalitarianism*, pp. 324, 384–387, and Alan Bullock, *Hitler: A Study in Tyranny*, rev. ed., New York 1961, pp. 356, 724.

26. Eleonore Sterling, *Er ist wie Du: Aus der Frügeschichte des Antisemitismus in Deutschland (1815–1850)*, München 1956. A revised edition appeared recently under the title *Judenhass*, Frankfurt am Main 1969.

27. Fritz Stern, "The Political Consequences of the Unpolitical German," reprinted in his recent volume of essays *The Failure of Illiberalism*, New York 1972, pp. 3–25.

28. Fritz Stern, *The Politics of Cultural Despair*, Garden City 1965. The book had first appeared in 1961.

29. Quoted by Stern, *The Politics of Cultural Despair*, p. 326.

30. George L. Mosse, *The Crisis of German Ideology*, New York 1964.

31. Werner Jochmann, "Die Ausbreitung des Antisemitismus," *loc. cit.*

32. *Ibid.*, pp. 457, 466.

33. *Ibid.*, p. 494.

34. *Ibid.*, p. 441.

35. Uriel Tal, *Judaism and Christianity in the "Second Reich" 1870–1914* (in Hebrew), Jerusalem 1969.

36. Eliyahu Tscherikower, *Jews in Periods of Revolution* (in Hebrew), Tel Aviv 1957, pp. 23–103. Arthur Hertzberg, *The French Enlightenment and the Jews*, New York 1968, pp. 248–268. Shmuel Ettinger, "Jews and Judaism as seen by the English Deists of the 18th Century" (in Hebrew), *Zion*, XXIX (1964), pp. 182–207; *idem*, "The Roots of Antisemitism in the Modern Era" (in Hebrew), *Molad*, new series II (1969), pp. 323–340. Jacob Katz, *Out of the Ghetto*, Cambridge, Mass. 1973; *idem*, "Judaism and Jews in the Eyes of Voltaire" (in Hebrew), *Molad*, new series V (1973), pp. 614–625. Uriel Tal, "Liberal Protestantism and the Jews in the Second Reich 1870–1914," *Jewish Social Studies*, XXVI (1964), pp. 23–41. The critical assessment of German liberalism by Jewish scholars has been supported from the German side by the exemplary monograph by Reinhard Rürup, "Die Judenemanzipation in Baden," *Zeitschrift für die Geschichte des Oberrheins*, CXIV (1966).

37. Jacob Katz, *Jews and Freemasons in Europe 1723–1939*, trans. by Leonard Oschry, Cambridge, Mass. 1970.

38. *Ibid.*, pp. 164–165.

39. Tal, *Judaism and Christianity,* pp. 225–234. Geoffrey G. Field, "H. St. Chamberlain: Prophet of Bayreuth" (unpublished Columbia University doctoral dissertation, 1972). See now also Field's "Antisemitism and Weltpolitik," in *LBIYB XVIII* (1973), pp. 65–91.

40. Hermann Greive, *Theologie und Ideologie,* Heidelberg 1969.

41. Hans-Helmuth Knütter, *Die Juden und die deutsche Linke in der Weimarer Republik 1918–1933,* Düsseldorf 1971. George L. Mosse, "German Socialists and the Jewish Question in the Weimar Republic," in *LBIYB XVI* (1971), pp. 123–151. Long before, Massing had detected some of the ideological and strategic factors which inhibited Social Democrats from defending Jews specifically. (Massing, *Rehearsal for Destruction,* pp. 151, 157–169, 180–183.) While one might raise objections to the method and organization, Donald L. Niewyk's *Socialist, Anti-Semite, and Jew,* Baton Rouge 1971, does provide a counterbalance to the critical conclusions of Knütter and Mosse.

42. The formulation is that of A.J.P. Taylor, quoted by Stern, *The Politics of Cultural Despair,* p. 353.

43. Wilhelm von Humboldt, "Regarding the Draft of a New System of Legislation for the Jews, July 17, 1809," trans. by Max J. Kohler, *Publications of the American Jewish Historical Society,* XXVI (1918), p. 104. The translation has been slightly revised.

44. Jochmann, "Die Ausbreitung des Antisemitismus," *loc. cit.,* p. 425.

45. Certainly the few studies that have been undertaken in this area justify an intensification of effort. See Helmut Neubach, *Die Ausweisungen von Polen und Juden aus Preussen 1885/86,* Wiesbaden 1967; Horst Fischer, *Judentum, Staat, und Heer in Preussen im frühen 19. Jahrhundert: Zur Geschichte der staatlichen Judenpolitik,* Tübingen 1968 (Schriftenreihe wissenschaftlicher Abhandlungen des Leo Baeck Instituts 20); Ernest Hamburger, "Jews in Public Service under the German Monarchy," in *LBIYB IX* (1964), pp. 206–238; Marjorie Lamberti, "The Prussian Government and the Jews: Official Behaviour and Policy-Making in the Wilhelminian Era," and Werner T. Angress, "Prussia's Army and the Jewish Reserve Officer Controversy before World War II," both in *LBIYB XVII* (1972), pp. 3–18 and 19–42.

Thinking Historically

$\mathscr{e}\mathscr{o}$ 8

Wissenschaft and Values

The centennial of The Jewish Theological Seminary of America ought to prompt some reflection on the legacy of modern Jewish scholarship, for the rabbinical schools founded by Zacharias Frankel, Sabato Morais, and Solomon Schechter played pioneering roles in the history of the discipline. The Breslau Seminary constituted the first institutional framework in Germany and, in truth, in Europe for the academic study of Judaism and, no less importantly, dared to make of it the bedrock of rabbinic education. At the turn of the century, Breslau's American counterpart, especially under the leadership of Schechter, served as one of the main conduits for transplanting the new learning to these shores. Both seminaries were part of a small number of Jewish institutions that nurtured a field of study long deemed unworthy of admission to the halls of the university. In the process they set a high standard for applying the canons of Western scholarship to the sacred texts of Judaism and created a rabbinic leadership equipped with startlingly new conceptions of the Jewish past.

The continued exclusion of Judaica from the university bespoke a view of Judaism that still accorded with the unequal and separate political status of medieval Jewry. A new political status for Jews begged for a reevaluation of Judaism. It made little sense to invite a minority into the body politic for whose religion one had only contempt, unless the ultimate expectation was to free them of that religious legacy. With nearly prophetic insight, Leopold Zunz argued that respect for Judaism was the very precondition for emancipation.

So let us grant the spirit its right. Approval of the individual will follow from approval of his spirit. We should perceive and respect in Jewish literature an organic spiritual activity, which accords with world developments and is thereby of general interest, which inspires empathy by virtue of its struggles. This always exposed literature, never subvented, often persecuted, whose authors never belonged to the mighty of the earth, has a history, a philosophy, a poetry which makes it the equal of other literatures. If this be granted, must not then these Jewish authors and in

Reprinted from *Tikkun Magazine* (July/August 1987), a bi-monthly Jewish critique of politics, culture and society. Subscriptions are $31.00 per year from *Tikkun*, 251 West 100th Street, 5th floor, New York, NY 10025.

fact the Jews themselves attain to the citizenship of the spirit? Must not then a spirit of humanity pour out over the land from the font of scholarship, paving the way for understanding and harmony? The extension of equality to the Jews in society will follow from the extension of equality to the academic study of Judaism.[1]

It is no historical accident that in the country of its birth, where *Wissenschaft des Judentums* (the scientific study of Judaism) never gained entry into the university, emancipation would eventually be revoked.

I stress this political import of Jewish studies to highlight the significance of what has happened to the field in America since the 1960s. The proliferation of courses, professors, and programs in the university attests to the unheralded political security of Jews in American society. The theoretical right to be different had been anchored in a high regard for Judaism. Emancipation required of Jews to explain themselves to a Christian society pervaded by the prejudice of centuries. In 1949 Louis Finkelstein wrote in the foreword to his ambitious collaborative synthesis entitled *The Jews* "it is no extravagance to call Judaism the unknown religion of our time."[2] Nearly four decades later we can declare that the ever-broadening study of Jews and Judaism at the pinnacle of the educational system has diminished that ignorance, enhanced the dignity of the discipline, and above all solidified the place of Jews in American society. The contribution of the Seminary, especially under Dr. Finkelstein, played a vital role in that process of mediation and quest for respect.

The scientific study of Judaism is more than footnotes, variant readings, and bibliographies. These are but the fearsome trappings of the field. They are not to be taken as the tools of a burial society or the diet of fallen angels. Every serious intellectual and artistic enterprise has its arcane mode of expression which eludes and irritates the uninitiated. At the core of modern Jewish scholarship there is a new way of thinking about Judaism. Emancipation exposed Jews inexorably to the historical perspective: to understanding the present in terms of the past and the past in terms of itself. A religious tradition indifferent to the category of time in comprehending itself, that indeed made a virtue of leveling chronologically all its literary strata—*ein mukdam u-meuhar ba-Torah*—was suddenly confronted with a mode of cognition that rested on contextual interpretation. Dating became the key to eliciting the meaning of a text and no contemporaneous piece of evidence—Jewish or non-Jewish—could be arbitrarily dismissed in the interpretive exercise. The title of Krochmal's early and seminal response to the challenge of history, *Moreh Nevukhei ha-Zeman*, adroitly alludes to his audience—Jews perplexed by the intrusion of time.

It was not the first era in which a new consciousness had ruptured the continuity of Jewish thinking. The midrashic thought processes of the Second Commonwealth had transformed the literary legacy of the First Commonwealth. The precedence of sage over prophet signaled not only the end of Scripture but its subordination to a method of reading pioneered by the Greeks. The sustained exegetical genius of the rabbis eventually lifted the Oral Law to the rank of gate keeper, the final arbiter of the meaning of the Written Law. Similarly, by the tenth century Islam had begun to imbue Jews with a new philosophic sensibility. The anthropomorphic language which gives the Bible its pathos and immediacy was suddenly felt to be offensive. Jews were acutely reminded of God's unfathomable transcendence, and whether in philosophical or mystical terms, they struggled to restore God to His rightful grandeur without losing access to His presence. Against the backdrop of these earlier encounters with Greek thought, Zunz located his own age of *Wissenschaft*. "Three times did Jews encounter the Hellenic spirit, the emancipator of nations."³ Each time an infusion of consciousness had rendered the natural painfully problematic. Each time it had provoked a confrontation that led to an outburst of creative cultural transmission. Confrontation, it seems to me, is one of the wellsprings of the still undiminished creative vigor of the Jewish people.

Wissenschaft des Judentums, therefore, is the most important legacy of German Jewry, a community that served as both cutting edge and laboratory for the emancipation experiment. In its transcending of constraints, modern Jewish scholarship is the intellectual counterpart to the political freedom of emancipation. It embodies a basic shift in perspective from the dogmatic to the undogmatic, from the exegetical to the conceptual, from the acceptance of unexamined knowledge to a deep concern with method, from resting content with the normative texts of Ashkenazic Jewry to an ever-widening canvass of Jewish creativity. *Wissenschaft* as ethos bespeaks a profound respect for the integrity of the individual entity—be it fact, text or person. It bitterly contests the essentially disjointed and disjunctive way of reading texts sanctified by rabbinic tradition.

Above all, *Wissenschaft* venerates the importance of details. In the memorable motto of Abby Warburg, "God is to be found in details." For all his antagonism toward the *Wissenschaft* of his predecessors, Gershom Scholem personified its spirit when he wrote in 1945:

We have sought to submerge ourselves in the study of details and of the detail of the detail. . . . We have sought the light of the scientific idea, which illuminates the welter of details like sunlight dancing on the water, and yet we know . . . that it dwells only in the details themselves."⁴

Attention to details, a maddening degree of facticity, became the scalpel by which Zunz and his disciples cut through the miasma of errors and the overgrowth of *derash* which obliterated the original and literal sense of a text. Not unlike the circle of the Vilna Gaon, the practitioners of *Wissenschaft* were in hungry pursuit of the *peshat*, the plain meaning of ancient texts. What distinguished the two groups was the equipment they were prepared to use in the chase. With their receptivity to gentile wisdom, Western scholars were uninhibited about adding to the cache of internal tools already available.

In fact, I have long felt that the single-minded quest for the literal meaning of the text is what rendered *Wissenschaft* scholars deaf to the mystic chords of *Kabbalah*. To be sure, questions of authorship also got in the way. The traditional and often untenable claims for the antiquity of mystical texts provoked the scholarly wrath of historical positivists crusading for truth. But, in the final analysis, as champions of the long-neglected *peshat*, they were unable to appreciate even the distortions of *midrash*, let alone the exegetical violence of the *Kabbalah*. The source of their revulsion was not a rational bent per se, because some of the bitterest critics of *Kabbalah*, like Luzzatto and Graetz, had a pronounced romantic streak, but rather an obsession with what they held to be the sanctity of the literal sense of the text. It was only the rare scholar like a Landauer, a Joel, or a Jellinek who rose above these alien and confining categories of analysis to approximate a more sympathetic understanding of the Jewish mystical tradition.

But the real evaluative question is not what is *Wissenschaft des Judentums* but, rather, what has it accomplished? The European founders of the academic study of Judaism suffer from a notoriously bad press. The stature of Scholem as a scholar has given his highly charged indictment an authority which seems to settle the matter. He could not forgive his forerunners for their denigration of what he believed to be the lifeblood of rabbinic Judaism. And yet the basis of his judgment was far too narrow. For all his achievements, he tended to minimize their contributions to his own field. No less significant, the resounding impact of his own career is irrefutable evidence of the continuing centrality of scholarship in the shaping of modern Judaism. Would the strains of Jewish mysticism beckon our attention if not for the gargantuan labor of excavation and reconstruction performed by Scholem?

One way of understanding *Wissenschaft des Judentums* is as a collective act of translation, a sustained effort to cast the history, literature, and institutions of Judaism in Western categories. Emancipated Jews quickly lost access to the language, wisdom, and symbols of their religion. Mendelssohn's translation of the Torah proved to be emblematic. Luther's translation would not do, for Jews and Christians read Scripture differently. Mendelssohn's fidelity to the plain sense of the text and interest in Hebrew grammar and literary style adumbrated emphases of modern scholarship. More important, his work bespoke the need to retain contact with the past through a new medium. Without translation, sacred texts would soon have become sealed for all except the cognoscenti. The Hebrew Bible would be translated at least ten more times into German during the next one hundred and fifty years, telling evidence of a broad and lively religious sentiment, with the Zunz Bible alone going through some eighteen editions.

But of course I am not speaking of translation merely in the literal sense. The whole gigantic enterprise to impose a semblance of system on an untidy traditional Judaism, to recover the contours of Jewish creativity, to reconstruct Jewish history, to study normative religious texts from fresh perspectives, and to mediate the burgeoning results in a variety of popular forms constituted a rendering of the Jewish experience in terms comprehensible to the Western mind. In the process vast changes in self-perception occurred. To give but one example, Mordecai Kaplan is inconceivable without Zunz and Steinschneider, who expanded the conception of Jewish literature to include religious and secular works by Jews in any language. While Zunz unfurled the unimagined fecundity of Jews in Hebrew, Steinschneider demonstrated their deep involvement in the literature of other languages. The conception of Judaism as a religious civilization rested squarely on a century of prodigious scholarly excavation.

The effective translation of Judaism into Western categories, in turn, served to inculcate Jews with a sense of historical consciousness that at least partially offset the loss of communal constraints and personal piety. At the end of the nineteenth century Dubnow, who sought to replicate the achievements of German Jewish scholarship in the Russian empire, could write "in these days the keystone of national unity seems to be the historical consciousness."[5] In an age of individual freedom and growing secularism, scholarship had become the ground for consent. Accordingly, Zunz detested Jewish scholars who disparaged their subject matter. "It is better to praise Israel's antiquity two or three times than to traduce it once," he declared in 1846. "Where art goes under (i.e., of Jewish scholarship), the artists have preceded it."[6] And of course no scholar contributed more directly to fortifying and fertilizing Jewish consciousness than Heinrich Graetz, whose extraordinary blend of narrative vigor and scholarly depth stirred a legion of readers, including men as diverse as Hess, Dubnow, Scholem, and Rosenzweig.

To be sure, much of that consciousness was filled with the history of Jewish suffering. The martyrdom of past generations laid claim to the loyalty of their descendants. A common fate united Jews even in an age of unprecedented individualism. But the undue attention given to persecution is precisely what linked the modern mentality to older layers of Jewish consciousness. The memory of misfortune is a dominant thought pattern in the history of Jewish consciousness. The modern historian merely had more tools at his disposal to carry out the ancient rabbinic injunction of *mahabevin et ha-zarot*—to cultivate the memory of the community's affliction. Each new misfortune amplified ancient strains. In the aftermath of the decimation of eastern European Jewry in World War II, Simon Bernfeld produced his majestic if funereal anthology entitled *Sefer ha-D'maot*—The Book of Tears—the literary remains of Jewish suffering through the ages. Our own preoccupation with the Holocaust is fueled not only by the horrendous uniqueness of the event itself but also by the affinity of the subject to very deep constructs of the Jewish mind.

Finally, the emergence of *Wissenschaft* had made historical thinking the dominant universe of discourse among modern Jews. Reading the past correctly has become the key to future planning. The countless programmatic debates which punctuate the history of the emancipation era are redolent with historical rhetoric. At the threshold of the classical age of German historicism, the German philosopher

Schelling spoke of the historian as a "backward-looking prophet." The stuff of prophecy was historical research; to look forward one had to look backward. "The child is father of the man." The most formidable thinkers of modern Judaism were its historians, with the example of Scholem being merely a case in point. To restrict the history of modern Jewish thought to philosophers or theologians is to impoverish the field. It was Jewry's great historians who provided the values and verities, the constructs and consolations, the programs and paradigms that informed Jewish identity and prompted Jewish action. At the end of the first edition of his *Social and Religious History of the Jews,* Baron intoned the normative role of his work.

To put it in a nutshell: the interpretation and reinterpretation of the history of the people, a kind of *historic Midrash,* is now to serve as a guidance for the future. A new divine book has opened itself before the eyes of the faithful: the book of human and Jewish destinies, guided by some unknown and unknowable ultimate Power. This book, if properly understood, would seem to answer the most perplexing questions of the present and the future.[7]

Written a few years after the ascendancy of the Nazis, the book placed the most dispassionate scholarship at the service of Jewish survival. It was by no means the first time in the history of Jewish studies that historical perspective had turned into consolation.

Modern scholarship has permanently affected the way we think about Judaism. It constitutes the necessary point of departure. To ignore its insights and discoveries is to return to a state of dogmatic thinking. That was the fatal flaw in Franz Rosenzweig's alluring conception of Judaism as ahistorical. In his rejection of *jüdische Wissenschaft,* he embraced a static view of Judaism that posited its exit from world history after 586 B.C.E. and argued for its quotidian embodiment of the final messianic goal. On the contrary, the cumulative evidence of modern scholarship and the achievement of a Jewish state suggest the extraordinary ability of Judaism to contend with survival in the very midst of the historical maelstrom. It is simply a starry-eyed reading of Jewish history to assert that Judaism promoted a surrender of engagement and creativity in this world for a mundane foretaste of ultimate redemption.

Entirely at odds with the romantic mood of Rosenzweig, the great accomplishment of The Jewish Theological Seminary, long a center for the study of rabbinics, has been to reveal the degree to which rabbinic Judaism was an integral part of the Greco-Roman world. It was not the presumptuous fabrication of schoolmen insulated from the dilemmas of life, but rather the concerned and resourceful response of men who understood the challenges posed by their time. Witness the declared intent which informed Saul Lieberman's *Greek in Jewish Palestine*:

In the present book the author tries to develop the subject of the relation between the Jewish and non-Jewish cultural spheres in Palestine. This undertaking, I feel is justified and desirable in view of the opinion to which my very learned colleagues, the Talmudists, persistently adhere, namely that the Rabbis were very little influenced by the outside Hellenistic world.[8]

It is worth recalling in this regard that the renowned Yeshiva of Volozhin was closed by the Russian authorities in 1892 for refusing to introduce the most elementary level of secular education. In contrast, emancipation sensitized Jewish scholars to dimensions undreamed of in the most well-mined Jewish texts. Lieberman's dictum and the massive scholarship behind it project a paradigm of dynamic rabbinic leadership unafraid to face the bullying and blandishments of a triumphant civilization. The survival of Judaism, historically considered, bespeaks an unceasing dialectic between provincialism and responsiveness, constancy and innovation.

NOTES

1. Leopold Zunz, *Zur Geschichte und Literatur* Berlin 1845), p. 21.
2. Louis Finkelstein, ed., *The Jews*, 3rd. ed., I (Philadelphia 1960), p. xxvi.
3. Leopold Zunz, "Essay on the Geographical Literature of the Jews" in A. Asher, *The Itinerary of Rabbi Benjamin of Tudela* (London and Berlin 1841), p. 303.
4. Gershom Scholem, *Devarim be-Go* (Tel Aviv 1975), p. 401.
5. Simon Dubnow, *Nationalism and History,* ed. by Koppel S. Pinson (Philadelphia 1958), p. 266.
6. Leopold Zunz, *Gesammelte Schriften,* II (Berlin 1876), p. 190.
7. Salo W. Baron, *Social and Religious History of the Jews,* 1st ed., II (New York 1937), p. 457.
8. Saul Lieberman, *Greek in Jewish Palestine* (New York 1942), p. vii.

The Ethos of Modern
Jewish Scholarship

I

The application of the historical and critical mode of cognition to the study of Judaism is the most profound expression of the process of Westernization touched off by emancipation. It eventually effected a conceptual translation of Judaism into nineteenth-century categories of thought, transformed the nature of Jewish consciousness, and generated the substance for the formation of a Diaspora Jewish subculture. *Die Wissenschaft des Judentums* heralded a revolution in self-understanding that prompted Heinrich Graetz, when he came to write of his own era, of the age from Mendelssohn to the Revolution of 1848 in the final volume of his comprehensive *Geschichte der Juden*, to call it "the period of growing self-awareness."[1] The terminology echoed the spirit in which Hegel had written his epochal *The Phenomenology of Mind* back in 1807:

It is surely not difficult to see that our time is a time of birth and transition to a new period. Spirit has broken with the world as it has hitherto existed and with the old ways of thinking, and is about to let all this sink into the past; it is at work giving itself a new form.[2]

History is more than a commitment to recording "the transactions of the past, for the instruction of future ages." It is also a mode of perception and a method of operation. Knowledge of the past alone does not begin to exhaust the complexity of modern historical thinking. Pre-emancipation Jews were certainly not bereft of historical information. The radical import of the academic study of Judaism, which I think is the best English rendition of the pompous German nomenclature, is not to be found in the quantum accumulation of new historical data, but rather in the way the past was now perceived and studied. The discontinuity of Jewish thought was a function of the shift from *Wissen* to *Wissenschaft*, from the ready acceptance of a sanctified body of facts to the concern for methodological rigor.

Unimpeded historical research is exactly what Judaism had repudiated at the end of the sixteenth century. A responsible case for a limited version of it had been made in 1573 in northern Italy by Azariah de Rossi with the publication of his

Meor Einayim (The Light of the Eyes). No one realized more acutely than this wary and pedantic Italian scholar the disorientating novelty of his wide-ranging collection of essays on biblical literature and ancient Jewish history. Accordingly, he adroitly garbed his offspring with the nimbus of a divine mandate by suggesting subliminally that the earthquake he survived in Ferrara in 1570 delivered a personal summons from on high to bring his studies to completion.[3] And throughout the book he interspersed a brief for the validity of historical research that restricted the authority of the talmudic sages to matters of Jewish law and countenanced the cautious use of Gentile authors to clarify scientific and historical questions raised in sacred texts but beyond rabbinic competence.[4] The citation of nearly 100 non-Jewish works spanning classical literature, the New Testament and the Church Fathers, and contemporary publications is testimony to de Rossi's vast erudition.[5] It also points to his deep awareness that the study of the biblical and talmudic canon could no longer be conducted in "splendid isolation," impervious to all other sources of knowledge on the subjects treated therein. There was in fact vital information to be garnered from Jewish authors like Philo who had written in languages other than Hebrew. For example, de Rossi's Hebrew translation of *The Letter of Aristeas* introduced his audience to a version of the origin of the Septuagint that greatly deviates from the descriptions of the events recorded in rabbinic literature.[6] De Rossi sensed, as did few of his Jewish contemporaries, that the recovery of antiquity by the Renaissance dictated a recognition of discrepancies between Hebrew and non-Hebrew sources and offered the prospect of studying texts and events contextually.

Beyond this general intellectual problem, de Rossi was exercised, in the spirit of Renaissance historians, by a distinctly pragmatic consideration. The bulk of his melange is devoted to a minute examination of the system of Jewish chronology based on a calculation of the years since creation (*minyan yeẓirah*). On the basis of internal evidence, he was able to cast some doubt on several of the biblical links in the chain. But clearly the weakest link related to the era of Persian suzerainty over Judea, which the rabbis had compressed untenably into a period of thirty-four years, whereas the cumulative evidence of other ancient sources indicated a span of more than two centuries.[7] Moreover, in good historical fashion de Rossi took up the problem of when counting by creation might first have arisen and concluded that the system was not at all Sinaitic, prevailing in neither of the two temple periods, but seemed rather to have been officially promulgated along with the liturgical calendar somewhere in the middle of the fourth century, or even later.[8] The analysis, to be sure, was often dense and quite arid, and yet beneath the surface beat an existential impulse. De Rossi was determined to dampen the widespread messianic fervor kindled by the Spanish expulsion by undermining the chronological base on which all messianic speculations were predicated, including the high hopes entertained for the year 1575.[9] While Spanish exiles like Joseph ha-Kohen and Samuel Usque enlisted historical discourse in the service of mes-

sianic consolation, de Rossi, a sober man hailing from a different culture, ingeniously turned the medium against the message.[10]

But de Rossi's limited experiment in critical history did not inaugurate an age
of undogmatic scholarship. On the contrary and despite his precautions, the book
was greeted by a wave of denunciations that in due course spread across the Jewish
world from Venice to Safed to Prague. In 1574 the Venetian rabbinate persuaded
some eight other Jewish communities in Italy to deny any Jew access to the book
without prior approval from the local rabbinic authority.[11] The most substantive,
as opposed to vituperative, response to de Rossi's challenge came in 1592, exactly
ten years after Pope Gregory XIII had shaken the Christian world by the introduction of the calendar named in his honor, in David Gans's *Zemah David* (The
Shoot of David). No less a polymath than de Rossi though much more of a scientist,
Gans had studied in Cracow with the renowned Ashkenazic talmudist Moses Isserles and now belonged to the circle of enlightened pietists around the charismatic
figure of Jehuda Loew ben Bezalel in Prague.[12] That Gans fully appreciated the
twofold threat posed by de Rossi and wrote essentially to repudiate him, despite
an abundance of misleading favorable citations from his work, will become clear
only once we understand the enigmatic structure of the book. The structure of a
text is often a key to its meaning, and in this instance agreement on details most
assuredly did not betoken agreement in principle.

Zemah David is a chronicle that narrates by year according to the Jewish calendar
the events of Jewish and Gentile history in two parallel and largely unintegrated
sections. Each organizational strategy—that is the chronological framework and
division of subject matter—is designed to rebut a different attack. Gans opted for
the antiquated straitjacket of a chronicle to reassert the validity of the Jewish system of chronology. Though too good a historian to deny the lateness of the entire
system (even admitting a tenth-century date), he manfully countered each of de
Rossi's specific arguments.[13] On the extent of the Persian dominion, he finally took
refuge in the primacy of tradition. "My intention is not to seek innovation. For we
possess only what we have inherited from our ancestors and the tradition and
customs of our ancestors shall remain for us Torah, never departing from our
mouths or the mouths of our children."[14] Gans knew that active eschatology rested
on chronology and his book gives sufficient evidence of his own lively messianic
yearning.[15]

It was also the primacy of tradition that led him to divide his chronicle into
sacred and profane history. For Gans the knowledge of Jewish history, which he
narrated in part one, was a function of Hebrew sources written by Jews and sanctified by tradition. In part this dogmatic principle expressed a legitimate degree of
skepticism about the reliability of all historical sources. In an imperfect world
where testimonies and records of the same event abound in discrepancies, Gans
was prepared to construct Jewish history (and especially its earliest strata) only
on inspired sources certified by tradition.[16] That principle not only justified his

retention of the Jewish calendar but also dissolved the confusion from the explosion of knowledge that beset de Rossi. Integration of unequally reliable sets of information was uncalled for. Hence Hellenistic Jewish literature, except for what was known from the early medieval Hebrew *Josippon*, was relegated to the domain of profane history.[17] Gans certainly believed that it was incumbent upon Jews to be conversant with the history of the world in general and the history of Bohemia in particular, for all the pragmatic reasons listed in his introduction to part two, and his own knowledge of both was astonishing, but not because these subjects were a source of truth about the history of the Jews.[18] The realm of the profane could never illuminate the path of the sacred. Thus Gans had articulated a subtle dogmatic posture that devalued Gentile knowledge without dismissing it, a distinction that would disappear entirely with the subsequent triumph of Lurianic *Kabbalah*.[19]

In the light of this retrospective, it is hard to argue for an internal Jewish provenance for *Wissenschaft des Judentums*. The promise of *Meor Einayim* was cut down by *Zemah David*, with an intellectual strategy of separate and unequal that was only reinforced by the deepening insularity of Ashkenazic culture. Though Zunz admitted later in life that his interest in Jewish scholarship was first awakened by reading Gans and by Johann Christoph Wolf's *Bibliotheca Hebraea*, the ethos of nineteenth-century *Wissenschaft* was nothing if not a resounding protest against the dogmatic history conjured up by Gans.[20] Growing political emancipation and cultural integration leveled such arbitrary intellectual barriers and spread a profound malaise of cognitive dissonance. In the life of the individual Jew, abrupt immersion in the world of the West often induced an intellectual mutation, as captured in the poignant testimony of Zunz on the moment in 1807 when the enlightened Samuel Ehrenberg became the director of the traditional school in which he (the orphaned Zunz) and Jost had languished for some four years.

We literally moved from the medieval to the modern age in one day, along with the emergence from Jewish slavery to civil freedom. One must remember clearly everything which I lacked till then: parents, love, instruction, educational materials. Only in mathematics and Hebrew grammar was I ahead of everyone else. . . . But of the world and what filled it, of all the subjects that by the age of 13 boys today have already studied for some three or four years, of people and social graces, I knew nothing.[21]

As the sonorous name *Wissenschaft des Judentums* implies, the emergence of historical thinking in modern Judaism is unimaginable outside the German context. The intellectual equivalent of political emancipation, it was a direct offshoot of the renaissance of the German university after the humiliation of Prussia by Napoleon in 1806. Nearly three-quarters of a century later, after the Franco-Prussian War of 1870, Ernest Renan would single out that vaunted intellectual bastion as the primary cause of Prussia's shattering victory on the battlefield, and young French academics who had studied in Germany in the 1860s would set about revitalizing the French historical profession according to the German paradigm.[22] What they ruefully acknowledged in their despair was the central role played by German scholarship in transforming a welter of territorial fragments into a single, powerful, and self-confident national state. The thousands of American students who streamed to Germany in the course of the nineteenth century to study at its universities, regardless of how little they may have absorbed, offer equally cogent evidence of the international preeminence of an institution founded in defeat.[23] Jewish emancipation, therefore, coincided with the classical age of the German university, and as early as 1830 the percentage of Jewish students at several institutions already began to exceed the percentage of Jews in the general population. By 1886/ 1887 Jews attending Prussian universities constituted nearly 10 percent of the student body.[24]

The University of Berlin was opened in 1810 to replace the fateful loss of Halle in the war, but what it really came to replace was the eighteenth-century concept of a university as the pedantic transmitter of a static body of knowledge with a faculty often employed elsewhere and not expected to advance the frontiers of knowledge.[25] The educational reform promoted by visionaries like Schelling, Fichte, Humboldt, and Schleiermacher was imbued with a research imperative and preoccupied by method.[26] It denigrated the memorizing of ready-made knowledge by students and stressed the individual developmental benefits of witnessing and undertaking scholarship.[27] The ideal function of the new university was not to prepare one for a career (pejoratively called *Brotstudium*), but rather "to awaken the idea of *Wissenschaft* in the young," a function which was institutionally expressed by the elevation of the faculty of philosophy from the very bottom to the top of the academic hierarchy.[28] Knowledge was conceived as organically united and ever unfolding and the student was never to be allowed to lose sight of the whole.[29] The instrument of philology went well beyond a mere dissection of words "as the anatomist dissects bodies."[30] The key to knowledge of the past and the basis of the claims of objectivity, philology embraced a threefold process of subjecting primary sources to linguistic analysis, textual exegesis, and historical signification.[31] For Schelling, the philologist was an artist and philosopher as well as a scrupulous scientist.[32] In brief, the scholarly ethos as embodied in Berlin drew much of its inspiration from the philosophic discourse of German Idealism and the Greek revival of neo-humanism.[33] In time, it professionalized the practice of scholarship, created a disciplinary community, and infused the individual scholar with a deep sense of vocation. *Wissenschaft* as method had achieved the capability of generating vast new bodies of *Wissen*.[34]

II

To rethink Judaism in terms of the historical canons of the German university was no less of a rupture in Jewish continuity than it had once been to rethink Judaism in terms of Greek philosophy under the impetus of Islam. But despite the noble quest of reconstructing the past "wie es eigentlich gewesen" (as it actually was), utilization of the same method hardly assured agreement in results. For what the historian ends up "seeing" is not only the product of his technique and instruments, but also the function of his location. It is that slippery factor of perspective that makes so much of our writing about the past a refraction of the present. And if rigorous method and a high degree of self-awareness may spare us from sheer arbitrariness, they will never wholly offset the subtle and unconscious influences of the space we occupy. To be sure, the discovery of new sources and the refinement of our disciplinary tools help in approximating a consensus on an ever-growing body of facts, but the structuring and interpretation of those facts remain the battleground of conflicting vantage points. These self-evident strictures on the nature of historical truth relate all the more to the historians of an embattled minority, where space is anything but tranquil.

Modern scholarship on Judaism betrayed all the urgent concerns raised by the long-contested venture in emancipation. They impacted on the formation of research agendas and intruded on the reading of the evidence. The scholarly rhetoric often vibrated with timeliness and where the connection to internal or external controversy lies concealed, personal correspondence helps to uncover it. For this reason alone, the ever-expanding circle of *Wissenschaft* scholars in Europe must not be construed as a single, undivided school. It is precisely their duels and divisions as they unfolded dialectically that requires careful tracking. But what they did share, for all their discord over results, was a common scholarly ethos, a secular research imperative that had shunted aside the ancient validation of piety for the study of sacred texts. To abstract its presuppositions may render the ideology somewhat purer in theory than it worked in reality, but it will serve to deepen our understanding of the intellectual revolution called *Wissenschaft des Judentums.*

The first thing to notice about the study of Judaism in the nineteenth century is that it was a field taken over by Jews. Till then Jews had felt little compulsion to explain themselves to a society on whose periphery they were barely tolerated. They wrote largely in Hebrew for internal consumption and abdicated the task of making sense of their religion and history for outsiders to Christian humanists whose partisanship compromised their erudition. Since the sixteenth century a library of Christian scholarship on Judaism had been amassed, including Latin translations of many an important ancient and medieval Hebrew text. The best of these works—the immense annotated bibliography of Hebrew literature by Wolf or the comprehensive history of the Jews by Basnage—were profitably consulted by later Jewish scholars and certainly enabled the founders of the *Wissenschaft* movement to launch their challenge at an advanced level. The worst—such as Eisenmenger's *Entdecktes Judentum* (Judaism Disclosed) with its huge inventory of well-ordered rabbinic quotations in both Hebrew and German—would provide generations of modern antisemites with ammunition to denigrate Judaism.[35] In

1818 in his opening gambit, the young Zunz bitterly characterized the quality of this Christian scholarly legacy:

In the field of religion, [the canons of scholarship] are completely violated, wittingly and systematically. Rarely has the world been presented with more damaging, erroneous, and distorted views than on the subject of the Jewish religion; here, to render odious has been turned into a fine art.[36]

It was this monopoly that Jewish scholars were eager to break. Emancipation had ended Jewish indifference to Christian opinion and precipitated a Jewish protest to the pre-eminence of Christian studies on Judaism. The dispassion of modern scholarship would replace the passion of religious polemics, as historical method vanquished theological animus.[37] It was in this spirit that Jost offered in 1820 the first volume of what by 1828 would distend into a pioneering nine-volume *Geschichte der Israeliten* from the Second Commonwealth to the *Haskalah*.

Scholarship gains nothing from wretched controversies fueled by passion and partisanship. It is time to close the files on the merit or lack of merit of Jews and Judaism, and to begin with the study of the phenomenon itself, its origin and development, in order to come to know its nature, and if it be found necessary, to change it [i.e., the phenomenon].[38]

Wissenschaft des Judentums signified a sustained effort by Jews to recount their history, to expound their religion, to register their achievements, and to dissipate the miasma of Christian ignorance and distortion that usually attended these subjects. Scholarship had social consequences: research would lead to respect and finally acceptance, setting Jews free. In the trenchant words of Zunz: "Will not a spirit of humanity pour out over the land from the font of scholarship, paving the way for understanding and harmony? The extension of equality to Jews in society will follow from the extension of equality to the academic study of Judaism."[39]

If, then, Christian scholarship on Judaism in the pre-emancipation era had validated either the exclusion of Jews from or their isolation within the body politic, modern Jewish scholarship fought for admission on equal terms. In the nineteenth century, the scholars of both camps continued to serve conflicting political ends and approached each other's research with all the distrust of adversaries. Thus, in 1877, even a Steinschneider, who certainly frowned upon the frequent lack of dispassion among his Jewish colleagues, was forced to concede that "the greatest injustice of Christians consisted and still does in the fact that they have never studied Judaism either then or now for its own sake, but only because of its relationship to Christianity."[40] The unrelenting exclusion of the study of post-biblical Judaism from the German university, a bitter symbol of second-class citizenship, only confirmed the suspicions of Jewish scholars. It was this inescapable social function that lent the *Wissenschaft* movement its periodic stridency and pervasive apologetic tone. Nothing illustrates more graphically the problematic entanglement of Jewish scholarship in the predicament of German Jewry than the conflicting counsels of Franz Rosenzweig. In 1917 he reiterated the battlefield metaphor of Jewish scholarship and warned against a takeover of the study of rabbinic Judaism by a resurgent Protestant academic elite, whereas in 1923 he abandoned this belligerent rhetoric in a penetrating analysis of the inherent limitations of all apologetic thinking.[41]

Most deleterious for Jewish scholarship was a visceral distrust of a century of Protestant research on the composite character of the Mosaic books of the Bible. Though Rosenzweig fully shared that sentiment, he did not hesitate to condemn the compartmentalized treatment of biblical subjects according to various traditions of learning in his review of the first volume of the *Encyclopaedia Judaica* in 1928. "The unity which the Orthodox insist on in the name of tradition, we moderns must insist on for the unity of scholarship which admits no long term separate accounts."[42] And a year later Ludwig Feuchtwanger, the learned editor of the *Bayerische Israelitische Gemeindezeitung*, amplified Rosenzweig's criticism. Addressing the insignificance of the Jewish contribution to biblical studies, he chided Jewish scholars for preserving a confessional approach:

A Jewish, Catholic, or Protestant Bible scholarship is completely untenable in terms of the nature and concept of scholarship. For this reason, the only possible locus and framework for the study of the Old Testament is not the theological faculty, but rather Semitic philology, ancient history, and the comparative study of religion.[43]

The deep engagement of *Wissenschaft des Judentums* in the affairs of the present expressed itself religiously as well as politically. From the outset, the luminous power of scholarship was to serve as a beacon through the shoals of emancipation. If on the one hand historical truth would advance the cause of integration, on the other it would assist in the formulation of religious policy in its wake. By the nineteenth century, the revolutionary insight of Giovanni Battista Vico had become a commonplace: "The nature of institutions is nothing but their coming into being at certain times and in certain guises. Whenever the time and guise are thus and so, such and not otherwise are the institutions that come into being."[44] Accordingly, access to the meaning and authenticity of a religious practice or institution seemed to lie in the nature of its origins, and the very essence of Judaism, as opposed to its present state, appeared definable through historical inquiry. The recovery of the Jewish past challenged the authority of the *halakhic* expert no less than that of the Protestant theologian. Cognizant of that role, the young Zunz, in 1818 in the founding document of the movement, enunciated a research project that would occupy him for the better part of his productive life. "A history of the synagogue liturgy on the basis of the sources would be, precisely at this time, a desirable if difficult undertaking."[45] In the introduction to his first major scholarly publication, Zacharias Frankel, a scholar of a different stripe, expressed the same conviction in the religious utility of *Wissenschaft*, more broadly and with less restraint.[46]

In sum, what basically distinguished the practice of Jewish scholarship from the venerable discipline of *Altertumswissenschaft*, the study of Greek and Roman antiquity, was its vital connection to a living community. Judaism constituted a present reality and the scholars emerging from its midst were consciously linked to its fate. Neither antiquarian nor funereal, they addressed the outside world as insiders and their own world as the bearers of new knowledge. For all its significance to German neo-humanists, *Altertumswissenschaft* was not the unbroken cultural legacy of an ancient community that had survived the tempests of time. A century after the founding of the *Verein für Cultur und Wissenschaft der Juden*, Ismar Elbogen, Weimar's premier Jewish historian, accentuated this existential dimension of *Wissenschaft des Judentums* by choosing to define it as "the academic study of a vital Judaism, standing within the stream of development, as a sociological and historical unity." Its proper academic analogue, claimed Elbogen, was not the study of Greece or Rome but the civilization of Islam.[47] As a new universe of discourse for Jews, *Wissenschaft* was inextricably both academic and practical, recondite and relevant.

But utilitarian considerations do not exhaust the ethos of modern Jewish scholarship in the century of its birth. Intellectual integrity as well as engagement prompted troubled Jews to critical self-examination. Historical thinking is quintessentially time-oriented and nothing challenged traditional Jewish culture more fundamentally than exposure to the factor of time. For good reason Nachman Krochmal insisted on the very use of the word in the title of his posthumously published "unfinished symphony":[48] it was the source of greatest dissonance and the leitmotif of his book. *Moreh Nevukhei ha-Zeman* as title conveys a sense for both the audience and the problem and is hence best rendered as a guide for contemporaries perplexed by the problem of time. Only a paraphrase can capture the subtlety of the *double entendre*.[49]

It is truly remarkable how Krochmal, who died in 1840 without ever setting foot outside Eastern Galicia or inside a university, grasped the full extent of the conflict between the claims of time and tradition. His book opens with a blunt dismissal of the flagrantly ahistorical mode of classical rabbinic exegesis. Imbuing an old rabbinic homily with a dynamic thrust quite alien to it, he argued that the tradition acknowledged the need of each generation to have its own teachers and interpreters because states of consciousness change. A method of instruction ideally suited for one generation could well wreak havoc on another. By way of example, he cited the rabbinic penchant for dating the contents of the Hagiographa early. The sages' religious intentions were noble and effective, but to continue to claim in our day that Psalm 137 is an awesome exercise of Davidic prophecy rather than an anguished testimony of exilic experience is to discredit the tradition and alienate the young. In an age rife with historical research readily available to young Jews leaving the ghetto, the tradition must be reworked from the historical perspective, namely "to examine, study, and date each and every text in terms of its precise period of composition."[50] Krochmal was confident that reading sacred texts contextually would yield layers of undetected and uplifting meaning.

Despite a definite historicizing trend in ancient Judaism and a large measure of collective memory, the presuppositions of the traditional mode of studying Scripture were distinctly unhistorical. Rabbinic literature posited a unity of divine authorship for Scripture which endowed the text down to the smallest fragment with infinite significance and an unlimited range of meanings. Moreover, the corpus of Oral Law derived by exegesis from the Written Law became, by extension, equally divine. Put differently, the principle of immanence reduced historical change to textual interpretation: later legal innovations that could be grounded in Scripture were regarded as implicit from the outset. The belief in a single divine author also permitted a radical disjunctive reading of biblical texts even as it lent the entire edifice—foundation and superstructure—an essential consistency that precluded basic contradictions. Finally, rabbinic literature posited an absence of chronological order in the structure of Scripture and tended to pattern and comprehend historical events according to moral considerations. Although these operative assumptions by releasing texts from their contextual moorings provided the rabbinic mind with a canvas of unbounded plasticity, they also worked to harmonize differences, submerge individuality, and subordinate earlier texts to later ones.[51]

In contrast, at the heart of the modern historical sensibility there ticks a conception of time finely attuned to the uniqueness of the individual. In the Heraclitean flux of existence there are no re-runs or repetitions; every person, event, and text is a distinct product of its time and place and must be understood on its own terms. To study history is to value the particular in all its particularity and to repudiate the ordering urge to subordinate the individual to universal constructs. According to Herder, the apostle of this new historical ethos: "Nothing in the whole of God's kingdom . . . is a mere means; all is both a means and an end . . ."[52] The attitude opened up for discovery a human world of untold variety and inspired Ranke's celebrated formulation of 1854:

Every epoch is immediate to God, and its worth is not at all based on what derives from it but rests on its own existence, in its own self. In this way the contemplation of history, that is to say of individual life in history, acquires its own particular attraction, since now every epoch must be seen as something valid in itself and appears highly worthy of consideration.[53]

That attitude, as Zunz clearly realized, vindicated the claim of *Wissenschaft des Judentums* for equal attention from the German academic establishment. "Just as for genuine scholarship no knowledge is insignificant, so is no individual for a true love of mankind."[54]

The disruptive import of that attitude for the reading of sacred Jewish texts had been stunningly adumbrated by Spinoza in the third quarter of the seventeenth century in his *Theologico-Political Treatise*. In his effort "to separate faith from philosophy" and religion from affairs of state, he assaulted the non-literal, allegorical mode of reading the Hebrew Bible basic to both Church and Synagogue.[55] Toward that end, he proposed to transfer the method of science from the scrutiny of God's handiwork to His word. The text was to be severed from all preconceptions and its meaning elicited inductively. "We are at work not on the truth of passages, but solely on their meaning."[56] The concept of truth implied accordance with an immutable body of wisdom external to the text, whereas the search for meaning was governed primarily by internal criteria of analysis. Biblical books were not empty vessels capable of bearing almost any content. Their elucidation could not be detached from a history of the Hebrew language, the literary and thematic integrity of the book in question, the author's historical context and a record of the text's transmission. The key to understanding a text lay in recognizing its time-bound singularity.[57]

In consequence, the dating of data erupted into a consuming passion for many of the early critical students of a tradition largely indifferent to the value of chronological order. Before a text could be subjected to a useful content analysis, its provenance had to be established, and sweeping works like Zunz's history of the Jewish sermon often devoted only a passing paragraph to the content of the texts they were quarrying out of the chaos. Krochmal spoke for the entire movement when he cleverly reversed a well-known rabbinic dictum to read: "Without differentiation there can be no knowledge."[58] And the knowledge that came with temporal distinctions interjected a profoundly alien dynamic into the tradition itself. For all their theological differences, Geiger, Frankel, Krochmal, Israel Lewy, and David Hoffmann committed much of their energy and ingenuity to the same research agenda—to recover the stages in the evolution of rabbinic law. In the somewhat fulsome words of Frankel, such a reconstruction would comprise

... an analysis that would show how the individual elements of the *halakhah* came into being and how the *halakhah* itself grew from a trickle into a rich and raging river; an investigation through which we would come to know what belongs to each period, furthermore, what sprang from the needs of the day and what owed its emergence to uninhibited study; an inquiry into the study techniques of different periods and how one derived from the other and then intermingled with each other, and, finally, how the diverse conglomeration of techniques was forged into a single system.[59]

The history of *halakhah*, in short, requires the individualization of an undifferentiated corpus.

A third component of the *Wissenschaft* ethos, fundamental to a history of *halakhah* and to the entire scholarly enterprise, was the right of free inquiry, the very principle denied de Rossi by his generation. Undogmatic scholarship was predicated on investigating questions without preconceived answers, on submission to the weight of the evidence—all of it—and not to the authority of the tradition, which abounded in historical claims. The issue was vividly if gently raised as early as 1807 by Salomon Jacob Cohen of Hamburg in the pages of the *Sulamith*. Whereas de Rossi had already given the nod to Roman over rabbinic sources on the matter of Titus's death, Cohen pondered the larger question of which portrait of the emperor the Jew was obliged to accept—that construed by Josephus (and supported by other sources) of a man of compassion who took every measure to avoid the destruction of the Temple, or that preserved by rabbinic literature of a bloodthirsty tyrant bent on the eradication of Judaism? To prefer Josephus, Cohen appreciated, was to impugn not only the historical veracity but the moral integrity of the rabbis—pietists guilty of fabrication. That painful implication, in fact, induced Cohen to back off from any resolution, content with having formulated the problem. Nevertheless, he did not hesitate to include the unequivocal view of Bendavid with whom he had consulted on the matter. In addition to the obvious reasons for treating the rabbinic testimonies with skepticism, Bendavid claimed that they were preserved in texts redacted some six hundred years after the fact and thus subject to a steady process of dilution and adulteration. Their value, Bendavid suggested in a mixture of insight and spite, resides not in the information transmitted about Titus, but rather in the hints offered about the state of mind of those who composed them and of those who continued to believe in them.[60]

Bendavid's example of uninhibited independence was soon to be followed by others. By 1824 his disciple Isaak Jost in the preface to volume four of his expanding history equipped the still small and battered band of *Wissenschaft* "subversives" with a classical definition of the freedom necessary for the modern research imperative:

No prejudice should blind the historian; no universally held dogma should darken his views; no apprehension should intimidate him from revealing the truth as he sees it. He must be able to look around freely, to examine clearly the subjects of his field, to illuminate the dark, to bring out what is hidden. Anyone who might take offense at this should retreat into the darkness and refresh himself in indolent slumber.[61]

Although social and religious constraints, especially outside Germany, were often to compromise this theory in practice, contracting the parameters of permissible departures, emancipation had, without a doubt, foreclosed the option of dogmatic history as a viable intellectual posture.

The exercise of free inquiry informed a variety of *Wissenschaft* pursuits. To begin with, there was a determination to clear away the litter of historical myth, error, imprecision, and ignorance allowed to accumulate by a tradition with so little regard for the value of historical knowledge, and in consequence of which the tradition had become a purveyor of falsehood. It was not the mere correspondence of the opening letters of two successive verses of Psalm 34 with the last two letters of Krochmal's Hebrew name, Nachman, that prompted him or his editor to place them prominently on the front page of his book.

> Who is the man who is eager for life,
>   who desires years of good fortune?
> Guard your tongue from evil,
>   your lips from deceitful speech.[62]

Those verses not only summed up the mandate of the age but also bestowed a semblance of divine sanction on the quest for truth. A flagrant disregard of historical truth threatened to discredit all of Judaism. The initial tack was to ascertain and assemble the facts, and the often maddening facticity of a Zunz or a Steinschneider, later misprized as mere antiquarianism, masked a moral fervor to demythologize.[63] Most reprehensible to them were the contemporary scholars who recycled old errors or manufactured new ones. The beginning of historical wisdom was the fear of error, no matter how insignificant. Truth could not be weighted.[64] At the University of Berlin Zunz had embodied the ideal of a revitalized German scholarship as enunciated by Wilhelm de Wette, his professor of Old Testament. "Truth is the first great law of history and love of truth the historian's first obligation."[65]

Nor could truth be restricted to texts by Jews in Hebrew. As de Rossi had rightly sensed, the reconstruction of past events and the plumbing of ancient meanings required the consulting of every piece of relevant evidence, irrespective of origins. Nineteenth-century Jewish scholars may have harbored the conviction that they were better equipped by experience and knowledge than Christians to understand Judaism, but they never discounted on principle the information to be garnered from non-Jewish sources. Moreover, much precious data survived only in those sources. By 1850 Selig Cassel, who was to convert some five years later, had impressively demonstrated for the first time the plethora of germane non-Jewish sources available to the Jewish historian in his compact but comprehensive political and social history of Diaspora Jewry. The distance that separates the compartmentalized *Wissen* of Gans from the integrated *Wissenschaft* of Cassel is memorably encapsulated in the epigram of Steinschneider: "For the spirit there is no ghetto."[66]

From the study of non-Jewish sources to the detection of non-Jewish influences was but a small step, and Jewish historians quickly, if vaguely, detected the presence of Persian, Greek, Roman and Islamic patterns in the changing garb of Judaism. Minimal evidence (and a good dose of antirabbinic bias) convinced Jost that Athens inspired the introduction of the Oral Law, and Rome the adoption of many of its legal concepts and the first codification of its sundry regulations.[67]

Nevertheless, the largest part of the Jewish past was to emerge from Jewish sources, and in the expansion of their number Jewish scholars registered their most astounding gains of the century. The truncated curriculum of the Ashkenazic *yeshivah,* with its exclusive focus on works of *halakhah* had all but obliterated any inkling of the depth and diversity of Jewish literature. Against this background, the emphasis on biblical literature by the German *Haskalah* must be seen as a preference laden with protest. The sudden illumination of the unexpected range of "rabbinic literature" delivered by Zunz in 1818 transformed that protest into a scholarly agenda.

This conceptual enlargement of what constitutes Jewish literary creativity went beyond the thrilling discovery of unknown texts like the *Siddur* of Saadia, the diary of David Reubeni, the Arabic original of Maimonides's *Guide*, the divan of Yehudah Halevi, the memoir of Glückel of Hameln, or the staggering number of some 100,000 literary fragments from the Cairo *Geniza* carted to Cambridge by Solomon Schechter in 1897.[68] A passing comment by the gifted young David Kaufmann in 1878 in one of his letters to the by then aged and revered Zunz conveys a sense of the exuberance of the results of this collective excavation. "The resurrection of our history out of the grave of manuscripts has for me a dramatic fascination."[69] But expansion of the canvas also took the form of reappropriating substantial texts like the Palestinian Talmud, *midrashic* collections, philosophic discourses, and liturgical compendia, which had hovered on the edges of Jewish consciousness, and submitting them to critical historical analysis. No less productive was the scrutiny of well-minded normative texts from the vantage point of new perspectives. If Zunz's history of the Jewish sermonic tradition from the late biblical period to his own day delivered an inspiring example of the former, then Rapoport's sparkling biographical essays on early medieval rabbinic luminaries displayed the awesome potential of the latter. In truth, much of the subsequent research into the biographies of *mishnaic* and medieval rabbis, the evolution of rabbinic law and literature, and the social and religious history of medieval Jewry rested on little more than the yield harvested by poring over sacred texts with new questions. For most practitioners of *Wissenschaft* it was not a matter anymore of reading texts "right" in the dogmatic sense, but reading the right texts for data and insight related to fresh concerns.

The enlarged category of available Jewish sources also included works written by Jews in languages other than Hebrew or Aramaic. In writing the history of the Second Commonwealth, Jost consistently preferred to rely on Josephus (and not the *Josippon* as Gans had) rather than the historical fragments embedded in rabbinic texts; Frankel wrote extensively if unsympathetically about the literary remnants of Hellenistic Jewry; and Esriel Hildesheimer made his scholarly debut with a study of the textual variants in the Septuagint related to biblical chronology.[70] The recognition of Jewish literary productivity in many languages would eventually culminate in a totally new view of Jewish creativity. The twentieth-century conception of Judaism as a religious civilization is directly indebted to the enlargement of the canvas of Jewish creativity by the *Wissenschaft* movement in the nineteenth century.

The fourth and final component of the ethos of *Wissenschaft* related to its con-

ceptual mode as an instrument of cognition, underscoring again its Western provenance. The traditional form of Jewish thinking, as shaped in the rabbinic period,
tended to be exegetical; commentary became the quintessentially Jewish genre of
intellectual expression. A sacred text called for explication, application, and renewal, and *midrash* evolved into a mode of cognition, an expression of piety, and
a vehicle for revitalization. But textually oriented thinking is essentially concrete,
circumscribed, and episodic. Its very specificity induces a minimal level of abstraction and a bewildering absence of systematic analysis. For all their anticipation of
modern scholarship, the ground-breaking Hebrew commentaries that accompanied Mendelssohn's translation of the Torah and Heidenheim's edition of the German cycle of festival prayerbooks, both adhered to the standard exegetical mode,
which bespoke the centrality of sacred texts and a static body of knowledge.

The confrontation with Western scholarship in the nineteenth century, like that
with Greek philosophy in the Islamic world of the tenth century, injected a liberating conceptual mode of thought into Judaism. In consonance with the more
secular temper of the age, *Wissenschaft* rendered the text subordinate to larger issues
that called for thematic and synthetic treatment. If the heart of the scholarly enterprise is "the power to frame questions susceptible of scholarly enquiry," then
Wissenschaft des Judentums, as distinct from traditional exegesis, was problem-
oriented, systematic, and ultimately synthetic.[71] Loosened from the text, it could
operate with a dynamic concept of knowledge, what Bacon called the "advancement of learning."[72] No one searched for new sources more zealously or read old
ones more incisively than Zunz, but primarily in the service of questions and
constructs that defied the limitations of disjointed analysis. The best proof for the
transformation in progress comes from Eastern Europe: the *Wissenschaft* of its autodidacts, steeped in the thought patterns of rabbinic culture, often failed to reach
the level of conceptualization, coherence, and systematization achieved by Jewish
scholars in the West with the benefit of a *Gymnasium* and university education.

The last word on the ethos of modern Jewish scholarship should rightly come
from the man who founded the field and set the standards. In his introduction to
Krochmal's *Guide*, an unhewn *Wissenschaft* classic rescued from oblivion by his
selfless act of editing, Zunz felt obliged to distill for its Hebrew readership in Eastern
Europe the spirit of the new learning emanating from the West. His threefold formulation remains unsurpassed in the power and clarity of its articulation. First,
the study of Jewish life must comprise all its expressions. The totality and continuity of Jewish consciousness shapes the substance of individual efforts, and later
stages will elude comprehension if earlier ones go unstudied. Second, the fabric of
Jewish life is always colored by the light of its non-Jewish surroundings, and a
wholly internal perspective will fail to appreciate the formative influence of context. Finally, the ultimate purpose of critical and emphatic scholarship is to better
the human condition. The asceticism of the solitary scholar must be tempered and
leavened by social commitment.[73]

In that ideal, especially as embodied in the careers of men like Krochmal and Zunz, emancipated Jewry had acquired the means to face the challenge of modernity.

NOTES

1. Heinrich Graetz, *Geschichte der Juden*, 11 vols., 2nd ed., Leipzig 1863–1900, XI, p. 1.

2. Quoted by John Edward Toews, *Hegelianism*, Cambridge–London–New York 1985, p. 30.

3. Azariah de Rossi, *Meor Einayim*, ed. by David Cassel, Vilna 1866, pp. 5–23. There is absolutely nothing innocent about de Rossi opening his historical work with an autobiographical chapter. The very resonant title of "God's Voice" must be read as an invocation of divine sanction.

4. De Rossi, *Meor Einayim*, pp. 81–90, 151–180, 196, 207–228, 269–270.

5. Salo W. Baron, *History and Jewish Historians*, Philadelphia 1964, p. 227.

6. De Rossi, *Meor Einayim*, pp. 28–69; Baron, *History and Jewish Historians*, pp. 220–221. The various rabbinic traditions on the translation of the Septuagint are assembled, edited and translated by Moses Hadas, *Aristeas to Philocrates (Letter of Aristeas)*, New York 1951, pp. 79–84.

7. De Rossi, *Meor Einayim*, pp. 310–325.

8. *Ibid.*, pp. 254–259, 336.

9. *Ibid.*, pp. 367–378. On the charged messianic atmosphere, see David Tamar, "The Messianic Expectations in Italy Concerning the Year 5335" (in Hebrew), *Sfunot*, II (1958), pp. 61–88.

10. Yosef Hayim Yerushalmi, "Messianic Impulses in Joseph ha-Kohen," in *Jewish Thought in the Sixteenth Century*, ed. by Bernard Dov Cooperman, Cambridge, Mass. 1983, pp. 460–487. Samuel Usque's Consolation for the Tribulations of Israel, trans. and introd. by Martin A. Cohen, Philadelphia 1965, pp. 18–29.

11. Baron, *History and Jewish Historians*, pp. 167–173; David Kaufmann, "Zur Geschichte der Kämpfe Azarja dei Rossis," in David Kaufmann, *Gesammelte Schriften*, 3 vols., Frankfurt am Main 1908–1915, III, pp. 83–95; Robert Bonfil, "Some Reflections on the Place of Azariah de Rossi's *Meor Einayim* in the Cultural Milieu of Italian Renaissance Jewry," in *Jewish Thought in the Sixteenth Century*, pp. 23–48.

12. On Gans, see the introduction by Mordechai Breuer to his new edition of *Zemah David*, Jerusalem 1983.

13. *Ibid.*, p. 61.

14. *Ibid.*, p. 64.

15. *Ibid.*, pp. 24, 48, 137, 138.

16. *Ibid.*, pp. 163, 181, 187.

17. *Ibid.*, p. 183. The Book of Judith is introduced into part one because Jewish tradition associated the slaying of Holofernes with the festival of Hanukkah, *ibid.*, pp. 70, 188–189.

18. *Ibid.*, pp. 163–167.

19. Thus, for example, at the very threshold of the emancipation era, Shneur Zalman of Lyada, the founder of the *Habad* (Lubavitch) *Hasidim* denies Gentiles any trace of a divine spark. In his popular ethical reformulation of Lurianic *Kabbalah* first published in 1796—*Likkutei Amarin*—he concedes them only a one-dimensional animalistic soul which emanates from the darkest regions of existence. In consequence, for a Jew to indulge in secular learning is a twofold sin—a diversion from the study

of Torah and a pollution of his divine attributes, and is therefore permitted only for the sake of a livelihood or to enhance the glory of God and His teachings. [Chapters 1, 6–8.] The theory is well suited to thwart a shift toward integration.

20. Marcus Brann, "Mittheilungen aus dem Briefwechsel zwischen Zunz und Kaufmann," *JJGL*, V (1902), p. 183.

21. Leopold Zunz, "Mein erster Unterricht in Wolfenbüttel," *JJGL*, XXX (1937), pp. 136–137.

22. William R. Keylor, *Academy and Community: The Foundation of the French Historical Profession*, Cambridge, Mass. 1975, pp. 19–54.

23. Carl Diehl, *Americans and German Scholarship 1770–1870*, New Haven–London 1978.

24. Monika Richarz, *Der Eintritt der Juden in die akademischen Berufe: Jüdische Studenten und Akademiker in Deutschland 1678–1848*, Tübingen 1974 (Schriftenreihe wissenschaftlicher Abhandlungen des Leo Baeck Instituts 28), pp. 93–94.

25. Roy Steven Turner, "University Reformers and Professorial Scholarship in Germany 1760–1806," in *The University of Society*, ed. by Lawrence Stone, 2 vols., Princeton 1974, II, pp. 495–531.

26. Ernst Anrich (ed.), *Die Idee der Deutschen Universität*, Darmstadt 1956.

27. F. W. J. Schelling, *On University Studies*, trans. by E. S. Morgan, Athens, Ohio 1966, pp. 34–36.

28. Roy Steven Turner, *The Prussian Universities and the Research Imperative, 1806 to 1848*, unpub. Ph.D. diss., Princeton University 1973, pp. 256, 259, 371ff.

29. Eduard Spranger, *Wilhelm von Humboldt und die Reform des Bildungswesens*, Tübingen 1960, pp. 200–203.

30. Leonard Krieger, *Ranke: The Meaning of History*, Chicago–London 1977, p. 359, n. 2.

31. Friedrich August Wolf, *Vorlesungen über die Altertumswissenschaft*, ed. by J. D. Gürtler and S. F. W. Hoffman, I, Leipzig 1839, pp. 22–25.

32. Schelling, *On University Studies*, p. 39.

33. Turner, *The Prussian Universities*, pp. 250–253.

34. *Ibid.*, pp. 306–308, 362; Krieger, *Ranke*, pp. 45–46.

35. Johann Christoph Wolf, *Bibliotheca Hebraea*, 4 vols., Hamburg–Leipzig 1715–1733; Jacques Basnage, *L'histoire et la religion des Juifs, depuis Jésus-Christ jusque'à présent*, 6 vols., Rotterdam 1706–1711; Johann Andreas Eisenmenger, *Entdecktes Judenthum*, 2 vols., Königsberg 1711. None of these works has received the attention of modern scholars that they deserve. In the meantime for Basnage, see Miriam Yardeni, "Jews and Judaism in the Eyes of the French Protestant Exiles in Holland" (in Hebrew), in *Mehkarim be-Toldot Am Yisrael ve-Erez Yisrael*, Haifa 1970, pp. 178–183; for Eisenmenger, see Jacob Katz, "Eisenmenger's Method of Prooftexts from Talmudic Sources" (in Hebrew), in *Proceedings of the Fifth World Congress of Jewish Studies*, II, Jerusalem 1972, pp. 210–216.

36. Leopold Zunz, "Etwas über die rabbinische Literatur," in *Gesammelte Schriften*, 3 vols., Berlin 1875–1876, I, p. 8.

37. Leopold Zunz, *Zur Geschichte und Literatur*, Berlin 1845, p. 20.

38. Isaak Markus Jost, *Geschichte der Israeliten*, 9 vols., Berlin 1820–1828, I, pp. viii–ix.

39. Zunz, *Zur Geschichte*, p. 21.

40. Moritz Steinschneider, *Hebräische Bibliographie*, XVII (1877), p. 35.

41. Franz Rosenzweig, *Kleinere Schriften*, Berlin 1937, pp. 31–42, 70–71.

42. *Der Morgen*, IV (1928), p. 291.

43. *Der Morgen*, V (1929), pp. 177–178. Also pp. 184–185. On Feuchtwanger,

see Max Gruenewald, "Critic of German Jewry: Ludwig Feuchtwanger and his Gemeindezeitung," in *LBIYB XVII* (1972), pp. 75–92.

44. *The New Science of Giambattista Vico*, trans. by Thomas G. Bergin and Max H. Fisch, Ithaca–London 1984, p. 64.

45. Zunz, "Etwas über die rabbinische Literatur," p. 8.

46. Zacharias Frankel, *Vorstudien zu der Septuaginta*, Leipzig 1841, pp. x–xi.

47. Ismar Elbogen, "Ein Jahrhundert Wissenschaft des Judentums," in *Festschrift zum 50jährigen Bestehen der Hochschule für die Wissenschaft des Judentums*, Berlin 1922, pp. 141–142.

48. The honorific comes from Simon Rawidowicz, *Studies in Jewish Thought*, ed. by Nahum N. Glatzer, Philadelphia 1974, p. 391.

49. As to the patrimony of the book's title, see Ismar Schorsch, "The Production of a Classic: Zunz as Krochmal's Editor," in *LBIYB XXXI* (1986), pp. 289, 294, 301.

50. *The Writings of Nachman Krochmal*, ed. by Simon Rawidowicz, Waltham, Mass. 1961, part 2, Krochmal's Introduction. The *locus classicus* of the *midrash* "dor dor ve-dorshav" is the *Babylonian Talmud*, *Avodah Zarah*, p. 5a.

51. Yizhak Heinemann, *Darkhei ha-Aggadah* (in Hebrew), Jerusalem 1954.

52. Friedrich Meinecke, *Historicism*, trans. by J. E. Anderson, London 1972, p. 339. The rise of this historical outlook in the West is the dominant focus of Meinecke's classic.

53. Leopold Ranke, *The Theory and Practice of History*, ed. by Georg G. Iggers and Konrad von Moltke, Indianapolis–New York 1973, p. 53.

54. Zunz, *Zur Geschichte*, p. 19.

55. *The Chief Works of Benedict de Spinoza*, trans. by R. H. M. Elwes, 2 vols., New York 1951, I, p. 183 (for the quotation).

56. *Ibid.*, p. 101.

57. *Ibid.*, pp. 98–103.

58. *The Writings of Nachman Krochmal*, part 2, p. 211. The *locus classicus* of the dictum "im ein dei'a havdalah minayin?" is the *Palestinian Talmud*, *Berakhot*, 5:2.

59. Frankel, *Vorstudien*, p. xii.

60. De Rossi, *Meor Einayim*, pp. 214–219; *Sulamith*, II (1807), pp. 281–290. On Cohen, see Reuven Michael, "The Contribution of *Sulamith* to Modern Jewish Historiography," *Zion*, XXXIX (1974), p. 96.

61. Jost, *Geschichte der Israeliten*, IV, Vorwort, p. iii.

62. *The Writings of Nachman Krochmal*, part 2, following Zunz's introduction. The translation is that of *The New JPS Translation of the Holy Scriptures*, 3 vols., Philadelphia 1962–1982, III, *The Writings*, p. 33.

63. Hermann Cohen, *Jüdische Schriften*, ed. by Bruno Strauss, 3 vols., Berlin 1924, I, p. 332.

64. Zunz, *Gesammelte Schriften*, III, p. 100.

65. Wilhelm Martin Lebrecht de Wette, *Beiträge zur Einleitung in das Alte Testament*, 2 vols., Halle 1896–1807, II, p. 1.

66. Selig Cassel, "Juden (Geschichte)," in *Allgemeine Encyklopädie der Wissenschaften und Künste*, zweite Section, vol. 27, Leipzig 1850, pp. 1–238; Moritz Steinschneider, *Die hebräischen Übersetzungen des Mittelalters*, 2 vols., Berlin 1893, I, p. xxii.

67. Jost, *Geschichte der Israeliten*, IV, pp. 100–101, 108, 114–115; Anhang, pp. 235–240.

68. Solomon Schechter, *Studies in Judaism*, 3 vols., Philadelphia 1945, II, p. 9.

69. *JJGL*, VI (1903), p. 127.

70. Hildesheimer's essay appeared in *Der Orient* (1847), pp. 357–360, 362–364, and in *Literaturblatt des Orients* (1848), pp. 131ff., 152ff., 161ff., 190ff., 203ff., 232ff., 253ff., 267ff., 317ff., 346ff.

71. The quotation is from Diehl, *Americans and German Scholarship*, p. 43. Cf. Rawidowicz, in *Studies in Jewish Thought*, pp. 45–80.

72. Franklin L. Baumer, *Modern European Thought*, New York–London 1977, p. 32.

73. *The Writings of Nachman Krochmal*, part 2, end of Zunz's introduction.

∾ 10

The Emergence of
Historical Consciousness
in Modern Judaism

The emergence of historical consciousness in modern Judaism is a subject that transcends the restricted focus and technical vocabulary of historiography. Conceived as an intellectual revolution, it comprises a fundamental change in mentality and epitomizes the dialectic process of Westernization that transformed medieval Ashkenazic Judaism. More concretely, historical thinking facilitated the urgent and agonizing effort to rethink the nature of Judaism. It quickly became the primary vehicle for translating the ideas, institutions, and values of an ancient oriental religion into equivalent or related Western categories, and beyond that served as the arbiter of what is authentic Judaism and the source for new and diverse self-perceptions. In short, *Wissenschaft des Judentums*, which is best rendered as the academic study of Judaism, lies at the very heart of nineteenth-century Jewish intellectual history.

To impose some conceptual order on a vast and amorphous body of material, this essay will study the formative period of *Wissenschaft* from the second to the eighth decade of the century in a twofold manner. The first part will attempt a synchronic and conceptual analysis of what might be termed the ideology of *Jüdische Wissenschaft*, that is the set of intellectual norms shared to some extent by nearly all its practitioners. The identification of this ideology will, it is hoped, serve to underscore the discontinuity in Jewish thinking effected by historical consciousness. The second part will examine the practice of *Wissenschaft* diachronically with a view to demonstrating that the endless divergence and disagreement on topics and issues of scholarship can best be understood dialectically. By the mid-seventies, when that extraordinary cluster of first- and second-generation *Wissenschaft* scholars completed its revolutionary work, modern Jewish scholarship had found an institutional base and history permeated the corridors of Jewish thought.

I

History is more than a commitment to recording "the transactions of the past, for the instruction of future ages."[1] It is also a mode of perception and a method of operation. Knowledge of the past alone does not begin to exhaust the complexity of modern historical thinking. Pre-emancipation Jews were certainly not bereft of historical information. The revolutionary import of *Wissenschaft* is not to be found in the geometric accumulation of new historical data, but rather in the way the past was now perceived and studied.

The ideology of *Wissenschaft* shattered a venerable dogmatic type of historical thinking which had received its classical formulation in the 1592 chronicle of David Gans entitled *Zemah David* (The Shoot of David). A polymath of truly Renaissance proportions, Gans composed a two-part Hebrew chronicle that hermetically sealed off Jewish from Gentile history and thereby delivered an ingenious response to the explosion of historical knowledge that marked his age in general and the seminal collection of historical essays published by Azariah de Rossi some nineteen years before in particular.[2] In contrast to de Rossi who cautiously strove for integration, Gans insulated Jewish history from outside contamination in two ways. Structurally, he relegated the history of Jews and Gentiles to separate sections of his book, despite the chronological inelegance, and methodologically he drew his information about Jewish history solely from Hebrew sources written by Jews. Jewish works written or preserved in languages other than Hebrew received mention only in the framework of Gentile history, and events in Jewish history that rested on both Hebrew and non-Hebrew sources were treated awkwardly in both sections.[3] Against de Rossi, Gans reasserted the messianic thrust and sacred character of Jewish history by restricting its study to texts hallowed by tradition.[4] Dogmatic compartmentalization neutralized, or better, permitted an astounding mastery of general history.

This intellectual strategy of separate and unequal collapsed in the face of the profound experience of intellectual dissonance created by the vast educational opportunities of the emancipation era. In truth, it was viable only as long as deep secular learning was alien to most ghettoized Jews. But emancipation coincided with a magnetic rejuvenation of the German university and by 1830 the percentage of Jewish students at several schools already began to surpass the percentage of Jews in the general population. By 1886–1887, Jews at Prussian universities constituted nearly 10 percent of the student body.[5] No Jewish figure understood more presciently the futility of persisting in a policy of cerebral segregation and literary censorship, giving the penetration of Western learning into Jewish consciousness, than Nachman Krochmal. Born in Brody in 1785, utterly self-taught, and never having been outside his native Galicia, Krochmal sternly warned in his posthumously published *Moreh Nevukhei ha-Zeman* (Guide for Those Perplexed by Time in Our Day) (1851) that nothing was more destructive than attempting to conceal what was readily available and widely known.[6] Intellectual dissonance begged for reconciliation and Krochmal devoted his vast learning and incisive mind to showing that many of the ideas of contemporary scholarship and philosophy were anticipated by the esoteric traditions of rabbinic Judaism.

In this context of discord, the ideology of *Wissenschaft* embodied a profound alienation from the intellectual posture of David Gans, even where a superficial resemblance appears to exist. The very title of Krochmal's book with its stress on the word "time" illuminates the chasm. The term embraces a *double entendre* which alludes simultaneously to the book's audience and to its central problem. Krochmal wrote for contemporary Jews confused and distressed by the introduction of time into Judaism. If, according to Marc Bloch, history is minimally the study of men in time, the pervasive non-literal exegesis (midrash) of traditional Judaism was intrinsically and flagrantly ahistorical.[7] Even Gans, who was preoccupied with dates, ordered his annals of the Jews according to the chronology of *anno mundi* primarily to vindicate the traditional frame of reference for purposes of messianic calculation against the attacks of de Rossi.[8] Krochmal fully realized that his generation would be ill-served by such arbitrariness and dogmatism. He made clear from the opening page of his book that the mandate of his age was "to investigate, to research, and to date each and every text in terms of its precise period of composition."[9] The meaning of a text could not be understood outside its time.

More profoundly still, the concept of time infused an alien dynamic factor into the perception of Judaism. Eternal verities and timeless institutions were suddenly cast into a Heraclitean flux where incessant change was the law of life. Regardless of whether *Wissenschaft* scholars wrote about rabbinic Judaism in eighteenth-century terms of decline and degeneration or nineteenth-century terms of growth and development, all were part of an intellectual revolution which no longer approached reality as a category of changeless being. The modern mind perceived existence as a function of becoming. In 1852 Ernest Renan, who had personally traversed the road from medieval scholasticism to modern scholarship, summed up the essence of the modern mind: namely, "to substitute the category of becoming for the category of being, the conception of the relative for that of the absolute, of movement for immobility."[10]

The ideology of *Wissenschaft* comprised a second fundamental component: the right of free inquiry. Predicated on a declaration of independence from the cognitive part of tradition, critical scholarship complemented the process of emancipation in the intellectual realm. This too was an unabashed repudiation of Gans, for if *Wissenschaft* stood for anything it was an openness of mind willing to accord equal status to Gentile sources in the pursuit of historical truth. The historian's craft dictated an exhaustive study of all extant sources for the comprehension of past events and ancient texts, and by 1850 Selig Cassel (who was to convert some five years later) had resoundingly demonstrated for the first time the plethora of germane non-Jewish sources available to the Jewish historian in his compact but comprehensive political and social history of Diaspora Jewry.[11] The discontinuity dividing the bifurcated *Wissen* (learning) of Gans from the integrated *Wissenschaft* of Cassel is best caught by the memorable epigram of Moritz Steinschneider: "For the spirit there is no ghetto."[12]

It was but a short step from the study of non-Jewish sources to the detection of non-Jewish influences, and historians quickly if dimly sensed the presence of Persian, Greek, Roman, and Islamic patterns in the changing garb of Judaism. Minimal evidence (and a good dose of antirabbinic bias) convinced Isaak Markus Jost that Athens inspired the introduction of the Oral Law and Rome, the adoption of many of its legal concepts and the first codification of its sundry regulations.[13]

Beyond the integration of sources and the search for influences, the eviction of dogma from the halls of *Wissenschaft* also entailed the freedom to challenge claims and conclusions long sanctified by tradition. In his programmatic essay of 1818, which vibrated with new sources and questions, Leopold Zunz tactfully presented the internal evidence from the text of the Zohar which cast doubt on its traditional attribution.[14] Similarly, Krochmal rejected a number of rabbinic attributions for biblical books, and even Zacharias Frankel, not known for his enthusiasm for biblical criticism, acknowledged the existence of two Isaiahs, two Zechariahs, and at least twenty-five post-exilic psalms.[15] Perhaps most contested, given the acrimonious debate over changes in the *halakhic* system necessitated by emancipation, was the assertion by scholars as religiously dissimilar as Abraham Geiger and Shlomo Yehudah Rapoport that talmudic exegesis was far from infallible in explicating the meaning of the mishnaic text.[16] In theory then, *Wissenschaft* was incompatible with prejudgment and compared to Gans it was so even in practice.

A third component of *Wissenschaft* ideology may perhaps best be described as a quantum jump in the conception of Jewish sources available for a study of the past. The truncated curriculum of the Ashkenazic *yeshivah*, with its exclusive focus on works on *Halakhah*, had all but obliterated any inkling of the depth and diversity of Jewish literature. Against this background, the emphasis on biblical literature by the German *Haskalah* must be seen as a preference laden with protest. The sudden illumination of the unexpected range of "rabbinic literature" delivered by Zunz in 1818 transformed that protest into a scholarly agenda.

This conceptual expansion of literary creativity and sources of knowledge went far beyond the obvious but thrilling discovery of unpublished texts like the *Siddur* of Saadia, the diary of David Reubeni, the Arabic original of Maimonides's *Moreh Nebukhim*, and the divan of Yehuda Halevi.[17] The personal correspondence of *Wissenschaft* scholars with each other, still largely unpublished, is replete with inquiries, reports, and discussions on the discovery and nature of unknown manuscripts. Expansion also took the form of reappropriating substantial texts like the Jerusalem Talmud, midrashic collections, philosophic discourses, and liturgical compendia, which had hovered on the periphery of Jewish consciousness, and subjecting them to critical historical analysis. No less fertile was the scrutiny of well-mined traditional texts from the vantage point of new questions. If Zunz's sweeping yet searching reconstruction of the synagogue's unbroken homiletical tradition delivered an inspiring example of the former, then Rapoport's sparkling biographical essays of early medieval rabbinic luminaries displayed the awesome potential of the latter.[18] In truth, much of the subsequent research into the biographies of mishnaic and medieval rabbis, the evolution of rabbinic law and literature, and the social and religious history of medieval Jews rested on little more than poring over known traditional texts with new questions. Information is as much a function of interest as insight is of perspective.

The enlarged category of valid Jewish sources, of course, now included works written by Jews in languages other than Hebrew or Aramaic. In writing the history of the Second Commonwealth, Jost consistently preferred to rely on Josephus (and not the *Josippon* as Gans had) rather than the historical fragments preserved in rabbinic texts, and Frankel wrote extensively if unsympathetically about the literary remnants of Hellenistic Jewry.[19] The willingness to master and utilize such non-Hebrew texts gradually culminated in a totally new conception of Jewish literary creativity.

Since Johannes Buxtorf's *Bibliotheca Rabbinica* of 1613, "the very first scientifically organized bibliography of Jewish literature," Christian scholars of Judaism had expressed their theological conception of the field with the term "rabbinic."[20] Jewish literature comprised only Hebrew works written by rabbis or concerned with rabbinics. In the title of his "Etwas über die rabbinische Literatur" Zunz retained the term, but the substance of the essay argued cogently for understanding its scope to include all works on any subject by a Jewish author (lay or rabbinic) as long as Hebrew was the medium of expression. That process of secularization was completed by Steinschneider. His dazzlingly erudite survey of Jewish literature published in 1850 rested explicitly on a conception that had been stretched to cover the literary productivity of Jews in any language.[21] It is that secular conception which later informed the elegant two-volume history of Jewish literature published by Gustav Karpeles in 1886 and created the substance for eventually conceiving of Judaism as more than a religious phenomenon.[22]

In fact, conceptual thinking as a mode of cognition lies at the very heart of the ideology of *Wissenschaft* and reflects yet another aspect of its Western provenance. The traditional mode of Jewish thinking, as shaped in the rabbinic period, tended to be exegetical, and commentary became the quintessentially Jewish genre of intellectual expression. A sacred text called for elucidation, application, and renewal, and midrash evolved into a mode of cognition, an expression of piety, and an instrument of revitalization. But textually oriented thinking is essentially concrete, circumscribed, and episodic. Its very specificity induces a minimal level of abstraction and a bewildering absence of systematic analysis. The confrontation with Western *Wissenschaft* in the nineteenth century, like the confrontation with Greek philosophy in the Islamic world of the tenth century, injected a conceptual mode of thought into Judaism. If the essence of the scholarly enterprise is "the power to frame questions susceptible of scholarly enquiry," then *Jüdische Wissenschaft*, as distinct from traditional exegesis, was problem-oriented, systematic, and ultimately synthetic.[23]

This emphasis on the conceptual character of the new thinking is not meant to play down the role of philology, which was undoubtedly crucial. Identifying, dating, understanding texts would have been inconceivable without the finely honed sensitivity of scholars to the historical development of Hebrew, and Zunz's *Gottesdienstliche Vorträge* is nothing if not a sustained exercise in rigorous philological analysis. But it is important to appreciate that historical and comparative philology was only an exegetical instrument for the solution of problems posed by a conceptual mode of thinking. Nothing was more alien to the exegetical mode of traditional Judaism than the style and categories of German idealism, which transformed the German university into a unique institution for original and systematic research. What often distinguished the *Jüdische Wissenschaft* of Eastern European autodidacts, who never benefited from the neo-humanistic training of a German *Gymnasium* and university, was the degree to which their scholarship was still marred by the lack of system and generalization inherent in the exegetical mode.

If the emergence of historical consciousness, then, can best be understood as an aspect of the Westernization of Judaism, it is equally apparent that *Wissenschaft* was never far removed from the arena in which that process occurred, namely the struggle for emancipation, and the final component of its ideology relates directly to that struggle. Objectivity did not preclude involvement and Jewish scholarship gave sustained expression to a sense of engagement in the fate of its subject. In an era in which the pursuit of Jewish scholarship exacted a heavy price in material comfort and psychic equilibrium, when that link snapped, as in the cases of gifted young scholars like Eduard Gans, Philip Jaffé, and Selig Cassel, the flight from the field and Judaism were usually never far apart.[24] Despite frequent bouts of ambivalence, antipathy, and despair, scholars who refused to convert placed their scholarship in the service of the present.

That quality of engagement was made manifest in two ways. First in Germany where the medium was predominantly German, *Wissenschaft* scholars were imbued with a determination to wrest the field of Judaism from the theologically drenched hands of generations of Christian savants. For the first time in many a century, Jews undertook systematically to recount their past and to explain their religion for a non-Jewish audience, and their work laid claim to the greater reliability of the insider. This challenge had nothing to do with idle academic competition. The founders of *Wissenschaft* knew that it had been theological contempt which had exiled the adherents of Judaism to the periphery of the body politic, and only a radical change in the Christian appreciation of Judaism would eventually secure complete political integration.[25] As Zunz often intoned with controlled vehemence, political status was ultimately a consequence of the level of intellectual respect for Judaism.[26]

But, *Jüdische Wissenschaft* was not pitched solely for a Christian audience, particularly if written in Hebrew. It was also intended to imbue Jews with the self-knowledge needed to reconcile an archaic and all-embracing religion to the pressures, opportunities, and tastes of a new social context. Faith in the normative power of historical research was shared by Christian and Jewish scholar alike. In the very decades in which Friedrich Karl von Savigny created a historical school of jurisprudence to forestall the arbitrary formulation of a unified code of German law resting on principles of natural law rather than historical research, a generation of Jewish intellectuals across Central Europe, neither unattached nor uninterested, set about to unearth the historical evolution of Judaism in order to inform and determine present policy.[27] As a vehicle of consciousness, *Wissenschaft* was inextricably both academic and practical, recondite and relevant.

II

It should be abundantly clear by now that *Wissenschaft des Judentums* posed a fundamental challenge to the assumptions, interests, and methods of traditional Jewish learning. As an expression of alienation induced by the penetration of Western culture, it was both inherently and historically reformative. Accordingly, its provenance is to be found among young, alienated German intellectuals uninterested in pursuing the rabbinate as a career and seething with resentment against talmudic Judaism and especially its contemporary rabbinic spokesmen. *Wissenschaft* was seized as the cutting edge of a concerted effort to revamp Judaism to accord with a new legal and social context.

But equally important is the fact that *Wissenschaft* did not long remain the preserve of scholars pushing for religious reform. While its ideology and method could be ignored only at the peril of obscurantism, its programmatic implications were by no means self-evident. Scholarship could be used to advance different religious positions. Within a few decades a countervailing style of conservative *Wissenschaft* emerged intent on fortifying Jewish loyalties in an age of collapsing self-confidence by composing a more favorable historical assessment of rabbinic Judaism. Critical of all scholarship in the service of religious objectives was yet a third posture that crystallized by mid-century and avowed to raise *Wissenschaft* above the dictates of religious controversy. In sum, the practice of *Wissenschaft* developed dialectically, coming to mirror the polarization of the community it served.

The brief and poignant history of the *Verein für Cultur und Wissenschaft der Juden* illustrates vividly that the campaign for religious reform and the cultivation of *Wissenschaft* share the same patrimony. Founded in Berlin on 7th November 1819, in the aftermath of the "*Hep! Hep!*" riots, by a tiny band of Jewish intellectuals, the

Culturverein energetically pursued a varied course of practical and scholarly projects designed to facilitate the transvaluation of Judaism.[28] As an organization, it was explicitly forbidden by the Prussian government to enter the area of *Kultus* (the synagogue);[29] yet the rhetoric of its meetings bristled with hostility toward "rabbinism," and several of its members were in the forefront of a widespread effort to create a "German synagogue" which, in the words of Zunz, would reconcile "the genuine piety of the East with the genuine culture of the West."[30]

That the recent outbreak of popular antisemitism provided the impetus for the formation of the *Culturverein* is evidenced by the fact that from November 1816 to July 1817 many of the same young men had participated in a scholarly circle which met for thirty-two lectures, with but one devoted to a specifically Jewish topic.[31] Now, aggrieved by rejection, they struggled to formulate a conceptualization of Judaism which would allow for a reconciliation of family and fatherland, Judaism and Europe. Emerging from the dungeon of non-history, the Jew was doubly alienated, from Judaism and from German culture. Henceforth, Jewish unity would rest on an inner idea rather than external pressure and Jews would be able to assimilate without disappearing. Whatever there was of Judaism that could not be given conceptual articulation was not worth preserving. Central to that process of conceptualization was the claim for an essence of Judaism, whose unchanging yet unfolding spiritual presence bestowed a vital sense for the continuity of Jewish history. At the same time, the category of essence reduced dominant features of traditional Judaism rendered offensive by the new social context to mere accidents of history.[32]

It was in this charged atmosphere saturated by Hegelian rhetoric that both the term and conception of *Wissenschaft des Judentums* were born. During 1823 the *Culturverein* published the first and only three numbers of its now famous *Zeitschrift für die Wissenschaft des Judentums*, which exhibited both the theory and practice of the new discipline. In the opening essay, Immanuel Wolf, despite an *a priori* definition of the essence of Judaism, set forth a truly comprehensive agenda for empirical research. *Wissenschaft des Judentums* was to embrace the totality of Judaism studied from the perspective of philology, history, and philosophy as well as the state of contemporary Jewry. The journal presented a potpourri of sixteen essays, five written by Eduard Gans, the president of the *Culturverein*, and three by Zunz, who served as editor and chairman of the scholarly seminar in which most of the essays had been previously delivered. The essays by Gans and Zunz gave dramatic promise of the extent to which the methodology of historical thinking could transcend the vehement antirabbinic animus in which it had been generated.[33]

By February 1824 the *Culturverein* had disintegrated. A dwindling membership, the utter indifference of the Berlin Jewish plutocracy, and the rising tide of political reaction had crushed the sense of fervor, mission, and elitism which sustained its frenetic activity. In his presidential address of 28th October 1821 Gans had expressed his conviction that if the *Verein* were to fail it would prove that its vision and intent were at fault and not its energy and commitment.[34] But Zunz, who unlike Gans persevered in that vision and commitment, offered a more trenchant assessment of the *Verein's* importance some forty years later: ". . . nearly all the advances by Jews in the scholarly, political, and civil sectors as well as the achievements in reforming school and synagogue have their roots in the activity of that *Verein* and some of its members."[35]

The first major achievement of the turn to *Wissenschaft* was the nine-volume *Geschichte der Israeliten* (1820–1828) produced single-handedly by Isaak Jost, a young Jewish teacher in Berlin and former member of the *Culturverein* turned bitter critic. A strong desire to free Jewish history from its bondage to Christian theology impelled and sustained Jost in this first Jewish effort at a comprehensive history from the Maccabean period to 1815 in a European language. Nevertheless, though critical in its use of sources, it was hardly objective. An adversarial relationship to rabbinic Judaism, which he fully shared with the *Culturverein*, pervaded his scholarship to a far greater extent than it did the essays of Zunz and Gans. As the historian of the radical wing of the Berlin *Haskalah*, Jost wrote about the decline and fall of Judaism in a manner fully reminiscent of Gibbon.

The theologian may indulge the pleasing task of describing Religion as she descended from Heaven, arrayed in her native purity. A more melancholy duty is imposed on the historian. He must discover the inevitable mixture of error and corruption which she contracted in a long residence upon earth, among a weak and degenerate race of beings.[36]

For Jost the destruction of the First Commonwealth in 586 B.C.E. terminated the validity of biblical law. Diaspora Jewry should have been reconstituted solely on the unobtrusive and inoffensive basis of the Bible's rational and ethical proposition.[37] Instead, the fateful triumph of rabbinic Judaism saddled the historian with the melancholy task of studying the progressively debilitating impact of an ever more presumptuous and insular religious leadership. Unlike the *Culturverein*, Jost refused to endow his Judaism with a continuous essence of universal mission which might inspire personal action. Not hope for the future of Judaism as much as ties of memory and kinship preserved in him a stoic but productive loyalty.

If Jost's history still echoed the mood, method, and knowledge of the eighteenth century, then the work of Zunz, his sometime friend and the sparkplug of the *Verein*, brilliantly inaugurated the scholarship of the nineteenth century. No less sweeping in scope, his *Gottesdienstliche Vorträge* (1832) rested on a far more searching philological study of all relevant texts, both published and unpublished. It also rested squarely on the concept of development which had been so obscured by Jost's preoccupation with decline. Zunz reassembled with rare architectural virtuosity the plethora of new data generated by the philological method into a history of Jewish exegetical literature, vibrant with organic growth. The cause of religious reform would be better served by demonstrating the inherently evolutionary character of Judaism than debunking the purported villains of degeneration. Specifically, Zunz depicted the variety of midrashic modes developed and deployed by Judaism, beginning as far back as the early centuries of the Second Commonwealth, to ensure the continuous revitalization of its sacred texts. The new German sermon was but another worthy link in a venerable and innovative tradition of public edification.[38]

In his foreword Zunz took occasion to express his indebtedness to Shlomo Yehudah Rapoport of Lemberg, whom he had cited more than 110 times in his book. Rapoport's six Hebrew biographical essays of tenth- and eleventh-century rabbinic scholars (1828–1831), perhaps inspired by Zunz's own masterful biography of Rashi (1823), had begun to penetrate the obscurity of Gaonic history. But the accomplishment was marred by the literary form. The didactic biographical mode of the *Haskalah* hardly constituted an adequate principle of organization for the myriad results produced by his awesome command of Hebrew literature and his thorough use of the bibliographies compiled by earlier Christian scholars.

Nevertheless, the cumulative effect of Rapoport's massive scholarship, which, given the Galician ambience, was *ipso facto* revolutionary, was to advance inconspicuously an alternate mode of Judaism. For Rapoport had succeeded in rooting the ideal of the Spanish Jewish gentleman, so dear to Ashkenazic intellectuals since the eighteenth century, in Gaonic soil. Every one of his subjects lived under the invigorating influence of the Islamic world and exhibited a style of rabbinic Judaism tempered by the dictates of reason, antagonistic to mystical excesses, and open to secular learning.[39] Rapoport had reinforced the Maimonidean paradigm, so critical of contemporary Ashkenazic Judaism, by discovering a legitimizing Gaonic prototype.

The most sustained linkage, however, between the cause for religious reform and the study of the past came in the seminal career of Abraham Geiger.[40] Despite the honor of a prize-winning dissertation which identified for the first time many of the Jewish sources of early Islam, Geiger was forced to satisfy his deep love for Jewish scholarship in the pulpit rather than in the ivory tower.[41] He refused to follow his close friend Joseph Derenbourg or Salomon Munk across the Rhine where they successfully transplanted *Jüdische Wissenschaft* on French soil. As a young rabbi in Wiesbaden, Geiger represented one of the first exemplars of a new type of rabbinic leadership, distinct from its medieval namesake in terms of education, function, and authority. In 1835 he founded a journal of Jewish theology which would advocate and legitimize a program of major reforms in the vocabulary of the new historical idiom. The nine years during which the journal appeared irregularly coincided with a period of theological turbulence in Geiger's own thinking in which he often bordered on despair over the worth, viability, and future of Judaism.[42]

Accordingly, it is not surprising to discover in Geiger's essays on rabbinic exegesis from this period a preoccupation with degeneration that still echoes the rhetoric of Jost. More specifically, the two-part essay on "Das Verhältniss des natürlichen Schriftsinnes zur thalmudischen Schriftdeutung,'' which nearly jeopardized Geiger's position in Breslau, addressed the very same question over which Michael Creizenach and Samson Raphael Hirsch had so fundamentally disagreed during the preceding decade: namely, the validity of the exegetical base which supports the sprawling superstructure of rabbinic Judaism. Geiger's contribution to this debate added a historical dimension in support of Creizenach's rationalistic analysis. Proceeding from Mishnah to Talmud, Geiger depicted rabbinic exegesis as utterly arbitrary and generally oblivious to the existence of a historically conditioned meaning of the text. What did separate Mishnah from Talmud was the programmatic intent of the Amoraim, in contrast to the Tannaim, to ground every post-biblical *halakhic* innovation in Scripture with a rigidity impervious to time. Thus the decline of Judaism was not the product of external oppression but rather internal corruption.[43]

What made Geiger eventually the ideological spokesman for German Reform was the fact that as a mature man he abandoned this negatively charged approach to the study of rabbinic Judaism, and the break enabled him to construct a developmental model which identified his own cause with its very mainstream. As his intimate letters to Steinschneider reveal, Geiger began in 1854 to work on his *Urschrift* (1857) with an absorbing enthusiasm fueled by a chain reaction of fresh insights.[44] The *Urschrift* and its subsequent reformulations argued with ingenuity and power that the arbitrary biblical exegesis of the Pharisees and their descendants was precisely the innovative instrument which enabled them to challenge the tradition-bound hegemony of the priestly Sadducean aristocracy with a democratic religious program. A new appreciation of the historical function of Pharasaic Midrash and *halakhah* opened the way for Geiger to rehabilitate the Pharisees as a party of the people and of progress.[45] On the basis of this historiographical breakthrough, Geiger was soon able to integrate the disparate data of his penetrating research into an incomparable synthetic history of Judaism that bestowed reform with the indispensable seal of authenticity.[46]

But the reform monopoly of *Wissenschaft* was broken long before the publication of the *Urschrift* in 1857. In fact, the appearance of Geiger's *Wissenschaftliche Zeitschrift* and especially his early deprecatory essay on rabbinic exegesis contributed directly to a dissolution of the ranks. Unlike Hirsch, who on principle rejected the historical method as an instrument of analysis alien to Judaism, a cluster of young *Wissenschaft* scholars, with a more conservative religious bent than Geiger's and offended by the debunking litany against Judaism on which reform till then was predicated, began to use the instrument to accentuate the virtues, vitality, and achievements of traditional Judaism, to moderate the pace of change, and to stem the tide of defections. The same medium could be made to yield different messages.[47]

The deep religious differences which separated Geiger from Rapoport and Samuel David Luzzatto soon manifested themselves publicly. In the third volume of

Kerem Hemed, which from 1833 to 1846 provided a lively Hebrew forum in which a cohort of Central European scholars could share and test their results, Luzzatto vigorously rejected Geiger's claim that R. Yehudah ha-Nasi in editing the Mishnah had also reduced it to a written text. Whereas Geiger was eager to demonstrate how early the process of petrification had set in to the *halakhic* system, Luzzatto tried to defend its essential responsiveness to changes in time and place by averring the protracted fluidity of the Oral Law. Astutely he quickly took the offensive. Luzzatto, who was far less enamored of Sephardic superiority than most of his enlightened contemporaries, used the issue of written codification to redirect the charge against Maimonides and to add a general critique of his intellectual elitism that distressed both Krochmal and Rapoport.[48]

Rapoport also quickly distanced himself from Geiger. In consequence of his decision in 1837 to secure his livelihood henceforth as a rabbi, Rapoport felt obliged to give public expression to his withdrawal from the published list of contributors to Geiger's journal.[49] But that was at most a precipitating cause. As his letters to Zunz from the 1830s make clear, Rapoport objected to purely negative *Wissenschaft* and refused to move far beyond what the Jewish masses found religiously acceptable. Time, moreover, was the proper vehicle for effecting the changes warranted by responsible scholarly research.[50] In 1845 Rapoport briefly took the lead in attempting to frustrate the radical designs of the Frankfurt rabbinical conference.[51]

The dismay at the tone and tendentiousness of reform *Wissenschaft* was fully shared by Michael Sachs, whose stirring presentation of the religious poetry of Spanish Jewry (1845) was written under the direct influence of both Luzzatto and Rapoport.[52] Sachs served as *Prediger* of the liberal *Tempelverein* in Prague from 1836 to 1844, where he befriended Rapoport, who guided, stimulated, and eventually ordained him. Since his translation of the Psalms (1835), Sachs had been casting about for a scholarly project which would allow him to do more than trace the course of Judaism's decrepitude. As the volume neared completion, Sachs wrote to Zunz on 21st January 1844, of his purpose.

I know I have written without prejudice and blind preference. But I do wish to counteract through deed and without overt polemics that unfortunately prevailing effort, which poses as criticism and impartial judgment, to besmirch and dishonor everything which Judaism has produced, that heartless insolence which soon becomes genuine betrayal . . .[53]

With the generous help of Luzzatto, who provided him with hitherto unknown specimens of Hebrew poetry, Sachs composed an uplifting tribute to the cultural creativity of Spanish Jewry. Yet ironically, he too was victim of the Spanish bias of his adversaries, and despite the stern counsel of Luzzatto, he chose to omit any sample of Ashkenazic religious poetry.[54] To his German translation of Sephardic poetry, Sachs added a long historical essay which he read to Rapoport as it was being composed. The approbation was unreserved and the reason is obvious, for the essay included an evocative depiction of midrash utterly at odds with the disdainful rationalism of Geiger. Sachs made of midrash the precursor of religious poetry and a distillation of the unreflective voice of the still effusive spirit of biblical literature.[55]

Two prolix volumes on the nature of *halakhic* (1840) and *aggadic* exegesis (1847) by H. S. Hirschfeld constituted yet another scholarly response by the emerging conservative bloc to the varied attacks against the exegetical foundations of Jewish law.[56] Born in Inowroclaw, West Prussia, and the holder of a Berlin doctorate, Hirschfeld had become one of the very first academically trained rabbis in the whole of Poznań when in 1840 he was elected to serve in Wollstein. His subsequent marriage to the daughter of Salomon Eger, the Chief Rabbi of. Poznań, allied him with one of the leaders of traditional Orthodoxy in Germany, though for a time he continued to work with Frankel against Reform.[57] Hirschfeld attempted in a highly original manner to explicate and defend the integrity of rabbinic exegesis phenomenologically rather than historically using an array of Hegelian categories to deflect the problems raised by critical scholarship. He contended that all exegesis was inherently subjective and analyzed the assumptions and techniques of rabbinic exegesis as expressions of Jewish consciousness. Despite grudging respect for his learning and ingenuity, Levi Herzfeld and Geiger dismissed his first book with its unhistorical method and excessive Hegelian framework as falling short of the standards of *Wissenschaft*.[58]

But the importance of Hirschfeld's work transcends its flawed originality. It points to an uncoordinated effort by *Wissenschaft* scholars to explain the Jewish legal system by recasting it in the legal and conceptual categories of the Western world. Although that effort was brilliantly launched by Eduard Gans back in 1823 in a wide-ranging comparative legal study of Jewish inheritance law, it languished till a conservative scholarly cadre in the 1840s felt the need to advance a proper understanding of Jewish law among Christian and Jewish critics alike.[59] No one doubted that a German translation of the Talmud would do little toward achieving that goal. In 1856 David Cassel, a member of the conservative camp, restated the consensus

that a correct, clear translation of the Talmud into the German language borders on the impossible, that the interests of Judaism would in no way be served by that kind of work, even if undertaken by the most learned of men, because, given the huge gulf which separates the world of our modern European views from that of Palestine and Babylonia in the third to the fifth century, misunderstanding, distortion, and disparagement of the sacred book would inevitably follow.[60]

Hirschfeld himself had intended to organize a cooperative venture to produce a Latin commentary to the entire Babylonian Talmud, though only the volume on *Makkot* (1842) was ever published.[61] An abiding love for Talmud tempered by embarrassment at its foreignness and excesses prompted *Wissenschaft* scholars to skirt the unpredictable exposure of literal translation till 1896 when the much criticized German translation of Lazarus Goldschmidt began to appear.[62]

Typical of this countervailing genre of conceptual analysis was the scholarship of Hirsch Bär Fassel, the rabbi of Prossnitz, Moravia, till 1851 and then, till his death in 1883, of Nagykanizsa, Hungary. His avowed commitment to the preservation of rabbinic Judaism did not blind him to the need for change. In the 1840s the lack of a doctorate cost him a German pulpit, but did not deter him from undertaking a series of books in which he arranged and expounded the non-religious sections of Jewish law in terms of Western legal and philosophic traditions.[63] His study of Jewish civil law was even structured according to the Austrian civil law code with innumerable comparisons enriching his exposition. With disarming candor Fassel acknowledged how his own understanding of Jewish law had been deepened by his comparative legal studies.

I studied Talmud before I occupied myself with the law codes of the modern period, and I know that rabbinic law became clear to me only by way of the latter. The authors of rabbinic law lacked the technical terms to make the various nuances, gradations, and differences clear and distinct.[64]

The dialectic alluded to by Fassel comprises the very essence of the *Wissenschaft* enterprise: a degree of alienation increased self-knowledge. To make Judaism comprehensible to the non-Jew required much more than a literal translation of ancient texts. The texts and institutions, the value system and thought patterns of Judaism had to be expounded and mediated in conceptual terms indigenous to the intellectual world of the West, and it was precisely this activity of conceptual translation which in turn illuminated many a facet of Judaism to which the insider had up to now been utterly oblivious. To dismiss such expositions as apologetics, written merely with a view to advancing the cause of emancipation, is to obscure the insight that comes with distance, the understanding that results from the application of new conceptual tools to a subject hitherto dominated by a well-entrenched mode of study.

Certainly the most competent *Wissenschaft* scholar to study Jewish law comparatively was Zacharias Frankel. During the course of a prolific career as pulpit rabbi and seminary director, he treated monographically the topics of oaths (1840), judicial procedure (1846), and marriage (1860) in Jewish law from the vantage point of historical jurisprudence. To be sure, each was occasioned by particular Jewish legal disabilities, and the homiletical tone at times grew rather excessive, yet all abounded with instructive comparisons. At its best, as in *Der gerichtliche Beweis*, Frankel's comparative method combined a breadth, thoroughness, and analytic power which could not fail to discredit the vertical and rationalistic approach of Geiger.[65]

Nevertheless, Frankel's historical significance rests on still more noteworthy accomplishments. In the 1840s as the forces for religious Reform in Germany registered dramatic gain, he moved to organize the inchoate conservative bloc around a journal which would counter the antihistorical rationalism of reform rhetoric. He recruited contributors vigorously by personal suasion and managed for a brief three years (1844–1846) to provide a rostrum from which a conservative point of view on the contemporary and historical issues could be disseminated. Every one of the conservative scholars previously mentioned, except Luzzatto, plus others like Bernhard Beer, Heinrich Graetz, Wolf Landau, Fürchtegott Lebrecht, Salomon Steinheim, and Moritz Steinschneider gave public expression to their sympathy for Frankel's outspoken antireform posture by contributing essays. Like Geiger, Frankel aimed his journal, for which he wrote voluminously, at a literate but non-rabbinic Jewish audience, with scholarship subordinate to ideology. Only with the second year did he add a small section of disinterested *Wissenschaft*. When Frankel re-entered the field of periodicals in October 1851 with his better known *Monatsschrift für Geschichte und Wissenschaft des Judentums*, the rubric of *Geschichte* was to comprise essays whose evocative, heroic style of popularizing Jewish history would intensify the ties to the past. Not surprisingly, many of those popular essays during the first decade came from Frankel, whose pen never ran dry.[66]

Equally unconventional was Frankel's intent to restrict the term *Wissenschaft des Judentums* to the study of rabbinic literature in the limited sense rejected by the aforementioned revisions of Zunz and Steinschneider. Frankel deftly equated the new term, with all its resonances, to the traditional study of sacred texts. It was the unbroken centrality of *Wissenschaft des Judentums* which illuminated the mystery of Jewish survival and dispelled all fear for the future. In consequence, the scholarly fare of the *Monatsschrift* expanded only gradually to include subjects unrelated to the history of the rabbinic period and its sacred texts.[67]

It is, of course, Frankel's sustained devotion to a history of Jewish law that gives his own scholarly career its unity. Several ebullient letters to Zunz from the 1830s suggest that Frankel was inspired by Zunz's sweeping external history of midrashic literature to conceptualize an analogous venture for *halakhah*, though with more attention to content. Both in his *Vorstudien zu der Septuaginta* (1841), which represented the first Jewish study of the Septuagint since Azariah de Rossi, and in *Der Gerichtliche Beweis* (1846) he articulated his proposal to put the study of Jewish law on a historical basis, and during the next thirty years, Frankel produced a shelf of monographs that studied with varying degrees of thoroughness the major strata and sources of *halakhic* development from the Septuagint to medieval *responsa*. Through Frankel the historical jurisprudence (*geschichtliche Rechtswissenschaft*) of Savigny entered the realm of Jewish scholarship.[68]

In Heinrich Graetz, Frankel gained a worthy ally whose visceral contempt for Reform played a formative role in the determination of his own scholarly agenda. A different reading of the past vindicated an alternate response to the pressures of emancipation. The timeliness of Graetz's doctoral dissertation on *Gnosticismus und Judentum* (1846) was not missed by Hirschfeld in his complimentary if critical review in Frankel's *Zeitschrift*. [69] For Graetz had imbued rabbinic Judaism with a positive valence: a religion open to the world but cognizant of where to draw the line. Unconventionally Graetz pictured R. Akiva as the farsighted and resourceful leader who had blunted the challenge of gnosticism. [70]

The same year Graetz locked horns with Reform again in a bold attempt to formulate a philosophy of Jewish history that would do equal justice to Judaism's layers of historical experience. In contrast to the selective and progressive philosophic pronouncements of Reform ideologues, in which earlier phases were transcended, Graetz tried to construct an all-inclusive conception in which the essential attributes of each of the major periods of Jewish history were preserved. Each attribute was but the realization of a latent characteristic present from the beginning and collectively they constituted the full and legitimate scope of Judaism. A theory of immanence had replaced that of essence and progress was confined to the realm of consciousness. [71]

If *Die Construction* argued the claims of the past philosophically, *Die Geschichte der Juden* (1853–1874) did so with vivid historical concreteness. More than any other work, it embodied the message of the Historical School founded by Frankel and Graetz: a proud and uncompromising loyalty to rabbinic Judaism rooted in the suffering and creativity of Jewish history. To deliver that message to the largest audience possible, Graetz divided his quintessentially national history, in the manner of the *Monatsschrift*, into *Geschichte* and *Wissenschaft*. Concentrating the arcana of his scholarship into systematic excurses at the end of each volume enabled him to craft a consummate narrative text punctuated with moral judgments.

What distinguished Graetz's accomplishment from a historiographical point of view is that he was the first *Wissenschaft* scholar to integrate the external and internal history of ancient and medieval Jewry into a single work of scholarship. Members of the *Wissenschaft* circle, regardless of their disagreements, fully shared the view that the Jews had no external history, other than a morbid record of unbroken persecution which hardly inspired painstaking research. [72] Accordingly, *Wissenschaft* scholars much preferred to direct their energies to studying the internal history of the Jews, or more narrowly still, the expressions of Jewish culture, where freedom, dignity, and creativity visibly abounded. While Jost had tended to concentrate on external Jewish history, or at best written the political history of the Second Commonwealth and the emergence of rabbinic Judaism as if they were hermetically sealed from each other, Zunz, Rapoport, Luzzatto, Sachs, Frankel, and Steinschneider focused almost exclusively on literary texts. Typical of this conceptual bifurcation were the pioneering essays by Selig Cassel and Steinschneider on Jewish political and cultural history (1850) for the renowned *Allgemeine Encyklopädie der Wissenschaften und Künste*. Though each scholar convincingly demonstrated the conceptual scope and primary sources of his respective field, the results remained unrelated. The breakthrough effected by Graetz was methodological: to integrate the fields of political and cultural history, or put differently, the history of Jews and Judaism in the same volume. Neither could be understood without systematic reference to the other. Two years before the first volume of his history appeared, Graetz had already enunciated his conviction, in an oblique attack against Jost, that

the external events of the time [i.e., of Hillel] and the development of the law (Lehre) stand in an unbroken reciprocal relationship to each other. In the presentation of this historical era and subsequent ones, whoever treats the history of Judaism apart from the history of the Jews can hardly advance beyond the basic requirements of a pragmatic historical approach.[73]

It is indeed ironic that the usual indictment of Graetz's history as little more than a "Leiden- und Gelehrten-Geschichte" (a history of suffering and learning), when put into historiographical perspective, points precisely to his achievement. Without doubt, his notion of Jewish political history, especially for the medieval period, was still skewed and truncated, but the principle of integration had been firmly established. In sum, the combination of structural innovation, basic research, and pulsating narrative made of Graetz's didactic scholarship the most effective vehicle for reinvigorating the waning identity of a disintegrating community with the power of historical memory.

It has been argued till now that *Wissenschaft des Judentums* was born in battle, forged by the detractors of rabbinic Judaism and then appropriated by its defenders. However, it did not stay subordinate to religious ideology for long. From the outset the desire to recover the past was coupled with a powerful need to right the commissions and perversions of Christian scholarship, sanctified by repetition. A typical example was the extensive exhibition on the history of printing held in Berlin in October 1840 which had conspicuously failed to display even a single Hebrew printed book. An outraged Zunz pondered over the coincidence of the exhibition with the revival of the blood libel in Damascus.

If the law of the outsider [das Ausnahmegesetz] applies to us in Damascus, it applies no less in the celebration of the printed book. One remembers mendacious accusations but not illustrious achievements. The Jews are self-evidently excluded from the homage lavished on the first printers.

The neglect of Jewish literature was a disservice to scholarship, to Jews, and to progress itself.[74]

To pursue Jewish history, therefore, was both an act of justice as well as self-interest: the success of emancipation no less than the integrity of scholarship required a new appreciation of Jewish history. Though certainly susceptible to self-censorship, this motive force by virtue of its target group and its allegiance to the academic ethos produced a breadth of Jewish scholarship that transcended the issues of religious accommodation. Pursued primarily by "laymen" as opposed to pulpit rabbis, this brand of *Wissenschaft* contained the seeds of scholarship for its own sake.

In the spirit of this orientation Julius Fürst founded and edited *Der Orient* from 1840 till 1851. Fürst had served as the Hebrew instructor of Franz Delitzsch and provided indispensable assistance in the preparation of his brilliant but distinctly Christian study of Hebrew poetry (1836).[75] As a *Privatdozent* in Oriental languages at Leipzig, he refused to convert for promotion and had to wait until 1864 for the unsalaried title of honorary professor, the first *Wissenschaft* scholar in Germany to gain that hollow distinction.[76] Though his own prolific scholarship was often less than rigorous and he soon managed to alienate most of his associates, he did create in the columns of his weekly and especially in its scholarly supplement a dynamic forum for the unveiling of new ideas, sources, and interpretations that ran the gamut of an emerging discipline—poetry, philosophy, literature, history, exegesis, philology, and biography. It was precisely his university ambience that gave him a clear sense of the scope, development, and subdivisions of an academic discipline, and it was not fortuitous that he described his literary forum in the conventional metaphor for the German university as "eine Pflanzstätte der Wissenschaft" (a seedbed for scholarship). In accord with the academic ethos, he tried to raise the level of Jewish scholarship above the constraints of religious partisanship.[77]

It was in the pages of the *Orient* in 1843 that David Cassel and Steinschneider first published a tentative conceptualization for an encyclopedia of *Wissenschaft des Judentums*. The idea for this daring venture, given the embryonic state of the field, had originated with Baer Loew Monasch, a publisher of Jewish books in Kroto-schin (Poznań) and later the father-in-law of Graetz.[78] He persuaded Cassel to assume the general editorship and Cassel in turn, his close friend Steinschneider to handle the section on *Literaturgeschichte*. It was clearly a project of a young second generation of *Wissenschaft* scholars undaunted by its intimidating difficulties. More established scholars like Zunz, Jost, Geiger, and Frankel preferred only a peripheral involvement. That initial description of the encyclopedia netted a major conceptual advance, for in it Cassel forced Steinschneider to move beyond the restricted notion of Hebrew literature to a non-linguistic definition, which, as we have seen, Steinschneider used in his subsequent essay on Jewish literature.[79]

Offended by the untoward criticism of their conceptualization by Fürst, Cassel and Steinschneider published the actual prospectus for the encyclopedia as a separate pamphlet several months later. They stressed their concern over the degree to which the emancipation debate had made of Jews and Judaism a subject of public, often vulgar discourse and over the lack of objective scholarship available on either. *Wissenschaft des Judentums* was a political necessity.

Whoever is cognizant of the terrible blunders and outrages against Judaism, from which practically no work of this sort [i.e., scholarly books and encyclopedias] is free . . . will certainly agree with us that the time has come for Jews themselves to take action to bring their downtrodden literature, their maligned faith before the bar of justice. No apologies, only a presentation of the truth![80]

Despite the fact that Cassel's zeal bore no fruit, it should be noted that the later essays by Steinschneider on Jewish literature and Selig Cassel on Jewish history were both conceived and started within the framework of that abortive project.

The same political note was struck by Zunz in 1845 in the opening chapter of his *Zur Geschichte und Literatur.* The widespread debate over a new and comprehensive Jewry law in Prussia intensified the awareness of a connection between emancipation and Jewish scholarship. As long as the venerated tomes of Christian theologians constituted the final authority on the nature of Judaism, government policy would continue to be determined by theological biases, as it had been throughout the Middle Ages. Full citizenship for Jews could only follow the emancipation of Judaica from its theological fetters.[81]

But theological fetters could be imposed by Jewish as well as Christian scholars, and this seminal volume of essays, devoted largely to aspects of medieval Ashkenazic culture, also represented Zunz's final break with reform *Wissenschaft.* For several years in a series of popular essays Zunz had been admonishing his contemporaries, with the same moral fervor he had once displayed in the early twenties as a *Prediger* (preacher), not to abandon their religious and cultural heritage. In the same vein Zunz now condemned the *Wissenschaft* aversion to the history of Ashkenazic Jewry. Jewish history stood little chance of winning the Christian respect it deserved if Jewish scholars themselves treated large chunks of it with contempt. Furthermore, such arbitrary selectivity violated the very canons of scholarship itself, which called for "a comprehensive, coherent, and fair knowledge" of the past. And finally, contemporary Jewish life in Europe could hardly be understood without a thorough grasp of its Ashkenazic roots.[82]

That break did not put Zunz for very long in the camp of the conservative bloc, despite the similarity in rhetoric. He soon came to regard it as but another form of *Glaubenswissenschaft* (dogmatic history) and his own scholarly posture was quite distinct from that of Geiger and Frankel.[83] What the break does show, however, is the extent to which the practice of *Wissenschaft* must be understood dialectically. A fluid political and religious context could hardly give rise to a single undifferentiated style of scholarship.

The renewed concerns of objectivity did not make Zunz an antiquarian, no matter how excessive his attention to detail. On the contrary, his final trilogy on liturgical poetry culminated a life-long preoccupation with the synagogue, the institution which he regarded as "the expression of Jewish nationality, the guarantee of its religious existence."[84] In an age of religious disaffection and antagonism toward the parochial, Zunz became the premier historian of the synagogue. A spirit of empathy, loyalty, reverence, and piety permeated his meticulous studies of its sermons and liturgy. Without the synagogue Judaism had no future and without a sense of continuity the reform of the synagogue would fail. It is certainly true that his later works on the liturgy lacked the special pleading for reform which marked *Die gottesdienstlichen Vorträge*; yet the pervasive liturgical fluidity, responsiveness, and variety which they irrefutably established constituted the most persuasive legitimation for liturgical Reform.[85]

Despite Zunz's plea, Ashkenazic culture continued to suffer from "benign neglect" until the next generation of *Wissenschaft* scholars, and even beyond. By 1871 when Abraham Berliner published his modest vignette of Ashkenazic popular religion, several local histories by Breslau students and others, the *Regesten* (1862) collected by Meir Wiener, and the sympathetically comprehensive history of Otto Stobbe (1866), a Christian historian at the University of Breslau who worked closely with Graetz, had reconstructed the political history of medieval German Jewry on the basis of an abundance of non-Jewish sources.[86] The turn to social history appeared to be merely a natural progression from external to internal history. But the shift by Berliner and Moritz Güdemann in the 1880s implied much more. Social history was the only way to write of Ashkenazic Jewry positively, for it could certainly not compete with individual Sephardic accomplishments poetically, philosophically, or culturally. Only on the level of social history could Berliner and Güdemann marshal the evidence to show a religious culture which never became barbarized. In the face of insecurity and oppression, that culture generated a nobility of character that compared favorably with the Spanish nobility of mind. German-Jewish life exhibited a spiritual tranquillity, ethical sensitivity, familial stability, and dignified piety that could instill a contemporary Jew with pride in his origins. In the case of Güdemann, who shared the pulpit with Jellinek in Vienna, the rising tide of German antisemitism injected a pronounced apologetic tone into his work and eventually diverted him permanently from further scholarship.[87]

No *Wissenschaft* scholar epitomized the ethos of value-free scholarship more than Moritz Steinschneider, who revered Zunz as his mentor and model. During a scholarly career that spanned more than six decades of unbroken productivity, he fought, with varying degrees of acerbity and stridency, for the exclusion of all partisan considerations from Jewish scholarship. From the bench of his bibliographical journal (1859–1865, 1869–1882), which he edited and filled with his reviews, he passed severe judgment on friend and foe alike for falling short of the rigorous standards of his scholarly vision.[88]

That vision was shaped in the tempestuous decade of the 1840s when the campaigns for emancipation and Reform intensified and converged. For a time the gifted young Steinschneider prepared himself for a career in the rabbinate, worked actively for the rejuvenation of Judaism, supported the efforts of Frankel, and gave somewhat free rein to his romantic leanings.[89] But he soon changed course to devote himself to the cause of gaining Jewish scholarship its rightful place in the world of German academia. His determined defense of method—of disinterested, philological, and contextual scholarship—was a direct function of this goal. Only the most exacting standards of research free of all extraneous subjectivity could eventually gain the respect of university scholars. The two-tier style of Breslau *Wissenschaft* repeatedly drew his scorn: "the combination of edifying and strictly scholarly purposes is a hermaphrodite."[90] In contrast Steinschneider wrote solely for the scholar. "There are fields which can never be popularized, because comprehension presupposes a certain preparation [and] interest in them, a special intellectual bent."[91]

Whatever the personal roots of his legendary hostility toward the rabbinate, it was, as it had been for Zunz and the *Culturverein,* an aspect of a scholarly vision.[92] A secular and egalitarian conception of Jewish cultural creativity could be subject to historical investigation only within a university setting with its intellectual openness and critical method. The only flaw with that program was that with regard to Judaism such a university did not exist in Germany. Steinschneider's principled contempt for all modern rabbinical seminaries, the only form of institutionalization available to Jewish scholarship in nineteenth-century Germany, allowed him to ignore the Christian ethos which continued to prevail in the German university.[93] The vicious attack on Zunz by Paul de Lagarde, the Teutonic-touting Göttingen Semitist, in the 1880s may have justified Steinschneider's caustic remark that "one cannot teach Jew-haters, least of all through history." But if their views were to dominate academic policy, the intellectual openness of the university would be no more than a painful platitude. The greatest achievement of *Wissenschaft des Judentums* is that it matured into an academic discipline entirely outside the framework of the German university.[94]

Steinschneider indeed contributed mightily to establishing the general historical importance of medieval Jewry. In three encyclopedic bibliographic works he documented the central role played by Jews in every stage of the involved transmission of Greek culture to Europe. These inexhaustible works emerged from a life-long fascination with the impact of Islam on Jewish consciousness and the creative intersecting of two cultural worlds.[95] Steinschneider was undeterred by Frankel's displeasure in 1846 at his "Arabomanie," a rebuke which he never forgave, and by 1850 he was arguing in his essay on Jewish literature for a new periodization of Jewish history along cultural rather than political lines.[96] The Jewish Middle Ages began not with the destruction of the Second Temple but with the end of midrashic thinking, a change in mentality that did not occur until the rise of Islam, and Jewish cultural creativity abated only after the disordering expulsion from Spain.[97] As for the following three centuries, Steinschneider portrayed them as monotonously unoriginal in accord with conventional wisdom, though his own appreciation of the impact of printing on the Jewish world fully belied that assessment.[98] Still, a self-respecting modern age requires a preceding and validating period of benightedness.

Aside from solidifying the practice of *Wissenschaft*, the massive and meticulous output of Steinschneider served to deepen the Sephardic bias of his contemporaries. His vaunted objectivity was not free of the pervasive revulsion for the allegedly unrelieved physical oppression and intellectual narrowness of medieval Ashkenazic Jewry. In the foreword to his *Die arabische Literatur der Juden* (1902), he let fly with a malevolent stereotyping of Ashkenazic Jewry worthy of the crudest polemicist. Steinschneider, like most emancipated German Jews, thought to discover in the diverse religious and cultural vitality of medieval Spanish Jews kindred souls who had resoundingly mastered the challenge of living in two conflicting worlds. As early as 1847 Luzzatto had warned Steinschneider of becoming part of the fashionable historical enterprise "of glorifying and flaunting those Jews whose being was not truly Jewish but rather Greek or Arabic." Even the scholarship of a Steinschneider was susceptible to the lure of resemblance and a touch of projection. In the profound words of Goethe: "You resemble the spirit which you comprehend." Historical insight and error may, paradoxically, flow from the same source.[99]

III

With the publication of the final two volumes of Zunz's *Gesammelte Schriften* in 1876, the first period in the history of *Wissenschaft des Judentums*, which he himself had opened in 1818 with a single essay, comes to an end. During the preceding two years Geiger and Frankel had died within a few months of each other and Graetz had published the final volume of his history. Without institutional support from either the universities or the Jewish community and despite the loss of the two greatest Jewish libraries in Germany to England in 1829 and 1848, a generation of pioneers had created the modern academic discipline of Judaica.[100] In the process they had displaced Christian scholarship from its once unchallenged domination of the study of Judaism, an accomplishment that would provoke a determined counter-attack in the next generation. More important, they had created a historical consciousness that could serve as a base for a voluntaristic and secular Jewish community.

NOTES

1. Edward Gibbon, *The History of the Decline and Fall of the Roman Empire*, 1st ed., London 1776, vol. I, ch. XVI, p. 633.

2. On Gans as a historian, see Mordecai Breuer, "The Objectives of *Semah David* by David Gans" (in Hebrew), *Ha-Ma'yan*, V, No. 2 (1965); *idem*, "R. David Gans, Author of the Chronicle *Semah David*" (in Hebrew), *Annual of Bar-Ilan University, Studies in Judaica and the Humanities*, XI (1973); Jirina Sedinova, "Non-Jewish Sources in the Chronicle by David Gans, *Tsemah David*," *Judaica Bohemia*, VIII (1972), No. 1; *idem*, "Czech History as Reflected in the Historical Work by David Gans," *ibid.*, No. 2; B. Z. Degani, "The Structure of World History and the Redemption of Israel in R. David Gans' *Zemah David*" (in Hebrew), *Zion*, XLV (1980). The standard text of *Semah David* is that published by Hayim Hominer, Jerusalem 1966. On Azariah de Rossi, see the three essays by Salo W. Baron in his *History and Jewish Historians*, Philadelphia 1964.

3. Thus the Apocrypha are mentioned only in part two (Hominer, *op. cit.*, p. 98)

while the translation of the Septuagint (*ibid.*, pp. 42, 104) and the Maccabean rebellion (*ibid.*, pp. 43–44, 106) are discussed in both parts.

4. Breuer, "The Objectives of *Semah David* by David Gans," *loc. cit.*, pp. 17–18; Hominer, *op. cit.*, p. 102.

5. Monika Richarz, *Der Eintritt der Juden in die akademischen Berufe: Jüdische Studenten und Akademiker in Deutschland 1678–1848*, Tübingen 1974 (Schriftenreihe wissenschaftlicher Abhandlungen des Leo Baeck Instituts 28), pp. 93–94.

6. *Kitvei Rabi Nachman Krochmal*, edited with introduction by Simon Rawidowicz, 2nd ed., London–Waltham, Mass. 1961, p. 144.

7. Marc Bloch, *The Historian's Craft*, New York 1953, pp. 27–29. Yishak Heinemann has trenchantly called the conception of the past on which the midrashic mode of thought was predicated as unhistorical or creative historiography. (Yizhak Heinemann, *Darkhei Ha-Aggadah*, Jerusalem 1954, pp. 1, 13).

8. Hominer, *op. cit.*, pp. 39–40, 102. Gans's basic defense of Jewish chronology (Minyan Yesirah) is not that it is ancient (a tribute to his acute historical sense) but rather that it has been sanctified by tradition. Accordingly, Gans is even prepared to accept the egregious rabbinic calculation of but thirty-four years for the Persian period despite the overwhelming non-Jewish evidence to the contrary.

9. Rawidowicz, *op. cit.*, Korchmal's introduction.

10. Franklin L. Baumer, *Modern European Thought*, New York–London 1977, p. 20.

11. Selig Cassel, "Juden (Geschichte)," *Allgemeine Encylopädie der Wissenschaften und Künste*, zweite section, vol. 27, Leipzig 1850.

12. Moritz Steinschneider, *Die hebräischen Übersetzungen des Mittelalters*, 2 vols., Berlin 1893, I, p. xxii.

13. Isaak M. Jost, *Geschichte der Israeliten*, 9 vols., Berlin 1820–1828, IV, pp. 100–101, 108, 114–115; Anhang, pp. 235–240.

14. Leopold Zunz, *Gesammelte Schriften*, 3 vols., Berlin 1875–1876, I, pp. 12–14.

15. Rawidowicz, *op. cit.*, Sha'ar 11, pp. 113–164; Zacharias Frankel, *Ueber den Einfluss der palästinischen Exegese auf die alexandrische Hermeneutik*, Leipzig 1851, pp. 30, 50n., 232–237.

16. Abraham Geiger, "Ueber selbständige Mischnaherklärung," *Literatur–Blatt: Beilage zum Israeliten des 19. Jahrhunderts*, No. 6, December 14, 1845; *idem, Nachgelassene Schriften*, 5 vols., Berlin 1875–1878, V, pp. 13–14; Shlomo Yehudah Rapoport, *Sefer 'Erekh Milin*, Prague 1852, pp. viii–ix.

17. Henry Malter, *Saadia Gaon: His Life and Works*, reprint, New York 1969, pp. 329–330; Leopold Zunz, "An Essay on the Geographical Literature of the Jews," in *The Itinerary of Benjamin of Tudela*, trans. and edited by A. Asher, 2 vols., London–Berlin 1840, II, pp. 271–274; Salomon Munk, *Le Guide des égarés par Moise ben Maimoun*, 3 vols., Paris 1856–1866; Morris B. Margolies, *Samuel David Luzzatto: Traditionalist Scholar*, New York 1979, pp. 54–55.

18. Leopold Zunz, *Die gottesdienstlichen Vorträge der Juden*, Berlin 1832; Shlomo Yehudah Rapoport, *Toldot Gedolei Yisrael*, 2 vols., reprint, Jerusalem 1969.

19. Jost, I, Anhang, pp. 10–11; II, Anhang, pp. 55–73, 101; III, Anhang, pp. 147–148, 156, 167–170, 185–191. Zacharias Frankel, *Programm zur Eröffnung des jüdisch-theologischen Seminars zu Breslau "Fränkel'sche Stiftung,"* Breslau 1854, pp. 27–42; *Monatsschrift für Geschichte und Wissenschaft des Judentums* (hereafter cited as *MGWJ*), III (1854), pp. 149–150; VII (1858), p. 298; VIII (1859), pp. 241–254; XVI (1867), pp. 241–252, 281–297.

20. The quotation is from Shimeon Brisman, *A History and Guide to Judaic Bibliography*, Cincinnati–New York 1977, p. 4.

21. Moritz Steinschneider, "Jüdische Literatur," *Allgemeine Encyklopädie der Wissenschaften und Künste,* zweite Section, vol. 27. The essay opens with the following inclusive definition: "The literature of the Jew in the broadest sense comprises actually everything which Jews from antiquity to the present have written, irrespective of content, language, and homeland" (p. 357). Why Steinschneider omitted this crucial definition in the English translation of this essay, which he personally revised, is perplexing. (*Jewish Literature,* reprint, New York 1965, p. 1).

22. Gustav Karpeles, *Geschichte der jüdischen Literatur,* 2 vols., Berlin 1886, I, pp. 1–14, II, p. 1138. See also the revealing critique of this new conception of Jewish literature by S. Levy, in *The Jewish Quarterly Review* (original series), XV (1903) and XVI (1904).

23. The quotation is from Carl Diehl, *Americans and German Scholarship 1770–1870,* New Haven–London 1978, p. 43. On the subject of commentary, cf. Simon Rawidowicz, *Studies in Jewish Thought,* Philadelphia 1974, pp. 45–80.

24. On Gans, see Hanns Günther Reissner, *Eduard Gans: Ein Leben im Vormärz,* Tübingen 1965 (Schriftenreihe wissenschaftlicher Abhandlungen des Leo Baeck Instituts 14). In the 1840s Jaffé, a student of Ranke and a promising medievalist, published some 27 medieval Latin documents related to Jewish history. See "Urkunden zur Geschichte der Juden im Mittelalter," *Der Orient,* 1842, pp. 366–368ff.; 1843; 1844.) Frustrated and embittered by career disappointments, he took his own life in 1870.

25. Eduard Gans, *Zeitschrift für die Wissenschaft des Judentums* (hereafter ZWJ), pp. 45–46.

26. Zunz, *Gesammelte Schriften,* I, pp. 5, 32–40, 59, 213–214; II, pp. 265–267; III, p. 1.

27. Friedrich Karl von Savigny, *Vom Beruf unsrer Zeit für Gesetzgebung und Rechtswissenschaft,* 2nd ed., Heidelberg 1828.

28. On the *Culturverein,* see Sinai (Siegfried) Ucko, "Geistesgeschichtliche Grundlagen der Wissenschaft des Judentums," *Wissenschaft des Judentums in deutschen Sprachbereich: Ein Querschnitt.* Mit einer Einführung herausgegeben von Kurt Wilhelm, Tübingen 1967 (Schriftenreihe wissenschaftlicher Abhandlungen des Leo Baeck Instituts 16/I), pp. 315–352. Also Reissner, *op. cit.,* pp. 59–83.

29. JNUL, 4°792, B-6, B-11.

30. Leopold Zunz, *Predigten,* Berlin 1846, pp. vi–vii.

31. JNUL, 4°792, B-1.

32. See the "Drei Reden" of Eduard Gans published by S. Rubaschoff (Shazar), in *Der jüdische Wille,* I (1918–1919), pp. 30–42, 108–121, 193–203. (Hebrew translation in Shneur Z. Shazar, *Orei Dorot,* Jerusalem 1971, pp. 351–384.) Also Immanuel Wolf, "On the Concepts of a Science of Judaism (1822)," trans. by Lionel E. Kochan, in *LBIYB II* (1957), pp. 194–204.

33. ZWJ (reprint, Hildesheim–New York 1976). Wolf, *loc. cit.,* pp. 201–202.

34. Gans, "Drei Reden," *loc. cit.,* p. 41. That conviction may have facilitated Gans's personal decision to convert in 1825. (Reissner, *op. cit.,* pp. 103–113.)

35. Letter to Adolf Strodtmann dated 4th May 1863 in JNUL, 4°792, G-27. Strodtmann's sympathetic chapter on the *Verein,* which he demonstratively entitled the "junge Palästina," in his *H. Heine's Leben und Werke,* 2 vols., Berlin 1867–1879, is still worth reading.

36. Gibbon, *op. cit.,* vol. I, ch. XV, p. 536. On Jost see below, pp. 237–242. Also Baron, *History and Jewish Historians,* pp. 240–262.

37. Jost, III, Anhang, pp. 158–159; VI, pp. 358–359.

38. On Zunz, see Schorsch, *loc. cit.* Also Fritz Bamberger, "Zunz's Conception

of History," *Proceedings of the American Academy for Jewish Research* (hereafter *PAAJR*), XI (1941); Luitpold Wallach, *Liberty and Letters: The Thoughts of Leopold Zunz*, London 1959 (Publication of the Leo Baeck Institute); Samuel S. Cohen, "Zunz and Reform Judaism," *Hebrew Union College Annual* (hereafter cited *HUCA*), XXI (1960); Nahum N. Glatzer, *Leopold Zunz: Jude—Deutscher—Europäer*, Tübingen 1964 (Schriftenreihe wissenschaftlicher Abhandlungen des Leo Baeck Instituts 11), pp. 3–72; and Michael A. Meyer, *The Origins of the Modern Jew*, Detroit 1967, pp. 144–182.

39. This was true as well for R. Natan ben Yehiel (Rapoport, I, pp. 10, 31–33) and R. El'azar Ha-Qalir (*ibid.*, pp. 210–211). On Rapoport, see Isaac Barzilay, *Shlomo Yehudah Rapoport and his Contemporaries*, Israel 1969, as well as Gerson D. Cohen, "The Reconstruction of Gaonic History," in Jacob Mann (ed.), *Texts and Studies*, 2 vols., reprint New York 1972, I, pp. xiii–xvii.

40. Among the best treatments are Ludwig Geiger (ed.), *Abraham Geiger: Leben und Lebenswerk*, Berlin 1910; Felix Perles, *Jüdische Skizzen*, 2nd ed., Leipzig 1920, pp. 24–41; Max Wiener, *Abraham Geiger and Liberal Judaism*, Philadelphia 1962, pp. 3–80; Hans Liebeschütz, *Das Judentum im deutschen Geschichtsbild von Hegel bis Max Weber*, Tübingen 1967 (Schriftenreihe wissenschaftlicher Abhandlungen des Leo Baeck Instituts 17), pp. 113–132; and Michael A. Meyer, "Jewish Religious Reform and Wissenschaft des Judentums: The Positions of Zunz, Geiger and Frankel," in *LBIYB XVI* (1971), pp. 19–41.

41. Abraham Geiger, *Was hat Mohammed aus dem Judenthume aufgenommen?* Bonn 1833; English trans., *Judaism and Islam*, prolegomenon by Moshe Pearlman, New York 1970.

42. *WZJT*, 6 vols. (1835–1847). Geiger's fascinating correspondence with Derenbourg (*Allgemeine Zeitung des Judentums*, 1896, *passim*, and in Wiener, *op. cit.*, pp. 83ff.) richly document his period of *Sturm und Drang*.

43. Abraham Geiger, "Das Verhältniss des natürlichen Schriftsinnes zur thalmudischen Schriftdeutung," *WZJT*, V (1844). Geiger's indictment of rabbinic law as "the product of an extremely muddled exegetical sense" (p. 81) jarred his contemporaries and formulated the scholarly agenda right down to Heinemann's *Darkhei Ha-Aggada*, pp. 1–14, 198n. Michael Creizenach, *Schulchan Aruch*, 4 vols., Frankfurt am Main 1833–1840. Samson Raphael Hirsch, *Horeb*, trans. by I. Grunfeld, 2 vols., London 1962.

44. Archives of the Jewish Theological Seminary of America, Steinschneider collection, Geiger (letters dated 23rd November 1854, 18th December 1854, 18th March 1855).

45. Abraham Geiger, *Urschrift und Uebersetzungen der Bibel*, 2nd ed., Frankfurt am Main 1928, esp. Book II. See Daniel R. Schwartz, "History and Historiography: 'A Kingdom of Priests' as a Pharisaic Slogan" (in Hebrew), *Zion*, XLV (1980), pp. 111–116. On the contemporary political and academic influences on Geiger's treatment of the Pharisaic–Sadducean conflict, see Liebeschütz, *op. cit.*, pp. 123–125.

46. Abraham Geiger, *Das Judentum und seine Geschichte*, 3 vols., Breslau 1865–1871.

47. See below, pp. 266–286.

48. *Kerem Hemed*, III (1838), pp. 61–76. Geiger had articulated his view in *WZJT*, II (1836), pp. 475–476, whereas Luzzatto had already adumbrated his stance in 1825 in his study of Targum Onkelos. (*Ohev Ger*, 2nd ed., Cracow 1895, introd., pp. vi–vii.) On Luzzatto, see the recent biography by Margolies.

49. Barzilay, *op. cit.*, pp. 146–147; Shimon Bernfeld, *Toldot Shir*, Berlin 1899, pp. 78–79; *WZJT*, IV (1839), pp. 473–475.

50. *Allgemeine Zeitung des Judentums*, 1895, pp. 236–237.

51. [S. Rapoport], *Tokhahat Megullah*, Frankfurt am Main 1845. On the genesis and German translation of this pamphlet, see the correspondence with Raphael Kirchheim published by Dinaburg in *Kiryat Sefer*, III (1926/1927), pp. 222–235, 309.

52. Michael Sachs, *Die religiöse Poesie der Juden in Spanien*, Berlin 1845. Shimon Bernfeld, *Michael Sachs* (in Hebrew), Berlin 1900.

53. JNUL, 4°792, G-21.

54. *Iggrot Shadal*, ed. by Eisig Gräber, 9 vols. in 2, reprint, Jerusalem 1967, pp. 766–767, 778–781.

55. Sachs, *op. cit.*, pp. 159ff. Cf. Heinemann, *op. cit.*, pp. 1–4.

56. H. S. Hirschfeld, *Der Geist der talmudischen Auslegung der Bible: Halachische Exegese*, Berlin 1840; *idem*, *Der Geist der ersten Schriftauslegungen: Die hagadische Exegese*, Berlin 1847. On him, see Richarz, *op. cit.*, p. 99n; *Der Orient*, 1841, pp. 1–2; and the charming description by his Christian physician and friend published by Ulla Wolff-Frank, *Jahrbuch für jüdische Geschichte und Literatur*, XXII (1919), pp. 132–158.

57. See his essay "Die Rabbinerversammlung, wie sie sein sollte," in Frankel's *ZRIJ*, III (1846).

58. *Literaturblatt des Orients*, 1841, cols. 609–616, 625–631; *WZJT*, V (1844), pp. 53–55.

59. Eduard Gans, "Die Grundzüge des mosaisch-talmudischen Erbrechts," *ZWJ*.

60. David Cassel, *Die Cultusfrage in der jüdischen Gemeinde von Berlin*, Berlin 1856, p. 46.

61. See the review in *Literaturblatt des Orients*, 1843, cols. 371–376.

62. Erich Bischoff, *Kritische Geschichte der Thalmud-Uebersetzungen*, Frankfurt am Main 1899, pp. 61–62.

63. *TZW*, 1847, p. 30; Hirsch B. Fassel, *Die mosaisch-rabbinische Tugend- und Rechtslehre*, Gross-Kanizsa 1862, p. xiii. In the Geiger–Tiktin controversy, Fassel took a moderate position. (*Der Orient*, 1843, Nos. 5–8.) See also Hirsch B. Fassel, *Das mosaisch-rabbinische Strafgesetz*, Gross-Kanizsa 1870, Vorwort.

64. Hirsch B. Fassel, *Das mosaisch-rabbinische Civilrecht*, 2 vols., Wien–Gross Kanischa 1852–1854. The quotation is from volume II, pp. 7–8.

65. Zacharias Frankel, *Die Eidesleistung der Juden*, Dresden–Leipzig 1840; *idem*, *Der gerichtliche Beweis*, Berlin 1846; *idem*, *Grundlinien des mosaisch-talmudischen Eherechts*, Leipzig 1860. See also Frankel, "Mosaisches Recht und Hindurecht," *MGWJ*, IX (1860). On Frankel, see Shaul Pinchas Rabinowitz, *R. Zecharia Frankel*, Warsaw 1898 (in Hebrew), and below, pp. 255–265.

66. *ZRIJ*, 3 vols. (1844–1846).

67. See below, pp. 260–261.

68. Zacharias Frankel, *Vorstudien zu der Septuaginta*, Leipzig 1841, p. xii; *idem*, *Der gerichtliche Beweis*, pp. 99–100. Schorsch, "Zacharias Frankel," below, p. 267.

69. Hirsch Grätz, *Gnosticismus und Judenthum*, Krotoschin 1846. Hirschfeld, *ZRIJ*, III (1846), pp. 317–320, 352–360.

70. Below, pp. 280–282. For bibliography on Graetz, see Schorsch, "Ideology and History," pp. 319–320.

71. Below, pp. 282–286.

72. See, for example, David Cassel, *ZRIJ*, III (1846), pp. 19–21; Z. Frankel, *MGWJ*, I (1852), pp. 203–207, 403–409; *MGWJ*, III (1854), pp. 5–9; L. Zunz, *Die synagogale Poesie des Mittelalters*, Berlin 1855, pp. 9ff.; M. Steinschneider, *Jahresberichte der Geschichtswissenschaft*, I (1878), pp. 38–39, and *Jewish Quarterly Review* (original series), XV (1903), pp. 302–311; A. Geiger, *Nachgelassene Schriften*, II, pp. 35–43.

73. Graetz, *MGWJ*, I (1852), p. 158. See also his *Geschichte der Juden*, III, 1st ed., p. 3.

74. Zunz, *WZJT*, IV (1844), pp. 35–36. See also Zunz in A. Asher, *op. cit.*, II, pp. 313–314.

75. Franz Delitzsch, *Zur Geschichte der jüdischen Poesie*, Leipzig 1836, pp. 124–125.

76. *Allgemeine Zeitung des Judentums*, 1873, pp. 139–141, 144–146; 1905, pp. 224–226.

77. Jacob Grimm and Wilhelm Grimm, *Deutsches Wörterbuch*, XVII, Leipzig 1889, col. 1721.

78. *Der Orient*, 1843, pp. 465–471, 491–494, 500–504. On Monasch see Peter Fraenkel, "The Memoirs of B. L. Monasch of Krotoschin," in *LBIYB XXIV* (1979), pp. 195–223.

79. Archives of the Jewish Theological Seminary of America, Steinschneider collection, David Cassel. *Der Orient*, 1843, pp. 491–492.

80. [David Cassel], *Plan der Real-Encyclopädie des Judenthums*, Krotoschin 1844, p. 22.

81. Leopold Zunz, *Zur Geschichte und Literatur*, Berlin 1845, pp. 1–21.

82. Zunz, *Gesammelte Schriften*, II, 172–203.

83. Glatzer, *Leopold Zunz*, p. 364.

84. Zunz, *Die gottesdienstlichen Vorträge*, p. 454. The trilogy consisted of *Die synagogale Poesi*; *Der Ritus des synagogalen Gottesdienstes*, Berlin 1859; and *Literaturgeschichte der synagogalen Poesie*, Berlin 1865.

85. This is particularly true of *Der Ritus*.

86. Abraham Berliner, *Aus dem inneren Leben der deutschen Juden im Mittelalter*, Berlin 1871; Meir Wiener, *Regesten zur Geschichte der Juden in Deutschland während des Mittelalters*, Hannover 1862; Otto Stobbe, *Die Juden in Deutschland während des Mittelalters*, Braunschweig 1866. On the relationship between Stobbe and Graetz, see Reuven Michael (ed.), *Heinrich Graetz: Tagebuch und Briefe*, Tübingen 1977 (Schriftenreihe wissenschaftlicher Abhandlungen des Leo Baeck Instituts 34), p. 407.

87. On Güdemann, see Ismar Schorsch, "Moritz Güdemann. Rabbi, Historian and Apologist," in *LBIYB XI* (1966), pp. 42–66.

88. *Hamazkir-Hebräische Bibliographie*. See Brisman, *op. cit.*, pp. 139–143. On Steinschneider, see Alexander Marx, *Essays in Jewish Bibliography*, Philadelphia 1947; Paul Oskar Kristeller, *PAAJR*, XXVII (1958); Franz Rosenthal, *ibid.*; Baron, *History and Jewish Historians*.

89. N. M. Gelber, *Zur Vorgeschichte des Zionismus*, Wien 1927, pp. 202–212. See also M. S. Charbonah (Steinschneider), *Herev be-Zion oder Briefe eines jüdischen Gelehrten und Rabbinen über das Werk Horev*, Leipzig 1839; M. Steinschneider, *Manna*, Berlin 1847.

90. *Hebräische Bibliographie*, II (1859), p. 100.

91. Steinschneider, *Die hebräischen Uebersetzungen*, I, p. xxiv. Also *Hebräische Bibliographie*, XVII (1877), p. 121.

92. Steinschneider, *Die hebräischen Uebersetzungen*, I, p. xxiii, George Alexander Kohut, "The Steinschneider Letters and Some Reminiscences," *Studies in Jewish Bibliography in Memory of A. S. Freidus*, New York 1929, p. 115 n.89.

93. Alexander Marx, "Steinschneideriana II," *Jewish Studies in Memory of George A. Kohut*, New York 1935, pp. 520–521.

94. "Lipman Zunz und seine Verehrer," *Mittheilung von Paul de Lagarde*, 4 vols., Göttingen 1884–1891, II, pp. 108–162.

95. Kristeller, *loc. cit.*, *pp. 62–64.*

96. ZRIJ, III (1846), p. 466; and *Hebräische Bibliographie*, V (1862), p. 118. For adumbrations of this periodization, see *ZRIJ*, II (1845),pp. 388–389; III (1846), pp. 409–410.

97. Steinschneider, "Jüdische Literatur," *Allgemeine Encyklopädie*, pp. 358, 360, 384, 386, 393–394, 448.

98. *Ibid.*, pp. 453, 455–457, 460–467.

99. Steinschneider, *Die arabische Literatur der Juden*, Frankfurt am Main 1902, pp. vii–viii; Luzzatto, *Iggrot*, p. 1031. Julius Goebel, *Goethes Faust: Erster Teil*, 2nd rev. ed., New York 1946, p. 27 (Du gleichst dem Geist, den du begreifst . . .)."

100. Brisman, *op. cit.*, pp. 38–42, 48–49.

Breakthrough into the Past: The *Verein für Cultur und Wissenschaft der Juden*

The city of Berlin is the birthplace of modern Jewish scholar-ship. Toward the end of the second decade of the nineteenth century, in the shadow of its fledgling university, a gifted and alienated coterie of young Jewish intellec-tuals assembled to revamp Judaism for a drastically altered and still unsettled so-cial context. The legacy of their assault was a new way of thinking about Judaism, enshrined in the name coined by them: *Wissenschaft des Judentums*.

The events of the preceding two decades had been as momentous for Jews as the Germans. Napoleon's presence on German soil had not only redrawn the checkered map of Central Europe but had also shaken Jewish life from its medieval moorings. In 1812 a vanquished but revitalized Prussia at long last extended a qualified citizenship to its approximately 32,000 Jewish inhabitants and in the ensuing three years as many as 1,300 Jews fought as volunteers in the Wars of Liberation, with seventy-two combatants earning the Iron Cross.[1] The display of patriotism notwithstanding, the fall of Napoleon unleashed a reaction that quickly imperiled Jewish advances. A renewed alliance between throne and altar and a highly charged romantic nationalism, joined to intone the Christian character of the emerging German state. In 1815 the Congress of Vienna refused to universalize emancipation throughout Germany or even to confirm those Jewish rights that derived from the French occupation, and a crescendo of antisemitic rhetoric even-tually erupted in riots against Jews and their property in the late summer of 1819. Leap-frogging from town to town across southern and western Germany from Würzburg to Hamburg, the disorders correlated to locations where some degree of emancipation had been tendered and reflected broad resentment at the change.[2] On the Jewish side, the prospects for a retraction of emancipation spurred intensive political lobbying and proposals for internal reform.

Amid this foreboding atmosphere, a cluster of seven men gathered in Berlin on 7th November 1819 to found "a society for the improvement of the Jewish condition in the German states" with the hope of meeting weekly for two hours on Sunday mornings.[3] In addition to Isaak Markus Jost and Leopold Zunz, the group included Joseph Hillmar, Joel Abraham List, Isaac Levin Auerbach, Eduard Gans, and Moses Moser. Collectively they were young, with an average age of 30.7 years, only recently settled in Berlin, and barely able to eke out a living. At twenty-two Gans, the only native Berliner, was the youngest, with List at thirty-nine and Hillmar at fifty-one the only members above the age of thirty. In terms of employment, Hillmar and Moser worked as bookkeepers, List and Jost conducted small private schools, and Auerbach served as a preacher in the "German synagogue" of the wealthy and naturalized (in 1809) Jacob Herz Beer, while Zunz was still completing his studies at the university and Gans was about to embark on an academic career. Though at the time Gans was the only member of the group to hold a doctorate, all except Moser, Hillmar and perhaps List had already studied at both a *Gymnasium* and a university. In short, the composition of the society was fairly homogeneous, entirely marginal, and decidedly bookish.[4]

As students they stood at the cutting edge of the emancipation experiment—immersed in the best of German culture, alienated from traditional Judaism, and vulnerable to the counter-attack of the resurgent Right. The antisemitic violence of August and September abruptly reminded them of their vulnerability, plunging them into a flurry of Jewish activity which till then they had generally avoided. Five of the founders, for example, had been among the participants of a scholarly circle of some twenty-three members, predominantly Jewish, that had met over a period of nineteenth months from November 1816 to July 1817 to hear and debate presentations on thirty-one topics, only one of which related directly to a matter of Jewish substance.[5] But the intensifying assault on Jewish aspirations shattered their equanimity. According to Gans's later reconstruction:

In many of the cities of the German fatherland those terrifying scenes had occurred which suggested to some an unforeseen return to the Middle Ages. We came together to help, wherever the need might arise, to consider the means how best to get at deeply rooted faults. Our intention was no more refined than that. At that time we stood at the very beginning of our struggle . . .[6]

Indeed, during the next five years this disaffected band of visionaries struggled manfully to articulate and implement a program for an emancipated Judaism, with little to show in the end. Their unfavorable social status, their fiercely intellectual bent, and their impervious elitism all militated against arousing the confidence of the plutocracy which governed Berlin Jewry. Their meager institutional success is testimony of the failure to persuade the larger community that their individual dilemmas were but the harbinger of a pending collective fate.

Thus the external history of the society is filled with pathos. From the outset it was determined to form a "think-tank" which would "unite the Jewish intelligentsia" with the unsurprising result that membership grew slowly.[7] The Berlin chapter eventually reached a maximum of twenty-five members and a Hamburg chapter founded in 1821 comprised a top figure of twenty-three members. But the totals belie the diminutive proportion of active participants. The nearly weekly meetings of the chapter in Berlin, the only one that really mattered, were rarely attended by more than ten members, often in fact canceled for lack of a quorum, and in recognition of that reality, the chapter decided on 8th September 1822 to reduce the quorum necessary for a meeting from a majority of the members living in Berlin to a figure of five.[8]

The name under which the society would eventually become known, *Der Verein für Cultur und Wissenschaft der Juden,* was not decided upon till 5th July 1821. At first, on 27th May 1821, Gans had boldly suggested "The Maccabees" as the most suitable name for the society, a choice which alluded in allegorical fashion to its goal of revitalization. But the political and military overtones of the allusion were regarded as extraneous to the intent of the society, and Gans's second suggestion was later adopted unanimously as more clearly conveying its purpose and program.[9] The pointed retention of the noun "Jew" in the name of the society, at a time when assimilating Jews were casting about for a less burdened nomenclature, also evinced the temerity and pride of its founders. Nevertheless, when the *Verein* soon after applied for official incorporation to secure its existence and enhance its prestige, the government, increasingly suspicious of all religious reform, misread the world "Cultur" in the name for "Cultus" and expressed its displeasure. Despite prompt clarification from Gans, who had submitted the original petition, and government approval of its instructional program, the *Verein* was denied the advantageous privileges of an incorporated society.[10]

The publication of its statutes at long last in 1822 did little to increase the society's visibility. They did, however, serve to articulate its fervor to lead the Jewish world out of its unbearable isolation. A new age necessitated an internal transformation of Judaism to be effected by enlarging the number of Jews conversant with German culture. Higher education and economic restructuring were to be the bridges across which Jews would gradually integrate into German society. To husband its slim resources and to assure some results, the society announced that it would restrict its own activities to the creation of a scholarly institute, an archive on contemporary Jewry, the production of a broadly conceived intellectual journal, and a tutoring program free of charge to facilitate the entrance of the children of the impecunious into the outside world.[11] The practical program, in other words, carried through in the society's name: the dissemination of German culture and the cultivation of a new type of Jewish learning would help to redefine the place of the Jew in Gentile society.

On 11th March 1821, nine years to the day after Prussia's emancipation edict, Gans finally assumed the presidency and presided over a thirty-month period of frenetic activity. In truth, the precocious, self-confident, and aspiring Gans, endowed with a booming voice and more than a dash of organizing talent, appears to have provided the inspiration and drive for the society from the beginning. The son of a well-to-do Berlin banker and Court Jew who had died in 1813 impoverished and in debt, Gans was a gifted legal historian and enthusiastic Hegelian. His determination to attain an academic appointment had already begun to founder on the opposition of Hegel's academic adversary and the leading advocate of the historical approach to the study of law, Friedrich Karl von Savigny, and on the reluctance of the government to carry out its promise of equal academic opportunity for Jews.[12] In a bitter petition to the government on 3rd May 1821, Gans lamented: "I belong to that unfortunate class of people that is hated because it is uneducated and persecuted because it seeks education."[13] As his personal campaign dragged on, the cause of the *Verein* offered Gans consolation, sublimation, and an instrument of battle.

Gans's three surviving presidential addresses reflect the quickened pace. On 28th October 1821 he could report that during the previous seven-month period the society had met a total of seventeen times and the scholarly institute, comprising many of the same people, had convened twelve times.[14] During the subsequent six months the society held some twenty-five meetings, the scholarly institute an unspecified number, and twelve students had been tutored by nine different members. Plans were also afoot to offer instruction to young Polish Jews coming to Berlin, to assemble a scholarly Jewish library, and to determine on a regular basis which students might be worthy of Jewish financial assistance to study at the university.[15]

The final address of 4th May 1823, which reviewed the activities of the preceding year, reported some forty-two meetings of the society, seventeen sessions of the scholarly institute and tutorials for fourteen students. It also made mention of the appearance of the second number of the institute's scholarly journal, edited by Zunz, printed in quarto size, and bearing the title *Zeitschrift für die Wissenschaft des Judentums*.[16] The first number of the journal had come out in the spring of 1822 in a run of 500 copies at a cost of 124 talers and the third and final number of this first and only volume would appear in the spring of 1823.[17] Given these circumstances, the journal reached relatively few hands. As late as 1839 Zacharias Frankel was to admit to Zunz that despite strenuous effort he had never seen the journal and no one in Dresden, including his good friend Bernhard Beer who possessed a large Jewish library, owned a copy.[18] To inform the scholarly world of the new journal, Zunz sent free copies of the first number to a selection of academics and merited in return at least one noteworthy response from Silvestre de Sacy, the doyen of French orientalists. In his cordial letter of 7th October 1822 de Sacy expressed some doubts as to the feasibility of the new field. The paucity of sources—both Jewish and Gentile—for large periods of Jewish history would constitute a major difficulty and the use of the term "Judaism" suggested to him a temptation to replace facts with theoretical speculation. Prophetically, he added "that Germany was hardly the place where any one will appreciate the usefulness and difficulty of the work to which you are dedicating yourself."[19] On the other hand, Heinrich Heine, who had joined the society on 4th August 1822 and the scholarly institute a few weeks later, was appalled by the literary style and some of the contents of the journal.[20] After reading the third number, he wrote to Zunz sarcastically:

I have studied all kinds of German: Saxon, Swabian, Franconian—but our Journal-German I find the most difficult of all. If I did not happen to know what Ludwig Marcus and Dr. Gans want to say, I would not understand a word of what they have written.[21]

Heine did not fail to note the irony of a society dedicated to infusing Jews with culture which seemed unable to express itself with any degree of stylistic elegance.[22]

Gans had concluded his first presidential address on 28th October 1821 with a rousing call to all the free and idealistic spirits of German Jewry to join the ranks of the society. "I see in the close fraternization of such noble people the approach of the messianic era, of which the Prophets speak, and which only the common decadence of our generation has turned into a fairy-tale."[23] And indeed under Gans's leadership the society set abut to enlarge its membership. Already a few months before, at the end of August, Gans, together with Zunz and Julius Rubo, had journeyed to Hamburg, among other reasons, to assist in the formation of a small chapter there. The composition of the party evoked a memorable specimen of Zunz's flashing wit: "Three doctors tightly packed into a coach about to take a journey, each one bearing a name of four letters, without a single medical doctor among them!"[24] But the humor masked a painful premonition: that it was precisely the Jewish doctors of law and philosophy who would be most adversely affected by the incipient retreat from emancipation. During the next two years, the Berlin chapter affiliated eleven new regular members and twenty-one associated members within and outside Berlin including prominent older activists such as Joseph Perl, Israel Jacobson, Gottlob Euchel, Joseph Wolf, David Fränkel, David Friedländer, and Lazarus Bendavid.[25] But their involvement proved to be either nominal or detrimental. Heine in his aforementioned letter to Zunz astutely dismissed Bendavid's deep foray into biblical criticism in the last number of the journal as vintage 1786, utterly inappropriate for the post-rationalist era.[26]

Yet despite Gans's vigor and imagination, the society was unable to break out of its isolation. The journal failed to mediate its ideology or scholarship to a large audience, expenses ran well ahead of income as the wealthy withheld their backing, and there existed almost no contact with the leadership of the Jewish community of Berlin. If anything, the dissatisfaction of the board with Zunz's performance as *Prediger*, which forced his resignation in September 1822, only deepened its suspicions.[27] As for its part, the society steadfastly refused to compromise its elitism. At a meeting on 23rd February 1823, the membership by a vote of seven to three turned aside the idea of editing a textbook on Judaism for children (a kind of catechism) in an effort to be of some use to a larger constituency, a decision with which Heine, who protested against serving up Judaism in the manner of modern Protestantism, concurred.[28] By 6th June 1823 Gans finally learned of the government's decision—some three-and-a-half years after his initial request for an appointment—to exclude all Jews from teaching and academic posts in contravention of its own edict of 1812 and, instead, to offer him a two-year stipend for retraining.[29] Although as late as 26th November 1823, the society still held its annual public celebration before an audience of invited guests at which Gans, Rubo, and Zunz read learned papers, dissolution was imminent. The last meeting of the society seems to have taken place on 1st February 1824 with an attendance of five members, though without any official decision to disband.[30] On 20th April 1825, before he left Berlin in search of another career which ended with his conversion to Christianity in Paris on 12th December 1825—some six months after Heine, Gans turned over the records of the society to Zunz with a note that implied the omission of any formal interment: "Since I regard the society as being dissolved de facto, I also regard my presidency as ended. If you are of another opinion, you may as the acting president [Zunz had been vice president] assume the reins at your disposal. Be well."[31] The transfer of those precious documents to Zunz ensured their survival and enabled future historians to reconstruct the history and ideology of the *Verein*.

II

Nearly forty years after the collapse of the *Verein für Cultur und Wissenschaft der Juden*, Zunz succeeded in persuading Adolf Strodtmann, Heine's first biographer, that the history of the society deserved serious attention. Its significance was not to be measured in terms of accomplishments but rather with reference to its foresight: ". . . nearly every advance made by Jews in the scholarly, political, and civil arenas as well as the achievements of the Reform movement in matters of school and synagogue have their roots in the activity of that society and a few of its members."[32] That positive assessment along with the documents of the society put at his disposal by Zunz induced Strodtmann to compose a long and sympathetic chapter on the subject, which he pointedly titled "The Young Palestine." The name resonated with associations to the small and loosely knit group of radical political writers of the 1840s known as "The Young Germany," which included Heine, and was meant to conjure up an image of comparable revolutionary idealism.[33] The truth is that the society's importance is a function of intangibles. The strident and abstruse rhetoric of its endless deliberations contained the first full-fledged articulation of the emancipation dilemma—the pursuit of individual integration without the loss of a distinct collective identity. In their search for a solution, "the young Palestinians" fully anticipated many an idea and project to be raised independently later in the century.

What distinguished the *Verein* from the older and far more successful *Gesellschaft der Freunde* (Society of Friends) was its determination to work out a cogent intellectual justification for its two-fold program of integration and apartness. The *Ge-sellschaft der Freunde*, founded in Berlin in 1792 under the leadership of Joseph Mendelssohn, the oldest son of Moses, was essentially a fraternal organization of dissident Jews, at first restricted to gainfully employed bachelors. Eager to soften the heavy hand of Orthodox Jewish leadership, they banded together to support each other, to advance the cause of enlightenment among other Jews, and also to procure from the community the right to request a delay in burial without penalty (which they actually won by 1794).[34] Membership soon comprised the prosperous, the assimilated, and even on occasion the converted.[35] During the first year it rose from 78 to 118 and in 1828 it stood at about 400.[36] Gans, Moser, and Zunz were admitted in January 1820 and Jost probably not long thereafter—an affiliation which endowed them with a measure of social status.[37] As late as 1836 Gans was still apparently a member in good standing.[38] Yet for all its talent, prestige, and longevity, the *besellschaft* never set itself the task to defend its pervasive religious laxness with any kind of ideological vindication.

The eruption of antisemitism had driven the exposed intellectuals of the *Verein* to confront their secular aspirations with their religious loyalties. Could they collectively formulate an idea of Judaism that would resolve their inner torment and keep them from spurning the claims of the past for the promise of the present? They had lost the inner repose and wholeness which came with living in seclusion on the fringes of society, precisely what Heine so admired in the impoverished and uncultured Jews of Prussian Poland he had seen in the summer of 1822, just before he joined his friend Gans in the *Verein*.

Despite the barbarous fur cap that covers his head and the still more barbarous ideas that fill it, I value the Polish Jew much higher than many a German Jew who wears his hat in the latest Simon-Bolivar fashion and has his head filled with quotations from Jean Paul. In rigid seclusion that Polish Jew's character became a homogeneous whole; when breathing a more tolerant air it took on the stamp of liberty. The inner man did not become a composite medley of heterogeneous emotions . . .[39]

As host of the first meeting on 7th November 1819, Joel Abraham List opened the discussion by casting the challenge of the new era in nationalistic terms. In ages past, Jews as a nation had been held together by the force of external circumstances—exclusion from civil society, a solidarity of persecution, and a religion that stressed individual salvation in the afterlife—and not by a compelling inner idea. The force of all three was now being rapidly eroded by the combined onslaught of enlightenment and emancipation. Yet, List contended, those present were deeply conscious of the uniqueness of the Jewish nation, which was not a temporal phenomenon. The passing of outward forms must not obscure the existence of an eternal inner substance. Accordingly, the agenda of this group should be the articulation and dissemination of the character and nobility of that essence. "As Jews our national worth must be our highest good, or it is not worth a penny to bear the name [of Jew]." In terms reminiscent of later secular Zionism, List called on his friends to dedicate themselves to the restoration of Jewish nationhood ... *Volkstümlichkeit*) in all its dignity and to the eradication of a decadent rabbinic Judaism (*(Rabbinismus)*.[40]

In his elaboration of the society's intellectual mission on that occasion, Moser took as his point of departure the dichotomy between European and Jewish culture. Unlike many Jews of his day, Moser rejected out of hand a reconciliation (*Aufhebung*) so complete as to entail conversion. He distinguished between the secular and religious strands of European culture and insisted that Jews had only to embrace the former. "In other words: ideal Judaism must appear to us as completely reconciled with the State, insofar as it is determined by secular culture (*bürgerliche Kultur*), but in total opposition to the dominant Church as such and in reference to its dogmas." The consciousness of a distinctive national essence prompted Moser to fight for the survival of a Judaism to be transformed through a fresh study of its sacred texts. *Wissenschaft* would mediate between the essence of Judaism and its current reality. Regarding the Bible, Moser conjectured that only four types of material would be relevant for the future—the charming historical narratives of Genesis, the sublime specimens of biblical poetry, the lofty set of religious teachings, and even some dated legal practices that are still important "for the preservation of national unity." Regarding the Talmud, Moser likewise inveighed against its destructive influence, though he stopped short of a total renunciation. And lastly, he called for a thorough study of the neglected and error-riddled history of the Jews in the Diaspora.[41]

Gans appears to have first addressed the group formally at its third meeting on 21st November 1819, a date commemorated thereafter as the official founding of the society, on the topic "How Can an Improvement of the Jews Be Conceptualized?"[42] At the outset, he drew a basic distinction between the eras of the Enlightenment and Nationalism, which bespoke an acute awareness of his own age. In the age of reason, to improve the Jews meant to raise them to a universal standard, unrelated to Christianity, that ignored their immediate surroundings and condemned only that which was deemed inferior. By contrast, the framework of the *Verein* is neither rationalism nor ethics but history and therefore quite particularistic. In consequence, its mission is not to improve the Jews but to change them, to bring them into harmony with the values and ideas of the nation in which they live, even to the point of discarding what might be virtuous. Each Jewish community in the Diaspora must be infused with the national sentiments of its neighbors. But Gans immediately added that "out of higher considerations" this did not include their religion. What this conceptualization did imply was a program to transform the Jewish state of mind which viewed everything non-Jewish with alarming suspicion. A product of Jewish political and religious history, that state of mind could be altered only by a radical change in the factors that gave it rise. With the process of political amelioration well under way, Jews must be diverted from trade and directed into wholesome pursuits. Equally urgent was "the demolition of rabbinism and the return to pure Mosaism, which properly understood, does not stand in the way of merging (*Verschmelzung*) with the inhabitants of the country."[43]

Exactly one year later, on the occasion of its first anniversary, Gans gave unabashed expression to the society's sense of elitism and mission.

Representatives of Israel, unelected by the silent voices of the people, but summoned here by virtue of greater intelligence and a deeply felt need and out of an authority that is legitimately yours, fulfill the task you have set for yourselves. . . . No revolution is more difficult than the overturning and recasting of a state of mind. Here no force or movement from outside is effective; a psychic malady requires a psychic remedy. You will bring it about.[44]

The presumption that fuels this rhetorical flourish is a measure of personal desperation. In seeking to remake German Jewry, the members of the society were struggling to fortify their own attenuated and strained links to Judaism.

It is abundantly clear from these early statements that their affirmation of Judaism entailed a large amount of rejection. There could be no continuity without discontinuity. Born in a flurry of anticlericalism, the society envisioned itself as the rallying point for all the laymen, teachers, and preachers across Germany already on the battlefield. When the government misread "Cultus" for "Cultur" in the name of the *Verein*, it committed no error. The society rested on the conviction that social and cultural assimilation dictated religious reform, and some of its members fought simultaneously on both fronts. Zunz was as wedded to the creation of a Western mode of Jewish worship as to a Western mode of Jewish scholarship, and his early career is marked by denunciation of contemporary rabbinism. In a key note toward the end of his essay in 1818 on rabbinic literature, to which we shall soon come, he called for an end to the reign of what he termed "vulgar rabbinism" and especially its sophistic method of studying Talmud.[45]

Coincidental with the founding of the society a year later, he published two impassioned attacks on rabbinism. The first was an anonymous review in a Berlin paper, pulsating with anger and sarcasm, of the set of *responsa* against the "German synagogue" (*Eileh Divrei ha-Brit*) collected by the Hamburg rabbinate. The review attracted wide attention, even catching the eye of Hardenberg, the liberal chancellor of Prussia, and ran to a second printing. In addition to some choice examples of the rabbis' alleged benightedness, Zunz declared his intention to publish a work on the "spirit of the rabbis" in which he would demonstrate "that rabbinism as presently constituted is a decadent institution of ignorance, arrogance and fanaticism, diametrically opposed to the better efforts of some Jews and the humanitarian measures of the government." But at the same time, Zunz insisted on a distinction he would make for a lifetime: that contemporary rabbinism was not to be confused with its talmudic and medieval namesake, but rather should be seen as the nadir of a long decline beginning with the period of the Reformation.[46]

The second attack was published under the name of Levi Lazarus Hellwitz, a teacher in Westphalia, but drafted entirely by Zunz.[47] Far more substantial, systematic, and restrained, it offered a reasoned program for the religious restructuring of German Jewry. The basic argument for dismantling the cumbersome and separatistic structure of much of rabbinic Judaism was the lateness of its origins. In its present form it consisted of the accumulated deposits of countless generations. To avert anarchy but ensure progress, Zunz proposed replicating the process of religious and communal reorganization in France. The Prussian government should convene an assembly (Sanhedrin) of learned and enlightened Jews to undertake a revision of the entire corpus of Jewish law still in effect, which would eventually yield a religious code suitable for an emancipated Jewry. Every post-biblical institution of Jewish life would be subject to the assembly's examination, and the sum total of its work would someday be administered by a new type of religious leadership unrelated to the traditional judicial role.

The rabbi must be a morally good and enlightened man, equipped with courage, determination, and solid learning. He must be entirely familiar with the state of his diocese (Sprengels), enjoy the confidence of his community, and be able to deliver a useful, comprehensible, and stirring public address.[48]

Despite such strong views on Judaism, the society never threw itself openly into the campaign for religious reform. To be sure, its deliberations periodically focused on proposals of a religious nature—to organize the *Prediger* of the various "German synagogues" into a special group, to select a *Prediger* for the "German synagogue" which annually graced the Leipzig fair, or to undertake a new German translation of the Hebrew Bible—but each time the society shied away. One of the consequences of the attempt to incorporate had apparently been a specific warning from the government not to meddle in religious affairs, and the society was not eager to incur any official displeasure. Under these circumstances, the members also refused, in their meeting of 22nd December 1821, to introduce the teaching of Judaism from the perspective of religion into their educational program for adolescents. Still, the discussion is worth examining for the additional light that it throws on their personal views of Judaism.

The proposal itself came from Auerbach, who pleaded that the society must also do its part to stem the widespread defection from Judaism through conversion. The root of the problem, he felt, lay in an abysmal ignorance of Judaism, and hence the society should offer its students some "congenial instruction in the Mosaic religion." Immanuel Wohlwill (Wolf), one of the three Hegelians in the group (Gans and Moser being the others), did not think the suggestion contradicted the original commitment of the society to "teach a pure national Judaism." The hitch was that there was simply no consensus about how best to teach religion. If, indeed, Judaism is a revealed religion which ought to be preserved, then it must be taught and the society could actually assume a pioneering pedagogic role. However, Gans objected strongly. The larger purpose of the *Verein* was to curb the all-inclusiveness of religion in traditional Judaism and to create an independent realm for reason. In this regard, the society was actually "anti-religious." Then too, a special course devoted just to religion was a blatant imitation of Christianity, unknown among the peoples of antiquity. On the basis of the wisdom dispensed by philosophy on such problems as God and immortality, each person should formulate his own subjective religious position.[49]

Zunz spoke twice on the subject and sided with Gans for reasons that had nothing to do with the latter's secularized conception of Judaism. On the contrary, Zunz held the teaching of religion to be so fundamental to the character and life of the child that it transcended the competence of the society. With a perspicacity born of want, Zunz understood the primacy of affective education: the imbuing of a child with love for Judaism can be achieved only at home. At best the society could dispense instruction aimed at the child's intellect, an explanation of the ritual exterior of Judaism. Nearly two years before, Zunz had had occasion to elaborate his thinking when he applied to the Jewish community of Königsberg for a post as its teacher of religion. Zunz argued that at present the teaching of Judaism suffered from the superstitions of the pietists and the sophistry of the skeptics.

Pure religious instruction does not subject children to dry history, silly fairytales or hatred of Christianity. . . . It does not consist of a dreadful memorizing of passages or a hollow defense of mystical superstitions. Rather it seeks to enthuse the spirit of the child for religion with words of inspiration and by even more inspiring example, to give children a staff for the storms of life, to implant in their hearts the gentle virtues of love and thus to endow them with the happiness which the believer in divine providence enjoys.[50]

As the child matures, fortified by such emotional attachment, he can gradually be exposed to the systematic, cognitive study of Judaism—its laws, beliefs, and history. In sum, the essential task of the religious teacher is not to fill the child's head but his heart; not to offer a few weekly hours of religious instruction, but to ensure a lifetime of religious practice.[51] Zunz's vision of Jewish education throbbed with all the passion of a genuine calling, though he failed to receive the position in Königsberg.[52]

The most complete articulation of the society's ideology belongs to Gans. His three aforementioned presidential addresses cohere as a single sustained effort at clarifying its purpose. Redolent with Hegelianism, they define the challenge of the age for Judaism, prescribe a suitable Jewish response, and unveil the means by which to effect it. Gans spoke in a mood of excitement at the momentous change in the status of Prussian Jewry, as a citizen of the Prussian state and a proud and grateful member of the body politic. For Jews a thousand-year period of insecurity and humiliation, of admission through backdoors and confinement to cellars, had been mercifully brought to an end, and the progress of history was irreversible, not subject to the protests and outbursts of Christian adversaries still rooted in the medieval world. Jews did not need to approach their new freedom with all the wariness and trepidation of a long incarcerated prisoner. Citizenship did not require a surrender of deep-seated religious loyalties. Every member of the *Verein* was connected to the Jewish community by ties of birth, family, friendship, education, and, above all, childhood memories. To rupture those ties was not merely an act of ingratitude but of betrayal. The goal of the society had to be to hold aloft the ideal of reconciliation, to think through the relationship of a double set of loyalties.[53]

Toward that end, Gans devoted his second address to an analysis of the present. In the spirit of Hegel, he posits a historical development guided by reason and free of the fortuitous that has at last arrived at an all-encompassing union of many diverse parts, past and present. Historically speaking, the union is a composite of the monotheism of the Orient, the ideals of beauty and freedom of Greece, the Roman concept of statehood, the Christian notion of humanity, medieval feudalism, and modern philosophy, all preserved therein long after their moment of exclusive domination has passed. In terms of the present, each diverse part is complete in itself, but derives significance alone from its integration into the whole. "That is the good fortune and meaning of European man, that within the manifold estates (*Stände*) of civil society he may freely choose his own and that in that choice he can feel all the other estates of society."[54] The strength and power of contemporary Europe is to be found "in the richness and abundant variety of countless particularities and formations (*Besonderheiten und Gestaltungen*), which nevertheless find their unity in the harmony of the whole."[55]

If it is hard to recognize the reality of Restoration Europe in Gans's glowing abstractions, it is possible to catch a glimpse of a social vision both integrationist and pluralistic. The emphasis may have been on unity and conformity, but there is a notion of the right to be different. Without it, Gans and his friends would have converted immediately. When that vision did founder in the face of government retraction and Jewish resistance, Gans was prepared to concede that the vision itself was flawed.[56] In the meantime, he labored to formulate the legitimate parameters of Jewish existence after emancipation.

What the present offered Jewry, according to Gans, was a chance to leave their state of quarantine and to re-enter the civilized world. But at a price: "Where the organism (i.e. the whole) demands a wavy line, there a straight line is an abomination."[57] Concretely that meant the discarding of all otherness and particularity. The protective walls of separation must come down. Only that which is universal in Judaism and serves the whole may retain its distinctive identity, though without any claim to exclusive truth.[58] Nothing impairs the harmony of the social order more than intolerance. The particular must become subordinate to the whole without necessarily disappearing. "Thus neither will the Jews vanish nor Judaism disintegrate, but rather appear submerged in the great movement of the whole while still surviving, as the current survives in the ocean."[59] The mandate of the age was absorption without dissolution.

Gans's third address rightly takes up the instrument by which this transformation of Jewish life is to be wrought. Gans invokes the supreme achievement of his day, the category of consciousness, the embodiment of reason as self-reflection. "The Jewish world must be conceptualized."[60] It must become the object of systematic, critical, and comprehensive reflection. Whatever can no longer be understood, justified, and related to an immutable and unifying core has lost not only the right but also the ability to exist. Continued existence becomes a function of rationality, and in the form of *Wissenschaft*, its purest expression, consciousness must assess the rational content of every aspect of Judaism. With history as the key to meaning, nothing could be more practical than the scholarly enterprise, though for Judaism it did not exist as yet. That was the mission of the society: to create a scholarship free of the limited horizons and prejudgments of traditional rabbinism or Christian humanism, a scholarship grounded in respect for the uniqueness and independence of the phenomenon.[61]

The salient point of these discourses, as Gans reiterates in his peroration, is that the society represents a return to Judaism. It is not to be confused with the enlightened disciples of Mendelssohn who never transcended their unrelieved negativism. As traditional Judaism lost its moorings and inner directedness, they fled headlong into the outside world to pursue their own interests. They died metaphorically like old bachelors, unmourned because unconnected. In contrast, Gans and his circle personify a state of genuine freedom, in which one voluntarily reconnects with his origins. Their goal is to discover a new form of cohesion to replace the spiritual and communal ties of their ancestors.[62]

But not everyone in the *Verein* was brought to his feet cheering by Gans's high-flown rhetoric. No one had deeper reservations about this evaporation of an unbroken historical reality into a Hegelian idea than Heine, whose letters in the weeks before and after Gans's third address on 4th May 1823 simply bristle with sardonic contempt. Not that Heine was then any more religious than Gans. A day before the address, he described his own attachment to Judaism as consisting primarily in a profound antipathy for Christianity. His animus for all positive religions notwithstanding, he respected "the crassest Rabbinism" as an effective polar opposite. Unlike the prevailing sentiment in the society, he valued its tenacity and resilience, its fighting spirit, irrespective of content.[63] In that vein, he had exploded a month earlier in a letter to Wohlwill over the constant blood-letting of Judaism by rationalists "eager to pour that world-wide ocean into a pretty basin of *papier-mâché.*" "We no longer have the strength to wear a beard, to fast, to hate, and to endure out of hate. That is the motive of our Reformation."[64]

Since Heine left Berlin for Lüneburg only a few days after 4th May, it is most likely that he was in attendance when Gans spoke. And his letter of 23rd May 1823 to his dear friend Moser, whom he affectionately regarded as "the epilogue to Nathan the Wise," has all the earmarks of a violent reaction.[65] As so often, Heine ingeniously cast his criticism in the form of an outlandish dream. Taunted by a mob of children, Heine ran fuming into Moser's open arms, only to be greeted with the reassurance that he was merely an idea. Jeers could not harm him. To convince him, Moser seized a volume of Hegel's logic and pointed out a totally confusing passage, while Gans knocked on the window. But Heine became enraged instead and ran around the room screaming, "I am not an idea, and know nothing about any idea, and never even had an idea." Gans kept raising his voice and the diminutive Ludwig Marcus sitting on his shoulders belted out a chorus of quotations.[66]

It is in this state of revulsion that Heine resolved to write an essay for the society's journal on the tragedy of Jewish history (*der grosse Judenschmerz*), a resolve which would eventually yield, piecemeal and truncated, his justly famous *The Rabbi of Bacherach*. In his next letter to Moser, dated 18th June 1823, he made mention of his plan in conjunction with another witty diatribe against the emasculating philosophic Idealism of Gans that turns deadly earnest. "For heaven's sake, don't tell me again that I am only an idea. It makes me raving mad. As far as I am concerned, you can all become ideas; just leave me my beard. Because you and the old Friedländer and Gans have become ideas, you want to seduce me and make me over into an idea."[67]

For all his religious impiety and Judaic ignorance, Heine felt unerringly the travesty of dismantling a venerable and proven religion down to a set of theological maxims. Emancipation on such terms was merely another form of servitude. Gans had fatally chosen to minimize the illiberalism of the Prussian state. Intuitively, Heine grasped hold of the same weapon for battle in the cause of Judaism—the study of history. In a setting of partial emancipation and progressive Westernization, the study of Jewish history could serve to pare down or shore up, to vindicate radical reform or plead for preservation. The inchoate skirmish between Gans and Heine was a harbinger of confrontations to come.

III

There was nothing "academic" about the centrality of *Wissenschaft* and in the program of the society. Its ideology accorded the study of the past a normative role formerly reserved to Jewish law alone. The historian was to replace the rabbi as the expert on Judaism, as the mantle of religious authority passed to the master of a new universe of discourse. For all the urgency and presumption of the impetus, the few lasting scholarly achievements of the society managed to unveil the enormous potential of the discipline.

By the spring of 1820 the society had begun to consider the organizational form of its academic activity, and a year later its scholarly seminar bearing the official name of the *Institut für die Wissenschaft des Judentums* and led by Zunz was fully operative. Membership was by invitation and predicated on participation, with the result that it never rose above fourteen. Only a handful of the members of the society actually belonged to the seminar also, but those few were thus committed to at least one society function a week. In conception the seminar was a collective effort at "doing" Jewish scholarship, obliging each member to offer periodically a paper for discussion. According to the minutes of the seminar preserved by Zunz, some twenty-five papers were presented during the course of the seminar's existence, including six each by Gans and Zunz, five by Moser, three by Marcus, and two by Rubo. A goodly number ended up in the society's journal, for which the seminar was responsible and served as a splendid laboratory. At the last meeting of the seminar on 7th January 1824 with an attendance of three, Zunz read a revised version of his essay on Rashi that had appeared a year before in the journal. Many years later (1846), Zunz added the following poignant codicil to the minutes of the seminar: "After forty-five meetings the seminar was buried by its three founders, its last gasp being Rashi. Since then Gans and Moser have also died. The individuals and their forms disappear, the idea lives on."[68]

The decision to place a new type of Jewish scholarship at the heart of the society's agenda had been made possible by the publication of a revolutionary tract just a year before its founding. Zunz's *Etwas über die rabbinische Literatur* has long been justifiably revered as the cornerstone of the *Wissenschaft* edifice. Without it the *Verein* would have been just another Jewish fraternal or cultural organization; with it the *Verein* became the testing ground for the viability and application of rethinking Judaism historically. In a single majestic sweep, a twenty-three-year-old university student had succeeded in transferring the canons of Western scholarship to the study of Judaism and conceptualizing it afresh.[69] Yet it was not the cognitive anomalies of an outmoded paradigm that brought Zunz to formulate his vision of a new Jewish learning, but rather the challenge of academic antisemitism.

We know from Zunz's cryptic diary that in his first semester at the University of Berlin in the winter of 1815–1816, he dropped a course in ancient history by Friedrich Rühs because "he writes against the Jews."[70] The reference is to Rühs's assault on the basic liberal argument on behalf of Jewish emancipation entitled *Ueber die Ansprüche der Juden an das deutsche Bürgerrecht* (On the Claims of the Jews for German Citizenship), which went through two quick editions in 1815 and 1816. The prestige of a revitalized professoriate lent credence to an inherently important contention: that current Jewish depravity, which no one denied, was the product not of endless Christian abuse but of Judaism itself. Rühs assembled a welter of historical data from pre-Christian times through the Iberian experience down to his own day to demonstrate the unbroken continuity of Jewish traits. Diverse historical settings failed to alter the basic identity of Second Commonwealth, Spanish, Polish, and recently emancipated Jews. Rühs posited three decidedly internal factors that accounted for a national character impervious to outside influence: the supremacy of the rabbinic aristocracy which killed any prospect for religious development; a sense of chosenness that inculcated unbridled national arrogance; and a theologically rooted abhorrence of physical labor that gave rise to a parasitic economic profile. The conclusion followed incontrovertibly that as long as Jews adhered to Judaism they could not conceivably qualify for German citizenship. Their obnoxious religion, and not their allegedly dolorous history, condemned them to be an economic blight and an alien national body.[71] Whatever else this attack may have signified, it served to rivet attention once again on the need to study Judaism.

An unpublished manuscript among Zunz's papers confirms the young student's agitation over Rühs's entry into the emancipation debate. Dated 31st March 1816 and signed "Maskil," the eight-page manuscript is written in Zunz's tell-tale minuscule script and bears the title "To the Wise Counsellor of the Wise Directors of Germany" along with the bracketed subtitle "Against Rühs." The essay addresses Rühs directly and throughout in the familiar style and abounds with apparent praise and admiration for his singular achievement in having brought the classical period of the eighteenth century to an end.

Where can I find the words to portray properly my rapture over your refutation of Jewish claims? Only some future age, at a more advanced stage of enlightenment than we obtuse contemporaries, will immortalize you in its chronicles in recognition of your services. It is a pity that Lessing and Mendelssohn did not live to witness their defeat.[72]

These opening lines are sufficient to convey the real intent: to disarm through irony. To the very end Zunz sustains the pose of a fulsome, if clever, expositor eager to amplify and confirm the vilifications of his chosen text. Adroitly he interlaced his own flowing discourse with countless quotations from Rühs, always taking the trouble to underline the words and note the page references in the margin. The resulting mosaic pulsates with wit and consternation.

Yet Zunz withheld his outburst from publication for good reason, and not merely because he was a vulnerable university student. The essay was susceptible to easy misinterpretation. Irony did not always disguise an underlying sympathy for much of Rühs's criticism of Judaism and the distance between agreement and disagreement often seemed to blur into consent. Zunz yearned "to become an instrument to arouse the lost tribe of Israel," as he swore to Rühs.[73] But confused and disgruntled, he had not yet found his true voice. Dissembling was an ineffectual retort, perhaps no more than a desperate substitute for the inability to articulate a conception of Judaism distinct from those espoused by archaic rabbinists, Jewish deists, and the new romantic German nationalists.

It was in this agitated state of mind that Zunz composed his famous essay on rabbinic literature. Completed in December of 1817, it was not an expression of cognitive dissonance brought on by the first flush of enthusiasm for university studies but an inspired response to Rühs. Zunz had seized the weapon of *Wissenschaft* and turned it on his academic adversary. If the heart of the emancipation matter was the nature of Judaism, then the key to its proper evaluation lay in subjecting it to the same critical scholarship being applied in the university to other bodies of knowledge. Though Rühs had raised the right issue, he had simply recycled old stereotypes. Enlightened political action could flow only from informed understanding. Hasty and ill-conceived legislation merely entrenched archaic practices and institutions.

Thus to be able to recognize and separate what is old and useful, what is outmoded and detrimental, what is new and desirable, we must sensibly approach the study of a people and its history, both political and spiritual. But this is precisely what creates the greatest obstacle, that the matter of the Jews is handled like its literature. People tackle both with biased passion, assessing them either too low or too high.[74]

Zunz lamented the fact that in an age when scholarship deemed no language or culture unworthy of serious study, the content of rabbinic literature remained singularly ignored. Thus by continuing to brood on the import of Rühs's challenge, Zunz eventually forged a weapon whose immense power and utility transcended and concealed the circumstances of its birth.[75]

The emancipation debate also determined the parameters of the discipline as set down by Zunz in 1818. What was conspicuously omitted was any discussion of biblical literature, although in his initial response to Rühs he had seen fit to touch upon this realm of Jewish creativity as well. But Zunz knew that Judaism had been decisively reshaped by its long rabbinic phase and that much of the opposition to the admission of its adherents into civil society stemmed from its rabbinic character. Moreover, the non-Jewish world was far more in the dark about rabbinic literature than its biblical foundation. Hence the practical urgency for a "scientific" study, reinforced by internal Jewish developments. Zunz was convinced at the time that integration spelled the end of Judaism's rabbinic phase. Traditional institutions of higher Jewish learning were fast disappearing from the landscape of Central Europe, German Jews were appropriating the language and culture of their society, and Hebrew as a literary idiom was about to vanish. Passing from the scene, rabbinic culture in all its amplitude deserved to be given a scholarly assessment, a process that had to begin as long as its literary products and aficionados were still accessible.[76]

The enduring value of Zunz's departure was his dramatic enlargement of what comprised the field of rabbinic literature and how it ought to be studied. Properly understood, it was not restricted to works by rabbis or on rabbinics. Zunz bristled at the theological overtones of the very term "rabbinic literature," coined and defined by seventeenth-century Christian savants of Judaism, and much preferred the more neutral and comprehensive rubric "neo-Hebraic" or "Jewish literature."[77] Beyond nomenclature, Zunz exhibited with stunning detail a vast expanse of literature written in Hebrew by literate laymen as well as practicing rabbis that matched all the literary genres of a living people. And in accord with the study of classical literature, philology alone, in this case a grammatical and historical command of Hebrew and its cognates, had the power "to divest the past of its veil."[78] No less important than analytic dissection was an eye for synthesis, a sense for how the minutiae of any given text might relate to all of Jewish literature and, indeed, to the common spiritual legacy of all mankind. Above the numerous workshops of the scholarly craft, Zunz assigned, in the spirit of German Idealism, pride of place to philosophy—"the most exalted guide . . . in recognizing and disseminating the intellectual greatness of a people. In this spirit, every historical fact becomes . . . a contribution to the understanding of man, the noblest purpose of all research."[79]

In the span of a single essay of unbelievable richness, compression, and fervor, Zunz had enlisted scholarship in the service of progress. A new conception of Judaism as a religious civilization would lead to religious reform within and political rehabilitation without. As the revival of classical learning in the Renaissance had paved the way for the Reformation, so a new mode of Jewish scholarship would secure emancipation for a transformed Judaism.[80] Toward that end, Zunz invited others to join him in the publication of critical editions of worthy specimens of rabbinic culture. His own choice of a Spanish philosophic text from the end of the thirteenth century conveyed unmistakably the impression that such were not to be found in the world of medieval Ashkenaz. More broadly still, Zunz's essay implied a direct threat to the rabbinic leadership of his own age. Knowledge was power and henceforth the most reliable spokesman for Judaism was no longer the traditional rabbi, who at best presided over a single literary expression of rabbinic culture, but the modern scholar with his encompassing knowledge and critical method. By mediating the past, he offered a new source of direction for the present.[81]

If then the genesis of Zunz's essay may be attributed to Rühs, its transcendence comes from his teacher Friedrich A. Wolf, of Homeric fame. At the university Zunz attended four of his courses on the legacy of Greece and Rome and confided to his diary that "Wolf attracts me." In fact, Zunz seems to have composed his rebuttal during the very semester he heard Wolf discourse on the *Encylopaedia der Altertumswissenschaft*.[82] A decade earlier, after a teaching career of nearly a quarter of a century, Wolf had attempted in a single essay to provide a conceptual and methodological overview of classical studies, which provided Zunz with a model for the definition of an untidy academic discipline. For all their specific differences, Wolf's "Description of the Academic Study of Antiquity" (*Darstellung der Altertumswissenschaft*) and Zunz's "On Rabbinic Literature" faced the same problem—to reconceptualize a well-mined field from a fresh vantage point. Nothing signifies discontinuity more vividly than a new nomenclature, and Wolf insisted on replacing the sundry names in use for the field of classical studies with the term "Altertumswissenschaft," with "antiquity" in his judgment reserved exclusively for the Greeks and Romans, who alone of all ancient peoples had risen to the level of culture.[83] While Zunz only half-heartedly proposed a name change for "rabbinic literature" in 1817, a few years later in the context of the *Verein* he unfurled his chosen terminology of *Wissenschaft des Judentums* in the name of the scholarly institute and its journal. In both substance and structure, the term is analogous to

Wolf's own designation, whose genitive form was occasionally reversed into "Wissenschaft des Alterums."[84] Similarly in the deliberations of the institute, one did not hesitate to speak of "Judentumswissenschaft."[85]

The dimensions of the now full-blown field of Jewish studies were depicted for the first time by Immanuel Wohlwill (Wolf) in his seminal introductory essay to the journal. Wohlwill had joined the *Verein* in June 1820 while an impoverished student at the university, where Hegel agreed to admit him to his lectures without the requisite fees, provided he pay him or his heirs within five years. The gesture of respect for his talents furnished the society with another convinced Hegelian, at least until January 1823 when he moved on to Hamburg to begin a long teaching career at its Jewish Free School.[86]

Wohlwill's essay is a two-tiered statement comprising an *a priori* theory of Jewish history and a program of empirical Jewish studies. On the level of speculation, he employs German Idealism to posit an essence of Judaism, a religious idea that powers and unites Jewish civilization through the millennia. The idea, which is a gift of revelation, is the recognition of a single, unifying divine presence amid the diversity of existence and is best expressed in the four-lettered Hebrew name of God. The first benefit yielded by this essence is that it grounds the sense of continuity in Jewish history in an identifiable, ever-present core idea. The second is that everything else in Judaism is of limited duration, at best a temporary measure necessitated by historical circumstances. The third benefit is the grant of universal significance to Judaism, even after Christianity has become a vehicle for the dissemination of the unity idea. In embryonic form, Wohlwill had combined here for the first time the main ingredients of what would soon coalesce into a full-fledged reform theory of Jewish history. Diaspora-oriented, Wohlwill identified with the Jews who refused to return to Palestine after Cyrus, transvalued Jewish statehood and talmudic law into prophylactic institutions, reduced medieval Messianism to a function of persecution, embraced the idea of a Jewish mission, and held up Spinoza as a supreme expositor of Judaism.

The theory, of course, was an affront to the research imperative. Scholarship had not yet begun to generate the empirical evidence to support such metahistorical claims, if it ever could. The urgency of the moment had prompted Wohlwill and his comrades to put the proverbial cart before the horse, to venture in miniature a phenomenology of the Jewish spirit prematurely. Nevertheless, the horse itself was a healthy animal. Remarkably, Wohlwill formulated a balanced and coherent research program far more comprehensive than what Zunz had proposed earlier. While the object remained Judaism as a religious civilization, its study was to reach back to the biblical period and forward to the present. A philological analysis of the literary texts of each period, now demarcated by the changes in the form of Judaism's central idea, would yield the evidence for a broad external (relating to the religious, political, and literary) and internal (relating to the unfolding of its inner idea) history of Judaism. Despite a nod to the non-partisanship of modern scholarship, Wohlwill intoned the relevance of *Wissenschaft des Judentums*, to the state as well as to contemporary Judaism, and closed with a special plea to Jews to enter its ranks.[87]

The tension between method and relevance is thus a consequence of the ongoing character of Judaism. Moreover, as conceived by the society, Jewish scholarship was not to ignore the present state of the Jews. According to Wohlwill, the study of contemporary Jewry in the various lands of its dispersion was fully as important as the study of Jewish history. It was precisely this interconnectedness between past and present which informed Zunz's own methodological contribution to the journal. As the last substantive essay therein, his "Grundlinien zu einer künftigen Statistik der Juden" (Guidelines to a Future Statistical Study of the Jews) bequeathed a conception of the discipline so all-encompassing that it was not even approximated until the twentieth century.[88]

The term "statistics" derived from the eighteenth-century German version of political science and connoted an all-inclusive description of a country in its present state. Applied to the past by the Göttingen universal historian August Ludwig von Schlözer, it meant halting the historical continuum at a given point to depict a single cross-section. If history was the study of man along a dynamic vertical axis, then "statistics" (in a sociological sense) was the horizontal study of a society at a static moment.[89] In the words of Zunz, who proposed to transfer the distinction to Jewish studies: "A statistical study of a human group deals with its existence in a single moment, an existence which is the consequence of a preceding history . . . and conversely history is the result of an unending series of statistics."[90] Zunz suggested treating Judaism as a construct equivalent to the State and subjecting it to a series of exhaustive sociological studies along the course of its historical trek. Each "statistical" exposure was to be built stereoscopically from both Jewish and non-Jewish sources and include some fourteen different foci. The cumulative result would be a profound understanding of contemporary Jewry "which should be the culmination of this immense statistical edifice."[91] In short, not sterile antiquarian interests but deep engagement in the present motivated the projection of this awesome vision of what today we would call "total history."

An earlier essay by Zunz in the journal acquires added significance when read from the perspective of this "statistical" program. His effort to collect and identify Iberian place names mentioned in some twenty-five medieval Hebrew sources corresponded to one of the topics to be covered by any static depiction of a specific Jewish community. Zunz recognized that Judaism exhibited distinctive features in every regional setting and that initially any sociological sounding should be restricted to a single regional community. One of the first steps toward such a study was to assemble the names of all localities in which Jews had resided.[92] From Wolf, Zunz had learned that geography is an indispensable part of history.

Nothing is more necessary than first to familiarize yourself with the area in which the known peoples of antiquity lived and traded, in order to appreciate the variety of conditions over time which marked their places of settlement. Much that is distinctive to the nature of man in antiquity becomes explicable thereby.[93]

The attention to geographical detail by Zunz epitomized the centrality of context for the proper understanding of historical phenomenon.[94]

But traces of present-mindedness seeped even into a subject as concrete as Spanish toponyms in Hebrew literature. Cognizant of his pioneering effort, Zunz affixed a theoretical introduction to his essay. He lists therein the larger geographical blocs in which Jews were to be found, including America and Australia, classifies the types of Jewish sources that might contain geographical information, and reflects on the methods of extracting it. He also issues a sterling declaration on the extraordinary combination of attributes necessary for Jewish scholarship. Its practitioner must embody

not only objectivity and a disregard for acquired and fashionable prejudices, not only a majestic view capable of obliterating solitary, incidental, and momentary [phenomena], not only a favorable disposition toward that which has proven itself true by surviving all the arenas of world history, but also that many-sided knowledge that attunes the eye to the developmental path of Judaism—namely, a command of detail and a firm grasp of the whole along with great erudition in Jewish literature.[95]

Yet the ethos patently does not extend to a study of his own immediate cultural legacy. Quite oblivious to his own standards, Zunz soon slips into a jarring invocation of the Spanish bias. He has chosen to begin his excavations on Spanish soil, because its literary treasures are unpublished and unknown in the Ashkenazic world. While "every piece of trash from the Polish period is printed . . . good Spanish works gather mold in libraries, without anyone interested in redeeming them."[96] For all its dry technicality, Zunz's essay shares the prevailing zeal to expose Ashkenazic Jewry to a nobler brand of Judaism.

In this regard, Zunz's celebrated biography of Rashi, the acme of early medieval Ashkenazic Judaism, bespoke an honest awareness of precisely this shortcoming.[97] By abandoning the tactic of whipping contemporary rabbinism with the rod of Spanish rationalism, Zunz achieved a triumph of the scholarly ethos. The essay marks the first time since the *Haskalah* began to cultivate the genre of didactic biography that an Ashkenazic Jew, other than Mendelssohn, was deemed fit for biographical treatment.[98] As Zunz was later to explain, what prompted his choice was the realization that the aversion of the *Maskilim* simply confirmed the prejudice of Christian scholars. If the written record of mankind all too often bore the scars of human passion, then modern scholarship entailed an act of self-transcendence. But the *Maskilim* were ensnared by the vices of the Enlightenment; they had little stomach for a Jewish culture totally dominated by religion. To the extent that Jews had been excluded from Christian society, Judaism came to embrace all forms of Jewish self-expression. The greater openness of Moslem Spain allowed for the common cultivation of a religiously neutral cultural legacy.[99] In protesting the Sephardic bias, Zunz mustered the courage to face the centrality of religion in the Jewish historical experience and the empathy to treat it fairly.

To focus on Rashi permitted Zunz also to demonstrate the difference between fact and fiction. As the exegete par excellence, Rashi was not exactly a peripheral figure to Jewish consciousness. But indifference to historical thinking had obscured him behind a veil of legend. According to Zunz, the last two hundred years in particular had created a bogus Rashi, bereft of spirit and laden with nonsense. Even such elementary facts as the date and place of his birth or his actual name had been subject to corruption. To assault that citadel of ignorance, Zunz drew all his information about Rashi's life, intellectual world, linguistic competence, religious views, and literary works only from sources written by Rashi himself. He showed that Rashi was wholly a product of the rabbinic culture of his time, that he was part of a living exegetical tradition, that in both sets of commentaries (biblical and talmudic) he aspired to elucidate the plain meaning of the text, "to serve as Aaron for a mute Moses," and that he often revised his work.[100] And not to lose sight of the larger scholarly landscape, Zunz presciently pointed out the inestimable value of Rashi's commentaries for a host of other worthy topics. The practical import of Zunz's painstaking research echoed audibly throughout: contemporary rabbinism had betrayed its own noble heritage.[101] Scholarly integrity had induced him to switch tactics, but the adversary remained the same.

No less significant for the introduction of historical thinking into Judaism were the three major contributions by Gans to the journal.[102] His role in the *Verein* was by no means restricted to the heady realm of ideology. If Zunz unearthed the wealth and diversity of Hebrew sources available for the recovery of the Jewish past, Gans revealed just how vital was the consultation of non-Jewish sources, and in tandem the two of them imbued the journal with a solid balance of alternative modes of Jewish scholarship. Incomparably less learned in Jewish sources than Zunz, though not Hebraically incompetent, Gans was far more attracted by the intersection of Jewish and general history.[103] The history of Judaism could no longer be studied apart from its Gentile environment or in ignorance of its legal status. Thus he opened his first essay, in consonance with the emancipation struggle of his own age, with a brilliant proposal of staggering proportions—to collect systematically all laws and regulations pertaining to Jews ever issued in Europe.[104]

By way of illustration, the essay itself deals with the legal status of Jewry in the Roman Empire and makes a crucial distinction between the pagan and Christian periods in reference to their treatment of Jews. The novelty of his method did not signify a break with the deep-seated medieval Jewish perception of Diaspora history as saturated with suffering and persecution. Gans too regarded the precariousness of Jewish existence in both periods as a constant. What he did argue for was the recognition that the source of the danger changed. In pagan Rome, persecution derived from social tensions and not legal discrimination. The widespread anti-Jewish sentiment was rather a consequence of friction engendered by Jewish allegiance to Jerusalem, pagan ignorance of Judaism, and a tendency to view the early Christians as Jews. In contrast the triumph of Christianity with its conviction of a single truth turned law into an instrument of religious coercion. Only Christian reverence for the Hebrew Bible and the expectation of an ultimate conversion stayed the wrath of the Church. This indictment of the Church as the direct cause for the steady deteriation of Jewish status in the empire after the conversion of Constantine was to become a staple of *Wissenschaft* scholarship.[105] A peroration by Gans at the end of this section of the essay, censored in some copies of the journal, underscores the connection between past perception and present reality.

How long will that pernicious half-heartedness go on? Has history not sufficiently taught that one can only choose between two paths: Either to take as your point of departure the principle of the only saving Church and then in a completely logical manner (and thereby at least praiseworthy) wipe the Jews off the planet and fill the resulting gap with their interred bodies, or to forget in all matters of law that there may be Jews and thus fill the gap with their resurrected spirits. Only that which lies in the middle is evil.[106]

Apart from the ideological thrust, this essay is a grand example of integrative scholarship. Gans measures the impact of Christianity on Jewish status in terms of the office and authority exercised by Jewish communal leaders in the Roman Empire and in conjunction with that study tried to match up titles of leadership mentioned in the Hebrew sources with what appear to be their equivalents in the Roman legal codes.[107]

But the integration of disparate sources was not only of utility for communal or political history. In another major essay, Gans unfurled the benefits to be gained from studying the institutions of Jewish law comparatively and within the context of the Roman legal system. His pioneering study of "Die Grundzüge des mosaisch-talmudischen Erbrechts" (The Fundamentals of the Mosaic-Talmudic Law of Inheritance) was part of his majestic four-volume history of inheritance law worldwide and thus published twice in quick succession.[108] The larger project was conceived as a historical illustration of Hegel's philosophy of law, with the chronological order and cultural development of the specific legal institution of inheritance accounted for by rational necessity rather than historical accident. In accord with Hegelian periodization, biblical law is placed squarely within the oriental stage of the human spirit, though to be sure its highest form of expression.[109] But more important for Gans is to demonstrate the process of Westernization that biblical institutions underwent by virtue of talmudic exposition. Studied from the perspective of Greco-Roman law, talmudic legal practice can be shown to exhibit development, outside influence, and a decided resemblance to the West. Gans identified examples of substantive and linguistic affinities which bespoke cultural interaction and credited the rabbis with transforming the fragmentary injunctions of biblical law on inheritance into a coherent and advanced legal system.[110] Ironically, the rehabilitation of talmudic law had been launched by one of its "cultured despisers." The intellectual counterpart of political emancipation, integrative scholarship, illumined a landscape of new meaning.

The contribution which Gans might have made to the course of Jewish scholarship is amply adumbrated in these forgotten essays. Conversion terminated his engagement as it would that of others whose career aspirations foundered on the religious intransigence of the German university. *Wissenschaft des Judentums* constituted the society's most important legacy, a new weapon forged in a two-front war—for emancipation and against rabbinism, but with limitless utility for future crises. Its eventual perfection would be effected largely through the defiant and selfless dedication of Zunz. Despite bouts of abject despair, he emerged from the fiasco of the *Verein* with the resolve to pursue that vision as a vocation. In a searing flashback on the society thirty years after its demise, Heine bedecked Zunz with an unexaggerated accolade for his solitary perseverance.

This excellent, eminent man, who stood firm, constantly and unshakably, in a period of transition, hesitation, and vacillation; and who, despite the sharpness of his intellect, his scepticism, and his learning, remained faithful to the promise he had made himself, to the generous caprice of his soul. A man of words *and* a man of action, he worked unceasingly, he did what needed doing, at a time when others lost themselves in dreams and sank to the ground, bereft of courage.[111]

NOTES

1. Martin Philippson, "Der Anteil der jüdischen Freiwilligen an dem Befreiungskriege 1813 und 1814," *MGWJ*, L (1906), pp. 1–21, 220–247; Horst Fischer, *Judentum, Staat und Heer in Preussen im frühen 19. Jahrhundert: Zur Geschichte der staatlichen Judenpolitik*, Tübingen 1968 (Schriftenreihe wissenschaftlicher Abhandlungen des Leo Baeck Instituts 20), pp. 47–53.

2. Jacob Katz, "The Hep-Hep Riots in Germany of 1819: The Historical Background" (in Hebrew), in *Zion*, XXXVIII (1973), 62–108; Uriel Tal, "Young German Intellectuals on Romanticism and Judaism. Spiritual Turbulence in the Early 19th Century," in Saul Lieberman (ed.), *Salo Wittmayer Baron Jubilee Volume on the Occasion of his Eightieth Birthday*, American Academy for Jewish Research, 3 vols., Jerusalem–New York–London 1974, II, pp. 919–938.

3. Hanns Günther Reissner, *Eduard Gans: Ein Leben im Vormärz*, Tübingen 1965 (Schriftenreihe wissenschaftlicher Abhandlungen des Leo Baeck Instituts 14), p. 50.

4. *Ibid.*, pp. 31, 50, 174–175; Jacob Jacobson, *Die Judenbürgerbücher der Stadt Berlin 1809–1851*, Berlin 1962, pp. 57, 206.

5. Reissner, *Eduard Gans*, pp. 31–34; JNUL, 4°792/B-1.

6. S. Rubaschoff, " 'Erstlinge' (Drei Reden von Eduard Gans im Kulturverein," *Der jüdische Wille*, I (1918–1919), p. 113.

7. Nahum N. Glatzer, *Leopold Zunz: Jude—Deutscher—Europäer*, Tübingen 1964 (Schriftenreihe wissenschaftlicher Abhandlungen des Leo Baeck Instituts 11), p. 103.

8. Reissner, *Eduard Gans*, pp. 174–185; JNUL, 4°792/B-3.

9. JNUL, 4°792/B-2. Cf. Sinai (Siegfried) Ucko, "Geistesgeschichtliche Grundlagen der Wissenschaft des Judentums," reprinted in *Wissenschaft des Judentums im deutschen Sprachbereich: Ein Querschnitt.* Mit einer Einführung herausgegeben von Kurt Wilhelm, Tübingen 1967 (Schriftenreihe wissenschaftlicher Abhandlungen des Leo Baeck Instituts 16/I and 16/II), I, pp. 335–336.

10. JNUL, 4°792/B-2, B-6, B-10, B-11.

11. *Entwurf von Statuten des Vereins für Cultur und Wissenschaft der Juden,* Berlin 1822. For a partial English translation, see Paul R. Mendes-Flohr and Jehuda Reinharz (eds.), *The Jews in the Modern World,* New York–Oxford 1980, pp. 188–189.

12. S. Prawer, *Heine's Jewish Comedy,* Oxford 1983, pp. 10–43.

13. Reissner, *Eduard Gans,* p. 65.

14. Rubaschoff, *op. cit.,* pp. 40–41.

15. *Ibid.,* pp. 115–118.

16. *Ibid.,* pp. 199–201.

17. JNUL, 4°792/B-13.

18. JNUL, 4°792/G-12.

19. Ludwig Geiger, "Aus Leopold Zunz' Nachlass," in *ZGJD,* V (1892), pp. 259–260. Apparently the letter addressed to Zunz arrived during his absence from Berlin. In a covering note to Zunz, Moser confessed that he and Gans were so eager to learn of de Sacy's reaction that they committed the indiscretion of opening the letter. "We were curious as to the man's opinion. Nevertheless, we should have expected that the Frenchman would barely be able to grasp our idea. Still, he is at least more courteous than the Germans: Eichhorn, Paulus, and Vater." (JNUL, 4°792/G-18.)

20. Reissner, *Eduard Gans,* p. 94.

21. Prawer, *op. cit.,* p. 30.

22. *Heinrich Heine: Säkularausgabe,* 27 vols. (in progress) (Berlin and Paris 1970–), XX, pp. 102–103.

23. Rubaschoff, *op. cit.,* p. 42.

24. CAHJP, P 17/127 (Letter dated 28th August 1821 from Gans to Moser).

25. Reissner, *Eduard Gans,* pp. 180–184.

26. *Heine: Säkularausgabe,* XX, p. 103. For an analysis of Bendavid's essay within the context of his work, see Jakob Guttmann, "Lazarus Bendavid," *MGWJ,* LXI (1917), pp. 176–181. The correspondence between Bendavid and the *Verein* is in JNUL, 4°792/F-3.

27. JNUL, 4°792/B-3. See also the letter by Zunz to Mannheimer, dated 22nd August 1822 published by M. Brann and M. Rosenmann, "Der Briefwechsel zwischen Izak Noa Mannheimer und Leopold Zunz," *MGWJ,* LXI (1917), pp. 96–97.

28. JNUL, 4°792/B-3.

29. Reissner, *Eduard Gans,* pp. 92–93. A copy of the memorandum dated 18th August 1822 from King Frederick William III to Chancellor Hardenberg in which the decision against Gans is rendered is preserved in CAHJP, P 17/634.

30. JNUL, 4°792/B-3.

31. Reissner, *Eduard Gans,* p. 102.

32. JNUL, 4°792/G-27.

33. Adolf Strodtmann, *H. Heine's Leben und Werke,* 2 vols., Berlin 1867, I, p. 252.

34. Ludwig Lesser, *Chronik der Gesellschaft der Freunde in Berlin,* Berlin 1842, pp. iv, 9–10, 17, 26–27.

35. Hanns Günther Reissner, "Correspondence," in *LBIYB VI* (1961), pp. 287–288.

36. Isaak M. Jost, *Geschichte der Israeliten*, 9 vols., Berlin 1820–1828, IX, p. 94; Lesser, *op. cit.*, p. 17.

37. Reissner, *Eduard Gans*, pp. 54–55; Lesser, *op. cit.*, p. 66. The admission fee to the *Gesellschaft* cost Zunz the substantial sum of 15 taler. (JNUL, 4°792/C-13, p. 34b.)

38. Lesser, *op. cit.*, p. 81.

39. Prawer, *op. cit.*, p. 62.

40. Ucko, *op. cit.*, pp. 324–326 (quotation p. 326). Ucko's splendid essay, written in the early 1930s, treats the *Verein* as a secular expression of ethical nationalism.

41. *Ibid.*, pp. 328–332 (quotation on pp. 328, 331). The original text is in JNUL, 4°792/B-10.

42. JNUL, 4°792/B-11.

43. JNUL, 4°792/B-10.

44. JNUL, 4°792/B-11.

45. Leopold Zunz, "Etwas über die rabbinische Literatur," in *Gesammelte Schriften*, 3 vols., Berlin 1875–1876, I, p. 29 note 1.

46. *AZJ*, 1916, pp. 413–414.

47. Moritz Steinschneider, *Die Schriften des Dr. L. Zunz*, Berlin 1857, p. 11, note 23.

48. Levi Lazar Hellwitz, *Die Organisation der Israeliten in Deutschland*, Magdeburg 1819, p. 29. See also Zunz's letter to Ehrenberg, dated 5th January 1821, in Glatzer, *op. cit.*, p. 117. ("Meine Wirksamkeit gehet jetzt grossenteils dahin, den ganzen Rabbinismus zur stürzen.")

49. Ucko, *op. cit.*, pp. 333–335; JNUL, 4°792/B-2.

50. Hermann Vogelstein, "Beiträge zur Geschichte des Unterrichtswesens in der jüdischen Gemeinde zu Königsberg i. Pr.," *Sechs und dreissigster Bericht über den Religions-Unterricht . . . zu Königsberg . . .* Königsberg i. Pr. 1903, pp. 12–13.

51. *Ibid.*, p. 15.

52. *Ibid.*, pp. 16–17. Zunz could hardly expect to attack rabbinism with impunity. When the leadership of Königsberg inquired of Simon Weyl, the traditionalist rabbi of Berlin, about Zunz, it apparently received an unfavorable opinion, which seems to have put an end to his candidacy.

53. Rubaschoff, *op. cit.*, pp. 37–39.

54. *Ibid.*, p. 111.

55. *Ibid.*, p. 112.

56. *Ibid.*, p. 41.

57. *Ibid.*, p. 112.

58. *Ibid.*, p. 112.

59. *Ibid.*, p. 113.

60. *Ibid.*, p. 196.

61. *Ibid.*, pp. 114, 195–196.

62. *Ibid.*, pp. 197–198.

63. *Heine: Säkularausgabe*, XX, p. 122.

64. *Ibid.*, p. 72.

65. *Ibid.*, p. 133.

66. *Ibid.*, p. 86.

67. *Ibid.*, p. 97.

68. JNUL, 4°792/B-7, p. 15. In his first paper to the seminar, Moser urged that it be conceived "als einen Verein zum gemeinsamen *Studium* der Judenthumswissenschaft." (CAHJP, P 47.)

69. Zunz, *Gesammelte Schriften*, pp. 1–31. Zunz reached the age of twenty-four only on 10th August 1818 and the essay had been completed the previous December. (See *Das Buch Zunz*, ed. by Fritz Bamberger [n.p., n.d.], p. 20.)

70. *Das Buch Zunz*, p. 9.

71. Friedrich Rühs, *Ueber die Ansprüche der Juden an das deutsche Bürgerrecht*, Berlin 1816. See also Jacob Katz, *From Prejudice to Destruction: Anti-Semitism, 1700–1933*, Cambridge, Mass. 1980, pp. 76–82.

72. JNUL, 4°792/D-1, p. 1.

73. The passage is worth quoting in full. "Und heute, an diesem doppelt gefeierten Sonntage, auf dem Tage, der Paris gedemüthigt (1813 [sic], 31 März) und eine halbe Million ungläubiger Juden dem Elende preisgegeben (1492, 31. März, Ferdinands Edict) sah, schwöre ich in deinen Händen, du grösserer denn *Talavera* [sic], auch *ein Werkzeug zu werden, um den verlorenen Stamm Israels zu erwecken*" (p. 6.).

74. Zunz, "Etwas über die rabbinische Literatur," *op. cit.*, p. 5.

75. There is but a single, brief reference to Rühs in the entire essay, and this at the very end in a note in which Zunz delivers a mild reproof of his harsh assessment of rabbinic literature in a historical handbook. ("Etwas über die rabbinische Literatur," *op. cit.*, p. 31, note 1).

76. *Ibid.*, p. 4.

77. See above, p. 181.

78. Zunz, "Etwas über die rabbinische Literatur," *op. cit.*, p. 17.

79. *Ibid.*, p. 27. See Fritz Bamberger, "Zunz's Conception of History," *Proceedings of the American Academy for Jewish Research*, XI (1941), p. 4, note 14 for possible influence of August Boeckh.

80. Zunz, "Etwas über die rabbinische Literatur," *op. cit.*, p. 4.

81. *Ibid.*, pp. 26–27.

82. *Das Buch Zunz*, pp. 19–21. Cf. Bamberger, *op. cit.*, p. 4.

83. F. A. Wolf, "Darstellung der Altertums-Wissenschaft," in *Museum der Altertums-Wissenschaft*, I (1807), pp. 15–19, 30.

84. *Ibid.*, p. 6.

85. See above, note 68.

86. Reissner, *Eduard Gans*, p. 174; Albert Friedlander, "The Wohlwill–Moser Correspondence," in *LBIYB XI* (1966), p. 280.

87. Immanuel Wolf, "Ueber den Begriff einer Wissenschaft des Judenthums," in *ZWJ*, I (1822–1823), pp. 1–24. For an English translation, see *LBIYB II* (1957), pp. 194–204. On the sources of Wolf's thinking, see Luitpold Wallach, "The Beginnings of the Science of Judaism in the Nineteenth Century," in *Historia Judaica*, VIII (1946), pp. 39–43.

88. *ZWJ*, pp. 523–532.

89. Luitpold Wallach, "Ueber Leopold Zunz als Historiker," in *ZGJD*, V (1935), pp. 251–252.

90. *ZWJ*, p. 523.

91. *Ibid.*, p. 532.

92. Leopold Zunz, "Ueber die in den hebräisch-jüdischen Schriften vorkommenden hispanischen Ortsnamen," in *ZWJ*, pp. 114–176.

93. Wolf, *Museum der Altertums-Wissenschaft*, p. 50.

94. *ZWJ*, pp. 118–119.

95. *Ibid.*, p. 117.

96. *Ibid.*, p. 129.

97. Leopold Zunz, "Salomon ben Isaac, genannt Raschi," in *ZWJ*, pp. 277–384.

98. See below, p. 245.

99. *Ibid.*, p. 125.

100. *ZWJ*, p. 325.

101. *Ibid.*, p. 377 ("Das Erschweren [in *Halakhah*] nimmt zu mit der Ignoranz"), p. 380.

102. Eduard Gans, "Gesetzgebung über Juden in Rom, nach den Quellen des Römischen Rechts," pp. 25–67; "Vorlesungen über die Geschichte der Juden im Norden von Europa und in den slavischen Ländern," pp. 95–113; "Die Grundzüge des mosaisch-talmudischen Erbrechts," pp. 419–471.

103. Cf. Reissner, *Eduard Gans*, p. 105. There is no mention whatsoever in Gans's essay on Jewish inheritance law that he received help from Zunz. My impression from internal evidence is that Gans certainly read Hebrew and probably could handle the Jewish legal sources in the original.

104. *ZWJ*, p. 25.

105. *ZWJ*, pp. 27–51. For a recent challenge of this "reading," see Jeremy Cohen, "Roman Imperial Policy Toward the Jews from Constantine until the End of the Palestinian Patriarchate (ca. 429)," in *Byzantine Studies*, III (1976), pp. 1–29.

106. *Ibid.*, pp. 50–51.

107. *Ibid.*, pp. 51–67. Unfortunately, the essay was never completed.

108. Eduard Gans, *Das Erbrecht in weltgeschichtlicher Entwicklung*, 4 vols., Berlin 1824–1835.

109. *ZWJ*, pp. 420, 428, 430–431.

110. Some of Gans's etymological derivations for rabbinic terms such as *parna* (*ZWJ*, p. 437) and *diyyatiki* (*ZWJ*, pp. 465–466) were accepted by later rabbinic lexicography. (Jacob Levy, *Neuhebräisches und chaldäisches Wörterbuch*, 4 vols., Leipzig 1876–1889, I, p. 404; IV, p. 119.)

111. Prawer, *op. cit.*, p. 470. See also Michael A. Meyer, *The Origins of the Modern Jew*, Detroit 1967, pp. 180–181.

∾ 12

From Wolfenbüttel to *Wissenschaft:* The Divergent Paths of Isaak Markus Jost and Leopold Zunz

I

From 1803 to 1807 Isaak Markus Jost (b. 1793) and Leopold Zunz (b. 1794) languished as orphans in the decrepit Samson Talmud School (*Bet ha-Midrash*) of Wolfenbüttel in the Duchy of Brunswick. Amid poverty, filth and disorder, they endured a heartless regimen of talmudic studies, interspersed with three hours of weekly instruction in German and one in mathematics. On Thursdays and Fridays, the Pentateuch with Mendelssohn's translation was added. But the reading of German books was forbidden, and with the language of instruction being "the most frightful jargon," most students could scarcely understand spoken high German. At the age of eleven, aside from a small mathematics book, Zunz had not read a single book in German, and Jost was not to write his first German letter until the age of seventeen. Intellectual curiosity could be satisfied only through the reading of Hebrew books. Lonely and stifled, the two boys found affection and stimulation in their friendship with one another.[1]

I should like to express my gratitude to those institutions and individuals whose gracious assistance has aided my work immeasurably: The Memorial Foundation for Jewish Culture for its subvention of my larger project, a social and intellectual history of the first phase of the *Wissenschaft* movement, of which this essay constitutes the first fruits; Professor Nahum N. Glatzer and The Franz Rosenzweig Archive for making available to me the rich collection of Jost letters to Ehrenberg, which has since been transferred to the archives of The Leo Baeck Institute; The Central Archives for the History of the Jewish People and The Jewish National and University Library in Jerusalem for placing their rich archival holdings at my disposal during my sabbatical (1974–1975); The Leo Baeck Institute for use of the Ehrenberg correspondence to Jost; Professor David Weiss Halivni for reading and criticizing an earlier draft of this essay; Professor Michael A. Meyer for inviting me to read that earlier draft at the Seventh Annual Conference of the Association for Jewish Studies in Boston in December 1975 and for sharing with me his reactions; and Chancellor Gerson D. Cohen for finding the time to read my final draft and to enhance it with his counsel.

Release from this repressive setting came unexpectedly in April 1807 when Samuel Meyer Ehrenberg, a thirty-four-year-old educator who had himself been a student at the Samson School from 1789 to 1794, became the director. For years Ehrenberg had struggled to acquire the secular education of which he was deprived as a child, and now as director he moved swiftly to modernize the curriculum and humanize instruction.[2] He also quickly enriched the intellectual fare of his two gifted students and thereby opened the way to *Gymnasium* and university. Years later Zunz observed that on the day that Ehrenberg assumed the directorship of the school, its students had literally passed from the Middle Ages into the modern era, and looking back in 1833, Jost implored the hostile Prussian bureaucrat Karl Streckfuss not to forget how far his generation had come: "All of us who were still children thirty years ago can testify to the incredible changes that have occurred both within us and outside us. We have traversed, or better still, flown through, a thousand-year history." The trek from Wolfenbüttel to *Wissenschaft* bespoke a psychic transformation that had compressed the passage of a millennium into less than a lifetime.

The magnitude of this achievement stands out still more fully when we compare the disordered youth of Jost and Zunz to the secure childhood and adolescence of Leopold Ranke, who was born in 1795 into a respected old Lutheran family in a prosperous Thuringian valley. As the eldest son among nine children and destined for the ministry, Ranke received the finest humanistic classical education available at the famous *Gymnasium* of Schulpforta. At the University of Leipzig, where he had matriculated as a theological student, religious doubts cooled his ardor for the ministry though not his piety. History would soon replace the Bible for him as a text for the study of God's word and will. After finishing his dissertation on the political doctrines of Thucydides, he accepted a position teaching Latin and Greek at a *Gymnasium* in the Prussian town of Frankfurt on the Oder, where he remained until 1824, when the publication of his first history (*Geschichte der romanischen und germanischen Völker von 1495 bis 1514*) earned him a coveted invitation to teach at the University of Berlin.[4] The contrast in backgrounds was to be matched by the contrast in careers. In 1824 Jost, who had already completed four volumes of his *Geschichte der Israeliten*, was running a private Jewish boarding school in Berlin, and Zunz was dissipating most of his strength on the *Haude- und Spenersche Zeitung*, where he worked as an editor in the mornings.[5]

II

Despite their common hardships and early friendship, Jost and Zunz went on to produce such different types of scholarship that later generations saw fit to honor Zunz alone as the founder of *Wissenschaft des Judentums*. But the accolade is not quite as self-evident as it may appear. From a chronological point of view, by 1832 when Zunz finally found the time to complete his *Die gottesdienstlichen Vorträge der*

Juden, Jost had already published a nine-volume history of the Israelites from the Maccabean era to 1815 and a subsequent two-volume compendium which added an uncritical and tedious survey of the biblical period.[6] But the novelty of Jost's achievement is not to be gainsaid. It bore all the earmarks of the new medium: a secular spirit, source criticism, philological method and extensive utilization of non-Jewish sources. Not only was Jost the first Jew since Josephus to write a comprehensive history of his people, but more important, he was also among the first since Azariah de Rossi to risk using Josephus for the study of Jewish history.

Moreover, his broad synthesis was not always constructed at the expense of penetrating analysis. At times Jost anchored his narrative in the kind of source criticism which became the trademark of German historiography. Perhaps the most original example was his seminal analysis of the reliability of Josephus for the events in which he participated. Jost contended in a long excursus that the first-century historian had intentionally blamed the rebellion against Rome on brigands and their like in order to absolve the Jewish masses in Roman eyes.[7] No less important was Jost's recognition of and attempt to reconcile Josephus's conflicting accounts of his career in the Galilee during the early stages of the rebellion in *The Jewish War* and *The Life*.[8]

Of course, in retrospect it is easy to point out the price that Jost was to pay for daring to write a general history of the Jews prematurely. While Jost hurried to assemble an uneven and faulty narrative out of sources long published, Zunz patiently recovered, collected, dated, and analyzed the fragments of lost works preserved in known sources and the manuscripts of countless others buried in archives and private libraries. Nor could Jost begin to match Zunz's appreciation of new types of sources such as legal and exegetical commentaries, place names and personal names, homiletical literature, liturgy, tombstones, and coins to illuminate the recesses of the Jewish past. In fact, Zunz was among Jost's harshest critics, as Jost confided to Ehrenberg in a letter on 14th March 1830. He reproached him "for having immaturely put out such a long-winded work," whose deficiencies he must have realized. In response Jost insisted that the state of the field precluded perfection and scholarship stood to benefit even from his errors. Perfection had eluded far greater scholars, whose works were nevertheless superseded by later research. This difference in style and standards certainly contributed to turning their former adolescent intimacy into a strained and fluctuating relationship.[9]

But Zunz's criticism may also have been tinged with envy and many contemporaries disagreed with his appraisal. Among the most important was Jost's former teacher in Göttingen, the biblical scholar and historian Johann Gottfried Eichhorn. In a reserved but favorable review of his first two volumes, Eichhorn praised Jost for emphasizing the universal aspect of his subject at the expense of its national dimension and for wisely omitting the biblical period, which required a different set of tools. Eichhorn acknowledged that to open a new field with a comprehensive history was unorthodox. Yet despite the paucity of sources and the dearth of specialized studies, he urged Jost to continue. The merit of his work would be to clarify what has to be done.

How long has the scholarly world waited in vain for these preliminary studies! Why should we not try the reverse: to arouse enthusiasm for such monographs by an overview of the scattered sources, as far as one diligent scholar can bring them together, even though from the viewpoint of method they should first be worked over piecemeal by individual scholars?[10]

Certainly in terms of immediate impact, as far as this elusive factor can be measured, Jost's nine-volume history fared no worse than Zunz's one-volume *Die gottesdienstlichen Vorträge*. To be sure, neither became a best-seller, but at least by 1841 some 950 sets of Jost's work had been sold, whereas the 760 copies of Zunz's book printed in 1832 would not be sold out till 1851.[11] Likewise in terms of personal correspondence, each man became the center of a far-flung network of scholarly correspondents. In an undated letter from 1830, Jost told Ehrenberg that in the preceding six weeks he had sent out some seventy-five letters, mostly of a scholarly nature, and in 1841 he bemoaned that he was composing about 500 letters a year in five different languages.[12] That staggering quantity certainly compares favorably with the rich correspondence preserved in the Zunz Archive.[13] After 1832 aspiring young scholars and rabbis turned to Zunz for guidance, encouragement, and approval. They shared their insights and plans, sent along copies of their first published works, and longed for a review in print from the master. During the 1830s Zunz became the scholarly mentor of men as different as Geiger, Frankel, Sachs, Dukes, Holdheim, Fürst, Herzfeld, Beer, Samuel Hirsch, and Steinschneider. But there is little reason to assume that the non-extant correspondence of Jost with students and colleagues would not reveal the same respectful relationships.

In sum, Jost's achievement transcended its faults and earned him at least passing recognition. What eventually cost him his rightful place in the pantheon of the *Wissenschaft* movement was not the quality of his scholarship so much as its programmatic intent. Beneath a veneer of historical objectivity, he restated the older program of the radical wing of the Berlin *Haskalah* in a new medium.[14]

In his harsh and tendentious critique of nineteenth-century *Wissenschaft*, Professor Gershom Scholem has stressed the grave doubts among its practitioners about the prospects of Jewish survival beyond emancipation and pointed out with gusto the presence of a strong destructive intent. But to substitute such a sweeping charge with the chance remark of an aged Steinschneider to a student is dubious method at best, akin to writing a biography of Zunz on the basis of his despondent letters to the young David Kaufmann, written in the years of unconsolable grief which followed the death of his beloved Adelheid.[15] If the motive of giving Judaism a decent burial is verifiable anywhere in the *Wissenschaft* movement, it is only in the early work of Isaak Jost, where the mood fluctuates between animosity and ambivalence. It is this pervasive antagonism toward so much of the Jewish experience, which is so conspicuously absent from the work of Zunz, and not merely the difference in method and substance that curtailed Jost's long-term impact and destined his achievement for oblivion.

III

Thanks to the extensive and revealing Jost–Ehrenberg correspondence which has survived, it is possible to reconstruct the state of mind in which Jost turned out the volumes of his history at a truly incredible pace. Personal emancipation came during three exhilarating semesters spent at the nearby University of Göttingen in 1813–1814, where Jost matriculated as a "pauper" free of charge and from which he would receive a doctorate in 1828 upon the completion of the ninth and final volume of his history.[16] Two long unpublished letters by Jost to his "dearest friend" Zunz, who was still teaching for Ehrenberg back in Wolfenbüttel, provide a rare glimpse of his social, academic, and intellectual transformation. New Year's eve was spent in rowdy celebration with fellow students, to the dismay of many townspeople. Through the study of Arabic and the Old Testament, Jost drew quite close to Göttingen's renowned Professor of Theology, J. G. Eichhorn. Above all, his views on Judaism were subjected to rapid modification, as he reported at the end of his letter on 1st January 1814.

Frequent, reasonable, non-partisan debates with my friends on religion constantly enlighten my own ideas and increasingly motivate me to devote my greatest attention to this important subject. Therefore I am now carefully studying the sources of our religion and reading the Talmud. Two days ago I finished *Berachot*. . . . Also I am now busy working out something on the purity of our religion and the proper method to study and teach it.

In his next letter exactly three months later, Jost set forth his new attitude toward Hebrew, a language which both friends loved and wrote fluently. Jost now rejected the goal of reviving and modernizing Hebrew as utterly futile. The study of Hebrew should rather be directed to illuminate the obscurities of the biblical text and to correct the ideas of Judaism accordingly.[17] Forty years later Jost still spoke with enthusiasm of his liberation at Göttingen, a formative period in which he had scraped off the grime of the ghetto and embraced the thought patterns and civic virtues of his adopted fatherland.[18]

In 1814 Jost switched to the University of Berlin to join his benefactor Israel Jacobson who had settled in the Prussian capital the year before, after the fall of Westphalia. According to his own later testimony, Jost was quickly inspired by the encouragement of Friedländer and Bendavid to undertake a history of the Jews, and by 16th September 1815 he could proudly report to Ehrenberg that "My compilation [*Bearbeitung*] of Jewish history excites the young scholars and many have sought my company out of curiosity. Everything inspires me to continue this project diligently."[19] Ehrenberg's unpublished letters to Jost from this early period display a keen interest in the character and salability of the work in progress. When Jost surprised him by effusively dedicating the first volume to his teacher and friend, Ehrenberg was overcome with emotion, but recovered quickly enough to chide him for having wasted the opportunity of currying favor with some important public figure.[20]

Jost used the introduction to declare his intentions. He had worked with three types of reader in mind: Christian intellectuals and government officials who respected truth and justice and Jews intent on self-improvement. With the arrival of an enlightened age, the objective study of the origin and development of Judaism could begin with a view to understanding its character and improving its condition.[21] But despite the calm and dispassionate pose, Jost wrote in a mood beset by grave doubts over the worth and viability of his subject. The very year in which volume one appeared, he admitted to Ehrenberg his preference for pristine Christianity. The comment came in the context of a long and often critical description of the conversion activities of a recently founded and flourishing English missionary society. "I am far from admiring clerical Christianity [*Pfaffenchristentum*], although I cannot withhold my approval from New Testament Christianity, because it is a pure and purged Judaism and our Judaism only a debased Christianity."[22] Two years later, with more than a third of his history completed, Jost gave vent to his mood of resignation in a remarkably candid letter to Ehrenberg, which alludes again to the same missionary efforts.

Furthermore the Jews stand today in the midst of a dilemma. University students simply can not find employment and only baptism saves them for mankind. If we don't push the crafts, our entire next generation will turn Christian. And rightly so, for what should tie them to the religion of their fathers? Only childhood memories still hold us together, no more. Our children live in another world, and they have no reason to give up their entire life just to be called Jews, when they no longer are. Why do we vex ourselves? All efforts in this regard remain fruitless. The proselytizers here are fools because they try to achieve with lots of money and noise a goal which will come of its own. The state can not recognise Jews as legitimate as long as they will not marry the inhabitants of the country. The state exists only by virtue of its people and its people must constitute a unity. Why should it elevate an association whose main principle is that it alone possesses the truth and therefore must avoid all integration with the inhabitants of the country? . . . This is the way our children will reason and they will gladly abandon a coercive church to gain freedom, a sense of belonging to the Volk, love of the fatherland and service to the state—the highest possessions of earthly man. . . . I am no friend of desertion but the history of our day makes it general and justifies it.[23]

That outburst with its grim prognosis was written in the context of a bitter attack against the *Verein für Cultur und Wissenschaft der Juden* and what Jost considered its presumptuous program of revitalization. Jost himself had withdrawn from the *Culturverein* on 14th May 1820 out of personal pique when the members voted after seven sessions of debate to reject his lengthy memorandum on what form the *Verein*'s scholarly journal should take.[24] Two years later on 22nd August 1822, just six days after his profuse denunciation to Ehrenberg quoted above, he curtly rejected an invitation from the *Verein*'s scholarly seminar headed by Zunz to become a member.[25] In short, Jost had chosen to divorce himself from every single action taken by that small circle of idealistic young intellectuals to salvage and rehabilitate Judaism both inside and outside the synagogue, preferring instead to restrict himself to his small Jewish school which he had received permission to open in the autumn of 1816. Thus in an age pulsating with change, Jost opted for the *vita contemplativa*, while his former friend Zunz plunged with near messianic fervor into the *vita activa*.

The stance of observer, however, did not mean that Jost succeeded in elevating his history above the concerns of the day. On the contrary, it was permeated by the same sense of worthlessness and futility openly acknowledged in the letters to Ehrenberg. Far more fatal than the inelegance of style, which prompted Zunz to quip after the appearance of volume one that perhaps it was so abominably written in order to make subsequent volumes look good, was a consistent lack of empathy for the subject matter.[26] Jost dwelt at length on what he regarded as the flaws and defects of Judaism. Like Mendelssohn in part, and Friedländer and Bendavid in full, he had internalized much of the secular critique of Judaism, which derived from Spinoza and gained currency and enrichment through the polemics of the deists and philosophes.[27] His history amounted to a pedantic and passionless plea for the interment of rabbinic Judaism.

Several related themes loosely strung together formed an inchoate theory of history intended to vindicate the radical program of the Friedländer–Bendavit wing of the German *Haskalah*. To begin with, Jost retained the prevailing periodization which posited a basic discontinuity in Jewish history. Like Spinoza, Mendelssohn, Friedländer, and Bendavid before him, he contended that the destruction of the First Commonwealth, and not that of the Second, constituted the fateful turning point in antiquity.[28] Since Spinoza, the Enlightenment had come to evaluate the achievement of Moses in primarily political terms. As the founder of a state and author of its constitution, he had used religion to further his political ends.[29] The *Maskilim* were thus compelled to counter by assuring their Christian audience that Judaism had abandoned its political character millennia ago. The year 586 B.C.E. marked the end of Judaism's political experiment. Jost merely expanded the argument. The pious Jews of the Second Commonwealth never produced a religious replica of the First. On the contrary, they differed radically in the spirit of their constitution, the means of administration, the rites for gaining divine favor, and their ethical norms and language.[30]

Periodization is rarely a value-free exercise. Just as the needs of emancipation dictated focusing on the year 586 B.C.E., so the needs of survival, as the century progressed, evoked another periodization. By the middle of the century the emphasis had shifted to the destruction of the Second Temple, a calamity which Jewish historians now proceeded to invest with the mandate of the mission theory. To the preparatory but negative stage of 586, they added a powerful affirmative climax which not only justified the lands of exile as the proper locus of Jewish life but bestowed universal significance on Jewish survival.[31] It is no accident that Jost never embraced the mission theory.[32] As a disciple of Friedländer and Bendavid, his theological thinking never progressed much beyond their negative terms. With age his fatalism intensified and he scoffingly dismissed the futile illusions of a Jewish mission.[33]

Aside from these broader implications, the insistence on a total break in Jewish history served immediate ends. It cleared the way for Jost to portray the Pharisaic–rabbinic Judaism created out of the rubble of Israelite religion as a vast historical aberration. Taking his cue from a famous passage in Spinoza, Jost declared at the very outset of volume one: "If the charge that the Jews destroyed themselves is true, then the Pharisees bear the greatest guilt."[34] In line with this thesis, Jost traced the rise to power of an arrogant and ambitious class of clerics, indifferent to the dictates of life and obsessed with the sanctity of religious law. The steady expansion of that law obstructed the pursuit of an honest livelihood and rendered secular learning abhorrent. In an outburst worthy of Voltaire, Jost depicted the early sages not as philosophers but as teachers who like merchants disperse the wares that come their way without ever creating anything themselves.[35] In volume one, Jost held the Pharisees responsible for the death of Jesus and closed with the plea that the time might soon come when "the Pharisaism of all religious parties will cease."[36] Two volumes later he pointedly placed a chapter on the rise of Christianity on the heels of a lengthy indictment of rabbinism, opening the chapter itself with a diatribe against the Pharisees.[37] Thus Jost's repeated assault on rabbinism signified the Jewish counterpart to the Enlightenment's campaign against the "infamy" of Christianity.

Within the medieval world, Jost's conspicuous preference for Sephardic culture fully reflected the prevailing prejudice of emancipation spokesmen. Since the debates provoked by the English Jew Bill of 1753, proponents of amelioration had emphasized the existing economic and social differences that distinguished Sephardism from Ashkenazim, tending to appeal only on behalf of the former.[38] To project this contemporary disparity back into the past provided inferiority-ridden Ashkenazic intellectuals with an effective critique of their own tradition and a respectable cultural claim for political equality. Just two weeks before Jost pulled out of the *Culturverein*, Eduard Gans, its president, had read at a meeting a lengthy memorandum that he intended to submit to the Ministry of Interior, in which he underscored the different historical experience of Sephardic Jewry and cited its cultural integration into Moslem society in order to allay the fear of many that Jews were congenitally or religiously unfit for citizenship. Even after 1492, he contended, this cultural legacy prevented the uprooted Sephardic Jews who resettled in France, Holland, Italy, and England from ever becoming as unlike their Christian neighbors as their Ashkenazic co-religionists.[39] Jost wrote in the same spirit. The secure legal status, economic diversity, and intellectual stimulation enjoyed by Spanish Jews relieved the one-sidedness and fanaticism of their religion. These same factors, Jost asserted in a typical subjective flare, also rendered the trauma of expulsion so much more painful for Spanish Jews than for the restricted, isolated, and ignorant Jews of France.[40]

When it came to the treatment of medieval Ashkenazic Jewry, Jost lost all restraint. To move from Spain into Northern Europe was to enter a world of insecurity, oppression, persecution, narrow-mindedness, ignorance, and moral depravity. Again Jost read back into history the concerns of the day. Uncritically, he accepted the unrelieved condemnation of the Jewish masses by both sides of the emancipation debate and projected the stereotypes onto their ancestors. A legal status that excluded Jews from society, rendering them less than men, had created a condition in which all the inherent flaws of rabbinism could flourish. Jost applauded the noble intent of diverting Jews away from their useless preoccupation with talmudic study which lay behind the burning of the Talmud in 1240. That the Church failed was due only to the ill-chosen violence of its means, which proved counterproductive.[41] Jost considered the transference to Spain of the Ashkenazic brand of rabbinism with its "brutal" legal system by R. Asher ben Yehiel at the end of the thirteenth century as an unmitigated tragedy.[42] About the most favorable thing that he could say about Ashkenazic Jewry was that it was not entirely to blame for its ethical and moral depravity. Jost systematically employed the already well-developed emancipation argument that a steady diet of oppression and persecution had inflicted untold damage on the character and religion of the Jews.[43]

Enough has been said to warrant the contention that not only was Jost's *Geschichte der Israeliten* inspired by Freidländer and Bendavid but also that it was consistently written in their spirit. A decade after Mendelssohn's *Jerusalem*, Bendavid had proclaimed an alternate Jewish approach to the prospect of emancipation. Whereas Mendelssohn had reasserted the divinity of Jewish law and dismissed the idea of a trade-off, Bendavid called for a wholesale repudiation of the law and a return to the pure teachings of Moses, the Jewish version of natural religion. Only then would the state be ready to extend equality and integration. The alternative would be death by attrition: the loss of the wealthy, the educated, and the young.[44] Six years later in his well-known letter to Teller, Friedländer deepened the pragmatic argument of Bendavid with a skeletal and speculative theory of Jewish history, though the universe of discourse remained predominantly rationalistic.[45] It was Jost's achievement to legitimize the program of total assimilation with an elaborate historical argument. Twenty-three hundred years of Jewish history were shown to be an egregious mistake, a period deformed by a religious monstrosity. Never again in the history of the *Wissenschaft* movement would a study be produced with so little sympathy for its subject.

As a historian, however, Jost never shared the simplistic belief in the possibility of a return to a disembodied Mosaism. As he made clear in 1830 to Chiarini, the purported Italian authority on Polish Jewry, Mosaism must be conceived of as that religious core articulated ideally in the Bible but developed by later generations. Nevertheless, in its pure state Judaism is "nothing else than Mosaism in the idea."[46] It was this attraction to the Mosaic core which may have induced Jost into the indefensible decision to call his work a history of the Israelites, with the obvious biblical allusion, when in fact he was writing nothing but a history of the Jews. What is beyond dispute is that like Friedländer and Bendavid, Jost harbored a strong aversion for the epithet "Juden." When Gabriel Riesser in 1832 audaciously called his ephemeral periodical *Der Jude*, Jost was sufficiently distressed to write him so.[47]

Equally clear from Jost's intimate correspondence with Ehrenberg is that he never mustered much faith in the future of Judaism. While the intemperate tone of his early scholarship subsided, his basic views remained unchanged. Despite his investment of several years into the editing of a punctuated text and German translation of the Mishnah, Jost continued to express nothing but contempt for the corpus of rabbinic literature.[48] One volume of Goethe, he declared in 1848, contained more genuine learning and healthy reasoning than 300 talmudic folios.[49] The efforts to reform Judaism earned only his scorn. The bitter truth, he wrote in 1852, was that the once unique character of Judaism had been irreparably damaged. Only the experiences of childhood, he confessed, still tied him to Judaism. The formative influence of European civilization on his development could not offset the weight of having experienced the world first as a Jew. But the children of the next generation would lack such Jewish roots with the inevitable result that they would abandon Judaism. With all its imperfections, the world was still immensely attractive, and the Jewish component in their lives too shallow to enable them to resist its lure or endure its wrath.[50] What is remarkable about Jost's later scholarship is the extent to which it belies the dark prognosis of his own correspondence. What eventually emerged in the 1840s in three parts as the tenth volume of his *Geschichte der Israeliten* covering the developments of the first half of the nineteenth century was a balanced, incisive and sanguine panorama with a profound sense for the whole.[51]

IV

Influence, like education, can work two ways, either positively or negatively. In the case of the young Zunz the model provided by Jost proved unacceptable. Though the two men were to live in the same city from 1815 to 1835, when Jost left Berlin for Frankfurt am Main to teach at its Philanthropin school, the physical proximity only exacerbated their estrangement.[52] For Zunz, *Wissenschaft* never became a tool for interment. To read *Die Gottesdienstlichen Vorträge* today, with its awesome command of the primary sources, its refined sense for structure, and its spirit of empathy, is still an inspiring experience. In a single stroke Zunz had provided his bewildered generation with an astonishing display of the power of *Wissenschaft* to steer Judaism through the shoals and rapids of emancipation. A meticulous and unprejudiced study of the past could become a force for revitalization. On each of the themes which made up Jost's antirabbinic diatribe, Zunz eventually took a different tack, and it is hard to avoid the impression that his final stance was not at least in part adopted in protest to the spirit to which Jost's early scholarship was subordinated.

The absence of that spirit is the more remarkable because Zunz too was battling the ogre of rabbinism. In 1819, for example, he lent his hand to the composition of an elaborate programmatic statement published by L. L. Hellwitz designed to enlist government support to break the hegemony of the rabbis. The Talmud was described as a late body of literature of human authorship whose exclusive authority in Jewish life could be reduced only through the convening of a Sanhedrin and the formation of a consistorial system. The revision of Jewish law and the creation of an enlightened rabbinic leadership, on which the prospects of emancipation depended, required government intervention.[53] Zunz's letters to Ehrenberg also bristle with antagonism and convey a sense of urgency. On 5th January 1821 he reported that most of his energy was now directed toward toppling the entire edifice of rabbinism.[54]

But by rabbinism Zunz meant primarily what passed for it in his day. His fury was vented against the vulgarization of rabbinic Judaism brought on by more than two centuries of narrow-minded and sophistic study of the Talmud. He had specifically identified his enemy as early as 1818 in the essay on rabbinic literature, and he never committed the mistake Jost did in projecting that animosity back into history.[55] Until their control was broken and they were replaced by learned but enlightened leaders in tune with the times, no significant improvement in Jewish life could be effected. Unlike Jost, Zunz threw himself into the revolt of young intellectuals. From the autumn of 1819 to the beginning of 1824 he stood in the forefront of a small, self-conscious élite who toiled with a sense of mission and incredible zeal to transform the face of Berlin Jewry through the twin institutions of the *Culturverein* and the "deutsche Gottesdienst." Paradoxically, his deep engagement in the issues of the present sharpened his perception of the past.

The opening salvo was fired in 1818. Read in the context of the emancipation struggle, *Etwas über die rabbinische Literatur* was a political tract calling for a change in Jewish leadership.[56] A radical redefinition of an accepted term is usually put forward for a purpose. Rabbinic literature, Zunz contended, was not confined to the Talmud and its expositors and codifiers, but covered the whole vast range of literature written by Jews in Hebrew in the Middle Ages. The authentic spokesmen for Judaism, therefore, could only be its historians, who had explored its cultural diversity, and not its contemporary rabbis, who had restricted themselves to but a single branch of its literature. Without denigrating the Talmud or maligning its students, Zunz had undercut the legitimacy of the ruling rabbinic class to speak for Judaism. Nor did the demise of Hebrew signal the end of Judaism; it merely underscored the urgency of studying its long Hebraic phase historically. And Zunz made it quite clear that he did not expect his generation to be the last to study the subject.

For even equipped with all the requisite ability, knowledge, and tools, we always produce in the study of ideas new ideas and new subject matter. Bibliography, critical method, and history are produced not only by scholarship but also by history itself. And thus as we seek to incorporate objectively into the world of scholarship material already available which once was the subjective treatment of an older idea, so our own manner of mastering the world of scholarship will be rendered for us and posterity into new material to be reworked again.[57]

In sum, *Wissenschaft des Judentums* was born in the battle to unseat the rabbis who stood in the way of emancipation. Only those who understood the past were qualified to lead the way into the future.

Toward the end of this first essay, the twenty-four-year-old Zunz also exhibited the prevailing preference for Spanish Jewry. He announced his intention to publish a scholarly Latin edition of the only known manuscript of *Sefer Ha-Ma'alot* (*The Book of Ethical Degrees*), a thirteenth-century ethical treatise by the Spanish philosopher and poet Shem Tob ibn Falaquera, plus a separate Hebrew synopsis. His objective, he said, was twofold: to encourage others to join in salvaging the treasures of rabbinic literature from oblivion and to rehabilitate that literature in the eyes of the world by publishing its finest examples.[58] By implication Zunz was conceding that these were to be found in the Sephardic and not the Ashkenazic world.

In his next major essay in 1822 on the Spanish place names in Hebrew literature, Zunz delivered a veritable encomium on the uniqueness of Spanish Jewish literature. He chose to begin the arduous task of recovering the data to date and place books and authors in Spain, because compared to the cultural desert in Germany and Poland it was simply an oasis. There Jews had achieved a cultural level they had not known since the loss of political independence and which often left Christian Europe far behind. When they sought refuge in Germany from the Inquisition they enriched Ashkenazic culture in the process.[59]

On the issue of discontinuity in Jewish history the young Zunz likewise still saw eye to eye with Jost. In the same essay on Spanish toponyms, Zunz emphasized the break that had occurred with the end of the First Commonwealth. The Jews may have been the lineal descendants of the former inhabitants of Judah, but with a closed codex in hand they differed fundamentally in speech, morals, orientation, and theology.[60] Thus up to 1822, on the key issues of Sephardic superiority and the discontinuity of the Jewish past, Zunz and Jost were in complete agreement, while on the historical assessment of rabbinism their deep differences were submerged beneath their mutual antagonism toward its contemporary exponents. The disparity in their historical method was as yet unaccompanied by an equal disparity in historical interpretation.

With the publication of his essay on Rashi that same year, Zunz struck out boldly in an unexpected direction. Indeed, a biography of Rashi was certainly a strange topic for a man who detested the present generation of rabbis and who preferred the oasis of Sephardic culture. Instead of publishing his doctoral dissertation on ibn Falaquera and the single manuscript of *Sefer Ha-Ma'alot,* neither of which incidentally were ever to be published by Zunz, he abruptly turned now to study a figure who epitomized both rabbinic Judaism and Ashkenazic culture.[61] Still more significant, Zunz never used his subject as a foil to attack either. His purpose was not to debunk or denigrate, but on the contrary to strip off layers of legend and to get at the historical reality by using data drawn only from Rashi's own writings. With amazing empathy, Zunz was able to reconstruct the specific quality of a Franco-German Jew of the twelfth century. Rashi was not a northern mirror of a Spanish Jew. He was neither worldly nor multi-lingual. At most he knew the French of his day, for which he remains a major source of information. As a witness of the First Crusade, he harbored no love for Christianity. But Zunz neither blushed nor apologized. Rashi's creativity could be understood and measured only within the world of rabbinic Judaism, which constituted his immediate and primary environment.

To appreciate the full import of the Rashi biography, it must be remembered that aside from a few exemplary contemporaries no Ashkenazic Jew from the past had ever merited treatment by the *Maskilim* in the pages of *Hame'asef* and *Sulamith.*[62] The *Maskilim* made use of the biographical genre mainly for didactic purposes, to provide the young with exemplars whose piety did not preclude worldliness.[63] Moreover, the models they projected were not always constructed with an adequate respect for facts. In their biographies of Maimonides and Abravanel the *Maskilim* were quite ready to bevel the rough edges which they found offensive.[64] It is true that in 1810 *Hame'asef* published the opening section of Jacob Emden's autobiography in which he described his saintly father, Zevi Hirsch Ashkenazi, at length, but then the famous Hakham Zevi had spent much of his life in the Sephardic orbit.[65] Thus Zunz's essay on Rashi with its rigorous method, immense learning, and fierce honesty was not only a harbinger of *Wissenschaft* methodology at its best but also a declaration of independence from the tendentious spirit which distorted the research and restricted the horizon of *Haskalah* historiography.

Years later in his *Zur Geschichte und Literatur,* a volume of essays likewise devoted to the study of Ashkenazic literature, Zunz explained what prompted him to write the biography of Rashi. Troubled by the prevailing ignorance of Christian scholars of medieval Jewish literature, Zunz felt that the *Haskalah* with its exclusive concentration on the luminaries of the Spanish milieu was partly to blame. It was neither the brilliance of the Spanish period nor the lack of manuscripts which blinded the *Maskilim* to the literary achievements of Franco-German Jewry, but rather their aversion to everything specifically Jewish. They were also offended by the comprehensiveness of Judaism in the North. In Moslem society in the South a neutral, non-religious sector had prevented Judaism from attaining the all-embracing character which distinguished both it and Christianity in the rest of Europe.[66] Jost's later unequivocal endorsement of this pro-Spanish bias could only have reinforced Zunz in the justice of his cause. He was destined, however, to remain for decades the lonely and embattled expositor of the more particularistic mode of medieval Jewish culture.

The essay on Rashi should not be construed to mean that Zunz had abandoned his commitment to religious reform. Since its writing coincided with his controversial and abortive career as a *Prediger,* this hardly seems likely. What the essay did represent was a major effort to show how far rabbinic Judaism had deviated and degenerated from the cultural creativity it had achieved in the twelfth century. After briefly tracing the path of its decline in the centuries which followed the Reformation, Zunz summed up his case. "Neither the religious (rabbis) nor the civil (Parnasim) leadership maintained itself on the level of the best of Rabbinism, let alone the best of the age."[67] It is thus apparent that historical research could attack the present in two ways: by denigrating its pedigree or by exalting what preceded it. Either technique effectively impugned the legitimacy of what existed. While Jost had set out to demolish rabbinism by smearing its origins, Zunz sought to reform it by confrontation with the wholesomeness of an earlier age. Both men were in search of a usable past. The merit of Zunz's method was that it struck much closer to the historical truth.

The collapse of the *Verein* in January 1824 left Zunz exhausted and demoralized. Its intense idealism and ambitious program had utterly failed to elicit the support or even the interest of Berlin Jewry. Historically, it clearly had anticipated the major intellectual and religious developments of the next half-century, but at the time it died it was almost unknown and certainly unmourned.[68] For Zunz, the years that followed were to be among the most arduous, lonely, and depressing of his long life. But while he despaired of the Jews who denied him generosity or recognition, he never lost his faith in the survival of Judaism and the power of *Wissenschaft.* During that dark decade he continued to emancipate himself from the biases of *Haskalah* historiography.

The culmination of that process came in 1832, with the publication of *Die Gottesdienstlichen Vorträge der Juden,* a book which unfurled *Wissenschaft* for the first time in all its power and potential. It faced in a constructive and feasible way the major issue of the emancipation era, namely, what was to be done with the legacy of the past. A program like Jost's that called for the interment of rabbinic Judaism and the eradication of twenty-three hundred years of Jewish history was the petulant folly of a Jewish *philosophe.* It stood about as much chance of success as Robespierre's cult of the Supreme Being. In contrast, Zunz, despite his deep-seated political liberalism and penchant for rationalism, shared with the romantics of his day a healthy respect for the restricting reality of the past. In place of Jost's unrelieved emphasis on denigration, Zunz introduced the polyphonic theme of organic growth. With the concept of development, Jewish historiography had come of age.

The message of the book was that rabbinism could not be wiped out nor, properly understood, need it be. Central to his argument was the repudiation of Jost's insistence on the discontinuity between Mosaism and rabbinism. To begin with, the basic exegetical instrument of rabbinic Judaism was as old as the canon itself. With deep insight, Zunz showed the process of reinterpretation already in evidence in the work of the Chronicler at the beginning of the third century B.C.E. The instrument of Midrash eventually gave rise to three types of literature: translations, laws, and homilies. But Zunz insisted that the latter two—Halakhah and Aggadah—represented a continuation of the regimen of biblical law and the freedom of prophecy, and together they constituted the two basic strands of Jewish national life. Zunz portrayed Aggadah as the voice of the people, an anonymous, patriotic expression of the deepest national sentiments. The relationship between rabbinic Judaism and Israelite religion, therefore, bespoke an underlying unity, which Zunz would never relinquish.[69]

It was not fortuitous, of course, that Zunz chose to concentrate on the dimension of freedom. His design was to project a new image of rabbinism that challenged the existing caricature. What emerged from his prodigious learning and rigorous analysis was the vision of a vibrant religious culture responding creatively to the dilemmas posed by each new age. Without special pleading, Zunz marshaled the irrefutable evidence: like any living organism Judaism exhibited flexibility, experimentation, and development. With customary vigor he summed up the first 1,500 years of rabbinic literature:

This is the nature of the terrain from Chronicles to European Jewish literature: not a desert whose sudden forms—Talmud, Midrash, Targum, Masorah, Kabbalah—frighten the traveler rather than guide him, but an extraordinary road of development strewn with countless works and ruins, testimonies to intense passion, fighting concern, and inspiring ideas.[70]

The decay and rigidity which marked the present was a travesty of rabbinic Judaism brought on by the ever increasing isolation and oppression of Ashkenazic Jewry during the last few centuries.[71]

The understanding and warmth of Zunz's portrait were the achievement of disciplined engagement. Zunz's lifelong personal mission was to revitalize the synagogue, the one institution which, he felt, expressed the essence of the Jewish people and guaranteed its existence. In his very first essay in 1818 he had underscored the immediate usefulness of a historical study of the liturgy based on the sources.[72] His brief career as a *Prediger* merely shifted the approach; the goal remained the same. In 1832 Zunz took recourse to the métier in which he was most effective. *Die Gottesdienstlichen Vorträge* delivered a mountain of precedents to legitimize enriching the service with the introduction of the spoken word. In the

1850s and 1860s he culminated his commitment with a trilogy which effected the vision conceived at the very outset of his career. The national theater of the Jews, the synagogue, had found its historian, a man whose selfless perseverance was testimony to his deep faith in its future.

In the final analysis, what distinguished Zunz from Jost was the impact of Herder, who was to teach so many alienated intellectuals to rediscover the beauty and value of their different national traditions. Jost continued to write in the spirit of Voltaire, that is, judgmentally rather than empathetically. Like Voltaire, who was conscious and proud of being a member of the French bourgeoisie, he measured the past in terms of the present. The spokesman of reason in its eternal conflict with unreason, the historian came to judge, to condemn errors, and to applaud anticipations. Consequently, neither Voltaire nor Jost could muster much sympathy for the field of religion. In his rebellion against the Enlightenment, Herder stressed the uniqueness of the individual. There were no universal standards of beauty and good, because every historical collectivity was inimitable. In the challenging words of Herder: "Every nation has in itself its own centre of happiness, just as every sphere has its centre of gravity." The function of the historian is only to understand, and the method, that of sympathetic identification, was an idea so revolutionary that Herder had to invent the term *Einfühlung* to convey its meaning.[73]

Jost may have read Herder, but the young Zunz alone applied his teaching, as early as 1822, to be exact, in his biography of Rashi which he concluded with a cryptic reference to Herder.[74] His treatment of rabbinism was an achievement of extraordinary self-transcendence, given his animosity for its nineteenth-century form. Where the Jewish *philosophes* could see only error and degeneration, Zunz revealed creativity and growth. The sustained empathy of his work not only served to uncover the nature of the past, but also to influence the shape of the present. The mood and tone in which he wrote transformed *Wissenschaft* from an esoteric discipline into a powerful social force.

NOTES

1. The biographical data is culled from the following sources: LBIA, letter by Jost to Philipp Ehrenberg dated 12th May 1843; I. M. Jost, "Vor einem halben Jahrhundert," *Sippurim*, III (1854), pp. 150–157; L. Zunz, "Mein erster Unterricht in Wolfenbüttel," *JJGL*, XXX (1937), pp. 131–140. In a note to his *Geschichte der Is-raeliten*, IX (Berlin 1828), p. 64, Jost included himself among those Jewish teachers who had learned their German from Mendelssohn's translation of the Pentateuch.

2. L. Zunz, *Samuel Meyer Ehrenberg: Ein Denkmal*, Braunschweig 1854, pp. 9–15.

3. Zunz, *JJGL*, XXX, p. 136; I. M. Jost, *Offenes Sendschreiben an K. Streckfuss*, Berlin 1833, p. 65.

4. Theodore H. Von Laue, *Leopold Ranke: The Formative Years*, Princeton 1950, pp. 9–10, 31; Ernst Simon, *Ranke und Hegel*, München and Berlin 1928, pp. 1–15.

5. In the autumn of 1816, after lengthy delays, the Minister of Interior finally granted Jost permission to open a Jewish *Mittelschule*. The recommendation of the Berlin municipality had apparently broken the log-jam. While it certainly was de-

sirable to have Jewish children attend Christian schools, the memorandum pointed out that this eventually was unlikely for the foreseeable future. Consequently, to prevent Jewish children from attending the traditional institutions of Jewish education, the government should encourage the opening of enlightened Jewish schools (CAHJP, P17-498). The Prussian edict of September 1819, which forbade Christian children from studying in Jewish schools, put Jost's school out of business. (LBIA, Jost to Ehrenberg, 22nd December 1819.) It took him more than eighteen months to recover his economic equilibrium. (LBIA, Jost to Ehrenberg, 15th April 1821.) By 1825 both his school and pension were flourishing again. (LBIA, Jost to Ehrenberg, 6th June 1825.) Regarding Zunz's career as editor, see S. Maybaum, "Aus dem Leben von Leopold Zunz," *Zwölfter Bericht über die Lehranstalt für die Wissenschaft des Judenthums*, Berlin 1894, p. 12. While Zunz could not compete with Ranke in terms of status, his annual salary of 800 taler certainly compared favorably with Ranke's official salary of 500 taler. (LBIA,, Jost to Ehrenberg, 16th January 1824; Max Lenz, *Geschichte der Königlichen Friedrich-Wilhelms-Universität zu Berlin*, 4 vols., Halle 1910–1918, I, pp. 257–258.)

6. I. M. Jost, *Geschichte der Israeliten*, 9 vols., Berlin 1820–1828; *idem, Allgemeine Geschichte des Israelitischen Volkes*, 2 vols., Berlin 1832. Why Jost should have immediately followed his nine-volume opus with another two-volume survey is cleared up by his correspondence with Ehrenberg. Even before he had finished volume nine, it was suggested that at 600 taler it would be well worth his while. He eventually sold it for 640 taler. (LBIA, Jost to Ehrenberg, 8th March 1828; 6th March 1829; 28th May 1829.) In the summer of 1841 Jost took a sixteen-day trip to London to explore the prospects for an English edition, but nothing came of the venture. (LBIA, Jost to Ehrenberg, 1st November 1841.)

7. *Geschichte der Israeliten*, II, Anhang, pp. 63–64.

8. Shaye J. D. Cohen, *Josephus in Galilee and Rome: His Vita and Development as a Historian*, Columbia University doctoral dissertation, 1975, pp. 43–45.

9. LBIA, Jost to Ehrenberg, 14th March 1830. Jost reiterated his defense to Ehrenberg in a letter dated 10th March 1833. To be sure, there is ample evidence in the Jost–Ehrenberg, Zunz–Ehrenberg, and Jost–Zunz correspondence (JNUL, 4° 792/G-15) to document the ticklish relationship between the two men. But a unique and precious description by a third party is offered by Philipp Ehrenberg, the son of Samuel Meyer, to his brother Moritz in a letter dated 20th November 1829 (LBIA, 4025/272a). That autumn Philipp had joined his cousin Meyer Isler in Berlin to study at the university. As a frequent guest in the home of his father's former students, he quickly penetrated the façade of civility which masked their true feelings.

> The longer and more closely one gets to know him [i.e., Zunz] the more learning he reveals. Without a doubt he is a man of great feeling, a quality he strangely seeks to hide, usually tucking it away behind his wit. In this way I could live with these people [i.e., the Zunzes] quite comfortably and contentedly, except that the rivalry with Jost gets in the way, involving the mutual acquaintances and close friends of both families, so that we are almost the only ones [i.e., Philipp and his cousin] who remain completely neutral, not paying much attention to either side or party. The worst is that when they visit each other they are excessively polite and exchange compliments, especially the wives. Indeed, no *friendship* [underlined in the original] can exist between them; they can merely socialize. This, dear brother, is my opinion. I may see some things too grimly, but this is the truth, and Berlin would certainly be intolerable for me, especially during this first semester, if I did not have Meyer. . . .

10. *Göttingische gelehrte Anzeigen*, 1821, vol. I, pp. 137–141. The quotation is on p. 141. Although the review was published anonymously, Eichhorn had written Jost in advance that it was coming (LBIA, Jost to Ehrenberg, 25th July 1820), and on 2nd February 1821 Ehrenberg informed Jost that it had just appeared. (LBIA, 4025/121.) The Jost–Ehrenberg correspondence from the 1820s is rich in references to favorable reviews of and reactions to Jost's work. Among Jost's early admirers was Salomon Rapoport, who became disenchanted with Jost only in the 1840s. (Isaac Barzilay, *Shlomo Yehudah Rapoport and His Contemporaries*, Israel 1969, pp. 106–115.) Although Geiger's estimate of Jost also soon declined, his early letters do display an affirmative attitude toward his work. (Abraham Geiger, *Nachgelassene Schriften*, V, Berlin 1878, pp. 76, 81, 90.) On the other hand, Samuel Luzzatto was outraged from the very beginning by Jost's biblical criticism and treatment of rabbinic literature. (Eisig Gräber, ed., *S. D. Luzzatto's hebräische Briefe*, Przemysl 1882, reprinted Jerusalem 1967, pp. 178–180, 190–193.)

11. LBIA, Jost to Ehrenberg, 1st November 1841; "Das Buch Zunz," JNUL, 4° 792/C-13, p. 73d.

12. LBIA, Jost to Ehrenberg, 1830; 1st November 1841. See also Jost's letter dated 25th February 1827.

13. JNUL, 4° 792. For a description of the contents of this unique collection see Gotthold Weil, "Das Zunz-Archiv," in *Bulletin des Leo Baeck Instituts*, 2 (1959), No. 7, pp. 148–161.

14. In 1928 Salo Baron in a perceptive analysis of Jost's *Geschichte der Israeliten* argued that he still belonged primarily to the Enlightenment. My own assessment, as will become clear, confirms that thesis, though for very different reasons. That essay has been reprinted in Baron, *History and Jewish Historians*, Philadelphia 1964, pp. 240–262. See also the somewhat less critical but informative essay by Reuwen Michael, "I. M. Jost und sein Werk," in *Bulletin des Leo Baeck Instituts*, 3 (1960), No. 12, pp. 239–258. The older biography by Heinrich Zirndarf, *Isaak Markus Jost und seine Freunde*, Leipzig and New York 1886, is still useful.

15. Gerschom Scholem, *Explications and Implications: Writings on Jewish Heritage and Renaissance* (Hebrew), Tel Aviv 1975, pp. 385–403; *idem, The Messianic Idea in Judaism*, New York 1971, pp. 304–317. The Steinschneider story appears in both essays. The Zunz–Kaufmann correspondence was published in part by Markus Brann, *JJGL*, V (1902), pp. 159–209, and VI (1903), pp. 120–157.

16. Monika Richarz, *Der Eindritt der Juden in die akademischen Berufe: Jüdische Studenten und Akademiker in Deutschland 1678–1848*, Tübingen 1974 (Schriftenreihe wissenschaftlicher Abhandlungen des Leo Baeck Instituts 28), p. 124.

17. JNUL, 4° 792/G-15.

18. Jost, *Sippurim*, p. 161.

19. I. M. Jost, *Geschichte des Judenhass und seiner Sekten*, 3 vols., Leipzig 1857–1859, III, p. 319. Despite the prominence of universal history in the Göttingen tradition (Kurt Hunger, *Die Bedeutung der Universität Göttingen für die Geschichtsforschung am Ausgang des achtzenten Jahrhunderts*, Berlin 1932, pp. 37–43) including a *Weltgeschichte* published by Jost's favorite professor, J. G. Eichhorn, in 1799 (p. 41), I have found no evidence to support what I had conjectured earlier (Heinrich Graetz, *The Structure of Jewish History and Other Essays*, trans. by I. Schorsch, New York 1975, pp. 6–7) that Göttingen may have prompted Jost to try his hand at a Jewish version of a world history. Moreover, if that had been the genesis of his work, why should Jost have seen fit to conceal the fact in 1859 by crediting two *Maskilim* whose radicalism had long been discredited? The quotation in the text is taken from LBIA, Jost to Ehrenberg, 16th September 1815.

20. LBIA, 4025/100, Ehrenberg to Jost, 7th April 1820. The dedication read in part "to his revered and beloved foster-father, educator, teacher, and friend" and was followed by a two-page expression of gratitude.

21. *Geschichte der Israeliten*, I, Vorwort.

22. LBIA, Jost to Ehrenberg, 25th July 1820. On 21st August 1820 Ehrenberg registered his disagreement.

> What you say regarding Judaism and Christianity is partially true. But there is in the Christian world just as little pure Christianity etc. [*sic*] and the New Testament contains even more nonsense than the Old. Even the good stuff in it is to be found in the Old, if one only takes the trouble to look for it. As desirable as a reformation might also be for us, it must not lead through Christianity. The reformed Jew, as I envisage him, will be far more precious than a Christian. (LBIA, 4025/108.)

23. Nahum N. Glatzer, ed., *Leopold and Adelheid Zunz: An Account in Letters 1815–1885*, Publications of the Leo Baeck Institute, London 1958, pp. 34–35.

24. JNUL, 4° 792/B-1. See also Zunz's letter to Adolf Strodtmann, the biographer of Heine, dated 6th March 1863. (JNUL, 4° 792/G-27.) In an article in the *Allgemeine Zeitung des Judentums*, 1859, p. 176, Jost claimed he had withdrawn because of the demands of his scholarship, but the minutes of the *Verein* do not bear out his version of the event.

25. JNUL, 4° 792/B-13.

26. The source for Zunz's opinion is Heine's letter to Zunz, dated 2nd June 1823, in which Heine cleverly applied what Zunz had said of Jost's first volume to the first volume of the *ZWJ*. (JNUL, 4° 792/G-27.)

27. For the most recent contribution to the study of this secular critique, see Jacob Katz, "Judaism and Jews in the Eyes of Voltaire" (in Hebrew), *Molad*, new series, V, 1973, pp. 614–625.

28. B. Spinoza, *A Theologico-Political Treatise*, translated by R. H. M. Elwes, New York 1951, pp. 72, 236, 247–248; Moses Mendelssohn, *Jerusalem and Other Jewish Writings*, translated by Alfred Jospe, New York 1969, pp. 99–104; David Friedländer, *Sendschreiben an . . . Teller*, Berlin 1799, pp. 26–43; Lazarus Bendavid, *ZWJ*, I (1823), p. 208.

29. Spinoza, *A Theologico-Political Treatise*, pp. 218–236; Julius Guttmann, *Religion and Knowledge* (in Hebrew), translated by Saul Esh, Jerusalem 1955, pp. 195–196; Shmuel Ettinger, "Jews and Judaism as Seen by the English Deists of the 18th Century" (in Hebrew), *Zion*, XXIX (1964), pp. 182–207.

30. *Geschichte der Israeliten*, I, pp. 39–48; III, pp. 18–33; *Allgemeine Geschichte*, I, pp. 438–450. Like his mentors, Jost also spoke of Moses' work in political terms. "Moses did not give his people a religion, but a political constitution. At that time, all peoples tied religion to the constitution with unbreakable bonds." (*Geschichte der Israeliten*, I, p. 40.)

31. Graetz, *The Structure of Jewish History*, pp. 15–16.

32. In fact, he publicly rejected it as speculative and unnecessary. (Jost, *Culturgeschichte der Israeliten der ersten Hälfte des 19. Jahrhunderts*, Breslau 1846, p. 270.)

33. Nahum N. Glatzer, "Aus Unveröffentlichten Briefen von I. M. Jost," in *In Zwei Welten: Siegfried Moses zum Fünfundsiebzigsten Geburtstag*, edited by Hans Tramer, Tel Aviv 1962, p. 404.

34. *Geschichte der Israeliten*, I, p. 57. The passage in Spinoza (p. 56) reads: "Nay, I would go so far as to believe that if the foundations of their religion have not emasculated their minds they may even, if occasion offers, so changeable are human affairs, raise up their empire afresh, and that God may a second time elect them."

35. *Geschichte der Israeliten*, III, p. 64.

36. *Ibid.*, I, pp. 297–300.

37. *Ibid.*, III, pp. 145–160.

38. Thomas W. Perry, *Public Opinion, Propaganda, and Politics in Eighteenth-Century England*, Cambridge, Mass. 1962, pp. 11–12, 16, 21, 111; Antoine Guénée, *Letters of Certain Jews to Monsieur de Voltaire*, translated by Philipp Lefanu, 2 vols., Dublin 1777, I, pp. 21–77. Among these letters (pp. 29–57) is also the translation of Isaac de Pinto, *Apologie pour la nation juive*, Amsterdam 1762.

39. JNUL, 4° 792/B-10.

40. *Geschichte der Israeliten*, VI, pp. 84–85, 122–123, 257, 285, 291–292, 327. This Jewish preference for Sephardic Jewry, I think, has little to do with the enthusiasm generated by the romantic movement for Moorish Spain. It was fed by indigenous Jewish factors, though no doubt reinforced by the cultural climate. The convergence of both set the stage for the extraordinary role played by Jewish scholars in the development of Islamic studies in the nineteenth century (see Bernard Lewis, *Islam in History: Ideas, Men and Events in the Middle East*, New York 1973, pp. 20–21, 123–137.

41. *Geschichte der Israeliten*, VI, pp. 285–286.

42. *Ibid.*, pp. 334–339.

43. *Ibid.*, pp. 220–225.

44. Mendelssohn, *Jerusalem*, pp. 61, 106–110; Lazarus Bendavid, *Etwas zur Charakteristick der Juden*, Leipzig 1793, pp. 45, 56–66. It is worth noting that already in 1793 Bendavid bemoaned the many lacunae in the knowledge of Jewish history (p. 11).

45. Friedländer, pp. 25–43.

46. Jost, *Was hat Herr Chiarini in Angelegenheiten der europäischen Juden geleistet?*, Berlin 1830, pp. 87–88. See also *Geschichte der Israeliten*, III, Anhang, p. 158, where Jost declared:

> It probably is not advisable to break lightheartedly the chains of religion adopted long ago. But certainly the time has come to convene assemblies which would erect a truthful structure on the basis of holy Scripture in which the Mosaist (*der Mosait*) could live with dignity faithful to the principles of his synagogue.

47. David Friedländer, *Akten-Stücke die Reform der jüdischen Kolonieen in den Preussischen Staaten betreffend*, Berlin 1793, p. 8; Ludwig Geiger, "Aus Zunz's Nachlass," *Zeitschrift für Geschichte der Juden in Deutschland*, V (1892), p. 261; LBIA, Jost to Ehrenberg, 12th July 1832. In his review Eichhorn had already questioned the propriety of Jost's title (*Göttingische gelehrte Anzeigen*, 1821, vol. I, p. 139.)

48. Published in Berlin in six volumes from 1832 to 1834, it was officially put out by a "society of lovers of Torah and science in Berlin, the capital." But the last volume as well as Jost's correspondence leave no doubt that Jost was the editor. With its German translation printed in Hebrew characters, the project has all the earmarks of a mishnaic parallel to Mendelssohn's translation of the Pentateuch. Ehrenberg chided Jost for its innumerable printing errors. (Glatzer, *Leopold and Adelheid Zunz*, p. 79.)

49. LBIA, Jost to Ehrenberg, 9th February 1848. See also the Jost letters of 14th March 1830 and 2nd June 1844.

50. Glatzer, in *In Zwei Welten*, pp. 400–413.

51. Jost, *Neuere Geschichte der Israeliten von 1815 bis 1845*, 3 vols., Berlin 1846–1847. In a deeply felt obituary, Raphael Kirchheim, who lived in Frankfurt and was on intimate terms with Jost during his last years, indicated a basic shift in Jost's

orientation to Judaism. (*Allgemeine Zeitung des Judenthums*, 1860, pp. 720–721.) It is difficult to reconcile this opinion with the somber letters to Ehrenberg in 1852.

52. LBIA, Jost to Ehrenberg, 17th April 1835; 29th July 1835. Jost left Berlin without even saying good-bye. Nahum N. Glatzer, ed., *Leopold Zunz: Jude—Deutscher—Europäer. Ein jüdisches Gelehrtenschicksal des 19. Jahrhunderts in Briefen an Freunde*, Tübingen 1964 (Schriftenreihe wissenschaftlicher Abhandlungen des Leo Baeck Instituts 11), p. 182.

53. L. L. Hellwitz, *Die Organisation der Israeliten in Deutschland*, Magdenburg 1819, pp. 48–65. Although Zunz never claimed full credit for this pamphlet (unlike Luitpold Wallach, *Liberty and Letters: The Thoughts of Leopold Zunz*, Publications of the Leo Baeck Institute, London 1959, p. 145. See Zunz, *JJGL*, XXX, p. 166), the terse, direct style and rich historical insight confirm the extent of his contribution.

54. Glatzer, *Leopold Zunz*, p. 117. See also, for example, *idem, Leopold und Adelheid Zunz*, pp. 22–23.

55. Zunz, "Etwas über die rabbinische Literatur," *Gesammelte Schriften*, 3 vols., Berlin 1875–1876, I, p. 29, n. 1. It is noteworthy that in the curriculum revision for the Berlin teachers' seminary (*das jüdische Seminar Talmud Torah*), which Zunz submitted in December 1838, he proposed to devote eight of the thirty hours of weekly instruction in each year of the four-year program to the study of Talmud. Aside from Bible, which was allotted four hours per week, no other subject merited even half that amount of time. (Ludwig Geiger, "Zunz und das Berliner Provinzialsschulkollegium," *Liberales Judentum*, VII [1915], pp. 107–113.)

56. *Gesammelte Schriften*, I, pp. 1–31.

57. *Ibid.*, pp. 26–27.

58. *Ibid.*, pp. 29–30.

59. *ZWJ*, p. 128.

60. *Ibid.*, pp. 114–117.

61. Zunz, "Salomon ben Isaac genannt Raschi," *ZWJ*, pp. 277–385. *Sefer Ha-Ma'alot (Das Buch der Grade)* was eventually published in Berlin, 1894, by Ludwig Venetianer on the basis of four manuscripts.

62. During the first years of *Hame'asef*, when biography received much more attention than later, essays appeared on such Sephardic luminaries as Abravanel (1784), Yoseph Shlomo Delmedigo (1784), Moses Raphael de Aquilar (1785), Maimonides (1786), Menasseh ben Israel (1788), Isaac Orobio de Castro (1788), and Jacob Yehudah Leon (1788). The biographies of Mendelssohn and Wessely were published in 1788 and 1809 respectively. *Sulamith*, which carried both the spirit and program of *Hame'asef* into the first half of the nineteenth century, likewise devoted its historical biographies to model Sephardic figures. (Siegfried Stein, "Die Zeitschrift *Sulamith*," *Zeitschrift für die Geschichte der Juden in Deutschland*, VII [1937], pp. 217–218.)

63. See the programmatic statement which introduced the series entitled "Histories of the Great Men of Israel," *Hame'asef*, I (1784), pp. 25–30.

64. See the penetrating essay by James H. Lehmann, "Maimonides, Mendelssohn and the Me'asfim: Philosophy and the Biographical Imagination in the Early Haskalah," in *LBIYB XX* (1975), pp. 87–108.

65. *Hame'asef*, 1810, pp. 79–97.

66. Zunz, *Zur Geschichte und Literatur*, Berlin 1845, pp. 158–159. In his review of this book, Zunz's close friend, Bernhard Beer, stressed Zunz's determination to rectify the imbalance by rehabilitating the image of Franco-German Jewry. (*Zeitschrift für die religiösen Interessen des Judentums*, III [1846], pp. 347–348.)

67. *ZWJ*, p. 380.

68. This was also Zunz's estimate of the historical significance of the *Verein*. (See his letter to Strodtmann dated 4th May 1864 in JNUL, 4° 792/G-27.)

69. Zunz, *Die Gottesdienstlichen Vorträge der Juden*, Berlin 1832, pp. 1, 3, 36, 98, 311, 321–322. In 1855 Zunz elaborated his perception of the inherent unity of Jewish history. The genres of prophecy and psalmody constitute the basic forms of Jewish expression. As the prophets brought the wisdom of God to the people so the psalmists gave wings to their pain and prayers. In the post-biblical era these contrasting functions were assumed by the rabbis and the poets, who converged on the synagogue to intensify the religious experience of the entire nation. (*Die synagogale Poesie des Mittelalters*, Berlin 1855, pp. 1–8.)

70. *Die Gottesdienstlichen Vorträge*, pp. 307–308.

71. *Ibid.*, pp. 436ff.

72. *Gesammelte Schriften*, I, p. 8.

73. Friedrich Meinecke, *Historism*, translated by J. E. Anderson, London 1972, chapters on Voltaire and Herder. The quotation is on p. 340.

74. *ZWJ*, p. 381. The correspondence suggests that Herder was regarded highly in the Zunz household (Glatzer, *Leopold and Adelheid Zunz*, p. 82; *idem*, *Leopold Zunz*, p. 178.)

Zacharias Frankel and the European Origins of Conservative Judaism

It has long been observed that ideological ambiguity is the hallmark of Conservative Judaism. Passion appears to substitute for clarity. In part, at least, the fault inheres in occupying the center. Extremes lend themselves to dogmatic clarity, if not cogent thinking. As perceived from the middle, the complexity of reality is hardly susceptible to explanation in terms of a single principle. Compounding this difficulty is the fact that the middle is caught in the crossfire of a two-front war. It must produce an arsenal of arguments for use against both left and right which, of necessity, often include ideas that are barely compatible.

No Conservative thinker has been indicted more often for ideological ambiguity than Zacharias Frankel, who founded and shaped European Conservatism through the force of his personality, the scope of his scholarship, and the power of his pen. Descended from a line of rabbis and raised in the Jewish metropolis of Prague, Frankel faced the challenge of modernity in all its intractable complexity. He was an energetic, emotional, combative man who combined a deep knowledge of rabbinics with a firm command of the classics. In 1836 he came to serve the nascent Jewish community of Dresden as the representative of a new type of rabbinic leadership that was distinguished from its premodern counterpart in terms of function, education, and authority. Indeed, his reputation had already far transcended the borders of Saxony. For the next eight years Berlin courted Frankel to occupy its long vacant position of *Oberrabbiner*, the last time, in fact, that the community entertained the idea of appointing a supreme rabbinic authority. But Frankel preferred to fight for his vision of Judaism from the more tranquil corner of Dresden.[1] Finally, in 1854, when invited to head the newly opened modern rabbinical seminary of Breslau, the first in all of Germany, Frankel had a unique chance to institutionalize and disseminate that vision. He did not fail. By 1879, some four years after his sudden death, the seminary had offered instruction to a total of 272 students, while graduating and placing in the most important Jewish communities of

Europe nearly 120 teachers, preachers, and rabbis.[2] Frankel's conception of Judaism was well on the way to capturing the majority of German Jewry.

Though institutionalized in Breslau, that conception originated in Dresden where, during his eighteen years there, Frankel had labored to crystallize his views on the overwhelming dilemma of his generation: how to accommodate consciously an ancient, non-Western religion to the inescapable consequence of a radically new legal status without destroying its sense of integrity and continuity. With unsparing discipline, Frankel wrote voluminously to stem the tide of radical Reform, and though his German style tended to be prolix and passionate, with verbal precision often yielding to the urgency of the moment and the novelty of the challenge, his corpus is informed by a coherent religious position, clarified and deepened by frequent reformulation.

Since Frankel first entered the public arena during the heyday of German radical Reform, the meaning of his elusive terminology is rooted in his perception of his adversaries. Basically, Frankel regarded the Reformers as *Vernunftmenschen*, uncompromising rationalists determined to bring Judaism before the bar of reason. On the theoretical level, they attacked the entire legal edifice of Judaism by impugning its exegetical base. The arbitrary exegesis of the rabbis repeatedly did violence to the plain sense of Scripture. On the practical level, the Reformers stood ready to abandon every ritual practice which they condemned as irrational or obstructing integration. Unfeeling, irreverent, and Jewishly unlearned, they arrogated to themselves the right to impose Reform from above, with a view to reducing Judaism to a set of abstract, enlightened, and innocuous propositions.[3] Whatever the historical validity of this undifferentiated perception of contemporary Reform, there is no doubt that it exerted a decisive influence in shaping Frankel's own religious views.

There are five key terms in his rhetoric that require careful exposition: two adjectives, "positive" and "historical" and three nouns, *Volk, Geschichte* (history), and *Wissenschaft des Judentums* (the scholarly study of Judaism). Frankel invoked these terms repeatedly and only systematic textual analysis within the framework of his time can yield the full range of their meaning.

Perhaps the term least understood is "positive." What did Frankel intend to convey when he used the full phrase "positive, historical Judaism" for the first time during his brief and demonstrative attendance at the Frankfurt Rabbinical Conference of 1845?[4] To be sure, the term immediately suggests the opposite of "negative," and, often enough in his writing Frankel condemned the program of radical Reform for being utterly negative, preoccupied with cutting and curtailing. But the word "positive" also carried a well-established technical connotation, implying either law in general or posited law as opposed to natural law. For example, the young Hegel wrote an essay, first published in 1907, entitled "The Positivity of the Christian Religion," which indicted Christianity along Kantian lines for preserving, against the intent of its founder, Israel's bondage to law. Though Kant had preferred to use the word "statutory" in his own critique of Judaism, it was its positivity that summed up the ethically abhorrent legal nature of classical Judaism and, in Jewish circles, radical Reformers like Michael Creizenach and the young Abraham Geiger employed the term with precisely that meaning before Frankel did.[5]

Equally pertinent to our analysis is the fact that, one year after the Frankfurt conference, Frankel published a seminal book expounding rabbinic judicial procedure in terms of Western legal categories. Throughout this study, which marks the finest early effort at such conceptual translation, Frankel used the designation "positive" in its legal sense.[6] Consequently, during the very years when he was articulating his conception of Judaism, he was also working in another context with the word "positive" as a technical term.

By choosing the adjective "positive" to describe his conception of Judaism, Frankel defiantly reasserted its fundamentally legal character and rejected any effort to dilute it. In Judaism, religious sentiments and eternal truths were expressed in prescribed behavior. Unabashedly, Frankel spoke of Judaism as *"eine Religion der That"* a statutory religion of action rooted in revelation.[7] In so doing, he provided a striking example of his persistent demand for *Selbständigkeit*, by which he meant a pursuit of equality based on self-respect that entailed no denigration of authentic Judaism.[8] Despite the weighty critique of German luminaries from Kant to Bruno Bauer, law—as Mendelssohn had insisted to the embarrassment of his radical disciples—remained central to the Jewish religious experience. Moreover, Frankel scorned efforts to mute and transcend the concreteness of the *halakhic* mode through excessive symbolic interpretation. Philo, *kabbalah*, and Samson Raphael Hirsch were all equally guilty of devaluing the individual *mitzvah* by dwelling on its symbolic import.[9]

Yet it is quite apparent that Frankel never politicized classical rabbinism, for which he spoke, by denying its inherent responsiveness to the dictates of the age. Utilizing creative biblical exegesis, the rabbis were able to preserve an inner dynamic that ensured legal growth and flexibility.[10] Rigidity set in only when increasing dispersion necessitated recording and codifying the Oral Law and thereby curbing the freedom of opinion which marked the mishnaic and talmudic stages of development.[11] To regain that legal vitality was the challenge of the age. Frankel's work gives ample evidence of a personal willingness to alter specific practices. He was prepared to allow autopsies under certain conditions, to delay burial, to modernize the procedure for circumcision, to introduce a program of religious education for girls, to make changes in the prayerbook, and even to study the possibility of dropping the second day of the three pilgrimage festivals (*yom tov sheni*).[12] In sum, he advocated what he called "moderate reform" or a "thinking faith" and never opposed *halakhic* change in principle.[13]

Furthermore, Frankel never regarded *halakhah* as exhausting the realm of the sacred in Judaism. If *halakhah* was one source of sanctity, history was most assuredly another, and it is this non-*halakhic* dimension of Judaism that is designated by the term "historical" in Frankel's classic phrase. The occasion for Frankel's resounding withdrawal from Frankfurt was not a *halakhic* dispute. The overwhelming majority, including Frankel, had agreed that there were no *halakhic* impediments to dropping Hebrew as the language of public prayer, but, unlike a much smaller majority, Frankel did feel that the weight of history dictated retaining Hebrew on objective grounds and not for merely sentimental reasons.[14] Three years earlier, in 1842, in the controversy over the revised Hamburg prayerbook, he had protested against substituting Sephardic for Ashkenazic *piyyutim*, because the switch offended the historical consciousness of German Jewry.[15] Ancient custom, nourished by continuous practice and often sanctified by martyrdom, constituted a commanding voice. The past was a source of values, inspiration, and commitment. Though a secular category, history obligated no less than did *halakhah*, and both stood athwart the revolutionary and leveling path of reason.

To mediate the commands of *halakhah* and history, Frankel introduced the novel idea of the *Volk* as a formative agent in defining Jewish practice. Both the intent and source of this concept were manifestly conservative. If the Reformers sought to relieve the growing alienation from Judaism of educated and upwardly mobile Jews, Frankel spoke for the rural masses inside and outside Germany who were less affected by the fact or promise of emancipation. The elaborate rituals of Jewish life were not just partitions erected to shelter Jews in hostile climes; for countless Jews they remained the vital means of experiencing the divine. Rabbinic Jacobins could not unilaterally overthrow the realm of the sacred as long as it still enjoyed the benefit of popular support. The ultimate arbiter of the holy was the *Volk* itself. As long as it still possessed a vibrant religious consciousness, it represented a source of indirect revelation. Its piety exercised a legitimate veto over religious schemes imposed by a self-selected, rationalist elite.[16]

Frankel's emphasis on the people as a central component of the legal process was an idea adapted from Friedrich Carl von Savigny, who inaugurated the historical study of jurisprudence in Germany in 1814. In the wake of the French collapse, Savigny rejected the intoxicating proposal of fostering German unification through a single law code that would terminate the jungle of legal diversity which epitomized and reinforced the prevailing political fragmentation. Such a rationalistic effort could only do violence to the organically developed legal traditions and institutions of a given society. The *Volk* constituted the historical source of a society's legal system. Law, like language, was the spontaneous, unwritten, progressive emanation of a people's innermost spirit. With a brilliant Kantian twist, von Savigny implied that law was a form of self-legislation, and not a set of arbitrary constraints imposed from without. Only jurists and statesmen rooted in the midst of their people could give genuine expression to the collective will. Good legislation was little more than custom codified, while systematic codification usually signified social disintegration. In short, the key to jurisprudence lay in the study of history, which alone could identify the authentic components of a legal tradition.[17]

Given the centrality of rabbinic leadership in the traditional self-conception of *halakhah*, Frankel could hardly assign to the *Volk* the same dominant role in the genesis of law as did Savigny, though he did concede it a minor one. However, as early as 1841, he acknowledged that some Jewish practices had sprouted from popular soil: "An institution may also have become normative without benefit of higher authority, arising from ordinary life, from that which the piety of the people had elevated as a guiding principle. And once it struck root, it gained permanence."[18] But, essentially, Frankel was interested in underscoring the role of the *Volk* at the other end of the process: in maintaining the legal system. Living institutions could not be uprooted by fiat. The appeal for respect of public sentiment was raised to curb the freedom of rabbinic initiative. Only a duly elected synod of communal representatives could legitimately approximate the will of the people.[19]

Despite the immediate conservative benefit of this line of argumentation, Frankel was not unconscious of its liberal implications. Practices and institutions no longer firmly planted in the life of the community were destined to fade into oblivion. Frankel alluded to the example of R. Yehudah Nesia who, in the third century, had terminated the ancient prohibition against using Gentile oil because it had apparently failed to gain widespread acceptance.[20] Frankel admitted that if, someday, Jews would cease to regard covering the head and praying in Hebrew as instruments of the sacred, he would be ready to abandon these practices formally.[21]

But Frankel had no intention of waiting until indifference became normative. The *Volk* is susceptible to influence through instruction and example. Its religious consciousness can be raised.[22] If the final verdict lies with the jury, the rabbis still play the role of advocates. Thus, the direction that Judaism eventually takes is the outcome of a dialectical relationship between rabbinic leadership and the community. The need of the hour was not drastic reform but edifying instruction. Judaism stood in desperate need of intellectual rehabilitation. It had been the victim of a "bad press" for so long that uninformed, assimilating Jews were stripped of all self-confidence and self-respect. Frankel could not forgive the Reformers for internalizing that Gentile critique of Judaism and seeking to rebuild it along alien lines.

For this reason, he never restricted his scholarly journal, begun in the fall of 1851, to pure *Wissenschaft*. At first glance, the title, *Monatsschrift für Geschichte und Wissenschaft des Judentums*, conveys a certain redundancy, as if *Geschichte* and *Wissenschaft* were utterly unrelated rather than largely overlapping fields of inquiry. But, as carried out in the pages of the *Monatsschrift*, the distinction proved to be quite apparent, though in terms of tone and method rather than in subject matter. Frankel intended to address two distinct, and often antagonistic, audiences through the same medium. While the section of *Geschichte* was pitched toward an educated but non-scholarly body of readers and contained translations of sources and synthetic essays that were meant to edify and uplift, the section of *Wissenschaft* disseminated the tentative results of basic research to the scholarly community. In December 1851, Frankel gently chided Steinschneider in a letter for sending him a historical piece primarily of antiquarian interest and abounding in footnotes. He besought Steinschneider, who had published extensively in Frankel's short-lived journal of the mid-1840s, to remember

that the historical part, as I said at the beginning of the first issue, is intended actually more for the educated rather than the scholarly reader, and you know how much the unscholarly reader is frightened by scholarly notes. Consider still further that "men of understanding lack bread" and if I wanted to put out my journal only for scholars, it would barely count a hundred subscribers.[23]

It was, therefore, no accident that the first eight volumes of the *Monatsschrift* contained twelve biographical essays about early rabbinic sages, all printed in the section set aside for *Geschichte*. Not specimens of critical scholarship but rather of heroic history, these essays were clearly meant to restore respect for a much maligned elite. The function of biography, Frankel contended, should be to capture the spirit of a man and the character of his work. To restrict the canvas to recording the external facts was lifeless pedantry.[24]

In general, it was hoped that empathetic history would engender reconciliation, loyalty, and even love. With the past as one source of the sacred in Judaism, certainly the study of Jewish history could serve to revitalize the sacred. The historian had to be steeped in the life of his people to penetrate to the deepest layers of connective tissue linking its experience, creativity, and character. The innermost sources of national strength were spiritual and eluded the grasp of non-Jewish observers.[25] In Heinrich Graetz, Frankel found his high priest.

The terms *Geschichte* and *Wissenschaft* in the *Monatsschrift*, however, have still other connotations. Frankel did not apply them only to contrasting popular and critical genres of scholarship. On occasion, it appears as if *Geschichte* was restricted to the external history of the Jews, the unedifying tale of Jewish persecution and passivity, whereas *Wissenschaft des Judentums* was meant to designate the internal realm of cultural and spiritual creativity. Frankel readily concurred with the widely held conviction that the Jews had no history in the conventional sense of the word. External history written on the basis of non-Jewish sources amounted to little more than a history of Gentile animosity. The meaning and secret of Jewish existence inhered in how Jews lived and what they wrote, rather than what was done to them. Genuine *Wissenschaft* concerned itself with the realm of cultural history which revealed the vigor, originality, and resilience of the Jewish spirit.[26]

More precisely still, Frankel regarded the study of rabbinics as the core of Jewish intellectualism. Since law expressed the essential character of Jewish piety, it followed that the study of the law constituted the authentic form of Jewish scholarship. *Wissenschaft* had never been alien to classical rabbinism. As a unique mode of religious worship, talmudic study infused the external forms of Judaism with vitality and flexibility and kept rigidity at bay. Learning sustained piety, growth, and responsiveness. In an age of exploding historical consciousness that threatened to submerge the religious core of Jewish culture, Frankel defended the unpopular idea that authentically Jewish *Wissenschaft* still consisted of the undistracted study of rabbinic texts. By appropriating the vaunted term *Wissenschaft des Judentums* for traditional Jewish learning, Frankel not only deepened his notion of positivity, but minimized the discontinuity of the entire modern experience. The identification tended to mute the methodological break while retaining the order of priorities.[27]

In Breslau, Frankel created the ambience to realize his priorities. He had long doubted whether the German university with its Christian ethos, its contempt for post-biblical Judaism, and its own priorities could serve as the institution to train the modern rabbi. Within the confines of his seminary, Frankel stressed the importance of personal observance, devoted more than half of the curriculum to a broad and systematic study of rabbinic literature, and tried to counteract the lure of the doctorate, though the curriculum definitely allotted time for university attendance. Perhaps most interesting is the fact that, in his own teaching, Frankel shied away from introducing modern critical tools, preferring that students first master the material in the traditional manner. Responsible critical scholarship required a high degree of prior textual competence.[28]

The study of rabbinic literature absorbed Frankel's personal attention during a lifetime of unflagging research. In the process, he laid down the foundation for a new discipline. Profoundly influenced by the work of Savigny and his school of historical jurisprudence, Frankel conceived of, and created, the historical study of *halakhah*, or as Savigny's famous journal called the method, *geschichtliche Rechtswissenschaft*. The point of departure for both men was eminently practical. The organic principles which generate and inform a legal system could be recovered only chronologically, by tracing concepts and institutions back to their origins. Without knowledge of these principles and the identification of those contemporary institutions which still embody them, all legal reform would be premature. The course for the future had to be set by the nature of the past. When Frankel berated his adversaries for lacking such historically grounded principles, he could easily have invoked the clever allegory put forth by Savigny in 1814 against the French-inspired dream of a German code. "Because the Jewish people at Mount Sinai could not wait for the divine law, they impatiently made a golden calf, and thereby the true tablets of the law were smashed."[29]

The genesis of Frankel's scholarly agenda goes back to his first years in Dresden. As early as December 1836, shortly after coming to the Saxon capital, he wrote a letter to Leopold Zunz joyfully noting his ambition to reconstruct the emergence of talmudic literature by identifying the influences of time and place and characterizing the distinctive contribution of each sage. The results, he believed, would lead to the purification of contemporary Judaism. By March 1838, he had begun to conceptualize what, twenty-one years later, would appear as *Darkhei ha-*

Mishnah, and, in 1841, he announced and described publicly his vision of "a developmental history of *halakhah*" which would demonstrate how the individual components of the system emerged, proliferated, and interacted. Like Savigny, Frankel began by returning to the earliest and most obscure strata of the system.[30]

In brief, Frankel set out to introduce the concept of time into the study of *halakhah*, thus paralleling Zunz's brilliant work on the evolution of *midrashic* literature. Toward that revolutionary end he claimed the right of free inquiry, used both Jewish and non-Jewish Greek sources, carefully ordered his material, and wrote extensively on many of the stages and literary deposits of *halakhic* history. The results of this prodigious effort may have seemed timid and inconsistent to Geiger, who dismissed Frankel's *Darkhei ha-Mishnah* as the work of a deeply ambivalent scholar, half critical and half Orthodox, but there is no gainsaying the radical secularization inherent in the enterprise.[31] Despite his deep personal piety and his profound reverence for the subject matter, Frankel had transformed the *halakhic* system into the product of human hands. Unlike Krochmal, however, Frankel provided no theological superstructure to offset the implications of the developmental approach. The quotient of divinity in the *halakhic* system had been sharply and unambiguously reduced.

It was precisely this threatening consequence which prompted the bitter frontal assault of Hirsch and his circle on Frankel in 1861, two years after the publication of *Darkhei ha-Mishnah*.[32] The fluid lines of a blurred religious spectrum had finally hardened. Though Frankel had begun his public career some two decades earlier by defending traditional Judaism against the left, he now faced a determined attack from the right. As the differences between left and center dissolved with the decline of radical Reform, the disagreements between right and center deepened. The roots of the controversy go back to the 1840s when Frankel refused to sign the resounding Orthodox condemnation of the first rabbinical conference.[33] A decade later, at the opening of the Breslau seminary, Frankel judiciously ignored a public inquiry from Frankfurt that sought to establish the seminary's position on revelation, Scripture, tradition, and custom.[34] Within two years Hirsch informed German Jewry of his contempt for the brand of scholarship practiced at Breslau with a blistering review of Graetz's history of the talmudic period, though the attack was primarily restricted to challenging the results of his research.[35]

Frankel's pioneering reconstruction of the early stages of *halakhic* evolution raised the controversy to the level of principle. Hirsch's circle correctly perceived and denounced the implication that the historical method had recast the rabbis from transmitters of the *halakhic* system into its progenitors. To abandon the tradition's dogmatic version of its divine origins implied unmistakably that what men had created men could change.[36] Frankel's book, it was said, deserved to be titled *Darkhei ha-meshaneh*, the ways of the changer.[37] Hirsch, at least, had the benefit of consistency. On principle, he repudiated the legitimacy of free critical inquiry, substituting a mode of intuitive exegesis that Frankel considered a reversion to Alexandrian allegory. For Hirsch, statements of historical fact preserved in rabbinic literature were pronouncements of dogmatic truth beyond critical examination.[38] Judaism and modern *Wissenschaft* faced each other as irreconcilable antagonists.

To the chagrin of Rapoport, who wrote in his defense, Frankel adamantly refused to deliver the dogmatic confession which Hirsch demanded.[39] In one elliptic public declaration, Frankel reasserted that his work, which pulsated with love and loyalty, had critically demonstrated the antiquity of the *halakhic* system.[40] But that response was neither perfunctory nor peripheral. On the contrary, it pointed to the ultimate source of commitment in Frankel's conception of Judaism: Jewish history itself. With remarkable accuracy, that conception, as it gained adherents across Germany, became known as historical Judaism. The name embodied the essence of Frankel's accomplishment: harnessing the power of Jewish history for the preservation of Judaism. In large measure, antiquity had become a surrogate for divinity. Though more intuitive and less systematic, the program stands comparison with the historic reconciliation of Judaism and philosophy that was begun in tenth-century Baghdad.

Frankel boldly proposed to ground loyalty to Judaism in the very force which challenged its integrity: historical consciousness. His program offered a distinct alternative to both left and right. Whereas radical Reform cavalierly used history to legitimate its course of action and Hirsch continued to obligate through the dogma of a single act of exhaustive revelation, Frankel transmuted history into a conserving force, a generator of commitment. The intent was no longer to revamp Judaism by abandoning the past but to deepen Jewish consciousness by absorbing it. Studied with compassion and understanding, Jewish history could provide a source of inspiration, meaning, and renewal. The past was seen as the arena in which the collective will of Israel became manifest. Much of Judaism that was neither divine nor perfect had been rendered sacred by history, and the verdict of history obligated no less than the voice of revelation. Freed from the shackles of dogmatic history on the one hand and the pressure to subordinate the past to the present on the other, the Breslau school was able to achieve a creative symbiosis between traditional piety and modern scholarship.

Notes

1. See the fascinating correspondence between Frankel and Joseph Muhr pertaining to the Berlin position, published by S. Bernfeld, *AZJ*, 1898, pp. 343ff.

2. M. Brann, *Geschichte des jüdisch-theologischen Seminars in Breslau* (Breslau n.d.), pp. 31–32.

3. *ZRIJ*, I (1844), *passim*.

4. *Protokolle und Aktenstücke der zweiten Rabbiner-Versammlung* (Frankfurt am Main 1845), p. 19.

5. G. W. F. Hegel, *Early Theological Writings*, trans. T. M. Knox (Philadelphia 1971), pp. 67–181; Immanuel Kant, *Religion within the Limits of Reason Alone*, trans. T. M. Greene and H. H. Hudson (New York 1960), pp. 115–128; M. Creizenach, *Schulhan*

Arukh, II (Frankfurt am Main 1837); Abraham Geiger, *Der hamburger Tempelstreit* (Breslau 1842), pp. 34–35. Just a few of the many passages in which Frankel uses the term "positive" in its legal sense: *ZRIJ*, I (1844): 13; *ZRIJ* II (1845): 173–174; *ZRIJ*, III (1846): 201; *Protokolle*, p. 19; *MGWJ*, IV (1855): 10. I am grateful to my late friend Chancellor Gerson D. Cohen for suggesting this line of investigation to me years ago by bringing to my attention the discussion of the term in Shlomo Avineri, *Hegel's Theory of the Modern State* (London 1972), pp. 13–33.

6. Z. Frankel, *Der gerichtlische Beweis nach mosaisch-talmudischem Rechte* (Berlin 1846), pp. 5, 39, 54–55.

7. *ZRIJ*, I (1844): 9; *ZRIJ*, II (1845): 178.

8. *Der Orient* (1842): 63–64; *Literaturblatt des Orients* (1842), cols. 358–366; *ZRIJ*, I (1844): 227; *ZRIJ*, II (1845): 17. See also Rivka Horwitz, "The Idea of Jewish Independence in the Land of Israel of R. Zechariah Frankel in 1842" (Hebrew), *Kivvunim*, no. 6 (Feb. 1980): 5–25.

9. *ZRIJ*, I (1844): 94–95; *MGWJ*, I (1852): 245, 535; *MGWJ*, II (1853): 62–64; *MGWJ*, XVI (1867): 241–252, 281–297; *AZJ*, (1861), Beilage zu no. 8: 3.

10. *Der gerichtliche Beweis*, pp. 37–62.

11. *ZRIJ*, II (1845): 179–180.

12. *ZRIJ*, II (1845): 16, 265ff.; *MGWJ*, I (1852): 426; *MGWJ*, VI (1857): 13–14.

13. *ZRIJ*, I (1844): 14, 27.

14. *Protokolle*, pp. 18–54.

15. *Literaturblatt des Orients*, 1842, col. 381.

16. *ZRIJ*, I (1844): 19–21, 292; *ZRIJ*, II (1845): 15–16, 180.

17. Friedrich Carl von Savigny, *Vom Beruf unsrer Zeit für Gesetzgebung und Rechtswissenschaft*, 2nd ed. (Heidelberg 1828), pp. 8–15); *idem*, "*Über den Zweck dieser Zeitschrift*," *Zeitschrift für geschichtliche Rechtswissenschaft*, I (1815): 4; *idem*, *System des heutigen Römischen Rechts*, 3 vols. (Berlin 1840), I, pp. 14–50.

18. Z. Frankel, *Vorstudien zu der Septuaginta* (Leipzig 1841), p. xiii.

19. *ZRIJ*, II (1845): 181.

20. *ZRIJ*, I (1844): 21.

21. Z. Frankel, "Über das Wesentliche der Function und Qualification des Rabbiners . . . ," The Central Archives for the Jewish People, Jerusalem, P17/991.

22. *ZRIJ*, I (1844): 24.

23. *MGWJ*, I (1852): 3, 246, 526. The Frankel letter to Steinschneider, dated December 26, 1851, in the archives of The Jewish Theological Seminary of America, Steinschneider collection, probably marks the final break between these two men of fundamentally conflicting views on *Wissenschaft des Judentums*. The biblical quotation, which is in Hebrew in the original, comes from Eccl. 9:11, though Frankel, obviously quoting from memory, mixed up *Hahamim* and *Nevonim*.

24. *MGWJ*, IV (1855): 74.

25. *MGWJ*, IX (1860): 125.

26. *MGWJ*, I (1852): 5, 203–205, 243–244, 483–499, 523–524. See also *ZRIJ*, III (1846): 214–215, 382–383.

27. *MGWJ*, I (1852): 207, 421–422, 443–445.

28. Frankel, "Über das Wesentliche der Function und Qualification des Rabbiners . . ."; *MGWJ*, II (1853): 13–22; Brann, Beilage I; M. S. Zuckermandel, *Mein Lebenslauf*, reprint (n.p. 1915?), pp. vi, xvii–xviii.

29. Savigny, *Vom Beruf unsrer Zeit*, p. 134.

30. The Jewish National and University Library, Jerusalem, 4°792/G12; Frankel, *Vorstudien*, p. xii.

31. Geiger letter to M. Steinschneider dated April 17, 1861, The Jewish Theological Seminary of America archives, Steinschneider collection.

32. *Jeschurun*, VII (1860–1861); *passim*; L. Dobschütz, *Zacharias Frankel. Gedenkblätter*. . . , ed. by M. Brann (Breslau 1901), pp. 80–86.

33. *Der treue Zions-Wächter* (1846): 249–250; ibid. (1847): 81–83.

34. *AZJ* (1854): 245.

35. *Jeschurun*, II (1855–1856) and III (1856–1857): *passim*.

36. *Jeschurun*, VII (1860–1861): 252–269, 364–368; Zvi Benjamin Auerbach, *Ha-Zofeh al Darkhei ha-Mishnah* (Frankfurt am Main 1861).

37. *Jeschurun*, VII (1860–1861): 252.

38. *Jeschurun*, VII (1860–1861): 441–442.

39. Solomon Yehudah Rapoport, *Divrei Shalom ve-Emet* (Prague 1861), pp. 29–30; *Kirjath Sefer*, IV (1927–1928): 169.

40. *MGWJ*, X (1861): 159–160.

14

Ideology and History in the Age of Emancipation

Heinrich Graetz was the most energetic, versatile, and durable practitioner of *Wissenschaft des Judentums* in the nineteenth century. His comprehensive eleven-volume *History of the Jews*, published from 1853 to 1876, at the torrid pace of approximately a book every two years along with numerous other monographs and several revised editions of earlier volumes, still remains, a century later, the best single introduction to the totality of Jewish history. That is no mean achievement in a field where the discovery of new sources, the development of different tools and perspectives, the proliferation of original monographs, and the construction of new syntheses have continued unabated. And yet the extraordinary combination of narrative skill and basic research which was the hallmark of Graetz's work has never been matched.

Historians may be read in several ways: simply for information on a given subject, or in terms of the advance which their work represents in our understanding of that subject, and finally as part of the social and intellectual history of the period in which they wrote. For this essay, our reading of Graetz will be limited primarily to the interplay between his conceptualization of the Jewish past and the issues agitating his own generation. No man can be understood fully outside the context of his time; in the case of Graetz, a tempestuous personality deeply involved in the crises of a transitional age, even a partial glimpse is denied those who ignore the contemporary scene.

Emancipation, its prospect, the arduous and extended effort required to win it, and the partial and tenuous quality of its achievement, constituted the overriding concern of German Jewry in the nineteenth century. As in earlier periods of Jewish history, a fundamental change in the legal status of the Jews dictated substantial modifications in the practice of Judaism. The varied legal conditions under which Jews lived in the Babylonian exile, the Second Commonwealth, the Baghdad caliphate, medieval Christian Europe, and seventeenth-century England inevitably effected communal and religious adjustments. But very few shifts in legal status were as far-reaching and as bitterly contested as the emancipation of German Jewry.

The major instrument for altering the structure and image of Judaism so as to accord with the legal status eagerly sought by certain sectors of the Jewish community and grudgingly held out by a deeply ambivalent Christian society was *Wissenschaft des Judentums*. In nineteenth-century Germany the study of Jewish history functioned as both authority and medium. Construed as authority, a proper reading of Jewish history could yield the indispensable guidelines and validating principles to determine the future shape of Judaism. Invoked as medium, Jewish history could readily provide an interpretation of Judaism in terms of the idealistic idiom of the century. In the Middle Ages these two functions were fulfilled by different disciplines: a rich and flexible legal tradition generally served as sole authority for changes within the Jewish community, while philosophy offered the common idiom in which Judaism could be expounded for Jew and non-Jew alike. In the wake of emancipation, with the repudiation of Jewish law and the historicization of philosophy, history assumed the role of both. It became the functional equivalent of *halakhah* and philosophy in the medieval world. Scientific history alone transcended the passions and partisanship of a turbulent age, and it alone had access to the truth that would accord a revamped Judaism its rightful place in the century of self-cognition.

Invested with such power, *Wissenschaft des Judentums* soon became the most potent intellectual force on the German Jewish scene. Its devoted band of practitioners steadily increased, and the accumulated results of their investigations revolutionized the understanding of Judaism and the self-image of the Jew. Very few were able to resist the compelling appeal of the historical approach. Perhaps the most notable exception was Graetz's former teacher, Samson Raphael Hirsch, whose highly personal brand of allegory was far closer to the medieval than the modern idiom. When Esriel Hildesheimer, his Neo-Orthodox associate, finally opened a modern rabbinical seminary in Berlin in 1873 where *Wissenschaft* would be practiced no less assiduously than at Breslau or the Hochschule, Hirsch refused to extend the slightest support.[1]

However, the near universal use of *Wissenschaft* produced no universal agreement as to the nature of Judaism. Like most instruments, *Wissenschaft*, too, could be used in different ways. It could be wielded radically or conservatively, to reshape traditional Judaism or to defend it, to legitimize religious reform or to resist it. The intellectual leadership of the nascent Reform movement perceived the study of Jewish history as a liberating force, the means by which to bury the burdensome legacy of an insufferable past. By the 1840s, the exclusive and often reckless use of history in the cause of religious reform provoked a spontaneous counter-attack by a cluster of historians, appalled at the price of emancipation, who began to wield *Wissenschaft* in defense of traditional Judaism. Both sides shared a common idiom. The dilemmas posed by the emancipation struggle were to be resolved by a proper reading of Jewish history. The bitter disagreement over that reading derived not from differences in method but from prior religious positions that were deeply antagonistic. *Wissenschaft* history was programmatic history.

II

The first program in the field came in the guise of a full-blown theory of Jewish history which marked as sharp a departure in self-perception as did the emancipation in legal status. Long before Abraham Geiger's brilliant summation of this Reform theory of Jewish history in the 1860s in his *Das Judenthum und seine Geschichte*, it had become the regnant interpretation of the Jewish past. In the name of this novel theory, the spokesmen for religious reform advocated overhauling the major institutions and beliefs of Judaism. Graetz detested the program and formulated his own philosophy of Jewish history to challenge that prevailing in Reform circles.

The revision of Jewish history by the intellectuals of the Reform movement rested on two conceptual assumptions which often merged into substantive conclusions. Like every living phenomenon, Judaism was subject to the law of development. Its ideas and forms were part of a historical continuum, emerging gradually and constantly changing. The Talmud itself offered the most convincing proof of this, for it amounted to a vast reworking of biblical Judaism. The spirit of Judaism had always appropriated new forms, since old ones condemned to the rubbish heap of history could never be revived. This vitality of growth in the past was the guarantee that Judaism could also meet the dictates of the present.[2]

What saved Jewish history from the fate of pure historicism was the concept of essence. Behind the panorama of events existed and operated the essence of Judaism. It was this unchanging though ever unfolding idea which provided the continuity as well as the motive power of Jewish history. Present from the very outset, the idea was locked in combat with its materialistic adversaries. With each round it managed to assume a higher form more appropriate to its nature. But every resolution was merely temporary, for the very assumption of material form marked a compromise of the idea.[3]

On the basis of these assumptions, the architects of Reform designed a comprehensive reinterpretation of Jewish history whose general outline had been sketched as early as 1822 by Immanuel Wolf on behalf of the ephemeral Verein für Cultur. Its point of departure was the a priori identification of the essence of Judaism, and later ideologues felt no need to repudiate Wolf's bold formulation.

What is this idea that has existed throughout so much of world history and has so successfully influenced the culture of the human race? It is of the most simple kind and its content can be expressed in a few words. It is the idea of unlimited unity in the all. It is contained in the one word *Adonai* which signifies indeed the living unity of all being in eternity, the absolute being outside defined time and space. This concept is revealed to the Jewish people, i.e., posited as a datum.[4]

Monotheism thus constituted and exhausted the idea of Judaism. To be sure, men like Geiger and Samuel Holdheim later acknowledged the centrality of ethics, though even for them the irreducible and eternal core remained a unique vision of God. They also continued to acknowledge the divine source of this vision.[5] Moritz A. Stern, the Göttingen *Dozent*, who contended that the ultimate task of Reform was to destroy the belief in positive revelation, failed to attract any rabbinic support.[6]

Beyond this essential idea, nothing in Judaism was permanent and some, like Sigismund Stern, the noted Jewish educator and one of the founders of the Berlin Reform Association, claimed that even the original Sinaitic revelation was subject to evolution. The implacable law of development governed everything.[7] Accordingly, the national dimension of Judaism was historicized and accounted for in terms of function. Many of the early advocates of enlightenment and reform had received their first taste of secular learning through the philosophic works of Maimonides. In the third part of his *Guide for the Perplexed*, Maimonides had revolutionized the attempt to explain the intention of the commandments by employing a historical approach for the first time. The significance of countless biblical institutions could be ascertained only by a knowledge of contemporary pagan practice, for their function was strictly prophylactic.[8] Adopting this line of thought, Reform historians now contended that the entire Jewish state along with many of its religious institutions had merely served to shield the fragile idea of monotheism from the unmitigated depravity of the pagan environment until it had become sufficiently rooted in the consciousness of ancient Israel.[9] The destruction of the First Commonwealth and the Babylonian exile produced a new exemplar: the Jew who recoiled from the opportunity to return to his homeland but retained his religious identity. Wolf considered the rejection of the opportunity afforded by Cyrus's edict by the majority of Jews

a remarkable event! Hundreds of thousands remained in the dispersion and were not incorporated a second time into the Jewish state. But everywhere they preserved the self-same idea on which their nationhood depended. They remained adherents of Judaism and thereby links in a chain.[10]

These expatriated Jews were harbingers of the irreversible turn which Jewish history would take with the destruction of the Second Temple. The final Reform interpretation of this event was a modified version of a view articulated at the dawn of the emancipation era by Spinoza, whose significance for Jewish history lies in the devastating secular critique of Judaism which he bequeathed to the Enlightenment. On the basis of philosophical argument and scriptural evidence, Spinoza claimed that Judaism should have rightfully perished with the demise of the Jewish state,[11] its illegitimate survival being due solely to Gentile hostility.[12] When Mendelssohn took up the argument in *Jerusalem*, he conceded only that the loss of political independence had transformed Judaism into a purely religious system which operated by means of persuasion alone.[13] Moving still closer to Spinoza's original position, Friedländer and later architects of Reform rendered explicit what Mendelssohn had left implicit: the demise of the Jewish state marked the liberation of Judaism from its national origins.[14] More than a century and a half after the *Theologico-Political Treatise*, Holdheim unmistakably echoed Spinoza when he declared that "everything connected with a state qua state must cease once this national entity is dissolved."[15]

In the nineteenth century this reinterpretation was coupled with the idea of mission, an idea still lacking in Jost's *Geschichte der Israeliten*.[16] What former generations had mourned as a national calamity was now celebrated as a providential summons to enter the world to espouse the true conception of God. Exile became the proper locus for Jewish existence. Against the backdrop of a long tradition of Enlightenment criticism of Judaism's particularism, the advocates of Reform harped on the universalism of its essence and the nature of its mission. The dissemination of monotheism as Judaism's unique mandate became the major line of defense against collective suicide.[17]

But the destruction of the Temple did not fully release the spirit of Judaism. As in an earlier period, it was again encrusted with separatistic institutions that derived from both internal and external causes. The prolonged disintegration of the state created a vacuum filled by the proliferating regulations of a clerical elite. Holdheim accused the rabbis of having failed to grasp the verdict of history by desperately clinging to the political fragments of a vanished state.[18] With far greater scholarship, the young Geiger tried to show how the rabbis forged new bonds of unity by freely applying an irrational exegetical method which repeatedly violated the simple sense of the biblical text. The result was a vast and stultifying legal system which, despite intensive rabbinic effort, enjoyed no objective biblical mandate.[19]

To handle the extended and diversified medieval experience of the Jews, Reform ideologues appropriated for their own use the long regnant view of the exile as an era of unrelieved persecution. Whereas ancient and medieval Jewish literature had always perceived the state of *Galut* as fraught with danger, Sephardic historians of the sixteenth century, traumatized by the calamitous end to Jewish life in Spain and Portugal, were the first to construct chronological histories of Jewish persecutions through the ages.[20] In the seventeenth and eighteenth centuries this perception of the past was utilized by the early advocates of emancipation to clear the Jews of responsibility for the reprehensible quality of their social condition.[21] In the biting words of Mendelssohn: "They tie our hands and then reproach us for not using them."[22] In the nineteenth century the Reform theory of Jewish history transferred this same deeply ingrained view of the past to account for the ailing condition of Judaism. Major facets of medieval Judaism were now rendered unessential, for they were no more than a natural reaction to intolerable pressure. The medieval Jew could survive only by living either in the past, in the future, or in a world of fantasy.

In this manner the spokesmen for reform evaluated the institutions of talmudic Judaism and the ideologies of messianic and mystical movements. In an era of relentless persecution, the need for consolation had replaced the free development of the spirit. The codification of the Mishnah was a typical though early expression of the medieval attachment to the past. Much of the material which it preserved was no longer applicable even at the time of codification.[23] Surrounded by a hostile society, medieval Jews increasingly withdrew behind the protective institutions of the Talmud, a kind of surrogate homeland and the functional equivalent of the Jewish state in pagan antiquity.[24] Holdheim contended that communal autonomy was an anachronism imposed on the Jews by governments which refused to incorporate them into the fabric of society.[25]

Messianism and mysticism fared little better. Here, too, history transvalued what former generations had cherished. Neither the longing for political redemption nor the pursuit of the mystical experience were regarded as authentic expressions of Judaism, for both could easily be explained as the obvious and unhealthy consequence of physical persecution and cultural isolation.[26]

In sum, the Reform theory of Jewish history offers ample evidence of the extensive interplay between the needs of the present and the perception of the past. It simply bristled with relevance. By historicizing whatever appeared to be a liability, it legitimized the religious accommodation often crudely dictated by German emancipation; its thrust accorded with the perceived mandate of the age. With the end of fanaticism and persecution, the idea of Judaism could be stripped of its institutional armor and delivered to a receptive world. The vision of Sigismund Stern inspired the hearts of many: ". . . and when once the pagan world will be destroyed, not only by Christianity, but within it as well, then the separation of both religions will cease, and I can't decide which name the religion of mankind will bear."[27]

III

The decade of the 1840s marked a turning point in the political fortunes of German Jewry and consequently also in the direction of *jüdische Wissenschaft*. Not only had emancipation failed to bring the millennium, in the 1840s emancipation itself came under severe attack. The political crisis produced five years of enormous ferment which served to clarify opposing religious positions as well as to underscore the continued struggle between rabbis and laymen over the religious leadership of the Jewish community.

In 1843 a population of 206,050 Jews made Prussian Jewry the third largest Jewish community in Europe.[28] But unlike its much larger counterparts in Russia and Austria, large sectors of Prussian Jewry had enjoyed nearly full emancipation since 1812, although as late as 1846, 36.7 percent of the Jews in Prussia, mainly in the border province of Posen, had still failed to attain citizenship.[29] At the end of 1841 the new king, Frederick William IV, who detested the Enlightenment and yearned to reestablish the divine order of the Holy Roman Empire, issued a cabinet order which sent shock waves through Prussian Jewry. Reasserting the long denied identity of Judaism with the Jewish nation, Frederick William IV contended that only legislation which posited this unity and its attendant Jewish separateness could be effective.

The efforts of those who seek an improvement in the social situation of the Jews through their individual assimilation into the civil life of the Christian population of the land can never be fruitful and salutary for the mutual relationship between Christians and Jews, since they stand in contradiction to that national type.

Accordingly, the king proposed to treat the Jews as a national minority by organizing them everywhere into separate corporations, whose corporate interests on the municipal level would be represented by Jewish deputies alone. Jews would no longer be allowed to represent a Christian constituency. In line with their loss of individual citizenship, the king also advocated releasing the Jews from the universal obligation of military service.[30]

Prussian Jewry translated its dismay at the pending renunciation of emancipation into vociferous protest, with the result that Frederick William shelved his original proposal. For the next five years the Prussian government deliberated on the draft of a new Jewish law. In 1845 it invited Moritz Veit, the president of the Berlin Jewish community, Julius Rubo, its syndic, Leopold Zunz, the director of its teachers' seminary, and Joseph Muhr, a banker, to offer their suggestions in person. Notables and rabbis from across the land also dispatched memoranda to the government. Finally, in 1847, the representatives of the provincial estates sitting in a United Diet ratified a modified version of the government's proposal.[31]

The agonizing wait kept Prussian Jewry in a state of unrelieved suspension. In 1843 Holdheim reported:

The very much feared law of incorporation which still threatens the civil and social life of Prussian Jews, or Jewish Prussians, has raised the nationality question of the Jews in general in many circles. In the past year it variously occupied the minds of many.

The views of the king were well known. In 1846, Veit, the learned publisher who served as president of the Berlin community from 1839 to 1848 and who lobbied successfully for the support of the city and provincial governments on behalf of the Jews, still felt that a law reflecting the king's sentiments was a real possibility. His consolation was that the setback would be temporary: laws were no longer legislated for eternity.[32]

An attack from an unexpected corner intensified Jewish anxiety still further. In 1843 Bruno Bauer, the "Robespierre of theology" who had just lost his job at the University of Bonn for trying to undercut the historicity of the Gospels, published an essay in which he declared the adherents of Judaism unfit for emancipation. A left-wing Hegelian, who despised Frederick William's retrogressive ideology of the Christian state no less than did the Jews, Bauer lampooned Judaism as a fossil reflecting the lowest stage in the history of religion. It survived only by fleeing the mainstream of history and immuring itself within its talmudic fortress. But the price was high. The Jew became incapable of any further development. The efforts at reform since the Parisian Sanhedrin in the name of Judaism were fraudulent, for they signified a break and not a return. In the quest for emancipation, the Jews sought only an extension of privilege to cultivate their tribal exclusiveness. Bauer summoned them instead to abandon their parochial concerns and to join in the struggle for universal freedom, a goal that entailed the emancipation of society from religion.[33]

This renewed antagonism toward Jewish political aspirations from both the right and the left unleashed a burst of activity within the Jewish community for religious reform. The response was only to be expected, for since the very outset of the emancipation struggle in Germany the underlying issue had always been the nature of Judaism and the fitness of its adherents for admission into the modern state. The initiative to speak on behalf of Judaism was seized by university-educated laymen in Frankfurt, Breslau, and Berlin who organized to issue declarations defining their conceptions of Judaism. Generally, they stressed what they had discarded: the authority of the Talmud, the dietary laws, the medieval hope for national redemption, and a day of rest different from that of the society in which they lived. In a more positive vein, they asserted the eternal truth of Judaism's concept of God as well as its capacity for limitless development. These declarations were intended to persuade the German public and its officials of the existence of a non-Orthodox Judaism, that was entirely commensurate with the duties of citizenship. Its adherents had offered public testimony that they had cleansed their religion of all national vestiges.[34]

But were they, in fact, qualified to testify on the nature of Judaism? Had they not preempted a strictly rabbinic prerogative? Seen in this light, the well-known rabbinic conferences of the mid-1840s constituted an organized effort to regain the leadership of the Jewish community. Since the onset of the emancipation struggle in Germany when Mendelssohn appealed to the rabbis to relinquish their power of excommunication, enlightened lay leaders and traditional rabbis had battled for control over the religious affairs of the community. Now a new generation of secularly educated liberal rabbis rose to claim their right as the legitimate spokesmen for Judaism. Even Samuel Holdheim, the most radical among them, sharply criticized the Frankfurt declaration issued by a circle of assimilated and antirabbinic intellectuals in 1843 as being so negative in character that it could never help generate a religious revival.[35] While laymen clamored for a synod in which both parties would deliberate in full equality, the Frankfurt rabbinical conference of 1845 refused to endorse the Berlin Reform Association, the major proponent of the synod idea, without a promise to abide by the principles set forth by the conference.[36] Although the same political issues that prompted the lay declarations also fed many of the debates at the rabbinical conferences, the rabbis generally accorded more weight to the legacy of the past.

The rash of lay and rabbinic pronouncements on radical reform soon elicited a counter-response. For the first time a handful of men, trained in universities and committed to the practice of *Wissenschaft*, began to challenge the excessive concern with the dictates of the time. In the mid-1840s Zacharias Frankel took the lead. He had served as rabbi in Dresden since 1836, was already hard at work on a lifetime study of the origins and development of Jewish law, and had dramatically walked out of the Frankfurt rabbinical conference in 1845 over the issue of Hebrew in the services. In 1844 he founded what proved to be a short-lived journal openly hostile to Reform in which he formulated a critique of the Reform program based on several grounds.

Politically, he accused the Reform leadership of bartering Judaism for emancipation. Basing his case on a theory of natural law that post-Napoleonic Prussia rejected as a French import, Frankel claimed that equality was a right and not a privilege. Like the tortured victim of the Inquisition who finally came to believe himself guilty of the crime of which he was accused, many weak-kneed German Jews had come to accept the oft-repeated argument that the teachings and practices of Judaism were the real reason for the continued denial of emancipation. But such demands by the state violated the principle of freedom of conscience. True emancipation entailed a triumph of justice and humanity.[37]

To this political argument Frankel added a deeply felt historical consideration. The willingness to purchase emancipation displayed an appalling callousness toward the countless sacrifices of earlier generations. How many Jews had withstood the unrelenting oppression of the Middle Ages! When forced to choose between the cross and the sword, how many Jews preferred to lay down their lives! And today this divine legacy sanctified by blood was sold for material advantage! Such an exchange undercut the very purpose of emancipation: to grant Jews the freedom and dignity to dedicate their spiritual and physical resources to the welfare of society and the state.[38]

Finally, Frankel attacked the Reform program on religious grounds. Jewish rituals and ceremonies could not be discarded high-handedly as mere devices to separate Jews from a hostile environment because they continued to articulate the religious sentiment of a living people. The majority of Jews were still able to satisfy their deepest religious needs through these ancient forms of expression. In their extreme rationalism, the leaders of Reform blindly refused to acknowledge the still high level of religious observance among the Jewish masses, whose religiosity delimited those areas of Jewish life which must not be tampered with.[39] By appealing to current religious practice, Frankel thus employed the same criterion as the spokesmen for reform; they merely differed in their judgment. While the latter tended to reflect the alienation of a rising middle class, Frankel spoke for the piety of the *Landjuden* for whom the process of assimilation had scarcely begun.

The attack against Reform soon engulfed its practice of *Wissenschaft* which, till the 1840s, had been primarily a Reform preserve in Germany. As early as 1840 Michael Sachs, a preacher in Prague and a student of Solomon Yehuda Rapoport, one of the luminaries of the Galician *Haskalah*, voiced his disapproval of the tone and direction of Reform scholarship in a personal letter to his close friend in Berlin, Moritz Veit. Trained as a classical philologian at the University of Berlin, Sachs deplored the rationalistic efforts to reduce Judaism to a mere formula. It must be experienced to be understood. Better to observe the minutiae of the ritual codes than to utter a formula which curdles the blood like a lie the moment it's pronounced! Sachs also condemned the thoroughly negative character of Reform scholarship. Its exhaustive catalogue of the sins of which the ancient rabbis were guilty was enough to kill the patient. Lacking any love for their subject, Reform scholars made no attempt to revive contemporary Jewry through positive history. Sachs envisioned an entirely different kind of enterprise.

This is what I am looking for: to recognize spirit and life, a higher idealistic aspect everywhere; to state the known; to present Judaism in its power and glory as a guide to this higher view of life; to make us conscious of its institutions as an expression of its ideas, of its history in all of its edifying and uplifting might, of the voices of its men of God in their profoundly creative and deeply stirring power, of its significance for the present and that of the present for us.[40]

In 1845, one year after he came to Berlin to occupy the pulpit of the Jewish community, Sachs published a specimen of what he meant by positive history. *Die religiöse Poesie der Juden in Spanien* attempted to present in translation the pathos and power of Spanish Hebrew religious poetry and thereby to engender some admiration for the creative talent of medieval Jewry. Sachs added a lengthy historical essay in which he offered an effusive appreciation of his subject. In the opening chapter, without ever referring to the name of his protagonist, he delivered a deepfelt refutation of Geiger's scholarly indictment of rabbinic exegesis as arbitrary, faulty, and tendentious. Sachs contended that *Midrash* was the product of unreflective immediacy. Of course the rabbis realized the plain sense of the biblical text, but culturally isolated and still spared the tyranny of foreign methods and ideas, they continued to inhabit the conceptual and emotional world of the prophets. This creative intimacy survived intact until the invasion of Islamic culture and usually yielded a far profounder understanding of Scripture than that gained by the application of an alien science.[41]

The disagreement between Geiger and Sachs was not merely the consequence of a rationalistic versus a romantic approach to the study of the past, but also derived directly from antagonistic views as to the validity and viability of a legalistic religious system that seemed to obstruct the attainment of full emancipation. History had become the arena for resolving the dilemmas that wracked the present.[42]

The ranks of the emerging conservative bloc were significantly strengthened by the addition of Leopold Zunz, whose career had begun a quarter of a century before in the cause of Reform, and whose pioneering history of the homiletic literature of the Jews, which appeared in 1832 also in the service of Reform, had inspired both Geiger and Holdheim with a vision of the social usefulness of modern scholarship.[43] But in the 1840s he became disillusioned with the thrust of Reform and the quality of its *Wissenschaft*. His private letters bristled with cryptic, caustic remarks about the leaders and activities of the movement. He considered Geiger to be merely a party man and not a scholar. Holdheim was in a class with some of Judaism's most illustrious enemies like Hegel, Paulus, and Bauer. His anti-Jewish program would destroy Judaism. The Berlin Reformers were led by ignorant and simple men, and they stood ready to offer the dietary laws and the messiah in return for emancipation. The statements issued by rabbinical conferences and Reform associations alike smacked of Christianity.[44]

The urgency of the moment drove Zunz to speak out publicly. The original intention of the Frankfurt Reform Association to include a renunciation of circumcision in its declaration had finally been abandoned under pressure, but the controversy continued to reverberate throughout Germany. In 1843 and 1844 Zunz plunged in with two terse, highly charged affirmations of the religious rites of *tefillin* and circumcision. He accused the spokesmen of Reform of being politically motivated. Not a single divine law must be sacrificed for equality, which was after all not man's highest goal and would be achieved in any event. Zunz bitterly attacked the distinction between the national and religious dimensions of Judaism upon which Holdheim rested his case. The dean of *jüdische Wissenschaft* rebuked Holdheim for his exclusive worship of history! The Reform ideologues had rejected the God of Abraham for the idol of history. Jewish symbols would soon wither under the new regime. But Judaism consisted of more than a few disembodied universalistic ideas. To discard the Talmud and the belief in the messiah was to repudiate the Jewish past and future; to renounce circumcision would destroy the act which united Jews in the present. The Reform program amounted to suicide.[45]

Geiger challenged Zunz's change of heart in a long private letter in which he candidly stated his preference for the dictates of the present. The controversy centered on what should be the decisive force in shaping contemporary Judaism, the cultural level of the present or the legacy of the past? Geiger mourned the loss of Zunz to those in favor of granting the past a normative role. Zunz responded laconically and with evident reluctance. The norms for religion must be purely religious. We must reform ourselves, not our religion. The hue and cry against the Talmud had always been the tactic of apostates.[46]

In breaking with Reform, Zunz, like Sachs, clearly perceived the validating function played by the study of history. In 1845 he published his second major work, *Zur Geschichte und Literatur,* in which he now rendered explicit a theory of *Wissenschaft* that he had adumbrated in his early essays on rabbinic literature and medieval exegesis, and which clashed sharply with that held by Geiger. The volume consisted of a series of essays that dealt primarily with the legal, liturgical, ethical, and exegetical literature of medieval Ashkenazic Jewry and was intended as a corrective to an unwarranted imbalance in the scope of current *Wissenschaft*. Zunz condemned the work of Reform ideologues as selective and tendentious. Brainwashed by the Enlightenment's debunking of Judaism, they defined Jewish literature as religious in character and concentrated only on periods like the Spanish with which they could readily identify. They shunned the literature of Franco-Germany because it seemed too different, too parochial, and too Jewish. In their abhorrence of contemporary clericalism, which Zunz incidentally shared, and in their eagerness for emancipation they had taken to deprecating their past. But if this be the attitude of Jews, would the judgment of Christian scholars ever be more favorable?[47] For Zunz had long believed that the legal emancipation of Jews could never effectively precede the scholarly emancipation of Judaism.[48] The prerequisite for all scholarship was objectivity. Yet so many works of Reform history were undertaken for political gain or to buttress a prior point of view.

Thus we spend time on subjects which appeal to us because they serve transitory ends, while we avoid periods entirely unresearched. And since we do not study men and their actions as an end in itself, but rather for the sake of our anticipated advantage, we remain sunk, no less than our scornful enemies, in unfair prejudice toward many works of the past.[49]

The heart of Zunz's critique was a different concept of *Wissenschaft*.

History and justice is not the knowledge of a single epoch, of a single stage, of a single event. It is a comprehensive, integrated, and fair understanding. Many a misunderstood century has provided the basis for contemporary life, but since this life no longer pleases those who have fallen away from Judaism, they disdain the men of that age and scorn their works.[50]

To counter the one-sidedness of this perception of the past, Zunz devoted the rest of his life to rehabilitating the vast liturgical literature of medieval Jewry. Defying the prevailing irreligious sentiments of his age, Zunz labored to present the synagogue as a national theater in which a living nation gave ample expression to its religious genius.[51]

It was only to be expected that Zunz's indictment of Reform *Wissenschaft* would draw fire from Abraham Geiger, its leading practitioner. In a typically extensive nineteenth-century review of Zunz's book, Geiger set forth his own position with clarity and vigor. Jewish literature did not merit the designation of national literature, for it had always been, even in the days of political independence, heavily weighted toward the religious. The secular subjects on which the Jews may have written in the Middle Ages, when they no longer ranked as a living people, were but a pale reflection of general culture. The fact that Jews wrote about them in Hebrew merely attested to their cultural isolation, for the simple truth was that as soon as Jews began to assimilate to a superior culture they adopted its language. The survival of Hebrew, therefore, signified a cultural lag and not the existence of any national consciousness. Jewish literature had to be defined by its spirit and not its language.

Geiger also candidly challenged Zunz's plea for comprehensiveness. Not all periods were equally important; only some had truly exerted a lasting influence on the course of history, even if all derived from the Spirit. The historian must have the courage to be selective and judgmental. Distortion was not the result of knowing only part of the story, but of knowing the wrong part. *Wissenschaft* turned to the seminal periods of the past to write the history of the spirit of Judaism and to instruct and rejuvenate the Jews of today, but only after the present state of consciousness, nurtured by emancipation, determined what it considered to be seminal. Unwittingly, Geiger had acknowledged that subjectivity lay at the heart of his enterprise.[52]

It should be abundantly clear by now that the 1840s marked a turning point in the history of German Jewish *Wissenschaft*. Under the impact of an intensified emancipation struggle, Reform had moved rapidly further left, with the inevitable result that a countervailing force began to form. While men like Frankel, Sachs, and Zunz did not work in tandem, they did simultaneously rise to denounce the accommodations preached by Reform. What's more, they began to condemn the manner in which *Wissenschaft* was used in behalf of Reform, not by repudiating the discipline as alien to Judaism, but by insisting that it be practiced differently. The emerging conservative bloc had sensed that *Wissenschaft* was an instrument that could be employed to preserve traditional Judaism as well as to revamp it, to resist the price of emancipation as well as to pay it. The Reform monopoly of *Wissenschaft* had been broken. A handful of historians had begun to formulate an alternative program based on a different reading of Jewish history. In the mid-1840s the young Heinrich Graetz threw in his lot with this conservative bloc in resounding fashion. In the following decades he profoundly deepened its perception of the past.

I V

Some men can be understood only by identifying their adversaries. Their views were forged in controversy and therefore can never be fully fathomed in isolation. There is no other way to study the work of Heinrich Graetz. His entire career from his earliest days as a university student in Breslau was marked by an unfailing antipathy toward the Reform movement. The evidence is abundant and best summarized by Graetz himself in a letter to Raphael Kirchheim, a remarkably learned Jewish businessman in Frankfurt with an important personal library, who had drawn close to Geiger in the 1860s while remaining on friendly terms with Graetz. In 1869 Graetz wrote him frankly:

The great question today is, will Judaism survive or disappear? For I regard it as disappearing if it is christianized, or as Heine says, if it spins its *tzitzit* from the wool of the Lamb of God. I will fight against the christianization of Judaism, which is entailed in the reform of Judaism, to my last breath and with all the weapons at my command.[53]

The most potent weapon in his arsenal was *Wissenschaft des Judentums*. In contrast to his dogmatic mentor, Samson Raphael Hirsch, Graetz challenged the proponents of Reform with their own weapons. His reading and writing of Jewish history were born of opposition and his scholarship was shaped by the determination to provide an alternative view of Jewish history, which would invalidate the claims of the Reform movement to historical legitimacy. If the leaders of Reform in many ways resembled the *philosophes* of the previous century, it is not forcing the analogy to suggest that Graetz assumed the role of Edmund Burke. Like his conservative counterpart, he approached the past with reverence and held reason in distrust. Human reason was to be tempered by the wisdom of the ages and change enacted in accord with tradition. Neither man accepted the polemical view of the Middle Ages put forth by his adversaries and a pronounced moral strain pervaded the work of both.[54]

Graetz was born in 1817 in a remote eastern village in the backwater of Prussia, the province of Posen, whose 52,000 Jews were still decades away from emancipation. When he arrived in Breslau some twenty-five years later to matriculate in that city's famous non-denominational university, he had not had the benefit of a single year of formal secular education. In contrast to his solid mastery of Jewish sources, which had been acquired with the benefit of some formal instruction, including three years of tutorial work with Hirsch, his broad secular knowledge and linguistic competence were attained entirely on his own through superhuman effort and unrelieved hardship. The intimate diary which he began to keep in 1833 reveals a highly emotional young man, often overcome by moments of religious fervor and afflicted with recurring sieges of self-doubt and feelings of inferiority, but driven at the same time by a burning desire to achieve recognition.[55]

The move to Breslau brought Graetz, the aspiring self-educated country bumpkin, face to face with Abraham Geiger, only seven years his senior but already one of the acknowledged leaders of the expanding Reform movement. The confrontation quickly turned into a permanent feud. The differences went far deeper than religious disagreement. Geiger hailed from Frankfurt, had won his academic spurs at Bonn with a prize essay and his doctorate at Marburg, and possessed a far more even temperament than his lifelong younger adversary. Unlike Graetz, Geiger also enjoyed the hard-to-acquire status of a Prussian citizen, for which he had been compelled to wait idly in Berlin for more than a year before it was finally granted in November 1839.[56]

The differences in development and disposition were already strikingly evident in the contrasting reactions of each man to the publication of Hirsch's apodictic

Nineteen Letters of Ben Uziel in 1836, an event that projected its twenty-eight-year-old author into the limelight as a significant spokesman for a new, modified Orthodoxy favorable to emancipation. The same book, which rescued Graetz's faith from the near fatal challenge of secularism and inspired him to study personally with Hirsch for three years from 1837 to 1840,[57] provoked Geiger to write a devastating review in which he condemned Hirsch for his total lack of any historical sense and for his utterly arbitrary exegetical method.[58] Although Graetz eventually also came to regard Hirsch as the antithesis of modern *Wissenschaft*, during his first stay in Breslau he was still very much under his influence and harbored a passionate grudge against Geiger for his hostile review.[59]

In the 1840s Breslau was the third largest Jewish community in Prussia (behind Berlin and Posen) and growing rapidly. With a steady influx of rural Jews from Silesia and Posen, the Jewish population jumped from 5714 in 1840 to 7384 in 1849. It was also wracked by the bitterest and most protracted religious controversy of the decade precipitated by the election of Geiger as the community's second rabbi in 1838.[60] By the time Graetz came on the scene, Geiger's forces had clearly gained the upper hand. In the spring of 1842 the board had suspended its first rabbi Solomon Tiktin, his determined Orthodox opponent, following an unseemly demonstration at a funeral at which Geiger was to officiate.[61]

Nevertheless, Graetz's antipathy for Geiger exceeded his aversion to the unenlightened, casuistic Orthodox of the Tiktin camp.[62] As the Breslau correspondent of the *Orient* of Julius Fürst, a *Privatdozent* at the University of Leipzig whom Graetz respected for his determination not to convert to Christianity for the sake of an academic appointment, Graetz quickly received the notoriety he sought as a talented and uncompromising critic of Geiger and his movement. His articles were personal, passionate, and pugnacious.[63] In short, long before Graetz was to make his mark as a scholar he had developed a profound abhorrence for the Reform movement, fed by an envious dislike for the man who embodied and led it. The key to understanding Graetz's philosophy of Jewish history lies in the nexus between this early anti-Reform bias and the scholarly positions he subsequently adopted. Ideology governed his reading of Jewish history no less than it governed Geiger's.

The interaction produced a head-on collision in 1844. Graetz's first published venture in the field of *Wissenschaft* was nothing less than a lengthy, vitriolic review of a pioneering study by Geiger on the development of mishnaic Hebrew. To be sure, Geiger's work was not strictly dispassionate either. Since his earlier assault on Hirsch's exegetical method, he had undertaken a critical study of the history of rabbinic exegesis, with an eye to undermining the exegetical basis of a legal system which he regarded as alien to the essence of Judaism.[64] Yet Graetz tore into the book with all the venom of a jealous protagonist who disdained the learning but longed for the fame of his adversary.

Aside from a deluge of criticism on details, Graetz challenged Geiger on three questions of fundamental import. First, he contested Geiger's assertion that during the Second Commonwealth Hebrew ceased to be a living language and that the Hebrew of the Mishnah constituted the artificial creation of rabbinic scholastics. Refusing to acknowledge that the prophets were the last Jews to speak Hebrew, Graetz valiantly marshaled the meager evidence then available, including the theory that some of the psalms in the Psalter dated from the period of the Maccabees, to argue that the Maccabean revolt produced a Hebraic revival. Along with Aramaic, Hebrew had again been taken up by the masses as a language of conversation. Second, Graetz denounced Geiger's presumption to expound the Mishnah objectively and rejected his contention that at times the Talmud itself failed to interpret the Mishnah properly. Like Sachs, whom he admired and quoted at length, Graetz proposed that for the full understanding of certain intellectual works a critical apparatus was insufficient. What gave the "unscientific" rabbinic expositors of the Mishnah a decided edge, he contended, was the benefit of a living tradition which united them spiritually and substantively with the world of the Mishnah. Finally, Graetz rejected Geiger's critical assessment of the Mishnah's biblical exegesis as an argument patently contrived to advance the anti-*halakhic* program of the Reform movement.

The review unequivocally identified Graetz with the small group of university-trained men who had begun to take up the cudgels of *Wissenschaft* on behalf of traditional Judaism. It also brought him the public recognition for which he longed. He proudly recorded in his diary that he received an invitation from Frankel to write for his journal as well as a highly complimentary letter from Sachs. He dreamed of bringing them together with Hirsch to join their efforts against the rabbinical conferences and Reform associations. Graetz was now more determined than ever to serve Judaism in its hour of need, to join the fight against "malice and sophistry," and he struggled hard to overcome his fears that the jump from a shy, awkward, and unschooled yeshiva *bochur* to an eloquent national spokesman might be too great.[66]

In 1845 Graetz earned his Ph.D. from the University of Jena for a dissertation on *Gnosticismus und Judenthum* which was published a year later and dedicated to Hirsch, "the profound fighter for historical Judaism, the unforgettable teacher, the fatherly friend."[67] Notwithstanding Graetz's apologies for the utter irrelevance of the subject to the problems currently tormenting German Jewry, the book does provide a subtle commentary on the contemporary scene. At face value Graetz's scholarly debut was a highly innovative attempt to explore the impact of Gnosticism on second-century Judaism. The very suggestion of any such interaction served notice of the extent to which Graetz was willing to study the history of the Jews in terms of the general context. By locating the most likely historical context, he dated a number of talmudic passages and identified several enigmatic terms and events as the product of gnostic influence. The method of dating on the basis of ideological similarity and historical reasoning, which Graetz used throughout his life, was not terribly refined. It often was arbitrary and hypothetical, with similarities accepted as influence and speculation replacing facts. But at its best, the method could illuminate an undated text brilliantly.[68]

On a symbolic level Graetz's doctoral dissertation mirrored the dilemma of his age. In the introduction Graetz asserted that just as Judaism in the second century had successfully handled the grave challenge of gnostic dualism, so in the nineteenth century it would also overcome the ominous danger of "modern pantheism." Graetz's penchant for reducing historical trends and intellectual currents to personalities was already well developed. The ideological conflict of the second century was embodied in the contrasting figures of Elisha ben Abuya and Akiva ben Joseph, the products of completely disparate backgrounds. The wealthy, well-educated Elisha proved unable to resist the intellectual appeal of gnostic antinomianism and became the prototype of the medieval renegade; the lowly born, uneducated Akiva dramatically surmounted his origins to provide Judaism with the ideological vitality to turn back the challenge.[69] Graetz's spirited and partisan treatment of these ancient protagonists strongly suggests that he may have perceived them in terms of his own bitter relationship with Geiger, whom he labeled in his diary as the "miserable spokesman" of an "empty deism."[70] Graetz identified with Akiva, whose creative response to Gnosticism, he felt, was merely one dimension of a career which securely laid the foundation of rabbinic Judaism.[71] Thus the religious turmoil of the present replayed the script of an earlier struggle, with Graetz defending traditional Judaism with novelty and daring against the Elisha ben Abuya of his day.

The book closed on a Hegelian note which would reappear more prominently in Graetz's next work. The confrontation of Judaism with Gnosticism in Graetz's view had had its positive side. It had compelled Judaism to begin reflecting on itself and thereby elevated it to a higher level of self-consciousness.[72]

V

Graetz's first formative period in Breslau also provided the setting for his initial attempt at a philosophy of Jewish history. Exactly one year after the completion of his doctoral work, the twenty-nine-year-old Graetz published a wide-ranging and coherent prolegomenon to his later history in Frankel's *Zeitschrift*.[73] Ostensibly "The Structure of Jewish History" was an overview to define the nature of Judaism historically. Actually the essay offered a new theory of Jewish history carefully designed to refute that constructed by the advocates of Reform during the previous quarter century. In nearly every significant aspect, Graetz's theory ran counter to that propounded by his adversaries, and the cumulative evidence indicates that Graetz alone among the members of the emerging conservative camp was the first to realize fully the nature and function of the Reform theory of Jewish history.

To be sure, Graetz used the same ideological equipment employed by his opponents: he remained securely grounded in the world of German idealism. Ideas were the true substance and motive power of history, although visible to the historian only in their actualized form. Thus the idea of Judaism could be discovered only in the history of Judaism. What Graetz condemned in earlier efforts was the tendentious selectivity, the refusal to take into account the entire spectrum of Jewish history. Whole periods had been treated as historical mishaps unrelated to the essence of Judaism. Yet if an idea had forged its way into reality and stamped its imprint upon an age, then it must represent a genuine dimension of Judaism's essence. In light of the totality of Jewish history and in contrast to Reform ideologues, Graetz proposed a multifaceted essence of Judaism whose different dimensions shaped different periods of Jewish history.[74]

At the very time when Reform spokesmen were apprehensively protesting the purely confessional character of Judaism, Graetz dared to come out publicly with the declaration that the essence of Judaism comprised both a religious and a political factor, a concept of God as well as a theory of the state. Neither alone could ever exhaust the nature of Judaism. With respect to its God concept, Graetz adopted a line of reasoning first developed by Salomon Steinheim, the only contemporary German Jewish thinker aside from his former mentor whom he regarded highly. In 1835 Steinheim had written a fervent but lucid attack against the prevailing rationalist tendency of the age to reduce religion to the truths of philosophy. The second half of his book juxtaposed what Steinheim felt to be the conflicting views of paganism (i.e., natural religion) and Judaism (i.e., revealed religion) on God, creation, and freedom. Similarly, Graetz posited a fundamental antithesis, arguing specifically that Judaism's perception of God as absolutely transcendent repudiated paganism's theology of immanence.[75] But in contrast to Steinheim and the common Reform view, Graetz insisted:

that the monotheistic idea is not even the primary principle of Judaism, as it has been widely believed by many up till now, but only the secondary consequence resulting from the extra-mundane concept of God, just as polytheism and idolatry are not the foundation of paganism. Therefore, the idea of monotheism in no way exhausts the entire content of Judaism; the latter is infinitely richer, infinitely deeper.[76]

Part of this wealth was produced by the unique manner in which Judaism strove to overcome the dualism inherent in a theology of transcendence and to bridge the chasm between man and God. Against Hegel's critique of Judaism as a "religion of transcendence," Graetz claimed that Judaism was not even a religion, if by that term one understands a relationship to God that will insure personal salvation. It was of the very essence of Judaism to focus on the group and not the individual by translating theology into social practice. The transcendence of God was overcome, Graetz implied, by rendering the idea of God into a suitable social structure. The goal of building a religiously imbued body politic was the way Judaism reunited the spirit with nature. Thus the idea of Judaism comprised a religious and a political dimension, which together constituted the twin axes around which all of Jewish history revolved. The Torah was the soul and the land of Israel the body of a unique political organism. In defending Judaism against the charge that it was guilty of an irremediable dualism between man and God, Graetz arrived at a national definition of Judaism which directly challenged the claims of the Reform movement.[77]

Jewish history, which reflects the idea of Judaism and tests its viability, was divided by Graetz into three distinct periods. Each period realized one aspect of its multifaceted essence. The first period ended with the destruction of Jerusalem and the Temple in 586 and was predominantly of a political character. The second period spanned the Second Commonwealth, and terminated with the destruction of the Second Temple in 70, manifesting a distinctly religious character. The long medieval period of dispersion, which covered some seventeen centuries down to the end of the eighteenth century, revealed still a third dimension of the idea of Judaism.

At first glance, Graetz's periodization did not appear to break new ground, either in the demarking or the characterization of the periods. In both respects it bore considerable resemblance to the scheme outlined just three years earlier by Holdheim who likewise had depicted the first period as mainly political and the second as religious. Graetz also resembled his Reform opponents in the common failure to depart from the regnant Christian periodization of Jewish history which posited the year 70 as a fateful turning point in Jewish history. Since the third century the Church had defended tenaciously the argument that the destruction of Jerusalem and the dispersion of the Jews which allegedly accompanied it were the swift divine punishment for the crime of deicide. In the nineteenth century, few Jewish historians challenged the historical validity of this weighty theological legacy; they merely reinterpreted the significance of this watershed in Jewish history.[78]

The novelty of Graetz's scheme lay precisely in his radical departure from the significance conventionally attributed by the Reform theory of Jewish history to the third period. The destruction of the Second Temple did not climax the demise of Jewish nationhood nor inaugurate Judaism's mission to the world. In an omission pregnant with meaning, Graetz completely ignored the mission concept so central to Reform thinking. Instead, appropriating a Hegelian category, he argued that the period of dispersion was marked by a distinct speculative dimension unknown in the earlier periods. Exposure to conflicting life-styles and ideologies compelled Judaism to reflect upon itself. Although the immediacy of the original religious experience was shattered, exile served to elevate Judaism to a higher level of consciousness. Ultimately the Jews would return to their homeland to translate their profounder understanding of Judaism into a new social reality.[79]

This interpretation of the period of dispersion made it quite evident that there was nothing accidental about Jewish messianism. It was not the natural consequence of persecution but rather, reflected the basic drive of Judaism to translate theory into practice. In a telling metaphor Graetz compared God's exile of the Jews to a father's education of his son.

Once a son has been educated and matured by his father's guidance and teaching, the father himself sends the boy away from the hearth and ships him out into the world to gather experience and to test his paternal teaching in the thousand conflicts of life. But the father has no intention of letting his beloved boy perish in a distant land. With the strength and independence that comes through bitter experience, the son will return to his house to inherit his father's estate.[80]

Thus Graetz refused unequivocally to historicize the messianic hope, for to abandon the belief in national redemption was to render the exile meaningless.

This Hegelian function of exile as the path to greater self-consciousness also enabled Graetz to challenge the treatment accorded talmudic Judaism by Reform historians.

There is nothing more absurd and unhistorical than to assert that a force which penetrated as deeply as did the talmudic system is the product of an error, of twisted exegesis, of hierarchical ambition, in short, of an historical accident.[81]

If the origins of Judaism lay in protest and true enlightenment came only by plunging into the world, then a certain amount of self-imposed distance and isolation were indispensable for sheer survival. Separation was not imposed by the hostility of an alien environment but counterbalanced the necessity to examine opposing principles at close range.

By implication, Graetz's vision of Jewish history also broke with the basic conceptual assumption of development upon which the Reform theory relied. There is no true notion whatever of development in Graetz. The argument for a multi-faceted essence of Judaism amounts to a theory of immanence in which the major changes of later eras are reduced to the logical unfolding of the original idea. The radical import of Graetz's position is that, unlike the Reform theory, earlier phases of Jewish history are never transcended. The national dimension of the first period or the talmudic system of the third are not abandoned in the wake of subsequent eras. Although every period is shaped by a different dimension of Judaism, and thereby illuminates a part of the whole, none of these dimensions is historicized. All facets continue to remain operative and valid. Even the self-consciousness acquired in exile, which seems to suggest a theory of progress, does not serve to diminish the validity of earlier realizations of the idea of Judaism. Graetz simply refused to accord a higher status to later periods. Thus the proto-Zionist note on which he closed his essay aptly summed up his non-developmental theory.

And since these three dimensions have assumed historical form, they must have lain in the original idea of Judaism, as the tree in the seed, and according to this view of history, it seems that the task of Judaism's God-idea is to found a religious state which is conscious of its activity, purpose, and connection with the world.[82]

What Graetz did propose was much more akin to a cyclical theory of history. His overview of Jewish history emphasized the formal similarities between periods no less than the substantive differences. The periods of the first two Commonwealths, for example, abounded in parallels. Both periods began with terms of exile, to be followed by a return to Palestine under the inspired leadership of the Judges and the men of the Great Assembly respectively. In each case, Jewish life came to be gravely threatened by the challenge of a foreign ideology, monarchy and Hellenism, while the heroic responses culminating in the reigns of David and John Hyrcanus were cut short by deep internal divisions, in the first era between the kingdoms of Judah and Israel, in the second between Pharisees and Sadducees.[83]

In the final analysis, what distinguished Graetz's theory of Jewish history from that of his Reform adversaries is what separated Humboldt from Hegel or the historian from the philosopher. In his adamant refusal to impose a rigid developmental scheme on the totality of Jewish history, Graetz heeded Humboldt's astute caveat against a teleological approach to the study of history. in 1821, one year before Hegel began lecturing on his philosophy of history, Wilhelm von Humboldt, the paragon of German humanism, had delivered a brilliant statement on the task of the historian in which he asserted:

Historical truth is, generally speaking, much more threatened by philosophical than by artistic handling, since the latter is at least accustomed to granting freedom to its subject matter. Philosophy dictates a goal to events. This search for final causes, even though it may be deduced from the essence of man and nature itself, distorts and falsifies every independent judgment of the characteristic working of forces.[84]

Although Humboldt certainly believed in the causal role of ideas and acknowledged the existence of an unknowable cosmic plan, he resisted the philosophic appeal of doing violence to the flux and variety of history. The distinct essence which inhered in every individuality did reveal an aspect of infinity and represented the final goal of all historical research, but the sum total of essences could never be forced into the straitjacket of a progressive model.[85] Humboldt's position, with its respect for the diversity of history, provided Graetz with a theory perfectly suited to take on the spokesmen of Reform who had used the teleology, if not the dialectics, of Hegel to free themselves from the legacy of earlier and lower stages of development.

VI

In 1853 Graetz offered the reading public volume four as the first installment of what was billed as a multivolume *History of the Jews from the Earliest Times to the Present*. In so doing, he defied the scholarly judgment of his day, for Zunz and others had long felt that any further attempt at a comprehensive history of the Jews was premature. The quarter century which had passed since the appearance of Jost's ninth volume in 1828 had certainly witnessed a proliferation of monographs on talmudic and medieval history, but the results merely provided some idea of the vast stretches of the Jewish past still to be explored. Too many documents and manuscripts still lay buried in archives and private libraries, unstudied and unpublished. Graetz himself was clearly aware, as he admitted to his intimate friend Moses Hess in a letter in 1864, of the inevitable shortcomings of his work.

I am not so modest as not to realize that my history is much better than Jost's which is really none at all. But I know best of all what deficiencies in material, treatment, organization, style attend my work. However, I can't help it. I am paving the way for a better work.[86]

Graetz defied the judgment of his peers because an effective refutation of the Reform theory of Jewish history required a shift away from speculative history. Heinrich Heine had once quipped against Hegel that "Life is neither a goal nor a means, life is a right."[87] The most formidable challenge to Hegel's reading of history came from the scientific history of Ranke, who spent a lifetime carrying out Humboldt's conception of a historian. Deeply sensitive to the infinite variety of history, he refused to subsume the wealth of data under a teleological superstructure. "Every epoch is equally close to God."[88] Similarly, Graetz turned to scientific history to undermine the teleology of Hegel's Jewish disciples. Geiger recognized the gulf that separated the two men. In reviewing Graetz's fourth volume in 1866, on the occasion of a second edition, he zeroes in on the fundamental difference:

The book contains stories [*Geschichten*] which are loosely strung together, but no history [*Geschichte*]. We gain no sense of development, of an inner driving power. I'm not asking for contrived pragmatic history, but just as little do I want a force devoid of ideas. Movements must arise from the depth of a totality rooted in distinct spiritual tendencies. The phenomenona must come forth according to an inner law and work their way toward a goal.[89]

That Graetz began with volume four, which covered the turbulent but seminal period from 70 to 500 c.e., was not only a proof of the extent to which he had already worked out his overall conception, but was also evidence of the highly controversial nature of the period itself. The emancipation struggle had seriously threatened the viability of the entire rabbinic system. Reform historians like Jost, Holdheim, Geiger, and the Galician *maskil* Joshua Heschel Schorr had long sought to undermine the divine mandate of rabbinic Judaism by exposing its historical origins.[90] In the 1850s, with the publication of four major works on this crucial period, the level of debate reached a new high. The decade had opened with the posthumous publication of Krochmal's long-awaited *Moreh Nevukhei ha-Zeman* by Zunz in 1851. In 1853 Graetz added his contribution, which was followed in 1857 by Geiger's *Urschrift und Uebersetzungen der Bibel,* and two years after that by Frankel's *Darkhei ha-Mishnah.*

Despite the audacity and ingenuity of Geiger's radical study of rabbinic exegesis, by the end of the decade the conservative scholarship of Krochmal, Graetz, and Frankel had succeeded in presenting a more sympathetic and favorable assessment of rabbinic Judaism. Graetz tried valiantly to portray the disembodied rabbis of the Mishnah and Talmud as vibrant men, each with his own style and philosophy and personal frailties, who collectively resisted the disintegrating forces of their age.[91] In contrast to Jost, who harped on the rise and triumph of clericalism, Graetz invoked the categories of recovery, regeneration, and consolidation. In the wake of national disaster, creative leadership forged new religious institutions to preserve and invigorate the bonds of unity. Graetz berated Schorr and his circle for depicting the founders of rabbinic Judaism like contemporary Polish rabbis.[92] He defended talmudic literature as a great national achievement of untold importance to the subsequent survival of the Jews.[93]

The proud and exuberant tone of Graetz's work was as new as the interpretations being expounded, and it reflected the second major reason behind his decision to undertake a comprehensive history. A year before the first volume appeared Graetz had come to Berlin, and in the winter of 1852–1853 he taught a course in Jewish history to aspiring students of Jewish theology who also studied the Bible with Sachs and rabbinic literature with Zunz.[94] When Sachs introduced Graetz to Zunz one evening in his home, he mentioned that his guest intended to publish a history of the Jews. "Another history of the Jews!" sighed Zunz. "Yes," retorted Graetz unperturbed. "But this time a Jewish history!"[95] The significance of this well-known anecdote is not only that it underscores the determination to write a national history, but even more, it suggests one of the sources of Graetz's inspiration.

From the fragmentary evidence which remains it would appear that Sachs exerted a formative influence on his younger colleague. Equally endowed with strong feelings, both men shared an instinctive aversion toward Reform. Graetz had quoted Sachs at length in his review of Geiger's *Lehr- und Lesebuch zur Sprache der Mischnah*, and when Sachs wrote him a highly complimentary letter, Graetz referred to him in his diary as "the hero of the day, who belongs to those people who make a symbolic impression."[96] In the final volume of his history, which covered the events of his own day with a jaundiced eye, Graetz allotted the extraordinary amount of six pages for a glowing encomium on Sachs.[97] Graetz first met Sachs in 1846 and then again in 1852 when Sachs introduced him to his learned and close friend Moritz Veit, who agreed to publish the first volume of Graetz's forthcoming history.[98] Above all, Graetz wrote the kind of history for which Sachs had been pleading. In the hands of both men *Wissenschaft* became a vehicle for the recovery of self-respect and a force for the preservation of the Jewish people. Both repudiated an approach to Jewish history that studied the past mainly to escape from its tutelage. The historian had the sacred task to fire his people with a love for the drama and glory of its past in order to strengthen its sense of unity and its resolve to survive.

In their vision of *Wissenschaft* Sachs and Graetz mirrored the prevailing nationalist spirit of contemporary German historiography. Since the frustration of German unity at the Congress of Vienna, German intellectuals led by the retired statesman Baron vom Stein, had begun to unfurl the glories of German history to create a ground-swell for unification. It was hoped that the rediscovery of a common national history would engender a sense of national consciousness. The mood in which two generations of nationalist historians from Georg Pertz to Heinrich Treitschke labored was foreshadowed in the motto which Stein chose for the *Monumenta Germaniae historica,* that vast collection of Latin sources on medieval German history conceived by Stein and carried out by Pertz and then Georg Waitz: *Sanctus amor patriae dat animum* (The sacred love of the fatherland gives courage). To generate that love among the masses became the responsibility of the historian.[99]

The nationalist quality of Graetz's history expressed itself in a variety of ways, quite apart from the open acknowledgment he made at the end of his preface to volume one (which appeared in 1874), that the love for the people to which he belonged by birth and conviction sustained him in the execution of his work.[100] To begin with, an unshakable belief in the continuity of Jewish history infused his entire enterprise. Graetz lashed out against Christian theologians and historians for depriving the Jews of any legitimate history beyond the destruction of the Second Temple.[101] He also rebuked Jost for denying any continuity between the prophets and the rabbis.[102] In contrast, Graetz emphasized the legal character of the Bible and claimed, without effectively proving his case, that medieval Jewish history continued to show a national dimension.[103] In brief, the substance of Graetz's work was the story of a single people, still very much alive, whose unique historical experience spanned some three millennia.

Second, Graetz fully identified with his subject. When the Jews endured defeat and persecution, he shared the agony of their fate. On occasion, his quill faltered in recounting the brutality of their hardships.[104] Not surprisingly, Graetz also harbored an ill-concealed hatred for the enemies of his people. His history is replete with outbursts and expletives against Roman, Christian, and German oppressors.[105] He measured the character of renowned non-Jews like Luther, Voltaire, and Fichte in terms of their attitudes toward Jews and Judaism.[106] Similarly, Graetz did not hesitate to pour his wrath on Jews whom he regarded as having betrayed the course of Jewish survival. He railed against Hellenized Jews, Herod, Josephus, apostates, Friedländer, and Holdheim among others.[107] As was frequently the case in nineteenth-century national histories, empathy ended in partisanship.

Coupled with such self-righteous indignation at national degradation and treason was an eloquent effort to accentuate the ideal of national recovery. The Maccabees had effected a national revival which made Hebrew again a living language.[108] Rejecting the invidious portrait of the Zealots by Josephus, Graetz depicted them as noble, brave, and idealistic men inspired by faith to regain national independence.[109] The subsequent revolts against Rome in the second and fourth decades of the next century were cast in terms that echoed the contemporary European scene. The Jews loathed subjugation. Filled with an indomitable spirit of freedom and memories of independence, they rose in an epic struggle against the Roman colossus. "The beginning resembled every national uprising."[110] Graetz believed that in his own day one could detect the first sign of yet another national revival in the universal Jewish outrage and action in the face of the Damascus blood libel of 1840 and that this turning point in modern Jewish history should have been commemorated annually in the synagogue.[111] As modern Greek and Italian nationalists were reviving the glories of Pericles and Scipio, Jews must rediscover the heroic moments of their own history. The road to the future led through the past.[112]

Finally, Graetz as a national historian mounted a subtle argument for the importance of Jewish history for the understanding of general history. This rather bold proposition was the reverse of the more widely acknowledged realization that a proper understanding of the Jewish history of any given period required careful attention to the larger canvas of general history. And Graetz from the very beginning of his scholarly career repeatedly tried, sometimes with striking success, to account for particular Jewish developments in terms of the non-Jewish world.[113] But as a proud, assertive Jew, Graetz also was eager to show the Jewish impact on general history. All too frequently, this meant a forced and unhistorical comparison between Jews and Christians or Moslems to the decided advantage of the Jews, as if for the moment Jews remained the sole carriers of civilization.[114] But on other occasions, his claims were more substantive. Rabbinic sources, for example, were indispensable for illuminating the origins and early history of Christianity.[115] The Jewish revolts in the Diaspora and Palestine during Trajan's Parthian campaign might seriously have threatened the survival of the Empire, if they had only been coordinated.[116] The Jewish tribes of the Arabian peninsula helped shape the character of Islam.[117] The expulsion of 1492 deprived Spain of its middle class and thus insured its imminent decline.[118] And the prolonged Pfefferkorn–Reuchlin battle over the nature of talmudic literature, which engulfed the Holy Roman Empire and the Church, paved the way for the Reformation by creating a state of mind in Germany that was receptive to Luther's revolt against Rome.[119] These attempts to explain significant aspects of general history in terms of Jewish history implied a confidence in the continued centrality and uniqueness of the Jews. Graetz had recast the religious concept of chosenness in secular terms.

Yet during the very decades when Graetz poured his energies into the production of a patriotic narrative history of the Jews to counterbalance the kind of history being written by Reform ideologists, his own theory paradoxically began to approximate that of his adversaries. To be sure, the emotional antagonism toward Reform remained as intense as ever; witness the overtly polemical treatment accorded the precursors and founders of the movement in the final volume of his history.[120] But ideologically Graetz moved somewhat closer to Reform's conceptualization of the past. Not all of Graetz's later views were articulated or adumbrated in his schematic essay of 1846. The occasional essays in which he subsequently speculated on the nature of Jewish history along with certain tendencies of his comprehensive work reflect several significant departures from his initial effort at conceptualization.

In 1846 Graetz had maintained a pregnant silence on the central issue of a universal Jewish mission, which dovetailed perfectly with the essay's particularistic tone. That silence was abandoned in 1853 in the introduction to his first published volume. Graetz now also invoked the standard Reform argument: the redemption of mankind hinged upon the dissemination by the Jews of their unique theological and ethical systems. The traumatic events in the closing years of the Second Commonwealth were now interpreted by Graetz in terms of an apostolic role which necessitated dispersion. A consciousness of their mission and a confidence in their ultimate success served to sustain the Jews through centuries of frustration.[121] This line of reasoning became steadily more prominent in Graetz's later essays, simply because within the hostile context of German society Jewish existence was not a self-evident right but a privilege to be justified. Ludwig Philippson, the pro-Reform editor of Germany's leading Jewish weekly, summed up the Jewish dilemma in 1847:

That which desires to exist will be asked about the causes and content of as well as the justification for its existence. And only in so far as it can legitimately establish its rights, is it acceptable. . . . Judaism exists; it desires to and will survive. Thus it must make clear to both its adherents and others why it exists and for what reason it hopes to survive.[122]

The tragedy of the Jewish predicament was that to make a case for continued group survival inevitably entailed denigrating the faith of the very society into which Jews sought to integrate. Judaism's right to survive could only be established at the expense of Christianity. In formulating his case Graetz was merely not as politic and tactful as the leaders of Reform.[123]

A second feature of the Reform theory which Graetz quickly came to adopt was the undue emphasis on persecutions.[124] Ironically this version of the medieval Jewish experience is most often identified with Graetz. And yet his undeniable preoccupation with Jewish suffering led to a radically different conclusion. While articulating the same position, men can sometimes intend wholly different meanings. Unlike Reform historians, Graetz's perception of exilic history in terms of humiliation, oppression, and violence did not stem from a desire to exonerate his contemporaries from any alleged character defects or to provide a rationale for discarding aspects of Judaism which now seemed to be a liability. In the case of Graetz, the vivid and charged narration of Jewish suffering was intended to intensify the attachment to Judaism, whose institutions and beliefs had been sanctified by the blood of countless martyrs.[125] Graetz believed that persecution strengthened the bonds of faith. Catholics were always more devout in countries swept by the Reformation.[126] By extension, Graetz hoped that the vicarious experience of degradation and martyrdom which he sweated to convey to his readers would fortify their commitment to Jewish survival.

It is altogether likely that Graetz's excessive attention to the precariousness of Jewish existence in the past was also intended to question the exuberant and facile faith of his fellow Jews in the promise of the present.[127] Graetz never lost the awareness of being in exile. His skeptical view of human nature denied him the comfort of the prevailing faith in progress and the perfectibility of man. In the opening chapters of Genesis he saw the inevitable fate that awaits men who confidently conduct their lives solely by the canons of reason, arrogantly rejecting divine counsel.[128] Reason alone would never overcome the passions—it certainly was not on the verge of success in the nineteenth century. Graetz decried the immorality and materialism of Western civilization and denounced the illiberalism and antisemitism of German society.[129] In 1866 he confided to Hess his desire to settle in Paris and to teach at the École Rabbinique de France.[130] Long before most of his optimistic coreligionists, he sensed the gravity of the antisemitic backlash which engulfed the newly founded Empire.[131] In sum, Graetz simply did not share the state of mind which gave rise to the Reform theory of Jewish history. His conception of man led to a modified cyclical theory of Jewish history based on the sober realization that the darkness of a former age could descend again.[132]

That realization turned into personal reality for Graetz in 1879 when he became the object of a public attack by Heinrich Treitschke, the *"praeceptor Germaniae."*[133] In truth, such a collision was inevitable, for sooner or later Graetz's one-sided history was bound to offend the sensibilities of German nationalists. Treitschke and Graetz were cut from the same cloth and used history for the same ends. Extremely apprehensive about the fragile sense of unity and inchoate sense of national purpose from which the Reich still suffered, Treitschke condemned the divisive prominence of Jews in German society. Their presumption and insensitivity were typified by Graetz's *History of the Jews*, a work that insulted the religion and the cultural giants of the German nation. The import of Treitschke's remarks, which not only tried to vindicate the current antisemitic resurgence but effectively intensified it, was clear: the time had come for German Jewry to keep its side of the emancipation agreement. Assimilation meant dissolution.[134]

The spate of Jewish responses to the portentous intervention by Treitschke serve only to underscore Graetz's isolation. No one dared to defend his work openly. In his own two immediate replies Graetz ignored the larger issues and chose to defend himself against Treitschke's specific charges.[135] Not until 1883, and then only anonymously, did he deliver an impassioned argument on behalf of Jewish survival. *The Correspondence of an English Lady on Judaism and Semitism* was Graetz's final reply to Treitschke. Against the background of a devastating indictment of the moral degeneracy of the nineteenth century, Graetz asserted that the unfinished mission of Judaism was to convince mankind to accept the rigorous ethical system that was the key to Judaism's survival. Furthermore, the maintenance of talmudic Judaism with its pronounced legal and ritual character was still essential. While conceding that ritual would no longer be of value in the days of the Messiah, Graetz insisted that there was nothing messianic about his own day. Talmudic institutions still protected Jews from the virulent hostility of the outside world. A certain amount of ritual was being sloughed off by life itself. But to interfere with this natural process would only shatter Jewish unity so vital in the face of a hostile society. On the positive side, Jewish ritual helped to preserve a sense of unity. Borrowing a page from Mendelssohn, Graetz added that it also functioned as a vast pedagogic system ever reminding Jews of the ethical core of their religion. Before Jews could carry their message to the world, they had to actualize it among themselves. Graetz appealed directly to the sense of responsibility of Jewish intellectuals, who felt that they had already internalized Judaism's ethical teachings. They must continue to subject themselves to the dictates of the ritual system for the sake of the masses for whom it remained indispensable.[136]

Graetz ended this deeply felt declaration on Jewish survival with a veiled allusion to the future possibility of a renaissance of Jewish life in Palestine. It was a typically defiant finale, for Treitschke had explicitly warned that Germany could not tolerate dual loyalty.[137] But Graetz was steeped in Jewish national sentiment. Despite his embrace of the mission theory, he never ceased to regard Judaism as anything but a national religion. He spoke for the ancient and traditional twofold character of Judaism with its capstone of national messianism. When Hess wrote in *Rome and Jerusalem* that "the pious Jew is above all a Jewish patriot," he pinpointed the source of Graetz's nationalism.[138] Graetz had first articulated his national conception of Judaism in 1846, and his final reply to Treitschke, in 1883, confirms that he could not be intimidated to relinquish it. German pressure could only force him to mute and disguise it.[139]

Above all, Graetz remained committed to the rejuvenation of his people. His faith in God's guiding presence throughout Jewish history, as witnessed by two earlier instances of national recovery, assured him of the future.[140] His own work, he hoped, would contribute to the revival of Jewish consciousness. He succeeded beyond measure. As a young man Graetz had once failed to acquire a rabbinic pulpit because he was unable to complete the delivery of his sermon.[141] There is more than a touch of irony in the remarkable fact that the reception accorded to Graetz's history by Jews around the world made him the greatest Jewish preacher of the nineteenth century.[142]

NOTES

1. Mordechai Eliav, *Rabbiner Esriel Hildesheimer Briefe* (Jerusalem 1965), pp. 207–216.

2. Abraham Geiger, *WZJT,* I (1835), p. 2; idem, *Nachgelassene Schriften.* 5 vols.

(Berlin 1875–1878), V, pp. 181–182; Sigismund Stern, *Zur Judenfrage in Deutschland*, I (1843), p. 154, and II (1844), pp. 26–41; idem, *Der Israelit des neunzehnten Jahrhunderts*, VIII (1847), pp. 377–379.

3. Geiger, *WZJT*, V (1844), pp. 56–57.

4. Wolf, *LBIYB*, II (1957), p. 194.

5. Abraham Geiger, *Das Judenthum und seine Geschichte*, 3 vols. (Breslau 1865–1871), I, pp. 27–36; Samuel Holdheim, *Geschichte der Entstehung und Entwicklung der jüdischen Reformgemeinde in Berlin* (Berlin 1857), p. 115.

6. Ludwig Geiger, *ZGJD*, II (1888), p. 69.

7. Stern, *INJ*, VIII (1847), p. 378.

8. Amos Funkenstein, "Gesetz und Geschichte: Zur historisierenden Hermeneutik bei Moses Maimonides und Thomas von Aquin," *Viator* I (1970), pp. 147–178.

9. Sigismund Stern, *Die Aufgabe des Judenthums und der Juden in der Gegenwart* (Berlin 1845), pp. 9–10; Geiger, *Das Judenthum*, I, pp. 37–39.

10. Wolf, *LBIYB*, II (1957), p. 196. For similar comments, see Jost, *Geschichte der Israeliten*, I, p. xii; Samuel Holdheim, *Ueber die Autonomie der Rabbinen und das Princip der jüdischen Ehe*, 2nd ed. (Schwerin 1847), pp. 16–17; Jakob J. Petuchowski, *Prayerbook Reform in Europe* (New York 1968), pp. 53–54 (referring to the Hamburg Temple Prayer Book of 1819).

11. *The Chief Works of Benedict de Spinoza*, translated by R. H. M. Elwes, 2 vols. (Dover Publications, New York 1951), I, pp. 57–68, 72, 245–248.

12. Ibid., pp. 55–56.

13. Moses Mendelssohn, *Jerusalem and Other Jewish Writings*, translated by Alfred Jospe (New York 1969), pp. 99–104.

14. Friedländer, *Sendschreiben an . . . Teller* (Berlin 1799), pp. 34–38.

15. Holdheim, *Ueber die Autonomie*, p. 45.

16. It seems to appear first in his subsequent *Allgemeine Geschichte des Israelitischen Volkes*, 2 vols. (Berlin 1832), I, pp. 8–9.

17. Stern, *Die Aufgabe des Judenthums*, p. 17; *Protokolle und Aktenstücke der zweiten Rabbiner-Versammlung* (Frankfurt am Main 1845), p. 74 (henceforth PAZR); Geiger, *Das Judenthum*, I, pp. 149–162. The origins and elaboration of the radically new mission theory of the nineteenth century, by which the significance of *Galut* was effectively transvalued, have yet to be traced. The essay by Max Wiener, "The Conception of Mission in Traditional and Modern Judaism," *Yivo Annual of Jewish Social Science*, II–III (1947–1948), pp. 9–24 represents no more than an unfinished start. Years before, Max Nordau, who frequently gave eloquent expression to the Zionist critique of emancipation, had contended that Reform ideologists worked out their theory under the influence of Christian theology which itself had long maintained that Jewish dispersion and survival were intended to provide a witness for the truth of Scripture. There may be more to this intuitive insight than mere polemics. (Max Nordau, *Das Judenthum im 19. and 20. Jahrhundert*, 2nd ed. [Cologne 1911], pp. 17–19. On the Augustinian origin of this Christian argument, see Bernhard Blumenkranz, *Die Judenpredigt Augustins* [Basel 1946], pp. 175–181.)

18. Holdheim, *Ueber die Autonomie*, pp. 38–49.

19. Geiger, *WZJT*, V (1844), pp. 58–81, 234–259.

20. Samuel Usque, *Consolation for the Tribulations of Israel*, translated by Martin A. Cohen (Philadelphia 1964); Solomon ibn Verga, *Sefer Shebet Yehudah*, edited by Azriel Shohet (Jerusalem 1947); Joseph ha-Kohen, *Emeq ha-Bakha*, edited by Meir Letteris (Cracow 1895). On the precursors and sources of these sixteenth-century historians of persecution, see the conflicting views of Graetz, *Geschichte*, VIII, 4th ed.,

pp. 393–399; Isidore Loeb, *Joseph Haccohen et les chroniquers juifs* (Paris 1888); Fritz Baer, *Untersuchungen über Quellen und Komposition des Schebet Jehuda* (Berlin 1923); Martin Cohen, pp. 277–287.

21. Jacob Meijer, "Hugo Grotius' Remonstrantie," *Jewish Social Studies*, XVII (1955), pp. 95–96; John Toland, *Reasons for Naturalizing the Jews in Great Britain and Ireland* (London 1714), pp. 14–16; Christian Wilhelm Dohm, *Ueber die bürgerliche Verbesserung der Juden* (Berlin and Stettin 1781), pp. 31–35, 107–109; Henri Grégoire, *Essai sur la régéneration physique, morale et politique des Juifs* (Metz 1789), pp. 1–13, 32–44.

22. Mendelssohn, p. 146.

23. Geiger, *Das Judenthum*, II, p. 31.

24. Stern, *Die Aufgabe des Judenthums*, p. 25.

25. Holdheim, *Ueber die Autonomie*, pp. 17–18.

26. Friedländer, p. 38; Wolf, *LBIYB*, II (1957), pp. 197–198; *PAZR*, pp. 74–75, 76, 94, 100; Geiger, *Das Judenthums*, II, pp. 14–15. This alleged connection between oppression and messianism had already been suggested by Grégoire, p. 32.

27. Stern, *Die Aufgabe des Judenthums*, p. 78.

28. *Vollständige Verhandlungen des ersten vereinigten preussischen Landtages über die Emancipationsfrage der Juden* (Berlin 1847), p. xvi. Among the German states, Bavaria with 62,830 Jews had the second largest Jewish population.

29. Heinrich Silberpleit, *Die Bevölkerungs- und Berufsverhältnisse der Juden im deutschen Reich* (Berlin 1930), p. 9.

30. *Der Orient*, 1842, p. 187.

31. Horst Fischer, *Judentum, Staat und Heer in Preussen im frühen 19. Jahrhundert* (Tübingen 1968), pp. 158–190. See also the highly interesting memorandum submitted by Michael Sachs and published by Ismar Freund in the *Festschrift zu Simon Dubnows siebzigsten Geburtstag* (Berlin 1930), pp. 251–258.

32. Holdheim, *Ueber die Autonomie*, Vorwort to 1st ed., p. iii; Ludwig Geiger, "Moritz Veit also Kämpfer für die Emanzipation der Juden," *JJGL*, XIII (1910), pp. 140–141.

33. Bruno Bauer, *Die Judenfrage* (Braunschweig 1843). See also Nathan Rotenstreich, "For and Against Emancipation," *LBIYB*, IV (1959), pp. 3–11. On Bauer's work in general see the fresh reexamination by Lothar Koch, *Humanistischer Atheismus und gesellschaftliches Engagement* (Stuttgart 1971).

34. *INJ*, 1845, pp. 131–132; Ludwig Geiger, *ZGJD*, II (1888), pp. 49–62; Holdheim, *Geschichte der Reformgemeinde*, pp. 59–63; David Philipson, *The Reform Movement in Judaism*, 2nd ed. (New York 1931), pp. 231–234. On the social composition of these Reform groups, a subject as yet almost entirely ignored, see the hints in Holdheim, *Geschichte der Reformgemeinde*, pp. 26, 40, 50, 52; also the significant evidence uncovered by Jacob Katz, *Jews and Freemasons in Europe* (Cambridge 1970), pp. 91–95.

35. Holdheim, *Geschichte der Reformgemeinde*, pp. 63–66.

36. Philipson, pp. 241–244; *Der Orient*, 1945, p. 142. Even Holdheim, the later rabbi of the Berlin Reform Association, opposed the synod idea. The two groups simply did not share the same commitment to the past. (Holdheim, *Geschichte der Reformgemeinde*, p. 122.)

37. *ZRIJ*, I (1844), pp. 208, 224–228, 283, 331–332; *PAZR*, pp. 34–35.

38. *ZRIJ*, I (1844), pp. 14, 60–73, 208.

39. Max Wiener, *Jüdische Religion im Zeitalter der Emanzipation* (Berlin 1933),

pp. 256–257; *ZRIJ*, I (1844), p. 302; II (1845), pp. 15–16, 173, 180–181; *PAZR*, pp. 19–20.

40. Ludwig Geiger, ed., *Michael Sachs und Moritz Veit: Briefwechsel* (Frankfurt am Main 1897), p. 37.

41. Michael Sachs, *Die religiöse Poesie der Juden in Spanien* (Berlin 1845), pp. 148–164, 195.

42. In another context, Geiger, in passing, rejected Sach's historical approach as superficial and romantic, as aesthetic rather than scientific. (*Literatur-Blatt zum INJ*, 1846, p. 67.)

43. Ludwig Geiger, ed., *Abraham Geiger: Leben und Lebenswerk* (Berlin 1910), p. 17; Holdheim, *Geschichte der Reformgemeinde*, p. 11.

44. Nahum N. Glatzer, ed., *Leopold and Adelheid Zunz: An Account in Letters 1815–1885* (London 1958), pp. 129, 132, 139, 159–160.

45. Zunz, *Gesammelte Schriften*, II, pp. 196, 199–200, 201, 203.

46. Geiger, *Nachgelassene Schriften*, V, pp. 180–185.

47. Leopold Zunz, *Zur Geschichte und Literatur* (Berlin 1845), pp. 1–4, 17, 158.

48. Leopold Zunz, *Die Gottesdienstliche Vorträge der Juden*, 2nd ed. (Frankfurt am Main 1892), Vorrede.

49. Zunz, *Zur Geschichte*, p. 28.

50. Ibid., p. 28.

51. Wiener, pp. 182–183.

52. *Literatur-Blatt zum Israelit des neunzehnten Jahrhunderts*, 1846, nos. 1, 2, 14, 15, 17, 18–19.

53. S. Unna, "Briefe von H. Grätz an Raphael Kirchheim," *Jahrbuch der jüdisch-literarischen Gesellschaft*, XII (1918), p. 320.

54. Edmund Burke, *Reflections on the Revolution in France* (The Library of Liberal Arts, Indianapolis, 1955), pp. 36, 39–40, 42, 62, 90, 99.

55. To date, important selections from Graetz's diary, which spans the twenty-three years of his life from 1833 to 1856, have been published by Markus Brann, *MGWJ*, LXII (1918), pp. 231–265; LXIII (1919), pp. 34–47, 343-363; Reuven Michael, *Kiryat Sefer*, XXXVII (1961–1962), pp. 523–531; *LBIYB*, XIII (1968), pp. 34–49; Shmuel Ettinger, ed., *Heinrich Graetz: Darkhe ha-Historiah ha-Yehudit* (Jerusalem 1969), pp. 243–265. A complete edition of the diary plus several hundred of Graetz's letters, many of which have already been published, are now available in Heinrich Graetz, *Tagebuch und Briefe*, ed. Reuven Michael (Tübingen 1977). The two best biographical essay on Graetz are still those of Philip Bloch in Graetz's *History of the Jews*, VI (Philadelphia 1956), pp. 1–86, and Josef Meisl, *Heinrich Graetz* (Berlin 1917).

56. The best biography of Geiger is still that written by his son Ludwig Geiger in the collective volume *Abraham Geiger: Leben und Lebenswerk* (Berlin 1910), pp. 1–231.

57. Brann, *MGWJ*, LXII (1918), p. 258; Bloch, pp. 17–22.

58. See in particular Geiger, *WZJT*, III (1837), pp. 77, 81–82. The first two installments were published the previous year. (Ibid., II [1836], pp. 351–359, 518–548.) *Horeb* fared no better. (See ibid., IV [1839], pp. 355–381.)

59. Michael, *LBIYB*, XIII (1968), p. 42. The year is 1844, not 1848.

60. Salomon Neumann, *Zur Statistik der Juden in Preussen von 1816 bis 1880* (Berlin 1884), p. 45. Ludwig Geiger, *Abraham Geiger*, p. 56.

61. Ibid., pp. 78–79.

62. Michael, *Kiryat Sefer*, XXXVII (1961–1962), p. 527; idem, *LBIYB*, XIII (1968),

p. 42. Graetz also had grown critical of Hirsch's fanatical religious observance and expressed some strong reservations about the supremacy of the *Shulhan Arukh*. See Brann, *MGWJ*, XLIII (1919), p. 356, and Michael, *Kiryat Sefer*, p. 525.

63. See, for example, his caustic remarks about Geiger in *Der Orient*, 1844, pp. 355–356; 1845, pp. 292, 321, 394; 1846, pp. 111–112. Also his condemnation of the current rabbinical conferences in *Der Orient*, 1844, pp. 179–181; 1846, pp. 229–230, 238, 294–295.

64. Abraham Geiger, "Das Verhältniss der natürlichen Schriftsinnes zur thalmudischen Schriftdeutung," *WZJT*, V (1844), pp. 53–81, 234–259.

65. Abraham Geiger, *Lehr- und Lesebuch zur Sprache der Mischnah*, 2 vols. (Breslau 1845), I, pp. 1–2; II, pp. viii, 4, 7–11, 14, 15, 21–22; Graetz, *Literaturblatt des Orients*, V, pp. 822–827; VI, pp. 631–635.

66. Michael, *LBIYB*, XIII (1968), pp. 45–49.

67. Hirsch Grätz, *Gnosticismus und Judenthum* (Krotoschin 1846).

68. Among the most successful instances of Graetz's method are the following: *Geschichte*, III, 2nd ed., pp. 494–502; V, 4th ed., pp. 446–471; VII, 4th ed., pp. 430–448.

69. Graetz, *Gnosticismus*, pp. 62–71, 83–85. In the final chapter, Graetz argued that *Sefer Yesirah* was a second-century philosophic work, perhaps from the hands of R. Akiba, designed to refute gnostic ideas. He later dated the book in the Gaonic period on linguistic grounds. (*Geschichte*, V, 4th ed., p. 297n. Cf. Gershom Scholem, *Major Trends in Jewish Mysticism*, 3rd rev. ed. [New York 1954], pp. 75–78).

70. Michael, *LBIYB*, XIII (1968), p. 42.

71. Graetz, *Geschichte*, IV, 4th ed., pp. 50–56.

72. Graetz, *Gnosticismus*, p. 131.

73. Heinrich Graetz, "Die Construction der jüdischen Geschichte," *ZRIJ*, III (1846), pp. 81–97, 121–132, 361–368, 413–421. It was republished again ninety years later (Ludwig Feuchtwanger, ed., *Die Konstruktion der jüdischen Geschichte* [Berlin 1936]). It was also recently translated into Hebrew in Ettinger, ed., *Darkhe ha-Historiah ha-Yehudit* and now rendered into English.

74. Heinrich Graetz, *The Structure of Jewish History and Other Essays*, trans. Ismar Schorsch (New York 1975), pp. 63–66.

75. S. L. Steinheim, *Die Offenbarung nach dem Lehrbegriffe der Synagogue*, I (Frankfurt am Main 1835), zweite Abteilung. On Graetz's admiration for Steinheim, see *The Structure*, pp. 67, 123. In his *Geschichte*, XI, 2nd ed., Graetz allotted Steinheim more space than any of his contemporaries (pp. 431–437). On Steinheim's work, see Joshua O. Haberman, "Salomon Ludwig Steinheim's Doctrine of Revelation," *Judaism*, XVII (1968), pp. 22–41; Nathan Rotenstreich, *Jewish Philosophy in Modern Times* (New York 1968), pp. 149–174.

I am somewhat dubious about Prof. Rotenstreich's contention that Graetz was also influenced by Solomon Formstecher, in light of the latter's well-known Reform leanings. Furthermore, Graetz utterly ignored the man and his work in the volume of the *Geschichte* devoted to his own century. Finally, Graetz's body of ideas, if not their terminology, can readily be derived from Steinheim alone. (See Rotenstreich, *ha-Mahshabah ha-Yehudit ba-'Eit ha-Hadashah*, 2 vols. [Tel Aviv 1966], I, p. 77; idem, *Tradition and Reality* [New York 1972], pp. 54–55.)

76. Graetz, *The Structure*, p. 69. In contrast, Steinheim had asserted that the unity of God was and is the fundamental proposition of Judaism. (Steinheim, p. 306.) Even Frankel was disturbed by the radicalism of Graetz's position. Witness his long critical note attached to Graetz's essay (*The Structure*, pp. 304–305). Despite Fran-

kel's claim that Graetz had changed his view by the time he finished the last installment of his essay, Graetz always remained reluctant to reduce the core of Judaism to the idea of monotheism (ibid., p. 309).

77. See ibid., pp. 70–71. On Hegel's view of Judaism, see Nathan Rotenstreich, "Hegel's Image of Judaism," *JSS*, XV (1953), pp. 33–52.

78. Holdheim, *Ueber die Autonomie*, pp. 38–49. On the history of the Church's interpretation, see Jules Isaac, *The Teaching of Contempt* (New York 1964), pp. 39–73. This interpretation was fully retained by Jacques Basnage, the early eighteenth-century Huguenot historian of the Jews, in his epoch-making *History of the Jews from Jesus Christ to the Present Time*, translated by T. Taylor (London 1708), pp. 2, 53, 61, 145. In the nineteenth century, Reform historians continued to regard the year 70 as the start of a new era. (Aside from Holdheim, see also Julius Heinrich Dessauer, *Geschichte der Israeliten* [Erlangen 1846], p. 165; and Abraham Geiger, *Das Judenthum*, I, pp. 150-162.) Jost, however, with his emphasis on the pre-70 emergence of rabbinism, deserves to be credited with freeing himself at least partially from the prevailing Christian view. (See his *Geschichte der Israeliten*, III, pp. 180–185.) A less theologically oriented and more historically determined periodization had to await the nationalist historiography of our own century. (See Gedalyah Alon, *Toldot ha-Yehudim be-Eretz Yisrael bi-Tqufat ha-Mishanh ve-ha-Talmud*, I [Israel 1958], pp. 1–11.)

79. Graetz, *The Structure*, pp. 94–96, 124.

80. Ibid., p. 98.

81. Ibid., p. 100.

82. Ibid., p. 124.

83. Ibid., pp. 84–92.

84. Wilhelm von Humboldt, "On the Historian's Task," translated in *History and Theory*, VI (1967), p. 64.

85. Ibid., pp. 57–71. See also Georg G. Iggers, *The German Conception of History* (Middletown, Conn. 1968), pp. 56–62.

86. Edmund Silberner, "Heinrich Graetz' Briefe an Moses Hess 1861–1872," Instituto Giangiacomo Feltrinelli, *Annali*, 1961, p. 355.

87. Franz Schnabel, *Deutsche Geschichte im neunzehnten Jahrhundert*, 4 vols. (Freiburg im Breisgau 1933–1937), III, p. 85.

88. Schnabel, p. 87. See also Iggers, pp. 76–80.

89. Geiger, *Jüdische Zeitschrift für Wissenschaft und Leben*, IV (1866), p. 146.

90. Wiener, pp. 229–231.

91. Jost had contended that he was unable to detect any coherent intellectual system among individual rabbis. (See Jost, *Geschichte der Israeliten*, IV, pp. 30–45, Anhang, p. 224.)

92. Graetz, *Geschichte*, IV, 2nd ed., p. 480.

93. Graetz, *Geschichte*, IV, 2nd ed., p. 412. See the favorable review in *Der israelitische Volkslehrer*, V (1855), pp. 35–39. Hirsch, on the other hand, bitterly contested the *halakhic* development depicted by his former student. He completely rejected the portraits of R. Yohanan b. Zakkai and R. Akiva as reformers and innovators who rescued Judaism. (*Jeschurun*, II [1855–1856], p. 64; III [1856–1857], p. 403.)

94. Graetz apparently took the occasion to attack Jost's work publicly. (See Glatzer, pp. 253–254.)

95. Bloch, pp. 45, 60.

96. See Graetz, *The Structure*, p. 36, as well as Michael, *LBIYB*, XIII (1968), p. 45.

97. Graetz, *Geschichte*, XI, 2nd ed., pp. 522–527. Salomon Steinheim was the only other contemporary who received the same enthusiastic treatment (pp. 431–437).

98. I am indebted to Dr. Reuven Michael for the information on 1846. See also *INJ,* 1846, p. 334 and Bloch, p. 45.

99. G. P. Gooch, *History and Historians in the Nineteenth Century* (Boston, Beacon Press, 1959), pp. 60–71, 122–146; Schnabel, pp. 101–105.

100. Graetz, *Geschichte,* I, 2nd ed., p. xiii.

101. Graetz, *The Structure,* pp. 93–94. *Geschichte,* XI, 1st ed., p. 581.

102. Ibid., p. 456.

103. Graetz, *Geschichte,* II, 1st ed., Part One, pp. 192–200, 300, 303. Also pp. 133–139.

104. Graetz, *Geschichte,* III, 2nd end., pp. 405–406; VIII, 4th ed., pp. 355–392. A notable exception to this identification is to be found in Graetz's handling of the Chmelniecki persecution of 1648. In fact his pronounced aversion toward Polish Jewish culture and society induced Graetz to suggest that the disaster was not entirely undeserved. Greed had blinded the Jews to the precariousness of their position in the Ukraine and the dangers inherent in abusing the Cossacks. The consequences of the ensuing pogrom transcended the immediate loss of life. The refugees from Poland, with their medieval ways, now swarmed westward at the very moment that the nations of the West were entering the age of Enlightenment. The Polonization of Western Jewry retarded its entry into the modern world for more than a century. (*Geschichte,* X, 3rd ed., pp. 49–76.) It is instructive to compare this treatment with Graetz's attempt to absolve German Jewry of the eleventh century of any responsibility in setting off the persecutions which attended the First Crusade. (*Geschichte,* VI, 4th ed., pp. 82–83.)

105. Graetz, *Geschichte,* III, 2nd ed., pp. 50–51, 136; XI, 1st ed., pp. 377, 514, 520, 537. M. Brann cleaned up this final volume somewhat for the second edition in 1900. (See ibid., pp. vii–viii.) The intimate correspondence with Hess provides ample evidence of Graetz's unmitigated hatred for the Catholic Church and the Germans. (See Silberner, pp. 349, 353, 369, 377, 384, 387–388, 395, 396.) Understandably, Graetz laid the blame for many of the misfortunes of medieval Jewry on the steps of the Church. (*Geschichte,* VII, 4th ed., pp. 176–182, note 11; VIII, 4th ed., pp. 105–106, 283–284, 343–344.)

106. Graetz, *Geschichte,* IX, 4th ed., pp. 297–302; XI, 1st ed., pp. 53–54, 246–248. At the end of his essay on Voltaire, Graetz reiterated his conviction that "one can test quite accurately the integrity of the apostles of freedom and of the philosophers by their relationship to the Jews." (*MGWJ,* XVII [1868], p. 223.)

107. Graetz, *Geschichte,* III, 2nd ed., pp. 49, 151, 376; XI, 1st ed., pp. 170–175, 377–378, 561–566.

108. Graetz, *Geschichte,* III, 2nd ed., p. 70.

109. Ibid., pp. 339–340. See also his ingenious reconstruction of the evidence for an alliance between the Zealots and the Shammaites in 66 c.e. (Ibid., pp. 494–502.) For recent confirmation of Graetz's theory, see Saul Lieberman, *Greek in Jewish Palestine* (New York 1942), pp. 179–184, and Gedalyah Alon, *Mehqarim be-Toldot Yisrael,* I (Israel 1957), pp. 44–45, 266 n.63.

110. Graetz, *Geschichte,* IV, 2nd ed., pp. 125–126, 149–151, 161. Quotation p. 126.

111. Graetz, *Geschichte,* XI, 1st ed., pp. 509–510, 553–554. In 1840, a depressed and inferiority-ridden Graetz had collected six thaler from the indifferent Jews of Ostrowo, where he was serving as a house tutor, for Moses Montefiore's efforts on behalf of Damascan Jewry. (Michael, *Kiryat Sefer,* XXXVII [1961–1962], p. 525.) Geiger, on the other hand, refused to consider the plight of Damascan Jewry as more than an isolated humanitarian problem. The plight of Judaism disturbed him far

more, and he believed it could be relieved only through the intellectual and religious revitalization of German Jewry. (Max Wiener, *Abraham Geiger and Liberal Judaism* [Philadelphia 1962], pp. 87–88.)

112. Graetz, *Geschichte*, XI, 1st ed., p. 581. This passage was omitted from the second edition. (Cf. ibid., XI, 2nd ed., pp. 530–531.)

113. Besides the aforementioned study of Jewish gnostics, see also, for example, his essay "Die mystische Literatur in der gaonäischen Epoche," *MGWJ*, VIII (1859), pp. 113–118, 140–144; *Geschichte*, V, 4th ed., pp. 464–471; VII, 4th ed., pp. 35–36.

114. Graetz, *Geschichte*, V, 2nd ed., pp. 268, 317; VI, 4th ed., pp. 2, 66, 67.

115. Graetz, *Geschichte*, IV, 2nd ed., pp. viii, 77–116, 455–458.

116. Ibid., p. 128.

117. Graetz, *Geschichte*, V, 4th ed., pp. 100–119. Geiger had been the first scholar to put this proposition on a sound historical footing in 1833 in his brilliant prize-winning book *Was hat Mohammed aus dem Judenthume aufgenommen?*, 2nd rev. ed. (Leipzig 1902). (See the prolegomenon by Moshe Pearlman to the English edition of Abraham Geiger, *Judaism and Islam* [New York 1970].)

118. Graetz, *Geschichte*, VIII, 4th ed., p. 351.

119. Graetz, *Geschichte*, IX, 4th ed., pp. 64, 171, 174, 179, 477. A somewhat similar argument had been put forth by Samuel Usque in the sixteenth century to the effect that the Lutherans stemmed from Jews who had been forced to convert to Christianity (Usque, p. 193).

120. In 1869 when Graetz became the editor of the highly respected *MGWJ*, its pages suddenly began to reverberate with anti-Reform polemics. In the light of this unexpected change in editorial policy, the Institut zur Förderung der israelitischer Literatur, which had assumed publication of Graetz's history with volume three, refused to commit itself to publishing the forthcoming eleventh volume, which was to deal with the emancipation era. The board of the Institute, headed by Adolf Jellinek and Ludwig Philippson, feared that Graetz's treatment of the Reform movement might fall far short of the dispassionate research required of a scholarly study. To reassure itself, the board requested Graetz to submit his manuscript in advance for examination. When Graetz ignored the request, the Institute withdrew its support. (On Graetz's editorial policy, see Silberner, pp. 391, 393; on the controversy itself, see Philippson's version in the *AZJ*, 1869, pp. 387–389 as well as Graetz's inadequate rejoinder in the *MGWJ*, XVIII [1869], pp. 284–286.)

121. See Graetz, *The Structure*, pp. 125–132. *Geschichte*, III, 2nd ed., pp. 131, 216, 281–282.

122. *AZJ*, 1847, p. 2.

123. See, for example, "The Significance of Judaism for the Present and the Future," Graetz, *The Structure*, pp. 275–302.

124. See the introductions to volumes IV, V, and VII of his *Geschichte*.

125. This had been the view of Frankel. See above, p. 274.

126. Graetz, *Geschichte*, III, 2nd ed., p. 458. See also pp. 49, 79.

127. *Verhandlungen der zweiten israelitischen Synode zu Augsburg* (Berlin 1873), p. 253. Also Ismar Schorsch, *Jewish Reactions to German Anti-Semitism, 1870–1914* (New York, 1972), pp. 69, 232.

128. Graetz, *Geschichte*, II, 1st ed., part one, pp. 166–174.

129. See Graetz, *The Structure*, "The Correspondence"; Silberner, pp. 375, 384, 387–388.

130. Ibid., p. 369.

131. Schorsch, p. 71.

132. Graetz, "Die Schicksale des Talmud im Verlaufe der Geschichte," *MGWJ*, XXXIV (1885), pp. 529–541. See especially p. 540.

133. The sobriquet is applied by Andreas Dorpalen, *Heinrich von Treitschke* (New Haven 1957), chapter 9. A convenient selection of essays from this far-flung literary debate is to be found in Walter Boehlich, ed., *Der Berliner Antisemitismusstreit* (Frankfurt am Main 1965).

134. Boehlich, pp. 7–14, 33–47.

135. Schorsch, pp. 11, 45–46, 62, 70; Boehlich, pp. 27–33, 47–54.

136. [Heinrich Graetz], *Briefwechsel einer englischen Dame über Judenthum und Semitismus* (Stuttgart 1883). Mendelssohn, pp. 73–94. The structure of the book, as the title implies, is an exchange of letters between an inquiring English Jewess and her male friend, a knowledgeable and committed Jew. Graetz may have been prompted to choose this English setting by George Eliot's ideological novel *Daniel Deronda* which had appeared in 1876. Eliot had startled the literary world with an unexpectedly moving portrayal of Jewish character and destiny, in the course of which she not only insisted on the right of Jews to retain their identity but boldly averred the inseparableness of Judaism's spiritual and national strands. Against the backdrop of European nationalism, she envisioned the creation of "an organic center" in Palestine which would revitalize the Jews and benefit mankind [George Eliot, *Daniel Deronda* (Penguin Books, 1967), pp. 575–599]. Graetz's enthusiasm for the book is well attested: as editor of the respected *Monatsschrift*, he published David Kaufmann's exuberant review [*MGWJ*, XXVI (1877), pp. 162ff., 214ff., 255f.] and in the *Briefwechsel* itself, he referred to it warmly [Graetz, *The Structure*, pp. 205, 213, 255, 258.]

137. Boehlich, p. 46.

138. Moses Hess, *Rome and Jerusalem*, translated by Meyer Waxman (New York 1945), p. 55. Hess's return to Judaism inaugurated an extraordinary friendship with Graetz, who had read the manuscript of *Rome and Jerusalem* with great excitement and without whose help it would probably have remained unpublished. Graetz's letters to Hess over the next eleven years reveal an affectionate, frank, and meaningful relationship. Both men shared a deep antipathy toward the Germans and the Catholic Church, conceived of Judaism in a similar manner, and longed for national regeneration. They also readily came to each other's assistance. Hess provided Graetz with a number of relevant passages from rare nineteenth-century French pamphlets for volume eleven of the *Geschichte*, which he selected and copied personally, since to have the pamphlets copied by someone else in their entirety was too expensive. Graetz repeatedly invited Hess to join him on his projected trip to Palestine, on one occasion expressing the hope that he would soon be able to offer his friend an advance to help defray the expenses. In sum, the rich correspondence bespeaks a lasting friendship which was securely based on a common world view. (See Silberner, pp. 326–400.)

139. The extent to which the German scene compelled Graetz to write in allusions, projecting his true sentiments on to the past, is strikingly evident in his two popular essays on Jewish messianism. At the very same time that Graetz was concealing his beliefs behind a guise of historical learning and religious rhetoric, Hess, living in Paris, was able to expound his national conception of Judaism without inhibition in one of the leading Jewish periodicals. (Cf. Hess, "Lettres sur la mission d'Israël," *Archives Israélites*, XXV [1864].)

Graetz's resignation in 1885 from the governing committee of the recently formed international organization of *Hibbat Zion* must also be understood in the context of the German setting. In his letter to Leon Pinsker, which he threatened to make public if his name were not removed immediately from the membership of the committee, Graetz articulated his opposition to the increasingly nationalistic tone of the program to settle Russian Jews in Palestine. German antisemitism did not permit Graetz the freedom to determine his public posture solely according to his personal convictions. (See A. Druyanov, *Ketavim le-Toldot Hibbat Zion ve-Yishuv Eretz Yisrael,* I [Odessa 1919], cols. 405–406; Moses Lillienblum, *Ketavim Autobiographim,* III [Jerusalem 1970], pp. 33–34.)

140. See Graetz's revealing letter to his Hebrew translator, S. P. Rabinowitz, published by Meisl, p. 179 as well as Graetz, *The Structure,* p. 263.

141. Bloch, p. 32. On Graetz's fear of the rabbinate, see Ettinger, ed., *Darkhe ha-Historiah ha-Yehudit,* p. 255.

142. Besides the bibliography of Graetz's work prepared by M. Brann, ed., *Heinrich Graetz: Abhandlungen zu seinem 100. Geburtstage* (Vienna and Berlin 1917), pp. 124–171, which lists the countless translations of his history, see also Hess, *Rome and Jerusalem,* pp. 37, 73–74; B. Rippner, *Zum siebzigsten Geburtstage des Prof. Dr. Heinrich Graetz* (Magdeburg 1887), pp. 4, 26, 27; Meisl, p. 69; Richard Lichtheim, *Toldot ha-Zionut be-Germania* (Jerusalem 1951), p. 72; Solomon Grayzel, "Graetz's *History* in America," in Guido Kisch, ed., *Das Breslauer Seminar* (Tübingen 1963), pp. 223–237.

∾ 15

Scholarship in the Service of Reform

I

Born in battle for a better world, *Wissenschaft des Judentums* entered Jewish consciousness in alliance with the cause for religious Reform. For at least the first two decades after the demise of the *Verein für Cultur und Wissenschaft der Juden*, its primary practitioners were to be found among the first generation of university-trained school teachers and rabbis who pressed for internal accommodations dictated by the change in external conditions. The new Jewish learning offered a powerful challenge to the hegemony of an entrenched rabbinate rooted in an older universe of discourse, and all the early salvos of *Wissenschaft* carried some programmatic load. Recovery of the past became the means for reconstituting the present.

But control of this new weapon did not long remain a monopoly of reform-minded scholars. By the 1840s a second generation of students, often from regions further East than Berlin, had passed through a German university to take up the defense of traditional Judaism in terms of undogmatic scholarship. Viewed comprehensively and functionally then, the emergence of *Wissenschaft* displays distinctive and unappreciated patterns of development: a large lay component, regional differences, and a research agenda existentially and dialectically determined. For all its early international character, the new Jewish scholarship was energized by the religious dilemmas first raised in the German states after 1815, where progress toward full emancipation was ground to a halt and even reversed by a resurgent mood of political conservatism. For aspiring Jews the insecurity of partial emancipation had made of traditional Judaism, reinforced by government sanction, a collective liability and a personal hindrance.

Despite deep engagement, the new Jewish learning staked its claim for serious attention on the reliability of its method. The difference between *Wissen* and *Wissenschaft* expressed itself in terms of critical method, and it is that factor which separated two ambitious works begun while the *Verein* was still daring to storm the future. In 1822, Peter Beer, since 1811 a teacher of morality at the modern Jewish communal school in Prague, published a two-volume history of Jewish sects, with a flamboyant dedication to David Friedländer.[1] The book was the end product of an essay that had appeared in 1806 in the very first number of the *Sulamith* in which Beer had tried to inject a dynamic element into the conceptualization of Judaism. The demonstration of religious diversity in the past should embolden contemporary critics of Judaism not to regard it as an immutable monolith.[2] This avowedly pragmatic intent imbues the comprehensive work throughout. The 14,000 regulations of the *Shulhan Aruh* (by his count) codify not the sum total of Sinaitic revelation but the accumulated overgrowth of unpruned *halakhic* proliferation.[3] Moreover, the purported leadership of Pharisees and talmudists in Jewish life is marked by repeated challenges from sectarian quarters, from the early Samaritans down to the recent eruption of the *Hasidim*. Perhaps the most telling slight is the basic design of the book which treats rabbinic Jews as merely one sect out of many. Historical evenhandedness helps to diffuse the notion of a normative Judaism.

And yet Beer hardly deserves inclusion in the history of *Wissenschaft*. Utterly missing from his work is any critical examination of his sources. His simplistic idea of a historian is that of a facilitator, an assembler of scattered and inaccessible sources for convenient perusal.[4] But the evidence itself is rarely submitted to scrutiny. Beer presented his documents with no more critical acumen than Machiavelli had once brought to bear on Livy. Both read history "attentively" for guidance and edification and not to establish the meaning and veracity of ancient texts.[5] To be sure, the search for wisdom outside a sacred text marked a liberalization of dogmatic constraints, but historical thinking also entails going beyond the sanctity of the written word.

That distinction belongs to the pioneering nine-volume *Geschichte der Israeliten* of Isaak Markus Jost, which appeared in rapid fire from 1820 to 1828.[6] To move from Beer to Jost is to traverse the distance between Machiavelli and Niebuhr in a single generation. For all its defects, avoidable and unavoidable, Jost's sweeping history from the Hasmoneans to the *Haskalah* rests on a solid foundation of source criticism and thus rightly deserves to be considered as the first major achievement of the new Jewish learning. Ironically, the message remains unchanged: the dismantling of rabbinic Judaism and a return to biblical monotheism. In fact, the very idea of delivering that message through the medium of historical research may have been planted in the mind of the young Jost upon his arrival in Berlin by the same gentleman to whom Beer had dedicated his own book.[7] What distinguished Jost from Beer, who was born nearly thirty years earlier, was his exposure to the philological laboratory of the German university.

Like Zunz, Jost had been born before the turn of the century (1794 and 1793 respectively), orphaned early, and sent to the run-down talmudic academy and boarding school in Wolfenbüttel. The physical and intellectual deprivation endured in its meager confines for some four years saddled Jost with a lifelong antipathy for rabbinic Judaism, summed up in a barb tossed out in 1848 that "a single volume of Goethe . . . contains more true learning and sound common sense than 300 talmudic folios."[8] Amid their common misery, the two boys found consolation in friendship and freedom in their mastery of Hebrew, which opened for them an avenue to Gentile culture. Jost learned German, like many of his generation, from Mendelssohn's Bible translation, and composed his first German letter only at the age of seventeen.[9] In the spring of 1807, the outmoded Samson School was reorganized into a modern pedagogic facility under the direction of Samuel Meyer Ehrenberg, whose own deep commitment to Hebrew expressed itself in a forty-year project to execute a Hebrew translation of a history of Rome.[10] Two years later, both boys were ready to enter a *Gymnasium* and, in the words of Jost, "the life of an autodidact had thereby pretty much come to an end."[11]

For Jost the process of cultural transformation continued in 1813 for three exhilarating semesters at the nearby University of Göttingen. Aided financially by the wealthy Israel Jacobson, he immersed himself in the study of Latin, Greek, and Arabic literature, philosophy, and various books of the Hebrew Bible. At the same time, as he wrote to Zunz on 1st March 1814, he had dropped their mutual vision of reviving Hebrew as a living language of Jewish expression and settled for its pursuit as an instrument for the study of ancient texts. Even as a scholarly language, Hebrew had never been an adequate vehicle for treating academic subjects clearly and philosophically; it had always been forced to enrich its vocabulary with terms borrowed from other languages. And even if dedication yielded success, who would be able to read the work? The goal should not be to impose German idioms and thought patterns on Hebrew, but rather to understand the classical language and its texts on their own terms.[12]

The Göttingen experience orientated Jost for life. The thrill of social, intellectual, and religious emancipation reinforced his anticlericalism but did not rupture his communal ties. Unlike many of his Jewish classmates, he refused to convert. Years later he would write of those student days:

For me the period of one-and-a-half years which I spent there [at Göttingen] was one of completely throwing off old shackles and of fully integrating myself into the German way of thinking and patriotic concerns. I could think of no nobler calling than to impart eventually the same attitudes to our religious cohorts and to free them of all the onesidedness of an insular education.[13]

In that spirit Jost soon ventured, with the encouragement of Friedländer and Bendavid, to compose the first comprehensive Jewish history by a Jew in a European language since Josephus. In October 1814 he had shifted his studies to the University of Berlin, courtesy of Israel Jacobson. Some two years later, he managed to secure permission from the Prussian government to open a progressive Jewish school, and Jewish education would ever remain his livelihood. Though among the founders of the *Verein*, Jost withdrew in May 1820 aggrieved at the rough treatment accorded his lengthy written proposal for its journal.[14] But, in truth, Jost was separated from his friends by temperament. He fully shared their radical diagnosis of what the age called for and their intolerance for religious hypocrisy, but not their messianic fervor.[15] Far more sober and skeptical, he had a healthy respect for the formidable power of tradition and incumbency. Even his once intimate friendship with Zunz fell victim to their diverging activities and commitments. In contrast to the *Verein*, Jost preferred to launch his personal attack against rabbinism with less fanfare but more substance.

Alienation led to undogmatic history. Jost's ambitious project teems with examples of source analysis, often packed in excursuses, which certainly preceded the synthesis of the narrative text. Thus he has no inhibitions about treating the Bible as an ancient archive of human documents composed over eight centuries and to be dated individually by means of the history of the Hebrew language. Respect for the antiquity and centrality of these books is best evinced by guarding them against all forms of mutilation.[16] To be specific, Jost accepts a version of the documentary hypothesis for the Pentateuch. Using a variety of criteria, he identifies different textual units, including some twenty-five fragments in Genesis alone, ineptly edited by someone long after Moses. Nevertheless, he quickly adds that he does not mean to impugn the veracity of their contents, but only their alleged unity and authorship, and his fairly uncritical and generally rationalistic presentation of biblical history in his later *Allgemeine Geschichte des Israelitischen Volkes* wholly confirms that distinction.[17]

More original than his biblical criticism, in which he relies heavily on Protestant academic scholarship of the day, is his analysis of the Talmud as a historical source, in which he is truly an innovator. In this case, Jost is obliged to stress not only that it be read as any other human record, but that in fact it really does warrant consultation. He reproves Basnage for presuming to write on the history of rabbinic Judaism without ever having read its indispensable primary source, the Talmud, and he dismisses a host of his assertions and conclusions.[18] Clearly the contribution of a Jewish historian is to formulate a method by which to evaluate the historical content of this quintessentially Jewish document. In the end, Jost is prepared to grant a substantial degree of reliability to data in the Babylonian Talmud (though less to that in the Palestinian one because of its poor state of preservation) relating to the period of its own formation from the second to the beginning of the sixth century. The legal debates appear to be recorded without tendentiousness and the disparate historical material, especially in Hebrew, may well be drawn from a single historical source. By answering the question fundamental to all research in the talmudic era affirmatively, Jost had challenged the neglect of the talmudic corpus by Christian historians of the period.[19]

True to its patrimony, Jost's reading of Jewish history produced a coherent elaboration of the ideology of the radical wing of the German *Haskalah*. While his method faced forward his interpretive model was indebted to the Enlightenment—rational, skeptical, anticlerical, and degenerative rather than developmental. The spirit if not the talent of Gibbon pervaded the work. In the words of the incomparable Englishman:

The theologian may indulge the pleasing task of describing Religion as she descended from Heaven, arrayed in her native purity. A more melancholy duty is imposed on the historian. He must discover the inevitable mixture of error and corruption which she contracted in a long residence upon earth, among a weak and degenerate race of beings.[20]

The very parameters of the project, despite its misleading title, suggest that Jost conceived his subject to be the history of rabbinism, from emergence to demise, and not a full-fledged history of the Jewish people. Intended for statesmen, philosophers, and enlightened Jews, the work offered solace in the ordered evidence of the aberrant nature of rabbinism.[21]

To begin with, the Second Temple period is not to be construed as a continuation of the Mosaism of the First. Moses had erected a political state to protect temporarily a monotheism for which the pagans were unprepared; what eventually emerges from the restoration under Cyrus is a wholly religious society based on a written canon already partly outmoded.[22] The rabbis gradually seize the reigns of leadership and steadily increase their social control through the proliferation of religious institutions like the calendar, festivals, and prayers.[23] Israel is transformed into a messianic polity, bursting with intolerance, bereft of aesthetic sensibilities, and hermetically sealed off from the outside world. Yet the legal shackles, Jost contends, owe much to foreign influence. The concept of an oral law is Greek, while the idea to codify it in the *Mishnah* as well as many of its legal terms and principles are Roman.[24]

Though reversed for a time by the hospitality of Islamic Spain, the degeneration of rabbinism is intensified amid the culturally barren and politically unstable conditions of Northern Europe.[25] Waves of persecution deepen Ashkenazic insularity and excite mystical excesses and messianic eruptions. Jost abhors the casuistry of the medieval talmudic glossators (the *Tosafot*) and even applauds the intent if not the act of having the Talmud burned in Paris in 1240.[26] Finally, Mendelssohn's *Jerusalem* is read by Jost as bringing this unrelieved history of religious deviance to an end. The sage from Dessau recognized the termination of Jewish law as a binding system with 586 B.C.E., defended its continued value solely in relative and pedagogic terms, and accorded the individual Jew the right to convert.[27]

Admittedly, the force of Jost's theory of Jewish history is accentuated by synthesis and compression, but there is little doubt that its pervasive and directing presence transforms the entire work into an original and powerful brief for the interment of rabbinic Judaism. Jost himself never exercised the right to abandon an "unregenerate" Judaism, but as late as 1852 he still despaired of its ability to survive emancipation. Its unique character had been damaged beyond repair, robbed of the power to inspire the loyalty of a new generation without benefit of the formative memories of a childhood in the ghetto.[28] His own stoic attachment seemed rooted in filial piety and sustained by an austere regimen of unbroken scholarship, marked by increasing balance and empathy.[29]

Zunz was anything but pleased with Jost's ground-breaking history. He regarded it as premature, poorly written, long-winded, and far too harsh in tone. He held a lifelong disdain for Jewish scholars who indulged in any form of public denigration of Judaism and its history.[30] In a popular essay in 1845, he inveighed against Jewish historians who write only with contempt for their subject. If Jews are indifferent to their heritage, it is because their historians have only an eye for Jewish defects and deficiencies. A Jewish historian has the responsibility to infuse his work with empathy, to arouse his readers for the accomplishments of Jewish luminaries. In a resounding climax, Zunz declaimed that it is "better to praise Israel's antiquity two or three times than to defame it once. . . . Where art has gone under, artists went under first."[31] Then too, Zunz was convinced that a cause had to be argued from its core, that only an internal history could vindicate Judaism before the bar of reason and justice.[32] Such principles surely informed Zunz's first major scholarly achievement in 1832, *Die gottesdienstlichen Vorträge der Juden* and set it wholly apart from Jost, though no less committed to a reform of Judaism.

For several years after the failure of the *Verein*, Zunz had been without scholarly focus. Much of his time was simply absorbed with earning a living. From 1824 to 1831, he served as the foreign editor of a Berlin newspaper, spending six mornings a week till 1 p.m. preparing articles from French, English, Italian, and German papers.[33] From January 1826 to October 1829, he also directed the Berlin Jewish community's first public school for boys and offered some sixteen hours of weekly instruction himself.[34] Hence it comes as no surprise to read in one of Jost's letters to Ehrenberg dated 25th February 1827 that Zunz had laid aside his scholarship. "He could have contributed a great deal."[35] According to his own diary, Zunz had decided by March 1829 to write a general introduction to the field of *Wissenschaft des Judentums*, though by August the project was dropped for "a book on the sermons of the Jews," along with the derisive comment that "one doesn't get very far with such decisions, but at least farther than the Bourbons with Polignac," a political prediction that proved to be quite astute.[36] A year later, Jost told Ehrenberg of his doubts about the wisdom of Zunz's choice, given the utterly barren nature of rabbinic literature.[37]

Thus under the most trying of circumstances, Zunz produced a classic of modern Jewish scholarship that galvanized a generation and launched a movement. In contrast to Jost, he demonstrated unequivocally that the goals of emancipation and Reform could be served without compromising the integrity of the new discipline. Erudition, philology, and vision had transformed a concrete and immediate issue—the legitimacy of the German sermon opposed by a coalition of royal and rabbinic reactionaries—into a totally fresh conception of Judaism.

At the heart of this conception, Zunz placed the institution of the synagogue, which he depicted as the dominant forum of Jewish expression, since the loss of statehood, and the guarantor of national consciousness.[38] The synagogue embraced the full expanse of Jewish history. It reached back to the earliest days of the Second Temple period when Jews first began to meet to hear and read the word of God and extended forward into the present with Jews still gathering for the same purpose. The sounds of Scripture reverberated in the synagogue and the readiness to translate and interpret preserved its relevance. *Midrash* became the heir to prophecy. It linked the revelation of an earlier age to the needs of a later one and in time gave rise to a vast, diverse, and highly inventive body of exegetical literature.[39]

As a conceptual construct, the synagogue bespoke a uniquely modern sensibility. Historically, it had never enjoyed the kind of supremacy which Zunz accorded it. In pre-emancipation Judaism, it was but one of several institutional expressions of Jewish consciousness, often slighted by a rabbinic elite with a consuming passion for study. It was rather the centrifugal forces set off by emancipation that elevated the importance of the synagogue in Jewish life. In an age intolerant of all non-religious (and many religious) forms of Jewish expression, the synagogue appeared as the most vital source of communal cohesion. Sooner than most contemporaries, Zunz understood the import of these developments and prepared to equip the synagogue with a historical legitimacy equal to its new role. Already in 1818 he had suggested the urgency of producing a history of Jewish liturgy and now fourteen years later he dared to make the synagogue the organizing principle for constructing the internal history of Judaism.[40]

The strategy enabled Zunz to transform the prevailing negative image of rabbinism. He countered the polemical and unproductive model of disjunction and degeneration furnished by Jost with one of continuity and development. Organic growth is what bridges the periods of the First and Second Temple and spans the history of the Diaspora. Philologically and historically, Zunz traces the evolution of the three dominant genres of ancient rabbinic literature—*targum, halakhah,* and *aggadah*—out of the Bible and subsequently the medieval genres of ethical, historical, and exegetical literature out of the *aggadah*.[41] It is a canvas of staggering proportions, stretching from Ezekiel and the Chronicler down to the nineteenth century and filled with unsuspected literary treasures.[42] Several lost works are even ingeniously and correctly reconstructed out of surviving quotations in other texts.[43] And the entire output is often portrayed as the anonymous voice of the collective will of the people. In terms redolent with nineteenth-century romanticism, Zunz treats *midrash* as the medium of popular self-expression in the Jewish national assembly, the synagogue.

The products of *midrash* should be seen much rather as the expression of an activity rooted in the life, ideas, and interests of the Jewish people, in which it plays a certain participatory role. It is for this reason that the outstanding works of *halakhah* and *aggadah,* just like biblical law and prophecy, are national texts before which a later generation would nearly always abdicate its independence. They are the property of everyone—the results of a thousand-year development, monuments of the life of the nation, the achievements of its best minds.[44]

In a single work, then, of incredible scope and specificity, Zunz had managed to show the religious nature of Jewish nationhood, the continuity of Jewish history, the centrality of the synagogue, and the inherent responsiveness and flexibility of rabbinism. The present low state of rabbinism is not evidence of any genetic damage but rather the outcome of a deterioration in Jewish status which set in at the end of the fifteenth century. A favorable reading of rabbinic history was entirely in consonance with the need to address the altered sensibilities of the emancipated Jew. The synagogue was the area where his allegiance would be retained or lost and thus to write its history was anything but antiquarian. With *Die gottesdienstlichen Vorträge* Zunz had reassembled its effervescent homiletical tradition; several decades later, as we shall see, he would return to exhume the unimagined wealth of its liturgical vitality.

II

For all its brilliance, Zunz's resurrection of *midrashic* literature did not address the most urgent problem of his generation—the reconciliation of a Judaism steeped in *halakhah* with emancipation. Religiously and temperamentally Zunz was better suited to handle the literary rather than the legal side of Judaism. But he surely understood the full religious import of the political changes underway. As he said toward the end of *Die gottesdienstlichen Vorträge*: "A complete emancipation requires a complete reform, which will be made manifest only in institutions that protect both faith and science and that transmit unspoiled the legacy of the fathers to the sons."[45]

While emancipation eventually would have an impact on Judaism wherever it was realized, in the German states of the first half of the nineteenth century pressure for Reform within the Jewish community was intensified by the denial of full civil equality. A state of partial emancipation focused attention on what appeared to be its primary impediment—the differentiating body of Jewish praxis—and thus turned an unobtrusive social process into a raging political controversy. A broad Jewish desire to enjoy all the opportunities of full citizenship was frustrated by the virulent suspicion of German bureaucrats that religious apartness betrayed a form of foreign allegiance.[46] Prior to 1848 in both German society and the Jewish community the ferment for religious Reform masked fundamental political issues.[47]

It is for this reason that much of the Reform *Wissenschaft* of the period turned to study the origin, basis, and evolution of Jewish law. As Samson Raphael Hirsch quickly perceived and protested against, to transpose *halakhah* to the historical continuum would render it susceptible to the needs of the hour.

As in the case of rabbinism, the pointed assault on *halakhah* of the 1830s was launched by a school teacher in a dated universe of discourse, soon to be abandoned for the new historical mode. Born in 1789, Michael Creizenach is intellectually still very much part of the eighteenth century. In 1828 he joined the faculty of the *Philanthropin* in Frankfurt, a staunchly modern Jewish school whose roots went back to the beginning of the century, and he assumed responsibility for the weekly religious services held under its auspices and open to the public. During the next two unsettled decades—both politically and religiously—the *Philanthropin*, strengthened by the addition of Jost in 1835, became the seedbed for radical Reform in Germany. In 1837 members of its faculty participated in a unique and short-lived ecumenical forum—the publication in Frankfurt of a paper devoted solely to the unbiased discussion of religious events and issues in modern Protestantism, Catholicism, and Judaism. Michael Hess, the school's energetic director, and Jost edited the Jewish section of the *Unparteiische Universal-Kirchenzeitung für die Geistlichkeit und die gebildete Weltklasse des protestantische, katholischen, und israelitischen Deutschlands*, till political reaction forced it to close down with number 104 at the end of the year.[48]

In this hopeful and stimulating atmosphere, Creizenach produced from 1833 to 1840 a four-volume attack against the edifice of Jewish law, demonstratively entitled *Schulchan Aruch oder encyclopädische Darstellung des Mosaischen Gesetzes*. Though poorly integrated and maddeningly repetitive, the work is a theoretical attempt to diminish the discord between Jewish ritual and civic society. The overall strategy is to strip the Talmud of its divine nimbus in order to allow for major *halakhic* modifications. Creizenach argues, primarily on rational grounds, that the Talmud is in fact merely an instrument of exegesis for the human elaboration of biblical law, that it abounds with instances of legal alteration, and that its welter of prescriptions were intended for its time alone.[49] Only the ignorance of later generations permitted "our religion to take on the external appearance of a mummy. . . . If the scholars of Scripture had made laws for eternity, then the question would arise why Moses himself had not introduced these laws from the beginning."[50] Creizenach delivers a brief for reading the Bible according to the plain meaning of the text and feels no obligation to retain any injunction based on a textual interpretation that violates reason.[51] In short, he aims to restore equal authority in religious matters to the leaders of every generation, without debunking the Talmud or espousing a return to some form of pristine Mosaism.[52]

Nevertheless, in terms of method Creizenach's work is still of pre-*Wissenschaft* vintage. The total absence of any critical apparatus means that assertions go unproven and analysis is a function of common sense. It is only with the fourth and final volume that Creizenach even attempted an historical survey of rabbinic law, governed by the trope of development rather than degeneration, though still devoid of any philological base. Cumulatively speaking, however, he had composed a systematic theology of *halakhic* Judaism—unflattering if not venomous—and thereby challenged the exegetical underpinnings of the entire legal structure.[53]

When a few years later Abraham Geiger recast Creizenach's challenge in the medium of modern scholarship, he paid tribute to his predecessor's pioneering labor. Despite its popular and often practical nature, the work had focused on the most problematic part of talmudic law, its biblical exegesis.[54] Geiger's preoccupation with this selfsame subject formed a leitmotif of his own brilliant scholarly career and the power and originality of his theories would continue to resonate deep into the twentieth century.

Like so many scholars of the *Wissenschaft* circle, Geiger came from a background of religious Orthodoxy and economic deprivation. Born in Frankfurt in 1810, he spent his early years immersed in the study of Talmud, along with a marginal cultivation of Hebrew grammar and mathematics. Secular learning came serendipitously, because his parents refused to send him to the *Philanthropin*, and in later years he lamented, somewhat melodramatically, the narrowness of his youth.[55]

Alas! alas! How have you escaped me, my years of childhood, in useless trifling! I was not shaped by moral instruction, my body was not strengthened through physical exercise, nor my soul ennobled through education and culture. Alas, they have flown away like dust. Come back that I might use you.[56]

But talent was not to be denied and Geiger went off to the university, much to the displeasure of his family, to return with a thorough grounding in philology, important friendships, a prize-winning essay on Mohammed's indebtedness to Judaism, and a deep commitment to the revitalization of Judaism through modern scholarship.[57] He did not forsake Germany for France, as did Salomon Munk or his intimate friend Joseph Derenbourg, to satisfy his hunger for an academic post, but instead prepared himself for a twofold career as rabbi and scholar. While still a student in 1831, he turned in admiration and candor to Zunz to enunciate his plan to work for an organic reform of Judaism on two levels.

Since my earliest childhood, I have entertained the idea to work for the religious and civil life of the Jews, and every time my mood and external need would alienate me from the rabbinate [*Theologenstande*], an inner compulsion and a vision [*Hoffnung*] of future activity would pull me back to the field. . . . My future activity as rabbi [*Theologe*] will certainly embrace only my community, but please God, to work as a scholar for the academic study of Jewish sources and as a Jew for the civil and religious improvement of our religious brethren is another matter and must also become my responsibility in addition to my rabbinic office.[58]

This long and eloquent letter conveys vividly the growing influence of Zunz, the nexus between the denial of emancipation and the drive for religious Reform, and the caution required of an aspiring rabbinical candidate. In a revealing postscript, Geiger added: "Since as a prospective rabbi I am not permitted to express such opinions freely, I beg of you to keep this letter secret."[59]

Without a doubt, Geiger looms as the premier exemplar in the nineteenth century of the modern rabbi *qua* scholar. The intellectual and professional constraints of the pulpit notwithstanding, his prolific and often seminal research even earned the respect of scholars like Zunz and Steinschneider, whose anticlericalism often savaged the *Wissenschaft* of less competent rabbinic practitioners. His central interest to fathom the exegetical nature of talmudic thinking, at first purely in negative terms and then more positively, went all the way back to a youthful fascination with the *Mishnah,* which early on had prompted him to begin a Hebrew commentary designed to interpret the *mishnaic* text apart from its later talmudic exposition and to compile a *mishnaic* dictionary that would bring out the post-biblical development of the Hebrew language.[60] Though neither project was ever completed, the line of investigation bore fruit in a series of early forays that connected directly with the crucial issues raised by Creizenach.

In 1836, Geiger published a modest essay in the pages of his new *Wissenschaftliche Zeitschrift für jüdische Theologie* on the intention and order of the *Mishnah* in which the study of its text would be divorced from its canonical interpretation. Rigorous philological research would recapture the original character of the book and illuminate the fortuitousness of its genesis. To illustrate, Geiger contended on the basis of both rabbinic and patristic sources that the *Mishnah* was neither the first nor last instance in that period of rabbis (*Tannaim*) who ignored the prohibition against reducing the Oral Law to written compendia. Moreover, the *Mishnah* teems with traces of haphazard and desultory editing. Even the arrangement of individual tractates within a single order (Seder) according to size—an electrifying insight by Geiger that solved a puzzle which had defied the ages—served to amplify the relative carelessness of composition. Hence not the inherent quality of the work, but the august reputation of its editor—the Patriarch of Palestinian Jewry, Rabbi Yehudah ha-Nasi—quickly turned a set of private notes into a venerated national code and thereby initiated a process of rapid legal rigidification.[61]

Geiger's assault on the prevailing Ashkenazic tradition that the editing and transmission of the *Mishnah* was effected without the benefit of writing immediately drew the fire of Samuel David Luzzatto, who a decade earlier had defended the accepted view in passing in his work on the Aramaic translation of the Torah by Onkelos.[62] Luzzatto now registered an angry protest in the pages of *Kherem Hemed*: the Oral Law remained unwritten at least until the age of the *Saboraim* in the sixth or seventh century. Geiger had not only done violence to the integrity of the numerous rabbinic injunctions against transcription but also to the cumulative weight of the circumstantial evidence. The controversy over the *Mishnah*'s redaction was to exercise scholars for the rest of the century, and for good reason. The issue, as Luzzatto declared unabashedly at the end, transcended purely academic interests.

. . . I have prolonged this analysis because of its grave importance in my eyes, for we live in an age in which knowledge of the principles of our religion is more urgently needed than ever before. And yet we are very far from having this knowledge. As long as we fail to realize that the sages refrained from preserving the Oral

Law in writing so that courts in every generation might correct and alter it according to the circumstances of time and place, we will have no inkling of the principle of the Oral Law.[63]

In this instance, Geiger and Luzzatto differed not so much on the final objective as on the means to attain it. For a scholar conservatively inclined, *halakhic* flexibility could be recovered without deprecating rabbinic literature.

But what actually quickened the pace of Geiger's exegetical studies was the challenge of Samson Raphael Hirsch. Their friendship, formed at the University of Bonn and sealed by Geiger's affectionate declaration in 1832 that "Hirsch can do to me whatever he pleases, I will remain his friend regardless," was sundered by their rapidly diverging religious views.[64] Piqued by Creizenach's project to impugn the validity of Jewish law, Hirsch erupted in 1836 and 1837 with a vigorous restatement of the divinity of both the Oral and Written Law.[65] *The Nineteen Letters of Ben Uziel* and *Horeb* formulated the ideology of what would soon become known as Neo-Orthodoxy—an unreserved acceptance of emancipation coupled with a tenacious defense of Jewish *praxis.* What clearly facilitated this union of opposites was the rejection of *Wissenschaft* as an alien mode of cognition. In the spirit of David Gans, Hirsch reaffirmed dogmatically the historical claims of the tradition.

Within the circle of Judaism, the Divine Law must be the soil out of which your intellectual and spiritual life is to grow, not *vice versa.* You must not from your intellectual and spiritual life produce the basis on which to establish a Divine Law.[66]

The very structure of *Horeb*—even more than the title—was intended to reassert the biblical, and hence divine, origins of all of Jewish law. Aside from Hirsch's own system of reclassification, each set of *halakhic* particulars was introduced by the relevant verses from Scripture to convey the unity of a seamless whole. And freed from critical constraints, Hirsch was able to expound the religious meaning embodied in the sundry details of Jewish law in a highly imaginative but utterly speculative fashion.

Geiger reacted with predictable consternation. In two long reviews he inveighed against the defiance of the *Wissenschaft* ethos. Hirsch's combination of dogmatism and subjectivity violate every philological and developmental canon of the new Jewish learning. His method, in fact, given its systematic impulse, is not only more arbitrary but more dangerous than that of the Talmud, because it renders the biblical text entirely plastic.

What cannot be made of Scripture if it falls under the control of the most baseless subjectivity? *Aggadah* and *midrash* operate with the same arbitrariness, though with some degree of self-awareness and often to the displeasure of serious teachers and without ever seeking to transform this playfulness into sacred truths or a system. In contrast, Ben Uziel takes this game with the utmost seriousness, and the child's toy is for him a matter of life and death.[67]

According to Geiger, and often illustrated in the pages of his journal, the function of modern Jewish scholarship is to examine the basic texts of Judaism critically, to reconstruct its development over time, and to utilize the results for the articulation of religious policy.[68]

By the mid-1840s Geiger's views had ripened into the most formidable assault of the century on the validity of rabbinic exegesis. In a quick series of related publications, Geiger established his scholarly trademark—a profusion of philological detail integrated into a broad historical conceptualization. The attack began with a two-part essay on the heart of the problem—"The Relationship of the Literal Meaning of Scripture to the Biblical Exegesis of the Talmud." What Geiger seeks to prove with a cluster of telling examples is that nearly all the sages of the *Mishnah* and the Talmud read Scripture without the slightest sense for the existence of a literal meaning. Their efforts to link and sanctify emerging *halakhic* institutions to specific biblical texts exegetically betrays no awareness of the violence of their readings. Naively they identify the satisfaction of their religious needs—to legitimate the products of historical development—with the actual import of the text, and in time the arbitrariness of their method comes to dominate rabbinic thinking. In the earlier period of the *Mishnah*, Geiger argues, the *Tannaim* did not yet feel compelled to ground every *halakhic* innovation in a scriptural base and were quite ready to admit the most tenuous of connections. That sense of naturalness and security is lost by the later period, and the *Amoraim* rush to find for every *halakhic* injunction a suitable biblical verse. The abandon wreaks exegetical havoc: "What began only modestly in the *Mishnah* now smothers every trace of a healthy exegetical sense; works and letters are interpreted in the most arbitrary fashion."[69] Geiger sees no essential difference between the *aggadic* and *halakhic* exegesis of the rabbis. Both run roughshod over the literal meaning of the biblical text, oblivious in most cases to its very presence. "We observe in this entire method only the product of an incredibly muddled exegetical sense."[70]

The aggressive intent of Geiger's research is self-evident, namely to discredit the authority of the *halakhic* system. If religious authority requires an aura of infallibility, then the *halakhah* has been shown to rest on an exegetical travesty. What is faulty is hardly binding. Judaism must be refashioned in consonance with the consciousness of an age which is acutely aware of the reality of a text's literal meaning. Rabbinic exegesis is ultimately an expression of an entirely subjective state of consciousness.

Geiger's essay, then, at its most profound level resembles the epochal work of David Friedrich Strauss. Geiger was an avid reader of Christian historical theology—the counterpart to *Wissenschaft des Judentums*. *The Life of Jesus* mesmerized him when it exploded onto the German scene in 1835 and he followed the ensuing controversy with deep interest.[71] Strauss helped Geiger to formulate the problem in Hegelian terms. The opening line of his book cogently put in terms of consciousness the problematic of a legacy born of naive faith.

Wherever a religion, resting upon written records, prolongs and extends the sphere of its dominion, accompanying its votaries through the varied and progressive stages of mental cultivation, a discrepancy between the representations of those ancient records, referred to as sacred, and the notions of more advanced periods of mental development, will inevitably sooner or later arise.[72]

The evolution of consciousness, in other words, reveals an ever greater degree of incongruity. As Strauss shattered the identity of the Christ of faith with the Jesus of the Gospels, so Geiger dissolved the identity of *halakhic* exegesis with the literal meaning of the Bible. In each case, the ancient texts were demoted from sources of truth to states of consciousness.

In 1845 Geiger brought the full weight of his philological expertise to bear on the subject of rabbinic exegesis. In two slender volumes, he published the first grammar of *mishnaic* Hebrew, a selection of forty-five *mishnaic* texts—*aggadic* and *halakhic*—explicated according to the canons of the new Jewish learning, and a modest glossary of *mishnaic* vocabulary. Clearly part of Geiger's long-standing interest in the *Mishnah*, the sample of philology and history was intended to identify the individuality of the text by severing it from what had preceded and followed it. In the spirit of *Wissenschaft*'s regard for the uniqueness of the particular, Geiger dared to sunder the seamless fabric of the Oral and Written Law. On the one hand, he showed that *mishnaic* Hebrew constituted a far-reaching development of biblical Hebrew that changed both forms and meanings. On the other, he repudiated the Talmud as a reliable guide to a correct understanding of the *mishnaic* text. Equally unconventional, Geiger claimed that the Palestinian Talmud, long ignored by Ashkenazic Jews, often came closer to the literal meaning of the *Mishnah* than did the Babylonian, probably because the two corpuses shared a common social and cultural matrix. Altogether, Geiger had substantially enlarged his canvas: the Talmud misread the *Mishnah*, just as often as it misread the Bible. The beginning of critical scholarship, and religious Reform, was to free the study of sacred texts from a tradition or exegesis no less sacred, though highly subjective.[73]

In the opening line of Geiger's final contribution of the decade on the subject of exegesis, he eloquently enunciated his central concern: "In the interpretation of the documents of the Bible, the religious consciousness of an age is most clearly delineated."[74] Written with all the enthusiasm of a discoverer, the piece focused on a small circle of North French exegetes largely inspired by the example of Rashi to fathom the biblical text on its own terms. Geiger was to write of the circle again in 1855 and in each instance he enhanced his analysis with the publication of illustrative manuscript fragments.[75] Geiger had uncovered a sophisticated sense of the literal meaning of Scripture not among acculturated Spanish Jews, where its presence had been manifest and long recognized, but unexpectedly in the heartland of Jewish piety. The phenomenon engaged Geiger because it illuminated the history of rabbinic consciousness and not because it allowed for a surreptitious foray into the "dangerous" field of biblical criticism, though to be sure the two were not unrelated.[76]

It is for this reason that Geiger opened his first essay with a highly schematized history of rabbinic consciousness measured by awareness of a literal sense, a reconstruction that wove together the research of more than a decade. In the period of the *Mishnah*, rabbinic activity consisted of translating the Bible rather than interpreting it. The age felt no discrepancy between the evolving praxis of Judaism and its biblical origins. Everything was still perceived to be but a natural extension of Scripture. In the talmudic period, however, a sense of unease sets in and exegesis replaces translation. Though a consciousness of discrepancy is still not apparent, there is an eagerness to unveil the biblical foundation of the *halakhic* edifice, and exegesis becomes wholly subservient to extraneous considerations. In turn, excess begins to trigger a limited sense for the integrity of the text. Toward the end of the first millennium, the influence of Islam raises Jewish consciousness to new heights, and the geonic heirs of rabbinic culture effect at least a partial emancipation of biblical exegesis from its *halakhic* constraints. But what truly intrigues Geiger is the fourth period of the school of Rashi, for here he detects an untrammeled and untroubled appreciation of the literal meaning of the Bible. Moreover, this level of consciousness is reached not by virtue of any alien influence, but in consequence of a piety so secure as to be unthreatened by intellectual freedom.[77]

In sum, the scholarship of the young Geiger is all of a piece. Produced during a period of his life marked by inner torment and external turmoil, it applied the Hegelian concept of consciousness reinforced by profound philological learning to the exegetical infrastructure of rabbinic Judaism. The battle for religious Reform was a confrontation between two states of consciousness, in which the key to victory lay in dismantling rabbinic Judaism by discrediting its exegetical system. Geiger had wedded the "science" of philology to the cause of theology, and that alliance was to stamp the quality of his mature work as well.

The *Urschrift und Übersetzungen der Bibel*, which appeared in 1857, for all its sparkling novelty, is best treated as a continuation of Geiger's central research agenda of the thirties and forties. What ultimately distinguishes it is not so much substance but tone. The early work is still governed by a decidedly negative valence, an indictment cast either in terms of naiveté or degeneration. It is that critical posture which unites Geiger the philologian with Creizenach the rationalist. A decade later Geiger had fully liberated himself from that judgmental tenor and was now able to reconstruct the history of rabbinic exegesis using a development rather than a degenerative trope. The switch was of momentous import, for it yielded a patrimony for Reform drawn from the ranks of normative Judaism.

The precise genesis of the *Urschrift* is difficult to recover. At the end of his first essay on the literal sense of the rabbis, Geiger had promised to carry his investigation into the field of *targumim* (the early Aramaic translations of the Bible), which is exactly what he did in the *Urschrift*.[78] On the other hand, in 1865 Geiger wrote to the Christian Semiticist Theodor Nöldeke that he stumbled into his book from a project on the Karaites, for whom the Reformers had a strong affinity.[79] Whatever the case, the surviving correspondence testifies that by 1854 Geiger had plunged into a systematic study of the early strata of rabbinic literature, propelled by the exhilaration of fresh insight. On 8th March 1855 he apologized to Stein-schneider, a close friend, for his undue silence: "How can you grumble with some-one in love. . . . No, my dear friend, I am really quite serious; I am in love. . . . I am in love with my work. I am so completely immersed in it, it absorbs me so fully that I neither hear nor see anything else."[80] The partial inelegance of the final structure actually betrays signs of the emotional intensity in which the book was conceived.

Like Zunz, Geiger had grasped the centrality of the Bible in the history of the Jewish consciousness. And the different ways Jews have read the Bible was not to be measured or judged according to extraneous canons of reason or philology, but understood as an expression of existential relationship.

The Bible is now and has always been an ever-living word, not a dead letter. It has spoken to all generations and imparted its teachings to them; it expressed the full-ness of its spirit in the living, spontaneous phrase. . . . The eternal word was never considered part of any one era; its validity could not be dependent upon the time at which it was composed; by the same token, it could not be construed to lack any of the newer truths and insights. This is the reason why every age, every move-ment and every personality in history has brought its own ideas to bear upon the Bible; hence the multitude of elaborations, interpretations, and typical and sym-bolic attempts at explanation. All efforts, notwithstanding, it seems impossible to achieve an objective interpretation of the Bible, and even the non-believer will infuse his own feelings of aversion into his attempts to explain this work. This may result in a good deal of instability in exegesis, but at the same time it points up all the more clearly the significance of the Bible as all things to all men.[81]

The mature Geiger had abandoned the narrow search for practitioners of *peshat* (the plain meaning of the text). Instead, he had come to view rabbinic exegesis as an instrument of liberation that mediated the tension between continuity and de-velopment. *Midrash* had been transvalued into a dynamic principle.

Geiger's *Urschrift*, then, is above all a study of how Jews during the period of the Second Temple and the *Mishnah* preserved the relevance of their sacred liter-ature. During the early centuries, while the text still possessed a degree of fluidity, Geiger contended, Jews did not hesitate even to rewrite passages that no longer accorded with their political needs or ethical sensibilities. Such frequent incursions help to explain the many divergences between our text of the canon and the first translations of it into Greek and Aramaic. It was the original that had been tam-pered with.[82] Once the text attained its unalterable form, the technique of *midrash* served to keep it contemporaneous, legally as well as homiletically. Geiger's most dramatic discovery was the detection of *halakhic* diversity and development. He marshaled impressive evidence from a multiplicity of ancient sources to suggest *halakhic* innovation in response to new values and priorities.

But what lends the *Urschrift* its supreme power is the combination of philological detail and historical sweep. Geiger succeeded in correlating the dense and esoteric subject of biblical exegesis to the internal and external history of Palestinian Jewry during a period of nearly eight centuries. The evidence of exegetical and *halakhic* change is the sediment of controversy between contending religious parties. The motive force is the struggle for political power within the Jewish polity, often exacerbated by foreign rule, and Geiger assiduously aligns religious positions with political parties.[83] If the rabbinic research of the young Geiger was fertilized by the work of Strauss, the *Urschrift* bears the impress of Ferdinand Christian Baur. The ongoing struggle between Sadducees and Pharisees in Second Temple Judaism is quite analogous to the struggle between Pauline and Jewish Christians during the first two centuries of Christianity.[84] And the reconstruction of both men echoes the intermingling of religion and politics in pre-unified Germany. In the skillful hands of Geiger, the Pharisees emerge as the Puritans of their day—democratic, nationalistic, and progressive—battling to unseat an entrenched, priestly aristocracy.[85] The Prophets had announced the idea of one God; the Pharisees fought to make Him accessible. A clerical hierarchy was inimical to a vision of religious democracy.[86] Geiger had good reason to be pleased with his results: not only had he demolished the static conception of a dynamic period, but he had also reclaimed the Pharisees for the forces of religious progress.

III

In 1859 at the end of a long letter of corrections to Steinschneider's catalogue of Hebrew manuscripts at the University of Leiden, Geiger sought the indulgence of his esteemed friend: "Overlook my lowly state, that I am a rabbi. If ever I am born a second time, I will not do it again."[87] This self-deprecating disclaimer belies Geiger's greatest professional achievement: to have preserved learning as the core of the modern rabbinate. If historical thinking was pioneered by intellectuals in flight from the traditional rabbinate, in the person of Geiger it was reunited with a transformed and rejuvenated type of rabbinic leadership. What is more, the new Jewish learning constituted a powerful idiom for accommodating an ancient religion to a radically different set of political and social circumstances. For rabbis of a Reform bent, it held out a non-*halakhic* and "scientific" means to determine what was authentically Jewish. The very title of Geiger's 1835 periodical—*Wissenschaftliche Zeitschrift für jüdische Theologie*—proclaimed the religious relevance of historical research. A new rabbinic leadership began to invoke the mantle of a new authority, which also proved to be a source of deep personal fulfillment.[88] A few examples should suffice to illustrate the rapid diffusion of that vision.

By 1856 Levi Herzfeld had finished the first edition of his three-volume *Ge-*

schichte des Volkes Jsrael which spanned the crucial but sparsely documented period from the destruction of the First Temple to the final victory of the Maccabees.[89] Born in 1810, the same year as Geiger, in the region of the Harz Mountains, Herzfeld had acquired his talmudic education from Samuel Eger, the *Landesrabbiner* of Braunschweig, and his secular education at the *Gymnasium* in Nordhausen. In 1833 he moved to Berlin to attend its renowned university and received his doctorate three years later with a dissertation on the chronology of the judges and early kings of Israel, dedicated to Zunz, with whom he had developed a warm relationship.[90] Upon graduation, Herzfeld had intended to spend a year in Italy pursuing his studies, but a sense of obligation called him back to Braunschweig to assist his aged and blind teacher. Yet, as he confessed to Zunz, the act of self-denial left him quite despondent: "Only one thing can I think through (at this time) and have thought through, that I am not where I ought to be." To which Zunz tartly remarked in his next letter, "Among Jews, Jewish scholarship is not now where it ought to be, but rather in Golus [exile]."[91]

Herzfeld was acutely sensitive to the risks attendant upon practicing critical scholarship in the pulpit. The prevailing alliance between throne and altar in Prussia imposed constraints even on the freedom of German academics. As a student in 1834, Herzfeld had been denied an academic prize by Ernst Wilhelm Hengstenberg, the leading theological conservative, because he dared to characterize a biblical story as a fable and because his knowledge of Hebrew, a language he had been studying for twenty years, was deficient![92] But the wound left him cautious. In his first publication, a translation of and critical commentary on *Ecclesiastes*, he refused to challenge overtly the traditional Solomonic authorship, for which Zunz chided him in an otherwise approving review.[93] Years later Herzfeld defended himself publicly: "My silence came simply from the fact that seventeen years ago a Jewish minister could not engage in biblical criticism without grave danger."[94] Even writing for Geiger's journal, he told Zunz at the time, was inadvisable for anyone seeking a pulpit. And, indeed, Geiger was no less cognizant, if less fearful, of the risks. As he confided to Derenbourg in 1837 in regard to his editorial policy, he had no intention of plunging into biblical criticism and even held back with talmudic criticism until the sixth number of his journal.[95] For Geiger personally the backlash would come in Breslau in the early 1840s, when his Orthodox adversaries took the stance, provoked by the growing independence of his research, that critical scholarship was utterly incompatible with the rabbinate.[96]

When Eger, an open-minded traditionalist, died in 1842, Herzfeld received his post and two years later was host at the first nationwide conference of modern German rabbis. He attended the next two as well and emerged with a deserved reputation for religious moderation. Neither as torn nor as restless as Geiger, Herzfeld was to remain in the same pulpit for forty-two years without ever abandoning his dedication to *Wissenschaft*.[97] In the foreword to the final volume of his history, which appeared in 1856, he confessed that the composition had taken some eighteen years of his life:

I labored on it in good days and bad. The good, this work helped to make even better; the bad, it helped to alleviate. With this compensation in hand, I am entirely satisfied and I thank God, in Whose service this work has been written, for the strength He has accorded me.[98]

Herzfeld's history has all the density of German academic pedantry. Its mix of lifeless narrative, technical excursuses, and brief notes is as inelegant as it is thorough. Nevertheless, that impenetrable façade conceals a subtle instance of *Wissenschaft* from a Reform perspective, all the more interesting for its divergence from Geiger's path. Herzfeld does not appear to have gone through a phase in which he wrote of rabbinic Judaism in a degenerative mode. The main agenda of his history is "to demonstrate the emergence of Judaism out of Hebraism" and the dominant figure of speech throughout is development and not degeneration.[99] For all his attention to non-Jewish sources, Herzfeld relies heavily on the evidence preserved in rabbinic literature and generally gives credence to rabbinic claims unless he has good reason to dispute them. In short, the text is noteworthy for its conspicuous lack of antipathy toward the ancient rabbis.

What marks it as a specimen of Reform scholarship is the very design to locate the genesis of rabbinic Judaism in a specific time and place. Somewhere in the four obscure centuries between 587 and 170 B.C.E. a profound religious metamorphosis was gradually effected: "Yahwism" evolves into Judaism. Herzfeld's frequent use of the Christian scholarly version of the Tetragrammaton of Israelite religion epitomizes his critical distance, as does his ready application of biblical criticism. He is prepared to concede, for example, that the Pentateuch is a pre-exilic book, but not that its beliefs or practices ever gained wide currency during the First Commonwealth.[100] The historical evidence of the Early Prophets suggests that henotheism and not monotheism was the order of the day. Furthermore, Herzfeld contends in Reform fashion, that the Later Prophets never came to regard ritual as anything but a vehicle to disseminate monotheism. "For the sentient masses, religious ceremonies are the best containers of religious ideas. Their deleterious side emerges only if these containers are not then smashed in time."[101] While the Babylonian exile finally erases all traces of idolatry from Israel's midst, monotheism still fails to become pervasive for centuries after the return. Herzfeld's proof is drawn from what he perceives to be a massive betrayal of Judaism during the religious persecution under Antiochus IV Epiphanes. "The entire subsequent history of the Jews shows no evidence of apostasy on such a scale . . . so that it must at least partially be explained in terms of the still-prevailing indifference toward the belief in Yahweh."[102] In fact, Herzfeld, not unlike Elias Bickermann, nearly a century later, attributes the persecutions in part to the counsel of hellenized Jews eager to facilitate national assimilation.[103]

For Herzfeld, religious institutions evolve gradually over time, often under foreign influence. The exile exposed Jews for the first time to Zoroastrianism, and Herzfeld believed that the libation ceremonies connected with the festival of Succot, the manifold laws of ritual impurity, and the belief in resurrection all derived from that exposure.[104] The expansion of the Torah begins under the leadership of Ezra and Nehemiah who create a school of exegetes, the *Sofrim*, which labors to validate new religious developments either by reading them into Scripture or simply projecting them back to Sinai itself (*halakhah le-Moshe mi-Sinai*).[105] But not everyone was willing to accept this emerging legal and unrecorded supplement to Scripture. Herzfeld reflects the pre-Geiger preference for the Sadducees, whom he portrays as rejecting *in toto* the arbitrary addition of an oral law. Geiger had boldly shifted the source of the controversy between Sadducees and Pharisees by claiming that both parties expanded Judaism through biblical exegesis. The issue for Geiger was not one of principle but one of choice: which oral law served Judaism better, the more ancient and aristocratic law of the Sadducees or the newer and more democratic one of the Pharisees?[106] Herzfeld completed his work one year before Geiger's *Urschrift* and cast the controversy in terms of the legitimacy of the oral law itself. The Sadducees repudiated the very instrument along with its attendant rigors as a departure from the past. Though Herzfeld did not indict the Pharisees for religious hypocrisy but only for mechanistic piety, his pro-Sadducean bias implied a deep-seated if unspoken predilection for Mosaism.[107]

A few years later, Geiger's reinterpretation of the Pharisees drew fire from a "Mosaist" of long standing. Since 1847 Samuel Holdheim had served as *Prediger* of the Reform synagogue in Berlin, the most radical pulpit in Germany. Its weekly Sabbath services were held on Sunday, almost entirely in German, with men and women seated apart but on the same floor, without headcovering or prayer shawls. Women participated in the choir. The New Year was celebrated without benefit of a Shofar, the Day of Atonement was interrupted by a long break in the services, and the annual commemoration of the destruction of the Temple was shifted in time and transformed in meaning. Holdheim had fully repudiated the Orthodoxy of his Poznań youth.[108] Born in 1806 he had early gained proficiency in talmudic studies, discovered the path to Reform through reading *Die gottesdienstliche Vorträge* of Zunz, and finally acquired a doctorate from the University of Leipzig.[109] His scholarly discourse is a loose medley of *halakhic* and historical arguments, uncontrolled by rigorous method and avowedly in the service of Reform.

What makes Holdheim the most extreme Reformer among the rabbis of his day is that he is a lifelong exponent of the distinction between the politically temporary and religiously permanent components of Judaism enunciated first by the Paris Sanhedrin.[110] His scholarly output, if it may be dignified as such, is designed to divest modern Judaism of every political vestige of an earlier age, a category so broadly conceived by Holdheim that it includes many a religious practice. His vision is one of total integration into the fabric of German society, for which he holds aloft the historical example of the ten lost tribes of Israel and the majority of the exiles from Judah who failed to return when permitted by Cyrus. Both demonstrate the ability of Jews to transcend their national origins.[111] Holdheim restricts the realm of religion to man's relationship to God; how he relates to his fellow-man is a matter for the body politic to decide.[112] The pronounced political character of traditional Judaism, Holdheim contends, is the result of Gentile neglect and rabbinic presumption. The message of the year 70 C.E.—to discard whatever political trappings Judaism had left amid its growing religious consciousness—was missed by both sides. Instead Gentile society continued to exclude Jews, and the rabbis fomented ever new expressions of national vitality. The present generation has been granted the historic opportunity to complete that ancient assignment and thus transform Judaism into a wholly religious phenomenon.[113]

Holdheim unfurled this reading of Jewish history by way of introducing his book, *Über die Autonomie der Rabbinen und das Princip der jüdischen Ehe* (On the Jurisdiction of the Rabbis and the Issue of Jewish Marriage), which appeared first in 1843. Clearly prompted by the likely possibility of a rescinding of Prussian emancipation, the book took up again, from a fresh perspective, two of Napoleon's questions of 1806 to French Jewry—Can Jews marry Christians and what judicial authority is still exercised by the rabbis?[114] Properly understood, Judaism granted the rabbis no legal jurisdiction, either in civil or in matrimonial matters. Holdheim argued that both types of rabbinic law had nothing to do with religion and were late developments in consequence of a life lived on the fringes of society. Political events of the last century had already effectively retired the practice of Jewish civil law in Western Europe: Holdheim advocated that the same now be done for Jewish marriage law. To insist that Jews could not marry Christians was to preserve Jewish national purity and was tantamount to replacing an isolation imposed externally with one generated internally.[115] Despite the torrent of criticism which Holdheim's book justifiably provoked, it is worth noting that the Braunschweig rabbinical conference of 1844 adopted a resolution endorsing mixed marriages if the state would permit the children to be raised as Jews, a position that went beyond the one taken by the Paris Sanhedrin and bespoke deep political anxiety. But Holdheim's principled advocacy is to be distinguished from the political pragmatism of his colleagues.[116]

Holdheim's final scholarly work, *A Treatise on the Status of Women*, written unexpectedly in Hebrew and published in 1861, a year after his death, argued that divorce in Jewish law was no less a civil ceremony than marriage. Although this subject is certainly part of his long-term agenda, the immediate impetus seems to have come from Geiger's *Urschrift*, which distressed Holdheim for two reasons. First, he was upset by the idea that the Sadducees also operated with an oral law and thus contested the Pharisees merely on the level of details. Secondly, he criticized Geiger's political analysis. If the controversy is devoid of religious content, the present generation can hardly turn to either party in its search for a model.

Without much evidence, Geiger had presumed to overturn a well-established scholarly tradition.[117]

Holdheim's specific point of departure was the question of divorce. Assuming an identity of practice between Sadducees and Karaites, despite a separation of many centuries, Holdheim claimed on the basis of Karaite sources that the Sadducees, as priests, countenanced divorce for no one, and that Jesus adopted their point of view. In contrast, the Pharisees desacralized the state of matrimony, with marriage comparable to a financial arrangement, and hence a man could divorce his wife for almost any reason. Sadducean stringency bespoke a desire to protect the position of women by making of marriage a sacred covenant of equals. Pharisaic practice, on the other hand, reflected a deteriorating status, with women subject to arbitrary divorce and a host of other inequities. While the Pharisees did lavish praise on the Jewish woman in their *aggadic* pronouncements, they hermetically sealed off the *halakhic* realm from ethical considerations. And Holdheim pleads for opening up once again the legal process in Judaism to an infusion of moral values.[118]

On a larger scale, Holdheim depicts the basic issue dividing the two parties as the Pharisaic innovation of the oral law. Not only are the Sadducees more ethical, they are also more rational. They resist the oral law because it violates the integrity and literal meaning of the biblical text. The technique of *midrash* threatens the older, venerated practice of interpreting Scripture according to its plain sense and therefore is anathema to the Sadducees, who condemn the method as well as its theological and *halakhic* consequences. In the final analysis, Holdheim answers Geiger by elevating the Pharisaic-Sadducean dispute to a matter of ultimate religious moment. The cause of Reform was better served by the Sadducean-Karaite axis with its commitment to Mosaism than by a Pharisaic pedigree essentially political and highly legalistic.[119]

The two modes of Reform scholarship which we have been tracking in Germany, with their respective emphases either on deviation and decline or on growth and development, appear by the middle decade of the century in East Central Europe as well. And our study must not close without some mention of the diffusion of *Wissenschaft* beyond the borders of Germany. Though Reform as a religious movement fared badly in regions untouched by emancipation, where the native Orthodoxy and insularity of the masses was fortified by the incursion of *Hasidism*, the new Jewish learning was quickly appropriated by a far-sighted and courageous cluster of young men attuned to the West and in contact with each other. Thus almost from the beginning, *Wissenschaft* is practiced on an international scale with Hebrew as important a vehicle of communication as German. Among the second generation of these scholars, Joshua Heschel Schorr in Galicia and Leopold Loew in Hungary battled for the reform of a pre-emancipation Judaism in the scholarly modes worked out in Germany.

Schorr was born in the important commercial center of Brody in 1818 into a merchant family of means, and earned his living as a man of business.[120] The financial independence facilitated his education, his academic freedom, and eventually the ability to dispense his views. A radical product of the Galician *Haskalah*, Schorr made his scholarly debut in 1839 in the pages of Jost's short-lived *Israelitische Annalen*, thanks to the editor's willingness to render his Hebrew articles into German. His very first contribution on "The Present Fight between Authority and Criticism" conveys a precocious appreciation of the religious import of critical scholarship and adumbrates his own research agenda. Schorr fully realizes that *Wissenschaft* holds out the prospect of circumventing and undermining the authority of the *halakhah*. Till now advocates of Reform have struggled to validate their proposals on *halakhic* grounds, but to no avail, because the system can always be made to yield opposing points of view.

As long as the Talmud itself is acknowledged as a perfect and infallible monument to the divine tradition, it cannot be used as a means for Reform. But why not start to uncover the inner perfections and the many undeniable errors in the Talmud. In this manner we would prove beyond any doubt that we possess here a flawed work of mortal men which is not pervaded by a single unified spirit.[121]

Critical history, in brief, is ideally suited to soften the *halakhic* incrustation of Judaism. Uncovering the all too human origins of the system tarnishes its infallibility and grants contemporary Jews an equal right to modify its contours.[122]

In 1852, with the prospects for emancipation in Galicia improving, Schorr began publication of a militant Hebrew periodical, *Hehalutz*, whose full title, based on a detail from Joshua's siege of Jericho, unfurled its program: "The vanguard which leads the people of Israel in the battle for religion and reasonableness." Modeled on Geiger's earlier *Wissenschaftliche Zeitschrift*, the periodical combined scholarship with journalism, dense research into rabbinics with polemical assaults on the present-day rabbinate. *Hehalutz* became a transfer station for the transmission of Reform *Wissenschaft* to Eastern Europe. Geiger not only inspired much of Schorr's research agenda, but graced the periodical with his own contributions. Despite his preference for German in prayer as well as scholarship, Geiger wrote Hebrew with rare felicity and used the early volumes of *Hehalutz* to deepen and disseminate the conclusions of his *Urschrift*.[123]

Schorr's role increased as his small band of comrades fell away, alienated as much by his personality as by his scholarship. The trope which pervades·much of his work is deviation and decline, with sarcasm and polemics often invading the realm of scholarship. For example, Schorr follows Geiger in the effort to discredit the talmudic exegesis of the *Mishnah*, by collecting some thirty-nine instances of misprision under the provocative rubric of "errors of the Talmud."[124] Similarly, he intensifies Geiger's attack on the Babylonian Talmud from the vantage of its Palestinian counterpart, long neglected in the *halakhic* process, by collecting further evidence of its exegetical superiority.[125] On the other hand, despite a lengthy and laudatory review of Geiger's *Urschrift*—"filled from cover to cover with wisdom, understanding, and learning, incredible erudition in ancient literature and a wonderfully penetrating mind"—Schorr is hesitant to embrace his interpretation of the Sadducees.[126] Without doubt, his governing trope becomes developmental at times, when he dramatically pushes for extensive Zoroastrian influence in the late books of the Bible and the rabbinic period, a thesis which even Geiger found unconvincing, or for the post-biblical origins and, much later still, acceptance of the liturgical rite of *tefillin*.[127] But the tone always remains charged with antagonism, betraying the desperateness of Schorr's cause in the context of Galicia.[128]

A more moderate scholar of far greater stature was Leopold Loew, who was born in Moravia in 1811 and served as a rabbi of Szeged, Hungary's second largest city, from 1850 till his death in 1875. If Schorr resembled Holdheim, Loew was akin to Geiger. In terms of native endowment, career, scholarship, and religious position the two men were kindred souls. Loew laid the foundation for his superb command of all layers of rabbinic literature in several Moravian *yeshivot*, without neglecting his secular education which culminated at the universities of Pest and Vienna. Though a master of German prose—the main medium of his scholarship—Loew was an outspoken Hungarian patriot. He was one of the first rabbis to preach in Hungarian, a spokesman for the immersion of Hungarian Jews in Hungarian culture, and a prime mover in the translation of the Hebrew Bible into Hungarian and in the founding of a modern rabbinical seminary in Budapest. In the same spirit, he wrote extensively on the history of Hungarian Jewry, especially in his own turbulent century.[129]

Like Geiger, Loew plunged into the maelstrom of religious controversy fragmenting the Jewish community of his adopted homeland. He led the camp of indigenous Reformers (called Neologs in Hungary) and edited a religious weekly in German in behalf of their cause.[130] Repeatedly the emergence of a Jewish press in the nineteenth century was closely linked to the proliferation of competing religious positions. Loew's general religious orientation, if not his moderation, derived from Aaron Chorin, Hungary's first liberal rabbi, who had provided both him and Zunz with rabbinic ordination.[131] In a work like *Iggeret El Assaf* (A Letter to Assaf), published in 1826, Chorin had recommended prayer without headcovering on the grounds of Jewish law as well as comparative religion. Ritual as a means to an end is culturally influenced. Jews in an Islamic orbit, he noted, will express reverence for God differently from co-religionists living in a Christian world. Loew's devotion to his embattled mentor and forerunner is made manifest in a richly stocked biography, and his own scholarship incorporates both Chorin's *halakhic* and his comparative perspectives.[132]

Above all Loew writes of Judaism as a student of religion absorbed with tracing the evolution of its ideas, values, rites, and institutions. He is impatient with the type of Jewish scholarship which fails to go much beyond dating and identifying the author of an ancient text. His own diverse work, pervaded by a profound sense of both continuity and development, is designed to show that "in and of itself," the Jewish national spirit offers cogent testimony of its creative power, of its capability and predilection for taking in foreign elements and blending them with its own products."[133]

Such an ever responsive portrait of Judaism is offered up by Loew in his two most enduring works of scholarship, *Die graphischen Requisiten und Erzeugnisse bei den Juden* and *Die Lebensalter in der jüdischen Literatur,* published in the last five years of his life and the obvious culmination of years of research. The specificity of the titles completely belies the range of topics and depth of sources brought together in these majestic studies of Judaism *qua* religion. With effortless erudition, Loew roams over the full expanse of Judaism from the biblical era to his own day to convey a sense of organic vitality.

What unites both works in a common agenda, for all their divergence in focus on *realia* and attitudes, is the use of *halakhic* literature as the main source of evidence. Like no other scholar of his age, Loew realized the untapped wealth preserved in the *halakhic* deposits of each age for reconstructing the twofold history of Judaism as a composite of both official and popular religion. Taken together, ancient and medieval *halakhic* sources yield the most cogent argument for modern Reform—the influence of non-Jewish belief and practice as in the case of Jewish marriage customs, the late development of certain Jewish rites like the *Bar Mitzvah,* the overturning of earlier prohibitions by later generations as in the admission of wax for use as Sabbath candles, the divergence between Sephardic and Ashkenazic practice as in the case of writing on the intermediary days of Succot and Passover, or the depiction of the twelfth-century French *halakhist* Jacob ben Meir Tam as an advocate of Reform.[134]

Moreover, it is no accident that Loew closed his trail-blazing *Graphische Requisiten* with an invaluable discussion of the problem of how the *Mishnah* was produced. By 1871 the scholarly literature on the subject had been richly expanded and one is tempted to conjecture that Loew's very interest in the history of writing among Jews—a superb fulcrum for a sweeping study of a literary culture—was triggered by the question. The end of the work suggested its genesis. Specifically, Loew distinguished between the conflicting medieval traditions of Sephardim and Ashkenazim on the transcription of the *Mishnah,* identifying the position of Geiger with that of the Sephardim and that of Luzzatto with the Ashkenazim. Personally he came down on the side of Luzzatto. But for Loew the precise moment when the practice of verbal transmission was abandoned no longer mattered. The irrefutable fact was that the *halakhic* system evinced change: at some point, circumstances compelled a rupture with the past.[135] Survival was a function of adaptation. In general, the enormous evidence assembled by Loew from the most normative texts of Judaism projected a lively and diverse religious system ever-responsive to the need to change. Loew—a far more harmonious personality and synthetic scholar than Schorr—imbued the study of *halakhah* with historical perspective and thus challenged the reigning but rigid *halakhists* of his day on their own turf.

By the last quarter of the nineteenth century, historical research had long ceased to be a Reform preserve. Its irrefutable power attracted practitioners from all camps, for the idiom of *Wissenschaft* had become the dominant medium for thinking through the nature of Judaism and facing the challenges of a new age. No one defended the vitality of its present-mindedness more ebulliently than its most accomplished master of our time, Salo W. Baron. In the heroic epilogue to the first edition of his *A Social and Religious History of the Jews,* written on the eve of the "resumption" of the Great War, he summed up the core conviction of the new Jewish learning:

The interpretation and reinterpretation of the history of the people, a kind of *historical Midrash* [italics in the original], is now to serve as a guidance for the future. A new divine book has opened itself before the eyes of the faithful: the book of human and Jewish destinies, guided by some unknown and unknowable ultimate Power. This book, if properly understood, would seem to answer the most perplexing questions of the present and the future.[136]

NOTES

1. Peter Beer, *Geschichte, Lehren und Meinungen aller bestandenen und noch bestehenden religiösen Sekten der Juden,* 2 vols., Brünn 1822–1823.

2. *Idem,* "Über einige bei der jüdischen Nation bestandene, und zum Theile noch bestehende religiöse Sekten," *Sulamith,* I (1806), p. 266.

3. *Idem, Geschichte,* I, p. 331. Also pp. 231–232.

4. *Ibid.,* "Vorrede," p. vii.

5. Niccolò Machiavelli, *The Prince and the Discourses,* New York 1950, p. 170. Also Beer, *Geschichte,* II, "Vorwort," p. iv.

6. Isaak Markus Jost, *Geschichte der Israeliten,* 9 vols., Berlin 1820–1828. For a reliable and useful Hebrew summary of its contents, see Reuven Michael, *I. M. Jost: Founder of the Modern Jewish Historiography* (in Hebrew), Jerusalem 1983, pp. 15–76.

7. See above, p. 237.

8. Leo Baeck Institute Archives (LBIA), Jost to Samuel Meyer Ehrenberg, 9th February 1848.

9. Jost, *Geschichte der Israeliten,* IV, p. 64; above, p. 233.

10. According to Zunz, who is the source of this information, Ehrenberg finished this lifelong project in 1851, but then was no longer able to find a publisher. "The times did not favor such initiatives." Nevertheless, his attachment to Hebrew was undaunted. "With resignation Ehrenberg accepted the frustration of his cherished dream and began, on the spot, a new project—the translation of Campe's [edition of] Robinson [Crusoe], which he had nearly completed by July 1853 (just a few months before his death)." (Leopold Zunz, *Samuel Meyer Ehrenberg,* Braunschweig 1854, p. 43.)

11. I. M. Jost, "Vor einem halben Jahrhundert," *Sippurim,* III, ed. by Wolf Pascheles, Prague 1854, p. 157.

12. JNUL, 4°792/G-15.

13. Jost, "Vor einem halben Jahrhundert," p. 161.

14. JNUL, 4°792/B-1, 4°792/G-27, Zunz to Adolf Strodtmann, 6th March 1863. For Jost's version of his withdrawal from the *Verein,* see *Allgemeine Zeitung des Judentums,* 1859, p. 176.

15. Nahum N. Glatzer, "On an Unpublished Letter of Isaak Markus Jost," in *LBIYB XXII* (1977), pp. 129–137.

16. Jost, *Geschichte der Israeliten*, III, "Excurs," p. 215.

17. *Ibid.*, "Anhang zum zehnten Buche," p. 120. Isaak Markus Jost, *Allgemeine Geschichte des Israelitischen Volkes*, 2 vols., Berlin 1832. Cf. Michael, *I. M. Jost*, pp. 83–109.

18. Jost, *Geschichte der Israeliten*, III, "Anhang," pp. 165–171.

19. *Ibid.*, IV, "Excurs," pp. 264–294.

20. Edward Gibbon, *The History of the Decline and Fall of the Roman Empire*, 6 vols., London 1766–1788, I, p. 536.

21. Jost, *Geschichte der Israeliten*, I, "Vorwort."

22. *Ibid.*, I, pp. 39–48; III, pp. 18–33.

23. *Ibid.*, III, pp. 127–145.

24. *Ibid.*, IV, pp. 101, 108, 114–115; "Anhang," pp. 235, 240.

25. *Ibid.*, VI, pp. 121–218.

26. *Ibid.*, VI, pp. 246–247, 285–286. Jost actually dates the event in 1254 ("Anhang," p. 379).

27. *Ibid.*, IX, pp. 76–77.

28. Nahum N. Glatzer, "Aus unveröffentlichten Briefen von I. M. Jost," in *In Zwei Welteln: Siegfried Moses zum Fünfundsiebzigsten Geburtstag*, ed. by Hans Tramer, Tel-Aviv 1962, pp. 400–413.

29. While Jost's treatment of rabbinism in his final work—*Geschichte des Judenthums*, 3 vols., Leipzig 1857–1859—is far less judgmental than in his earlier history (for a summary, see Michael, *I. M. Jost*, pp. 170–200), his willingness to write of Jesus solely on the basis of an uncritical reliance on the Gospels provoked many a Jewish reader. (See the letter by Bernhard Beer to Gerson Wolf dated 13th July 1857 in *JNUL*, Ms. Var. 236/#3; also H. Zirndorf, *Isaak Markus Jost und seine Freunde*, Leipzig–New York 1886, pp. 177–183.) The unguarded opinion of Zacharias Frankel is worth quoting in full. In an undated letter to his dear friend Beer shortly after Jost's death, he wrote:

> The departure of Jost surprised me greatly. The last prattler [*Schwätzer*] of the old school has returned home. You judge him too generously [*liebevoll*] if you detect him prattling [*Geschwätzigkeit*] only toward the end. Thoroughness was never his forte. His first work combined Jew-hatred with shallowness; his last combined this with a love for Christ [*Christusliebe*], awfully strange in the mouth of a Jewish historian and teacher. His enlightened contemporaries have judged him; so will a non-partisan posterity." (Jewish Historical Institute, Warsaw, Jewish Community of Breslau, #1167, correspondence of Frankel with Beer)

30. LBIA, Jost to Ehrenberg, 14th March 1830; JNUL, 4°792/G-27, Heine to Zunz, 2nd June 1823.

31. Leopold Zunz, *Gesammelte Schriften*, 3 vols., Berlin 1875–1876, II, p. 190.

32. Hans Joachim Schoeps, "Aus dem Briefwechsel Steinheim-Zunz," *Jahrbuch für jüdische Geschichte und Literatur*, XXXI (1938), pp. 283–284.

33. Sigmund Maybaum, "Aus dem Leben von Leopold Zunz," in *Zwölfter Bericht über die Lehranstalt für die Wissenschaft des Judenthums in Berlin*, Berlin 1894, p. 17.

34. *Ibid.*, pp. 13–14.

35. LBIA, Jost–Ehrenberg correspondence.

36. JNUL, 4°792/C-13, pp. 52–53.

37. LBIA, Jost to Ehrenberg, 14th March 1830.

38. Leopold Zunz, *Die gottesdienstlichen Vorträge der Juden*, 2nd edn., Frankfurt am Main 1892, pp. 1, 469.

39. *Ibid.*, pp. 1–13, 37–61.

40. Zunz, *Gesammelte Schriften*, I, p. 8.

41. Zunz, *Die gottesdienstlichen Vorträge*, pp. 103–104, 316–323.

42. A student of de Wette, the young Zunz also read the later books of the Hebrew Bible with a critical eye. On the basis of the language of Ezekiel, he was prepared to date large chunks of the book to the Persian period (*ibid.*, pp. 167–171). More important still, he was the first scholar to ascribe a single author to Chronicles and Ezra-Nehemiah (*ibid.*, pp. 22–32). Finally, in the winter of 1834/1835 Zunz delivered some thirty-four public lectures on the Psalms before a small but distinguished audience of scholars and friends. (Ismar Elbogen, "Von Leopold Zunz's Psalmen-Studien," *Festschrift: Armand Kaminka zum siebzigsten Geburtstage*, Vienna 1937, pp. 25–32.)

43. Zunz, *Die gottesdienstlichen Vorträge*, pp. 69–86, 195–237.

44. *Ibid.*, p. 335.

45. *Ibid.*, p. 469.

46. For a typical example of such a Jewish declaration of "at-homeness," see Isaak Markus Jost, *Neuere Geschichte der Israeliten in der ersten Hälfte des XIX. Jahrhunderts*, 3 vols., Breslau [n.d. 1847?], III, p. 6.

47. Max Wiener, *Jüdische Religion im Zeitalter der Emanzipation*, Berlin 1933, pp. 87, 110.

48. Arthur Galliner, "The Philanthropin in Frankfurt: Its Educational and Cultural Significance for German Jewry," in *LBIYB III* (1958), pp. 169–186; Eugen Mayer, "An Ecumenical Experiment," in *LBIYB XIII* (1968), pp. 135–141.

49. Michael Creizenach, *Schulchan Aruch*, 4 vols., Frankfurt am Main 1833–1840, I, pp. 110–111, 162–163; II, p. 4.

50. *Ibid.*, II, pp. 69–70.

51. *Ibid.*, I, p. 17; III, pp. 2, 6.

52. *Ibid.*, III, pp. 112–115.

53. On the career of Creizenach's son, who converted to Christianity in 1854, see Michael A. Meyer, "Alienated Intellectuals in the Camp of Religious Reform: The Frankfurt Reformfreunde, 1842–1845," *AJS Review*, VI (1981), pp. 61–86.

54. *WZJT*, V (1844), pp. 53–54.

55. Abraham Geiger, *Nachgelassene Schriften*, ed. by Ludwig Geiger, 5 vols., Berlin 1875–1878, V, pp. 3–7; Ludwig Geiger, *Abraham Geiger: Leben und Lebenswerk*, Berlin 1910, p. 11.

56. Geiger, *Nachgelassene Schriften*, V, p. 6. For a judiciously edited introduction to Geiger in English, see Max Wiener (ed.), *Abraham Geiger and Liberal Judaism*, Philadelphia 1962. Also the sensitive portrait by Michael A. Meyer, *Response to Modernity*, New York–Oxford 1988, pp. 89–99.

57. Abraham Geiger, *Was hat Mohammed aus dem Judenthume aufgenommen?*, Bonn 1833. The topic was suggested to Geiger by his professor of Arabic, Georg W. Freytag. (Geiger, *Nachgelassene Schriften*, V, p. 39.)

58. Ludwig Geiger, "Aus Leopold Zunz's Nachlass," *Zeitschrift für die Geschichte der Juden in Deutschland*, V (1892), pp. 244–245.

59. *Ibid.*, p. 247.

60. Geiger, *Nachgelassene Schriften*, I, pp. 302–303; V, pp. 13–14, 29, 37.

61. Abraham Geiger, "Einiges über Plan und Anordnung der Mischnah," *WZJT*, II (1836), pp. 474–492.

62. Samuel David Luzzatto, *Philoxenus* (in Hebrew), 2nd edn., Cracow 1895, introduction.

63. Reprinted in *Mehkarei ha-Yahadut*, 2 vols., Jerusalem 1970, I, pp. 159–164. The quotation is on p. 164.

64. Letter by Geiger to Hirsch dated 26th February 1832 published by Isak Markon, "Ein unveröffentlichter Brief von Abraham Geiger an Samson Rafael Hirsch" (n.p., n.d.). The original is in the Hirsch papers at the library of Bar Ilan University.

65. See Hirsch's caustic attack on the first two volumes of Creizenach's work in S. R. Hirsch, *Erste und zweite Mittheilung aus dem Briefwechsel*, 2nd edn., Frankfurt am Main 1920, pp. 14–33.

66. S. R. Hirsch, *Horeb*, trans. by I. Grunfeld, 2 vols., London 1962, I, p. clvii. See also Hirsch, *The Nineteen Letters of Ben Uziel*, transl. by Bernard Drachman, New York 1942, pp. 194–195.

67. *WZJT*, III (1837), pp. 74–91; IV (1839), pp. 355–380. The quotation is in III, pp. 81–82.

68. *WZJT*, IV (1839), p. 378.

69. Abraham Geiger, "Das Verhältniss des natürlichen Schriftsinnes zur thalmudischen Schriftdeutung," *WZJT*, V (1844), pp. 53–81, 234–259. The quotation is on p. 70.

70. *Ibid.*, p. 81.

71. *WZJT*, II (1836), pp. 199–208; Geiger, *Nachgelassene Schriften*, V, p. 96; *AZJ*, 1896, pp. 164–166, 371.

72. David Friedrich Strauss, *The Life of Jesus*, transl. by Mrs. Charles Hennell and George Eliot, 3 vols., London 1846, I, p. 1.

73. Abraham Geiger, *Lehr- und Lesebuch zur Sprache der Mischnah*, 2 vols., Breslau 1845. For a summary of Graetz's bitter review of this work, see above, pp. 280–281.

74. S. L. Heilberg (ed.), *Nitei Naamanim* with *Beiträge* by Geiger, Breslau 1847, German part, p. 1.

75. Abraham Geiger, *Parschandatha: Die nordfranzösische Exegetenschule*, Leipzig 1855.

76. Cf. Sarah Jafet, "On the State of the Field" (in Hebrew), *Newsletter of the World Union of Jewish Studies*, No. 25 (Summer 1985), pp. 3–17.

77. Heilberg, *Nitei Naamanim*, German part, pp. 1–7.

78. *WZJT*, V (1844), p. 81.

79. Geiger, *Nachgelassene Schriften*, V, p. 296.

80. Jewish Theological Seminary Archives (JTSA) Steinschneider Collection, Geiger correspondence.

81. Wiener, *Abraham Geiger*, p. 216. The original is in Abraham Geiger, *Urschrift und Übersetzungen der Bibel*, 2nd edn., Frankfurt am Main 1928, p. 72.

82. Geiger, *Urschrift*, pp. 74–100, 232, 244–245, 251, 257.

83. *Ibid.*, pp. 149–158.

84. Horton Harris, *The Tübingen School*, Oxford 1975, *passim*. Already Hans Liebeschütz, *Das Judentum im deutschen Geschichtsbild von Hegel bis Max Weber*, Tübingen 1967 (Schriftenreihe wissenschaftlicher Abhandlungen des Leo Baeck Instituts 17), drew attention to the influence of Baur and his circle on Geiger, pp. 122–125.

85. Geiger, *Urschrift*, p. 104.

86. These conceptions would be amplified subsequently in Geiger's elegant and trenchant historical survey of Judaism, *Das Judenthum und seine Geschichte*, 3 vols., Breslau 1865–1871, I, 92–107; III, p. 5.

87. JTSA, Steinschneider Collection, Geiger correspondence. Letter dated 24th May 1859.

88. For the general development, see chapter 2 above.

89. Levi Herzfeld, *Geschichte des Volkes Israel von der Zerstörung des ersten Tempels bis zur Einsetzung des Makkabäers Schimon zum hohen Priester und Fürsten*, 3 vols., Braunschweig–Nordhausen 1847, 1854, 1857. Second editions of volumes II and III were published in Leipzig in 1863 but numbered as volumes I and II. Volume I is cited from the first edition and volumes II and III from the second edition.

90. Levi Herzfeld, *Handelsgeschichte der Juden des Alterthums*, 2nd edn., with a biographical introduction by Gustav Karpeles, Braunschweig 1894, pp. iii–v. The Latin dissertation has the title *Chronologia Judicum et Primorum Regum Hebraeorum*, Berlin 1836. See also Salo W. Baron, "Levi Herzfeld: The First Jewish Economic Historian," in *idem, History and Jewish Historians*, Philadelphia 1964, pp. 322–343.

91. JNUL, 4°792/G-14, Herzfeld to Zunz, 10th April 1836; 4°792/F-1, Zunz to Herzfeld, 1st May 1836, Book II, p. 16.

92. Karpeles, pp. vi–vii.

93. Levi Herzfeld, *Kohelet*, Braunschweig 1838, pp. 1–23; *Israelitische Annalen*, I (1839), pp. 102–104. Zunz preferred to date the book as late as the second century B.C.E. Herzfeld had solicited Zunz to review this work and the latter agreed out of friendship. (JNUL, 4°792/G-14, Herzfeld to Zunz, 1st May 1836.)

94. Herzfeld, *Geschichte des Volkes Israel*, II (1863), p. 66.

95. *Allgemeine Zeitung des Judentums*, 1896, p. 188, Geiger to Joseph Derenbourg, 10th April 1837.

96. See above, pp. 23–26.

97. Karpeles, pp. viii, xxii–xxix.

98. Herzfeld, *Geschichte des Volkes Jisrael*, II (1863), p. vii.

99. *Ibid.*, I (1863), p. 219.

100. *Ibid.*, I (1847), p. 43.

101. *Ibid.*, I (1847), p. 45. For examples of biblical criticism on the dating of canonical books, see *ibid.*, I (1847), pp. 278–302; II (1863), pp. 25, 49–50, 67, 92.

102. *Ibid.*, II (1863), p. 2. Also *ibid.*, I (1863), p. 252.

103. *Ibid.*, I (1863), pp. 233–234; Elias Bickermann, *Der Gott der Makkabäer: Untersuchungen über Sinn und Ursprung der makkabäischen Erhebung*, Berlin 1937, pp. 126–139.

104. Herzfeld, *Geschichte des Volkes Israel*, II (1863), pp. 123–125, 147, 160–161, 180–181, 307–309.

105. *Ibid.*, II (1863), pp. 260–262, 357.

106. Geiger, *Urschrift*, pp. 126–158.

107. Herzfeld, *Geschichte*, II (1863), p. 359. It should be noted that Herzfeld often took issue with the work of Zacharias Frankel. (*Ibid.*, II (1863), pp. 61, 217–218, 382n., 383, 389.)

108. Samuel Holdheim, *Geschichte der Entstehung und Entwicklung der jüdischen Reformgemeinde in Berlin*, Berlin 1857, pp. 142–143, 209, 243 n. 2. For a recent treatment of Holdheim, see Jakob J. Petuchowski, "Abraham Geiger and Samuel Holdheim: Their Differences in Germany and Repercussions in America," in *LBIYB XXII* (1977), pp. 142–149; also Meyer, *Response to Modernity, op. cit.*, pp. 80–84.

109. Holdheim, *Geschichte der Reformgemeinde*, p. 11 note; Immanuel Heinrich Ritter, *Geschichte der jüdischen Reformation*, 3 vols., Berlin 1858–1865, III, p. 37.

110. *Décisions doctrinales du Grand Sanhédrin*, reprinted Jerusalem 1958, pp. 6–9.

111. Samuel Holdheim, *Über die Autonomie der Rabbinen und das Princip der jüdischen Ehe*, 2nd edn., Schwerin 1847, pp. 16–17.

112. *Ibid.*, p. 50.

113. *Ibid.*, pp. 21, 38–49.

114. M. Diogène Tama, *Transactions of the Parisian Sanhedrin*, London 1807, pp. 154, 193–194.

115. Samuel Holdheim, *Gemischte Ehen zwischen Juden und Christen*, Berlin 1850, pp. 6–7.

116. *Protocolle der ersten Rabbiner-Versammlung zu Braunschweig*, Braunschweig 1844, p. 73. *Décisions doctrinales du Grand Sanhédrin*, Paris 1812, pp. 24–27. For reviews of Holdheim's *Autonomie*, see Ritter, *Geschichte der jüdischen Reformation*, III, pp. 103–148.

117. Samuel Holdheim, *Maamar ha-Ishut*, Berlin 1861, pp. 146–153.

118. *Ibid.*, pp. 32–60.

119. *Ibid.*, pp. 76–106.

120. See Ezra Spicehandler, "Joshua Heschel Schorr: Maskil and Eastern European Reformist," *Hebrew Union College Annual*, XXXI (1960), pp. 181–222; XL–XLI (1969–1970), pp. 503–528.

121. The quotation appears in Spicehandler, XXXI (1960), p. 202. The original is in *Israelitische Annalen*, I (1839), pp. 171–172. I have taken the liberty of modifying Spicehandler's translation slightly.

122. *He-Halutz*, V (1860), p. 31.

123. On Geiger's attitude toward Hebrew, see his letter to Zunz dated 12th August 1834 in his *Nachgelassene Schriften*, V, pp. 83–84 and his remarks at the rabbinical conference in Frankfurt in *Protokolle und Aktenstücke der zweiten Rabbiner-Versammlung*, Frankfurt am Main 1845, pp. 32–33. In *He-Halutz*, VI (1861), pp. 13–30, Geiger enlarged on his seminal differentiation between the Sadducees and Pharisees in reference to their *halakhic* views.

124. *He-Halutz*, I (1852), pp. 56–64; II (1853), pp. 58–60; V (1860), pp. 54–66.

125. *He-Halutz*, VI (1861), pp. 47–56.

126. *He-Halutz*, IV (1859), p. 82.

127. *He-Halutz*, VII (1865), pp. 3–80, VIII (1869), pp. 1–82 (on Zoroastrian influence); V (1860), pp. 11–26 (on *Tefillin*).

128. For Geiger's review of the first six volumes of *He-Halutz*, see *Jüdische Zeitschrift für Wissenschaft und Leben*, IV (1866), pp. 67–80.

129. See the entries on him in the *Encyclopaedia Judaica*, X, Berlin 1934, cols. 1138–1139, and *ibid.*, XI, Jerusalem 1972, cols. 444–445. Also Leopold Loew, *Zur neueren Geschichte der Juden in Ungarn*, Budapest 1874.

130. *Ben-Chananja*, 10 vols., Szegedin 1858–1867.

131. Leopold Loew, *Gesammelte Schriften*, ed. by Immanuel Loew, 5 vols., Szegedin 1889–1900, II, pp. 368, 410–411.

132. A. Chorin, *Igereth El Assaf* (in Hebrew and German), Prague 1826; Loew, "Aron Chorin," in *Gesammelte Schriften*, II, pp. 251–420.

133. Leopold Loew, *Die Lebensalter in der jüdischen Literatur*, Szegedin 1875, p. 1.

134. *Idem, Die graphischen Requisiten und Erzeugnisse bei den Juden*, 2 vols., Szegedin 1870–1871, I, pp. 101–102; *Lebensalter*, pp. 211–212; *Graphische Requisiten*, I, pp. 103, 130–131.

135. *Idem, Graphische Requisiten*, II, pp. 108–136. For two later treatments of the same problem, see Hermann L. Strack, *Introduction to the Talmud and Midrash*, New York 1959, pp. 12–20, and Saul Lieberman, "The Publication of the Mishnah," in *idem, Hellenism in Jewish Palestine*, New York 1950, pp. 83–99.

136. Salo Wittmayer Baron, *A Social and Religious History of the Jews*, 3 vols., New York 1937, II, p. 457.

History as Consolation

Hermann Cohen once remarked to Franz Rosenzweig that Leopold Zunz "could have been a great historian but actually was only an antiquarian."[1] Not so. A tad of truth should never be taken for the whole. For all his attention to facts, Zunz was not a pedant. A pedant would never have chosen for his motto an affirmation as ringingly proactive as "echte Wissenschaft ist thaterzeugend" (genuine scholarship creates deeds).[2] Zunz left Judaism transformed. His work repositioned a faith awash in midrashic thinking on the firm foundations of historical knowledge. He softened the resistance to reform, forged alternate bonds of loyalty, and compelled respect for a long-disdained religion. In an era dominated by the institution of the synagogue, Zunz excavated the rich deposits of its literary creativity (both prose and poetry) and then portrayed it as the bearer of national consciousness. Crafted over the course of a lifetime of self-denial, his majestic and intricate history of the synagogue endowed emancipated Judaism with the certitude of unbroken continuity, a new center of religious gravity, and a revitalized sense of self.[3]

Whereas pedants are unerringly deaf to the human need for relevance, Zunz's work pulsated with relevance. In a climate of critical scholarship, meaning simply welled up from fresh springs. Even Zunz was not adverse to reaching beyond the facts and on one occasion ingeniously turned chronological sequence into theological solace. The unparalleled tragedy of the Spanish expulsion, for example, prompted him to allude to the presence of divine concern.

The day of departure on which the temporary delay (of three months) for Spanish Jewry ended, the 2nd of August 1492, was the fast day of *Tisha B'av,* long stamped as a day of calamity. But with the very next day consolation arrived, though inaudible to those suffering: on the 3rd of August, Columbus set sail to discover a new world and a new freedom.[4]

The focus of this essay is one of Zunz's last publications, an unheralded instance of his abiding exertion to nourish Jewish collective memory. In 1872, as his powers began to ebb, he produced a second enlarged edition of a small book of eighty pages, now called *Die Monatstage des Kalenderjahres* (The Days of the Month of the Calendar Year). The unwieldy title was surely a euphemism in place of the blunter title, *Sterbetage* (Days of Death), of the incomplete first edition, which had failed to defer to middle-class sensibilities, though the subtitle *Ein Andenken an Hinge-schiedene* (A Remembrance of Those Departed) in both served to convey a sense of the contents.[5] Arranged by the days of the secular year beginning with January 1, the volume records the *Yahrzeit* of nearly eight hundred Jews and non-Jews, including twenty-two women, as well as the dates of some seventy medieval persecutions of Jews. In most cases, the name is accompanied by a pithy, often piquant description of what made the person memorable. A synopsis of Jewish history, this highly personal assemblage of facts in the service of faith is a window on its author through which no one as yet has been curious enough to cast a glance.

The genesis of this project takes us back to a decade of intense scholarly and public activity, the 1840s, when Zunz stood at the height of his powers. Prussia was politically astir again, with its Jews on edge over impending legislation that threatened to curb their rights and reverse the movement toward full equality. As director of the teachers' seminary of the Jewish Community in Berlin, Zunz occupied an important public post, enhanced by his scholarly reputation, and filled it with the fullness of his being. He never let up on his basic research (publishing *Zur Geschichte und Literatur* in 1845 and completing the editing of Krochmal's *Moreh Nevukhei ha-zeman* in 1846) even as he taught, administered, counseled the government, and wrote a medley of vigorous popular essays on Judaism. In a letter from the summer of 1843, he sketched for Krochmal's impatient son-in-law a rare and vivid self-portrait.

Absorbed by my writing, holding an official post, and set upon by the events and battles of the day, I sometimes envy the lot of those tranquil souls who live in modest retirement with the good fortune to be forgotten by the world, free of trouble and without knowledge of the pain all over.[6]

In short, the record of that decade not only offers the most trenchant refutation of Cohen's characterization, but also forms the context of Zunz's memorial calendar.

The depth of Zunz's engagement bursts forth with unique clarity from his essays, which tackle artfully contemporary issues from the perspective of Jewish history. So, for example, on the occasion of the coronation of Frederick William IV in October 1840, Zunz delivered himself in the main synagogue of an earnest plea for religious renewal and self-respect without any trace of groveling patriotism.

There is so much yet to do for the awakening of our religious souls, for the honor of Israel, for the salvation of our children. Do not wait till the divine spark in them (your children) has died out and they turn coldly away from you and your faith, till they trample on God's covenant and seal a covenant with the world, because they are consumed by the thirst for your vanities, a thirst which nothing can slake, neither gold nor title. . . . If we are ashamed of our faith, if we betray it for base profit, then we are duplicitous with both God and fatherland. We will have sunk to the level of barbarians who trade a treasure for a toy.[7]

One month later Zunz opened the new seminary with an invocation of the spiritual alliance between school, synagogue, and seminary as curators of Jewish consciousness. Again he rose to speak for the supreme value of Jewish continuity.

That we are a single Israelite totality, wish to be and must be, that everyone of us should grow up and mature in this sentiment—for that purpose you need, as the bearer of this knowledge, spiritual institutions to preserve the holy fire, a fire that can bring individual coals to burn collectively even as it melts down the metallic hardness of many a heart. Hospitals alone contribute nothing toward that end.[8]

Nowhere did Zunz enunciate his conservative value system more forcefully than in an 1844 defense of circumcision, the nineteenth-century version of our current "who is a Jew" question. Political pressure and personal distaste combined to induce a growing number of assimilating Jews to reject the rite for their sons. Asked by Baron Amschel Mayer Rothschild of Frankfurt to address the problem publicly, Zunz did much more: he spoke of his conception of Judaism.

Nearly all of our ceremonial laws are in their form and in the living ideas which accompany them the product of history. The great foundation of this historical edifice that binds us to the Bible is called Talmud. But we teach our children that the Talmud is not sacred, is not a law book, is not folk literature, is not an instrument of education . . .[9]

His integrated view of Judaism sought to preserve the historical structure while doing justice to the welter of new historical information. It also explains why Zunz still allotted nearly one-third of the seminary curriculum to the study of Talmud. The canopy of Oral Law wedded development to continuity.[10]

Yet Zunz would definitely not have countenanced setting "the goddess of history . . . over the God of Abraham."[11] He repudiated the facile historicizing of radical Reformers that led to trashing much of Judaism by emptying it of all religious specificity.

Since circumcision is a sign of the unity and eternity of Israel, a visible act of conferring and bequeathing God's law—its omission would be decisive for the next generation: a son left uncircumcised on principle will hardly stay loyal to Judaism on principle. An abrogation of both the Talmud and the messiah (as was the case with the Frankfurt Reform Association), that is with a surrender of both past and present severs Judaism squarely in the middle. Suicide is no reform.[12]

For Zunz the entire class of ceremonial law was an expression of historical loyalty. "Not a single law," he declared in the truculent spirit of Mendelssohn, "was to be sacrificed for equality."[13]

In still another popular essay from that period, Zunz blamed his fellow historians for the indifference toward Jewish history of most literate Jews. Bereft of empathy and integrity, all too many of them cast Jewish history entirely in terms of degeneration. Their works bristled with contempt for their subject, disregarded or distorted the facts, and traduced the major players. As gatekeepers to the past, such historians wholly lacked the tools, knowledge, and disposition to unlock the grandeur of the Jewish saga.

If the ties of language, history, and religion, the idea and its national forms, are thus constantly sundered, don't be amazed if our fashionable Jews quickly sell or put away their Hebrew books and care not a whit about the heroes of our history. . . . It is far better to praise Israel's ancient history two or three times than to defame it once. . . . Wherever art goes under, the artists have preceded it.[14]

Similarly, then, the compilation of *Yahrzeit* dates was a product of that selfsame decade in which Zunz often addressed an audience far larger than that of his scholarly peers. In 1847 he published a first installment of his *Sterbetage* that went as far as March 29.[15] A second installment appeared a year or two later, but only in New York, reaching the end of June.[16] Finally, and surprisingly, the first slender book edition of 1864, which reprinted the first two installments, extended the days of death only down to September 30. Not till 1872 did Zunz seem to have actually completed the project by providing at least one *Yahrzeit* for nearly every single day of the year. In fact, by then the number of *Yahrzeit*s per day had also increased substantially. Zunz, thus, clearly persisted with this unusual project for a quarter of a century as his larger research agenda yielded the biographical and chronological data of Jewish history.

The originality of the work lies in the effort to turn the Gregorian calendar into an instrument of Jewish consciousness. Brilliantly, Zunz made of the traditional *Yahrzeit* a portal into the unfolding world of Jewish history. His memorial calendar of the ordinary year offered a poignant synopsis of the last two millennia of the Jewish experience. And it was no accident that the first installment was published in an annual pocket-size calendar and yearbook for Jews that contained a melange of religious and practical information, of short stories and light history.

The subject of death was very much on Zunz's mind in the 1840s. In 1845 he had published an absorbing essay of one hundred fifty pages, unequaled to this day, on the manner in which Jews historically sought to preserve the memory of the dead. Structured thematically and developmentally, "Das Gedächtniss der Gerechten" (The Remembrance of the Righteous) assembled a staggering amount of information on a vital range of topics, from honorifics used in conjunction with the dead, to the fate of the dead, to the question of whether Judaism admits of a life-after-death to righteous non-Jews, with Zunz concluding that most authorities do, to the evolution of tombstones, to the importance of their inscriptions for reconstructing family history. Amid a plethora of primary sources, philology became the key to unraveling the history of Jewish practice and theology in regard to the dead.[17]

Zunz himself had been orphaned at an early age. His father and first teacher died in 1802, when Zunz was but eight, and a year later, when he was shipped off to the archaic *yeshiva* of Wolfenbüttel, he saw his mother, who was to die in 1809, for the last time.[18] So one senses, beneath the hard surface of Zunz's compressed style, a scintilla of personal anguish when he came to write of what he most lacked as a child.

Parents occupy first place among the living as among the dead. The lofty position assigned to parents by the Law in the very middle of the Ten Commandments, was later emphatically preserved. . . . This religious dogma created in Israel a family life worthy of envy by the Caucasian race, which contributed so vitally to Jewish survival.[19]

I would like to imagine that Zunz's scholarly interest in the unexplored area of commemorating the dead had its deepest roots in his own deprived childhood.

But there is nothing funereal about this majestic survey. Its brisk pace vibrates with a mix of empathy, reverence, and anti-Christian animus, while its ultimate intent is decidedly practical—to prompt Jewish communal leaders to set about preserving the tombstones that have survived the ravages of Christian plunder and Jewish indifference.

Above all, Jewish communities themselves must invest greater care in the preservation of their monuments, an obligation they owe both to the dead and the living. Toward that end, the official registering of all tombstones along with a copy of their inscriptions would be a great initial act of both religious and scholarly piety.[20]

This pioneering and exhaustive piece of scholarship most likely triggered the idea of a memorial calendar. Zunz stressed the age-old duty in Judaism to venerate the names of the departed, with children often named after their parents.

In this manner, names were passed down as objects of veneration. In the Middle Ages, the names of relatives, of famous teachers and benefactors, of persons who had served their community well were formally blessed at public services. One would give charity in their behalf, offer prayers for their salvation, and record their names in the "memorial book."[21]

The specific reference to *Memorbücher* suggests that Zunz's memorial calendar may well have been intended as a modern, secular version of this well-known medieval Ashkenazic genre.

Liturgically inspired in the post-Crusade period and consisting of three distinct sections, the *Memorbuch* lay on the reader's *almemor* table in the middle of the synagogue (hence the name) for frequent public use. It contained the special prayers to be recited after reading the Torah, an ever-growing necrology of local and national leaders individually described, and a martyrology that preserved the names of places and people struck down by persecution. After the pogroms of the Black Death, the *Memorbuch* became a staple of German Jewish liturgy, a tool for socializing the young to the uncertainty of Jewish life and for enriching the content of collective memory.[22] Remarkably, the contents of Zunz's final memorial calendar correspond throughout to the necrology and martyrology of the *Memorbuch*.

Not so his first edition, which failed to record dates of persecutions or acts of martyrdom. What expanded the conception of the popular format was Zunz's monumental work on the liturgical poetry of the medieval synagogue. In 1855 he had published his elegant survey of the corpus known to him, with countless examples in translation. Unexpectedly, *Die synagogale Poesie des Mittelalters*, after a short introduction on the Psalms, starts off with a detour, a searing chronicle of Jewish suffering, whose memorable opening lines betoken its angry, elegiac mood.

If there is a ladder of suffering, then Israel has reached the top. If the span of pain and the patience with which it is borne ennoble, then Jews surely are a match for the nobility of any land. If a literature with but a few classic tragedies be deemed rich, what are we to make of a fifteen-hundred-year tragedy recorded in prose and poetry by the heroic victims themselves?[23]

Yet the reason for the detour is basic: the poetry of the synagogue mirrors the precariousness of reality. The poet often gave voice to the anguish and resentment of the oppressed. Political context alone, Zunz argued, explains the strange commingling of the purest religious sentiments with the most shuddering imprecations for revenge.[24]

In due time, then, Zunz's avocation, his memorial calendar, took on the character of a true *Memorbuch*, with a martyrology as well as a necrology. Of the seventy-odd persecutions entered, many were simply transferred from the chapter compiled for *Die synagogale Poesie*. For example, Zunz had recorded therein that "in the year 1481, in Seville, Jews were slaughtered four times, namely on January 10, March 26, April 21, and November 4."[25] In the later memorial calendar, each onslaught is listed separately under its appropriate day of the year, with the last accompanied by a typical specimen of Zunz's stinging sarcasm. "On November 4, 1481, in Seville, God was entertained with an auto-da-fé."[26]

Indeed, the memorial calendar depicted the reign of terror for Jews as extending well beyond the middle of the sixteenth century, at which point *Die synagogale Poesie* had stopped, by taking special note of the auto-da-fés of the seventeenth century. Witness the following two entries:

On May 5, 1624, the priests of Coimbra (Portugal) burned Dr. Antonio Homem along with three baskets of books, because he admitted to being a Jew. ·

On May 10, 1682, Abraham Lopez Pereira and Isaac de Fonseca were burned in Lisbon. This form of sacrifice, as is well known, did not fall into disuse until after the period of Bayle, Voltaire, and Frederick the Great.[27]

The contempt for Christianity is barely disguised. More important, the addition of the martyrological mode accorded with the traditional and still prevailing view of Jewish survival: a dialectic of suffering and learning, of torment and Torah.

The necrology, of course, addressed the spiritual side of the ledger. At the outset Zunz cautioned not to impute too much significance to the individual names salvaged from the wreckage of the Jewish past. Each fragment enlarged our picture of the whole, and the Jewish experience comprised a valuable part of the total human odyssey. The brief introduction, which went unchanged from 1847 to 1872, intoned his reverential and polemical design.

Since the muse of Jewish history seldom favors her devotees with the age of her heroes, how thankful must we be when the day of death is noted. Thus let us not press too hard as to why one person is considered and another more important overlooked. For where many are wronged and much goes unheard and some still lie buried waiting for a quickening love, there we should not seek to censure or judge, but rather to preserve the memory of those who, if not singlehandedly surely as partners, labored mightily for a common idea. Accordingly, the following pages of remembrance are given over to all those who do not choose to ignore the spokesmen of the spirit if they be Jews or individuals who admired or defended things Jewish.[28]

Nevertheless, the final mosaic bristles with subjectivity. The names chosen and the comments added offer a luminous view of Zunz's own value system. To begin with, his unique erudition is graced by an encompassing spirit of humanity. More than 5 percent of the names entered belong to non-Jews, who, often at great risk, had dared to study Judaism fairly, to defend it publicly, or to advance the cause of political emancipation. Thus Zunz paid tribute to his own teacher of Bible at the University of Berlin, Wilhelm de Wette, "in whose works an undogmatic critical spirit fought against mindless fundamentalism,"[29] and to the scientist Alexander von Humboldt who "bore the most famous name of our day and [who] regarded the Jews as his equal. His word, as his life, were a death knell to the exclusivism of the clerics and to the arrogance of an impoverished nobility."[30] Some like Columbus were listed because, as we saw, they benefited Jews indirectly,[31] and a few like Benjamin Franklin, simply because Zunz admired them: "For him it was enough to be a good man. By means of magnetism, he attracted both flashes of lightning and human hearts."[32] Even Luther's death was noted, though without comment, probably in gratitude for his early defense of Jews.[33]

The magnanimity of Zunz's spirit extended even to those who had chosen to abandon Judaism. A number he knew personally. His own view seemed to accord with that of Lazarus Bendavid, the freethinker who had directed the Jewish Free School of Berlin for twenty years without pay and whom he quoted approvingly. "They [i.e., the converts to Christianity] are splinters, that must be painfully extracted from a clumsy giant. The giant thereby will only get stronger."[34] More concretely, the attrition hurt, but was not life-threatening. On occasion, Judaism's loss became mankind's gain, and Zunz fearlessly honored their memory. Besides passing references to Spinoza, Heine, Josef von Sonnenfels (the Councillor to Joseph II), and the medieval historian Philipp Jaffe, Zunz singled out his lifelong friend Eduard Gans, "who converted to Christianity in Paris on December 12, 1825, but whose finest period of development fell between 1818 and 1823 [i.e., the period of the Verein für Cultur und Wissenschaft der Juden], a period entirely passed over by Laube in his biography."[35] The pathos of the past was intensified by the continued injustice of the present. The creation of a single German Reich in 1870 had failed to diminish the ubiquitous hostility toward Jews, as Zunz wittingly remarked while commenting on the converted writer Ludwig Börne, "On this day [February 13, 1837] L. Börne died in Paris. In 1821 he had written *Der ewige Jude* [a hard-hitting defense of the Jews], and if he were still alive in 1871, he could have written it once again."[36]

But in the final analysis, it is the Jewish cameos of Zunz's gallery that are most captivating. The study of Jewish history had begun to reshape the contours of collective memory. Zunz's empathy heralded the known and enfranchised the forgotten. Though his necrology bore a distinct German complexion, it also revealed a bias for Italian Jews and a steady interest in Jews around the world from Kovno (Abraham Mapu) to New Orleans (Gerson Adersbach).[37] In consequence, the gallery unveiled the bracing diversity of Jewish expression—political leaders and religious teachers, halakhists and aggadists, Karaites and Kabbalists, poets and philosophers, scientists and historians, preachers and printers, commentators and grammarians, and, remarkably, the names of over twenty women like Judith Montefiore, "the wife of Moses and the author of a diary of her trip to Palestine."[38] Throughout, Zunz is at pains to note what survives unpublished of their literary legacy: our knowledge remains so fragmentary.

As curator of this exhibit, Zunz achieves an admirable balance between piety and progress. He recalls the memory of rabbinists and reformers graciously by focusing on the positive. This is not a forum for settling scores. What does offend him deeply, though, is trifling with Judaism. "Already in the year 1813 Abraham Muhr [a prominent Prussian Jewish attorney who died in 1847] had admonished that in matters of religion we ought not tear down old pillars to replace them with the trivia of modernity."[39] Yet Zunz was no less exercised by the willful ignorance of coercive fundamentalists. "On the same day of the month [September 7, 1848], while in Germany, three parliaments proclaimed freedom of conscience, the respected preacher and author Abraham Cohn of Lemberg was poisoned by his pious enemies."[40] The passion lies in the juxtaposition.

The encomium Zunz penned for Naftali Herz Wessely, the finest Hebraic writer of Mendelssohn's circle, flashed a glimpse of his own quest for equilibrium. "A man aglow for beauty and human welfare, who dared to include his love for Israel. He taught his generation that orthodoxy need not consist of decay and ignorance, nor in hatred and intolerance for other religions."[41] Zunz drove home the same point in what he chose to stress in the life of Marcus Herz, the physician who fell under the spell of Immanuel Kant. "Herz had on more than one occasion reprimanded the exclusivists, who condemn or ridicule all knowledge outside their own. He regarded freedom of thought, that is the articulation of what is thought, as a key factor for imbuing whole nations with a measure of good taste."[42] Indeed, the affinity Zunz evinces for such catalytic figures as Rashi, Jacob ben Meir Tam, Abraham Ibn Ezra, David Gans, Efraim Lentschutz, Yomtov Lipman Heller, Nachman

Krochmal, Isaac Benjacob, Solomon Steinheim, and Shlomo Yehuda Rapoport is rooted in the conviction that insularity can only serve to warp a wholesome faith.

By the same token, Zunz displayed a firm reserve toward Kabbalah, enunciated with amusing subtlety. On occasion, facts are marshaled to deflate a myth, as in the case of Isaac Luria, who died in Safed on July 15, 1572. "The Kabbalists of the seventeenth century elevated him to a hero and wonder worker, in much the same manner as the authors of the Zohar had once done with Simeon ben Yohai. Yet his contemporaries, including R. Joseph Karo, had no inkling of such glory."[43] And where the facts were still unknown to Zunz, juxtaposition could serve the same purpose.

September 10, 1676 is the day of death of the alleged messiah Shabbatai Zevi, who left behind no other trace of his activity than the sarcastic and polemical tracts called forth by his following. Jewish literature does owe an eternal debt of gratitude to Edward Pococke [professor of Arabic and Hebrew at Oxford as well as biblical scholar], who died the same day [1691] in Oxford.[44]

Finally, Zunz saw fit to praise Jacob Emden, who merited an ambivalent entry, for undermining the traditional view which attributed the Zohar to R. Simeon ben Yohai. "To this powerful zealot [Emden] goes the honor of being the first to dethrone the mighty Zohar, which he did in the same year that Mendelssohn's *Phädon* appeared [1767]."[45]

In contrast, Zunz betrayed no estrangement from the Hebrew language. It had been his first writing medium back in the yeshiva of Wolfenbüttel. Samuel Meyer Ehrenberg, "his unforgettable teacher and mentor," loved the language deeply, and his own mastery of all its literary and linguistic strata was unrivaled.[46] In consonance with that background, Zunz wrote of the decline of Hebrew at the turn of the eighteenth century with felt emotion. Witness how he chose to etch the memory of Isaac Euchel, who had died in Berlin on June 14, 1804: "The biographer of Mendelssohn, the editor of [a new edition of] Maimonides' *Moreh Nevukhim*, and a co-founder of the epoch-making Hebrew periodical *The Collector* [*Hame'asef*] in April 1783. In the summer of 1800 he lamented already the growing neglect among Jewish youth of the study of Hebrew."[47]

More poignant still is the immediacy of the recollection of Adam Wolfssohn, who had passed away on March 23, 1835 in Fürth at the age of seventy-nine.

One of those men who in the last decades of the previous century worked for enlightenment through translations and Hebrew journals. At the end of 1797, *The Collector* had only 120 subscribers and closed down. Indeed, at the time Wolfssohn said: "It would truly be sad if we should find our hopes dashed and if among all the Jewish inhabitants in Germany there would not be 200 people who would be prepared to offer up two taler annually." Nevertheless, *The Collector*, after it had served its time, did close down and thus provided yet another example that individuals are only the servants of Providence but never Providence itself.[48]

The tone of resignation is nuanced by nostalgia. Zunz was clearly distressed by the erosion of Hebrew as a living language. In retrospect, his selfless decision to edit Krochmal's Hebraic torso should also be regarded as a valiant effort to sustain and enrich the ancient tongue.

Hopefully, our scrutiny of the memorial calendar has mounted a case for celebrating Zunz as one of the great servants of Providence. As Degas taught us, beauty is often viewed best obliquely. From the perspective of his occasional essays, Zunz emerges as anything but a mindless and indifferent pedant. Although he graciously crowned Rapoport as "the founder of the critical phase of Jewish scholarship,"[49] no one did more than Zunz himself in rethinking Judaism historically. By the time he finished, historical consciousness was well on the way to replacing revelation as the ground of Jewish existence. His memorial calendar sought to pour that new wine into old bottles—the institutions of the *Yahrzeit* and the *Memorbuch*—for large scale consumption.[50] Paradoxically, despite the change in *mentalité*, Zunz perpetuated the traditional bipolar vision of the Jewish past as consisting solely of victims and scholars.

NOTES

1. Hermann Cohen, *Jüdische Schriften*, 3 vols., Berlin 1924, I, p. 332. Recently Prof. Michael Stanislawski laid to rest the well-known version of a visit by Judah Leib Gordon to the aged Zunz that was fabricated to deliver the same charge (*For Whom Do I Toil?*, New York and Oxford, 1988, pp. 123–124).

2. Solomon Schechter, "Leopold Zunz," *Studies in Judaism*, 3 vols., Philadelphia 1945, III, p. 117.

3. In addition to the essay by Schechter and the early biography by Shaul Pinchas Rabinowitz, *R. Yomtov Lipman Zunz: His Life, Times, and Books* (Hebrew), Warsaw 1897, one may now consult the accumulating recent scholarship on Zunz: Nahum N. Glatzer, *Leopold Zunz: Jude—Deutscher—Europäer*, Tübingen 1964, pp. 3–72; Michael A. Meyer, *The Origins of the Modern Jew*, Detroit 1967, pp. 144–182; also above chapters 2, 11, and 12.

4. [Leopold] Zunz, *Zur Geschichte und Literatur*, Berlin 1845, p. 526. Cf. Yitzhak Baer, *A History of the Jews in Christian Spain*, 2 vols., Philadelphia 1961, II, pp. 439, 512.

5. L. Zunz, *Sterbetage*, Berlin 1864; *idem, Die Monatstage des Kalenderjahres*, Berlin 1872.

6. Ismar Schorsch, "The Production of a Classic: Zunz as Krochmal's Editor," *LBIYB*, XXXI (1986), p. 299.

7. [Leopold] Zunz, *Gesammelte Schriften*, 3 vols., Berlin 1875–1876, II, pp. 119, 124.

8. *Ibid.*, II, p. 127.

9. *Ibid.*, II, p. 198. On the genesis of Zunz's essay, see JNUL, 4°792/F2, p. 35.

10. See above, p. 253, n.55.

11. Zunz, *Gesammelte Schriften*, II, pp. 199–200.

12. *Ibid.*, II, p. 199.

13. *Ibid.*, II, p. 203.

14. *Ibid.*, II, pp. 186, 190.

15. L. Zunz, "Sterbetage," in Isidor Busch, *Kalendar und Jahrbuch für Israeliten auf des Schaltjahr (1848) 5608*, VI (1847–1848), pp. 87–94.

16. Listed by M[oritz] St[einschneider], *Die Schriften des Dr. L. Zunz*, Berlin 1857, p. 15.

17. *Zur Geschichte*, pp. 304–458.

18. M. Brann, "Mittheilungen aus dem Briefwechsel zwischen Zunz und Kaufmann," *JJGL*, V (1902), p. 190; David Kaufmann, *Gesammelte Schriften*, 3 vols., Frankfurt am Main 1908–1915, I, p. 334.

19. *Zur Geschichte*, p. 319.

20. *Ibid.*, p. 404.

21. *Ibid.*, pp. 318–319.

22. M. Weinberg, "Untersuchungen über das Wesen des Memorbuches," *JJLG*, XVI (1924), pp. 253–320.

23. [Leopold] Zunz, *Die synagogale Poesie des Mittelalters*, Berlin 1855, p. 9.

24. *Ibid.*, p. 58.

25. *Ibid.*, p. 51.

26. *Die Monatstage*, p. 60.

27. *Ibid.*, pp. 25, 27.

28. *Ibid.*, "Vorwort."

29. *Ibid.*, p. 34.

30. *Ibid.*, p. 26.

31. *Ibid.*, p. 28.

32. *Ibid.*, p. 20.

33. *Ibid.*, p. 9; see also *Die synagogale Poesie*, p. 55.

34. *Die Monatstage*, p. 15.

35. *Ibid.*, p. 26.

36. *Ibid.*, p. 8.

37. *Ibid.*, pp. 48, 52.

38. *Ibid.*, p. 53.

39. *Ibid.*, p. 33.

40. *Ibid.*, p. 50.

41. *Ibid.*, p. 14.

42. *Ibid.*, p. 4.

43. *Ibid.*, p. 40.

44. *Ibid.*, p. 50.

45. *Ibid.*, pp. 20–21.

46. Isaak M. Jost, "Vor einem halben Jahrhundert," *Sippurim*, III, pp. 150–152; Leopold Zunz, *Samuel Meyer Ehrenberg*, Braunschweig 1854, p. 43.

47. *Die Monatstage*, p. 33.

48. *Ibid.*, pp. 13–14.

49. *Ibid.*, p. 57.

50. Shaul Pinhas Rabinowitz, in his generally sympathetic biography of Zunz, roundly criticized him for omitting the Hebrew date of each *Yahrzeit*. To Rabinowitz, one of the great transmitters of German-Jewish *Wissenschaft* to the Jews of Eastern Europe, the use of the Hebrew calendar was a matter of national pride and religious integrity. While Rabinowitz deemed the rise of a sense for history as a vital step toward national revival, he abhorred the readiness to assimilate, as exemplified in the choice of calendars (pp. 327–328).

∾ 17

Jewish Studies from 1818 to 1919

Although Judaism has long valued the study of sacred texts as an instrument of piety, the field of Jewish studies as an academic discipline is a product of the emancipation process and the Westernization of Judaism in the nineteenth century. Born of a sense of the profound changes in the context of Jewish life and imbued with the academic ethos of the newly founded University of Berlin (1810) and with the philosophic rhetoric of German Idealism, *Wissenschaft des Judentums* heralded a series of disorienting intellectual shifts: from Christian to Jewish scholarship on Judaism; from dogmatic to undogmatic, but not value-free, scholarship on Judaism; from a partial to a comprehensive conception of Jewish creativity; and from an exegetical to a conceptual mode of thought. What stands out in the subsequent development of the discipline over the next century, beyond its ceaseless growth and bifurcation, is the continued centrality of the German provenance down to the 1930s.

EARLY ACADEMIC CONTEXT

As launched by Leopold Zunz (1794–1886) and his friends in the Verein für Cultur und Wissenschaft der Juden (1819–1824), the application of the historical method to the study of Judaism by university-educated Jews challenged the undisputed Christian monopoly on the subject. Since economic utility had largely dictated the peripheral legal status of pre-emancipation Jews, their spokesmen had scarcely felt the need to transcend the insularity of the ghetto with an "insider's" depiction of Judaism for Christian consumption. In consequence, according to Zunz, "Rarely has the world been presented with more damaging, erroneous, and distorted views than on the subject of the Jewish religion: here, to render odious has been turned into a fine art" (*Etwas über die rabbinische Litteratur,* 1818). Against this backdrop, *Wissenschaft des Judentums* embodies a novel and sustained effort by Jews themselves to recount their history and expound their religion for non-Jews, to dissipate the miasma of misconceptions and prejudice with facts and empathy. From the outset, Zunz intuited the political payoff of the enterprise: public respect for Judaism would be the only secure ground for lasting social integration.

Symptomatic of the prevailing denigration was the exclusion of ancient Jewry from the vaunted field of *Altertumswissenschaft*. Admission was restricted to the Greeks and Romans, for they alone of the nations of antiquity had achieved the level of a learned culture. In his lectures on the discipline, Friedrich August Wolf, famed Homer scholar and one of Zunz's teachers, dismissed Israel's historical claim to equal treatment:

The Hebraic nation did not raise itself to the level of culture, so that one might regard it as a learned, cultured people. It does not even have prose, but only half poetry. Its writers of history are but miserable chroniclers. They could never write in full sentences; this was an invention of the Greeks. (*Vorlesungen über die Altertumswissenschaft*, vol. 1, 1831, p. 14)

Thus, academically as well as philosophically, Judaism was relegated to a preliminary and long-surpassed stage of Oriental history, and hence was consigned to the periphery of Western consciousness.

The absence of any countervailing Jewish scholarship at the time is graphically illustrated by the plight of the young Heinrich Heine, then a member of the Verein when he tried to convey an image of the attractiveness and pathos of medieval Judaism through the medium of a historical novel. The reasons for his failure to complete *Die Rabbi von Bacharach* (1840) are no doubt many, but among them surely is the total absence of empathetical historical works by Jews in German. With the primary Hebrew sources closed to him, Heine, under Zunz's tutelage, was forced to feed on the standard Christian fare, with the result that his imagination soon foundered. By way of contrast, Michael Sach's evocative *Die religiöse Poesie der Juden in Spanien*, which appeared in 1845, did trigger Heine's poetic fantasy and led directly to his richly inventive and deeply felt collection, *Hebräische Melodien* (1851), an eloquent testimony to what he, and German academics, had lacked in 1824.

WISSENSCHAFT DES JUDENTUMS

In terms of method, *Wissenschaft des Judentums* raised an equally formidable challenge to the principles and parameters of traditional Jewish learning. Unfettered by dogmatic considerations, the alienated intellectuals of the Verein, at bitter odds with rabbinism but not prepared to convert, had formed "an association of consciousness" to begin conceptualizing Judaism afresh. Toward that end it embraced the research program enunciated in 1818 by Zunz in his profound, prescient, and determinative work *Etwas über die rabbinische Litteratur.* Convinced that emancipation spelled the end of the Hebraic-rabbinic period of Jewish history, Zunz called for its dispassionate historical assessment. In the process, he demonstrated with stunning detail its dimly realized cultural expanse and diversity. Postbiblical Hebrew literature was authored by Jews of all kinds, not only rabbis, and embraced all the interests of the human mind, not only matters of Jewish law. Given that scope, only the historian was equipped to speak of its genesis and character with any authority. The anticlerical thrust was unmistakable: the canons of modern scholarship were to be enlisted "in order to know and sort out the old which is useful, the antiquated which is detrimental, and the new which is desirable." History presumed to usurp the role of *halakhah* and philosophy as both the arbiter and expositor of Judaism. At issue was a grievously flawed method of learning overgrown with historical myth and error, indifferent to time and contextual analysis, hostile to all non-Hebraic and non-Jewish sources, and crippled by a truncated view of Jewish literature and a static concept of sacred texts.

The comprehensiveness of this vision of the Jewish experience extended into the present. As conceived by Zunz and amplified by Immanuel Wolf in his opening essay for the Verein's ephemeral *Zeitschrift für die Wissenschaft des Judentums* (1823), from whence the name, the field comprised not only the study of a remote past but of a living present. Both as an inner idea and a religious culture, Judaism was still of vital concern to a living community, which itself deserved scholarly attention. In the words of Wolf, "The history of the past is directly followed by the second main division of the subject, i.e., Judaism in the living form in which it lies before us—the general statistical position of the Jews in every country, with special reference to their religious and political circumstances" (*Leo Baeck Institute Year Book*, vol. 2, 1957, p. 202). It is precisely this sense of continuity and connectedness that distinguished the practitioners of *Wissenschaft des Judentums* from those of *Altertumswissenschaft*. For all its appeal and meaning to German neohumanists, *Altertumswissenschaft* was not the uninterrupted cultural legacy of a contemporary community. A century after the Verein, Ismar Elbogen (1874–1943), Weimar's premier Jewish historian, again emphasized this existential dimension of the field by defining it as "the academic study of a vital Judaism, standing in the stream of development, as a sociological and historical unity" (*Festschrift . . . der Hochschule für die Wissenschaft des Judentums*, 1922, p. 141). Its proper academic analogue, claimed Elbogen, was not the study of Greece and Rome but the world of Islam. Given this degree of contemporaneity, *Wissenschaft des Judentums* became the major medium for thinking through the dilemmas generated by Judaism's confrontation with modernity.

ZUNZ'S CONTRIBUTION

What facilitated that use was the shift to a conceptual mode of thought. For all their anticipation of modern scholarship, the pathbreaking Hebrew commentaries accompanying Moses Mendelssohn's translation of the Torah and Wolf Heidenheim's edition of the German cycle of festival prayerbooks both adhered to the traditional exegetical mode, which bespoke the centrality of sacred texts. In consonance with the secular temper of the age, modern scholarship would render the text subordinate to larger issues that required thematic and synthetic treatment. No one searched for new sources more zealously or read old ones more trenchantly than Zunz, but all in the service of questions and constructs that defied the limitations of disjointed analysis. The modern scholarship of eastern European autodidacts, steeped in the thought patterns of rabbinic culture, often failed to reach the level of conceptualization, coherence, and systematization achieved by university-trained practitioners of *Wissenschaft* in the West.

Of the original members of the Verein, Zunz alone remained true to the promise of *Wissenschaft*. Years later Heine would celebrate him as one "who stood firm, constantly and unshakably, in a period of transition, hesitation, and vacillation. . . . A man of words and a man of action, he worked unceasingly, he did what needed doing, at a time when others lost themselves in dreams and sank to the ground, bereft of courage" (quoted in S. S. Prawer's *Heine's Jewish Comedy*, 1983, p. 470). For much of his productive life, Zunz focused his scholarly energy on a history of the synagogue, the institution which he regarded as "the expression of Jewish nationality and the guarantee of its religious existence." In 1832, his *Die gottes-dienstlichen Vorträge der Juden* was published, which first exhibited the full sweep of Midrashic creativity in the synagogue from the third century B.C.E. down to his own day, and from 1855 to 1865 he complemented that work with three volumes: *Die synagogale Poesie das Mittelalters* (1855), *Die Ritus des synagogalen Gottesdienstes* (1859), and *Literaturgeschichte der synagogalen Poesie* (1865), which unveiled the synagogue's undreamed of liturgical richness. The final volume also included the treatment of some six thousand liturgical poems along with the identification of nearly one thousand poets.

That devotion to the history of the synagogue derived from Zunz's conviction that a culture deserved to be studied at its core, in its more quintessential expressions and not on the fringes of its creativity. Not only did he fearlessly refuse to dilute the "parochial" character of Jewish culture, but by portraying it with insight and warmth he meant to raise the self-respect and level of commitment of contemporary Jews. "Genuine scholarship," ran his motto, "gives rise to action." Historical consciousness could serve to augment the depleted forces for Jewish survival.

CONCEPT OF DEVELOPMENT

The upshot of Zunz's massive research on the synagogue was to introduce the concept of development, the trademark of modern historical thought, into the study of rabbinic literature. The urgency of the hour dictated the early agenda of *Wissenschaft* scholars: emancipation seemed to challenge the very nature of a Judaism more rabbinic than biblical. Could subjects entangled in a seamless web of ritual obligations meet the demands of citizenship? Scholars soon moved beyond the inviting freedom of aggadic exegesis to the more problematic realm of rabbinic law to explore its genesis, evolution, and authority. Within two decades, works such as Levi Herzfeld's *Geschichte des Volkes Israel* (3 vols., 1847–1857), Nahman Krochmal's *Moreh Nevukhei ha-Zeman*, edited by Zunz (1851), Heinrich Graetz's *Geschichte der Juden von den ältesten Zeiten bis auf die Gegenwart*, volume 4 (1853), Abraham Geiger's *Urschrift und Uebersetzungen der Bibel* (1857), Zacharias Frankel's *Darkhei ha-Mishnah* (1859), and Joseph Derenbourg's *Essai sur l'histoire et la géographie de la Palestine* (1867) had pierced the darkness of the Persian and Greco-Roman period of Jewish history to illuminate the dynamic origins of the *halakhic* system. For all the disagreement in detail and interpretation, the cumulative effect of their prodigious research was to dissolve a corpus of literature that had long been venerated as a single harmonious entity into its many historical components: namely, early sources, literary forms, exegetical modes, stages of complexity and composition, conflicting protagonists, and formative external influences. While it discomforted Orthodox spokesmen such as Samson R. Hirsch, and although it rested heavily on later rabbinic sources, the research served to show Christian scholars the unabated vitality of Judaism after the Babylonian exile and the responsive nature of rabbinic leadership.

JEWISH SECTARIANISM

At the same time, *Wissenschaft* chipped away at the static rabbinic monolith from yet another direction. As early as 1816, Krochmal, living in the midst of a still-unpunctured traditional society in eastern Galicia, had publicly defended the legitimacy of investigating the literature of the Karaites, who despite their *halakhic* deviance, had never distanced themselves from Jewish suffering. A few years later, Peter Beer of Prague published his *Geschichte, Lehren und Meinungen aller bestandenen und noch bestehenden religiösen Sekten der Juden und der Geheimlehre, oder Cabbalah* (2 vols., 1822–1823), an unabashedly antirabbinic history of Jewish sects (including medieval mystics), which provided a glimpse of the recurring resistance to Talmudic hegemony. At first, much of the interest in Jewish sectarianism focused on the era of the Second Commonwealth, but the steady publication of Karaite manuscripts in the ensuing decades, especially the rich cache by Simhah Pinsker in 1860, prompted works such as Isaak M. Jost's *Geschichte des Judenthums und seiner Sekten* (3 vols., 1857–1859), Heinrich Graetz's *Geschichte der Juden von den ältesten Zeiten bis auf die Gegenwart*, volume 5 (1860), and Julius Fürst's *Geschichte des Karärthums* (3 vols., 1862–1869), which reflect a renewal of the effort at a synthesis of Karaite history, though with insufficient attention to the Islamic ambiance. In Geiger's *Urschrift und Uebersetzungen der Bibel* (1857) and *Das Judentum und seine Geschichte* (3 vols., 1864–1871) the inherent link between sectarianism and *halakhic* development and the possible continuity of sectarian praxis were ingeniously integrated into a single overarching theory. Still more important, Geiger rehabilitated the Pharisees as the progressive party in ancient Judaism and claimed their patrimony for his own movement. The effect was to undercut the penchant among Reform leaders to connect their cause with the Sadducean-Karaite line, an affinity without much benefit.

RABBINIC AND BIBLICAL LITERATURE

The absorption with rabbinic literature was a function of conception as well as need. When Zunz unfurled the agenda of *Wissenschaft des Judentums* in 1818, it was restricted to *"neuhebräische oder jüdische Literatur."* By design he seemed to exclude, for the moment, the study of biblical literature, a subject firmly ensconced in the German university. If scholarship was to facilitate legislation, it had to concentrate on what was least known and most problematic: the nature and history of rabbinic Judaism. And, in fact, the modest amount of biblical scholarship produced by Jews in the nineteenth century bespeaks an avoidance intensified by dogmatic inhibitions but also born of political considerations.

Against this background, what was achieved, while not generally original, was not undistinguished. In *Die gottesdienstlichen Vorträge der Juden* (1832), Zunz already argued for a single author of *Ezra, Nehemiah,* and *Chronicles* and a postexilic date for *Ezekiel.* In later essays, he analyzed the Pentateuch in terms of numerous constituent sources with none earlier than 900 B.C.E. and *Leviticus* following *Ezekiel.* Though Geiger preferred to date *Leviticus* before *Deuteronomy,* he matched Zunz's documentary analysis of the Pentateuch and insisted on the fluidity of the biblical text long after composition. More conservative scholars like Krochmal and Graetz confined their research to the Prophets and the Writings, though often taking leave of traditional views.

The most substantial and lasting Jewish contribution of the century to biblical research, however, came not from Berlin or Breslau but from Padua, where Samuel David Luzzatto, with an unsurpassed knowledge of the Hebrew language, renewed the long-disrupted genre of medieval Jewish exegesis of the Bible. Independent of Protestant scholarship and rooted in the distinctive style of Italian Judaism, Luzzatto's Hebrew commentaries were anything but doctrinaire. Unfortunately, by the last quarter of the century the rising tide of German antisemitism also seeped into the halls of the university and retarded the acceptance of the documentary hypothesis by Jewish scholars for decades. In 1910, the rabbinical seminary in Breslau still excluded modern biblical criticism from its curriculum.

SPANISH JUDAISM

Zunz's modest proposal of 1818 ended with the charge to undertake the publishing of largely unknown but classical specimens of "rabbinic literature" in order to begin to banish the contempt in which it was held. By way of example, he declared his intention to bring out a scholarly edition with Latin translation of a Hebrew philosophical treatise by Shem Tob ibn Falaquera, a thirteenth-century Spanish Jew. The identification of the best of Hebrew literature with medieval Spain epitomized the Sephardic bias so vital to emancipated Ashkenazim in search of legitimacy. With roots going back to the seventeenth century, the attraction of Spanish Jewry and its descendants became a pervasive cultural force in nineteenth-century German Jewry, finding diverse expression in liturgy, synagogue architecture, literature, and, of course, scholarship.

Young scholars, whose own intellectual emancipation often started with Moses Maimonides' *Guide of the Perplexed* and the Hebrew literature of the *Haskalah*, gravitated naturally to the poetic and philosophical legacy of Spain. Ironically, the term *golden age*, which is used to highlight Jewish cultural creativity in Muslim Spain, is not of Jewish provenance. It was first bestowed by Franz Delitzsch, the greatest Christian scholar of Judaism in the nineteenth century, in his *Zur Geschichte der jüdischen Poësie* (1836), in which he depicted the two centuries from 940 to 1140 as the golden and silver ages respectively of Jewish poetic achievement. But the term accorded fully with the needs and perceptions of German Jewry, and despite the heroic effort by a penitent Zunz not to ignore the dissimilar but equally impressive cultural achievements of medieval Ashkenazic Jewry, the *Wissenschaft* of a long line of scholars served to deepen and solidify the bias. At the same time, their failure to generate much sympathy for the mystical side of Spanish Judaism was a consequence of their own rational bent, compounded by outrage at the unfounded historical claims of the mystics themselves.

The attraction to cultural history was reinforced by a decided aversion to political history. To work out a conceptualization that would have done justice to the unconventional political history of Diaspora Jewry would have produced more flak than self-esteem. The embattled position of German Jewry militated against the subject. When Michael Sachs decided to produce *Die religiöse Poësie der Juden in Spanien* (1845), a volume of medieval religious poetry in translation, he settled on Spain because of the widely held view, going back to Shlomoh Yehudah Rapoport, that Sephardic poets addressed God as lonely believers, whereas Ashkenazic poets only lamented the fate of the nation. Sachs specifically asked Luzzatto, who had agreed to supply him material, not to send any "national poems." Somewhat later, in volume five of his *Geschichte der Juden*, Graetz did declaim with courage that the medieval Jewish experience betrays a political dimension, but he failed completely to demonstrate it. Neither he nor his colleagues moved beyond the older Spanish conception of Jewish political history as one of recurring persecution, though they amplified it factually and emotionally. On occasion, isolated works of political history such as Selig Cassel's "Geschichte der Juden" in the *Allgemeine Encyklopädie der Wissenschaften und Künste* (1850), Otto Stobbe's *Die Juden in Deutschland während des Mittelalters in politischer, socialer und rechtlicher Beziehung* (1866), and a volume of *Regesten zur Geschichte der Juden in Deutschland während des Mittelalters* (1862) by Meir Wiener did reveal just how much the systematic use of non-Jewish archival sources could enlarge and enrich the conception of the subject, but Graetz, with whom Stobbe worked closely, remained skeptical about their large-scale utility.

INSTITUTIONAL STANDING

By the mid-1870s when the founders of jüdische Wissenschaft had completed most if not all of their work (only Zunz, Steinschneider, and Graetz were still living, though Zunz was no longer productive), the study of Judaism had all the signs of an academic discipline except one: inclusion in the structure of the German university, the premier research institution of the century. Though a direct product of its research imperative, *Wissenschaft des Judentums* matured entirely outside the framework of the university. Jewish scholars as its primary practitioners were never accorded the university's recognition and support. The occasional appointment of a *Privatdozent* or *Honorarprofessor* in a cognate field was but the trappings of academic respectability. Of course, that was exactly the kind of institutional affiliation, given their commitment to undogmatic scholarship and their resentment of rabbinic leadership, for which the founders yearned. Typical of faculty and bureaucratic resistance to the idea was the rebuff administered to Zunz in 1848 by the philosophy faculty of the University of Berlin to his request to create a chair in Jewish history and literature. Such a chair, it was felt, smacked of confessional interests and would merely strengthen Jewish parochialism. Misreading Zunz's intent, the faculty declared that it was not the function of the university to train rabbis. In the German context, such exclusion, which was, to be sure, experienced for a time by other nascent fields, meant the denial of the discipline's universal significance and doomed hardy aficionados to eke out a living in circumstances that were often trying. Increasingly, young scholars had little choice but to enter the ranks of a rabbinate in transition and to "make" the time for sustained research.

The creation of the Jewish Theological Seminary in Breslau in 1854 from the largess of a single Jewish benefactor finally provided an institutional base for the floundering field and cemented its connection with the modern rabbinate. With a curriculum informed by *Wissenschaft des Judentums*, a small faculty immersed in it, and a scholarly journal promoting it, Breslau became the model for all modern rabbinical seminaries established during the next half-century in central and western Europe and the United States. Despite denominational differences, these institutions determined the scholarly character of the modern rabbinate, until it was modified again at the turn of the century by the changing social and political needs of the Jewish community. Its graduates brought to the pulpit a lively commitment to deepen as well as to disseminate the new mode of Jewish learning.

But Zunz and Moritz Steinschneider viewed these developments with dismay, regarding much of the scholarship coming out of Breslau as dogmatic and pretentious. Twice in the 1870s, Steinschneider, a man of awesome learning, prodigious output, and extensive personal contacts with non-Jewish scholars, preferred to turn down invitations from new seminaries in Berlin and Budapest and to stay at his modest post as director of the girls' school of the Berlin Jewish community. In 1876, he reaffirmed the original integrationist vision with typical acerbity:

Institutions to preserve the rabbinate in the form acquired during the last centuries promote systematic hypocrisy and scholarly immaturity. What is scholarly about Jewish history and literature has no need to avoid the atmosphere of the university and must be made accessible to Christians. The task of our time seems to me, above all, to call for the temporary funding [obviously with Jewish money—I.S.] of unpaid instructorships for Jewish history and literature at philosophical faculties, so that governments will be prompted to create professorships and institutions in which matriculated Gymnasium students might prepare themselves for the study of Hebrew literature. (*Jewish Studies in Memory of George A. Kohut*, ed. Salo W. Baron and Alexander Marx, 1935, p. 521)

When Steinschneider shared his reasons for refusal with his old mentor and life-long friend, Heinrich L. Fleischer, Germany's leading Orientalist, the latter, sensing the futility of such expectations, chided him for his errant purism: "If men like you deny your cooperation, have you then still a right to complain about the new institution's lack of success? Why not get involved from the outset in the hope that in this way the better will triumph?" (letter of 1 July 1875, Fleischer correspondence from the "Steinschneider Papers," archives of the Jewish Theological Seminary).

No scholar among the *Wissenschaft* pioneers contributed more to validating the right to university admission for Jewish studies than Steinschneider himself. With his matchless command of unpublished sources, he painstakingly reconstructed the unsuspected and seminal role that medieval Jews in the Islamic world had played in the transmission of Greco-Roman culture to the Christian West. His oeuvre, especially his massive *Die hebraeischen Übersetzungen des Mittelalters und die Juden als Dolmetscher* (2 vols., 1893), demonstrated for the first time the existence of a cultural unity in the medieval world that transcended religious differences, a theme that would continue to exercise Jewish scholars in the twentieth century. For instance, at Harvard, Harry A. Wolfson would try to integrate the parallel traditions of medieval religious philosophy into a single universe of discourse that prevailed from Philo to Spinoza. And at Princeton, on the basis of the inexhaustible documentary wealth of the Cairo Geniza, Shlomo D. Goitein would portray the social, economic, and material contours of a medieval Mediterranean society through the prism of Jewish sources.

TURN OF THE CENTURY

The engagement of Jewish scholarship with the vital concerns of a dynamic community was, if anything, intensified by the unsettling events of Jewish history in the twentieth century. In particular, the resurgence and diffusion of antisemitism at the turn of the century added to the inherent momentum toward specialization and institutionalization which the discipline had already generated in the course of the century. Even without this intrusion, the remarkable sweep of early *Wissenschaft* works would hardly have survived the growing technical complexity of the field. In 1897 alone, Solomon Schechter brought back to Cambridge from the Cairo Geniza, which he had emptied, some 100,000 literary fragments pertaining to nearly fifteen hundred years of Jewish history in the Greco-Roman and Islamic worlds. Thus, new sources, interests, and anxieties expanded Jewish scholarship into a movement of international proportions.

HISTORICAL SOCIETIES

The last decades of the nineteenth century give evidence of a chain reaction across the Jewish world in the formation of national Jewish historical societies. With the overt intention of stimulating research on the antiquity, fate, and contribution of Jews in their respective lands of settlement, these societies betray all the anxiousness of insecurity. But they also testify to the emergence of a cadre of indigenous scholars. The first to be founded in Paris in 1880 was the Société des Études Juives, which published the triannual *Revue des études juives* (1880–), designed to accomplish two ends. By casting its net over the entire field of Jewish studies, the *Revue* served to challenge the German hegemony embodied in Breslau's *Monatsschrift für die Geschichte und Wissenschaft des Judentums* (1851–1939), a policy that accorded with the rancor sown by the Franco-Prussian War. At the same time, the *Revue* placed at the heart of its agenda the twofold intent of encouraging the study of Jews in the history of France and of French Jews in the history of medieval Judaism. By 1897 the new subfield could boast of a volume of universal Jewish import. In *Gallia Judaica* (1897) Henri Gross, Hungarian-born as were so many of the *Wissenschaft* circle, produced a geographical dictionary that listed, along with ample historical information, all French localities in which Jews are known to have lived according to medieval Hebrew sources. In the twentieth century, this accomplishment became the model for the *Germania Judaica* (1917–) of the Gesellschaft zur Förderung der Wissenschaft des Judentums and the *Sefer ha-Yishuv* (1939–) of the Palestine Historical and Ethnographical Society.

AMERICAN SCHOLARSHIP

In America too, Jewish scholarship was enlisted to stem the growth in antisemitism set off by the massive influx of eastern European Jews. Jewish notables exploited the occasion of the four-hundredth anniversary of Columbus's discovery of America in 1892 to create an American Jewish Historical Society, which would restrict its mission to assembling data on the role of Jews in "the discovery, settlement, and development of our land." Its president, Oscar S. Straus, who had served as the American ambassador to Constantinople a few years before, invited and funded a noted European scholar of Spanish Jewish history, Meyer Kayserling of Budapest, to write *Christopher Columbus and the Participation of the Jews in the Spanish and Portuguese Discoveries* (1894) to "bring to light the extent to which our race had direct part and share with Columbus in the discovery of our continent." Straus hoped that the historical confirmation of "this fact would be an answer for all time to come to anti-Semitic tendencies in this country."

Far more important than Kayserling's careful study of 1894 was the publication in 1901–1906 of the twelve-volume *Jewish Encyclopedia,* edited by Isidore Singer and Cyrus Adler, by the non-Jewish firm of Funk and Wagnalls. Produced in a land on the fringes of the *Wissenschaft* movement with no scholarly tradition of its own, this first Jewish encyclopedia represented a collective venture of huge proportions and astonishingly high quality, a magnificent summation of nearly a century of Jewish scholarship, and, above all, the transplantation of *Wissenschaft des Judentums* to America. But the level of scholarly attainment should not obscure the pragmatic concerns of its genesis. The preface alluded to the anxieties of the moment: ". . . the world's interest in Jews is perhaps keener than ever before. Recent events, to which more direct reference need not be made, have aroused the world's curiosity as to the history and condition of a people which has been able to accomplish so much under such adverse conditions." Accordingly, the editors were eager to present a balanced picture of Jews as both integrated and parochial, as both cosmopolitans and cultivators of their own traditions.

ANGLO-JEWISH SCHOLARSHIP

The founding of *The Jewish Quarterly Review* in 1888 and the Jewish Historical Society of England in 1893 certainly suggests a similar set of circumstances for Anglo-Jewry. The fact that Lucien Wolf launched the research program of the society in 1901 with his splendid edition of *Menasseh ben Israel's Mission to Oliver Cromwell* reflects the same need as felt in America for a "foundation myth" that intersects at a decisive juncture with the history of the nation. In one sense both Wolf's texts and the very idea of the society owed their patrimony to Heinreich Graetz, who in his address to the immensely successful Anglo-Jewish Historical Exhibition of 1887 had called for an organized scholarly effort to study local history. *The Jewish Quarterly Review,* on the other hand, became the academic organ for a talented cluster of English scholars who had gathered around the charismatic figure of Solomon Schechter. For two decades it not only encompassed the full panoply of Jewish studies, but also often protested the jaundiced scholarship on ancient Judaism coming out of Germany.

RUSSIAN SCHOLARSHIP

Under the guidance of Simon Dubnow, the small and ever more beleaguered liberal sector of Russian Jewry also began to display an interest in the study of local history to firm up its sense of belonging and distinctiveness. Fully aware of the social role of Jewish scholarship in the West, the young Dubnow transformed his own religious alienation into a lifelong program for the cultivation of historical consciousness. In 1891 to 1892, he issued appeals in Russian and Hebrew to set up a Jewish historical society that would coordinate a nationwide effort to collect the diverse sources, fast disappearing, related to the nine-hundred-year history of Jews in Poland and Russia. He pointed with envy to what had been accomplished in the West and berated Russian Jews for failing to realize the cohesive power of historical consciousness. However, his own conception of Jewish history had already begun to diverge from that of his *Wissenschaft* mentors. While he too stressed the greater importance of internal Jewish sources, he articulated for the first time a vision of Jewish political history in the Diaspora that went far beyond the passive endurance of persecution. In the institution of the *kahal*, Diaspora Jews, wherever they settled, had created a unique instrument of national self-government that preserved a large measure of political initiative. The still-unemancipated status and traditional character of Russian Jewry had sensitized Dubnow to the medieval political expression of Jewish nationhood, and he pleaded for the sources to study its history. In his *History of the Jews in Russia and Poland* (3 vols., Eng. ed., 1916–1920) and *Weltgeschichte des jüdischen Volkes* (10 vols., 1925–1929), Dubnow not only combined his many preliminary studies into a coherent narrative of a millennium of Jewish history in Poland and Russia, but also fully formulated and espoused his theory of Diaspora nationalism.

Dubnow's original proposal finally bore fruit in 1908 in Saint Petersburg with the founding of the Russian Jewish Historical Ethnographic Society by Maxim Vinaver and David Günzberg. Also at Saint Petersburg that same year, the scholarly, aristocratic Günzberg opened at his own expense an academy of Jewish studies in which Dubnow delivered public lectures on Jewish history and conducted seminars for advanced students, whose rank included some of the leading Zionist historians of the next generation. Most important of all, Dubnow's call to collect and record had become part of the credo of the nationalist Jewish renaissance emanating from Saint Petersburg. In the last three years before the war, the writer Solomon Anski led an ambitious ethnographic expedition sponsored by the society into the Jewish hinterland of the Ukraine to plumb its rich deposits of folklore and iconography, bringing back thousands of photographs, tales, folkways, manuscripts, and artifacts. In 1915, Issachar Ryback, a young art student, financed his own study of the wooden synagogues of White Russia, and in 1916 the society sent him and fellow artist El Lissitzky back to the Ukraine to do the same for its synagogues. In a far more somber vein, Anski in *Khurbm Galitsye* (1921) documented the agony of Galician Jewry inflicted by war in a monumental memoir of his heroic relief mission, and Eliyahu Cherikover, entirely in the spirit of Dubnow, organized and administered at great personal risk during the years 1918 to 1920 an archive to record the unparalleled slaughter of as many as seventy-five thousand Ukrainian Jews amidst the chaos of civil war.

FOLKLORE

The wholesale consumption of Jewish folklore in Russia exuded all the enthusiasm of the populist fervor unleashed by the socialist and Zionist rebellions at the turn of the century. But as an academic field, its origins lie in Germany, and as such it marked a sharp departure from the preoccupation with high culture that absorbed the founders of *jüdische Wissenschaft*. With fewer acknowledged luminaries than in the Sephardic world to distract them, the early students of Ashkenazic Judaism were forced to look at popular expressions of religious culture. The skein of development runs from the midcentury writers of ghetto novellas about central European Jewish life at the threshold of emancipation through the often overlooked collection of Judeo-German proverbs and expressions, *Sprichwörter und Redensarten deutsch-jüdischer Vorzeit* (1860) by Abraham Tendlau, the pioneering social histories of medieval Ashkenazic Jewry in Abraham Berliner's *Aus dem inneren Leben der deutschen Juden im Mittelalter* (1871), and Moritz Güdemann's *Geschichte des Erziehungswesens und der Cultur der abendländischen Juden während des Mittelalters und der neueren Zeit* (3 vols., 1880–1888), to Max Grunwald's work at the end of the century. A graduate of Breslau and rabbi in Hamburg, Grunwald delivered a manifesto in 1896 urging the creation of a society, museum, and journal of Jewish folklore, and two years later he began publishing the first number of the *Mitteilungen der jüdischen Volkskunde* (1898–1929), which he was to edit single-handedly in different formats for thirty volumes. That the first chair in Jewish folklore established at the Hebrew University in 1973 bears the name of this polymath is resounding testimony to his decisive role in launching the field.

The fascination with folklore signaled a broadly felt need to reconnect with the irrational, to reinvigorate an excessively cerebral tradition with the life-giving forces of imagination. Rabbinic Judaism as codified in the East or spiritualized in the West did not exhaust the record of Jewish lore and legend begun in the first decade of the twentieth century by scholars as diverse as Martin Buber, Hayyim Bialik and Yehoshua Ravnitzki, Louis Ginzberg, and Micha Josef Berdyczewski. Ginzberg's monumental *The Legends of the Jews* (7 vols., 1909–1938), elegantly designed for scholar and layman alike, not only revealed the popular wellsprings of rabbinic religion, but also demonstrated the extent to which Jewish legends preserved and mediated the folklore of antiquity.

ART

Jewish art, as cultural expression and scholarly discipline, was similarly invigorated by the discoveries of folklore. In no area of contemporary Jewish life did creativity require quite as urgently the validation and inspiration of a historical tradition. Jewish artists and historians faced the same deep-seated stereotype, shared by friend and foe alike, that Jews by virtue of religion and race were singularly bereft of any aesthetic sensibility. But dramatic historical evidence to the contrary began to mount: the exhibition of the Isaac Strauss collection in Paris in 1878, the publication of the Sarajevo Haggadah in 1898 along with the recovery of a Jewish tradition of manuscript illumination, the formation of Jewish art societies and collections, the publication in 1916 of *Antike Synagogen in Galilaea* by Heinrich Kohl and Carl Watzinger of the first study of Galilean synagogues, and, above all, the plethora of folk art unearthed in the wooden synagogues of Russia. For artists projecting a secular Jewish culture, historians were supplying the resources of an indigenous past. In the beautiful pages of *Rimon*, a lavish magazine of Jewish arts and letters published in Berlin after the war in both a Hebrew and Yiddish edition, the artistic and historical dimensions converged symbiotically.

SOCIOLOGY

From Jewish folklore to sociology was but a small step, for the interest remained primarily non-elitist. The impetus for this expansion of Jewish scholarship came directly from the nascent Zionist movement. Although Zunz had clearly foreshadowed the sociological study of the Jews in a programmatic essay in 1823, *Grundlinien zu einen künftigen Statistik der Juden*, it took the Zionist indictment of assimilation with all its putatively alarming consequences for Jewish survival to effect a scholarly shift to the present. At the fifth Zionist Congress in 1901, Max Nordau, who annually treated the delegates to a foreboding assessment of the Jewish situation, called for the systematic assemblage of data to confirm the Zionist consensus. The proposal took institutional form three years later in Berlin in the Bureau für Jüdische Statistik, manned by a small staff of unpaid Zionists, which for the next eighteen years would publish an invaluable journal for Jewish demography and statistics. Its first editor, till he went to Israel in 1908 to head the Palestine Office of the Zionist Organization, was Arthur Ruppin, who in 1904 had produced in his *Die Juden der Gegenwart* the first work of Jewish sociology. Not surprisingly, the first generation of scholars was drawn largely from the ranks of Zionists. By 1930 Ruppin's own research had grown into a sweeping two-volume *Soziologie der Juden* (1930–1931), and in 1938 he was the natural candidate for the Hebrew University's first professor of Jewish sociology.

EARLY TWENTIETH-CENTURY SCHOLARSHIP

The first century of Jewish studies ends where it began, in Berlin, with the formation of another association of young scholars still in rebellion against rabbinic ascendancy. In 1919 Eugen Täubler, this time with substantial Jewish backing, founded the Akademie für die Wissenschaft des Judentums. The idea was the outgrowth of a *cri de coeur* in 1917 by Franz Rosenzweig to German Jewry to revitalize its scholarly forces against the onslaught on ancient Judaism by the ever more confident scholarship of liberal Protestantism. Judaism's exclusion from the university remained unaltered, its incorporation into German society riddled with problems, and its laity unequipped for adversity. In final form, the academy, stripped of any polemical or educational intent, came to represent German Jewry's last attempt to bring *Wissenschaft des Judentums* out of its academic isolation and thereby to set its course for the twentieth century. In Täubler the academy had a classicist trained by Theodor Mommsen yet fully conversant with Jewish sources, a historical thinker of great conceptual power, and a proven administrator, who some years before had organized a national Jewish archive as the central repository for Jewish communal records.

As enunciated by Täubler, the mission of the academy was to end *jüdische Wissenschaft's* obsession with antisemitism and reliance on practicing rabbis and to reunite it with the highest standards of modern scholarship. This meant specialization, systematic use of non-Jewish archival sources, philological analysis broadly conceived, and contextual and comparative research. Talmudic research in particular still suffered from the absence of a firm philological basis. Täubler dreamed of creating eventually a library of critical editions of all Jewish texts prior to the eighteenth century. In the meantime, he divided the field of Jewish studies into nine distinct specialities, delineated the nature of ancillary instruments of resources, and funded the research of young scholars like Chanokh Albeck, Yitzhak Baer, David H. Baneth, Arthur Spanier, and Selma Stern.

Three years after Täubler died in 1950 in Cincinnati, he was eulogized in Jerusalem by Baer, Moshe Schwabe, and Benzion Dinur, three men whose lives he touched deeply. But the tribute signified more than personal indebtedness. The very conceptualization, ethos, and instruments of Jewish studies as they came to be embodied in the Hebrew University after 1924 were conceived by Täubler in Berlin. The professionalization of Jewish scholarship was under way, though communal concerns would continue to influence research agendas.

German Judaism: From Confession to Culture

Permit me to introduce my topic with an allusion to the scientific contribution of Niels Bohr. Years ago he defended the dual manner in which physicists spoke of light with a theory of complementarity.

So remote is that strange quantum world of the atom that, if we wish to visualize it, a single everyday picture will not suffice. We are reduced to using pairs of conflicting complementary images. Never mind that the wave and particle images are contradictory. We need them both. They merely complement one another.[1]

The profundity of that theory lies in the recognition that the complexity of certain phenomena defies reduction to a single theory or metaphor. The behavior of light at certain times is best accounted for in terms of waves, at others in terms of particles. The search for truth is best served by contradiction.

While I do not presume to understand the substance behind Bohr's theory, I have long felt that as a statement of method it has great relevance for the historian. The complex objects of our scrutiny are often not exhausted by a single focus, depiction, explanation, or theory. Like a stereoscope, they benefit from more than one perspective, without any promise of ultimate integration. In regard to a subject as involved and differentiated as the state of Weimar Judaism, no one sweeping generalization will do justice to the full reality. For in truth, Judaism on German soil in its final years of emancipation was riven by countervailing forces, by a rising rate of attrition and a spiritual resurgence that cannot be caught in a one-dimensional assessment. The conflicting religious patterns which appear bespeak the responses of individual Jews in the aggregate to the turbulence of Weimar Germany. Time constraints allow me to address my attention to only two of these patterns, mutually exclusive but not equally significant.

The first which quickly comes to mind is epitomized in the title of Felix Theilhaber's strident and bellicose book, *Der Untergang der deutschen Juden*, first published in 1911 and then again ten years later in a revised version to rebut his many critics. The book represented an early and extreme example of the largely Zionist-inspired scholarly discipline of Jewish sociology and drew an alarming picture of the disintegrating impact of emancipation and modernity on German Jewry as an organized group. A dwindling birth rate and ever larger numbers of exogamous marriages and conversions to Christianity foreboded an irreversible depletion of Jewish manpower. Constituted as a religious confession, German Judaism seemed unable to stem and therefore to survive the steady erosion of its demographic base. The primacy of group interests had fallen victim to rampant individualism.[2]

In 1920 Max Brod re-echoed the lament in softer and more personal terms. His "Elegie an die abgefallenen Juden" is a poetic depiction, laden with pathos, of the author's imaginary visit to a vast cemetery of living corpses, of Jews who have forsaken their ancestral ties. But to our astonishment, we are not treated to an outburst of self-righteousness against the unfaithful. On the contrary, the occupants of the cemetery are depicted mainly as youngsters failed by a stern and uncaring Judaism, by parents and teachers who did not reach out to attend to the varied spiritual needs of their children. Not social forces but spiritual deprivation is to blame for the alienation of the young. The poem is a powerful indictment of a community of adults whose shallowness and selfishness threaten to forfeit the Jewish future. Like Theilhaber, Brod was grim about the inner resources available to retain the allegiance of the individual Jew.[3]

But a surge of spiritual and cultural creativity was already well underway, and it is this second pattern that I wish to examine at greater length. National Socialism did not bury a Judaism on the brink of religious exhaustion. If one sector of the community is indeed best accounted for in terms of spiritual bankruptcy, the behavior of another sector constituted a dramatic polar opposite, whose singular achievement was to deepen and culminate the development of a distinct Jewish subculture in a relatively open and voluntaristic social setting. Though German Judaism did exhibit many of the ravages of assimilation, it also demonstrated the ability to generate new cohesion through cultural vitality.

The existence of this German-Jewish subculture can be most vividly illustrated in the eighty-three slim volumes published by the Schocken Verlag from the end of 1933 to 1938 under the rubric of *Bücherei des Schocken Verlags*. Probably conceived by Salman Schocken himself, the series was designed to select from the wellsprings of all of Jewish literature texts of peculiar relevance to Jewish readers in Nazi Germany. In the spirit of the very first title—Isaiah's prophecies of comfort in the new translation by Buber and Rosenzweig—each selection vibrated with levels of meaning that comprised consolation and instruction.[4] But what is most remarkable about this inspired series is its almost unbounded cultural range and the speed at which it was produced. The eighty-three titles convey a conception of Judaism as a religious civilization that spans the Bible, rabbinic literature, medieval and modern Hebrew poetry, philosophy and mysticism, folklore and popular culture, letters and memoirs, modern *belles lettres* and poetry in German and Yiddish, as well as works of Jewish history and historical sources. The format of the series made it somewhat difficult to do more than allude to the accumulating expressions of Jewish music and art.[5]

After the publication of the first five volumes in November and December of 1933, the plan was to put out two volumes a month or a total of twenty-four volumes a year, a figure which was in fact achieved only for one year, in 1935. Nevertheless, the production of a German library of ninety-two volumes of Jewish culture over a period of five years is testimony not only to the urgency of the hour and the dedication of Moritz Spitzer and Lambert Schneider, but also to the very existence of a living cultural legacy. Had that legacy lain inert and uncultivated in Germany since the emancipation, the *Schocken Bücherei* would hardly have managed to put out more than a few consolatory titles. But no *creatio ex nihilo* was called for; there already existed a vibrant subculture to sample and consolidate, because much of the past had steadily been appropriated by a present bent on adding its own distinct voice. In fact, a vast part of the Jewish output of the Schocken Publishing Company from 1931 to 1938—some 225 titles reflecting a dozen literary genres—reinforces the impression of a flourishing Jewish subculture in the German language.⁶

The creation of a dynamic religious subculture in an age dominated by centrifugal forces constitutes the greatest achievement of the Jews in modern Germany. On the basis of a reorganized local community and a growing network of national institutions, German Jewry erected a cultural superstructure that confuted the conviction that Jewish culture was a function of political and social exclusion. The Westernization of Judaism, first effected in Germany, was an exercise in creative cultural transmission, a dialectic between inner resiliency and external stimulation. Its rich cultural sediment yielded a Jewish version of German *Bildung*. To the atomized Jew, the most vulnerable victim of assimilation, it held out an infusion of memories and meanings that in moments of receptivity might renew his group consciousness and religious pride. Jewish culture provided the attuned individual with a sense of connectedness to the past, an awareness of other Jewish communities in the present, and a source of spiritual resistance for the future.⁷

There is no doubt that the extraordinary religious and intellectual ferment of Weimar Jewry contributed mightily to the cultural edifice of German Judaism, but it was not a building erected overnight. Since the days of Mendelssohn individual Jews had been producing works of mediation in the service of Judaism and works of confrontation that aired aspects of Judaism incongruent with the modern world. For all its originality, the cultural dynamism of Weimar Judaism is part of a gradual emergence of religious culture that spans the previous century. The rest of this essay will seek to give some evidence of its growth and manner of diffusion, for unmediated culture is of little social import.

The first cogent evidence for the phenomenon is to be found in the *Institut zur Förderung der israelitischen Literatur* formed by Ludwig Philippson in 1855. In February of that year Philippson had issued an appeal to "all German-reading Israelites to found an Israelite literary society" that would devote itself to the publication of works relating to some aspect of Judaism. The avowed purpose was to create the reading public for such books, to counter the absence of a market that destined Jewish works to single limited editions. By April Philippson had sprung a Jewish book club with nearly 1,100 members from across Western Europe, though mostly in Germany, each paying an annual fee of two talers for one copy of every publication.[8]

That the idea for German Jewry's first book club should have come from Philippson was not entirely fortuitous. As editor of the first national Jewish newspaper in Germany begun in 1837, the *Allgemeine Zeitung des Judentums,* he presided over a powerful new catalyst of Jewish culture. While its weekly pages were devoted to informed discussion of contemporary Jewish issues and to the reporting of Jewish current events from around the world, its monthly *feuilleton* generated a steady fare of Jewish *belles lettres,* poetry, memoirs, and translations. Philippson himself became one of the most prolific writers of Jewish historical novels of the century. In retrospect, he was the first of a versatile, energetic, and learned group of editors—men like Marcus Lehmann of *Der Israelit,* Hirsch Hildesheimer of the *Jüdische Presse,* Gustav Karpeles of the *Allgemeine Zeitung des Judentums,* Ludwig Feuchtwanger of the *Bayerische Israelitische Gemeindezeitung,* and Robert Weltsch of the *Jüdische Rundschau*—who transformed the Jewish press in Germany into a major vehicle for the stimulation and spreading of Jewish culture.

During the first three years of operation, the membership of the institute peaked at about 3,600, as it published some twenty titles and distributed a total of 90,000 copies. Altogether it functioned over a period of eighteen years until 1873 and brought out some eighty-seven titles, or on the average of nearly five books a year. The list included a *mélange* of fiction, poetry, travel, translations of Hebrew texts, theology, and a good sample of scholarly works by Graetz, Jost, Fürst, and Geiger. Philippson chaired a small executive committee of three and saw to it that the institute printed a total of nineteen books by him and three by his brother Phoebus, a record that no doubt eventually contributed to discrediting the project.[10]

Twenty years later, in 1893, the founding of the *Verband der Vereine für jüdische Geschichte und Literatur* in Hanover provides a second occasion to assess the growth and dissemination of Jewish culture in Germany. Like the institute, the *Verband* was the brainchild of the editor of the *Allgemeine Zeitung des Judentums,* this time in the person of Karpeles, a historian of Jewish literature, who had assumed the post in 1890 upon the death of Philippson. In words that bespoke the enveloping swirl of antisemitism, Karpeles declared that "spreading a knowledge of Jewish history and literature is the most urgent need of the hour."[11] Toward that end the *Verband* promoted the formation of local chapters that would assemble public Jewish libraries, conduct discussion evenings, and hold a series of public lectures each winter on topics connected with the Jewish experience. By 1900 this national effort could boast of some 1,000 annual lectures in about 150 Jewish communities as well as the active participation of the Hildesheimer wing of German Orthodoxy.[12] From 1898 the *Verband* distributed to each member a modest yearbook reviewing the year's Jewish events and scholarly publications along with a religious calendar and a medley of semi-scholarly essays. By 1913 the number of chapters had risen to 219 with an enrollment of more than 16,500 members.[13] It was not to be the last time in Germany that the achievements of Jewish scholarship would be enlisted in the cause of spiritual resistance. In the words of Ismar Elbogen, on the occasion of his election in 1911 to replace the deceased Karpeles as president of the *Verband*: "Only a community firmly rooted in the past can work for the future."[14]

Yet it is only in the brief span of the Weimar period that the full expanse of a viable ethnic subculture breaks into view. The panorama represents the culmination of an organic development that reaches back to Mendelssohn's translation of the Bible as well as a consequence of the intellectual currents of the twentieth century, the Zionist infusion, and the animating impact of war-related events. Judaism had progressively emerged from a lifeless set of theological platitudes into a vital force seeking expression in works of art and literature, history, and theology. The motto of the age seemed to be that nothing Jewish was alien and long-abandoned legacies—Hasidism, Jewish mysticism, the culture of Eastern Europe— were reappropriated with a vengeance. The Bible itself attracted renewed attention, as Jewish scholars and theologians began to challenge the uncontested dominance of Protestant scholarship. The remarkable cluster of Jewish literature journals that served both as cutting edge and mediator evince the vigor and scope of this cultural effusion. Joseph Wohlgemuth's *Jeschurun*, the *Neue Jüdische Monatshefte*, Buber's *Der Jude*, and Julius Goldstein's *Der Morgen* reflect not only the major sectors of German Jewry, but echo a common ethos that included the practice of critical scholarship, an expanding horizon of Jewish consciousness, and a thoroughly modern sensibility. A committed cadre of Jewish intellectuals and professionals sustained a level of discourse, vitality of mind, and diversity of subject matter that augured, as the title of *Der Morgen* implied, the dawning of a new cultural age.

Moreover, channels of transmission proliferated from the turn of the century, bringing the producers and consumers of Jewish culture ever closer. The *Gesellschaft zur Förderung der Wissenschaft des Judentums* (1902) and the *Encyclopaedia Judaica* (1928–1934) disseminated in different formats the results of a century of Jewish scholarship.[15] The *Gesamtarchiv der Deutschen Juden* (1906) involved at least a few people in each of hundreds of Jewish communities in the preparation of sources for future research.[16] The growth of institutions like the *Lehrhaus* and the *Jugendgemeinde* across Germany held out some promise of offsetting the consequences of a diluted system of Jewish education.[17] And finally an overlay of some 103 papers, periodicals, and annuals assured an uninterrupted flow of Jewish information and opinion.[18] The individual Jew may not have possessed a high degree of Jewish literacy, but the organized community had managed through a succession of distinguished personalities to generate a solid Jewish counterpart to the German tradition of *Bildung*. Despite a century of emancipation, German Jewry had not neared the threshold of dissolution. Indeed, a renewal of communal and cultural vigor had begun to redress the erosion caused by individual attrition. The instruments to deepen Jewish consciousness were in place.

If the German concept of *Bildung* was intimately connected with the revival of Greek classicism, its Jewish counterpart was no less rooted in the emergence of *Wissenschaft des Judentums*. The critical and historical study of Judaism, for all its novelty, was ultimately a vehicle of continuity. The recovery of the past served to shape Jewish consciousness in the present. Translation of either a literal or conceptual sort preserved access to the canon of sacred texts; the narration of Jewish suffering militated against defection; and the revelation of diverse forms of Jewish creativity in the past projected a paradigm for the future. Thus the emerging landscape of Jewish culture was constantly irrigated by the wellsprings of *Wissenschaft*. So too in dark times, when *Wissenschaft* became a source of profound solace. The final *Almanach des Schocken Verlags* which appeared for the year 1938–1939 opened with four small Hebrew poems of Yannai, a prolific liturgical poet in sixth-century Palestine utterly unknown at the beginning of the nineteenth century. They were taken from a magnificent volume of Yannai poems edited by Menahem Zulay and published by the Schocken Verlag just a few months before.[19] In Spitzer's faithful translation, Yannai's voice reached across the centuries with a note of inspired consolation.

> Nach Deiner Liebe vergehn uns die Augen.
> Der die vom Feindhaß Gehaßten Du liebst.
> O sieh auf das Elend drinnen bei uns,
> Blick auf den Haß, der von draußen uns trifft,
> Wie Lea Du ansahst, im Elend gebeugt,
> Blicktest aud den Haß, der ihr Elend erzeugt.
> Hasser hatte sie drinnen im Zelt,
> War draußen von Schürern des Hasses umstellt.
> Nicht jeder, der geliebt ist, ist geliebt,
> Nicht jeder, der gehaßt ist, ist gehaßt.
> Manch drunten Gehaßter ist droben geliebt.
> Gehaßt sind, die Du hassest, geliebt, die Du liebst.
> Weil Dich wir lieben, trifft uns der Haß, Heiliger![20]

NOTES

1. Banesh Hoffmann, *Albert Einstein: Creator and Rebel*, New York 1972, p. 186.

2. Felix A. Theilhaber, *Der Untergang der deutschen Juden*, 2nd rev. edn., Berlin 1921.

3. Max Brod, *Im Kampf um das Judentum*, Vienna–Berlin 1920, pp. 129–131.

4. *Die Tröstung Israels*, mit der Verdeutschung von Martin Buber und Franz Rosenzweig, Berlin 1933.

5. A complete list is to be found at the end of the *Almanach des Schocken Verlags auf das Jahr 5699*, Berlin 1938/1939.

6. Volker Dahm, *Das jüdische Buch im Dritten Reich*, 2 vols., Frankfurt am Main 1982, II, cols. 507–596.

7. Leo Baeck, "Kulturzusammenhänge," *Der Morgen*, I (1925), pp. 72–83.

8. *Die Allgemeine Zeitung des Judentums*, 1855, pp. 87–89, 223–224.

9. The typology of the editor of the German-Jewish press deserves to be studied. In the meantime, see Max Gruenewald, "Critic of German Jewry: Ludwig Feuchtwanger and his Gemeindezeitung," in *Year Book XVII of the Leo Baeck Institute*, London 1972, pp. 75–92.

10. *Die Allgemeine Zeitung des Judentums*, 1857, p. 624. For a complete listing of all the institute's publications see Aron Freimann, *Katalog der Judaica und Hebraica*, rep. Graz (Austria) 1968, pp. 29–30. Philippson's altercation with Graetz over volume II of his *Geschichte der Juden* must also have alienated many a subscriber. (See above, p. 300, n.120).

11. Mitteilungen aus dem Verband," *Jahrbuch für Jüdische Geschichte und Literatur,* 1910, p. 2.

12. Ismar Schorsch, *Jewish Reactions to German Anti-Semitism 1870–1914*, New York–London 1972, p. 112. "Mitteilungen aus dem Verband," *Jahrbuch für Jüdsiche Geschichte und Literatur,* 1912, pp. 2, 5.

13. *Ibid.*, pp. 11–16. Given the thrust of my analysis, I would like to believe that the personal experience of Arthur Ruppin was not altogether atypical. His participation from 1892 to 1893 in the Graetz Society for Jewish History and Literature in Magdeburg under Rabbi Mortiz Rahmer, a graduate of Breslau, was the most vital expression of an otherwise attenuated relationship to Judaism. The stimulation received therein brought him to reflect seriously on antisemitism and eventually to gravitate toward Zionism. (Alex Bein [ed.], *Arthur Ruppin: Memoirs, Diaries, Letters,* New York 1971, pp. 60–64.)

14. "Mitteilungen aus dem Verband," *Jahrbuch für Jüdische Geschichte und Literatur,* 1912, p. 5. See also the positive assessment by Israel Friedlaender, *Past and Present*, repr. New York 1961, pp. 203–204.

15. "Zum Jubiläum der 'Gesellschaft zur Förderung der Wissenschaft des Judentums,'" *Monatsschrift für Geschichte und Wissenshaft des Judentums*, LXXII (1928), pp. 1–5. See also the scintillating reviews of volumes 1–4 by Rosenzweig published originally in *Der Morgen* and collected in his *Kleinere Schriften*, Berlin 1937, pp. 521–538.

16. Eugen Taeubler, *Außätze zur Problematik jüdischer Geschichtsschreibung 1908–1950*, Tübingen 1977 (Schriftenreihe wissenschaftlicher Abhandlungen des Leo Baeck Instituts 36), pp. 1–20.

17. Rosenzweig, *Kleinere Schriften*, pp. 56–93, 100–105; Nahum N. Glatzer, "The Frankfort Lehrhaus," in *LBIYB, I,* London 1956, pp. 105–122.

18. Margaret T. Edelheim-Muehsam, "The Jewish Press in Germany," in *LBIYB, I,* London (1956), pp. 171–172.

19. Menahem Zulay, *Piyyute Yannai*, Berlin 1938. On the history of Yannai scholarship see Zulay's introduction.

20. *Almanach des Schocken Verlags aus das Jahr 5699*, p. 7. In Zulay's edition, p. 399. The following English translation comes from T. Carmi, ed., *The Penguin Book of Hebrew Verse* (New York 1981), p. 215.

> Our eyes are weak with longing for
> Your love, O Loving One, for we are
> hated by the enemy. Look how afflicted
> we are from within, see how hated we
> are from without—as You looked on

the afflicition of Leah and saw her
tormented by hate. She was hated
within the house and detested without.
But not every loved one is loved, nor
every hated one hated: there are some
who are hated below, yet beloved
above. Those whom You hate are
hated; those whom You love are loved.
We are hated because we love You,
O Holy One!

∽ 19

The Leo Baeck Institute:
Continuity amid Desolation

The twenty-fifth anniversary of the founding of the Leo Baeck Institute provides an appropriate occasion to ponder the source of its remarkable achievement, for in that time the Institute has attained an undisputed presence in the fractious world of academia. In a world that accords recognition primarily for creativity rather than longevity, the international reputation of the Institute rests firmly on a quarter-century of undiminished productivity. Twenty-five volumes of the English Year Book, thirty-six volumes of the *Schriftenreihe wissenschaftlicher Abhandlungen*, seventeen volumes of the German Bulletin, twenty-one volumes of biographies and memoirs in the Deutsche Verlags-Anstalt series, plus a number of special publications, which includes the incomparable Goldschmidt *Mahzor*, constitutes an unmatched scholarly output of well over 100 books, or an average of at least four books a year.

That publishing record in three languages (German, English, and Hebrew) has tended to overshadow the Institute's other major accomplishment: the creation in New York of the single largest library and archive pertaining to central European Jewry anywhere in the world. In retrospect, and without exaggeration, the Institute has succeeded beyond the most audacious fantasies of its founders. Intent to compile data and stimulate research with a view toward an eventual comprehensive history of the Jewish experience in modern Germany, the Institute has spawned a flourishing subspecialty of abiding interest to both Jewish and German historians.

A quick glance at the change in the composition of Year Book contributors conveys a sense of the vitality of the field. As the following table suggests, the ranks of the founders were gradually revitalized by a new generation of professional historians.

Year Book	Contributors	Ph.D.s	Academics	Average Age
1956	22	11	6	60
1966	13	7	6	53
1978	18	15	13	48.5

Furthermore, the contents of the Year Book show that the continued fascination with German-Jewish history goes well beyond a quest for the roots of the Holocaust, to a desire to understand the complex and paradigmatic nature of the German-Jewish confrontation with modernity. Today the Year Book serves as the international forum in which young American, Israeli, German, and English academics, whose own historical experience lies this side of 1933, exhibit and test the products of their craft.

The explanation for this track record, I believe, abounds in paradox. Without doubt, an acute sense of discontinuity, a painful realization that the Nazis had abruptly and brutally terminated a uniquely creative symbiosis stirred the founders to action. Yet the surprising success of their efforts is a direct function of continuity. They transcended the chaos of discontinuity precisely because they embodied the values, culture and style of German Jewry at its best. Beyond the proverbial German addiction to work and thoroughness, that continuity expressed itself in at least three identifiable ways.

In terms of organizational structure, the Institute was as comprehensive and flexible an institution as the German *Kultusgemeinde*. It too aspired to organizational unity by appreciating the reality and benefit of diversity. The Institute was able to harness the disparate and far-flung remnants of German Jewry because it allowed for geographic, political, and religious diversity. Three working centers in the dominant areas of German-Jewish immigration coordinated their individual agenda through the annual meetings of a central board. Within that structural framework, an atmosphere obtained which induced German Jews of all persuasions, Zionist and non-Zionist, religious and secular, orthodox and liberal, to cooperate in the sacred task of preserving the past. The Institute never became the preserve of a single faction nor was any one facet of German-Jewish life ever programmatically ignored, though to be sure many still await their historian. Diversity within unity was part of the communal ethos which the founders of the Institute had absorbed while still in Germany.

Equally important, continuity expressed itself also in terms of personnel. It did not take a generation before qualified historians would emerge to implement the Institute's threefold program of gathering material for the intellectual, social, and institutional history of German Jewry. From the outset, the Institute benefited from the energetic involvement of an extraordinary cluster of Jewish scholars trained in German universities and steeped in *jüdische Wissenschaft*. In fact, most had already made their mark in the world of Jewish scholarship. Their knowledge, vision, and scholarship informed the Institute's collective judgment and elevated its publications to the highest standards.

Beyond that academic nucleus, the Institute galvanized the support of a significant circle of lettered Jews. Well educated, once prominent in some phase of organized Jewish life in Germany, and often with a keen eye sharpened by dislocation for that which was distinctive in German Jewry, they were eager and able to record their experiences and reflections. By publishing in German, the Institute spared them the anxiety and shame of writing in a language not their own and thus kept them from falling silent, the usual lot of literary men and women forced to relocate into another cultural orbit. Future historians of German Jewry will be the richer for this policy.

At the center of this galaxy of academics and literati stood Robert Weltsch, the founder and editor of the Year Book. A product of the cultural fertility and Zionist idealism of Habsburg Prague and editor of the *Jüdische Rundschau* during its final two decades, Weltsch possessed a panoramic yet profound knowledge of Central European Jewry based on tumultuous experience tempered by voracious reading. His wisdom and integrity generated the distance so necessary for writing history at such close range. He demanded balance and empathy and repeatedly warned against writing history backward or imposing simple-minded deterministic interpretations on complex developments often confounded by the fortuitous. His own corpus of introductions to the Year Book, German essays and regular Hebrew articles for *Ha'aretz*, constitutes a sophisticated exposition of the dominant features of Central European Jewish history in the modern era. Weltsch's powerful presence graced the Year Book with stability, direction, and standards.

The third and final manifestation of continuity is perhaps the least tangible, yet, I believe, also the most decisive. The achievement of the Institute derives ultimately from a well-developed sense of history, cultivated for more than a century in Germany by *Wissenschaft des Judentums*. The program to understand the totality of Judaism historically, initiated by Leopold Zunz in 1818 and gradually implemented by an ever widening circle of scholars down to 1939, eventually shaped the conceptual equipment and self-definition of nearly every sector of the community. During the disorienting experience after 1933, *Wissenschaft des Judentums* became a major source of consolation in the organized effort at spiritual resistance. The nearly 100 small volumes of the famous *Bücherei des Schocken Verlags* are moving testimony to the vital communal role of *jüdische Wissenschaft* in those final difficult years. Yet no academic discipline can ever be enlisted as a social force in times of stress unless its method and meaning have not already gained some prior resonance outside the "ivory tower."

The historical consciousness of German Jewry likewise did not ignore the millennial presence of Jews in Central Europe. Since the early days of the *Monatsschrift*, Zacharias Frankel had encouraged his colleagues and students to study the origins of Jewish settlements in medieval German towns. The subject quickly received the competent attention of engaged *Wissenschaft* scholars, and by the end of the Weimar period the field of German-Jewish history could boast of a unique national archive, a special journal and a formidable amount of finished research.

In consequence, the founders of the Institute were imbued by a rich historiographical legacy marked by a lively sense of time and place and especially attuned

to the distinctiveness of German Jewry. Both the nature and success of their enterprise had deep roots in their own cultural ambience.

On a concrete level, this connection is transparent. The Institute reissued a few
scholarly books whose entire printing had been confiscated by the Nazis. More
important, the Institute acted, where possible, to complete the pre-war agenda of
a rejuvenated *Wissenschaft* movement as it pertained to the history of German
Jewry. With the turn of the century, a circle of young scholars had begun to wrest
control of the movement from the hands of a more apologetic, pulpit-oriented leadership. High on their priority list was the systematic search for new sources. While
some of the projects inspired by this effort were completed before the war, most
notably those of the young Yitzhak Baer, others still required large investments of
time and money. The support and publication of the two volumes of the *Germania
Judaica* and the eight volumes of Selma Stern's *Der Preussische Staat und die Juden*
are a lasting tribute to the Institute's sense of responsibility and historical
judgment.

On the deepest level, the founders of the Institute, like the founders of the *Wissenschaft* movement, were impelled by the same poignant need: to explain themselves to an alien world. Emancipation, no less than the Holocaust, had brought
to an end, albeit differently, the conditions that had sustained a distinctive and
vibrant community. In each case, an élite of proud but self-conscious survivors
refused to abdicate the preservation of their past and the exposition of their heritage to uninformed and even hostile outsiders. The inevitable estrangement inflicted by homelessness had in fact invigorated their powers of self-perception, and
the best of their work pulsated with insight and vitality. A tenacious effort at per-
petuation by a cluster of visionaries had not only helped to transcend the personal
reality of chaos and anomie, but also to enhance the prospects for collective Jewish
survival. Self-renewal has always depended on creative cultural transmission.

The Place of Jewish
Studies in Contemporary
Scholarship

Anyone acquainted with the contemporary academic scene must be impressed by the burgeoning of Jewish studies in colleges and universities across North America. In numerical terms alone the growth of Judaic studies as an academic discipline is astonishing. Well over a thousand courses in the field are presently offered in institutions of higher learning outside Israel. In addition to all this, we are witnessing the proliferation of new subfields and the appearance of new centers of scholarly productivity around the world. But a skeptic might still question how deeply the academic study of Judaism has filtered into the general scholarship of religious studies. A subtle but significant index of the secure place of Judaica in the contemporary study of religion is the recently published fifteen-volume *Encyclopedia of Religion*, edited by the late Mircea Eliade (Macmillan, 1987).

This majestic collective work uniquely confirms the status attained in our day by the field of Jewish studies within the American university and may even offer a clue as to the source of that incredible success. It is a work inspired by a generosity of spirit quite alien to the Christian bias and categories that colored its pedantic English predecessor, the thirteen-volume *Encyclopedia of Religion and Ethics*, edited by James Hastings from 1908 to 1926.

In the midst of that earlier venture, in 1921, Harry Austryn Wolfson, still an insecure and underpaid instructor of Hebrew literature and philosophy at Harvard, appealed to the pride of American Jewry to fund the publication of the classics of medieval Jewish philosophy. His justification of the project poignantly betrayed the unaltered peripheral status of Jewish studies within the scholarly world after a century of awesome productivity.

When I speak of the importance of this unpublished part of Jewish philosophic literature, I do not mean to imply that I consider medieval Jewish philosophy to be the most important field of Jewish study. Hardly that. For I believe, just as our pious ancestors believed, though for different reasons, that the Talmud with its literature is the most promising field of study, the most fertile field of original re-search and investigation. But I believe that medieval Jewish philosophy is the only branch of Jewish literature, next to the Bible, which binds us to the rest of the literary world. In it we meet on common ground with civilized Europe and with part of civilized Asia and civilized Africa. (*Menorah Journal*, 7 [1921], p. 32)

In other words, to get a hearing in the Western world, the study of Judaism had to start off-center, on a body of literature—no matter how glorious—that was tan-gential to its essential character. Admission to the academy imposed subordination to external values and perspectives. It is worth noting that back in 1818, Leopold Zunz, the young visionary founder of the academic study of Judaism in Germany, had proposed a strikingly similar project, though in terms far less conciliatory to traditional rabbinics and more overtly apologetic.

This is not to say that the Hastings *Encyclopedia of Religion and Ethics* willfully overlooked the role of Judaism in the history of religion. On the contrary, its editors invited serious Anglo-Jewish scholars like Israel Abrahams, Elkan Adler, and Her-bert Loewe and Christian authorities like Hermann Strack and Travers Herford to compose often substantial articles on Jewish subjects. Strack's lengthy treatment of antisemitism and Loewe's sympathetic survey of *kabbalah* are but two of the more memorable contributions. It may well be that the dramatic publication of *The Jewish Encyclopedia* in New York from 1901 to 1906—the first encyclopedic distil-lation of modern Jewish scholarship—served to induce Hastings and his colleagues to accord greater attention to Judaism.

Yet the overall coverage of Judaism proved to be sparse and subordinate, a vic-tim of the imperious Christian tone that marked Hastings's entire work. For all its historical erudition, the Hastings encyclopedia treated non-Christian religions from a developmental perspective that impeded empathy and encouraged invidious comparisons. Generally entries were authored by outsiders. Thus, Islam was ac-tually portrayed under the rubric "Muhammadanism," an inaccurate Western ap-pellation patterned after the formation of the name for Christianity. The forty-six page entry on "Jesus Christ" opened with a volley of aggressive assertions about the inferiority of Buddhism and Islam to Christianity. And the long article on Is-raelite history and religion, written by the Regius Professor of Hebrew at Cam-bridge, ended on a decidedly Christian note. The Maccabean martyrs, it said, pointed to the emergence of the universal church, the true heir of ancient Israel. In short, the Hastings encyclopedia cast the religions of humanity in a hierarchical, theistic, and ethical mode forged by the Christian experience.

Not so the new *Encyclopedia of Religion*. Its scholarly ethos is militantly non-evolutionary and consequently non-judgmental. Its authors do not speak of higher and lower forms of religion and steadfastly shun the use of such loaded terms as "primitive." The working definition of religion throughout is consciously non-theistic. "Religion is the organization of life around the depth dimensions of experience—varied in form, completeness, and clarity in accordance with the environing culture" (vol. 12, p. 286). From that definition flows an expansive and holistic spirit of inquiry that lavishes caring attention on the non-Western experience of the sacred and on the full scope of each religious experience—its social, ritual, and theological expressions.

The tone is set by the very manner of dating. Gone from every article, except those of manifestly Christian content, are the Christian calendrical referents B.C. (before Christ) and A.D. (*anno domini*—in the year of the Lord), which characterized Hastings's and even George Foot Moore's eminently fair study of rabbinic Judaism done in the 1920s. In deference to the religious sensibilities of non-Christians, the editors of the new encyclopedia chose to employ the more neutral referents B.C.E. (before the common era) and C.E. (of the common era). Their handiwork—a collective triumph of the contemporary study of religion—is firmly anchored in the seminal ecumenism of Mircea Eliade, its editor (who sadly did not live to see the child of his old age), as well as in the still vital legacy of Rudolf Otto, whose book *The Idea of the Holy* published seventy years ago first broke through to the non-rational core of the religious experience.

The coverage of Judaism is a direct beneficiary of that propitiously open-minded setting. Never before has a general encyclopedia devoted so much space to expounding the sundry deposits of Judaism's millennial religious dynamism. If this new work be compared to "a garden of nearly three thousand flowers, grown from seeds sown in scholarly fields around the globe" (vol. 1, p. xvii), then the variety called "Judaism" represents well over 10 percent of the vegetation, arranged in separate historical entries and in subdivisions of broadly thematic and synthetic entries. The presence of Judaism pervades the pages of the encyclopedia.

Even more important than quantity is the qualitative intent to survey Judaism from within, on its own terms. Criteria intrinsic to the nature and development of Judaism clearly determine the selection of topics. In consequence, a host of talmudic sages, medieval rabbis, and modern Orthodox leaders, who are not exactly household names even in the Jewish world, merit the honor of a biographical entry. Similarly, searching articles abound on religious institutions and bodies of literature that neither border on nor blend with Christian consciousness, but assuredly define the realm of the sacred in Judaism. How many general encyclopedias have devoted an article to the medieval Ashkenazic glossators of the Talmud, the *Tosafot*, or to the vital and multifaceted concept of Torah? A profound respect for the uniqueness of religious phenomena motivated Eliade and his circle to illuminate the central expressions of Judaism, as understood by the best of Jewish scholarship in our day.

No Jewish scholar contributed more to deepening the academic appreciation of Judaism as a religion than the late Gershom Scholem, and it is altogether apposite that Eliade singled him out for praise in his brief preface. But beyond the accolade, it was the readiness of the encyclopedia to involve Jewish scholars from start to finish that enabled it to do justice to Judaism. The appointment of Robert M.

Seltzer, professor of Jewish history at Hunter College and the author of a splendid one-volume history of the Jews, as one of the eight senior editors ensured that Judaism would be accorded an integral part in the very conceptualization of the project. And the energetic recruitment of Jewish scholars to write the articles, even in the area of Biblical scholarship, long a contested turf, gave "insiders" a generous chance to be heard. The result is a plethora of well-informed expositions equally sensitive to inner meanings and outer settings.

The *Encyclopedia of Religion* is resounding evidence that the field of Jewish studies is at last not only in the university but of it. The subject is no longer a mere structural appendage, the product of enlightened Jewish donors in an age of affluence and the insatiable academic need for fresh funds. It has finally been woven into the very fabric of American scholarship because of the inherent human value of the Jewish experience. Admission into the university has gradually culminated in scholarly acceptance.

Many developments have contributed to this historic achievement. Neither American society nor the Jewish world nor the university are what they were when Wolfson tactfully stressed what connected Judaism to the mainstream. But publication of the new encyclopedia should also alert us to the formative role played by the discipline of religious studies. Its successful entry into the university in the decades after World War II heralded not only the importance of religion generically for the humanities but also the value specifically of non-Western religions for an institution that presumed to be universal. Along with other factors, the discipline of religious studies, often spearheaded by emigré scholars, helped to expand the parochial horizon of the university, and led eventually to a greater receptivity for the study of Judaism. Many of the early positions in Jewish studies were located within departments of religion.

This encyclopedia—a dazzling specimen of the humanity that currently informs the discipline of religious studies—also reminds us of the paradoxical link between value-free scholarship and the creation of new values. Broadening the intellectual horizon through non-partisan, comparative scholarship surely helps to foster a respect for individuality and diversity and a spirit of kinship and interdependence vital to an ethos of ethnic and religious pluralism.

Above all, the achievement of this encyclopedia is meant to enlarge religious commitment, not erode it. In the words of Eliade, "Knowledge of the religious ideas and practices of other traditions better enables anyone to understand his or her own" (vol. 1, p. xi). A measure of distance yields a myriad of insights. Would that those tempted by the resurgent dogmatism abroad in the land permit themselves to savor of the wisdom so lovingly assembled in this encyclopedia. No gentler antidote has been devised.

↷ 21

The Lachrymose Conception
of Jewish History

The adjective "lachrymose" is not an everyday word, except for Jews. Salo Wittmayer Baron (1895–1989) has made it part of our daily vocabulary. It is, in fact, the word most often associated with his name, because since 1928, when he first applied the word to describe the entrenched view of Jewish history as a story of unending travail, he often returned to repudiate it. Ironically, the patrimony does not bespeak a theory he sired but rather one that he committed his professional life to correcting. To fight it, he first had to name it.

Nor is it a distortion of Baron's prolific career to rest his fame on this term. He closed his programmatic essay of 1928, on "Ghetto and Emancipation," declaiming that "Surely it is time to break with the lachrymose theory of pre-Revolutionary [i.e., French] woe, and to adopt a view more in accord with historic truth."[1] And he never let up in his own campaign to effect such a revision. The effort drove his vast historiographical enterprise and offers the best lens through which to see its underlying coherence.

With his nuanced erudition, Baron challenged the most basic assumption of all modern Jewish scholarship, indeed of all medieval and rabbinic thought as well. The diverse scope of Jewish history defied the lugubrious and undifferentiated religious category of *Galut,* or exile. To be sure, antisemitism was a given which he accounted for generically in his testimony at the Eichmann trial in 1961 as "the dislike of the unlike." But he refused steadfastly to regard it as the predominant and inevitable motif of the Jewish odyssey. As he told Robert Servatius, the defense attorney, when cross-examined:

I am not a historical determinist. Hegel and Spengler may be called idealistic determinists. Though they are sometimes right, I have never felt that their approach was correct. According to my opinion, history develops by reason of causes and changes within society, many of which are unpredictable. Accident is very important. Personality is very important. Together all these things create history.[2]

And yet, the unvarnished truth is that Baron failed. The Holocaust overwhelmed his lifelong agenda to present a version of Jewish history that would do justice to all the evidence. It reinforced the age-old sense of foreboding and precariousness. Only a world-class historian would have persisted against such odds, holding his ground to the very end, even at the risk of falling out of sync with his own time.

My argument is simply this: at the heart of Baron's legacy pulsated the conviction that Jews were always more than the hapless victims of persecution. And what better place to make it than at Columbia University, where he taught for thirty-three years, on the evening of *Kristallnacht*, against the backdrop of the Jewish Museum's "Convivencia" exhibition, which, in the spirit of Baron, commemorates the cultural heights of Sephardic Jewry on the Iberian peninsula rather than its brutal demise.[3]

II

We should not underestimate the courage needed for a young historian of thirty-three to call for a revision of the lachrymose theory. The modern experience, for all its departures from tradition and secularizing tendencies, had only strengthened its hold. First, it added the residue of the emancipation debate in which proponents had long excused Jewish traits, practices, and beliefs deemed to be offensive in terms of Christian intolerance. Unrelieved oppression always warped the character of the oppressed, or in the stinging formulation by Mendelssohn: "They tie our hands and then accuse us of not using them."[4]

Second came the contribution of the early advocates for religious reform who sought to relativize large chunks of Judaism by ascribing what they despised to dark times. Writing in terms of degeneration rather than development, they spoke of Talmud, messianism, and mysticism as protective aberrations born of relentless hostility.[5]

Third, and most importantly, the critical scholarship of the 1850s confirmed the polemical rhetoric. Within the span of a single decade, the publication of two path-breaking histories and four editions of medieval texts seemed to ground perception in reality. In 1851, Meir Halvei Letteris, a protégé of Nachman Krochmal and admirer of Samuel David Luzzatto, brought out the first edition of *Emek ha-Bakha* (Vale of Tears), the wide-ranging chronicle of Jewish suffering written in the wake of the Spanish expulsion by Joseph ha-Kohen, who was born in Avignon in 1496 but lived in Genoa. As manuscript, it had circulated in Italy alone. Luzzatto gave Letteris an extant copy, urged him to publish it, and even added notes of his own.[6]

Two years later the young Heinrich Graetz burst onto the scene with volume four of his incomparable *Geschichte der Juden*. Actually the first to appear, the volume depicted the emergence of rabbinic Judaism in the post-Temple period. It also enunciated what Graetz believed to be the twofold nature of the Diaspora experience. "To study and wander, think and persist, learn and suffer are the hallmarks of this long era." Indeed, the volumes to come in rapid order would not deviate from that defiant and constricted view.[7]

In 1855, Leopold Zunz joined his authoritative voice to the chorus with a sweeping survey of the history of Jewish liturgy. Like his earlier work on midrash, *Die synagogale Poesie des Mittelalters* celebrated the synagogue as the Jewish national theater, the religious forum for the millennial dialogue between God and Israel. Zunz read the poetry contextually; its pervasive tone of national anguish mirrored the perilous conditions of Jewish life in Christian Europe. Accordingly, he prefaced his work with a searing fifty-page chapter entitled "Suffering" which, in the spirit of Joseph ha-Kohen, chronicled the history of Jewish vulnerability from Constantine to Charles V, that is, from the triumph of Christianity over the Roman Empire to its unraveling in the Reformation era. Prayer served Jews as catharsis, a vehicle for solace, lament, vengeance, and even blasphemy. In the compressed words of Zunz: "Under pressure, a noble spirit gives voice to lofty sentiments, the pressed flower yields its fragrance, and the person enchained is freer than his tormentor."[8]

Meir Wiener, a scholarly and hard-working Jewish teacher in Hanover, concluded the decade with three more books on the subject of persecution. In 1855 he put out a new Hebrew edition of Solomon Ibn Verga's sixteenth-century historical tract *Shevet Yehudah* (Scepter of Judah), followed a year later by a German translation.[9] Ibn Verga may qualify as Spanish Jewry's equivalent of Hannah Arendt—an unfettered political thinker highly critical of contemporary Jewish leadership. Yet over the centuries his caustic, entertaining text, part chronicle, part dialogue, had been published often and widely read. Finally, in 1858, Wiener added a German translation of ha-Kohen's more funereal work, thus linking inextricably the historiographical legacy of Sephardic Jewry to the conceptual grid refurbished and reformulated by *Wissenschaft* scholars.[10]

The darkened political horizon in central Europe after 1848 may well have induced this sudden spirit of scholarly interest in the historical record of persecution. The quest for Jewish citizenship did suffer an immediate setback as the forces of reaction regained power. Nine German states simply abrogated the emancipation granted during the revolution, while Prussia curbed it constitutionally by declaring itself to be a Christian state. In Hanover, where Wiener lived, Jews lost the right to be elected to public office, and in Berlin, Zunz, a prominent figure in the uprising, returned to his research spent and dejected. For him the 1850s would become, politically speaking, "a decade of sleep."[11]

Fourth, even after the achievement of full citizenship in a united Germany, a quick resurgence of antisemitism on a truly continental scale denied emancipated Jews a sense of at-homeness. With government-aided pogroms in Russia, overtly antisemitic political parties in Germany and the Habsburg Empire, and the Dreyfus affair in France, the nineteenth century ended for Jews on a medley of distressing notes. The lachrymose theory remained apposite. No one caught the mood of foreboding more tellingly than the Lodz-born Jewish painter Samuel Hirszenberg in his turn-of-the-century epic paintings *Golus* (1898), *The Wandering Jew* (1899), and *Funeral of the Zadik* (1905). *Golus* and *Funeral* depict Jewish rootlessness in the stark form of black-garbed masses filled with fear or resignation moving across a bleak and timeless landscape. In contrast, *The Wandering Jew* portrays a single, almost naked, half-crazed man fleeing in a forest of crosses over ground strewn with corpses. The huge canvas rings with indignation: Christianity must bear the guilt for the frightful condition of the Jew.[12]

In sum, emancipation was surely still incomplete and perhaps impermanent and hardly conducive to rethinking Jewish history in more balanced terms. World War I and its aftermath would make the task only more difficult.

That it erupted on the Ninth of Av, the traditional fast day commemorating Jewish suffering, foreshadowed the waves of calamity to come. The Great War shattered "the prevailing Meliorist myth . . . and reversed the Idea of Progress," which meant for the centers of Jewish population in eastern Europe chaos and destruction on an unprecedented scale.[13] On January 1, 1915, in Warsaw, Peretz and Anski, in the spirit of the earlier ethnographic expedition into Ukraine, issued an appeal to fellow Jews "being dragged into the global maelstrom" to record the details of their suffering. "Woe to the people whose history is written by strange hands and whose own writers have nothing left but to compose songs of lament, prayers and dirges after the fact."[14] Ansky personally hastened to Galicia to recount the decimation of its still largely pious Jewry trapped between the warring armies of Russia and Austria-Hungary. In the devastated synagogue of Dembitz he found but two words still legible on a shard of the Ten Commandments, which symbolized for him the unfolding horror—"*tirzah* and *tinaf*, thou shalt kill . . . thou shalt commit adultery." Published in 1921, his classic *Khurbm Galitsye* served as both epitaph and inspiration, reaffirming the power of the pen in times of persecution.[15]

Nor did the collapse of the tsarist regime bring immediate relief. The rebirth of Poland after more than a century of oblivion was marred with a rash of pogroms in 1918–19 in more than 130 localities, which eventually drew official study missions from the United States and Great Britain. More devastating still were the Ukrainian pogroms which raged from 1918 to 1920, engulfing as many as 200,000 Jews or 10 percent of the total Jewish population. Chaos increased Jewish vulnerability. The combatants in this three-way power struggle seemed united in their violence against Jews. Repelled by the level of atrocities, a Parisian jury in 1926 refused to convict Shalom Schwartzbard, the Jewish assassin of Simon Petliura, the erstwhile leader of the ill-fated Ukrainian national movement.[16]

If Hirszenberg reflected the anxiety of European Jews at the turn of the century, Simon Bernfeld epitomized it after the war in a three-volume Hebrew anthology of primary sources on Jewish suffering from the time of Antiochus IV to the last quarter of the eighteenth century. A native of Galicia but long-time resident of Berlin, Bernfeld titled his morbid project *Sefer ha-Demaot* (The Book of Tears), alluding to the plea by the psalmist that God should collect the tears of his anguish in God's own flask (58:6). The set which appeared from 1923 to 1926 offered an unalloyed version of the lachrymose view, a worthy modern counterpart to ha-Kohen's *Vale of Tears*. Bernfeld took a rabbinic proverb to characterize the ancient view deepened by recent events: "Should the pitcher fall on the stone, the pitcher will break. Should the stone fall on the pitcher, the pitcher will break. Either way, woe to the pitcher."[17]

While the documents of each persecution, whether prose narrative or poetic lament, are of immense historical value, Bernfeld's simplistic introductions to the volumes bulge with present-mindedness. Torment and fury spill over into emotion-laden, sweeping generalizations. He insists, for example, that antisemitism is a constant of the Jewish experience, irrespective of the differences between medieval and modern, with its root cause in the sense of Jewish chosenness and superiority. To defame Jews has become a worldwide industry. At the end he admits unashamedly that he is too drained and exhausted to continue. His original design was to proceed all the way to the post-war wreckage in Ukraine, but "the work depleted my strength and left my eyes bereft of sleep."[18] Though Bernfeld wrote in Hebrew, his solution to "The Jewish Question" was decidedly non-Zionist, no more than an integral part of improving the human condition in general. The assistance he received in carrying out his complicated task from Ismar Elbogen, Simon Dubnov, and Hayyim Brody suggests just how entrenched was this rendition of the past among the leading scholars of his day.

III

Exactly two years after Bernfeld fell silent, Salo Baron, now in New York at Stephen Wise's Jewish Institute of Religion, raised his voice in protest. "Ghetto and Emancipation" makes it luminously clear why he had turned down an offer to accept the vacant post in Jewish history at the Breslau Seminary once held by Graetz, the master teacher of *Leidens- und Gelehrtengeschichte*, Jewish history as pain and piety. His own conceptualization differed too greatly from the regnant paradigm. Did he perhaps choose to come to America in 1926 because it gave promise of a Jewish existence that would better accord with his own paradigm?[19]

Whatever the combined weight of the historical and contemporary evidence, Baron, with rabbinic ordination from Vienna's *Beit ha-Midrash* and three doctorates from the University of Vienna, dared to enunciate a new conceptualization, quietly, confidently, and cogently. In particular, he aimed his firepower at the one-sided depiction of the Middle Ages by shifting the focus of research from change to continuity, from the periodic explosions of Jew hatred to issues of status, structure, and context. For example, he employed the tools of legal history to argue that the notion of equal rights was utterly alien to the period. Rights were a function of corporate membership and Jews enjoyed more than the villeins who made up most of feudal society. At best the peasants were serfs in civil law, subject to the barely curbed power of their overlord, while the Jews were serfs in public law protected from abuse by others by the authority of the ruler of the realm. It was an egregious misunderstanding of medieval law to view the legal term *servi camerae* (serfs of the chamber), which came to signify Jewish status, as a mark of inferiority.

Similarly, Baron intoned the benefits of the ghetto as a form of self-government freely sought by Jewish settlers in Europe to preserve their mores and identity. "There were locks inside the ghetto gates in most cases before there were locks outside."[20] Led by Dubnov, Jewish historians in eastern Europe with a much livelier sense of nationhood than that of the *Wissenschaft* scholars in Germany had stressed the vital role of communal autonomy throughout the Diaspora. Baron now built upon their results to temper the attitude that the ghetto was only emblematic of exclusion and oppression.

He also ventured to counter the terror conjured up in the Jewish imagination by the memory of the Spanish Inquisition. Its notorious procedures were no different from those employed in other juridical systems throughout the Middle Ages. Above all, he argued that it affected few Jews because its province was restricted to heresy among Christians.

Moving forward in time, Baron tried to soften the negative image of the centuries following 1492. He marshaled demographic evidence of dramatic growth in the Jewish population of Europe to contend that the period could not have been as perilous as generally maintained. Moreover, he displayed unusual sympathy for the case made by Werner Sombart that Jews played a significant role in the rise and diffusion of capitalism. He overlooked Sombart's antisemitic design, and used his facts and line of inquiry to lift the gloom associated with the period.[21]

Finally, Baron refused to glorify the benefits of emancipation. If Bernfeld had exaggerated the suffering of the Middle Ages, he did appreciate the unredeemed nature of the modern era. And so did Baron, who would not minimize the cost to Jews of their admission to the body politic as equal citizens. They gave up the exercise of communal autonomy and endured a fractured identity that could no longer blend effortlessly both the religious and national expression of Judaism. Despite those sacrifices, Jews remained the object of contempt and violence. In the spirit of Dubnov, he believed that full emancipation for Jews had ultimately to rest on an equal measure of individual freedom and group autonomy.

Overall, then, it can be said that Baron's revisionist essay upgraded the quality and stability of Jewish life in the Middle Ages even as it downgraded what had been accomplished by emancipation. Inevitably if only implicitly, his vision of the past challenged Reform and Zionist ideologues alike for leaning too heavily on a uniform history of Jewish martyrdom.

The boldness of Baron's reconceptualization stands out when compared to that put forth by Cecil Roth in 1934 in the same *Menorah Journal* which had published Baron's. His essay "The Most Persecuted People?" betrays an unease with the exclusive and excessive attention to Jewish martyrdom, but does not go much beyond a mechanistic argument that not every case of violence against Jews was an instance of persecution, that other groups suffered as much as the Jews, and that the Middle Ages were endemically unstable and disordered. More important, Roth did not stay with this anemic effort. His later work returns wholeheartedly to the conventional wisdom.[22] In contrast, Baron's revision expressed his root conviction as a Jewish historian and foreshadowed the leitmotif of his far-flung scholarship.

In the ominous year of 1937, Baron expanded his essay into a three-volume discourse on the nature of Jewish history bearing the title *A Social and Religious History of the Jews*. Whatever may have prompted this reflective synthesis in an age of synthetic and ideologically driven histories—and I continue to believe as I have written elsewhere that Baron intended it as part of the current debate over the roles and relationship of religion and ethnicity in Jewish history—it was also a vehicle for elaborating the argument against the lachrymose theory. Given the time, it was a work laden with irony and pathos; Baron fought the irresistible tendency to let the present color the past.[23]

As the Nazi regime reversed emancipation in Germany and threatened it elsewhere, Baron defiantly reasserted his conviction that

It would be a mistake . . . to believe that hatred was the constant keynote of Judeo-Christian relations, even in [medieval] Germany or Italy. It is in the nature of historical records to transmit to posterity the memory of extraordinary events, rather than of the ordinary flow of life. . . .[24]

He singled out Spanish Jewish chroniclers like Samuel Usque and ha-Kohen as being at least partly responsible for shifting the interest of Jewish historiography away from "the achievements of the rabbis and teachers" to "passionate accounts of Israel's woes and sorrows," and strikingly preferred the legacy of their contemporary Azariah de Rossi, "a solitary thinker in his day, [who] investigated the [distant] past of his people in a more detached and serene mood."[25]

Accordingly, Baron paid but scant attention to the insecurity of exile with its trials and tribulations. He stressed instead a bevy of interacting factors which yielded a deeper understanding of Jewish fate in medieval Europe. For example, he identified the Catholic Church, bound by powerful theological constraints, as serving to ensure Jewish survival. Against the widespread *Wissenschaft* hostility toward Catholicism, he declared: "It may be asserted that had it not been for the Catholic Church, the Jews would not have survived the Middle Ages in Christian Europe."[26] He also dwelled on the mutuality of interests between the central authorities of the feudal state and their Jewish subjects. When that alliance did break down, it was expulsion and not a pogrom which terminated the relationship. "In contrast to Czarist Russia," he wrote bitingly, "no medieval government ever countenanced pogroms. When the government felt it could no longer protect the Jews and preserve order, the result was not a pogrom but an expulsion."[27]

Though generally reliable, both of these institutions could be transformed by the process of national unification, which then as now created pressure, often from below, for the elimination of foreign elements. Baron, a long-time student of European nationalism, contended that that is precisely the dynamic behind the expulsions from England, France, and Spain. Incipient nationalism reinforced underlying economic and religious tensions. For this reason, he averred that medieval Jews fared best in multi-ethnic societies.[28]

In a remarkable epilogue of nearly 100 pages, in which Baron extrapolated the lessons of Jewish history as he saw them for his own beleaguered generation, he again toned down the redemptive rhetoric on emancipation and cautioned against casting the Nazis in terms drawn from the Middle Ages.

One must not, under any circumstances, allow emancipation or theoretical equality, to become a fetish, and to spend all available energies in its defense. The frequently heard identification of the German governmental discrimination with the Dark Ages is highly misleading. It has been pointed out here in various connections that during the European Middle Ages, the Jews belonged to the privileged minority of each country and that consequently, in comparison with the majority of Christians, modern equality was for them a relative (though by no means absolute) loss.[29]

The passage betrays respect for the medieval achievement. Baron was an avowed critic of the modern nation-state and envisioned protecting the individual and group rights of Jews through international arrangements like the post-war national minority treaties supervised by the League of Nations.[30]

Alongside these new points, Baron reiterated the ones already voiced in his original essay to give his overall work an untimely roseate hue. In the dark decade of the 1930s, he had authored anything but a history of gloom and doom filled with rage and self-pity. His was not an indictment of non-Jews for what they had inflicted on Jews throughout the ages, but rather a celebration of what Jews had done for themselves. The hero of this tale was the Jewish people itself, resourceful, resilient, and relentless in pursuit of its goal in history—"the reconciliation of its national and universalist ideologies, through a process of inner and outer growth as an ethno-religious unity beyond the boundaries of state and territory."[31] Baron had cast the Jewish people in epic terms, a fragile nation imbued with the mission to create a universal monotheism in which the spiritual values of history would prevail over the concrete limitations of nature.

Baron's distinctive voice quickly drew fire from the pen of an equally gifted historian with a totally different worldview. Yitzhak Baer had settled in Palestine in 1930 to join the faculty of the just-founded Hebrew University. A superbly trained medievalist, Baer was absorbed in a history of Spanish Jewry that would repudiate the bipolar value system of the Sephardic courtier class, precisely what had most appealed to emancipated German Jews in search of a valid integration model. His own preference was for the insular and pietistic Jews of medieval Ashkenaz (Germany), who, he felt, perpetuated the pristine ethos of rabbinic Judaism.

Anticipating the clash to come between them is the arresting fact that as young scholars, Baer was drawn to study Ibn Verga while Baron worked on Azariah de Rossi.[32]

In 1936 Baer had published in German a slender volume—sweeping, compressed, and melancholy—on perceptions of *Galut* in Jewish thought. Without letup, he argued that life outside Palestine was always regarded as exile, a temporary and unstable condition threatened by hostility. Antisemitism was inevitable because incited by "the Jews' exalted consciousness of religious superiority and of their mission among the nations, a consciousness all the more infuriating because it exists in a nation totally without power." In reference to 1492 he wrote that "the Jewish problem of fifteenth-century Spain indicates only the terrible inevitability of historical conflicts which apparently are constantly renewed in new forms." Nor did Baer hold out any resolution other than an occasional moment of mutual understanding by both sides, which means "an open clarification of the historical limitations of the situation and an alleviation of its difficulties by the exercise of a spirit of humanity."[33]

Two years later, in the new Hebrew journal of the Israeli Historical Society, Baer delivered himself of a twenty-three-page review of Baron which trashed the book in a torrent of criticism that welled up from the deepest recesses of his being. He condemned the lifelessness of the thematic method, the neglect of the Maccabean revolt and the Hasmonean kingdom, the prudential portrait of the Pharisees, the preference for the creativity of Diaspora centers, and the elitist, rational characterization of the Talmud. Baer was above all a *homo religiosus* in the garb of a historian and repeatedly censured Baron for missing the religious impulse at the heart of the Jewish experience.

By the same token he posited an unerodable religious essence to the worldwide dispute among Judaism, Christianity, and Islam which would forever deny the Jewish people safety outside their own homeland. "The root controversy remains what it was in the very first debate between the Old and New Testaments, namely, whether man's soul will be redeemed through keeping the commandments of the Torah or believing in the Christian messiah." Whatever validity might inhere in the other factors like medieval nationalism that Baron had raised, and Baer granted them a measure, "the incontrovertible fact remains," he wrote, "that Jewish history in the Middle Ages was an unbroken chain of persecutions, and that the absence of any sense of confidence in the permanence of Jewish existence was felt even in Spain and even in those moments when the demons were held in check."[34]

Baron never answered Baer in a direct rebuttal, except for an aside in a footnote to a long essay published at the height of the Holocaust in 1942. The essay itself, on "The Jewish Factor in Medieval Civilization," gave ample evidence that Baron had not let up on his determination to look at Jewish history from new perspectives and with far greater attention to the larger context. Precisely at the point where Baron reasserted his basic view that "medieval Jews at their worst were better off,

both politically and economically, than the masses of villeins who usually constituted the majority of each European nation," he stopped to defend himself against
Baer. He rejected outright Baer's slight that he might simply be following the lead
of certain antisemites who were the first to insist that the Jews had little to complain about. Revealingly, Baron wrote that he

is still unable to locate any anti-Semitic forerunners and, to the best of his knowledge, was the first to coin the term "lachrymose conception" [in the aforementioned essay in the *Menorah Journal*] when his scholarly conscience
[subconsciously, perhaps, also his pride in the Jewish heritage] made him impatient with the eternal self-pity characteristic of Jewish historiography.[35]

The rare reference to what motivated him may allude to Baron's own aristocratic roots in Tarnow under the Habsburgs. His father was both an Orthodox Jew
and a man of means, a private banker, an owner of property, and the president of
a Jewish community of some 16,000. The harmony of personal success and communal loyalty impressed itself on the son whose courtly manners, lifelong service
to the Jewish people, exalted sense of Jewish pride, and visceral aversion to self-
pity bore the stamp of the Galician Jewish aristocracy.[36] The resonant cadence of
his full name, which he preferred to use, bespoke a noble pedigree.

That selfsame year Baron also published his magnificent study of the institutions of Jewish self-government prior to the modern era, *The Jewish Community*. The
first comprehensive work on a subject placed on the agenda of Jewish scholarship
and politics by Dubnov, Baron's most conspicuous mentor, *The Jewish Community*
assembled the enormous amount of diverse data on the remarkable ability of Jews
to organize and administer themselves on alien soil. The very polar opposite of an
exercise in self-pity, this book celebrated the tenacity and ingenuity, the self-
discipline and group loyalty, the piety and political sagacity which gave concrete
form to what Dubnov and Ahad Ha-am had called the Jewish will to survive. That
singular record of ethnic autonomy underscored what Jews had surrendered in
return for emancipation, even as it offered a valuable resource in their urgent quest
for new communal structures. *The Jewish Community* should thus be read as an
indirect response by Baron to the challenge of Baer.

His decision to undertake a new edition of the *Social and Religious History of the
Jews* in 1952 at the age of fifty-seven should be seen in the same light. If anything,
the Holocaust, even at that early post-war date, had cast a pall rendering the lachrymose conception of Jewish history all but irrefutable. It confirmed on a scale
unimagined the age-old premonition of ineluctable doom. The prospect of a total
eclipse drove Baron to throw himself into a vast reaffirmation of his maverick
views.

The key question to be asked of his unfinished second edition is, what prompted
him to do it in the first place? He definitely did not return to his pre-war work and
format simply because of an exponential growth of knowledge. Something far
deeper and existential impelled him to recount again the worldwide odyssey of

his people, and this was the deleterious impact of the Holocaust on the Jewish state of mind. Undaunted by the task, he dared to write against the spirit of the Holocaust, against the stampede to generalize, against the impulse to turn a historical event into a worldview.

Along the way Baron dropped hints as to what it was that motivated him, as for example, in a note that concludes a nuanced discussion of the reasons for the expulsion from England in 1290, with special emphasis on the role of nationalism:

> To the adherents of the "lachrymose conception of Jewish history" the explanation was even simpler: the perennial martyrology of the Jewish people in exile. This school of thought, to which most Hebrew chroniclers of the Late Middle Ages and early modern times belonged, also found eloquent representatives among leading modern Jewish historians, including L. Zunz and H. Graetz. The holocaust under the Nazis necessarily reinforced this point of view.[37]

And it was to dispel that Nazi overlay of a far older predilection that Baron wrote.

The second edition then, like the first, was a sustained act of self-transcendence. Baron mobilized an awesome body of historical evidence to repel the noxious fumes of the Holocaust and preserve the individuality of early periods. His aversion to victimhood amplified the power of his arguments, yielding an endless variation on the irrepressible fortitude and creativity of the Jewish people. It is this focus which ultimately lends coherence to this sprawling work of eighteen volumes and helps to explain why he stayed for so long on the external side of Jewish history. While the excessive attention to Jewish foreign affairs in the last ten volumes broke the elegant balance between the social and religious, the external and internal components of the story, it did drive home the point that the Jews, even in the worst of times, like the late Middle Ages, were more than just objects, victims, and martyrs.[38]

There is poignant irony in the fact that the historian called to testify at the Eichmann trial on the world turned to ashes by the Nazis was also the scholar who devoted his formidable talents to rein in the demons of the Holocaust. Born in western Galicia, Baron rose above the blood-stained history of his region and his time. Like the great French-Jewish historian Marc Bloch whose life was ended by the Germans in 1944, Baron struggled to take the long view. And what Eugen Weber said of Bloch illuminates the contribution of Baron as well: ". . . the great historian contributes, not a model, but the suggestion of a new way of going about our business, not a vision, but a view; vision surviving at best as a document of its times, the view adding to historical understanding."[39] In the light of that distinction, we may conclude that while Baer restated a tattered vision with great force, Baron forged a new view for a less tormented age.

NOTES

1. Salo Baron, "Ghetto and Emancipation," *The Menorah Journal*, XIV (June 1928), p. 526.

2. Salo W. Baron, "European Jewry Before and After Hitler," *American Jewish Year Book* LXIII (1962), pp. 49, 51. See also *idem*, "Changing Patterns of Antisemitism: A Survey," *Jewish Social Studies*, XXXVIII (Winter 1976), pp. 5–38.

3. My essay is a revision of the one I delivered on November 9, 1992, at Low Memorial Library at the international conference commemorating the 500th anniversary of the expulsion of the Jews from Spain jointly sponsored by The Jewish Theological Seminary of America and The Center for Israel and Jewish Studies at Columbia University in collaboration with The Jewish Museum. For the catalogue of the concurrent exhibition see *Convivencia: Jews, Muslims, and Christians in Medieval Spain*, ed. by Vivian B. Mann *et al.*, New York 1992.

4. Moses Mendelssohn, *Gesammelte Schriften*, III, Leipzig 1843, p. 183.

5. See above, pp. 268–271.

6. See Letteris's introduction in ha-Kohen, *Emek ha-Bakha*, Cracow 1895, pp. 1–8.

7. Heinrich Graetz, *Geschichte der Juden*, IV, 4th ed., Leipzig 1908, pp. 1–2.

8. Leopold Zunz, *Die synagogale Poesie des Mittelalters*, Berlin 1855, p. 15.

9. R. Salomone Aben Verga, *Liber Schevet Jehuda*, ed. by M. Wiener, Hanover 1855; *Idem, Das Buch Schevet Jehuda*, trans. by M. Wiener, Hanover 1856.

10. R. Joseph ha-Cohen, *Emek habacha*, trans. by M. Wiener, Leipzig 1858. As one of the publications of the Institut zur Förderung der israelitischen Literatur, Wiener's translation enjoyed wide distribution.

11. Jacob Toury, *Soziale und politische Geschichte der Juden in Deutschland 1847–1871*, Düsseldorf 1977, pp. 299–313; Leopold Zunz, *Jude—Deutscher—Europäer*, ed. Nahum N. Glatzer, Tübingen 1964, p. 389.

12. Avram Kampf, *Jewish Experience in the Art of the Twentieth Century*, New York 1975, pp. 8–9; Norman L. Kleeblatt, *The Dreyfus Affair*, Berkeley, Los Angeles, London 1987, pp. 20–21.

13. Paul Fussell, *The Great War and Modern Memory*, London, Oxford, New York 1977, p. 8.

14. David G. Roskies, ed., *The Literature of Destruction*, Philadelphia, New York, Jerusalem 1988, p. 210.

15. *Ibid.*, pp. 218–219.

16. Ismar Elbogen, *A Century of Jewish Life*, Philadelphia 1953, pp. 496–99; Salo W. Baron, *The Russian Jew Under Tsars and Soviets*, New York and London 1964, pp. 217–222.

17. Simon Bernfeld, *Sefer ha-Demaot*, 3 vols., Berlin 1923–1926, I, p. 40.

18. *Ibid.*, III, p. 6.

19. Salo W. Baron, *History and Jewish Historians*, Philadelphia 1964, p. xiv.

20. "Ghetto and Emancipation," p. 519.

21. Paul R. Mendes-Flohr, "Werner Sombart's The Jews and Modern Capitalism: An Analysis of Its Ideological Premises," *LBIYB* XXI (1976), pp. 87–107.

22. Cecil Roth, "The Most Persecuted People," *The Menorah Journal*, XX (1934), pp. 136–147. For evidence of his retreat, see the chapters by Roth and Louis Finkelstein, ed., *The Jews*, 2 vols., 3rd ed., n.p., 1960, and *idem*, "European Jewry in the Dark Ages: A Revised Picture," *Hebrew Union College Annual*, XXIII, part 2 (1950–1951), pp. 151–169.

23. Ismar Schorsch, "The Last Jewish Generalist," *AJS Review*, VIII (Spring 1993).

24. Salo Wittmayer Baron, *A Social and Religious History of the Jews*, 3 vols., New York 1937, II, p. 40.

25. *Ibid.*, p. 31.

26. *Ibid.*, p. 85.

27. *Ibid.*, p. 37.

28. *Ibid.*, pp. 38–40.

29. *Ibid.*, p. 429.

30. *Ibid.*, pp. 423–426. Cf. Salo W. Baron, "Is America Ready for Ethnic Minority Rights?" *Jewish Social Studies*, XLVI (Fall 1984), pp. 189–214.

31. *A Social and Religious History of the Jews*, I, p. 240.

32. Fritz, Baer, *Undersuchungen über Quellen und Komposition des Schebet Jehuda*, Berlin 1923. Baron's essays on de Rossi from the late twenties were reprinted in his *History and Jewish Historians*, pp. 167–239.

33. Yitzhak F. Baer, *Galut*, New York 1947, pp. 9–10, 58, 46.

34. *Zion*, III (1937–1938), pp. 292, 291.

35. *Zion*, p. 291; Salo W. Baron, "The Jewish Factor in Medieval Civilization," *Proceedings of the American Academy for Jewish Research* XII (1942), p. 35.

36. Aryeh Gartner, *Zion*, LV (1990), p. 317; Michael Stanislawski, "Salo Baron and the Meaning of Jewish Emancipation" (unpublished lecture delivered at Stanford University, May 2, 1990), pp. 8–9.

37. Salo Wittmayer Baron, *A Social and Religious History of the Jews*, 2nd ed., XI, New York, London, Philadelphia, p. 388 n. 24. See also Gavin I. Langmuir, *Toward a Definition of Antisemitism*, Berkeley, Los Angeles, Oxford, pp. 48–49, 173.

38. Schorsch, "The Last Jewish Generalist," pp. 48–49.

39. Eugen Weber, "About Marc Bloch," *The American Scholar*, LI (Winter 1981–1982), p. 82.

Index